Digital System Design

Second Edition

Digital System Design

Barry Wilkinson
Department of Computer Science
The University of North Carolina, Charlotte

With a contribution by
Rafic Makki
Department of Electrical Engineering
The University of North Carolina, Charlotte

Prentice Hall
New York London Toronto Sydney Tokyo Singapore

First published 1992 by
Prentice Hall International (UK) Ltd
Campus 400, Maylands Avenue
Hemel Hempstead
Hertfordshire, HP2 7EZ
A division of
Simon & Schuster International Group

© Prentice Hall International (UK) Ltd, 1992

Typeset in 10 on 12 point Times
by Mathematical Composition Setters Ltd, Salisbury, England

Printed and bound in Great Britain by
Dotesios Ltd, Trowbridge, Wiltshire.

Library of Congress Cataloging-in-Publication Data

Wilkinson, Barry
    Digital system design/Barry Wilkinson, with a contribution by
Rafic Makki – 2nd ed.
        p.   cm.
    Includes bibliographical references and index.
    ISBN 0–13–220286–7 : $33.99
    1. Digital electronics. 2. Logic design. 3. Microprocessors.
I. Title
TK7868.D5W46 1992   91-45100
621.381–dc20   CIP

British Library Cataloguing in Publication Data

Wilkinson, Barry
    Digital system design. – 2nd ed.
    I. Title. II. Makki, Rafic
    621.39

    ISBN 0–13–220286–7

1 2 3 4 5 96 95 94 93 92

*To my wife, Wendy
and to my daughter,
Johanna*

Contents

Preface

This book introduces the fundamental topics in digital system design. It is divided into three parts. Part 1 is devoted to logic design. Part 2 is devoted to the components of a microprocessor system. Part 3 contains further aspects of digital system design, and extends topics introduced in Part 1 and Part 2. Overall, the purpose of the book is to provide a broad but comprehensive coverage in concise chapters.

The second edition retains this basic format of the first edition but opportunity has been taken to expand the treatment of logic design and to up-date the treatment of microprocessors. Also, a major new chapter on VLSI systems design and testing is included, written by Dr Rafic Makki of the University of North Carolina at Charlotte. The chapters on magnetic secondary memory and multiprocessor systems have been removed to focus more properly on logic design.†

Part 1 consists of Chapters 1 to 5. Chapter 1 considers the basic topic of binary numbers and codes which are used in digital systems. A new section on ANSI/IEEE floating point numbers is included. The ANSI/IEEE floating point standard has met with very wide acceptance and is implemented in many microprocessor systems. Chapter 2 introduces Boolean variables, expressions and simplification methods including both the Karnaugh map method and the Quine–McCluskey method. The Karnaugh map with map-entered variables is now introduced. Chapter 3 describes the function of fundamental logic devices in which outputs depend upon the present input values irrespective of any past values (so-called combinational logic circuits). Logic devices in the TTL family are quoted as examples. Chapter 4 presents sequential logic circuits (whose outputs may depend upon past input and output values). The concept of a state diagram is introduced early in this chapter first to derive flip-flop logic circuits (the basic sequential circuit building block), and subsequently for counters. ANSI/IEEE standard graphic symbols for logic circuits are now described. Electronic circuit details of logic devices are separated into Chapter 5. This chapter could be omitted if electronic details are not required, though essential electronic concepts are explained briefly where necessary.

---

† Multiprocessor system design can now be found extensively treated in my book *Computer Architecture Design and Performance*, published by Prentice-Hall, 1991.

Part 2 consists of Chapters 6 to 10. Chapter 6 outlines the basic stored program concept embodied in computer and microprocessor systems. Various possible instruction formats are described and the concept of a reduced instruction set computer (RISC) is introduced, with potential advantages. The general architecture of a microprocessor and a microprocessor system are then given. Chapter 7, a completely new chapter, discusses the instructions found in microprocessors. Examples are drawn from 32-bit microprocessors, and three processors have been selected for illustration purposes, namely the Motorola 88100 RISC processor, the Intel $80x86$ family, and the Motorola $680x0$ family. The Motorola 88100 is an example of a high performance RISC processor. The Intel $80x86$ family and Motorola $680x0$ family are very widely found in personal computers and continue to be enhanced by their manufacturers. Chapter 8 is devoted to semiconductor memory devices, as used in microprocessor systems and in computer systems. Chapter 9 deals with input/output circuits and operation, including interrupt and DMA operation. Chapter 10 considers the methods employed to manage the memory hierarchy in a computer system, including a microprocessor system. This chapter contains both main memory/secondary memory management schemes and the use of cache memory between the processor and the main memory.

Part 3 begins with Chapter 11, a continuation of Chapter 4 on sequential circuit design, and includes both synchronous and asynchronous sequential circuit designs. This chapter could be studied immediately after Chapter 4, or could be omitted if extra detail is not required. A substantial new section is included on designing with programmable logic devices (PLDs). Design examples are drawn from micro-processor interfaces, a common application of PLDs. Opportunity is taken to introduce an alternative form of state diagram which has become quite common and is applicable to interface design and to other systems with several logical variables. Chapter 12 considers the design of a central processor. The concept of a register transfer notation is introduced. Microprogramming is explained, using the Am29C300 32-bit microprogrammable family of devices for an example of a microprogrammed system (replacing the original description using the Am2901A and Am2910A devices). Finally overlap and pipelining are described as general techniques in processor design. Chapter 13 describes the factors and techniques used in VLSI logic design. Chapter 14 considers the engineering aspects of creating a working system. Assessment of transmission line reflections, cross-talk and noise are presented. In Chapter 15, the reliability of a digital system is calculated. Methods to increase the reliability are discussed.

This book can be used as a text for undergraduate electrical engineering, computer engineering, and computer science courses in logic design and micro-processor systems. The material covered in Chapters 1 to 4 inclusive could be used for a first course on logic design. Chapter 5 is available particularly for Electrical Engineering students but could be omitted without loss of continuity for Computer Science students. Material from Chapter 11 could be used for a more extensive logic design course or a second course in logic design. Similarly Chapters 13 to 15 inclusive are available for further engineering aspects. The chapters in Part 2, Chapters 6 to 10 inclusive, could form part of a combined logic design/microprocessor system course or could be used for a separate course. Processor design, Chapter 12, is a candidate for inclusion into these courses, especially for one concentrating on the logic design of processors. Problems are set at the end of each chapter. A Solutions Manual containing solutions to the problems is available from the publishers.

This book has been greatly improved by the introduction of the chapter on VLSI design (Chapter 13) written by Dr Rafic Makki. I wish to record my appreciation to Dr Makki. I also extend special thanks to Helen Martin, Viki Williams and Allison King of Prentice Hall International, for their support and guidance received throughout the preparation of this book.

Barry Wilkinson
Charlotte, North Carolina

About the Authors

Barry Wilkinson received the MSc and PhD degrees from the University of Manchester (Department of Computer Science), England, in 1971 and 1974 respectively. He is currently an Associate Professor in the Department of Computer Science at the University of North Carolina at Charlotte. He has previously held faculty positions at Brighton Polytechnic, England (1984–1987), State University of New York, College New Paltz (1983–1984), University College, Cardiff, Wales (1976–1983), and the University of Aston, England (1973–1976). From 1969 to 1970, he worked on process control computer systems at Ferranti Ltd. He is the author of *Computer Peripherals* (with D. Horrocks, Hodder and Stoughton, 2nd edn, 1987) and *Computer Architecture: Design and performance* (Prentice Hall, 1991).

Rafic Makki is an Associate Professor at the University of North Carolina at Charlotte. Dr Makki received the PhD degree in Electrical Engineering from Tennessee Technological University in 1983. His areas of interest include VLSI design, logic synthesis, fault modelling, test generation, and design for testability. Dr Makki is the author of over thirty research publications.

Part 1

Logic Design

| Binary Numbers

I.I Number systems

When a number such as:

259

is written, it is generally taken to mean:

$$2 \times 10^2 + 5 \times 10^1 + 9 \times 10^0$$

i.e. two hundreds plus five tens plus nine units. In this number system, the decimal number system, there are ten different characters or digits 0, 1, 2, 3, 4, 5, 6, 7, 8 and 9 and the position of each digit indicates the power of ten to multiply the value represented by the digit. Formally, the number is defined as:

$$(a_n, a_{n-1}, \ldots a_1, a_0)_b = a_n b^n + a_{n-1} b^{n-1} + \ldots a_1 b^1 + a_0 b^0$$

where a_n is the digit in position n and b is the base, ten in this case. Fractions are simply an extension of the above, i.e.

$$(0.145)_{10} = 1 \times 10^{-1} + 4 \times 10^{-2} + 5 \times 10^{-3}$$

Formally a number including a fractional part is defined as:

$$(a_n, \ldots a_1, a_0. \, a_{-1}, \ldots a_{-m})_b = a_n b^n + \ldots a_1 b^1 + a_0 b^0 + a_{-1} b^{-1} + \ldots a_{-m} b^{-m}$$

The subscript 10 is introduced to indicate that the base is 10, i.e. a decimal number. Using the base ten is only one possibility of this form of number representation. Whatever value we choose for b, there needs to be the same number of different symbols for the digits. For example, if $b = 8$, there need to be eight different digit symbols. The number system using the base 8 is known as the octal number system. The eight symbols used are 0, 1, 2, 3, 4, 5, 6 and 7. In the *octal* number system, the number:

$(257)_8$

would equal

$$2 \times 8^2 + 5 \times 8^1 + 7 \times 8^0$$

or

$$2 \times 64 + 5 \times 8 + 7 \times 1 = (175)_{10}$$

Notice even here we are using the decimal number system to represent the numbers in the calculation because we are familiar with decimal numbers. We use the decimal number system because we have ten fingers to count with. If the human race had been given eight fingers, perhaps the octal number system would be used.

If the base is 2, there are only two digit symbols, 0 and 1. This system is known as the *binary* number system. Each binary digit is known as a *bit*. The following are examples of the binary number system:

$$(101)_2 = 1 \times 2^2 + 0 \times 2^1 + 1 \times 2^0$$
$$(1.11)_2 = 1 \times 2^0 + 1 \times 2^{-1} + 1 \times 2^{-2}$$

The binary number system is always used within digital computers because of having only two symbols to represent. Each of the digits can be represented within the computer by one of two voltages, say 0 V to represent a binary 0 and 5 V to represent a binary 1. (In practice, a range of voltages would represent each digit, say 0 V to 0.8 V to represent a 0, and 2 V to 5 V to represent a 1.) For permanent storage purposes, magnetized surfaces can be used and the two states of magnetization can directly or indirectly represent the binary digits. In the past,

Table 1.1   Decimal, binary, octal and hexadecimal numbers

Decimal	Binary	Octal	Hexadecimal
0	00000	0	0
1	00001	1	1
2	00010	2	2
3	00011	3	3
4	00100	4	4
5	00101	5	5
6	00110	6	6
7	00111	7	7
8	01000	10	8
9	01001	11	9
10	01010	12	A
11	01011	13	B
12	01100	14	C
13	01101	15	D
14	01110	16	E
15	01111	17	F
16	10000	20	10
17	10001	21	11
18	10010	22	12
19	10011	23	13
20	10100	24	14

punched holes in paper tape or cards have been used for storage purposes. The presence of a hole in the tape or card represents a 1 and the absence of a hole represents a 0.

The number system using the base 16 is known as the *hexadecimal* number system, abbreviated to 'hex'. As we will see, this number system is sometimes used to represent binary numbers. In the hexadecimal number system, there are 16 different digit symbols, the numerals 0 to 9 and the first six letters of the alphabet, A, B, C, D, E and F. The letters are used to represent 10 to 15. For example:

$$(1AE)_{16} = 1 \times 16^2 + A \times 16^1 + E \times 16^0$$
$$= 1 \times 16^2 + 10 \times 16^1 + 14 \times 16^0$$
$$= 1 \times 256 + 10 \times 16 + 14 \times 1$$
$$= (430)_{10}$$

Table 1.1 lists the numbers from 0 to 20 in decimal and the equivalent binary, octal and hexadecimal numbers.

1.2 Conversion from one number system to another number system

1.2.1 Conversion between binary and octal or hexadecimal numbers

Conversion between binary and octal or hexadecimal numbers is particularly easy because the octal and hexadecimal bases, 8 and 16, are powers of the binary base, 2 (third and fourth powers respectively). This leads to a direct relationship between groups of digits in octal or hexadecimal numbers and binary numbers.

For octal, groups of three digits of the binary number are equivalent to one digit of the octal number. For example:

(i) Conversion of $(1100101)_2$ into octal. Dividing the binary number into groups of three:

    1 100 101

Encoding each group into one octal digit:

    1 4 5

Therefore

    $(1100101)_2 = (145)_8$

(ii) Conversion of $(011110111)_2$ into octal. Dividing the binary number into groups of three:

    011 110 111

Encoding each group into one octal digit:

    3 6 7

Therefore

$$(011110111)_2 = (367)_8.$$

Clearly the reverse process can be performed.

The hexadecimal base, 16, is the fourth power of the binary number and groups of four digits of the binary number become equivalent to one hexadecimal digit. For example:

(i) Conversion of $(1011101)_2$ into hexadecimal. Dividing the binary number into groups of four digits:

   (0)101 1101

Encoding each group into one hexadecimal digit:

   5 D

Therefore

$$(1011101)_2 = (5D)_{16}$$

(ii) Conversion of $(11110111)_2$ into hexadecimal. Dividing the binary number into groups of four digits:

   1111 0111

Encoding each group into one hexadecimal digit:

   F 7

Therefore

$$(11110111)_2 = (F7)_{16}$$

Fractional numbers can be converted using the same method, by taking groups of three or four as appropriate, working away from the 'point'. For example:

(i) $(111101.101111)_2 = (75.57)_8$
(ii) $(111101.101111)_2 = (3D.BC)_{16}$

Unless the same number of digits can represent a number in each base, the larger the base, the smaller the number of digits required to represent a particular number; for example

$$(1011001101010001010)_2 = (1315212)_8 = (59A8A)_{16}$$

This fact, together with the simple conversion, has led to octal and hexadecimal numbers being used to represent the binary numbers held within computers, especially for a close examination of stored numbers. It was convenient with computers using 24-bit numbers to represent each 24-bit number in documentation by eight octal digits. The symbol * has been used preceding the octal number for recognition purposes, i.e.

$$(10111101)_2 = *275$$

More recently, 8-bit, 16-bit and 32-bit microprocessor systems have been developed and in these cases, the hexadecimal number system is convenient, as two, four and eight hexadecimal digits can represent 8-bit, 16-bit and 32-bit numbers respectively. The letter H is sometimes used to indicate hexadecimal numbers, i.e.:

$$(10101111)_2 = AFH$$

The letter H is not a valid hexadecimal digit and thus does not cause confusion with the valid hexadecimal digits preceding it. Eight bits are called a *byte*.

Generally though, we would prefer to use decimal numbers in our documentation. Let us consider methods of converting numbers from one base to another base where one base is decimal. We shall consider integer numbers and fractional numbers separately. When a number consists of both an integer part and a fractional part, each part is converted separately using the appropriate method on each part.

1.2.2 Conversion from decimal to binary/octal/hexadecimal/other

(a) Integer conversion algorithm

By rearranging the formal representation of an integer, we obtain:

$$a_0 + b(a_1 + b(a_2 + b(a_3 + b(a_4 + \ldots b(a_n)\ldots)$$

Dividing by the base, b, we get:

$$a_1 + b(a_2 + b(a_3 + b(a_4 + \ldots b(a_n)\ldots) \text{ plus a remainder } a_0$$

By successive division of the resultant quotient by the base, the digits of the number can be extracted as the remainder digits and hence all the digits of the number can be found. This leads to a formal integer conversion algorithm, where b is the base of the converted number and the divisions are done using arithmetic of the original number system. It can be applied to any number system but unless the original number system is decimal, the arithmetic is not familiar.

For the conversion of a decimal number into a number of a new base the steps would be:

Step 1   Divide the decimal number, N, by the new base, b, giving the result as a quotient, Q_0 and a remainder, r_0
Step 2   Divide Q_0 by b, giving Q_1 and a remainder r_1
Step 3   Continue the process until Q_n is zero.

The remainders are the digits of the required binary number where r_0 is the least significant digit (rightmost digit). For example, to convert the decimal number 47 into binary we perform the following division processes:

$47 \div 2 = 23$ remainder 1; least significant bit
$23 \div 2 = 11$ remainder 1
$11 \div 2 = 5$ remainder 1
$5 \div 2 = 2$ remainder 1
$2 \div 2 = 1$ remainder 0
$1 \div 2 = 0$ remainder 1; most significant bit (left-most digit)

Therefore $(47)_{10} = (101111)_2$. Generally, the number of digits in a binary number is about three times that of the equivalent decimal number.

Let us take another example, decimal 862 into hexadecimal:

	Decimal	*Hexidecimal*	
$862 \div 16 = 53$ remainder	14	E	;least significant bit
$53 \div 16 = 3$ remainder	5	5	
$3 \div 16 = 0$ remainder	3	3	;most significant bit

Therefore

$$(862)_{10} = (35E)_{16}$$

(b) Fraction conversion algorithm

Starting from the formal definition of a fractional number:

$$(.a_{-1}, \ldots a_{-m})_b = a_{-1}b^{-1} + \ldots a_{-m}b^{-m}$$

we get the number equal to:

$$(1/b)(a_{-1} + (1/b)(a_{-2} + (1/b)(a_{-3} + \ldots (1/b)a_{-m})\ldots)$$

by rearrangement. Hence by multiplying by the base, b, we get:

$$a_{-1} + (1/b)(a_{-2} + (1/b)(a_{-3} + \ldots (1/b)a_{-m})\ldots)$$

This number consists of an integer part (a_{-1}) which is the first digit of the required number, and a fractional part. By repeated multiplications of the fractional part by the base, the required digits of the number are extracted. A comparison can be made with the integer method which uses division operations rather than multiplication operations. Again the method could be applied to any number system conversion but the arithmetic must be done in the original number system. Therefore it is particularly suitable for conversions from decimal numbers to other number systems. Describing the conversion as a series of steps we get:

Step 1   Multiply the decimal number, N, by the new base, b, giving a product consisting of an integer part I_0 and a fractional part F_0.
Step 2   Multiply F_0 by b, giving a product, $I_1.F_1$.
Step 3   Continue the process until a fractional part, F_n is zero.

The integer parts, I_n to I_0 are the digits of the required number, where I_0 is the most significant digit.

Consider for example, the conversion of the decimal number $(0.485)_{10}$ into binary:

Fractional parts		Integer parts
0.485	$\times 2 = 0.97$	0
0.97	$\times 2 = 1.94$	1
0.94	$\times 2 = 1.88$	1
0.88	$\times 2 = 1.76$	1
0.76	$\times 2 = 1.52$	1
0.52	$\times 2 = 1.04$	1
0.04	$\times 2 = 0.08$	0
	$\vdots$	

Therefore

$$(0.485)_{10} = (0.0111110\ldots)_2.$$

A finite fraction in one number system will not necessarily convert into a finite fraction in another system. Normally the process is terminated when a given number of digits is obtained. Consider another example, the conversion of $(0.347)_{10}$ into hexadecimal:

Fractional parts		Integer parts	
		Decimal	Hexadecimal
0.347	$\times 16 = 5.552$	5	5
0.552	$\times 16 = 8.832$	8	8
0.832	$\times 16 = 13.312$	13	D
0.312	$\times 16 = 4.992$	4	4
0.992	$\times 16 = 15.872$	15	F
	$\vdots$		

Therefore

$$(0.347)_{10} = (0.58D4F\ldots)_{16}.$$

The conversion of a large decimal number into binary can be shortened by first converting into octal and then to binary by inspection, because the number of divisions (or multiplications) of eight to convert into octal is less than the number of divisions (or multiplications) of two to convert into binary.

1.2.3 Conversion from binary/octal/hexadecimal/other to decimal

We could use the same methods as above using arithmetic of the original base for conversions to decimal (or between any base). However, it is rather inconvenient to use any base other than decimal for arithmetic. (The reader may care to perform the reverse conversions above using the general method.) Alternative algorithms exist using arithmetic of the new base.

(a) Integer conversion algorithm

The required number can be obtained directly from the formal representation given in section 1.1 by the summation of products of each digit multiplied by the base raised to the corresponding power. The calculation can be achieved from the rearrangement used in Section 1.2.2, leading to a process of successive multiplications. We can describe this method by the following series of steps using the arithmetic of the new base:

Step 1   Multiply the most significant digit by the old base, b.
Step 2   Add the result to the next most significant digit.
Step 3   Multiply the result by b.
Step 4   Repeat steps 2 and 3 in succession until the least significant digit is reached.

The final sum is the required decimal number, for example $(11010)_2$ into decimal:

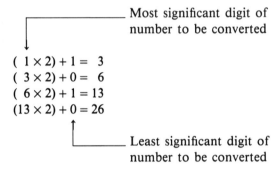

Most significant digit of number to be converted

$$(1 \times 2) + 1 = 3$$
$$(3 \times 2) + 0 = 6$$
$$(6 \times 2) + 1 = 13$$
$$(13 \times 2) + 0 = 26$$

Least significant digit of number to be converted

Therefore

$$(11010)_2 = (26)_{10}.$$

Another example, $(9CE)_{16}$ into decimal:

$$(9 \times 16) + C = 144 + 12 = 156$$
$$(156 \times 16) + E = 2496 + 14 = 2510$$

Therefore

$$(9CE)_{16} = (2510)_{10}.$$

(b) Fractions conversion algorithm

For fractions we have a process of repeated division beginning at the least significant digit (again using the arithmetic of the new base):

Step 1   Divide the least significant digit by the base, b.
Step 2   Add the result to the next least significant digit.
Step 3   Divide the result by b.
Step 4   Repeat steps 2 and 3 in succession until the most significant digit is reached. Include the final division.

The result is the required decimal number, for example $(0.1101)_2$ into decimal:

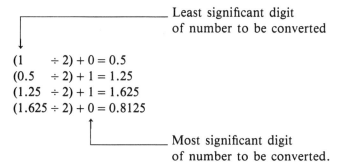

Least significant digit
of number to be converted

(1   ÷ 2) + 0 = 0.5
(0.5   ÷ 2) + 1 = 1.25
(1.25 ÷ 2) + 1 = 1.625
(1.625 ÷ 2) + 0 = 0.8125

Most significant digit
of number to be converted.

Therefore

$(0.1101)_2 = (0.8125)_{10}.$

Another example, $(0.4562)_8$ into decimal:

(2   ÷ 8) + 6 = 6.25
(6.25   ÷ 8) + 5 = 5.78125
(5.78125   ÷ 8) + 4 = 4.72265625
(4.72265625 ÷ 8) + 0 = 0.59033203125

Therefore

$(0.4562)_8 = (0.59033203125)_{10}.$

1.3 Binary arithmetic

1.3.1 Binary addition

In decimal arithmetic, we add two numbers as shown below:

A	1	7	4	3
$+B$	$_1$9$_1$	8	4	
Sum	2	7	2	7

Carry digits are generated as shown when the sum of the A and B digits (including any carry from the lower significant digit addition) is greater than nine. Similarly, carry digits may be generated when binary addition of two binary digits (including any carry from the previous digit addition) is greater than one, as shown in the addition of two numbers in binary shown below:

Augend, A	0	0	1	1	1	1	0	0	$(60)_{10}$
Addend, B	0	0$_1$	1$_1$	0$_1$	1$_1$	1	1	0	$(46)_{10}$
Sum	0	1	1	0	1	0	1	0	$(106)_{10}$

Leading 0's are introduced to form (positive) binary words of a defined length, in this case eight bits. Addition of binary numbers follow a similar procedure to decimal addition. First the digits in the furthest right-hand column are added together, in this case $0 + 0 = 0$. Only in one instance could the sum be greater than one digit, i.e. $1 + 1 = 10$. This would have caused a carry of 1 to be passed over to the next stage. (Compare with decimal arithmetic. When the sum is greater than 9, a carry is generated and there are many instances of this.) Other columns of digits are added working from right to left. When a binary carry is generated three digits need to be added in the next column, the A and B digits of the column and the carry digits from the previous column.

We can recognize two types of addition processes in the above. First there is the addition of two binary digits in the first column where there is no previous carry. Second there are the other additions when a carry from the previous addition requires three digits to be added together, the A digit, the B digit and the carry (in) digit. Both these forms of addition produce a two-digit result consisting of a sum digit and a carry (out) digit.

Two binary digits, A and B, can each take on one of two values, 0 or 1. Therefore there are four possible combinations of A and B. When $A = B = 0$, both the sum digit and the carry digit are a 0. When $A = 0$, $B = 1$ or $A = 1$, $B = 0$, the sum digit is a 1 and carry digit is a 0. Finally, when both A and B are a 1, the sum digit is a 0 and the carry digit is a 1. This can be given in tabular form:

A	B	Sum	Carry (out)
0	0	0	0
0	1	1	0
1	0	1	0
1	1	0	1

There are eight combinations of three binary digits, A, B and carry in. The sum digit alone is a 1 whenever only one of the three inputs is a 1 (including the carry in digit). The carry out digit is a 1 whenever two of the three input digits are a 1. Only when all three input digits are a 1 are both sum and carry out digits a 1 (i.e. $1 + 1 + 1 = 11$). In tabular form, we have:

A	B	Carry in	Sum	Carry out
0	0	0	0	0
0	0	1	1	0
0	1	0	1	0
0	1	1	0	1
1	0	0	1	0
1	0	1	0	1
1	1	0	0	1
1	1	1	1	1

Tables such as the above giving input values and corresponding output values are known as *truth tables*. Circuits to add together two binary digits A and B are known as *half adders*. Circuits to add together two binary digits and a carry (in) are known as *full adders*. These circuits will be considered in detail in Chapter 3.

1.3.2 Binary subtraction and negative numbers

Rules can be devised to achieve binary subtraction in a similar fashion to the rules of binary addition. For example to subtract $(46)_{10}$ from $(60)_{10}$ we have:

Minuend	0	0	1	1	^{1}1	^{1}1	^{1}0	0
Subtrahend	0	0	1	0_1	1_1	1_1	1	0
Difference	0	0	0	0	1	1	1	0

In cases where the subtrahend digit is greater than the minuend digit a borrow digit is required to complete the subtraction of one digit from another. However, we have the problem of dealing with negative numbers, as we do if negative numbers are to be manipulated generally. One way to incorporate negative numbers in the number representation is to assign one bit as a 'sign' bit set to a 0 if the number is positive and set to a 1 if the number is negative. The absolute value of the number is represented in pure binary separately. This representation is known as the *sign plus magnitude* representation. Though this representation is used for particular applications (for example floating point numbers, section 1.4), it is inconvenient for the central representation of numbers within a computer as it requires the sign bits to be examined before any arithmetic operation is performed.

It is very convenient if the process of subtraction can be considered as the addition of one number to the negative of the other number, i.e.:

$$A - B = A + [-B]$$

Where $[-B]$ is the negative of $+B$. Then circuits used to perform addition can also be used to perform subtraction, by presenting the negative of B to the addition unit.

One approach is to represent the negative number $[-B]$ by the result of subtracting B from a number one larger than the maximum number that can be represented by the digits provided. The largest number that can be represented by an *n*-digit number is $2^n - 1$. Therefore $[-B]$ would be represented in this system by:

$$[-B] \equiv 2^n - B$$

This is known as the *2's complement system*. For example, if $n = 4$ and $B = 0101$ (5_{10}), then:

$$[-B] \equiv 2^4 - 0101 = 10000 - 0101 = 1011$$

In the 2's complement system, all positive numbers must begin with a 0. In consequence, all negative numbers will begin with a 1. Zero is regarded as positive. Clearly, if we use this representation, addition of numbers must lead to the correct answer according to the representation.

Consider both A and B positive and A greater than B. If we now subtract B from A by using the equivalent for $-B$ and adding, we get:

$$A - B = A + [-B] = A + (2^n - B)$$
$$= 2^n + (A - B) \qquad (A \text{ greater than } B)$$

Truncating the result to n digits removes the 2^n to give $A - B$, the required answer. ($2^n = 100\cdots0$, i.e. 1 followed by n 0's. Adding this to an n-digit number does not affect the first n digits. The $(n + 1)$th digit simply becomes a 1.) If $A - B$ happens to be negative (i.e. B greater than A), the result is the appropriate equivalent negative number:

$$A - B = A + [-B] = A + (2^n - B)$$
$$= 2^n - (B - A) \qquad (A \text{ less than } B)$$

The reader may care to verify that all combinations of positive and negative numbers compute correctly (Problem 1.5). An example producing a positive result is $7 - 5$ (decimal):

$$7 - 5 = 0111 - 0101 = 0111 + 1011 = 10010$$
truncating gives $0010 \equiv 2$ in decimal

An example producing a negative result is $5 - 7$:

$$5 - 7 = 0101 - 0111 = 0101 + 1001 = 1110 \ (-2 \text{ in decimal})$$

Table 1.2 (third column) gives the number representation in the 2's complement system for 4-bit numbers, which gives a range from -8 to $+7$. If a greater number of bits were used, leading 0's are repeated in the positive numbers, e.g. $+5 = 0101 = 00000101$ for 8-bit numbers. For negative numbers, leading 1's are repeated, e.g. $-5 = 1011 = 11111011$. A quick method of obtaining the negative representation of a number is to invert all the digits of the positive number, i.e. change all occurrences of 1's to 0's and all occurrences of 0's to 1's, and then add 1 to the result. For example, -5 can be obtained as follows:

$$+5 \quad 0101$$
Inverting we get $\qquad 1010$
Adding 1 we get $\qquad 1011 = 5$ in the 2's complement system

This is because $2^n - 1$ is always $11\ldots11$ irrespective of the value of n, and subtracting any number from $11\ldots11$ inverts each digit. Adding 1 produces the same result as subtracting the number from 2^n.

An alternative representation, known as the *1's complement system*, represents negative numbers by:

$$[-B] \equiv (2^n - 1) - B$$

Generating the negative representation is particularly simple; all the digits are inverted. Using this representation to subtract B from A, we have:

$$A + (2^n - 1 - B) = 2^n - 1 + (A - B) \qquad (A \text{ greater than } B)$$

Table 1.2   4-bit binary, 2's complement and 1's complement numbers

Decimal	Binary	2's complement binary	1's complement binary
+7	0111	0111	0111
+6	0110	0110	0110
+5	0101	0101	0101
+4	0100	0100	0100
+3	0011	0011	0011
+2	0010	0010	0010
+1	0001	0001	0001
0	0000	0000	$\begin{cases} 0000 \\ \text{or} \\ 1111 \end{cases}$
−1	—	1111	1110
−2	—	1110	1101
−3	—	1101	1100
−4	—	1100	1011
−5	—	1011	1010
−6	—	1010	1001
−7	—	1001	1000
−8	—	1000	—

To obtain the correct result, $A - B$, 1 must be added. However, if A is less than B, we obtain the correct result:

$$A + (2^n - 1 - B) = 2^n - 1 - (B - A) \qquad (A \text{ less than } B)$$

It is found that whenever a final carry is generated during the addition process, a 1 must be added to the result (Problem 1.6). This process is known as *end-around-carry*. Table 1.2 (column 4) lists 1's complement numbers. There are two representations of zero, 0000 and 1111, and the range of 4-bit 1's complement numbers is from -7 to $+7$. Most computers employ the 2's complement representation.

Complement schemes can be applied to decimal numbers. The decimal 10's complement system is equivalent to the binary 2's complement system using 10^n rather than 2^n and the decimal 9's complement system is equivalent to the binary 1's complement using $10^n - 1$ rather than $2^n - 1$.

1.3.3 Range of binary numbers

The range of numbers that can be represented by a fixed number of bits is zero to $2^n - 1$ where n is the numbers of bits, if only positive numbers are represented (i.e. *pure* binary numbers). The largest number is 11 ... 111. Using the 2's complement system, the range of numbers is from -2^{n-1} through zero to $+2^{n-1} - 1$. The most positive number is 011 ... 11 and the most negative number is 100 ... 00. When two binary numbers are added together, there may be a final carry generated from the most significant column, for example:

A		1	0	0	1	0	1	0	1
$+B$	$_1$	0_1	1_1	1_1	1	0_1	1	1	0
Sum		0	0	0	0	1	0	1	1

This leads to a result with one extra digit, i.e. nine bits in our example, when the final carry is brought into the result. Usually a fixed number of bits is allowed to represent numbers in computers, and the final carry, if generated, is separated. If a carry is generated during an addition process with two pure binary numbers, the result without the final carry is of course incorrect. If we employ the 2's complement system, we discard any 2^n term appearing in the final result. This term appears as a final carry, which is not considered in the result. However, the final result without the final carry may still be incorrect if the desired result is outside the range permitted with a given number of bits. In the above example, it is correct using the 2's complement system. A is negative (-107_{10}) and B is positive ($+118_{10}$), leading to the correct positive number ($+11_{10}$). An incorrect result is obtained if we add two positive numbers which apparently give a negative result or we add two negative numbers which apparently give a positive result (without considering the final carry). A correct result is always obtained if we add a positive number and negative number together. In a computer, an incorrect result due to an insufficient number of digits (or other reason, for example in a division operation when an attempt is made to divide by zero) is indicated by an *overflow* bit or flag being set to 1.

1.4 Floating point numbers

We have highlighted above that there is a fixed number of binary digits provided in digital computers to represent an individual number. Microprocessors, for example, have commonly employed 8-bit, 16-bit and 32-bit numbers. The 2's complement number system is used almost universally which would allow any integer value from -128 to $+127$ for 8-bit numbers and any integer value from $-32,768$ to $+32,767$ for 16-bit numbers. A 32-bit number would give a range of $-2,147,483,648$ to $+2,147,483,647$. Fractions or numbers including a fractional part can be accommodated by including the notation of a binary point. The binary point has no effect on the internal arithmetic of the computer. All these types of number are known as *fixed point numbers*.

If we wish to represent a large or small number in decimal, such as two millions, it can conveniently be written as 2×10^6 rather than 2,000,000. This type of representation can be carried over to binary for numbers outside the range permitted by the fixed point representation. The representation is known as *floating point* representation and is composed of two parts, a *mantissa* and an *exponent*. The relationship between these parts and the actual number is:

$$\text{Number} = \text{mantissa} \times \text{base}^{\text{exponent}}$$

The base for binary is 2 or a power of 2, for example 8 or 16. The binary word representing the number contains two *fields*, one for the mantissa and one for the exponent. The number of bits assigned to each field depends upon the resolution required for the number and its range. Standards have been laid down to enable interchangeability of program data.

Both the mantissa and the exponent can be either positive or negative fixed point numbers. A negative mantissa enables negative numbers to be represented and a negative exponent enables very small numbers to be represented. The mantissa usually employs the sign plus magnitude convention where the first bit indicates the sign and the rest of the mantissa bits indicate the magnitude, usually a fractional number.

To utilize the maximum resolution, floating point numbers are *normalized*. In a normalization procedure, the number is arranged so that the first bit of the magnitude is always a non-zero digit. The exponent is then adjusted accordingly. We can compare the normalization process to the normalization of a decimal number such as 0.0000345×10^9. Leading zeros are removed to produce a non-zero first digit, i.e. 0.3450000×10^5. Hence we have more digits available to represent magnitude of the number. Similarly in binary, the number 0.0010101×2^{-7} normalized would be 0.10100×2^{-9}. If the base is, for example, 16, the normalization process would lead to a non-zero hexadecimal digit, though not necessarily a 1 in the first place, since we would only be able to adjust the number in powers of 16. For example, the floating point number 0.06E (i.e. 0.000001101110) $\times 16^{45}$ normalized would be 0.6E (i.e. 0.01101110000) $\times 16^{44}$. With the base 2, it is not necessary to store the most significant bit of the magnitude of a normalized number as it is always a 1. However, a larger base enables a larger range of numbers to be stored, at the expense of the precision of the mantissa, given a fixed number of bits for the sum of mantissa and exponent bits.

The exponent usually employs a *biased integer* notation. In this notation, a bias number is added to the exponent before it is stored, to make the stored exponent always positive. Therefore the number is represented by:

$$\text{Number} = \text{mantissa} \times 2^{\text{stored exponent} - bias}$$

For example, a bias of 2^{n-1} would be suitable with a 2's complement exponent (where n is the number of digits in the number). A bias of $2^{n-1} - 1$ is also used. Having only positive stored exponents simplifies comparison of exponents which is necessary during floating point addition and subtraction. Normally, zero has a special representation, for example with all bits of the mantissa and exponent set to 0. Numbers smaller or larger than can be represented lead to underflow and overflow conditions respectively.

1.4.1 ANSI/IEEE floating point standard 754-1985 [1]

The IEEE has created standard floating point number formats which have become widely accepted. The advantages of standard formats include exchangeability between systems, defined error conditions, user familiarity, and less likelihood of logic design problems. Logic designers producing IEEE standard floating point number arithmetic processors must conform to the standard. The IEEE standard specifies four formats for floating point numbers, each with different numbers of bits for the exponent, and mantissa, namely 32-bit single format, 64-bit double format, and two extended formats, single extended and double extended. The extended formats are not fully defined, though a double extended format using 80 bits is commonly implemented. All formats use a biased exponent and an implied most significant one in the mantissa. The binary point of the mantissa is immediately behind the implied one, so that the stored part of the mantissa represents the fractional part of the mantissa. The 32- and 64-bit formats match in length the 32- and 64-bit words found in most computer systems, and are given as follows:

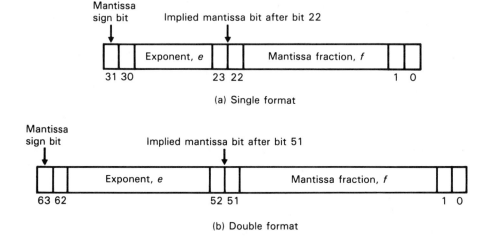

(a) Single format

(b) Double format

An exponent bias of $+127$ is used for the single format and a bias of $+1023$ for the double format.

The standard uses the minimum and maximum values of the stored (positive) exponent, e, and zero mantissa fraction, f, to indicate zero, infinity, denormalized numbers or invalid results. The minimum value of e is 0. Let the maximum value of e be e_{max}. Then $e_{max} = 255$ for the single format and $e_{max} = 2047$ for the double format. Valid normalized numbers are represented when $0 < e < e_{max}$ (f can be 0).

Zero is represented by $e = 0$ and $f = 0$. The sign bit gives $+0$ and -0, which can be significant in certain situations. Infinity is represented by $e = e_{max}$ and $f = 0$. Again, the sign bit gives $+\infty$ and $-\infty$, which are regarded differently. Notice that infinity could conceivably be used as an operand, though in most cases it is not allowed.

Denormalized numbers can be represented. Representation of denormalized numbers is a characteristic of the standard which allows 'graceful' reduction of values towards zeros, though with reducing precision. Denormalized numbers are represented using $e = 0$ and $f \neq 0$. The exponent of the represented number is assumed to be $-(e_{max}) + 1$, i.e. -126 in the single format and -1022 in the double format. Also there is no implied bit in the mantissa; the store fraction represents the full mantissa. The mantissa sign bit is used, leading to numbers given by $\pm(\cdot f) \times 2^{-126}$ for the single format and $\pm(\cdot f) \times 2^{-1022}$ for the double format. Normalized numbers would generally be used except when it is not possible to normalize a value because it is too small.

Results which cannot be produced for any logical reason (invalid operands, etc.) are indicated by $e = e_{max}$ and $f \neq 0$, and called *not-a-numbers* (NaNs). There are two types of NaNs: signalling NaNs which cause an external signal to be generated for activating user exception routines; and quiet NaNs (non-signaling NaNs) which do not so signal but carry through to the result the error condition for diagnostic purposes. Signalling NaNs and quiet NaN are given separate identifying binary patterns. Signalling NaNs could be used, for example, to show that uninitialized memory and registers are being used. Quiet NaNs are useful for representing invalid results.

Invalid operations are categorized as:

(i) Invalid operation with specified operands, for example addition with infinity
(ii) Division by zero (categorized separately from 1)
(iii) Overflow
(iv) Underflow
(v) Inexact result.

Overflow occurs where the result would be too large for the number representation. Underflow occurs where the result is too small for the normalized number representation. Inexact result occurs if rounding cannot be done properly. Floating point arithmetic is defined in the standard including how rounding is to be performed. Arithmetic is to be performed first assuming infinite precision, and then rounded to the nearest representable value. Rounding can also be specified as towards $+\infty$ towards $-\infty$, or towards zero.

SOME EXAMPLES

(a) The binary number 1101.001×2^{101} represented in IEEE format

The exponent 101 is binary and represents 5 in decimal. To normalize the mantissa, we need to shift the mantissa three places right and hence add three to the exponent to obtain:

$$1.101001 \times 2^{1000}$$

This particular number could easily be represented in the single precision format. The exponent needs to be biased before stored by adding 127, to get the biased exponent $01111111 + 00001000 = 10000111$. The final stored pattern without the leading 1 in the mantissa is:

0	1 0 0 0 0 1 1 1	1 0 1 0 0 1 0 0 0 0 0 0 0 0 0 0 0 0 0 0 0 0 0

31 30   23 22   0

(b) The smallest and largest normalized numbers (single precision)

The smallest normalized number is given by the smallest biased exponent together with the smallest normalized mantissa. The stored biased exponent of 00000000 is used to represent zero or a denormalized number. Hence we get the smallest number as:

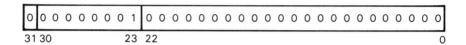

This corresponds to an exponent of 2^{-126} and a mantissa of 1.00000000000000000000000. Hence the smallest normalized (positive) number is 2^{-126}. The sign bit gives the smallest normalized negative number as -2^{-126}.

   The largest normalized number is given by the largest exponent together with the largest normalized mantissa. The largest stored biased exponent is 11111110 (as 11111111, i.e. e_{max}, is used to represent infinity or NANs). Hence we get the largest number as:

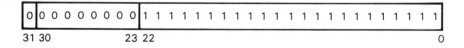

This corresponds to an exponent of 2^{+127} and a mantissa of 1.11111111111111111111111 about 2 decimal. Hence the largest normalized positive number is about 2^{+128}. The largest normalized negative number is -2^{+128}.

(c) The smallest and largest denormalized numbers (single precision)

Denormalized numbers use a stored biased exponent of 0 representing 2^{-127}. The implied digit of the mantissa is 0. The largest denormalized number is:

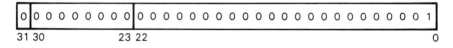

which corresponds to $0.11111111111111111111111 \times 2^{-127}$ or about 2^{-126}. The smallest denormalized number is:

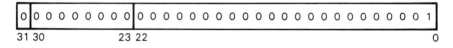

which corresponds to $0.00000000000000000000001 \times 2^{-127}$ or $2^{-23} \times 2^{-127} = 2^{-150}$.

Overall, we get the range of numbers:

Negative overflow	Negative normalized numbers	Negative denormalized numbers	Positive denormalized numbers	Positive normalized numbers	Positive overflow
	-2^{-128} ...... -2^{-126}		Zero 0	$+2^{-126}$ ...... $+2^{-128}$	

1.5 Binary coded decimal numbers

In some applications (e.g. calculators and check-out tills), decimal numbers are continually displayed or entered. Clearly, the decimal numbers can be converted to binary and vice versa as we have seen, and this can be done by computer. However, the decimal nature of the numbers can be retained within the computer using the *binary coded decimal* (BCD) number system. In BCD, each decimal digit is converted into a four-bit binary equivalent and each four-bit word is joined together to form the coding of the number. For example, the number $(259)_{10}$ in BCD is the 12-bit number:

0010 0101 1001

In the BCD coding system, the digits are not 'weighted' in the normal ascending power of the base as in binary or decimal numbers or in any other normal positional number system. The weighting in BCD is:

$$...,100 \times 2^4 \; 100 \times 2^2 \; 100 \times 2^1 \; 100 \times 2^0,$$
$$10 \times 2^4 \; 10 \times 2^2 \; 10 \times 2^1 \; 10 \times 2^0, \; 1 \times 2^4 \; 1 \times 2^2 \; 1 \times 2^1 \; 1 \times 2^0$$

Within each group, the binary combinations from decimal 10 to 15, i.e. 1010, 1011, 1100, 1101, 1110 and 1111 are not used and would be invalid if they occurred. Hence more digits are used to represent the number than are strictly necessary.

Two BCD digits can be held in one 8-bit word, four BCD digits can be held in one 16-bit word, and eight BCD digits can be held in one 32-bit word. BCD numbers with more than one BCD digit contained in a binary word are called *packed BCD* numbers. Microprocessors in particular, because of being suited for applications such as check-out tills and calculators and similar BCD applications, can manipulate and perform arithmetic operations on packed BCD numbers. For example, two 8-bit words, each holding two BCD digits, can be added together with the result as a packed 8-bit BCD word. Similarly, BCD numbers can be subtracted.

The addition process can be performed firstly without regard to the special nature of the BCD numbers and subsequently a correction process is performed when necessary to produce the correct BCD result. Firstly an example in which no correction is necessary, the addition of 25_{BCD} and 44_{BCD} shown below:

Binary coded decimal	Binary
$(2\ 5)_{BCD}$	0010 0101
$(4\ 4)_{BCD}$	0100 0100
$(6\ 9)_{BCD}$	0110 1001

We can see here that simply adding two binary words representing the BCD digits results in the binary pattern representing the correct BCD result. However, if a BCD digit in the result should be greater than 9, we will not obtain the correct result. Table 1.3 shows the results of adding two numbers, each in the range 0 to 9 inclusive, which produces a number up to 18. The second column in the table gives the result in pure binary, and the third column the required BCD representation. In all cases above 9, the correct representation can be obtained by adding six to the binary result. This leads to a BCD carry digit being passed on to the next stage, which must be included in the subsequent digit addition. We can identify two groups of incorrect results.

Firstly, one of the unused binary patterns from 10_{10} to 15_{10} will appear if we add together two BCD digits resulting in a sum between 10 and 15 inclusive. This is corrected in the following example:

Binary coded decimal	Binary
$(2\ 5)_{BCD}$	0010 0101
$(4\ 8)_{BCD}$	0100 1000
$6\ 13_{BCD}$	0110 1101
$+\ \ \ 6$	0110
$(7\ 3)_{BCD}$	0111 0011

A carry digit is passed to the second stage after the correction process. For the results 16 to 18 inclusive, a carry from the fourth stage will already have occurred in the binary addition as in:

Binary coded decimal	Binary
$(5\ 9)_{BCD}$	0101 1001
$(2\ 8)_{BCD}$	0010 1000
$8\ 1$	1000 0001
$+\ \ \ 6$	0110
$(8\ 7)_{BCD}$	1000 0111

One way to view the correction process is that of bypassing unused codes. Each of the six unused codes in each 4-bit group is bypassed by the addition of a +6 correction factor at each level of significance. Whether correction is necessary can be detected by recognizing an invalid pattern (10_{10} to 15_{10} inclusive in Table 1.3) or

Table 1.3 Correction in BCD addition

Decimal	Binary	Binary coded decimal	
0	00000	0000 0000	
1	00001	0000 0001	
2	00010	0000 0010	
3	00011	0000 0011	
4	00100	0000 0100	No correction
5	00101	0000 0101	
6	00110	0000 0110	
7	00111	0000 0111	
8	01000	0000 1000	
9	01001	0000 1001	
10	01010	0001 0000	
11	01011	0001 0001	
12	01100	0001 0010	
13	01101	0001 0011	Correction (add 6)
14	01110	0001 0100	
15	01111	0001 0101	
16	10000	0001 0110	
17	10001	0001 0111	
18	10010	0001 1000	

a carry being generated (16_{10} to 18_{10} inclusive in Table 1.3). BCD subtraction can be done, for example, by using a decimal complement representation.

1.6 Alphanumeric codes

People need to communicate with a computer through the medium of letters of their spoken and written language, in our case English. Therefore it is clear that some coding method of representing the letters of the alphabet needs to be provided within the computer. It would also be helpful if the same method were used for all computers to assist in information transfer between computers and between computers and their peripheral devices. One coding method that has emerged to gain widespread acceptance is called the *American Standard Code for Information Interchange* (ASCII). This is a 7-bit code capable of representing up to 94 printed characters and provides a representation for all of the upper-case (capital) letters and lower-case letters of the alphabet, the numerals 0 to 9 and various punctuation symbols. In addition, 32 special control codes are provided for the control of data transmission and peripheral devices. The complete ASCII specification is given in Table 1.4. Referring to the table, the bits are numbered b_7, b_6, b_5, b_4, b_3, b_2, and b_1. Bits b_7, b_6 and b_5 define a column in the table and b_4, b_3, b_2 and b_1 define a row. The first two columns define control codes which are described in the table with two- or three-letter mnemonics.

Table 1.4 ASCII code

b7 b6 b5					0 0 0	0 0 1	0 1 0	0 1 1	1 0 0	1 0 1	1 1 0	1 1 1
b4	b3	b2	b1	Column→ Row↓	0	1	2	3	4	5	6	7
0	0	0	0	0	NUL	DLE	SP	0	@	P	'	p
0	0	0	1	1	SOH	DC1	!	1	A	Q	a	q
0	0	1	0	2	STX	DC2	"	2	B	R	b	r
0	0	1	1	3	ETX	DC3	#	3	C	S	c	s
0	1	0	0	4	EOT	DC4	$	4	D	T	d	t
0	1	0	1	5	ENQ	NAK	%	5	E	U	e	u
0	1	1	0	6	ACK	SYN	&	6	F	V	f	v
0	1	1	1	7	BEL	ETB	'	7	G	W	g	w
1	0	0	0	8	BS	CAN	(	8	H	X	h	x
1	0	0	1	9	HT	EM	)	9	I	Y	i	y
1	0	1	0	10	LF	SUB	*	:	J	Z	j	z
1	0	1	1	11	VT	ESC	+	;	K	[	k	{
1	1	0	0	12	FF	FS	,	<	L	\	l	¦
1	1	0	1	13	CR	GS	—	=	M	]	m	}
1	1	1	0	14	SO	RS	.	>	N	^	n	~
1	1	1	1	15	SI	US	/	?	O	—	o	DEL

Control codes

Abbreviations:

NUL	Null	FF	Form feed	CAN	Cancel
SOH	Start of heading	CR	Carriage return	EM	End of medium
STX	Start of text	SO	Shift out	SUB	Substitute
ETX	End of text	SI	Shift in	ESC	Escape
EOT	End of transmission	DLE	Data link escape	FS	File separator
ENQ	Enquiry	DC1	Device control 1	GS	Group separator
ACK	Acknowledge	DC2	Device control 2	RS	Record separator
BEL	Bell	DC3	Device control 3	US	Unit separator
BS	Backspace	DC4	Device control 4	SP	Space
HT	Horizontal tabulation	NAK	Negative acknowledge	DEL	Delete
LF	Line feed	ETB	End of transmission block		
VT	Vertical tabulation	SYN	Synchronous idle		

1.7 Error detection

It is often necessary to be able to check whether any errors have been introduced during transmission to and from a computer and sometimes within a computer. Since a binary digit can only be either a 1 or 0, simple methods of detecting the presence of errors can be devised. Consider as an example, the transmission of an ASCII-coded character represented by seven binary digits. If one bit becomes corrupted and changes from a 0 to a 1 or from a 1 to a 0, the number of 1's in the whole word will change. If the total number of 1's in the correct number were odd it would become even, and conversely an even number of 1's would become odd. Therefore if the transmitted word was always arranged to have, say, an even number of 1's, all single bit errors could be detected by checking whether there was an even or odd number of 1's in the received word. Always having an even number of 1's at the source of transmission can be achieved by appending an extra bit to the code, in the case of ASCII making an eight-bit code and setting this eighth bit to a 1 or 0 so as to make the total number of 1's even. An odd number of 1's in the received word would indicate an error. The scheme of appending an extra bit to make the total number of 1's even is known as the *even parity* scheme. An alternative, known as the *odd parity* scheme, appends a bit with a value such that the total number of 1's is odd. Any subsequent single bit error would result in an even number of 1's and this can be detected in a similar fashion as previously. Both odd and even parity methods are used. Odd and even parity methods will also detect multiple odd numbers of errors.

   Some codes have an inbuilt error detection mechanism. For example, the now rather little used *2-out-of-5* code encodes the numerals 0 to 9 with five digits such that the total number of 1's in all codes is two. Consequently, any single bit error would corrupt this characteristic. Methods of detecting multiple errors and methods of automatically correcting errors are described in Chapter 15, section 15.4.2.

1.8 Gray code

A variety of codes has been devised for particular reasons. One code of some importance is *Gray* code. Gray code has the property that only one bit changes from one number to the next number in the sequence, as shown in Table 1.5 for four bits. Gray code reduces the likelihood of unwanted transient changes occurring when changing from one code to the next code. A particular application is the encoding of the position of a continuously revolving shaft. The shaft is marked at various angular positions. Figure 1.1 shows markings in 4-bit Gray code. As the shaft revolves, markings are sensed which enable the position of the shaft to be determined. If binary code is used, a totally incorrect code might occur due to mechanical misalignment of the sensors or delays in the circuits when several changes are necessary such as from 0111 to 1000, where all four bits must change. With Gray code, only single changes are necessary between adjacent codes, which limits errors to one position. We shall use Gray code in asynchronous sequential

Table 1.5   Gray code

Decimal	Binary	Gray
0	0000	0000
1	0001	0001
2	0010	0011
3	0011	0010
4	0100	0110
5	0101	0111
6	0110	0101
7	0111	0100
8	1000	1100
9	1001	1101
10	1010	1111
11	1011	1110
12	1100	1010
13	1101	1011
14	1110	1001
15	1111	1000

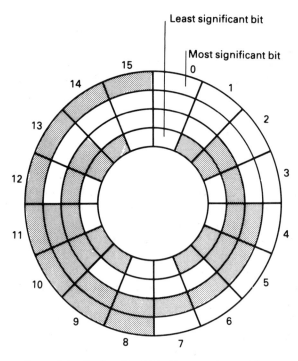

Figure 1.1   Shaft with 4-bit Gray code markings

circuit design (Chapter 11) to reduce the likelihood of unwanted transients occurring in logic systems designs. Gray code also occurs in the labelling of Karnaugh maps (Chapter 3).

Reference

1. *ANSI/IEEE Standard for Binary Floating-Point Arithmetic, Std 754-1985*, New York: IEEE, 1985.

Problems

1.1 Convert the following binary numbers into octal and hexadecimal:

(a) 101010101010
(b) 10000.000001

1.2 Convert the following hexadecimal numbers into octal:

(a) FE45
(b) 0.567
(c) F.FF

1.3 Convert the following decimal numbers into binary:

(a) 48729
(b) 666
(c) 0.7239
(d) 6.8941

1.4 Convert the following binary numbers into decimal:

(a) 11000
(b) 01010
(c) 0.00111
(d) 11.11

1.5 Verify mathematically that when two numbers in the 2's complement system are added, all combinations of positive and negative numbers, and combinations of relative magnitudes, compute correctly.

1.6 Verify mathematically that when two numbers in the 1's complement system are added, all combinations of positive and negative numbers, and combinations of relative magnitudes, compute correctly using the end-around carry mechanism (i.e. a 1 is added to the result if a carry is generated from the most significant stage).

1.7 Convert the following decimal numbers into binary and perform the operation shown using 2's complement arithmetic where appropriate:

(a) $67 - 5$
(b) $123 + 998 - 754$
(c) $45 - 124$
(d) $-78 - 23$

Confirm that the results are correct by converting them back into decimal.

1.8   Represent the following numbers in normalized floating point form, with a fractional sign plus magnitude mantissa and 7-bit unsigned biased exponent using the base of 2 and a bias of 64:

(a) 123567
(b) −45.89
(c) 0.00567

1.9   In a computer system, one floating point number employs two adjacent 24-bit words. The bits of these words are numbered B_0 through to B_{47}. B_0 is the least significant bit. B_{47} is the mantissa sign bit. B_8 to B_{46} is the mantissa considered as a binary fraction. B_0 to B_7 is an unsigned biased exponent using the base of 2 and a bias of 127. The floating point numbers are normalized and there is an assumed leading 1 in the mantissa. Deduce the approximate range of numbers that can be stored. What is the smallest number that can be stored? Give your answer in decimal assuming that 2^{10} is equal to 10^3.

1.10   Convert the following BCD numbers into binary and perform the operation shown, applying any correction process necessary to obtain the correct BCD result:

(a) 44 + 33
(b) 29 + 99
(c) 55 + 78

1.11   Deduce the value of an even parity bit added to the ASCII code for the character N. Repeat for the ASCII control operation NUL.

2 Boolean Algebra and Minimization

2.1 Boolean variables

We presented a study of number systems in Chapter 1 as this is fundamental to the design of digital systems. The binary number system is chosen for the number representation as this number system has only two types of digit, 0 and 1, which can be represented by two voltages. Having made this decision, we now need some mathematical methods to manipulate these binary quantities with a view to designing digital systems. Fortunately, such methods had been developed well before the advent of digital computers (the 1940s) by George Boole, a 19th-century mathematician. Boole [1] developed an algebra which we now call *Boolean algebra*. Claude Shannon [2] adapted this algebra for digital switching circuits. In (two-valued) Boolean algebra, variables only take on one of two values, 0 or 1, i.e. if a variable does not equal 0, it must equal 1 and if it does not equal 1, it must equal 0. The 1 value corresponds to binary 1 and the 0 value corresponds to binary 0. Sometimes a 1 is called *true* and a 0 called *false* from the earlier propositional (Boolean) algebra. (Propositional algebra could be used, for example, to determine whether a conclusion is correct following a series of statements. Such statements could be true or false.) Also two-value Boolean variables can be used to show whether a particular result of a computation has occurred and in this sense, 'true' and 'false' keep their original meaning. Boolean algebra does not itself restrict variables to two values, but this is done here as only two-valued Boolean algebra is applicable to digital systems.

As an example of a simple switching system, consider a heating system controlled by a room thermostat and an external frost thermostat. When the heating is switched on manually, heat is provided but only when the room temperature is below the setting on the room thermostat. Heat is also provided when the external frost thermostat indicates the external temperature is below $0\,^{\circ}\mathrm{C}$ and the room temperature is below the room thermostat setting (to protect against water in pipes freezing). We could allocate Boolean variables as follows:

(i) $H = 1$ if manual heating switch is on, otherwise $H = 0$
(ii) $R = 1$ if room temperature is below setting on room thermostat, otherwise $R = 0$

(iii) $F = 1$ if frost thermostat indicates external temperature below $0\,^\circ\text{C}$, otherwise $F = 0$

(iv) $S = 1$ if heat is to be supplied.

Therefore $S = 1$ when either $H = 1$ and $R = 1$ or when $F = 1$ and $R = 1$. We have Boolean notations to indicate the 'and' operation and the 'or' operation, namely $+$ and $\cdot$. The Boolean expression for S becomes:

$$S = H \cdot R + F \cdot R$$

From this expression we will be able to develop the appropriate switching circuit, as we shall see later.

Suppose we had defined F as:

$F = 1$ if frost thermostat indicates external temperature below $0\,^\circ\text{C}$, otherwise $F = 0$.

Then $S = 1$ when either $H = 1$ and $R = 1$ or when $F = 0$ and $R = 1$. In Boolean algebra, if a variable such as $F = 0$, the variable $\bar{F} = 1$ (and if $F = 1$, $\bar{F} = 0$). Hence $S = 1$ when either $H = 1$ and $R = 1$ or when $\bar{F} = 1$ and $R = 1$, i.e.

$$S = H \cdot R + \bar{F} \cdot R$$

As an example of Boolean variables applied to binary numbers, consider the addition of two binary digits as given in Chapter 1, section 1.3.1. SUM $= 1$ when either $A = 1$ and $B = 0$ or when $A = 0$ and $B = 1$. CARRY $= 1$ when $A = 1$ and $B = 1$. Hence the Boolean expressions for SUM and CARRY are:

$$\text{SUM} = A \cdot \bar{B} + \bar{A} \cdot B$$
$$\text{CARRY} = A \cdot B$$

Again we will be able to develop the circuits from these Boolean expressions. Circuits developed from Boolean expressions are considered in Chapter 3. Firstly, let us formally define the three fundamental Boolean (*logical*) operations.

2.2 Boolean operators and relationships

2.2.1 NOT, AND and OR operators

(a) NOT operator

The NOT operator operates on a single variable say A, and is defined as follows:

If $A = 0$ then 'NOT' $A = 1$
If $A = 1$ then 'NOT' $A = 0$

i.e. the operation produces the opposite binary state to that of A. 'NOT' A is written as $\bar{A}$. $\bar{A}$ is the *complement* or *inverse* of A. A truth table can be used to show a Boolean function. This table lists all the possible values of the variables and the results of the operation. A NOT operation truth table is shown in Table 2.1. Note

Table 2.1   Truth table of NOT operation

A	$\bar{A}$
0	1
1	0

that a single variable can take on only one of two values, either 0 or 1, so there are two entries in the table.

(b) AND operator

The AND operator operates on two variables, say A and B, and is defined as follows:

>   If A and B are both a 1 then A 'AND' $B = 1$
>   otherwise A 'AND' $B = 0$

A 'AND' B is written as $A \cdot B$. The operation is sometimes called Boolean multiplication and as in ordinary multiplication, the $\cdot$ is often omitted. We will include the $\cdot$ only where necessary for clarity. The AND operation truth table is shown in Table 2.2(a). Notice that in truth tables, the values of the 'input' variables are listed in increasing binary order. More variables can be introduced, for example $A \cdot B \cdot C$. The truth table for three variables is shown in Table 2.2(b). Three variables can take on any of eight combinations of values. Irrespective of the number of variables, the result is a 1 only if all the variables are a 1, otherwise the result is a 0, i.e.

>   If A and B and C and D and ... are all a 1, then $A \cdot B \cdot C \cdot D... = 1$
>   otherwise $A \cdot B \cdot C \cdot D... = 0$

The English word 'and' is taken literally, i.e. A and B and C, A and B and C and D, etc. The definition for several variables follows directly from the repeated application of the basic definition for two variables.

Table 2.2   Truth tables of AND operation

A	B	$A \cdot B$	A	B	C	$A \cdot B \cdot C$
0	0	0	0	0	0	0
0	1	0	0	0	1	0
1	0	0	0	1	0	0
1	1	1	0	1	1	0
			1	0	0	0
(a) Two variables			1	0	1	0
			1	1	0	0
			1	1	1	1

(b) Three variables

Table 2.3 Truth tables of OR operation

A	B	A + B
0	0	0
0	1	1
1	0	1
1	1	1

(a) Two variables

A	B	C	A + B + C
0	0	0	0
0	0	1	1
0	1	0	1
0	1	1	1
1	0	0	1
1	0	1	1
1	1	0	1
1	1	1	1

(b) Three variables

(c) OR operator

The OR operator operates on two variables A and B and is defined as:

If A or B or both are a 1 then A 'OR' $B = 1$
otherwise A 'OR' $B = 0$

A 'OR' B is written as $A + B$. This is sometimes called Boolean addition. The OR operation truth table is shown in Table 2.3(a). Again more variables can be introduced, for example $A + B + C$, $A + B + C + D$ i.e:

If A or B or C or D... is a 1 (including more than one) then
$$A + B + C + D + ... = 1$$
otherwise $A + B + C + D + ... = 0$

Table 2.3(b) shows the OR operation with three variables. Irrespective of the number of variables, the result is a 1 if any of the variables is a 1. The English word 'or' is taken literally, i.e. A or B or C, A or B or C or D. The definition for several variables follows directly from the repeated application of the basic definition for two variables.

2.2.2 Basic relationships and laws

(a) Relationships

The following can be easily proved from the definition of the operators or their truth tables:

1.   (i) $A \cdot \bar{A} = 0$
   (ii) $A + \bar{A} = 1$
   (iii) $\bar{\bar{A}} = A$
2.   (i) $A \cdot 1 = A$
   (ii) $A \cdot 0 = 0$
   (iii) $A \cdot A = A$

3.   (i) $A + 1 = 1$
     (ii) $A + 0 = A$
     (iii) $A + A = A$

The relationships can be proved by substituting all possible combinations of values of the variables and deducing the result in each case, i.e. proof by perfect induction. Proof by perfect induction is particularly suitable for Boolean expressions containing a few Boolean variables as each variable can only take on one of two values, and it is feasible to try each value. For example, in the first relationship 1(i), $\bar{A} \cdot \bar{A} = 0$, A can be a 0, and then $\bar{A} = 1$. In that case, we have $0 \cdot 1 = 0$ from the truth table of the AND operation. The alternative value for A, a 1, and hence $\bar{A} = 0$, leads to $1 \cdot 0 = 0$. Therefore irrespective of the value of A, the result is a 0. It is left to the reader to prove the other relationships in a similar fashion. Where appropriate, the relationships can be extended to more than one variable, for example relationship 3(i), $A + 1 = 1$, can be extended to $A + B + C + 1 = 1$.

(b) Laws

There are three general algebraic laws relating to the way expressions can be written and their interpretation. These laws can be applied to both $\cdot$ and $+$:

(i) Commutative law
This states that the order of variables is unimportant, e.g.:

$$A \cdot B = B \cdot A$$

and

$$A + B = B + A$$

(ii) Associative law
This states that the grouping of variables is unimportant, e.g.:

$$A \cdot (B \cdot C) = (A \cdot B) \cdot C = A \cdot B \cdot C$$

and

$$A + (B + C) = (A + B) + C = A + B + C$$

(iii) Distributive law
This states that an operator 'distributes' its operation throughout variables within parentheses, e.g.

$$A \cdot (B + C) = A \cdot B + A \cdot C$$
$$A + (B \cdot C) = (A + B) \cdot (A + C)$$

In the first instance above, the $\cdot$ operation operates on both B and C while in the second instance the $+$ operation operates on both B and C. The first instance is true in ordinary algebra but the second is not true in ordinary algebra.

(iv) De Morgan's theorem

De Morgan's theorem states that:

$$\overline{A + B + C} \ldots = \overline{A} \cdot \overline{B} \cdot \overline{C} \ldots$$
$$\overline{\overline{A} + \overline{B} + \overline{C}} \ldots = A \cdot B \cdot C \ldots$$

for any number of variables. De Morgan's theorem as given above can easily be proved for two variables by substituting all combinations of the variables. Then repeated substitution can lead to a proof for any number of variables. For example, let us assume the first form of De Morgan's theorem has been proved for two variables, then replacing $B + C$ for B in $\overline{A + B} = \overline{A} \cdot \overline{B}$, we get $\overline{A + B + C} = \overline{A} \cdot \overline{(B + C)} = \overline{A} \cdot \overline{B} \cdot \overline{C}$ by applying De Morgan's theorem with two variables. This process can be repeated for any number of variables. Alternatively, we can note that $\overline{A + B + C} \ldots$ to any number of variables can only be a 1 if all the variables are a 0. Similarly, $\overline{A} \cdot \overline{B} \cdot \overline{C} \ldots$ to any number of variables can only be a 1 when all the variables are a 0. Hence the two terms must be equivalent.

De Morgan's theorem is very useful in simplifying Boolean expressions, as we will see later. It can be generalized to:

$$f(A, B, C, \ldots +, \cdot) = \bar{f}(\bar{A}, \bar{B}, \bar{C}, \ldots, \cdot, +)$$

i.e. the inverse function can be obtained by complementing all the variables, changing all $\cdot$'s to $+$'s and all $+$'s to $\cdot$'s.

(v) Principle of duality

Each relationship, law or theorem has a dual, obtained by replacing every occurrence of 1 by 0, 0 by 1, $+$ by $\cdot$ and $\cdot$ by $+$. Duals have been given above. For example, the dual of $A + 0 = A$ is $A \cdot 1 = A$. Once we can prove one relationship, the dual relationship can be assumed to be true without proof. The existence of duality between the two operators AND and OR can be seen by changing all 1's to 0's and all 0's to 1's in the truth table of one operator, whereupon the truth table of the other operator is obtained. One must be careful not to confuse the principle of duality with De Morgan's theorem.

2.2.3 NAND and NOR operators

Of the three basic Boolean operators, AND, OR and NOT, either the OR operator or the AND operator is unnecessary. From De Morgan's theorem, $A + B = \overline{\overline{A} \cdot \overline{B}}$. Therefore all occurrences of $A + B$ can be replaced by $\overline{\overline{A} \cdot \overline{B}}$ and the OR operation can be eliminated. Alternatively, using $A \cdot B = \overline{\overline{A} + \overline{B}}$, all occurrences of $A \cdot B$ can be replaced with $\overline{\overline{A} + \overline{B}}$ and the AND operation can be eliminated. However, we cannot dispense with the NOT operator. An operator can be introduced which combines AND and NOT which is known as the NAND ('NOT-AND') operator.

(a) NAND operator

The NAND operator performs the AND operation followed by the NOT operation as described for two and three variables in Table 2.4. There is a special symbol for NAND, $\uparrow$, i.e. A'NAND'B is written as $A \uparrow B$ but this is rarely used in engineering. Normally A'NAND'B is written $\overline{AB}$.

Equally, the OR and NOT operations can be combined to created a 'NOT-OR' operator called a NOR operator.

(b) NOR operator

The NOR operator performs the OR operation followed by the NOT operation as described for two and three variables in Table 2.5. Again there is a special symbol, $\downarrow$, which is rarely used in engineering; A'NOR'B being written simply as $\overline{A + B}$.

2.2.4 Exclusive-OR/NOR operators

The OR operation is sometimes called 'inclusive-OR' because the result is true when either of the two operands A and B is a 1, including both A and B a 1. The

Table 2.4   Truth tables of NAND operation

A	B	$\overline{A \cdot B}$
0	0	1
0	1	1
1	0	1
1	1	0

(a) Two variables

A	B	C	$\overline{A \cdot B \cdot C}$
0	0	0	1
0	0	1	1
0	1	0	1
0	1	1	1
1	0	0	1
1	0	1	1
1	1	0	1
1	1	1	0

(b) Three variables

Table 2.5   Truth tables of NOR operation

A	B	$\overline{A + B}$
0	0	1
0	1	0
1	0	0
1	1	0

(a) Two variables

A	B	C	$\overline{A + B + C}$
0	0	0	1
0	0	1	0
0	1	0	0
0	1	1	0
1	0	0	0
1	0	1	0
1	1	0	0
1	1	1	0

(b) Three variables

'exclusive-OR' operator operating on two variables A and B is true if A or B is a 1 but not when both A and B are a 1, i.e. it excludes both A and B being a 1. A symbol for the exclusive-OR function is $\oplus$. The operation is described in Table 2.6. The operation can be derived as a function in terms of AND and OR from the truth table by examining the occurrences of 1's in the result. We can see that the result is a 1 when $A = 0$ and $B = 1$ or when $A = 1$ and $B = 0$. Therefore the exclusive-OR function is:

$$A \oplus B = \bar{A}B + A\bar{B}$$

The truth table of the inverse operation, 'exclusive-NOR', is given in Table 2.7. The exclusive-NOR function is true if both A and B are the same and is false if A and B are different. The function is also called 'equivalence' ($\equiv$) and performs the comparison function of two binary digits. It is given in terms of AND and OR as:

$$\overline{A \oplus B} = AB + \bar{A}\bar{B}$$

2.2.5 Logical devices

The electrical circuits which perform logical operations are called *gates*. The Boolean values are usually represented by voltages, one voltage to represent a 0 and another voltage to represent a 1. For example $+5V$ could represent a logical 1 and 0V could represent a logical 0. To give some immunity against electrical interference (noise, further details in Chapter 5 and Chapter 14) in the system, a voltage range is specified for each logic level. For example, a 0 could be represented by any voltage between 0V and 0.8V, and a 1 could be represented by any voltage between 2V and 5V. If a 1 is represented by a voltage which is more positive than the voltage representing a 0, the representation is known as *positive logic representation*. If a

Table 2.6   Truth table of exclusive-OR operation

A	B	$A \oplus B$
0	0	0
0	1	1
1	0	1
1	1	0

Table 2.7   Truth table of exclusive-NOR operation

A	B	$\overline{A \oplus B}$
0	0	1
0	1	0
1	0	0
1	1	1

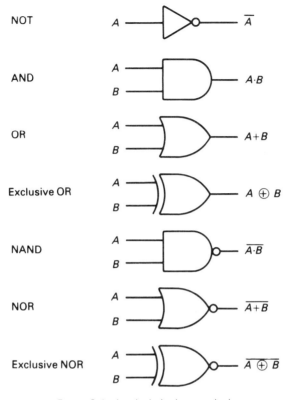

Figure 2.1 Logical device symbols

0 is represented by a voltage which is more positive than the voltage representing a 1, the representation is known as *negative logic representation*. In the past, some computers used negative logic representation but now computers, including microprocessors, generally use positive logic representation. However, logic representation is only a convention; changing from one convention to the other in the same system involves changing all 1's to 0's and all 0's to 1's. An AND gate with positive logic representation becomes an OR gate in negative logic representation, and an OR gate becomes an AND gate.

Symbols widely used for logic gates are shown in Fig. 2.1. The actual circuit details of the logic devices are described in Chapter 5.

2.3 Boolean expressions

2.3.1 Sum-of-product and product-of-sum expressions

A Boolean expression contains Boolean variables linked with Boolean operators. There are two standard forms of Boolean expressions, the *sum-of-product* form and the *product-of-sum* form. In the sum-of-product form, variables are connected with AND operators to create Boolean terms which are then connected together with OR operations as in:

$$ABC + DEF + GHI$$

where A, B, C, D, E, F, G, H and I are Boolean variables.

In the product-of-sum expression, variables are connected together using OR operators to form terms which are then connected with AND operators as in:

$$(A + B + C)(D + E + F)(G + H + I)$$

An expression with every variable appearing in each term is called a *canonical* expression. For example:

$$f(A, B, C, D) = AB\bar{C}D + A\bar{B}CD + A\bar{B}C\bar{D}$$

is a canonical sum-of-product expression. A sum-of-product expression can be converted to canonical form by multiplying each term by $(A + \bar{A})(B + \bar{B})(C + \bar{C})\dots$, where $A, B, C\dots$ are the variables not in the original term. Then the expression is expanded, for example the expression:

$$f(A, B, C) = AC + A\bar{B}$$

expands to:

$$= A(B + \bar{B})C + A\bar{B}(C + \bar{C})$$
$$= ABC + A\bar{B}C + A\bar{B}C + A\bar{B}\bar{C}$$
$$= ABC + A\bar{B}C + A\bar{B}\bar{C}$$

One method of converting a product-of-sum expression to canonical form is to first find the inverse function, $\bar{f}$, by De Morgan's theorem, apply the above procedure, and then convert back to f.

The product term in a canonical sum-of-product expression is called a *minterm*. For example, ABC is a minterm in the canonical sum of product expression above. The sum term in a canonical product-of-sum expression is called a *maxterm*. Minterms and maxterms can be given numbers for identification purposes. These numbers are obtained by considering variables as binary 1's and their complements as binary 0's as shown in Table 2.8. Sometimes the maxterms are numbered with the variables as binary 0's and the complements as binary 1's ('inverse numbering') as this leads to a simpler conversion between sum-of-product and product-of-sum expressions.

2.3.2 Conversion between canonical sum-of-product form and canonical product-of-sum form

Canonical sum-of-product terms and expressions can be converted into product-of-sum form and vice versa by algebraic means. Firstly, let us consider the conversion

Table 2.8   Minterm and maxterm notation

Minterm	Number	Product	Maxterm	Number	Sum
$\bar{A} \cdot \bar{B} \cdot \bar{C}$	000 0	P_0	$\bar{A} + \bar{B} + \bar{C}$	000 0	S_0
$\bar{A} \cdot \bar{B} \cdot C$	001 1	P_1	$\bar{A} + \bar{B} + C$	001 1	S_1
$\bar{A} \cdot B \cdot \bar{C}$	010 2	P_2	$\bar{A} + B + \bar{C}$	010 2	S_2
$\bar{A} \cdot B \cdot C$	011 3	P_3	$\bar{A} + B + C$	011 3	S_3
$A \cdot \bar{B} \cdot \bar{C}$	100 4	P_4	$A + \bar{B} + \bar{C}$	100 4	S_4
$A \cdot \bar{B} \cdot C$	101 5	P_5	$A + \bar{B} + C$	101 5	S_5
$A \cdot B \cdot \bar{C}$	110 6	P_6	$A + B + \bar{C}$	110 6	S_6
$A \cdot B \cdot C$	111 7	P_7	$A + B + C$	111 7	S_7

of individual terms:

(a) Relationship between minterms (product terms) and maxterms (sum terms)

By examining Table 2.8 we find that:

$$\bar{P}_0 = \overline{\bar{A}\bar{B}\bar{C}} = A + B + C = S_7$$

(For inverse numbering, $\bar{P}_0 = S_0$.) In general, the relationship between n variable minterms and maxterms is:

$$\bar{P}_i = S_{2n-1-i} \qquad (1)$$

(For inverse numbering, $\bar{P}_i = S_i$.)

(b) Minterm relationship

The Boolean summation (OR operation) of all minterms is given by:

$$\sum_{i=0}^{2^n - 1} P_i = 1 \qquad (2)$$

i.e.

$$\Sigma \text{ (all possible product terms)} = 1$$

because one of the minterms must equal 1. If the function is f, then $f + \bar{f} = 1$ (one of the basic relationships). Therefore

$$\bar{f} = \Sigma \text{ (minterms not in } f) \qquad (3)$$

(c) Canonical sum-of-product expression to canonical product-of-sum expressions

Taking an example, let us convert the three-variable canonical sum-of-product function:

$$f = \Sigma \ (P_0, P_2, P_3, P_4)$$

into canonical product-of-sum form. We shall reduce the canonical notation to:

$$f = \Sigma \ (0, 2, 3, 4)$$

From (3) we have:

$$\bar{f} = \Sigma \ (1, 5, 6, 7) = P_1 + P_5 + P_6 + P_7$$

Therefore

$$f = \overline{P_1 + P_5 + P_6 + P_7}$$

and by De Morgan's theorem:

$$f = \bar{P_1}\bar{P_5}\bar{P_6}\bar{P_7}$$

Hence, from (1) we have:

$$f = S_6 S_2 S_1 S_0 = \Pi \ (6, 2, 1, 0)$$

(or with inverse numbering:

$$f = \Pi \ (1, 5, 6, 7)$$

i.e. with inverse numbering, the equivalent product-of-sum expression contains the 'numbers' not in the sum-of-product expression).

(d) Maxterm relationship

The Boolean multiplication (AND) of all maxterms is given by:

$$\prod_{i=0}^{2^n - 1} S_i = 0 \tag{4}$$

i.e.

$$\Pi \ (\text{all possible sum terms}) = 0$$

because one of the maxterms must equal 0. Also we have the basic relationship, $f\bar{f} = 0$. Therefore:

$$\Pi \ (\text{sum terms in } f)(\text{sum terms not in } f) = 0$$

and

$$\bar{f} = \Pi \ (\text{sum terms not in } f) \tag{5}$$

(e) Canonical product-of-sum expressions to canonical sum-of-product expressions

As an example let us convert the three-variable canonical product-of-sum expression:

$$f = \Pi \ (1, 2, 3, 4)$$

to canonical sum-of-product form. From (5) we have:

$$\bar{f} = \Pi \ (0, 5, 6, 7) = S_0 S_5 S_6 S_7$$

Therefore:

$$f = \overline{S_0 S_5 S_6 S_7}$$

From De Morgan's theorem we obtain:

$$f = \bar{S}_0 + \bar{S}_5 + \bar{S}_6 + \bar{S}_7$$

From (1) we have:

$$f = P_7 + P_2 + P_1 + P_0 = \Sigma \ (7, 2, 1, 0)$$

(or with inverse numbering:

$$f = \Sigma \ (0, 5, 6, 7)$$

As in (c), with inverse numbering, the equivalent sum-of-product expression contains the 'numbers' not in the product-of-sum expression. Also we see that with this numbering, the inverse function ($\bar{f}$) in one form has the same numbers as the true function (f) in the other form.)

2.4 Boolean minimization

The aim of Boolean minimization is to reduce Boolean expressions to their simplest form. The simplest form is one with the least number of terms and the least number of variables in each term, if this is possible. There may be other criteria depending upon the application, for example number of gates required for the final implementation and how the gates are interconnected. It is usually preferable to have the number of gates between the inputs to the circuit and the outputs at a minimum to reduce the overall signal delay and the chances of unwanted transient signals occurring. The number of gates between the input and output defines the *levels of gating*. Two levels of gating is often a design aim, but may not always be feasible.

2.4.1 Boolean minimization by algebraic means

Minimization can be achieved through the use of Boolean relationships and theorems such as those given previously. The following are some methods that can be applied:

(a) Grouping of terms

Terms can be grouped together in a manner that leads to reduction through the use of a particular relationship, for example:

$$A + AB + BC = A(1 + B) + BC$$
$$= A + BC \quad \text{since } 1 + B = 1$$

Terms can be repeated in an expression without affecting the expression and grouping may then be applied repeatedly using the same term grouped together with more than one other term, for example:

$$AD + ABD + \overline{ADC} = AD + AD + ABD + \overline{ADC}$$

$$\text{because } AD + AD = AD$$

$$= AD(1 + B) + AD + \overline{ADC}$$

$$= AD + AD + C$$

$$= AD + C$$

(b) Multiplication of terms by redundant variables

The most common approach here is to multiply terms by $(X + \bar{X})$ where X is a variable not occurring in the term. This does not logically alter the expression and it may lead to simplification, for example:

$$AB + A\bar{C} + BC = AB(C + \bar{C}) + A\bar{C} + BC$$

$$= ABC + AB\bar{C} + A\bar{C} + BC$$

$$= BC(1 + A) + A\bar{C}(1 + B)$$

$$= A\bar{C} + BC$$

(c) Using De Morgan's theorem

Complex expressions can be often simplified by the repeated use of De Morgan's theorem, applied to various terms and groups of terms, for example:

$$\overline{(\overline{AB}C + \overline{ACD})} + B\bar{C} = (\bar{A} + B + \bar{C}) + (\bar{A} + \bar{C} + \bar{D}) + B\bar{C}$$

$$= \overline{(\bar{A} + B + \bar{C} + D)} + B\bar{C}$$

$$= \overline{(\bar{A} + B + \bar{C} + \bar{D})}$$

$$= A\bar{B}CD$$

It may also be possible to use the general form of De Morgan's theorem applied once to obtain the inverse function which may then simplify immediately.

(d) By substitution of all values

Sometimes it is easier to substitute all the possible values of variables in the expression and deduce the solution from the result. For example, the truth table of the expression $A + \bar{A}B$ is given in Table 2.9. From this, we can see that the expression, $A + \bar{A}B$, is a 1 when $A = 1$ or $B = 1$ or both A and B are a 1, so that the solution must be $A + B$.

Table 2.9 Truth table of function $A + \bar{A}B$

A	B	$A + \bar{A}B$
0	0	0
0	1	1
1	0	1
1	1	1

2.4.2 Karnaugh map minimization method

(a) The Karnaugh map

A *Karnaugh map* consists of a grid of squares, each square representing one canonical minterm combination of the variables or their inverse, e.g. $\bar{A}\bar{B}C$, $\bar{A}\bar{B}C$, $\bar{A}B\bar{C}$ etc. The map is arranged with squares representing minterms which differ by only one variable to be adjacent both vertically and horizontally. Therefore $A\bar{B}\bar{C}$ would be adjacent to $\bar{A}\bar{B}\bar{C}$ and would also be adjacent to $AB\bar{C}$ and $AB\bar{C}$. Figure 2.2 shows the Karnaugh map for three variables. Squares on one edge of the map are regarded as adjacent to those on the opposite edge. The squares are labelled by one of two means, both of which are shown in the figure.

Firstly, the top left corner is labelled with the variables as shown and the two edges from this corner are labelled with 1,0 combinations, 1 to indicate the variable is true and 0 to indicate the variable is false (complemented). For example, the top left square is allocated to $\bar{A}\bar{B}\bar{C}$ and all variables are false. Above the square, there is 00 to indicate that B and C are false and along the edge 0 to indicate A is false. We note that the numbers on the top edge are in Gray code (Chapter 1, section 1.7). This will be also the case for maps with larger numbers of variables, on both edges.

The second form of labelling groups those squares which have a common variable. For example, the middle four squares all have the variable C true, and this is labelled accordingly. The right four squares have B true as the common variable and the bottom row of four squares have A true as the common variable.

It is sometimes useful to know the minterm number associated with each square. Figure 2.3 shows two-, three- and four-variable Karnaugh maps with the minterm

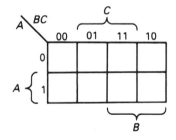

Figure 2.2 Three-variable Karnaugh map

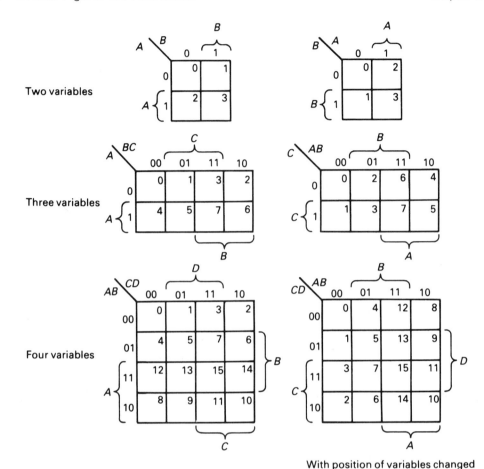

Figure 2.3 Two-, three- and four-variable Karnaugh maps with minterm numbers

numbers included. Variables can, of course, be transposed. Two common arrangements are shown in the figure.

(b) Minimization technique

The expression to be minimized should generally be in sum-of-product form. If necessary, the conversion processes described previously are applied to create the sum-of-product form. The expression need not be in canonical form but let us first assume that it is in canonical form. The function is 'mapped' onto the Karnaugh map by marking a 1 in those squares corresponding to the terms in the expression to be simplified. The other squares may be filled with 0's. Thus, the function is described on the map.

Pairs of 1's on the map which are adjacent are combined using the theorem:

$$P(A + \bar{A}) = P$$

where P is any Boolean expression. If two pairs are also adjacent, then these can also be combined using the same theorem. The minimization procedure consists of recognizing those pairs and multiple pairs. These are circled indicating reduced terms. Groups which can be circled are those which have two 1's, four 1's, eight 1's, etc. Figure 2.4 shows some possibilities on two-, three- and four-variable Karnaugh

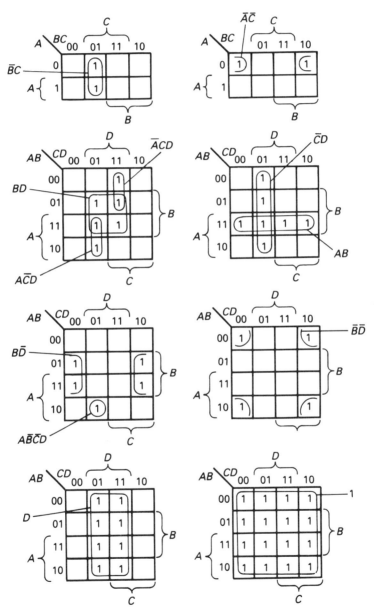

Figure 2.4 Examples of groupings on Karnaugh maps

maps. Note that because squares on one edge of the map are considered adjacent to those on the opposite edge, groups can be formed with these squares. Groups are allowed to overlap. The objective is to cover all the 1's on the map in the fewest number of groups and to create the largest groups to do this.

Once all the possible groups have been formed, the corresponding terms are identified. A group of two 1's eliminates one variable from the original minterm while a group of four 1's eliminates two variables and a group of eight 1's eliminates three variables. The variables eliminated are those which are different in the original minterms of the group.

For our first design problem, consider the problem of designing a combinational logic circuit which accepts two 2-bit numbers, A_1A_0 and B_1B_0, and generates a single output, Z, which is a 1 output only when A is greater than B. Table 2.10 can be derived from the problem specification. There are six instances when A is greater than B, namely when $A_1A_0 = 01$ and $B_1B_0 = 00$, $A_1A_0 = 10$ and $B_1B_0 = 00$ or 01, $A_1A_0 = 11$ and $B_1B_0 = 00$, 01 or 10. From the table, we can obtain the Karnaugh map for Z as shown in Fig. 2.5(a). This minimizes to:

$$Z = \bar{B}_1 A_1 + \bar{B}_0 A_1 A_0 + \bar{B}_0 \bar{B}_1 A_0$$

A circuit realization is shown in Fig. 2.5(b).

(c) Don't care conditions

If a certain combination of variables cannot occur or it does not matter what the outputs are if the combination does occur, the combination is known as a *don't care*

Table 2.10 Truth table of a comparator

A_1	A_0	B_1	B_0	Z
0	0	0	0	0
0	0	0	1	0
0	0	1	0	0
0	0	1	1	0
0	1	0	0	1
0	1	0	1	0
0	1	1	0	0
0	1	1	1	0
1	0	0	0	1
1	0	0	1	1
1	0	1	0	0
1	0	1	1	0
1	1	0	0	1
1	1	0	1	1
1	1	1	0	1
1	1	1	1	0

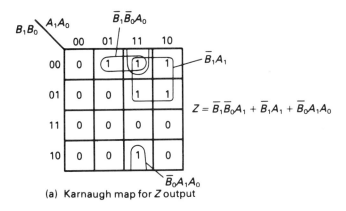

(a) Karnaugh map for Z output

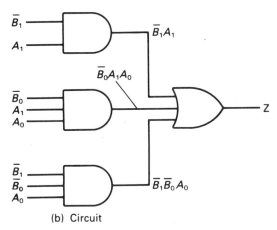

(b) Circuit

Figure 2.5 Comparator logic circuit design

condition. Don't care conditions are marked on the Karnaugh map as X's. Each X can be considered as either a 0 or 1, whichever is best for minimization. A function with one or more don't care conditions is called an *incompletely specified function*.

Don't care conditions come about because of some physical constraint in the system. For example, consider the design of a circuit which generates the even parity bit for a 4-bit binary coded decimal (BCD) digit. (In practice, parity bits are not normally added to less than 8-bit words.) The circuit has four inputs to enter the BCD digit and one output, the parity bit. Assuming that a valid BCD digit is entered, the combinations 1010 (10 decimal), 1011 (11 decimal), 1100 (12 decimal), 1101 (13 decimal), 1110 (14 decimal) and 1111 (15 decimal) do not occur and can be considered as 'don't cares'. The parity bit is a 1 whenever there are an odd number of 1's in the BCD number, which creates an even number of 1's in all. The parity function is shown in Fig. 2.6(a). This function is minimized taking some of the don't cares as 1's and some as 0's, resulting in the reduced expression shown, and the circuit in Fig. 2.6(b).

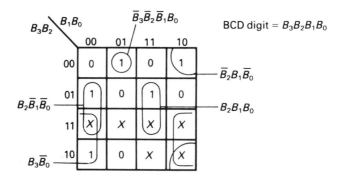

$$P = \bar{B_3}\bar{B_2}\bar{B_1}B_0 + \bar{B_2}B_1\bar{B_0} + B_2B_1B_0 + B_3\bar{B_0} + B_2\bar{B_1}\bar{B_0}$$

(a) Karnaugh map for output, P

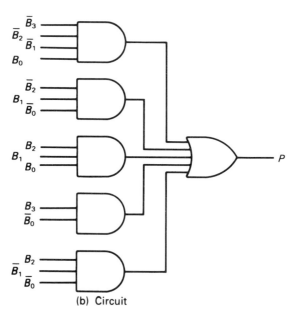

(b) Circuit

Figure 2.6 BCD parity generator logic circuit design

(d) Function not in canonical form

It is not necessary to convert the original function into canonical form before minimization. Each term in the function can be mapped onto the Karnaugh map directly, noting that a term with one variable missing maps onto two adjacent squares, a term with two variables missing maps onto four squares, etc., just as the minimization procedure identifies a term with one variable omitted for two squares, a term with two variables omitted for four squares, etc.

(e) Large Karnaugh maps

A property of Karnaugh maps is that an n-variable map can be a direct extension of an $(n-1)$-variable map. A 4-variable map can be composed of two 3-variable maps. One is a mirror image drawn below the other. The fourth variable is assigned to the mirror image. A 5-variable map can be drawn taking a 4-variable map and placing another mirror image map next to it (or below it). Thus any size of Karnaugh map can be constructed by drawing a mirror image map by the side of or below the original map. On 5-variable (and larger) Karnaugh maps, it is necessary to combine any squares in one half with squares in the mirror image as shown in Fig. 2.7. Generally it becomes increasingly difficult to recognize all possible groupings. The Quine–McCluskey method described in section 2.4.3 overcomes this problem.

(f) Technical terms

The following are some technical terms which can be applied to the Karnaugh map.

(i) Prime implicant
This is the name given to the groups formed on the map. This may include groups not actually necessary in the final solution.

(ii) Essential prime implicants
This is the name given to the groups which include at least one 1 not covered by any other group. It is clear that the solution must include the essential prime implicants.

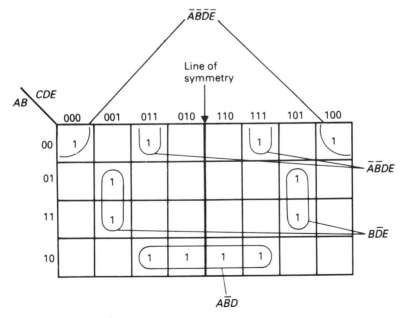

Figure 2.7 Five variable Karnaugh maps with examples of groups

(iii) Non-essential prime implicants

This is the name given to the prime implicants which are not essential but nevertheless cover 1's on the map. For example, it may be possible to cover a 1 in two ways, each with a different non-essential prime implicant. One of the non-essential prime implicants would be necessary in the solution to cover the 1.

(iv) Redundant prime implicants

Non-essential prime implicants which only cover 1's already covered by essential prime implicants are called *essentially redundant prime implicants* and are unnecessary. Sub-groups within a group are also redundant and need not be considered.

From these definitions, it can be seen that the minimal solution is given by all the essential prime implicants plus a careful selection of the non-essential prime implicants. An example is shown in Fig. 2.8. The expression to be minimized is:

$$f(A, B, C, D) = \bar{A}\bar{B}\bar{C}D + \bar{A}\bar{B}CD + \bar{A}B\bar{C}D + \bar{A}BC\bar{D} + \bar{A}BCD + A\bar{B}\bar{C}\bar{D}$$
$$+ A\bar{B}\bar{C}D + AB\bar{C}\bar{D} + AB\bar{C}D + ABC\bar{D}$$

The prime implicants are:

Essential prime implicants:	$A\bar{C}, \bar{A}D$
Non-essential prime implicants:	$\bar{A}BC, BC\bar{D}, AB\bar{D}$
Redundant prime implicant:	$\bar{C}D$

Complete cover of the 1's can be achieved by choosing the essential prime implicants together with the non-essential prime implicants $\bar{A}BC$ and $AB\bar{D}$ or the non-essential prime implicant $BC\bar{D}$. The minimal cover is obtained by choosing the non-essential prime implicant $BC\bar{D}$. Hence the minimal solution is given by $A\bar{C} + \bar{A}D + BC\bar{D}$.

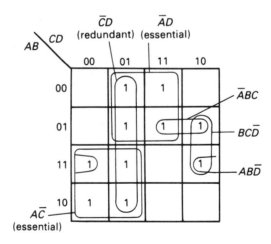

Figure 2.8 Prime implicants on a Karnaugh map

(g) Map-entered variables

The Karnaugh map method becomes quite difficult to use when there are more than about four or five variables, but it can be extended to cope with a few extra variables by using *map-entered variables* (MEVs). To take a simple example, suppose we have the four-variable function:

$$f(A, B, C, D) = \Sigma \ (3, 4, 5, 7, 8, 11, 12, 15)$$
$$= \bar{A}\bar{B}CD + \bar{A}B\bar{C}\bar{D} + \bar{A}B\bar{C}D + \bar{A}BCD$$
$$+ \ A\bar{B}\bar{C}\bar{D} + A\bar{B}CD + AB\bar{C}\bar{D} + ABCD$$

This function would normally be mapped onto a conventional Karnaugh map as shown in Fig. 2.9(a), leading to the minimized function:

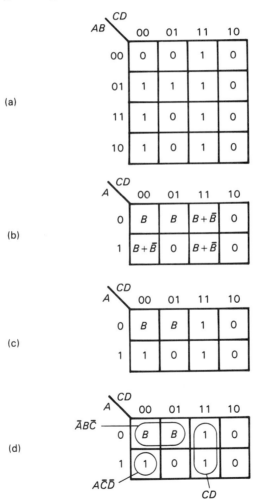

Figure 2.9 Minimization using map-entered variable method

$$f = A\bar{C}\bar{D} + \bar{A}B\bar{C} + CD$$

In the MEV method, one or more variables are identified to be *map-entered variables*. The MEV method is especially useful when some variables are 'infrequently used' (do not occur in most terms within the expression). For the function, f, we select the variable B as an entered variable, B being the least used. (However, a solution can be obtained after selecting any term, and the selection of terms may be simply from those that are most convenient.) A three-variable Karnaugh map will be used for A, C and D, mapping the appropriate B term on to squares of the map to complete the minterm identification. Doing this, we get the MEV map shown in Fig. 2.9(b), which reduces to Fig. 2.9(c) because $B + \bar{B} = 1$. Of course, we could have drawn Fig. 2.9(c) directly. In any event, it is important to read 1's entered on the MEV map as $B + \bar{B}$ in the following minimization procedure:

As with the conventional Karnaugh map, adjacent terms are grouped together in a 'looping', procedure. The MEV terms are considered first and the 1's afterwards. The procedure leads to Fig. 2.9(d). The reduced expression can be read off the map as in the conventional Karnaugh map but with the entered variables

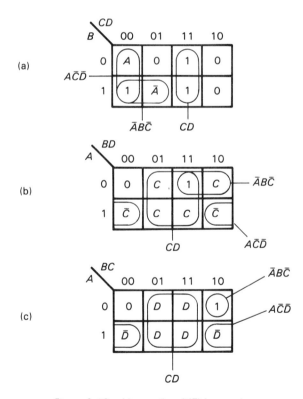

Figure 2.10 Alternative MEV mapping

included as necessary. The reduced expression in Fig. 2.9(d), $f = \bar{A}B\bar{C} + CD + A\bar{C}\bar{D}$, is obtained as follows:

$$f = \bar{A}B\bar{C} \qquad \text{(covering the two } B\text{'s)}$$
$$+$$
$$CD \qquad \text{(covering two 1's)}$$
$$+$$
$$A\bar{C}\bar{D} \qquad \text{(covering the remaining 1).}$$

In all cases, $B + \bar{B}$ implicit in a 1 must be covered.

Figure 2.10(a), (b) and (c) shows the solutions for f after selecting A, C and D respectively. In Fig. 2.10(a), a 1 is decomposed to A and $\bar{A}$ to obtain the terms $A\bar{C}\bar{D}$ and $\bar{A}B\bar{C}$. In Fig. 2.10(b), the single '1' after the CD group is in place still leaves a $\bar{C}$ to be covered by $\bar{A}B\bar{C}$.

Starting with an n-variable expression, the MEV method has reduced the map into one with $n - 1$ variables. The MEV method can further reduce the map into one with $n - 2$ variables, and so on into less variables. We can visualize the process by considering each square on the MEV map as a function described by a sub-map. For example, the sub-maps of the MEV map in Fig. 2.9(d) are shown in Fig. 2.11(a). The collection of sub-maps constitutes the original four-variable Karnaugh map (Fig. 2.9(a)). The sub-maps could cover more variables and reduce the size of the main map further. Figure 2.11 (b) shows the function, f, with B and D as MEVs. Again, the same minimized solution is obtained. The MEV method does not guarantee to produce the minimal solution in all cases, though the reduced solution obtained may be sufficient for some applications. The sub-maps can also describe a complex sum-of-product Boolean function, and this function is then entered into the MEV map. However, it is debatable whether it is worthwhile using the MEV method with complex sub-map functions.

Don't care conditions are handled in the same way as in a normal Karnaugh map, by considering them as 0's or 1's as appropriate to give the best solution. When a don't care condition occurs in a sub-map, the resulting function can be described as though the don't care condition is an additional variable, say ϕ, logically ANDed with the other variables identifying the square. For example, a single variable sub-map with the variable A and a don't care creates the term $A\phi$. The term is then considered as A or not used at all (i.e. ϕ is considered as a 1 or 0 as appropriate). For further details of this idea and use of more complex expressions, the reader can consult [3] and [4].

(h) Other uses of Karnaugh maps

The Karnaugh map can be used in a variety of other ways to obtain different reduced functions and alternative implementations.

(i) Inverse functions
The 0's on a Karnaugh map indicate when the function is a 0. We can minimize the inverse function by grouping the 0's (and any suitable don't cares) instead of the

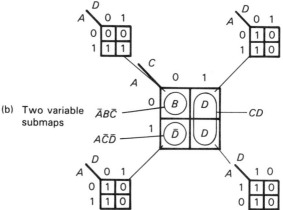

Figure 2.11   MEV sub-maps

1's. For example, the BCD parity generator shown in Fig. 2.6 could be designed by taking the 0's on the Karnaugh map as shown in Fig. 2.12, which leads to

$$\bar{P} = B_3 B_0 + \bar{B}_2 B_1 B_0 + B_2 \bar{B}_1 B_0 + B_2 B_1 \bar{B}_0 + \bar{B}_3 \bar{B}_2 \bar{B}_1 \bar{B}_0$$

This technique leads to an expression which is not logically equivalent to that obtained by grouping the 1's (i.e. the inverse of $\bar{P} \neq P$) because the don't cares are considered differently in each case, though they are equivalent for the allowable input values. Minimizing for the inverse function may be particularly advantageous if there are many more 0's than 1's on the map. We can also apply De Morgan's theorem to obtain a product-of-sum expression, i.e.:

$$P = (\bar{B}_3 + \bar{B}_0)(B_2 + \bar{B}_1 + \bar{B}_0)(\bar{B}_2 + B_1 + \bar{B}_0)(\bar{B}_2 + \bar{B}_1 + B_0)(B_3 + B_2 + B_1 + B_0)$$

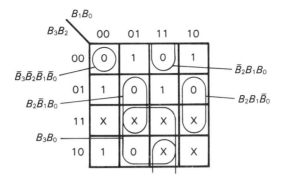

Figure 2.12 Selecting the inverse function for the BCD parity generator

(ii) Exclusive-OR/exclusive-NOR gate implementation

Since the exclusive-OR and exclusive-NOR gates are available, it is reasonable to design for these gates if this leads to an economical solution and satisfies speed requirements (Exclusive-OR/exclusive-NOR gates often have slightly longer propagation times than AND/OR gates.) Exclusive-OR/exclusive-NOR functions can be found from two Karnaugh map patterns:

(i) Diagonally adjacent 1's.
(ii) Pairs of 1's separated by one column or row.

Figure 2.13(a) shows the BCD parity function with diagonally adjacent 1's grouped together. The exclusive-OR and exclusive-NOR functions are identified by examining the variables. (Remember that $A \oplus B = \bar{A}B + A\bar{B}$ and $\overline{A \oplus B} = AB + \bar{A}\bar{B}$.) The parity function then becomes:

$$P = \bar{B}_3\bar{B}_1(B_2 \oplus B_0) + B_3B_1(B_2 \oplus B_0) + \bar{B}_3B_1(\overline{B_2 \oplus B_0}) + B_3\bar{B}_1(\overline{B_2 \oplus B_0})$$
$$= (B_3 \oplus B_1)(\overline{B_2 \oplus B_0}) + (\overline{B_3 \oplus B_1})(B_2 \oplus B_0)$$
$$= (B_3 \oplus B_1) \oplus (B_2 \oplus B_0)$$

which can be implemented with two levels of exclusive-OR gates as shown in Fig. 2.13(b). It so happens that the BCD parity function Karnaugh map has both diagonally adjacent and pairs of 1's separated by one column/row as shown in Fig. 2.13(c), and alternative exclusive OR/NOR functions, or even mixtures of exclusive OR/exclusive NOR and AND OR gates, can be derived.

(iii) Minimizing product-of-sum expressions

Occasionally a problem is initially specified in product-of-sum form, rather than the sum-of-product form normally associated with Karnaugh maps. A Karnaugh map can be used to minimize an expression given in product-of-sum form by mapping product terms directly onto the map. Logical adjacency of 1's on the map and the theorem:

$$(P + A)(P + \bar{A}) = P$$

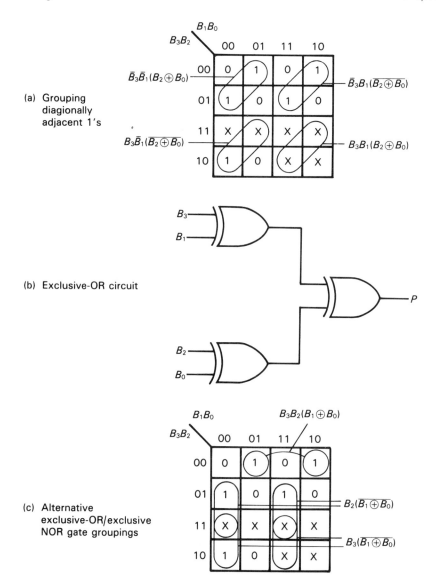

Figure 2.13 Minimizing for exclusive-OR/exclusive-NOR gates

are invoked, so that minimized product terms can be read off the map directly and combined into a product-of-sum expression.

2.4.3 Quine–McCluskey minimization

The Quine–McCluskey minimization method uses the same theorem to produce the solution as the Karnaugh map method, namely $P(A + \bar{A}) = P$. This theorem is applied repeatedly using a formal tabular procedure which is particularly suitable for minimization of an expression containing a large number of variables. The procedure is also suitable for being carried out by a computer as well as manually.

First, the expression is represented in the canonical sum-of-product form if not already in that form. An example will be taken to explain the procedure. Suppose that the function to be minimized is:

$$f(A, B, C, D, E, F) = \bar{A}\bar{B}\bar{C}D\bar{E}\bar{F} + \bar{A}\bar{B}\bar{C}D\bar{E}F + \bar{A}\bar{B}\bar{C}DE\bar{F} + \bar{A}\bar{B}CDE\bar{F}$$
$$+ \bar{A}B\bar{C}D\bar{E}\bar{F} + \bar{A}BC\bar{D}E\bar{F} + \bar{A}BCD\bar{E}\bar{F} + \bar{A}BCDE\bar{F}$$
$$+ A\bar{B}\bar{C}D\bar{E}\bar{F} + A\bar{B}CD\bar{E}\bar{F} + A\bar{B}CD\bar{E}\bar{F} + A\bar{B}CDE\bar{F}$$

The function is converted into numeric notation described in section 2.3.1, i.e.:

$$f(A, B, C, D, E, F) = \Sigma \ (4, 5, 6, 14, 20, 26, 28, 30, 36, 38, 44, 46)$$

The numbers are converted into binary form, i.e.:

$$f(A, B, C, D, E, F) = (000100 + 000101 + 000110 + 001110 + 010100$$
$$+ 011010 + 011100 + 011110 + 100100 + 100110$$
$$+ 101100 + 101110)$$

Then, the minterms are arranged in a column divided into groups. The minterm $00\cdots00$ (no 1's), if present, is placed in the first group. The minterms with one 1 in their numbers are placed in the second group. The minterms with two 1's in their numbers are placed in the next group, and so on until all the minterms are placed. The result of this operation for our example is shown in the leftmost column of Table 2.11.

The next step is the beginning of the minimization procedure proper. Starting with the first minterm of the first group, each minterm of one group is compared

Table 2.11   Quine–McCluskey minimization procedure

(4)	000100	✔	(4, 5)	00010X		(4, 6, 36, 38)	X001X0
			(4, 6)	0001X0	✔	(6, 14, 38, 46)	X0X110
(5)	000101	✔	(4, 20)	0X0100		(36, 38, 44, 46)	10X1X0
(6)	000110	✔	(4, 36)	X00100	✔		
(20)	010100	✔					
(36)	100100	✔	(6, 14)	00X110	✔		
			(6, 38)	X00110	✔		
(14)	001110	✔	(20, 28)	01X100			
(26)	011010	✔	(36, 38)	1001X0	✔		
(28)	011100	✔	(36, 44)	10X100	✔		
(38)	100110	✔					
(44)	101100	✔	(14, 30)	0X1110			
			(14, 46)	X01110	✔		
(30)	011110	✔	(26, 30)	011X10			
(46)	101110	✔	(28, 30)	0111X0			
			(38, 46)	10X110	✔		
			(44, 46)	1011X0	✔		

with each minterm in the group immediately below. Each time a number is found in one group which is the same as a number in the group below except for one digit, the pair of numbers is ticked and a new composite number is created. This composite number has the same digits as the numbers in the pair except the digit different which is replaced by an X. For example, 000100, the first and only number in the first group, can be combined with 000101 in the second group to form 0010X. The composite numbers are placed in the next column in groups as before. In our example, the number in the first group can be combined with all the numbers in the second group to form the first group of four numbers in the second column. Similarly, the four numbers in the second group of the first column combine with the numbers in the third group of the first column to produce the five numbers in the second group of the second column. The third and fourth groups of the first column combine to form the final group in the second column, and all terms in the first column have been ticked. Note that terms are compared with all terms of the group immediately below even though the term may already have been ticked from a previous comparison. Only one tick is shown on paired terms.

The above procedure is repeated on the second column to generate a third column. For pairs to be now ticked, the 'X's must be in the same position. For example, X00100 and X00110 combine to form X001X0. Subsequent columns are generated in the same manner until no more pairs can be found. In our case, three columns can be generated. Any repeated terms are deleted. The terms not ticked are the prime implicants of the expression. We have nine prime implicants, six in the second column and three in the third column.

The next step is to identify the essential prime implicants, which can be done by using a *prime implicant* chart. The prime implicants label the rows of the prime implicant chart and the original minterms label the columns as shown in Table 2.12. For identification purposes, prime implicants are called a, b, c, d, e, f, g, h and i. Where a prime implicant covers a minterm, the intersection of the corresponding row and column is marked with a cross. Those columns with only one cross identify

Table 2.12 Prime implicant chart

		Minterms											
Prime implicants		4	5	6	14	20	26	28	30	36	38	44	46
a	00010X (4, 5)*	$\otimes$	$\otimes$										
b	0X0100 (4, 20)	$\otimes$				X							
c	01X100 (20, 28)					X		X					
d	0X1110 (14, 30)				X				$\otimes$				
e	011X10 (26, 30)*						$\otimes$		$\otimes$				
f	0111X0 (28, 30)							X	$\otimes$				
g	X001X0 (4, 6, 36, 38)	$\otimes$		X						$\otimes$	$\otimes$		
h	X0X110 (6, 14, 38, 46)			X	X						$\otimes$		$\otimes$
i	10X1X0 (36, 38, 44, 46)*									$\otimes$	$\otimes$	$\otimes$	$\otimes$

* = essential prime implicant

the essential prime implicants labelling the corresponding rows. We have three such cases:

> a(4, 5)   due to the single cross on column for minterm 5
> e(26, 30)   due to the single cross on column for minterm 26
> i(36, 38, 44, 46)   due to the single cross on column for minterm 44

These prime implicants must be in the final answer. The single crosses on a column are circled and all the crosses on the same row are also circled, indicating that these crosses are covered by prime implicants selected. This procedure on our problem leads to circled crosses on minterm columns 4, 30, 36, 38 and 46 in addition to 5, 26 and 44. Once one cross on a column is circled, all the crosses on that column can be circled since the minterm is now covered. In our case this leads to crosses on all columns except 6, 14, 20 and 28 being circled. If any non-essential prime implicant has all its crosses circled, the prime implicant is redundant and need not be considered further. We have none of these.

Next, a selection must be made from the remaining non-essential prime implicants, by considering how the crosses not circled can best be covered. Generally one would take those prime implicants which cover the greatest number of minterms, that is, which have the most number of crosses on their row. If all the crosses on one row also occur on another row which includes further crosses, then the latter is said to *dominate* the former and can be selected. The dominated prime implicant can then be deleted. In our case, prime implicant c (01X100) dominates prime implicants b (0X0100) and f (0111X0). Similarly, prime implicant h (X0X110) dominates d (0X1110) and g (X00lX0). These two dominating prime implicants cover all the remaining crosses and give us the solution, i.e.

> a + e + i + c + h

or

> 00010X + 011X10 + 10X1X0 + 01X100 + X0X110

or

> $\bar{A}\bar{B}\bar{C}DE + \bar{A}BCE\bar{F} + A\bar{B}D\bar{F} + \bar{A}BD\bar{E}\bar{F} + \bar{B}DE\bar{F}$

If necessary, one can also look for *column dominance*. If one column contains all the crosses on another column and other crosses, it is said to dominate the column with fewer crosses. The dominating column can then be deleted rather than the dominated row previously. This is because if the minterm with the fewer crosses is covered, the other minterm is covered automatically.

The above procedures to obtain the solution from the prime implicants are rather complicated and a much simpler approach is available, due to Petrick (and developed by Pyne and McCluskey). In the Petrick method all the prime implicants are regarded as single Boolean variables and a sum-of-product expression is formed. To take our example, we can deduce from the prime implicant chart that to cover minterm 4, either prime implicant a or b or g is needed. To cover minterm 5, prime implicant a is needed. To cover minterm 6, g or h is needed. Continuing along these lines, we obtain the following Boolean expression:

$$\text{Function} = (a + b + g)(a)(g + h)(d + h)(b + c)(e)(c + f)(d + e + f)(g + i)$$
$$(g + h + i)(i)(h + i)$$

This function can then be manipulated using any of the standard Boolean minimization procedures. Using algebraic manipulation we get:

$$
\begin{aligned}
\text{Function} &= aei(g + h)(d + h)(b + c)(c + f) \\
&= aei(h + hd + hg + gd)(c + bc + bf + cf) \\
&= aei\,[h(1 + d + g) + gd]\,[c(1 + b + f) + bf] \\
&= aei(h + gd)(c + bf) \\
&= acehi + abefhi + acdegi + abefgi
\end{aligned}
$$

The minimized expression gives the possible combinations of prime implicants which would cover all the minterms. Normally, the combination with the smallest number of prime implicants would be taken, namely acehi, giving the same result as previously.

Don't care conditions can be handled in the Quine–McCluskey method. First, the don't care minterms are included in the function to be minimized and the normal procedure is followed. When the prime implicant chart is drawn, the don't care minterms are not included and are not considered further. Any prime implicants which cover only the don't care minterms can be deleted. Subsequent steps are as normal.

References

1. Boole, G., *An Investigation of the Laws of Thought*, New York: Dover Publications, 1954 (Reprint of original publication in 1854).
2. Shannon, C. E., 'A Symbolic Analysis of Relay and Switching Circuits', *Trans. Am. Inst. Elect. Engrs.*, 57 (1938), 713–23.
3. Fletcher, W. I., *An Engineering Approach to Digital Design*, Englewood Cliffs, NJ: Prentice Hall, 1980.
4. Tinder, F. R., *Digital Engineering Design. A Modern Approach*, Englewood Cliffs, NJ: Prentice Hall, 1991.

Problems

2.1   Suppose in the heating system described in section 2.1, heat is provided when the frost thermostat indicates the external temperature is below $0°C$ irrespective of the room temperature. Derive the Boolean expression for S.

2.2   Expand the following expressions to canonical form:
(a) $\bar{A}B + A\bar{B} + \bar{C}$
(b) $(\bar{A} + B)(A + C)$

2.3   Convert the following sum-of-product canonical expressions to canonical product-of-sum expressions:

(a) $f(A, B, C) = \Sigma\ (1, 4, 5, 6)$

(b) $f(A, B, C, D) = \Sigma\ (5, 7, 10, 15)$

2.4   Minimize the following expressions algebraically:

(a) $(\bar{A} + BC)(\overline{\bar{B} + C})(\bar{A}\bar{B}C + B\bar{C})$

(b) $(A + BC)(A + B\bar{C})(A + BC)$

(c) $X\bar{Y}\bar{Z} + XY\bar{Z} + X\bar{Y}Z$

2.5   Simplify the following by any method:

(a) $f(A, B, C)\quad = \bar{A}B + \bar{B}C + A$

(b) $f(A, B, C, D) = \Sigma\ (0, 4, 6, 8, 9, 10, 11, 15)$

(c) $f(A, B, C, D) = A(BC + CD + C + B + \bar{C}) + \bar{A}$

(d) $f(A, B, C)\quad = \overline{AC} + \overline{(\bar{A}\bar{B} + C)(\bar{A} + C)} + \overline{\overline{(\bar{A}\bar{B}C)}}(A + B)$

2.6   Determine whether the following Boolean identities are valid, by algebraic means:

(a) $A + \bar{A}B = A + B$

(b) $(A + B)(\bar{A} + C) = AC + \bar{A}B$

(c) $\bar{A}\bar{C}D + \bar{A}CD + ABD = \bar{A}D + BD$

(d) $\bar{A}\bar{B}C + \bar{A}B\bar{C} + A\bar{B}\bar{C} + ABC = C(\bar{A}B + A\bar{B}) + \bar{C}(\bar{A}B + A\bar{B})$

(e) $XY + XZ + YZ = \bar{X}\bar{Y} + \bar{X}\bar{Z} + \bar{Y}\bar{Z}$

2.7   Reduce the following expressions using De Morgan's theorem:

(a) $f = \overline{\bar{A}\bar{B}C} + \overline{\bar{A}BC}$

(b) $f = \overline{(\bar{A} + \bar{B} + C)(A + B + \bar{C})}$

(c) $f = \overline{\overline{(A + \bar{B} + C)(\overline{AB} + \overline{CD})} + \overline{ACD}}$

2.8   Simplify the following expressions using the Karnaugh map method:

(a) $f = \bar{A}B\bar{C}\bar{D} + \bar{A}B\bar{C}D + \bar{A}BC\bar{D} + A\bar{B}CD + AB\bar{C}D$

(b) $f = \bar{A}D + \bar{A}\bar{B}C + A\bar{B}\bar{D} + AB\bar{C} + \bar{A}B\bar{C}D$

(c) $f = ABD + ABCD + \bar{A}B\bar{C}D + AB\bar{C}\bar{D} + A\bar{B}D$

    Don't care $= \bar{A}B\bar{D}$

(d) $f = ABC + ABE + ABD + ADE + AE$

(e) $f(A, B, C, D) = \Sigma\ (1, 3, 4, 5, 9, 11, 12)$

(f) $f(A, B, C, D) = \Sigma\ (1, 2, 3, 5, 10, 11)$

    Don't cares $= 4, 9, 13$

(g) $f(A, B, C, D, E) = \Sigma\ (2, 7, 9, 10, 13, 15, 18, 19, 23, 26, 27, 28, 29, 31)$

2.9   Minimize the following functions using the Karnaugh map method:

(a) $f(A, B, C, D) = \Sigma\ (2, 3, 7, 12, 13, 14, 15)$

(b) $f(A, B, C, D) = \Pi\ (2, 3, 7, 12, 13, 14, 15)$

2.10   Extract the prime implicants from the Boolean expression:

$$f = \Sigma\ (10, 11, 15, 21, 24, 25, 26, 28, 29, 30)$$

using the Quine–McCluskey method. Obtain the minimal set of prime implicants to cover the expression, with the aid of a prime implicant chart.

2.11 The output of a logic circuit is a 1 only when any of the following 6-bit numbers is present at its six inputs:

$$1, 2, 3, 5, 7, 13, 15, 22, 23, 29, 31, 41 \qquad \text{(decimal)}$$

Obtain the minimal logical expression for the circuit output signal. All numbers between 0 and 63 are valid except $39, 45$ and 47 which do not occur and can be considered as don't cares. Use the Quine–McCluskey method to obtain the prime implicants and an algebraic method to obtain the minimal solution.

2.12 A logic circuit accepts three 2-bit (positive) binary numbers A, B and C on six input lines, and produces a single output, Z, which is set to a 1 only when $A + B - C$ is equal to or greater than 4 (decimal). ($+$ and $-$ are arithmetic operations.) Show that the output is given by the Boolean function:

$$f(C_0, C_1, B_0, B_1, A_0, A_1) = \Sigma \ (5, 7, 11, 13, 14, 15, 31, 39, 45, 47)$$

Where A_1, B_1 and C_1 are the most significant digits of A, B and C respectively. A_0, B_0 and C_0 are the least significant digits of A, B and C respectively. Minimize the above function using the Quine–McCluskey method.

3 Combinational Circuit Design

3.1 Combinational circuits

A *combinational logic circuit* is one which has output values dependent upon the values of the input signals applied at that instant, i.e. the output(s) depend upon the combination of input values and do not depend upon any particular condition in the past. This contrasts with a *sequential logic circuit* whose output or outputs depend upon the input signals applied at that instant and also input/output values in the past. Chapter 4 considers sequential circuit design. Boolean expressions as described in the previous chapter are implemented using combinational logic circuits.

3.2 Combinational circuit function implementation

3.2.1 TTL logic circuit family

Reference will be made to actual logic devices in the TTL (transistor-transistor-logic) logic family [1] which are widely used to implement digital systems. A full range of fundamental gates are manufactured, including those given in Table 3.1. Apart from the fundamental combinational logic circuit parts (AND gates etc.), other more complex integrated circuit parts exist for particular applications. The part numbers, apart from a manufacturer's prefix such as SN (semiconductor network), begin with the numbers 74 (for commercial versions; military versions use the numbers 54). These numbers may be followed by letters referring to particular internal circuit designs such LS (low-power Schottky), S (Schottky), AS (advanced Schottky), ALS (advanced low-power Schottky). These and other circuit designs are described in Chapter 5. The final numbers refer to the particular part within the logic family. Most of the devices in this family and similar families are manufactured in *dual-in-line* packages. The number of TTL gates fabricated within the package is often between 1 and 100. When the number of gates is less than 12, the technology is commonly called *small scale integration* (SSI). When the number of gates is between 12 and 100, the technology is called *medium scale integration* (MSI). (The term *large scale integration*, LSI, is used for devices with 100 to 1000

Table 3.1   Some gates in the TTL logic family

Gates		Number of gates in package	Device number
NOT		6 (Hex)	74LS04
AND	2-input	4 (Quadruple)	74LS08
	3-input	3 (Triple)	74LS11
	4-input	2 (Dual)	7421
OR	2-input	4 (Quadruple)	74LS32
NAND	2-input	4 (Quadruple)	74LS00
	3-input	3 (Triple)	74LS10
	4-input	2 (Dual)	74LS20
	8-input	1	74LS30
	13-input	1	74LS133
NOR	2-input	4 (Quadruple)	74LS02
	3-input	3 (Triple)	74LS27
	5-input	2 (Dual)	74LS260
EXCLUSIVE-OR	2-input	4 (Quad)	74LS86[*]
EXCLUSIVE-NOR	2-input	4 (Quad)	74LS266[*]
AND-OR-INVERT	2-wide 2/3-input	2 (Dual)	74LS51
	4-wide 2/3-input	1	74LS54

[*] Classified as MSI in reference [1].

gates and *very large scale integration*, VLSI, when there are thousands of gates in the device.) The dual-in-line packages used commonly have 14, 16 or 20 pins for connections on the two longer sides of the package. Figure 3.1 shows the 14-pin package and some connections. Sixteen-pin and 20-pin packages have the same 0.3 in. width and 0.1 in. spaced pins.

A logic 1 in TTL is represented by the voltage 3.4V nominally, though it can be generated between 2.4V and 5V. A logic 0 is represented by the voltage 0.2V though it can be generated between 0V and 0.4V. There are slight variations in the nominal voltages between device types. Voltages as low as 2V will be recognized as a logic 1 level by gates and voltages as high as 0.8V at the inputs of gates will be recognized as a logic 0 level, to allow extraneous electrical noise in the system. The overlaps between the recognized voltage ranges and the generated voltage ranges are shown in Fig. 3.2.

3.2.2 Using AND, OR and NOT gates

Circuit realization of any Boolean expressions can be done using the three fundamental gates, AND, OR and NOT gates. AND gates can be used where there are AND operations specified in the Boolean expression and OR gates used where there are OR operations. For example, a sum-of-product expression such as:

$$f(A, B, C, D) = \bar{A}BC + \bar{B}\bar{C} + AD$$

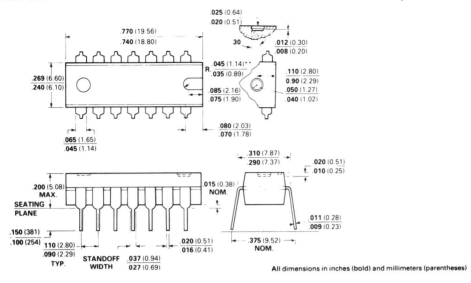

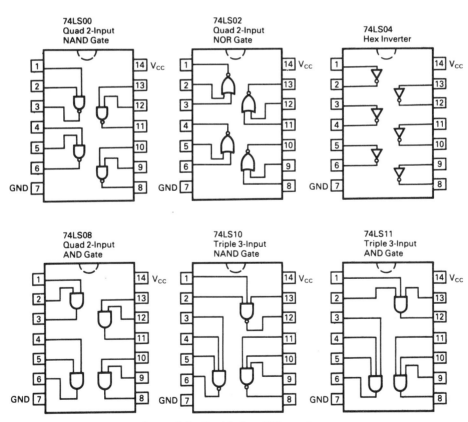

Figure 3.1   Dual-in-line TTL packages

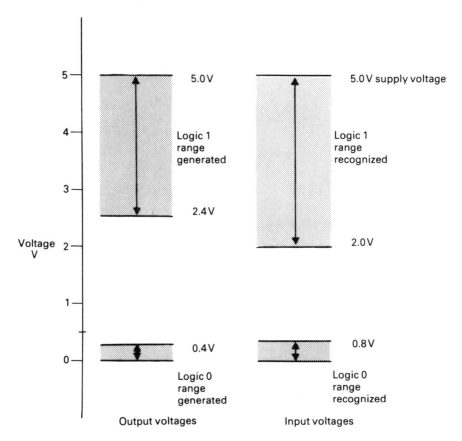

Figure 3.2   TTL voltages

can easily be realized as shown in Fig. 3.3(a). The inverse variables $\bar{A}$, $\bar{B}$ and $\bar{C}$ are generated using NOT gates. The first product term, $\bar{A}BC$, is realized using a three-input AND gate. The second and third product terms are realized using two-input AND gates. The overall OR operation is performed using one three-input OR gate.

The realization is *two level* because the signals pass through two gates from the input of the circuit to the output, if we ignore the gates for inverting the input signals. Alternative AND/OR implementations can sometimes be created by firstly factorizing the function. This may lead to less gates but a greater number of logic levels. Two-level implementations generally minimize the delay before a new output is generated. A further advantage of the implementation is that it is clear how the function has been implemented. This is particularly important to help any people other than the original designers subsequently working on the circuit, such as those making modifications or testing the circuit. Integrated circuit parts exist which contain composite two-level AND-OR/NOR gate combinations. In some applications, however, two-level implementations would require large numbers of gates and alternative schemes need to be produced, for example using iterative arrays (section 3.4.3).

3.2.3 Using NAND gates

NAND gates are universal in the sense that any logic function can be implemented using NAND gates only. A NAND gate implementation of the previous sum-of-product is obtained by rearranging the function as follows; firstly apply double inversion:

$$f = \overline{\overline{\overline{A}BC + \overline{B}\,\overline{C} + AD}}$$

Then by De Morgan's theorem, we get:

$$f = \overline{(\overline{\overline{A}BC})(\overline{\overline{B}\,\overline{C}})(\overline{AD})}$$

This can be implemented as shown in Fig. 3.3(b). Inversion of input signals can be obtained by using a NAND gate with all its inputs tied together. The terms in the equation enclosed in parentheses are generated in the next level of gating and the overall NAND operation in the final level. Notice that the general configuration

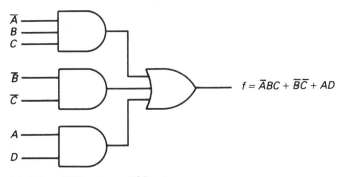

(a) Using AND gates and OR gate

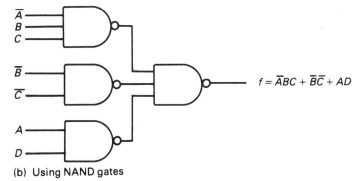

(b) Using NAND gates

Figure 3.3 Implementation of the function $f = \overline{A}BC + \overline{B}\,\overline{C} + AD$

and the signals applied to the circuit are the same as those applied to an AND-OR gate arrangement. Therefore an AND-OR gate implementation can be directly converted into NAND gate implementation by inspection.

3.2.4 Using NOR gates

NOR gates are also universal and any logic function can be implemented with NOR gates only. Rearranging the above function to:

$$\bar{f} = \overline{(\overline{A + \bar{B} + \bar{C}}) + (\overline{B + C}) + (\overline{\bar{A} + \bar{D}})}$$

using De Morgan's theorem leads to a NOR implementation of the inverse function with two levels of gates disregarding gates for inverting A, B and D. NOR gate implementations are not very common now: either AND/OR or NAND gates are used for simple functions.

3.2.5 Mixed logic representation

We have seen that AND, OR and NOT gates can be used to implement a sum-of-product expression directly without any manipulation, or NAND gates can be used or even NOR gates can be used solely. It is also possible to employ both NAND gates and NOR gates in various combinations. However, it is preferable to design a circuit that can be easily understood from the logic diagram. This can be achieved with a system of logic diagrams, known as *mixed logic representation*, which shows the logic function intended in the mind of the designer irrespective of the actual gates used. Alternative symbols are used for AND, OR, NAND and NOR gates where the logic operation intended is different, as shown in Fig. 3.4. A small circle is used to

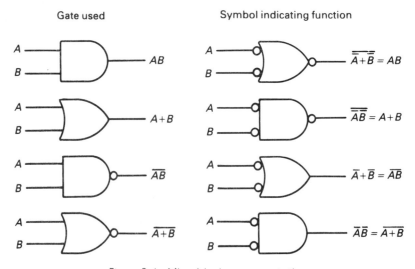

Figure 3.4   Mixed logic representation

indicate inversion as on the output of the NOT, NAND and NOR gate symbols. This circle is also applied to the inputs when the input variables are inverted before the main logical operation. For example, a two-input NAND gate has the function:

$$f(A, B) = \overline{AB}$$
$$= \bar{A} + \bar{B}$$

and so can be used as an 'OR' operation if the input variables are inverted as on the equivalent symbol shown. This symbol would be used if the designer had an OR operation in mind.

Figure 3.5 shows a mixed logic representation for the function $f(A, B, C) = \bar{A}BC + \bar{B}\bar{C} + AD$ implemented using NAND gates.

3.2.6 Multiple output combinational logic circuit design

In Chapter 2, two logic circuits were designed from a problem specification using the Karnaugh map minimization method (section 2.4.2). In each case, there are a number of logic inputs and one logic output. Now let us consider a circuit with more than one output. Suppose the three combinational functions:

$$f_1(B_3, B_2, B_1, B_0) = \Sigma \ (5, 7, 8, 12, 13, 15)$$
$$f_2(B_3, B_2, B_1, B_0) = \Sigma \ (0, 3, 4, 5, 7, 13, 15)$$
$$f_3(B_3, B_2, B_1, B_0) = \Sigma \ (3, 7, 8, 12, 13)$$

are to be implemented, where the inputs to the circuits are B_3, B_2, B_1 and B_0. We could minimize each function separately and create three separate two-level circuits (plus inverters where necessary). However, it may be possible to share one or more of the first-level gates between functions. It may sometimes be better not to fully minimize the individual functions to obtain greatest gate sharing.

An informal approach to identify the appropriate Boolean expressions is to map each function onto individual Karnaugh maps and look for possible gate sharing. The Karnaugh maps for our functions are shown in Fig. 3.6(a). We can see that the term B_2B_0 is common to both f_1 and f_2. Similarly, $\bar{B}_3B_1B_0$ is common to f_2 and f_3.

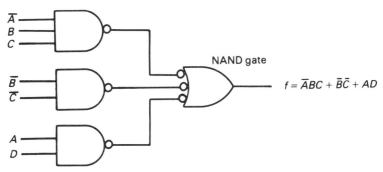

Figure 3.5 Mixed logic representation of the function $f = \bar{A}BC + \bar{B}\bar{C} + AD$ using NAND gates

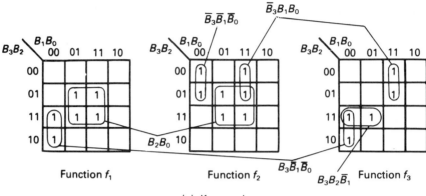

(a) Karnaugh maps

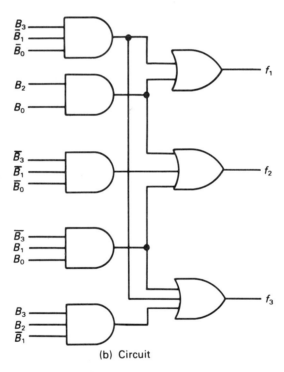

(b) Circuit

Figure 3.6 Circuit with three outputs

Finally, $B_3\bar{B}_1\bar{B}_0$ is common to both and f_1 and f_3. This observation leads to the design shown in Fig. 3.6(b), where three gates are shared.

A formal approach can be used which ensures that the greatest gate sharing is achieved. First, we find the following prime implicants by examining the Karnaugh maps or by more certain means using the Quine–McClusky method (Chapter 2):

(i) The prime implicants common to all the functions, that is of the function $f_1 f_2 f_3$

(ii) The prime implicants common to two of the three functions, that is, of the functions $f_1 f_2, f_1 f_3$ and $f_2 f_3$.

(iii) The prime implicants of the individual functions f_1, f_2 and f_3.

If there are more than three functions, the prime implicants of all combinations of functions must be found. In our case, the following prime implicants are found:

	Minterms	Prime implicants
$f_1 f_2 f_3$	7, 13	(7), (13)
$f_1 f_2$	5, 7, 13, 15	(5, 7, 13, 15)
$f_1 f_3$	7, 8, 12, 13	(7), (8, 12), (12, 13)
$f_2 f_3$	3, 7, 13	(3, 7), (13)
f_1	5, 7, 8, 12, 13, 15	(8, 12), (12, 13), (5, 7, 13, 15)
f_2	0, 3, 4, 5, 7, 13, 15	(0, 4), (3, 7), (4, 5), (5, 7, 13, 15)
f_3	3, 7, 8, 12, 13	(3, 7), (8, 12), (12, 13)

Then, a prime implicant chart is drawn with rows labelled with the prime implicants. The columns are divided into three groups, one for each function. One column is provided for each minterm within each group, as shown in Table 3.2. A cross is marked at the intersection of a row and a column if the prime implicant is in the function, i.e. if the minterm and all the other minterms in the prime implicant are included in the function.

Columns with only one cross identify essential prime implicants. Since essential prime implicants must be provided, all the crosses on essential prime implicant rows can be circled, indicating the associated minterms are covered. Once a cross has been circled, any other cross on the same column can also be circled as the minterms will be covered. In our case, we find four essential prime implicants.:

$$(0, 4), (3, 7), (8, 12), (5, 7, 13, 15)$$

Prime implicants (8, 12) and (5, 7, 13, 15) will cover f_1 completely and prime implicants (0, 4), (3, 7) and (5, 7, 13, 15) will cover f_2 completely. Prime implicants

Table 3.2 Prime implicant chart for circuit with multiple outputs

Prime implicants	Function f_1						Function f_2							Function f_3				
	5	7	8	12	13	15	0	3	4	5	7	13	15	3	7	8	12	13
(7)		⊗									⊗				⊗			
(13)					⊗							⊗						⊗
(0, 4)*							⊗		⊗									
(3, 7)*								⊗			⊗			⊗	⊗			
(4, 5)									⊗	⊗								
(8, 12)*			⊗	⊗												⊗	⊗	
(12, 13)				⊗	⊗												⊗	⊗
(5, 7, 13, 15)*	⊗	⊗			⊗	⊗				⊗	⊗	⊗	⊗					

* = essential prime implicant

(8, 12) and (3, 7) are necessary for f_3, but we are left with minterm 13 to be covered. This minterm can best be covered with the prime implicant (12, 13) rather than (13), leading to the same circuit as previously. If several non-essential prime implicants are present, it may be necessary to turn to Petrick's method (Chapter 2, section 2.4.3).

3.2.7 Iterative circuit design

There are some design problems which would require a very large number of gates if designed as two-level circuits. One approach is to divide each function into a number of identical subfunctions which need be performed in sequence and the result of one subfunction is used in the next subfunction. Consider the following design problem.

Design an even parity generator circuit which produces the parity bit (B_7) for a 7-bit code word $B_6B_5B_4B_3B_2B_1B_0$, i.e. produces an output set to a 1 only when the number of ones in the code word is odd so as to have an even number of 1's in the (8-bit) word including the parity bit. The code word might be an ASCII representation of characters, for example. The parity function has seven variables as shown in the Karnaugh map in Fig. 3.7 and does not minimize. (It will not minimize for any number of bits in the code word.) Therefore the output function consists of a seven-variable canonical sum of product expression with sixty-four minterms. A two-level implementation requires sixty-four 7-input AND gates and

$B_6B_5B_4B_3$ \ $B_2B_1B_0$	000	001	011	010	110	111	101	100
0000	0	1	0	1	0	1	0	1
0001	1	0	1	0	1	0	1	0
0011	0	1	0	1	0	1	0	1
0010	1	0	1	0	1	0	1	0
0110	0	1	0	1	0	1	0	1
0111	1	0	1	0	1	0	1	0
0101	0	1	0	1	0	1	0	1
0100	1	0	1	0	1	0	1	0
1100	0	1	0	1	0	1	0	1
1101	1	0	1	0	1	0	1	0
1111	0	1	0	1	0	1	0	1
1110	1	0	1	0	1	0	1	0
1010	0	1	0	1	0	1	0	1
1011	1	0	1	0	1	0	1	0
1001	0	1	0	1	0	1	0	1
1000	1	0	1	0	1	0	1	0

Figure 3.7   Karnaugh map of parity generator

a 64-input OR gate. Sixty-four input OR gates are not manufactured, so an equivalent configuration of cascaded OR gates would need to be formed, each OR gate having perhaps five to eight inputs. A NAND implementation would have the same difficulties.

A design based around the iterative approach is shown in Fig. 3.8(a). There are seven logic circuit cells. Each cell accepts one code word digit and the output from the preceding cell. The cell produces one output, Z, which is a 1 whenever the number of 1's on the two inputs is odd. Hence successive outputs are a 1 when the number of 1's on inputs to that point is odd and the final output is a 1 only when the number of 1's in the whole code word is odd as required. Each cell function can be described by the function:

$$O_i = B_i \bar{I}_i + \bar{B}_i I_i$$

where

$O_i = i$th cell output
$I_i = i$th cell input
$B_i = i$th bit of code word

Thus, the cell function is the exclusive-OR function and the parity generator requires seven cascaded cells as shown in Fig. 3.8(b).

To create an iterative design, the number of cells and the number of data inputs to each cell need to be determined and also the number of different states that must be recognized by the cell. The number of different states will define the number of lines to the next cell (usually carrying binary encoded information). The above parity generator cell has the minimum number of inputs, one data and one from the previous cell, which results in the simplest cell design. The problem may decompose naturally in such a way that each cell has more than one output and several inputs. In a parity generator circuit, we could have chosen pairs of code word inputs, $B_{n+1}B_n$. Again one output is sufficient to indicate the state that there is an odd

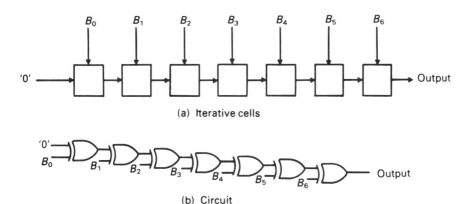

(a) Iterative cells

(b) Circuit

Figure 3.8 Parity generator using iterative cells

number of 1's so far, and hence one input to the next cell. The jth cell output function would now be:

$$O_j = B_{n+1}\bar{B}_n I_j + \bar{B}_{n+1}B_n I_j + B_{n+1}B_n \bar{I}_j + \bar{B}_{n+1}\bar{B}_n \bar{I}_j$$

3.2.8 Gate timing parameters

It will be useful at this stage to define some timing parameters of combinational circuits. The *propagation delay* is the delay between the application of new input signals to a logic gate or part and the generation of the resultant output. The propagation delay is typically measured at the 1.3V points, as shown in Fig. 3.9 for a NOT gate. The propagation time for a 0 to 1 output change is not normally the same as the propagation time for a 1 to 0 output change in the same device. The propagation time for a 0 to 1 output change is typically 9 ns and the propagation time for a 1 to 0 output change is typically 10 ns (1 ns = 10^{-9} s) for a 74LS04 NOT gate. The differential between the two propagation times is greater in some other TTL gates. Notice that in practice logic voltages take a finite time to rise from a 0 to a 1 and fall from a 1 to a 0. These times are called the *rise time* and *fall time* respectively, measured at 10% and 90% points as shown. Using nominal values, the 10% point will be at 0.2V + (1/10) × (3.4 − 0.2)V = 0.52V. The 90% point will be at 0.2V + (9/10) × (3.4 − 0.2)V = 3.08V.

Propagation delay time, in particular, will define the speed of operation of logic circuits. The rise and fall times will depend upon the output circuit of the gate and the circuits connected to the output. Generally the rise and fall times will increase

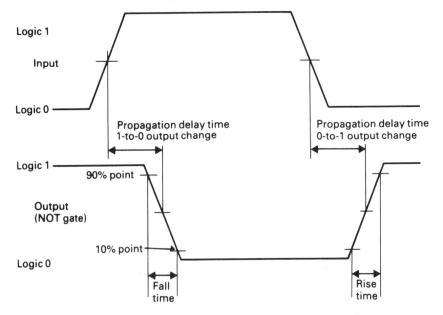

Figure 3.9 Rise time, fall time and propagation delay time

as greater loads are presented to the output and the propagation delay time will also be increased.

3.2.9 Race hazards in combinational circuits

A *race hazard* results in the generation of a 'logic spike', i.e. a transient logic signal, which may occur at the output of a gate when input signals change. It may be due to changes in signals passing through different paths to the output and experiencing different delays. A *static race hazard* is created by the delay between a signal and the complement signal. For example, a circuit implementation of the function $f(A, B) = AB + \bar{A}C$ is shown in Fig. 3.10(a). Consider the operation of the circuit when $B = C = 1$ and A changes state. $\bar{A}$ will be slightly delayed from A because of the extra gate delay of the NOT gate (ignoring the delay through the AND gates). During a 1 to 0 change, this extra delay causes both A and $\bar{A}$ to be at a 0 transiently, resulting in a transient 0 output as shown in Fig. 3.10(b).

Static hazards can be eliminated as follows: first the function is mapped onto a Karnaugh map and groups (prime implicants) formed to specify the minimal solution. Then groups which do not overlap any other group are identified. These indicate potential race hazards. Additional groups are introduced crossing over

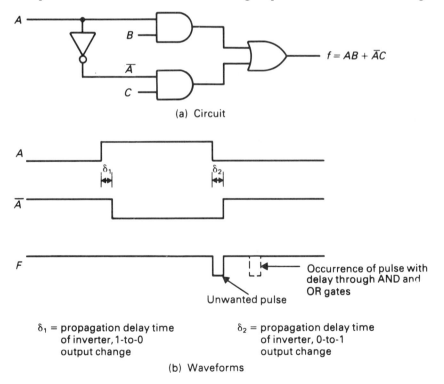

(a) Circuit

(b) Waveforms

δ_1 = propagation delay time of inverter, 1-to-0 output change

δ_2 = propagation delay time of inverter, 0-to-1 output change

Figure 3.10 Static race hazards

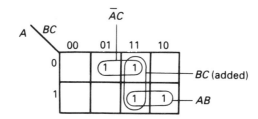

(a) Function with overlapping prime implicant added

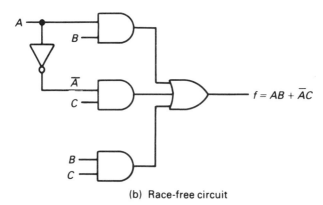

(b) Race-free circuit

Figure 3.11   Elimination of static race hazard in function $f = AB + \bar{A}C$

these groups so that no group is not overlapped by another group. In our case, this means that one extra group, *BC*, is necessary between the two original groups, *AB* and $A\bar{C}$, as shown in Fig. 3.11(a). Finally this extra term is incorporated into the circuit as shown in Fig. 3.11(b). The inclusion of the logically redundant term maintains a '1' output during the *A* transition.

In general, all prime implicants must be included in the solution to avoid static hazards and perhaps the best method of identifying all the prime implicants is by the Quine–McCluskey method. Other types of race hazards exist (see Chapter 11).

3.3 MSI combinational logic circuit parts

There are many MSI parts in the TTL family, including arithmetic circuits which we shall consider separately in section 3.4. Firstly, we shall consider two MSI parts, the decoder and the data selector, quoting part numbers in the TTL range.

3.3.1 Decoders/demultiplexers

A *decoder* is a logic circuit part which has a set of inputs, typically three or four, and a set of outputs. One output is activated for each possible binary pattern occurring on the inputs. Outputs are commonly *active low*, meaning that they are normally at a 1 and become a 0 to indicate that the corresponding input pattern has been generated. With three inputs, there are up to eight (2^3) different possible binary input patterns and therefore eight outputs. The first output is activated when the pattern 000 occurs on the three inputs, the second output is activated when the input pattern 001 occurs, the third output is activated when the input pattern 010 occurs, and so on. With four inputs, there are up to sixteen different possible patterns and sixteen outputs. A decoder with three inputs and eight outputs is known as a 3-line-to-8-line decoder (e.g. 74LS138) and a decoder with four inputs and sixteen outputs is known as a 4-line-to-16-line decoder (e.g. 74LS154). The decoder may have additional *chip select* or enable inputs which must be activated to activate any of the outputs.

A *demultiplexer*, a component similar to a decoder, has one data input which is fed to one of a set of data outputs depending upon select inputs, as shown in Fig. 3.12, with three select inputs to select eight data outputs. The first data output is selected when the pattern 000 occurs on the select inputs and the second data output is selected when the pattern 001 occurs on the select inputs, just as in the decoder. Whatever the logic level on the single data input, this occurs on the selected data output. The function of the data input is the same as the chip enable input of a decoder and consequently the two devices, decoder and demultiplexer, may be identical.

The truth table for a 74LS138 3-line-to-8-line decoder/demultiplexer is shown in Table 3.3 and the logic diagram is shown in Fig. 3.13. *A*, *B* and *C* are the binary encoded inputs. There are three enable inputs, G1, G2A and G2B shown on the decoder. The selected output is activated when $G1 \cdot \overline{G2A} \cdot \overline{G2B}$ is true. This expression becomes $G1 \cdot (\overline{G2A + G2B})$ by De Morgan's theorem. In Table 3.3, G2A + G2B is called G2 and hence the device is activated when $G1\overline{G2}$ is true (when G1 = 1 and G2 = 0, i.e. when G1 = 1, G2A = 0 and G2B = 0).

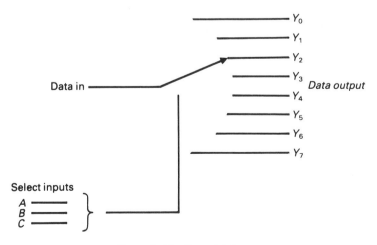

Figure 3.12 Demultiplexer

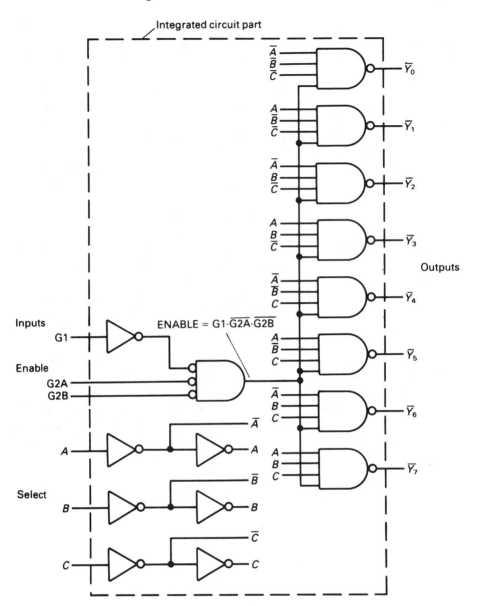

Figure 3.13   3-line-to-8-line decoder/demultiplexer

Some decoders are designed to generate outputs corresponding to BCD (binary coded decimal) inputs. This simply means that there are only ten outputs corresponding to the numbers 0 to 9 and the patterns 10 to 15 (decimal) are not recognized. These decoders are called *BCD-decimal decoders* (e.g. 74LS42).

Decoders can be used to implement combinational logic expressions and may lead to a reduced number of packages. Each output of a decoder corresponds to one

Table 3.3 Truth table of a 3-line-to-8-line decoder/demultiplexer (74LS138)

| Inputs | | | | | Outputs | | | | | | | |
| Enable | | | Select | | | | | | | | | |
G1	G2	C	B	A	$\overline{Y}_0$	$\overline{Y}_1$	$\overline{Y}_2$	$\overline{Y}_3$	$\overline{Y}_4$	$\overline{Y}_5$	$\overline{Y}_6$	$\overline{Y}_7$
X	1	X	X	X	1	1	1	1	1	1	1	1
0	X	X	X	X	1	1	1	1	1	1	1	1
1	0	0	0	0	0	1	1	1	1	1	1	1
1	0	0	0	1	1	0	1	1	1	1	1	1
1	0	0	1	0	1	1	0	1	1	1	1	1
1	0	0	1	1	1	1	1	0	1	1	1	1
1	0	1	0	0	1	1	1	1	0	1	1	1
1	0	1	0	1	1	1	1	1	1	0	1	1
1	0	1	1	0	1	1	1	1	1	1	0	1
1	0	1	1	1	1	1	1	1	1	1	1	0

G2 = G2A + G2B

X = don't care

minterm. For example, the outputs of our 74LS138 3-line-to-8-line decoder generate the following minterms:

$$Y_0 = \overline{C}\overline{B}\overline{A}$$
$$Y_1 = \overline{C}\overline{B}A$$
$$Y_2 = \overline{C}B\overline{A}$$
$$Y_3 = \overline{C}BA$$
$$Y_4 = C\overline{B}\overline{A}$$
$$Y_5 = C\overline{B}A$$
$$Y_6 = CB\overline{A}$$
$$Y_7 = CBA$$

assuming A is the least significant bit and C is the most significant bit. Therefore canonical sum-of-product expressions can be implemented by feeding selected outputs into an OR gate. For example, if the function:

$$F(C, B, A) = \overline{C}B\overline{A} + C\overline{B}\overline{A} + CBA$$

is required, Y_2, Y_4, and Y_7 are selected to feed in a three-input OR gate generating $Y_2 + Y_4 + Y_7$, as shown in Fig. 3.14. The decoder is permanently enabled. This solution requires two packages. The SSI solution using NAND gates would lead to two triple three-input NAND gate packages plus an additional package to generate all the complemented variables. In the decoder solution, the other decoder outputs are available, should several sum-of-product expressions be required, and it is easier to change a minterm. Also the enable inputs are available to generate more complex functions in conjunction with the ABC inputs.

Decoders are more often used in logic systems to recognize a particular binary pattern by selecting only the output associated with the pattern. They are commonly used in microprocessor systems to activate memory modules containing memory

3-line-to-8-line decoder/demultiplexer

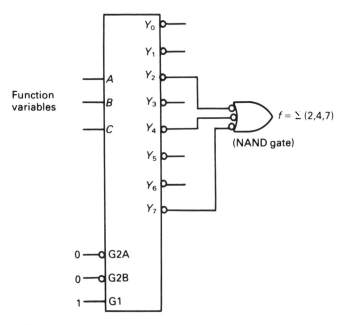

Figure 3.14   Generating a sum-of-product expression using a decoder

devices. We shall consider microprocessor systems in Part 2. Briefly, a unique address (a binary number) is given to each memory location holding information. The first memory location is given the address $0\ldots00000$, the second location is given the address $0\ldots00001$, the third location $0\ldots00010$, and so on. If a memory device contains 1024 (2^{10}) memory locations, 10 address bits would be necessary to identify the location within the device as there are 1024 different true and false combinations of 10 bits. The addresses would range from 0000000000 to 1111111111. There may be several memory modules. If there were eight identical memory modules, a further three address bits would be necessary to identify the module as there are eight combinations of three bits. The module addresses would be 000, 001, 010, 011, 100, 101, 110 and 111. Suppose each memory module contains one memory device with 1024 locations. Thirteen address bits would be needed in all, three to select the memory module and eight to select the location within the memory module.

A 3-line-to-8-line decoder can be used to identify the individual memory module as shown in Fig. 3.15. The decoder output corresponding to the address of the module connects permanently to the memory device. The address lines from the microprocessor connect to the *ABC* select inputs of the decoder and a signal from the microprocessor which indicates that the address is valid connects to an enable input of the decoder. When the data is to be obtained or changed, the address of the location is generated by the microprocessor and appears on address lines from the microprocessor with the memory unit. The appropriate decoder output is

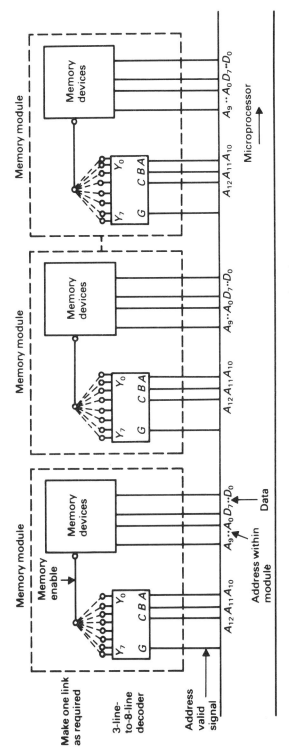

Figure 3.15 Memory module address decoder

activated which causes the data in the memory location to be transferred from the memory to the microprocessor and thus it can be obtained by the microprocessor. If new information is entered into the location, this is transferred from the microprocessor to the memory device. Different outputs of the decoder are necessary for different memory modules, and wire links can be provided between the decoder outputs and the memory device. Each module is then given a different link during manufacture or test. Alternatively, switches can be used. Eight switches are necessary in place of the wire links. Only one switch makes a connection, depending upon the address required.

3.3.2 Data selectors/multiplexers

A *data selector* or *multiplexer* is a logic circuit which allows one of several data inputs to be selected and fed to a single output as shown in Fig. 3.16. This is the reverse process to the data demultiplexer. As in the demultiplexer, the multiplexer has a set of select inputs, three if there are eight data inputs, four if there are sixteen data inputs. When one input is selected, the binary information on the data input is transferred to the output. The logic diagram of a 8-line-to-1-line data selector/multiplexer (74LS151) is shown in Fig. 3.17 and its truth table in Table 3.4 where D_0 to D_7 are the data inputs. A single enable input, $\bar{E}$, is shown. Other data selectors include the 74150, which is a 16-line-to-1-line data selector; the 74LS153, a dual (two in a package) 4-line-to-1-line data selector; and 74LS157, a quad (four in a package) 2-line-to-1-line data selector.

Though not its primary design application (which is to select data from several sources and send to one destination), a data selector can be used to implement a

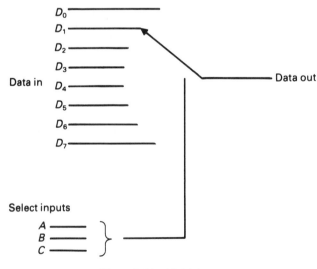

Figure 3.16 Multiplexer

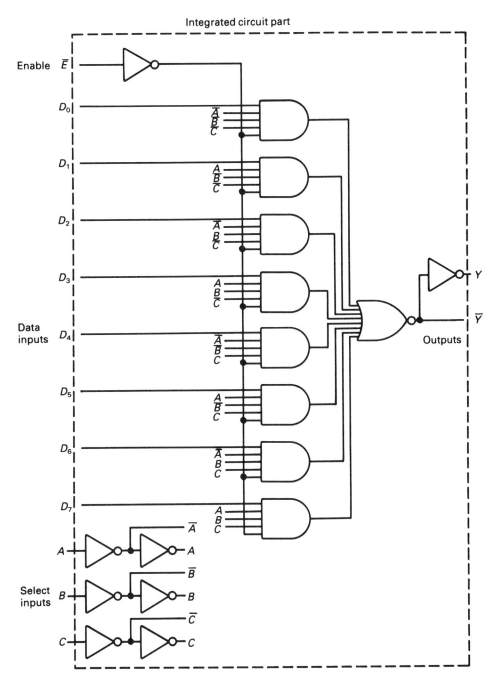

Figure 3.17   8-line-to-1-line data selector/multiplexer

Table 3.4 Truth table of an 8-line-to-1-line data selector/multiplexer

Inputs				Outputs	
Enable	Select				
$\bar{E}$	C	B	A	Y	$\bar{Y}$
1	X	X	X	0	1
0	0	0	0	D_0	$\bar{D}_0$
0	0	0	1	D_1	$\bar{D}_1$
0	0	1	0	D_2	$\bar{D}_2$
0	0	1	1	D_3	$\bar{D}_3$
0	1	0	0	D_4	$\bar{D}_4$
0	1	0	1	D_5	$\bar{D}_5$
0	1	1	0	D_6	$\bar{D}_6$
0	1	1	1	D_7	$\bar{D}_7$

D_n is the nth data input
X = don't care

8-line-to-1-line data selector/multiplexer

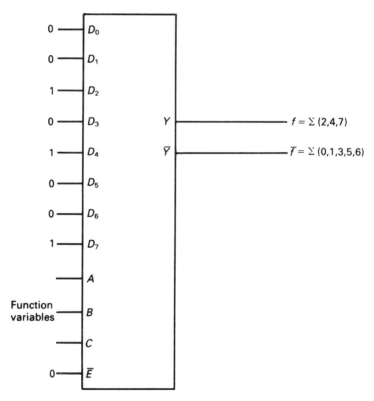

$$f = \Sigma\,(2,4,7)$$

$$\bar{f} = \Sigma\,(0,1,3,5,6)$$

Figure 3.18 Generating a sum-of-product expression using a data selector/multiplexer

combinational function by permanently connecting each data input either to a 0 or a 1 depending upon whether the associated minterm is required in the output function. The first data input is associated with the minterm, $\overline{C}\overline{B}\overline{A}$, the second with $\overline{C}\overline{B}A$, and so on. For example, the previous function:

$$f(C, B, A) = \overline{C}B\overline{A} + C\overline{B}\overline{A} + CBA$$

can be implemented using a data selector as shown in Fig. 3.18. The inputs associated with the minterms in the function (2, 4 and 7) are permanently set to 1 and the rest set to 0. If the 74LS151 data selector is used, both the true and inverse functions are available. If a data selector is used having only the inverse output, to obtain the true function $f = \Sigma\ (2, 4, 7)$ above, inputs 0, 1, 3, 5 and 6 are set to 1 and the rest are set to 0 because $\bar{f} = \Sigma\ (0, 1, 3, 5, 6)$ from Chapter 2, section 2.3.3. Functions with four variables can be implemented with the 8-to-1-line data selector by applying the fourth variable to selected data inputs instead of permanent logic 1 levels. An extra inverter is required should the fourth variable be complemented in the selected minterm. However, there is often a significant saving in packages by using a data selector rather than basic gates.

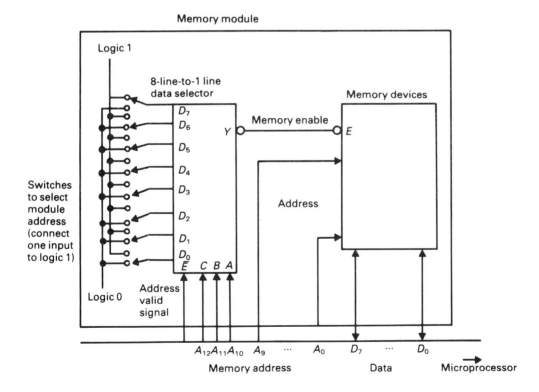

Figure 3.19 Memory module address decoder using data selector

A data selector can be used as a memory address decoder. Taking the previous memory module example, in Fig. 3.19 the three memory module address lines connect to the ABC select inputs of the decoder and the enable input as before to the address valid line from the microprocessor. The single output of the decoder activates the memory device. The data input corresponding to the address of the module is connected to a permanent 0 (assuming that this activates the memory device) and all other data inputs connect to a permanent 1. Again

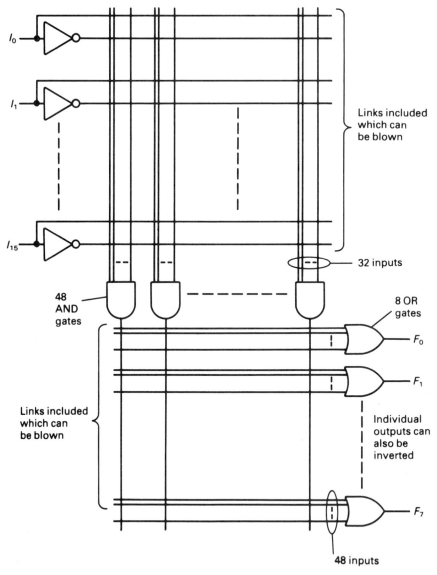

Figure 3.20 Field programmable logic array logic diagram

wire links or switches can be provided on the data inputs for different module addresses.

3.3.3 Programmable logic arrays (PLAs)

A *programmable logic array* (PLA) is a logic circuit part containing a number of AND gates and OR gates which can be interconnected internally to implement sum-of-product expressions. Links are provided internally which may be selectively broken at the time of manufacture or subsequently by the user. In the latter case, the links are formed with 'integrated circuit' fuses which can be selectively blown to break the connection, using special PLA programming units. These types of PLAs are known as *field programmable logic arrays* (FPLAs). Once a link is broken, it cannot be re-made.

A logic diagram of a typical FPLA is shown in Fig. 3.20. There are sixteen inputs. Both true and complemented signals are generated from the inputs, each of which is connected via links to the inputs of 48 AND gates. The outputs of these gates connect via links to the inputs of 8 OR gates which generate the 8 outputs of the part. The inverse outputs can also be selected. In the unprogrammed state, all the connections are made, and those which are not required are broken by passing current through the device during a programming sequence. With this particular device, each of the device outputs, F_0 to F_7, can be programmed to any sum-of-product expression each containing up to 48 terms and up to 16 true or inverse variables in each term.

The actual PLA implementation of Fig. 3.20 uses only one line where 32 are indicated into each of the 48 AND gates (48 lines in all) and every true and comple-ment variable connection is made to each line. (The link is a fuse and a diode or transistor; see Chapter 5 for details of diode and transistor logic.) Figure 3.21 shows the possible states for one pair of connections to a line. In the unprogrammed state, both connection links are made. In that case, both the true and complemented vari-ables are applied to the AND gate. Clearly this would result in the AND gate being disabled. Generally, this state is not used when the device is programmed for use. In Fig. 3.21(b), the true variable is selected. In Fig. 3.21(c), the complement variable is selected. In Fig. 3.21(d), neither variable is selected. This is a 'don't care' condition. During the programming sequence, one of (b), (c) or (d) can be produced for each input of each AND gate. The subsequent OR gate connections are simply left made or broken as required. State (a) and state (d) often produce the same logical result.

The PLA is used for the memory decode function, particularly if the memory module address contains many bits. In fact eight separate address decode functions could be implemented simultaneously with the above PLA, though this would then be sited in one place. Both canonical and non-canonical expressions can be implemented directly. Generally expressions are minimized to non-canonical expressions where possible because the number of gates available within the PLA is limited. For example, the problem in section 3.2.6 could be implemented using a PLA as shown in Fig. 3.22.

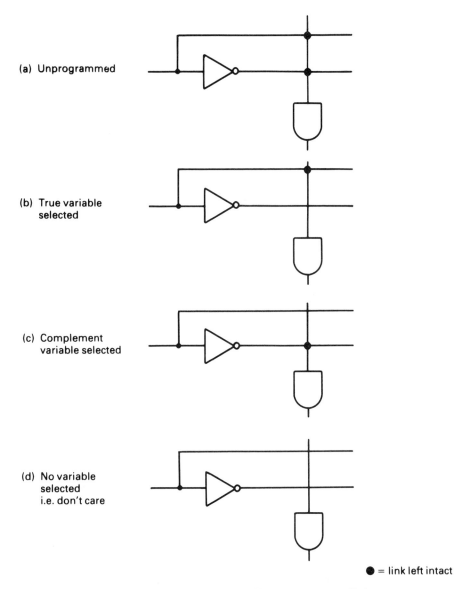

(a) Unprogrammed

(b) True variable
    selected

(c) Complement
    variable selected

(d) No variable
    selected
    i.e. don't care

● = link left intact

Figure 3.21   Conditions of AND gate links in a PLA

3.3.4 Read-only memories (ROMs)

A (semiconductor) integrated circuit memory is a logic part containing a circuit arrangement to maintain one bit of information. The circuit arrangement is repeated many times in the memory to store many bits. The primary use of a memory is to store programs and data in a computer system such as a microprocessor system. The

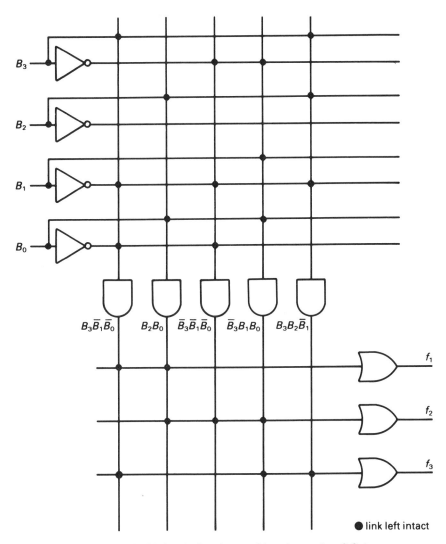

Figure 3.22 PLA solution for problem in section 3.2.6

bits stored in a semiconductor memory are organized so that one bit or a fixed number of bits (a word) can be accessed at a time. Each bit or word is given a unique identification number known as an *address*, as mentioned in section 3.3.1. This address is presented to the memory in order to identify the storage location for extracting the stored information (reading) or for inserting new information (writing). Semiconductor memories are considered in detail in Chapter 8.

One version of semiconductor memory called the *read-only memory* (ROM) has application as a combinational logic circuit. In a read-only memory, the information is defined during manufacture. In a variant of the read-only memory, the *field programmable read-only memory* (FPROM), the pattern may be defined by the user in much the same way as in a FPLA. The read-only memory has address inputs to select a particular memory location, data outputs carrying the information from the selected location, and enable inputs. For example, a read-only memory holding 1024 8-bit words requires a 10-bit address to identify one location (as $2^{10} = 1024$) and 8 data outputs. Typically there are two enable inputs, $\overline{CE}$, a general enable input, and $\overline{OE}$ which activates the data output circuits.

To use the device as a combinational logic circuit implementing a Boolean expression, the address inputs of the memory become the Boolean input variables and the data outputs become the required functions. Consider the previous function:

$$f(A, B, C, D) = \bar{A}BC + \bar{B}\bar{C} + AD$$

This function is described in truth table form in Table 3.5. The function has been expanded into canonical form as this is necessary for ROM implementation. Note that this is different from PLA implementation in which non-canonical form can be implemented. The truth table, if necessary, can be obtained from a Karnaugh map description of the function. The variables A, B, C and D specify the addresses of memory locations. The function output is the data at the addressed locations which can be programmed into the device. In our case, only one bit of each word is required to store the value of the function and only the first sixteen words of the memory, as there are only four variables A, B, C and D. Naturally, more complicated expressions can be realized, in particular multiple independent expressions. Figure 3.23 shows a read-only memory solution for the three-output problem in section 3.2.6. Sixteen words each of 3 bits are necessary in the memory.

Table 3.5   Truth table of function $f = \bar{A}BC + \bar{B}\bar{C} + AD$

D	C	B	A	Function
0	0	0	0	1
0	0	0	1	1
0	0	1	0	0
0	0	1	1	0
0	1	0	0	0
0	1	0	1	0
0	1	1	0	1
0	1	1	1	0
1	0	0	0	1
1	0	0	1	1
1	0	1	0	0
1	0	1	1	1
1	1	0	0	0
1	1	0	1	1
1	1	1	0	1
1	1	1	1	1

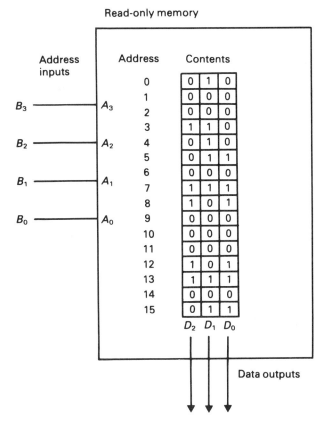

Read-only memory

Figure 3.23   Using a ROM as a combinational circuit

A 16 word × 4-bit memory could be used with one bit in each location not used. (Memory devices generally have 1-, 4- or 8-bit words.)

3.4 Binary addition circuits

Binary arithmetic was introduced in Chapter 1, being fundamental to digital computers. Now we shall study the basic logic circuits that perform binary addition. Binary addition circuits can be combinational circuits because the binary sum output depends only on the values of input operands at that instant and not on any past values. Some very early binary addition circuits shared one internal circuit over successive digit additions, and therefore the outputs of the circuit would depend upon the previous digit additions. This process is sequential in nature internally. Such an adder circuit is classified as a sequential logic circuit. Sequential or serial adders are not considered here.

3.4.1 Half adder

As mentioned in Chapter 1, section 1.3.1, the circuit to add together two binary digits is known as a *half adder*. The half adder circuit accepts two inputs, A and B, and generates two outputs, SUM and CARRY according to Table 3.6. The Boolean expression for SUM and CARRY can be derived from this truth table by examining the occurrences of 1's in the functions. For SUM there are two occurrences, when $A = 0$, $B = 1$ and when $A = 1$, $B = 0$. Therefore the SUM function is:

$$SUM = \bar{A}B + A\bar{B}$$

Similarly the CARRY function is obtained as:

$$CARRY = AB$$

The SUM function can be realized with two-level AND-OR gates and the CARRY function with a single AND gate as shown in Fig. 3.24. The SUM function,

Table 3.6   Half adder truth table

Inputs		Outputs	
A	*B*	SUM	CARRY
0	0	0	0
0	1	1	0
1	0	1	0
1	1	0	1

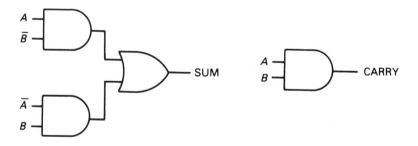

or: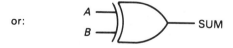

Figure 3.24   Half adder circuit

$\overline{A}B + A\overline{B}$, is the exclusive-OR function, and a single exclusive-OR gate could be used. Alternatively, the functions can be implemented using NAND gates as shown with NAND gate symbols in Fig. 3.25(a), and with mixed logic representation in Fig. 3.25(b).

3.4.2 Full adder

A *full adder* is also mentioned in section 1.3.1 as a circuit to add two binary digits A and B together with a 'carry-in' from a previous addition. This addition is necessary when two binary words are added together. A full adder has three inputs, A, B and 'CARRY IN' (abbreviated here to C_{in}), and two outputs, SUM and 'CARRY OUT' (abbreviated to C_{out}). The truth table of the full adder is shown in Table 3.7.

From this truth table, we can deduce the Boolean expressions for both SUM and C_{out} as:

$$\text{SUM} = \overline{A}\overline{B}C_{in} + \overline{A}B\overline{C}_{in} + A\overline{B}\overline{C}_{in} + ABC_{in}$$

$$C_{out} = \overline{A}BC_{in} + A\overline{B}C_{in} + AB\overline{C}_{in} + ABC_{in}$$

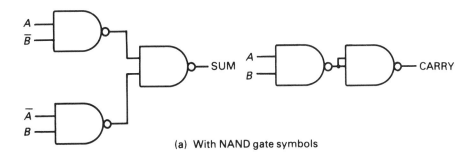

(a) With NAND gate symbols

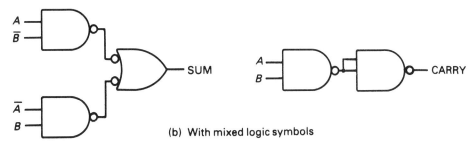

(b) With mixed logic symbols

Figure 3.25 Half adder using NAND gates

The C_{out} function can be simplified to:

$$C_{out} = AB + AC_{in} + BC_{in}$$

Both SUM and C_{out} can be implemented with two level gating as shown in Fig. 3.26, assuming the complements of the input signals are available.

A full adder can also be formed from two half adders. Starting from the basic full adder expressions, we can derive:

$$\begin{aligned}
\text{SUM} &= \bar{A}\bar{B}C_{in} + \bar{A}B\bar{C}_{in} + A\bar{B}\bar{C}_{in} + ABC_{in} \\
&= C_{in}(\bar{A}\bar{B} + AB) + \bar{C}_{in}(\bar{A}B + A\bar{B}) \\
&= C_{in}(\overline{\bar{A}B + A\bar{B}}) + \bar{C}_{in}(\bar{A}B + A\bar{B}) \\
&= C_{in}(\overline{A \oplus B}) + \bar{C}_{in}(A \oplus B) \\
&= C_{in} \oplus (A \oplus B)
\end{aligned}$$

where $\oplus$ is the exclusive-OR (not equivalence) half adder SUM output function. From the original C_{out} expression, we can derive:

$$\begin{aligned}
C_{out} &= \bar{A}BC_{in} + A\bar{B}C_{in} + AB\bar{C}_{in} + ABC_{in} \\
&= C_{in}(\bar{A}B + A\bar{B}) + AB(\bar{C}_{in} + C_{in}) \\
&= C_{in}(\bar{A}B + A\bar{B}) + AB \\
&= C_{in}(A \oplus B) + AB
\end{aligned}$$

C_{out} can be obtained by 'ORing' together the CARRY outputs of both half adders. Hence a full adder can be implemented as shown in Fig. 3.27. Though a well quoted design solution for a full adder, it has the major disadvantage that there are several levels of gate. For example, if each half adder requires three levels, the overall number of levels is seven.

Table 3.7   Full adder truth table

Inputs			Outputs	
A	B	C_{in}	SUM	C_{out}
0	0	0	0	0
0	0	1	1	0
0	1	0	1	0
0	1	1	0	1
1	0	0	1	0
1	0	1	0	1
1	1	0	0	1
1	1	1	1	1

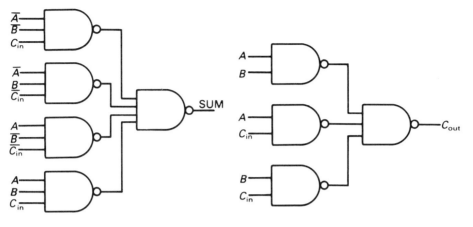

(a) With NAND gate symbols

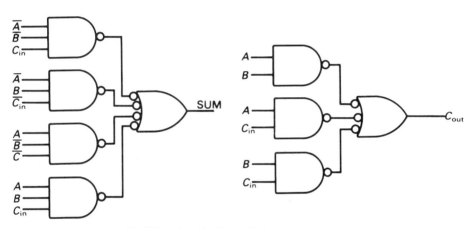

(b) With mixed logic symbols

Figure 3.26   Full adder using NAND gates

3.4.3 Parallel adder

A circuit arrangement to add two binary words with all the bits of the words presented and processed together (i.e. in parallel) is known as a *parallel adder*. Figure 3.28 shows the general arrangement of a parallel adder using one full adder for each pair of binary digits. The two numbers to be added together, A and B, have digits, $A_n \ldots A_1$ and $B_n \ldots B_1$ respectively. There are n full adders and each binary number has n digits. (In this section and the next section, the subscripts begin at 1 rather than the more conventional 0 to clarify the subsequent algebra.)

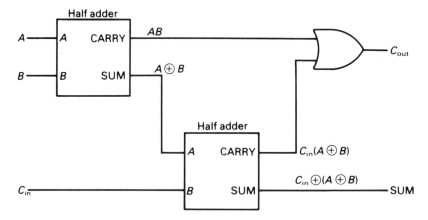

Figure 3.27 Full adder using half adders

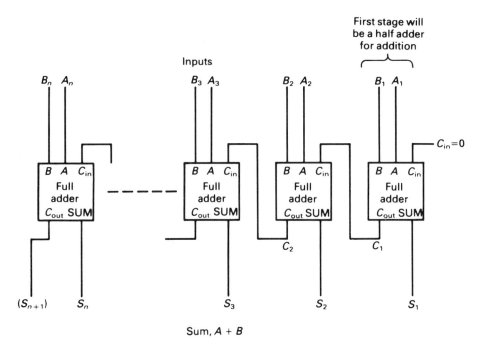

Figure 3.28 Parallel adder

The first pair of digits, A_1 and B_1, enter the first full adder to produce the first sum digit, S_1 and a carry output, C_1. The carry input to the first full adder is set to a 0. The second pair of digits, A_2 and B_2 enter the second full adder together with the carry output from the first stage to produce the second sum digit, S_2, and the second carry output, C_2. This arrangement is continued for subsequent pairs of digits, resulting in the required sum digits being produced, $S_{n+1} \dots S_1$. The final sum digit, S_{n+1}, is obtained from the carry output from the final state. (Note that the addition of two n-bit numbers leads to a possible $(n + 1)$-bit answer.) This parallel adder is an example of an iterative logic circuit, each iterative cell of the circuit being a full adder. Parallel adders such as the above are available as complete parts (e.g. 74LS83 4-bit full adder).

Since the first stage $C_{in} = 0$, the first stage could be a half adder. However, a full adder in the first stage allows for subtraction. Subtraction using 2's complement arithmetic is done by adding the 2's complement negative of one operand (B), which can be accomplished with the parallel adder by presenting the complement of B, i.e. $\bar{B}_n \dots \bar{B}_1$, to the adder rather than $B_n \dots B_1$ Simultaneously a 1 is applied to the first stage C_{in} input. Using a parallel adder for subtraction in this way is shown in Fig. 3.29 which follows from being able to produce the 2's complement of a number by inverting the digits and adding one. Hence the adder is easily modified into an adder/subtractor.

The parallel adder implements the addition directly as one would add binary numbers manually. The first digits are added, then the second digits with the carry from the first stage, continuing with subsequent stages in sequence. The second sum digit cannot be produced until the first carry digit has been produced. Similarly, the third sum digit cannot be produced until the second carry digit has been produced, and hence after the first carry digit has been produced. Therefore the overall addition time to produce the complete sum word will be the summation of each stage

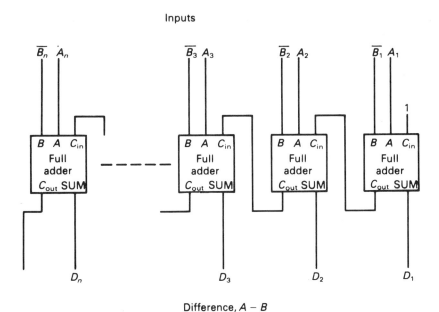

Figure 3.29 Subtraction using a parallel adder

addition time, as the addition of each stage must occur separately in order. Hence the overall time is given by:

$(n) \times (C_{out}$ propagation delay time of one full adder)

where there are n digits in each binary number and n full adders. If each full adder has three levels of gating between the inputs and the carry output, and each gate used in the full adders has a propagation delay time of t seconds, the total time taken for the parallel adder to operate is:

$(n) \times (3t)$ seconds

Common logic gates such as TTL gates operate with propagation delay times of the order of 5 to 20 ns. Using 20 ns gates, a 16-bit parallel addition would take 960 ns.

3.4.4 Carry-look-ahead adder

The aim of the carry-look-ahead adder is to increase the speed of operation of parallel addition by eliminating the 'ripple' carry between stages in the parallel adder. The full adders are still used, but separate logic is provided at each stage to generate each carry-in signal independently of the previous stages.

Table 3.8 shows the truth table of a full adder with two new output terms called *carry generate*, C_g, and *carry propagate*, C_p. C_g indicates that a C_{out} signal is generated by the adder stage itself, i.e. by A and B, which occurs when both A and B are a 1. C_p indicates that the value of C_{in} (1 or 0) is passed to C_{out} due to either A or B being 1. With the variables defined as described, we can see that:

$C_g = AB$

and

$C_p = A \oplus B$

Table 3.8   Truth table for carry propagate and carry generate terms

\multicolumn{3}{c}{Inputs}			\multicolumn{2}{c}{Outputs}		\multicolumn{2}{c}{New Terms}	
A	B	C_{in}	SUM	C_{out}	C_p	C_g
0	0	0	0	0	0	0
0	0	1	1	0	0	0
0	1	0	1	0	1	0
0	1	1	0	1	1	0
1	0	0	1	0	1	0
1	0	1	0	1	1	0
1	1	0	0	1	0	1
1	1	1	1	1	0	1

and

$$C_{out} = C_g + C_p C_{in}$$

An alternative definition for the carry propagate term includes the situation when both A and $B = 1$, overlapping the carry generate function. This definition leads to the same C_{out} and C_g functions but a simpler C_p given by:

$$C_p = A + B$$

The above expressions can be verified from the Karnaugh map of C_{out} shown in Fig. 3.30.

The carry generate and propagate terms are given by the inputs A and B of the stage. The C_{out} equation relates the carry out of the stage in terms of carry generate and carry propagate and from this, we can obtain the following carry out equations for each stage of a parallel adder:

For the first stage: $C_1 = C_{g1} + C_{p1}C_{in}$ (1)
For the second stage: $C_2 = C_{g2} + C_{p2}C_1$ (2)
For the third stage: $C_3 = C_{g3} + C_{p3}C_2$ (3)
$$\vdots$$
For the final stage: $C_n = C_{gn} + C_{pn} + C_{pn}C_{n-1}$ (n)

where C_{in} is the carry in of the first stage. $C_{in} = 0$ for addition. C_1 is the carry out of the first stage and carry in of the second stage, C_2 is the carry out of the second

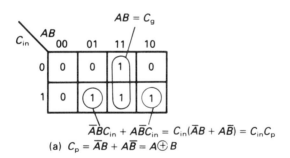

$$\overline{A}BC_{in} + A\overline{B}C_{in} = C_{in}(\overline{A}B + A\overline{B}) = C_{in}C_p$$

(a) $C_p = \overline{A}B + A\overline{B} = A \oplus B$

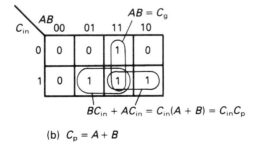

$$BC_{in} + AC_{in} = C_{in}(A + B) = C_{in}C_p$$

(b) $C_p = A + B$

Figure 3.30 Full adder C_{out} function on Karnaugh map showing C_g and C_p

stage and carry in of the third stage, C_3 is the carry out of the third stage and carry in of the fourth stage, etc.

Substituting (1) into (2) we get:

$$C_2 = C_{g2} + C_{p2}(C_{g1} + C_{p1}C_{in})$$

and then into (3):

$$C_3 = C_{g3} + C_{p3}(C_{g2} + C_{p2}(C_{g1} + C_{p1}C_{in}))$$

Continuing, we get an expression for the ith stage carry out as:

$$C_i = C_{gi} + C_{pi}(C_{gi-1} + C_{pi-1}(C_{gi-2} + C_{pi-2}(C_{gi-3}$$
$$+ C_{pi-3}(C_{gi-4}... + C_{p1}C_{in})...)$$

where

$$C_{gi} = A_iB_i$$
$$C_{pi} = A \oplus B \text{ or } A + B$$

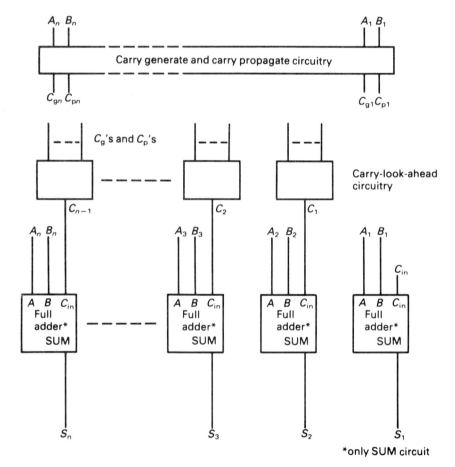

Figure 3.31   Carry-look-ahead parallel adder

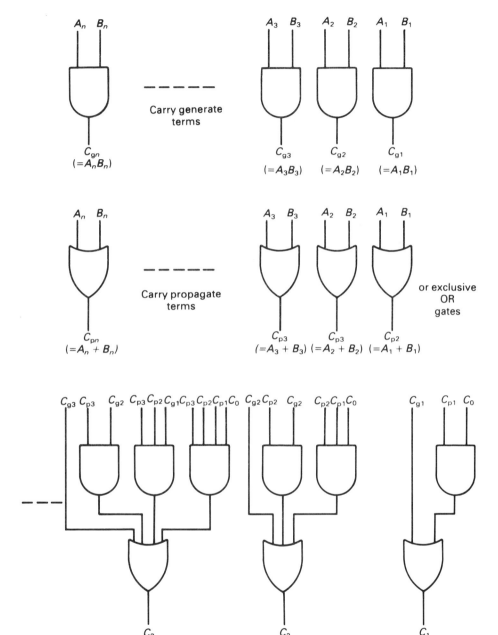

Figure 3.32 Carry-look-ahead logic

and A_i, B_i are the inputs of the ith stage. This expression can be expanded into:

$$C_i = C_{gi} + C_{pi}C_{gi-1} + C_{pi}C_{pi-1}C_{gi-2} + C_{pi}C_{p-1}C_{pi-2}C_{gi-3}$$
$$+ C_{pi}C_{pi-1}C_{p-2}C_{pi-3}C_{gi-4} \ldots + (C_{pi} \ldots C_{p2}C_{g1}) + (C_{pi}\ldots C_{p1}C_{in})$$

Consequently, the carry output for each stage can be generated from the C_g's and C_p's which are themselves generated from the inputs only. The logic required only needs these inputs with no ripple carry to slow the operation. The general scheme is shown in Fig. 3.31. The first three stages of carry out circuitry using AND and OR gates are shown in Fig. 3.32. The carry-look-ahead circuitry replaces the ripple carry connections of the parallel adder. Each carry generate term is produced with one AND gate and each carry propagate term is produced with one OR (or exclusive-OR) gate, resulting in one level of grating to generate these terms. The carry out terms can then be generated with an extra two levels of gating.

Normally, because of the considerable amount of logic required at the higher stages, not all stages are provided with true carry-look-ahead. One approach is to group, say, four stages together with carry-look-ahead within the group. The carry out from the group can be generated with look-ahead circuitry and connected to the carry in of the next higher group. Thus there is a form of 'ripple' carry between groups. The technique is employed in the 74LS283 '4-bit binary full adder with fast carry' logic part.

The ripple carry arrangement between stages can be replaced by group carry-look-ahead circuitry. The 'carry in' to each group is produced from 'group carry propagate' and 'group carry generate' signals from the carry-look-ahead adder groups. Each 'group carry generate' signals indicates that a carry is generated by the group, and the 'group carry propagate' signal indicates that a carry is propagated by the group. This technique is used in the 74S182 look-ahead carry generator and the 74LS181 arithmetic unit combination.

The outputs of a parallel adder depend upon the combination of inputs applied at that instant and hence the combinational implementations using PLAs or ROMs are possible. A single PLA solution requires (preferably) the minimized sum-of-product Boolean expressions for each output. We can develop these expressions from the look-ahead equations by substituting the carry generate and propagate expressions (AB and $A + B$ respectively) into the carry out expressions and substituting the result into sum expressions. However, the number of terms in higher expressions becomes excessive for a single PLA solution (see Problem 3.16). A ROM solution requires the result of every possible combination of input digits to be stored in the ROM. A 4-bit adder could be implemented using a ROM with $256(2^8)$ locations addressed by the two 4-bit operands (8 address bits).

3.5 Binary multiplication by combinational logic

3.5.1 Binary multiplication

As a further example of combinational logic design, let us consider binary multiplication by combinational logic. We shall assume that the numbers to be multiplied are positive binary numbers. The 'paper and pencil' method of binary multiplication of two unsigned binary numbers A and B, is shown in Fig. 3.33. The traditional method to implement this multiplication is to use a parallel adder to successively add A to an accumulating sum when the appropriate bit of B is a 1. Starting with the least significant bit of B and with the accumulating sum initialized to zero, A is added to the accumulating sum if the B digit is a 1 but not if the B digit is a 0. Then, either A is shifted one digit place left or the accumulating sum is shifted one place right, and the process repeated with the next B digit, until the final product is generated. This is a lengthy process. Since the final product is dependent only on the values of A and B at the instant they are applied, there must be a purely combinational logic solution. Here we will consider three combinational logic methods.

3.5.2 Carry-save method

The carry-save method is used to add more than two numbers together in a way that ripple carries are eliminated, except in a final parallel addition. It is particularly applicable to binary multiplication, though it can be applied whenever several numbers are to be added together. We use the fact that a full adder actually adds together three digits, which for the purposes of parallel addition, are called A, B and C_{in}, but it could be any three digits. Applying the carry-save method to the above binary multiplication of the numbers A and B, first we generate all the numbers to be added together. The digits of these numbers are given in Fig. 3.34(a) where A_n and B_n are the nth digits of A and B. Each of the above terms can be produced using AND gates.

Then, the numbers to be added together are divided into groups of three. We shall take the first three numbers of the six into one group and the remaining three numbers into the second group. The numbers in each group are added simultaneously using one full adder for each triplet of bits in each group without the carry being passed from one stage to the next. This process results in two numbers being generated for each group, namely, a sum word and a carry word, as shown in Fig. 3.34(b). Each carry word is shown moved one place right to give it the correct significance. The true sum of the three numbers in each case could be obtained by adding together the sum and carry words. The final product is the

```
         A  110101
         B  101011
            ──────
            110101
           110101
          000000
         110101
        000000
       110101
    ──────────────
    100011100111
```

Figure 3.33 Multiplication of two 6-bit numbers

$$A_5B_0 \ A_4B_0 \ A_3B_0 \ A_2B_0 \ A_1B_0 \ A_0B_0$$
$$A_5B_1 \ A_4B_1 \ A_3B_1 \ A_2B_1 \ A_1B_1 \ A_0B_1$$
$$A_5B_2 \ A_4B_2 \ A_3B_2 \ A_2B_2 \ A_1B_2 \ A_0B_2$$
$$A_5B_3 \ A_4B_3 \ A_3B_3 \ A_2B_3 \ A_1B_3 \ A_0B_3$$
$$A_5B_4 \ A_4B_4 \ A_3B_4 \ A_2B_4 \ A_1B_4 \ A_0B_4$$
$$A_5B_5 \ A_4B_5 \ A_3B_5 \ A_2B_5 \ A_1B_5 \ A_0B_5$$

(a) Step 1 Generation of partial product digits

	110101		110101
Group 1	110101	Group 2	000000
	000000		110101
Sum 1	01011111	Sum 2	11100001
Carry 1	01000000	Carry 2	00101000

(b) Step 2 Carry-save addition of two three-word groups

Sum 1	01011111
Carry 1	01000000
Sum 2	11100001
Sum 3	11100010111
Carry 3	00010010000

(c) Step 3 Carry-save addition of three words from step 2

Sum 3	11100010111
Carry 3	00010010000
Carry 2	00101000
Sum 4	11011000111
Carry 4	01000100000

(d) Step 4 Carry- save addition of two words from step 3
and one word from step 2

Sum 4	11011000111
Carry 4	01000100000
Final sum	100011100111

(e) Step 5 Final normal addition of two words from step 4

Figure 3.34 Multiplication of two 6-bit numbers by the carry-save method

summation of Sum 1, Carry 1, Sum 2 and Carry 2. Taking three of these numbers, the carry-save process is repeated to produce Sum 3 and Carry 3 as shown in Fig. 3.34(c). Sum 2 is shown moved three places right to give the number the correct significance. The process is repeated taking Sum 3, Carry 3 and Carry 2 to produce Sum 4 and Carry 4 as shown in Fig. 3.34(d). Finally, the two numbers, Sum 4 and Carry 4, are added together using a parallel adder (Fig. 3.34(e)). To eliminate any ripple carry delay, the final parallel adder can use a carry-look-ahead scheme.

The method requires a considerable amount of logic but results in a substantial increase in speed of operation. In the above example, the traditional method could use one 6-bit parallel adder for five sequential additions plus an accumulator for storing the intermediate results. The carry-save method could be implemented as shown in Fig. 3.35 which would lead to the following operating delay:

> one AND gate delay

plus

> three full adder delays

plus

> one 8-bit carry-look-ahead adder delay

3.5.3 Binary multiplication using iterative arrays

An array of iterative cells can be used for the design of a binary multiplier. This approach is particularly suitable for integrated circuit construction. To take an example of the method, consider the multiplication of two 4-bit numbers, A and B, as set out in Fig. 3.36. The summation of the partial products is done by cells, each of which performs the following three-bit addition:

$$A_iB_j(+)K(+)M$$

where A_i, B_j, K and M are inputs to the cell. A_i and B_j are the ith and jth digits of the numbers A and B respectively. The AND operation with these digits is performed within the cell. The symbol $(+)$ represents binary addition and the three-bit addition is simply the full adder function. Two outputs are generated, SUM and CARRY.

The cells are interconnected as shown in Fig. 3.37. Each cell has been drawn for convenience with the A and B inputs at the top corners of the cell, the M input at the middle of the top and the K input at the middle of the right side. The A input also passes through, leaving at the bottom left corner to connect to other cells. In this application, $M_3M_2M_1M_0$ and $K_3K_2K_1K_0$ are set to 0000.

Each cell performs the summation of three digits, i.e. one partial product digit (A_iB_j), the output of another cell of the same significance but immediately preceding (partial product) word, and a carry output from the cell one significant place lower of the same word. The resultant sum is passed to the next cell of the same significance but one word further in the list of words to be added together. The carry output of the cell passes to the next cell of the same word but one greater in significance.

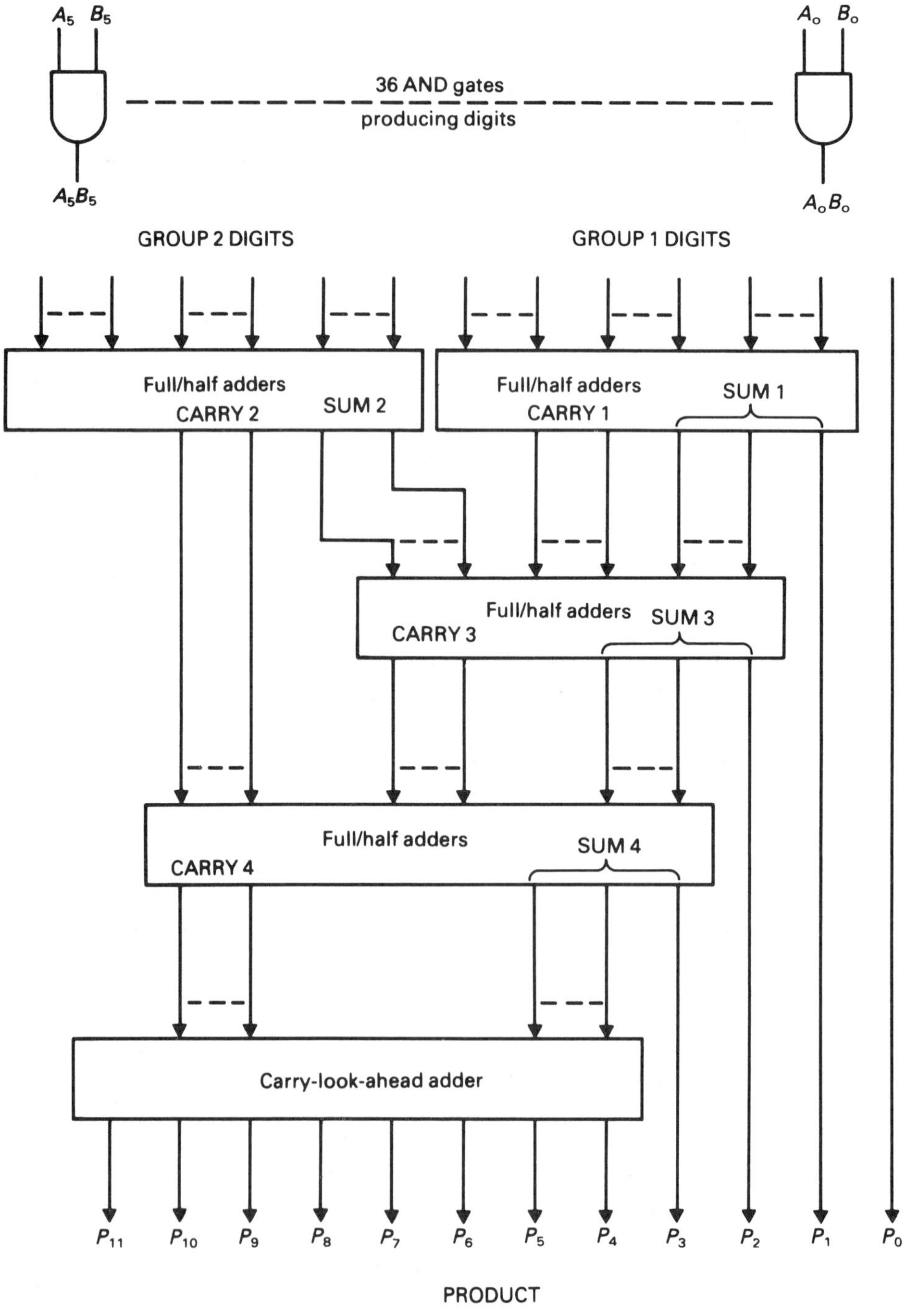

Figure 3.35   6-bit × 6-bit carry-save multiplier logic

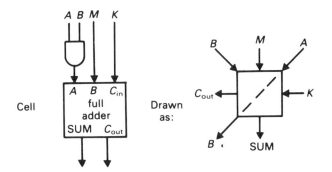

Figure 3.36   Multiplication of two 4-bit numbers

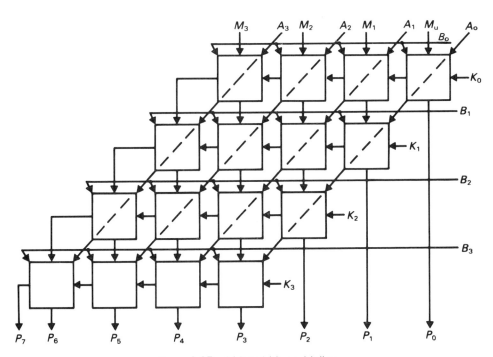

Figure 3.37   4-bit × 4-bit multiplier

The time for the multiplier to produce the final product is given by:

$10 \times$ (time for one cell to produce valid summation)

or for the multiplication of two n-digit numbers:

$(3n - 2) \times$ (time for one cell to produce valid summation)

3.5.4 Simultaneous multiplier

The simultaneous multiplier implements multiplication by considering the multiplication functions as a normal combinational logic function, i.e. the outputs are given by the particular combination of inputs applied at that instant. The input combinations and corresponding output values can be listed by truth tables from which simplified Boolean expressions can be developed. This approach is only practical for numbers with a few bits. Take, for example, the multiplication of two 2-bit numbers, A_1A_0 and B_1B_0. The resultant product is the four-digit word, say $P_3P_2P_1P_0$. There are seven different valid values of the product word dependent upon A and B, which are given in Table 3.9. From this table, we can derive the Boolean expressions for each output by plotting the 1's on Karnaugh maps. The minimal expressions for the product digits are:

$$P_0 = A_0B_0$$
$$P_1 = \bar{A}_1A_0B_1 + A_1A_0\bar{B}_0 + A_1\bar{B}_1B_0 + A_1\bar{A}_0B_0$$
$$P_2 = A_1\bar{A}_0B_1 + A_1B_1\bar{B}_0$$
$$P_3 = A_1A_0B_1B_0$$

Table 3.9   Truth table of a 2-bit $\times$ 2-bit multiplier

	Inputs				Product		
B_1	B_0	A_1	A_0	P_3	P_2	P_1	P_0
0	0	0	0	0	0	0	0
0	0	0	1	0	0	0	0
0	0	1	0	0	0	0	0
0	0	1	1	0	0	0	0
0	1	0	0	0	0	0	0
0	1	0	1	0	0	0	1
0	1	1	0	0	0	1	0
0	1	1	1	0	0	1	1
1	0	0	0	0	0	0	0
1	0	0	1	0	0	1	0
1	0	1	0	0	1	0	0
1	0	1	1	0	1	1	0
1	1	0	0	0	0	0	0
1	1	0	1	0	0	1	1
1	1	1	0	0	1	1	0
1	1	1	1	1	0	0	1

The functions can be realized with two-level logic assuming the complements are available, or alternatively by PLA or ROM.

3.5.5 Two's complement multipliers

We introduced the multiplier to show combinational logic design. However, it should be noted that both the multiplier and multiplicand are considered as positive numbers. If the numbers employ the 2's complement notation, there are four possible combinations of A and B, namely:

(a) Both A and B positive

This produces the correct result.

(b) A positive and B negative

Here we obtain:

$$A(2^n - B) = 2^n A - AB$$

(Adjacent terms are multiplied, not logically AND'ed.) The correct answer is $2^{2n} - AB$, i.e. the negative representation of AB to $2n$ digits.

One correction process is to add the difference between the required result and that obtained, i.e. add $2^{2n} - 2^n A$ to $2^n A - AB$ to obtain $2^{2n} - AB$. Since $2^{2n} - 2^n A$ is the negative representation of $2^n A$ to $2n$ digits, we could subtract $2^n A$ from the multiplier result.

An alternative correction process is to 'sign extend' B by n digits, i.e. produce $2^{2n} - B$, before multiplying the numbers. Then we obtain:

$$A(2^{2n} - B) = 2^{2n} A - AB$$

The term $2^{2n} A = 2^{2n}(A - 1) + 2^{2n}$. Therefore we obtain $2^{2n}(A - 1) + 2^{2n} - AB$. $2^{2n}(A - 1)$ is beyond the range of numbers in the computation, and therefore can be ignored, leaving the correct result, $2^{2n} - AB$.

(c) A negative and B positive

Here we obtain:

$$(2^n - A)B = 2^n B - AB$$

The correct answer is $2^{2n} - AB$. One of the two correction factors in case (b) could be applied, with A and B transposed.

(d) Both A and B negative

Here we obtain:

$$(2^n - A)(2^n - B) = 2^{2n} - 2^n A - 2^n B + AB$$

The correct answer is AB. In this case, we can ignore 2^{2n} as it is outside the range of numbers in the computation, leaving a correction factor of $2^n A + 2^n B$ which could be added to the result. Alternatively, we could sign extend A to get:

$$(2^{2n} - A)(2^n - B) = 2^{3n} - 2^{2n} B - 2^n A + AB$$

Removing the first two numbers which are out of range of the computation, we get $-2^n A + AB$. This can be corrected to AB by adding $2^n A$.

Note that in each case, the sign of the multiplier and multiplicand need to be examined before any correction process is performed. The reader is referred to Lewin [2] for a description of another method of signed multiplication known as Booth's algorithm.

3.6 ANSI/IEEE standard graphic symbols for logic functions

A standard called ANSI/IEEE Std 91 – 1984 [3] has been developed by the American National Standards Institute (ANSI) and the Institute of Electrical and Electronic Engineers (IEEE) for logic function symbols. The standard provides a framework to represent virtually all logical functions. However, it becomes complex and not very readable, even for common logical functions. We will describe the essential features of the standard, though not all of its esoteric facets nor will we apply it throughout the text because of the added complexity of the standard. Knowledge of it is helpful but certainly not essential.

The outline of a logic component is usually rectangular. The general symbol outline is shown in Fig. 3.38. Input lines enter from the left and output lines leave

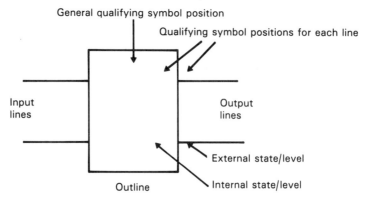

Figure 3.38 General symbol outline

from the right. The reverse direction is allowed if marked with arrows showing the direction. A *general qualifying symbol* is placed inside the outline near the top. Some general qualifying symbols are shown in Table 3.10. Symbols for highly complex functions are supplemented with an indication of the function. Memory element symbols must be supplemented with an indication of their size, e.g. PROM $1K \times 8$.

Figure 3.39 illustrates the equivalent rectangular IEEE symbols for the combinational gates. The standard also allows the *distinctive-shape* symbols shown previously in Fig. 2.1 The distinctive shape symbols are 'not preferred', though they are still very much used. Notice that the 'bubble' is still used to indicate negated output (or input).

In more complex logic components, the inputs and the outputs have *qualifying symbols* usually within the outline, and possibly also outside the outline. An important distinction is made between external logic levels and internal logic levels. External logic levels or states are assumed to exist outside the outline. Internal logic levels/states are assumed to exist inside the outline. A signal entering (or leaving) the outline may have different external and internal levels. Notably an inversion 'bubble' causes the internal level to be the inverse of the external level. Input/output qualifying symbols for combinational circuits are shown in Table 3.11.

Symbol outlines can be combined or placed touching ('embedded and abutted') to conserve space, or to show a logical link between elements, the latter with a vertical common border. A simple AND-NOR element using the standard is shown in Fig. 3.40. Small horizontal lines can be placed across the vertical common borders to indicate specific logical connections.

The outlines of more than one identical element can be pushed together as an *array of elements*; then the general qualifying symbol need only be on the top

Table 3.10   General qualifying symbols for combinational circuits

Symbol	Meaning
&	AND
$\geqslant 1$	OR
$= 1$	XOR
=	Equivalence
'1'	Input must be 1 or output always a 1
$> n/2$	Majority element
$2k$	Even number of inputs must be active to active output
$2k + 1$	Odd number of inputs must be active to active output
X/Y	X to Y Code converter (X and Y replaced with appropriate description, e.g. decimal/BCD)
MUX	Multiplexer
COMP	Comparator
S	Adder
P	Multiplier
ALU	Arithmetic logic unit

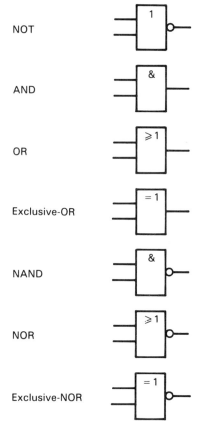

NOT

AND

OR

Exclusive-OR

NAND

NOR

Exclusive-NOR

Figure 3.39   ANSI/IEEE standard symbols for gates

Table 3.11   Input/output qualifying symbols for combinational circuits

Symbol	Meaning
—o|	Negated input
|o—	Negated output
—| ⊓	Input with hysteresis
◇ |—	Open circuit output (e.g. open collector)
▽ |—	Three-state output
EN	Enable input

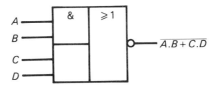

Figure 3.40 AND-NOR element

element. The *common control block* symbol can be attached to the top or bottom of an array of elements to show control of inputs and outputs by common signals. An example is shown in Fig. 3.41.

Sometimes a set of outputs may depend upon the input/outputs of an array of elements. For this application, the *common output element* outline can be used which consists of a rectangle with a double line on the border nearest the array (unless embedded in a control block, then the double line is set on the edge away from the array).

The standard introduces a *dependency notation*. In the previous array of elements, control signals affect all the duplicated elements in the same way. The dependency notation enables the relationship between specific inputs, outputs or inputs and outputs to be shown. A signal (the *affecting signal*) causing an effect on other signal(s) (the *affected signals*), is labelled with Lm where L is one of various capital letters indicating the type of relationship and m is an integer identifying the affected signals. The affected signal is similarly labelled with the same integer, m. It is possible for an affecting output to affect an affected input in circuits with feedback. Having to label affected inputs and outputs with an integer generally requires that different integers must be used for each type of dependency (except address dependency, A, given in Table 3.12). Two affecting inputs can have the same identifying number if there is an OR relationship between the affecting inputs. A bar over an integer label indicates that the complement of the affecting input/output causes the effect. Often a common control block has dependencies.

Eleven dependencies are identified as given in Table 3.12. Control (C), enable (EN) and mode (M) are similar; when the affecting input is at a 1 state, actions are

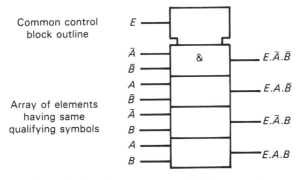

Figure 3.41 Common control block example

Table 3.12   Dependency notation

Letter type		Result on affected input/outputs	
		Affecting input = 1	*Affecting input = 0*
C	Control		
EN	Enable	Permits action	Prevents action
M	Mode		
G	AND	Permits action	Imposes 0 state
V	OR	Imposes 1 state	Permits action
N	Negate (NOT)	Complements state	No effect
S	Set	Set state	No effect
R	Reset	Reset state	No effect
A	Address	Permits action	Prevents action
X	Transmission	Path established	Path not established
Z	Interconnection	Imposes 1 state	Imposes 0 state

permitted on the affected input/outputs and conversely when the affecting input is at a 0 state, action is prevented. Control is used specifically when the affecting input produces actions as clock signals of flip-flops. Enable is used when the affecting input activates (enables) outputs. When action is prevented (affecting input at a 0 state) three-state outputs enter their high impedance state. Mode is used when one or more than one mode of operation is possible and the affecting input selects the mode. Address (A) is similar but applied to address lines, the permitted action being that associated with an address of a memory location. AND (G) specifies the logical AND of the affecting input and the affected input/outputs. OR (V) specifies the logical OR operation. Negate (N) specifies the logical NOT operation. R and S dependencies are provided essentially to show the effect of $S = R = 1$ on flip-flops and latches (see Chapter 4). An example of the dependency notation is shown in Fig. 3.42. This element produces at its outputs true or complement values of the data inputs dependent upon N3. G2 indicates that each data input is logically ANDed with the enable input.

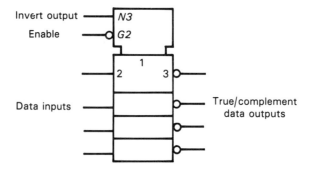

Figure 3.42   Example of dependency notation

References

1. *The TTL Data Book for Design Engineers* (6th European edn.) Dallas, TX: Texas Instruments, Inc., 1983.
2. Lewin, D., *Theory and Design of Digital Computers*, London: Nelson, 1972.
3. *ANSI/IEEE Standard Graphic Symbols for Logic Functions, Std. 94-1984*, New York: IEEE, 1984.

Problems

3.1 Design a logic circuit to realize the function $f = AB + ACD + BCD$ using NAND gates.

3.2 Repeat Problem 3.1 using NOR gates.

3.3 Using the formal method described in section 3.2.6, derive the Boolean expressions to realize the following functions to enable greatest gate sharing:

$$f_1 = \Sigma \ (0, 1, 2, 3, 6, 9, 11)$$
$$f_2 = \Sigma \ (0, 1, 6, 8, 9)$$
$$f_3 = \Sigma \ (2, 3, 8, 9, 11)$$

Draw a gate realization.

3.4 Design an iterative logic circuit which detects when all of 32 data inputs are set to a logic 0.

3.5 A logic circuit accepts two 3-bit numbers and generates a logic 1 output only when the two 3-bit numbers applied to the circuit are equal. Design a two-level realization assuming that the complements of the inputs are available.

3.6 Repeat Problem 3.5 using an iterative logic circuit arrangement.

3.7 Design a circuit free of static hazards to implement the function

$$f = \bar{B}\bar{C}\bar{D} + AB\bar{C} + BC\bar{D}.$$

3.8 A logic circuit accepts two 3-bit positive numbers and generates a logic 1 output only when one 3-bit number is greater than the another 3-bit number. Design a two-level logic circuit realization assuming that the complements of the inputs are available.

3.9 Design a two-level combinational logic circuit which will produce a 1 only when the number of 1's in a set of three input variables A, B and C is even (i.e. a parity checker). The complements of the inputs are available.

3.10 A *majority* gate is a digital circuit whose output is a 1 if the majority of the inputs are a 1, otherwize the output is a 0. Design logic circuits for a 3-input majority gate and a 5-input majority gate.

3.11 The *excess-three* code, used to represent decimal digits, is a 4-bit code similar to binary code except that each code has a binary value three greater than the decimal number it represents. For example, the excess-three code for the binary number 0101 (5) is 1000 (8).

(a) Design a logic circuit which will convert a 4-bit binary code to the equivalent 4-bit excess-three code. The binary codes 1010 to 1111 inclusive can be considered as don't cares.

(b) Design a logic circuit which will produce a 1 only when the four output variables form a code which is not an excess-three code representing any of the decimal digits 0 to 9.

3.12 Design a 4-bit binary to Gray code converter using two-level logic.

3.13 Realize the functions in Problem 3.3 using a 4-line-to-16-line decoder and NAND gates.

3.14 Realize the functions in Problem 3.3 using a PLA.

3.15 A priority encoder logic circuit has eight inputs and produces three outputs according to Table 3.13. Obtain the minimal Boolean expression for each output.

Table 3.13   Priority encoder logic circuit truth table

Inputs								Outputs		
B_7	B_6	B_5	B_4	B_3	B_2	B_1	B_0	D_2	D_1	D_0
0	0	0	0	0	0	0	X	0	0	0
0	0	0	0	0	0	1	X	0	0	1
0	0	0	0	0	1	X	X	0	1	0
0	0	0	0	1	X	X	X	0	1	1
0	0	0	1	X	X	X	X	1	0	0
0	0	1	X	X	X	X	X	1	0	1
0	1	X	X	X	X	X	X	1	1	0
1	X	X	X	X	X	X	X	1	1	1

X = don't care

3.16 Develop sum-of-product expressions from the carry-look-ahead equations to implement the first three stages of a parallel adder using a PLA.

3.17 Devise a logic scheme to multiply two 8-bit binary numbers using the carry-save technique.

4 Sequential Circuit Design

4.1 Synchronous and asynchronous sequential circuits

In Chapter 3, we noted that combinational logic circuits have output values dependent upon the values of the input variables at a particular instant. For example, an AND gate has an output value of 1 only when at that instant the inputs are all at a 1. When the output depends upon not only the present values of the inputs but also on the past values of the inputs and outputs, the circuit is called a *sequential logic circuit*. Therefore sequential circuits must be capable of remembering information about the previous values.

Sequential circuits can exist in one of a defined number of *states* and can change from one state to another state when new input values are presented to the circuit. The states are presented by variables from which the outputs are derived. It may be that the output and state variables are the same, which is the case for all sequential circuits described in this chapter. However, this correspondence does not always apply (see Chapter 11).

There are two classes of sequential circuit:

(i) Synchronous sequential logic circuit
(ii) Asynchronous sequential logic circuit.

A *synchronous sequential logic circuit* is one in which all changes in state (and output) are initiated directly by a clock signal applied to the circuit. The clock signal is a logic signal which changes from 0 to 1 and from 1 to 0 at fixed intervals. One type of clock transition (either 0 to 1 or 1 to 0) normally activates state and output changes.

An *asynchronous sequential logic circuit* is one in which the changes in state (and output) occur after inputs change and the changes do not depend upon an additional clock signal. In an asynchronous sequential logic circuit, changes in more than one output do not necessarily occur simultaneously. Changes in outputs may depend upon other output changes and propagation delays will occur.

Many digital systems are made to be synchronous in nature, for example a digital computer overall, though there may be particular instances of asynchronous operation internally. To create a synchronous system, a repetitive clock signal must be generated.

4.2 Flip-flops

The basic sequential logic circuit is the *flip-flop*. The flip-flop is used as the logic storage device in more complex sequential circuits. Flip-flops have two or more inputs dependent upon the type of flip-flop, and one or two outputs, Q and $\bar{Q}$. When the flip-flop is one operating normally, $\bar{Q}$ always takes on the inverse logic value of Q, i.e. if $Q = 0$, $\bar{Q} = 1$ and if $Q = 1$, $\bar{Q} = 0$. The outputs remain permanently in a 0 or 1 state until new input values are applied. Then the output may 'flip' to a 1 if originally at a 0 or 'flop' to a 0 if originally at a 1 or remain at the original state.

There are three fundamental types of flip-flops, the *R–S flip-flop* the *J–K flip-flop* and the *D-type flip-flop*. The letters in the names are derived from the letters identifying the inputs.

4.2.1 R–S flip-flop†

The $R–S$ flip-flop has two basic inputs, the R input and the S input, abbreviated from reset and set. The R (reset) input is used to make the Q output become a 0 while the S (set) input is used to make the Q output become a 1. Just as a combinational logic circuit such as an AND gate can be described by a truth table, the operation of a flip-flop can be described by a truth table. The truth table of the $R–S$ flip-flop is shown in Fig. 4.1(a). $R–S$ flip-flops can be synchronous and incorporate an additional *clock* input for synchronizing output changes, or they can be asynchronous without the extra clock input. The truth table is the same in both cases, though in the synchronous flip-flop, the stated outputs are not attained until an activating clock transition has occurred.

It is necessary to describe present and past values in a sequential circuit such as flip-flop. We shall do this by appending the variable name with a subscript + to indicate the value after new inputs have been applied (including the clock in synchronous flip-flops), otherwise the past value (before the clock has been activated in synchronous flip-flops) is assumed. Therefore Q_+ is the Q output after the stated inputs are applied, including the clock if present, while Q is the Q output before the stated inputs are applied. X marks an undefined output condition. In the $R–S$ flip-flop, there is an undefined output when $R = S = 1$, an invalid combination of input values. Note that X is not a don't care (or cannot happen) condition. If $R = S = 1$, an output will be generated, but it is not defined and may be inconsistent (e.g. $Q = \bar{Q} + 0$). Normally, the input combination giving rise to an undefined condition would not be used.

A rectangular box symbol is used to represent flip-flops, with inputs and outputs labelled. Figures 4.1(b) and (c) show possible synchronous and asynchronous $R–S$ flip-flop symbols. The clock input may be additionally marked to indicate the form of logic transition required to activate the device, and any restrictions. A restriction found in certain flip-flop implementations is that the other inputs should not alter

† Also called an *S–R* flip-flop.

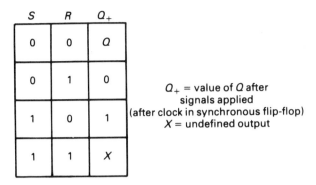

S	R	Q_+
0	0	Q
0	1	0
1	0	1
1	1	X

Q_+ = value of Q after
signals applied
(after clock in synchronous flip-flop)
X = undefined output

(a) Truth table

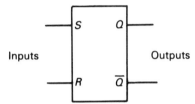

Inputs   Outputs

(b) Asynchronous R–S flip-flop symbol

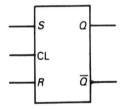

(c) Synchronous R–S flip-flop symbol

Figure 4.1   R–S flip-flop

while the clock is high. The actual flip-flop activation mechanism will be considered later when the internal flip-flop design is examined.

4.2.2 J–K flip-flop

The J–K flip-flop is always synchronous. In addition to the clock input, the flip-flop has two inputs, J and K, which when activated independently cause the flip-flop to operate in the same manner as the S and R inputs of a R–S flip-flop, i.e. when $J = 1$ and $K = 0$, the Q output sets to a 1 and when $J = 0$ and $K = 1$, the output resets to a 0. The stated outputs are only attained after the device is 'clocked'. The undefined R–S flip-flop condition, $S = R = 1$, has been replaced in the J–K flip-flop with a specified action. With $J = K = 1$, the Q output complements, i.e. if $Q = 0$, $Q_+ = 1$ and if $Q = 1$, $Q_+ = 0$. The full J–K flip-flop truth table and symbol are shown in Fig. 4.2 (a) and (b) respectively. Remember that the first three entries in the truth table are the same as the first three entries in the R–S flip-flop truth table.

J	K	Q_+
0	0	Q
0	1	0
1	0	1
1	1	$\overline{Q}$

(a) Truth table

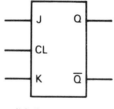

(b) Symbol

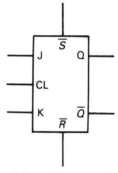

(c) J–K flip-flop symbol with
asynchronous set and reset inputs

Figure 4.2 J–K flip-flop

The $J–K$ flip-flop is a very useful device in practice. By setting the $J–K$ inputs to a 1 permanently, the output 'toggles' (changes state after each activation). This toggle operation is used in the design of binary counters. Counters are sequential circuits which produce defined output sequences when input pulses are applied. Sometimes mention is made of a *toggle* or T-type flip-flop as a device having a single input, T, in addition to the clock input. A T-type flip-flop can be created from a $J–K$ flip-flop by connecting the J and K inputs together and calling this connection the T input. Actual T-type flip-flops are not usually manufactured as such.

Asynchronous independent set and reset inputs can be incorporated into any synchronous flip-flop as shown in Fig. 4.2(c) for a $J–K$ flip-flop. These inputs will set or reset the output irrespective of the signals applied to the J, K and clock inputs. The asynchronous set and reset inputs are commonly active low (action occurs when the signal is taken to a 0). This fact may be indicated by labelling the inputs as $\bar{S}$ and $\bar{R}$ or by marking each input with a small circle. Other features can be incorporated into the $J–K$ flip-flop, for example several J and K inputs can be provided which are combined logically (either AND'ed or OR'ed or a combination) within the device. Occasionally, the K input is active low while the J input is active high, i.e. a $J–\bar{K}$ flip-flop. (This particular arrangement allows a $J–\bar{K}$ flip-flop to be easily configured as a D-type flip-flop by connecting both J and $\bar{K}$ together to form the D input; see next section.)

4.2.3 D-type flip-flop

The D-type flip-flop is always synchronous and is also used to store one binary digit. The flip-flop has one input, D (for data or delay), in addition to the clock input. The binary value applied to the D input at the time of the clock activation is transferred to the Q output. This action can be described in the very simple truth table shown in Fig. 4.3(a). The symbol of the D-type flip-flop is shown in Fig. 4.3(b).

4.3 Flip-flop implementation

In this section, the internal design of the major flip-flops is considered. We shall introduce some formal techniques of sequential circuit design. The finer technicalities of formal sequential circuit design will be considered in Chapter 11.

4.3.1 Asynchronous R–S flip-flop implementation

In designing an asynchronous $R–S$ flip-flop, we are designing an asynchronous sequential logic circuit. This asynchronous sequential circuit has two inputs, R and S, and two outputs, Q and the complement, $\bar{Q}$. The first step we shall take in the design procedure is to draw a state diagram from the problem specification. A *state diagram* is a graphical representation of the logical operation of a sequential circuit.

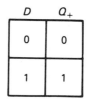

(a) Truth table

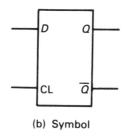

(b) Symbol

Figure 4.3   D-type flip-flop

The diagram indicates the various states that the circuit can enter and the required input/output conditions necessary to enter the states.

A state diagram of the $R-S$ flip-flop is shown in Fig. 4.4(a). This type of state diagram is known as a *Moore model state diagram*. Each large circle indicates a state. Inside each circle is the state number and the associated output of the circuit for that state. The lines between states indicate transitions from one state to the other state and the numbers next to the lines give the required input conditions. The effects of all input conditions must be considered in each state. Some input conditions cause no change in state which is indicated by a 'sling' line around the state circle. The states with sling lines around them are the stable states in an asynchronous sequential circuit. Stable states remain until an input condition occurs which causes a transition to another state which may be an unstable state. Transitions occur until another stable state is entered.

A state table is constructed from the information described in the state diagram. A *state table* lists the present states and the next states for each possible new input condition and the corresponding output. The state table for the $R-S$ flip-flop is shown in Fig. 4.4(b). The two states are given in the first column. The next four columns give the new (next) state for each possible new input condition marked above the columns, i.e. $R = 0$, $S = 0$; $R = 0$, $S = 1$; $R = 1$, $S = 1$ and $R = 1$, $S = 0$. The input variables are labelled in this order to match the labelling of a Karnaugh map which will be constructed from the state table. There is only one independent output, Q, and this output corresponds directly to the two states. One state corresponds to the Q output being a 1 and one state corresponds to the Q output being a 0. A state table giving the variables representing the states, rather than the state numbers, is known as an *assigned state table*. The assigned state table for the

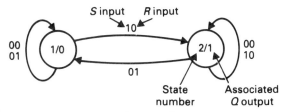

S input   R input

00
01   1/0   2/1   00
                                        10

State   Associated
number   Q output

(a) Moore model state diagram

Present state	Next state S R inputs			
	00	01	11	10
1	1	1	X	2
2	2	1	X	2

(b) State table

Present state	Next state S R inputs			
	00	01	11	10
0	0	0	X	1
1	1	0	X	1

(c) Assigned state table

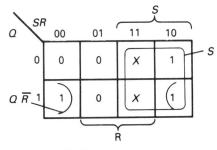

(d) Q_+ function

Figure 4.4   R–S flip-flop design procedure

R–S flip-flop is shown in Fig. 4.4(c). In our case, the state variable is the same as the output Q.

We next require a Boolean expression for the output. This expression can be derived from the assigned state table. The output function can be extracted directly as a Karnaugh map describing Q_+, as shown in Fig. 4.4(d), because for convenience the state table is labelled with the relevant variables, R, S and Q, in the same order as a three-variable Karnaugh map. The Boolean expression becomes:

$$Q_+ = Q\bar{R} + S$$

which is known as the *characteristic equation* of the R–S flip-flop. The characteristic equation of a flip-flop describes the relationship between the new output in terms of the inputs applied and the current output.

Finally, a circuit realization is drawn from the Boolean characteristic expression. The circuit can use AND and OR gates as shown in Fig. 4.5. Though the procedure leads to a design, we have not taken into account possible malfunction due to new signal changes being fed back from the output to the input. Therefore it is now necessary to check that the circuit will operate under all valid input and output conditions and that the appropriate stable outputs are generated. It is possible with our circuit to list all valid input and output combinations and then deduce the corresponding new output, which is always correct. It is left to the reader to perform this verification.

A more common circuit realization uses NAND gates solely, as shown in Fig. 4.6, which follows from applying De Morgan's theorem to the characteristic equation, i.e.:

$$Q_+ = \overline{(\overline{Q\bar{R}})\bar{S}}$$

The complement output expression is found from the Karnaugh map of Q_+ by grouping the 0's, i.e.

$$\bar{Q}_+ = \bar{Q}\bar{S} + R = \overline{(\overline{\bar{Q}\bar{S}})\bar{R}}$$

(Note that input combinations for the X's do not occur.) Active high inputs require extra NAND gates. Sometimes, active low R and S signals are used, in which case gates are not necessary to invert the input signals. If the undefined condition, $S = R = 1$, is applied, both Q and $\bar{Q}$ become a 1. If both S and R are then altered to a 0, the behaviour of the circuit is unpredictable. Extra set and reset inputs can

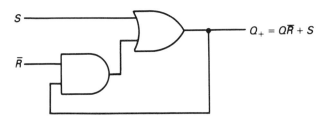

Figure 4.5   Asynchronous R–S flip-flop circuit

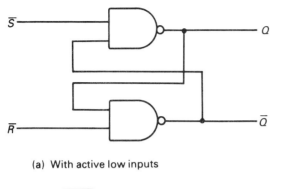

(a) With active low inputs

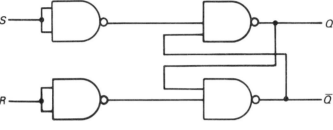

(b) With active high inputs

Figure 4.6   Asynchronous R–S flip-flop using NAND gates

be incorporated by adding further R and S inputs to the cross-coupled NAND gates, leading to a very economical circuit design. Consequently, the circuit has been widely used, especially when the number of gates available in one package was low and hence it was particularly important to keep the number of gates in a system design to a minimum.

NOR gates alone can be used. Starting from the characteristic equation, by De Morgan's theorem we obtain:

$$\bar{Q}_+ = \overline{Q\bar{R} + S}$$
$$= \overline{(\overline{\bar{Q} + R}) + S}$$

which leads to the circuit shown in Fig. 4.7. Notice that the R and S input signals are not complemented.

One application of the $R-S$ flip-flop is as a *switch debouncer* for a switch used to generate logic 0 or logic 1 depending upon the position of the switch. The contacts of most switches when the switch is operated have a tendency to vibrate, making and breaking contact several times over a period of perhaps a few milliseconds. This vibration can create transient 0's and 1's rather than a single logic transition. Figure 4.8 shows a simple circuit using a switch to generate a logic signal and the effect of switch contact bounce. Notice that there are several changes in the output when the switch is closed.

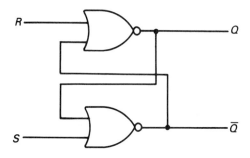

Figure 4.7   Asynchronous R–S flip using NOR gates

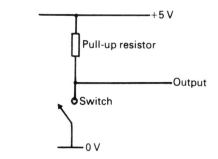

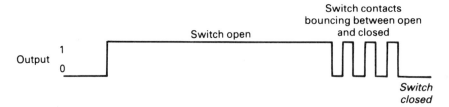

Figure 4.8   Switch bounce

To avoid these transient changes in output, a switch debouncer circuit such as that shown in Fig. 4.9(a) can be employed. In this circuit, the R–S flip flop consists of NAND gates and a two-way switch is necessary. When the switch connects 0V (accepted as a logic 0 voltage in TTL) to the $\bar{S}$ input, the Q output becomes a 1 and the $\bar{Q}$ output becomes a 0. Conversely, when the switch connects 0V to the $\bar{R}$ input, the Q output becomes a 0 and the $\bar{Q}$ output becomes a 1. The resistors ensure a logic 1 level in the open-circuit input condition. If the switch contacts vibrate during the change of switch position, assuming that the vibration is not sufficient to cause the switch arm to touch both contacts alternately, the output of the flip-flop will change only on the first contact made, as shown in Fig. 4.9(b). For this application, a pair of NOT gates can be used, as shown in Fig. 4.9(c). The switch connects 0V to one input. In this circuit, the output of one of the two NOT gates will always be

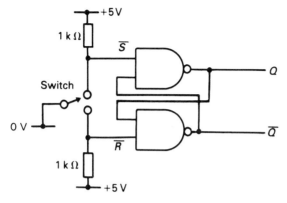

(a) Circuit using NAND gates

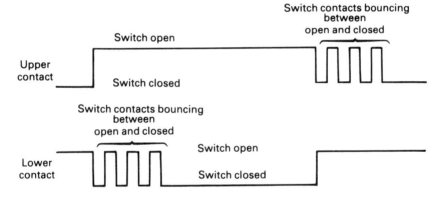

(b) Waveforms

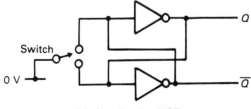

(c) Circuit using NOT gates

Figure 4.9 Switch debouncer circuits

connected to 0V, depending upon the position of the switch. This is acceptable since at the same time the input of the gate is at a 1 and no conflict occurs between the output level and the voltage from the switch.

4.3.2 Synchronous R–S flip-flop implementation

A synchronous $R–S$ flip-flop can be created by the simple modification to the asynchronous $R–S$ flip-flop design shown in Fig. 4.10. In this design, the clock signal controls the $R–S$ input NAND gates so that when the clock signal is a 0 ('low'), the state of the flip-flop cannot be altered by any change in the $R–S$ inputs. When the clock becomes a 1 ('high'), the $R–S$ input signals are allowed to enter the flip-flop and the outputs change if a change is specified by the flip-flop truth table. By limiting the $R–S$ input changes to when the clock is a 0, all changes in the output will occur as the clock signal changes from a 0 to 1, i.e. the output changes are synchronized by the rising transition of the clock signal.

It is important to note that the $R–S$ input signals must not change while the clock input is a 1 if the synchronous operation is to be preserved. We will see later that this restriction can be removed by alternative circuit arrangements which are normally applied to $J–K$ and D-type flip-flops. The particular merit of the $R–S$ design presented here is the simplicity and economy of gates. Additional active low set and reset inputs can be incorporated as shown in dotted lines in Fig. 4.10.

4.3.3 J–K flip-flop implementations

Again the first step we shall take is to draw the state diagram. A Moore model state diagram of the $J–K$ flip-flop is shown in Fig. 4.11(a). From the diagram, we can derive the state table shown in Fig. 4.11(b) and the assigned state table shown in

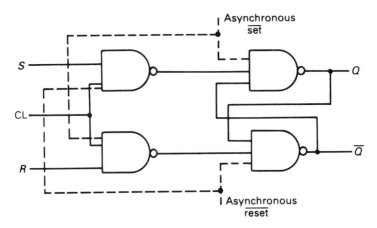

Figure 4.10   Synchronous R–S flip-flop

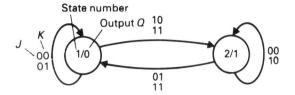

(a) Moore model state diagram

Present state	Next state J K			
	00	01	11	10
1	1	1	2	2
2	2	1	1	2

(b) State table

Present state	Next state J K			
	00	01	11	10
0	0	0	1	1
1	1	0	0	1

(c) Assigned state table

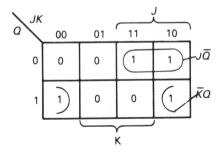

(d) Q_+ function

Figure 4.11   J–K flip-flop design procedure

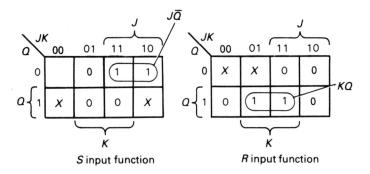

S input function   R input function

(e) *R–S* flip-flop input function

Figure 4.11 continued

Fig. 4.11(c). This leads to the Karnaugh map shown in Fig. 4.11(d) and the characteristic equation for the *J–K* flip-flop given by:

$$Q_+ = J\bar{Q} + \bar{K}Q$$

It is important to note that the state diagram given describes a synchronous sequential circuit, and we shall design a synchronous sequential circuit, as opposed to the asynchronous sequential circuit (such as the asynchronous *R–S* flip-flop circuit in section 4.3.1). State changes occur due to clock signal transitions. Given a synchronous *R–S* flip-flop, the *J–K* flip-flop can be designed by adding extra gates to the *R–S* flip-flop so that it behaves as a *J–K* flip-flop. The clock applied to the circuit is applied to the clock input of the synchronous *R–S* flip-flop.

Let us firstly consider the effect of the inputs of an *R–S* flip-flop on flip-flop output, which can be one of four possible types: the output can remain at a 0 ('0 to 0'), the output can change from a 0 to a 1 ('0 to 1'), the output can change from a 1 to a 0 ('1 to 0') or the output can remain at a 1 ('1 to 1'). The required inputs to an *R–S* flip-flop to achieve these effects, as deduced from the *R–S* flip-flop truth table, are shown in Table 4.1. There are two possible *R–S* input combinations to achieve a '0 to 0' effect, either $R = 0$, $S = 0$ or $R = 1$, $S = 0$, so the value of R does not matter and is entered in the table as a don't care *X*. Similarly, there are two

Table 4.1 Q/Q_+ table for an *R–S* flip-flop

Required output change		Inputs	
Q	to Q_+	S	R
0	0	0	X
0	1	1	0
1	0	0	1
1	1	X	0

possible $R-S$ input combinations to achieve a '1 to 1' effect, either $R = 0$, $S = 0$ or $R = 0$, $S = 1$, so the value of S does not matter and is entered in the table as a don't care X.

The required inputs to the $R-S$ flip-flop can be found by applying Table 4.1 to the Q_+ function described in the Karnaugh map of Fig. 4.11(d). For example, when $J = K = Q = 0$ in Fig. 4.11(d), the output is to remain at a 0 ('0 to 0'), and the required inputs are $S = 0$ and $R = X$. These values are entered on Karnaugh maps describing the reset and set functions. By continuing with this procedure, the two functions can be mapped totally, as shown in Fig. 4.11(e). Simplifying, we obtain:

$$\text{Set } = J\bar{Q}$$
$$\text{Reset} = KQ$$

Therefore the circuit implementation would appear to be as shown in Fig. 4.12. The true output, Q, and the inverse output, $\bar{Q}$, are cross-coupled to the input gates to produce the two input functions above. However, when checking for possible malfunction of the circuit, by examining all possible input and output conditions, we find while the clock is high, the input gates are enabled, allowing changes in J, K and Q to subsequently affect the flip-flop. In particular, if $J = K = 1$, the circuit would oscillate continuously. Therefore the circuit must be modified to prevent incorrect operation. The fundamental problem is the type of $R-S$ flip-flop used, namely the type which must not have the R or S inputs changed when the clock is at 1. There are two principal methods which can be employed, namely the *edge-triggered* design and the *master-slave* design. Both of these designs alter the basic $R-S$ flip-flop design.

(a) Edge-triggered flip-flop design

An edge-triggered flip-flop is activated by a logic transition on the clock input, say a 0 to 1, or alternatively a 1 to 0, but not both in one device. The former is called *positive edge-triggered* and the latter *negative edge-triggered*. The timing diagram

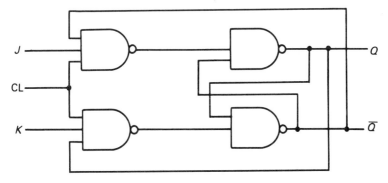

Figure 4.12 Incorrect J–K flip-flop design

for a negative edge-triggered J–K flip-flop is shown in Fig. 4.13. The shading indicates that the logic level does not matter.

The edge-triggered mechanism could be implemented by inserting a circuit in the flip-flop between the clock input and the original clock inputs of the AND gates to have the effect of producing one positive narrow logic 'pulse' (a signal which changes from 0 to a 1 and then back to a 0, staying at a 1 for a very short time) on every positive clock transition. The pulse causes the flip-flop to operate. It is necessary for the duration of the pulse to be less than the time it takes for the output signals to be generated and fed back to the inputs. Figure 4.14 shows a simple design using the delay through a NOT gate to produce a pulse. It is necessary to ensure that the pulse width is less than the delay around the flip-flop loop under all conditions. The implementation actually used in integrated circuits is usually a variant on the above.

(b) Master–slave flip-flop design

In the master–slave flip-flop, the single R–S flip-flop above is replaced by two R–S flip-flops, one called the master flip-flop, and the other called the slave flip-flop. These are connected together as shown in Fig. 4.15. The J–K inputs enter the master flip-flop with the usual clock gating. The outputs of the master flip-flop are connected to the inputs of the slave flip-flop with additional gates and the outputs of the overall circuit are taken from the slave flip-flop. The cross-coupling between the inputs and the outputs of the overall circuit is provided as defined by the J–K

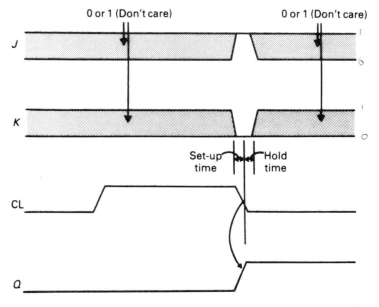

Figure 4.13   Timing diagram of a negative edge-triggered J–K flip-flop

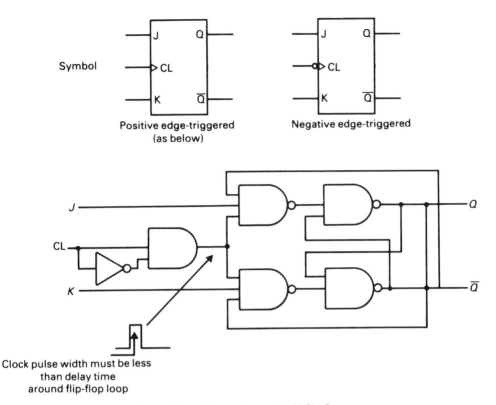

Figure 4.14   Edge-triggered J–K flip-flop

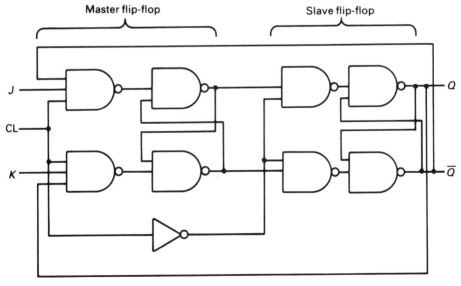

Figure 4.15   Master–slave J–K flip-flop

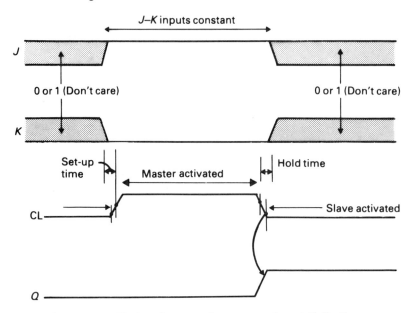

Figure 4.16 Timing diagram of a master–slave J–K flip-flop

flip-flop design. However, the overall feedback loop is broken by arranging that the J–K inputs enter the circuit when the clock is high (say) but only pass to the slave flip-flop when the clock is low. While the clock is low, the J–K inputs are inhibited from the master flip-flop but the master flip-flop can set or reset the slave. It is assumed that the J–K signals do not change when the clock is high. It is necessary for the NOT gate connecting to the slave flip-flop to have a higher switching threshold than the input NAND gates, so that there is no overlap between the master activation and the slave activation. The timing diagram for the master–slave flip-flop is shown in Fig. 4.16.

If the J–K inputs did change the high clock level, the master flip-flop would respond and the final result would depend upon the final input values rather than the states of the J–K inputs at the instant of the rising edge of the clock, losing the synchronous nature required. It is possible to modify the master–slave design to incorporate a *data lock-out* mechanism which allows the J–K inputs to change while the clock is high. However, most modern flip-flops are now edge-triggered. Examples of J–K flip-flops in the LS-TTL family include the 74LS109 dual positive edge-triggered J–K flip-flops, the 74LS73, 74LS76, 74LS78, 74LS112, 74LS113 and 74LS114 dual negative edge-triggered J–K flip-flops. Some of the edge-triggered flip-flops were master–slave in the original standard TTL series (e.g. 7473, 7476 and 7478 were master–slave J–K flip-flops).

4.3.4 D-type flip-flop implementation

For uniformity of approach, the procedure to implement a *D*-type flip-flop using an *R*–*S* flip-flop is shown in Fig. 4.17, performed in the same manner as for the *J*–*K*

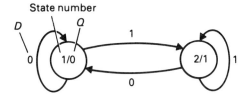

(a) Moore model state diagram

Present output Q	Next output D	
	0	1
0	0	1
1	0	1

(b) Assigned state table

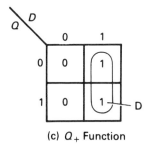

(c) Q_+ Function

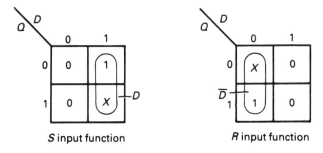

S input function   R input function

(d) R–S flip-flop input functions

Figure 4.17 D-type flip-flop design procedure

flip-flop. The characteristic equation is:

$$Q_+ = D$$

and the inputs to the R–S flip-flop are:

Set $= D$
Reset $= \bar{D}$

Hence a D-type flip-flop can be created from an R–S flip-flop by connecting a NOT gate from the S input to the R input, using the S input as the D input. The same arrangement can create a D-type flip-flop from a J–K flip-flop, connecting a NOT gate from the J input to the K input and using the J input as the D input. With these configurations, the clock activation mechanism of the resultant flip-flop will be the same as that of the original flip-flop.

Figure 4.18 shows a D-type flip-flop based on a synchronous R–S flip-flop employing cross-coupled NAND gates. In this implementation, the output would follow the data input while the clock is high and data would be stored at the instant that the clock falls to a low. The circuit is known as a *transparent* latch. Example in the TTL family include the 74LS75 quad transparent latch and the 74LS373 octal transparent latch. In the 74LS75, pairs of latches share the same clock input and the 74LS373 all eight latches share a common clock. D-type flip-flop are also edge-triggered. Examples include the 74LS74 dual D-type positive edge-triggered D-type flip-flop and the 74LS534 octal D-type flip-flop, the latter with a common clock.

4.3.5 Timing considerations

In the edge-triggered flip-flops, the R–S, J–K or D input signals must be applied before the activating clock transition for the circuit to operate correctly. The period before the transition during which the inputs must be stable is defined as the *set-up* time. Typically the set-up time of TTL flip-flops is in the regions of 20 ns. Also these signals may need to be maintained at a steady level for a short period after the clock

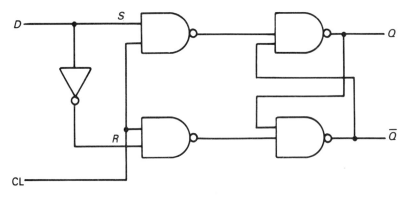

Figure 4.18 D-type flip-flop circuit (transparent latch)

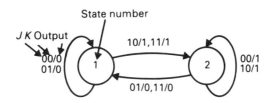

Figure 4.19 Mealy model state diagram of J–K flip-flop

transition has occurred. The period after the clock transition during which the input must be stable is known as the *hold* time. The hold time is in the region of 5 ns for TTL. Some devices have no hold time, i.e. a hold time specified as 0 ns. Similar timing constraints exist for traditional master–slave flip-flops with the added constraint that the inputs must not change between the two clock transitions used to load the master and slave flip-flops (unless a data lock-out mechanism is incorporated into the flip-flop).

If the inputs do change during the set-up time or hold times, the resultant output could not be predicted. Worse, the flip-flop might enter a non-stable state with the output not at a defined logic level but at some intermediate voltage. Theoretically, this condition could, depending upon when exactly the inputs change, last for ever. In practice, the condition very occasionally lasts for several tens of nanoseconds. This is a particular problem when flip-flops are used with randomly occurring input signals.

4.3.6 Mealy model state diagram

Another type of state diagram is known as a *Mealy model state diagram*. In a Mealy model state diagram, the outputs are not associated with the states within the state circles. Instead, the new output is given next to the input values on the lines leaving the states. Thus in this type of state diagram, it would be admissible to have a state having more than one possible output value. The two types of state diagram for flip-flops are very similar and one particular output is associated with each state. Figure 4.19 shows a Mealy model state diagram for the *J–K* flip-flop. In this chapter we will restrict our state diagram to the Moore type in which the output values are given within the state circles. However, Mealy model state diagrams can be used, as shown (with implications) in Chapter 11. In the following, each state generally has different output values. The state numbers correspond to particular output values and are omitted, for clarity.

4.4 Sequential circuit design and parts

In this section we will examine common sequential circuits including those often fabricated in MSI technology. Rather than simply present circuits, where appropriate we shall introduce the common circuits via digital system requirements and specifications using state diagrams. The circuits presented are mainly synchronous sequential circuits.

4.4.1 Registers

A *register* is a logic circuit capable of storing a number of binary digits and is normally implemented with a number of flip-flops. The most suitable flip-flop is the *D*-type flip-flop, and the discussion will concentrate on the use of *D*-type flip-flops for registers. Of course, other types of flip-flops can be used to store binary digits and can be made to behave as *D*-type flip-flops (for example as explained in section 4.3.4).

A *parallel-in parallel-out data register* stores a number of binary digits which are entered into the flip-flops of the register together and all digits are extracted from the flip-flops of the register together. A clock signal is used to cause the input data to be stored and the stored data becomes available at the outputs after the flip-flops have responded. Reset circuitry can be provided to clear the information held in the register, by using asynchronous reset inputs on the flip-flops, or synchronously by gating at the flip-flop inputs. Parallel-in parallel-out registers in the TTL family include the 74LS374 8-bit register (eight *D*-type flip-flops with a common clock).

4.4.2 Shift registers

Once we use a data register to store a binary pattern, possibilities exist by moving bits within the register. For example, we can multiply a binary number by two by moving all the digits one place left, e.g.:

Number before operation	$= 00000110$ (6_{10})
Number after digits moved one place left	$= 00001100$ (12_{10})

Here the least significant digit is set to 0. Similarly, moving the digits one place right divides the number by two, e.g.:

Number before operation	$= 00011101$ (29_{10})
Number after digits moved one place right	$= 00001110$ (14_{10})

Here the fractional part is lost, given an 8-bit register.

A data register configured to move the digits left or right is known as a *shift register*. In a shift register, all the digits can be moved from being stored in their current flip-flop to the adjacent flip-flop on application of a clock signal. The logic circuit arrangement is probably now obvious to the reader from the above, but let us develop it formally. A state diagram and state table can be produced to describe the operations required, as given in Fig. 4.20 for a 3-bit shift register. If the state table, all possible values that could be held in the register are listed and the values that would appear after a clock pulse is applied. Only the outputs are shown in the

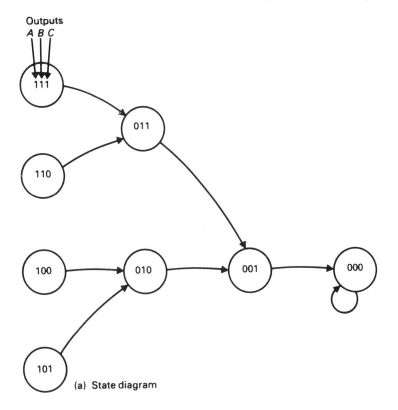

(a) State diagram

Present state			Next state		
A	B	C	A_+	B_+	C_+
0	0	0	0	0	0
0	0	1	0	0	0
0	1	0	0	0	1
0	1	1	0	0	1
1	0	0	0	1	0
1	0	1	0	1	0
1	1	0	0	1	1
1	1	1	0	1	1

(b) State table

Figure 4.20   Shift register sequence

state diagram as there is a direct correspondence between output and states. The circuit can exist in one of eight states corresponding to the eight possible values held in the register. The initial values held in the register are applied before the shifting operation.

Clearly we need three flip-flops to hold the 3-bit number and generate the outputs. We have specified D-type flip-flops although any synchronous type can be used. The appropriate signals need to be applied to the three D inputs of the flip-flops to cause the states given in the state table to be entered when clock pulses are applied. Since a D-type flip-flop takes on the value presented to the D input after the clock is applied, it is only necessary to apply the appropriate next state functions to each input. Figure 4.21(a) shows the Karnaugh maps of these functions taken directly from the next state columns of the state table. Minimizing, we obtain the functions shown and the circuit realization in Fig. 4.21(b).

The basic configuration of a shift register connects the output of each flip-flop to the input of the adjacent flip-flop. The data may be entered serially (one bit at a time) as shown in Fig. 4.22(a), or in parallel (all bits together) as in the parallel-in register using extra gates. In the serial input shift register, every time a clock signal is applied, each digit is moved ('shifted') to the adjacent flip-flop. In the shift register shown in Fig. 4.22(b) the shifting process is one place right, though the shift process may of course be configured for moving left. The values of the input applied to the first flip-flop at the time of each clock activation are shown as D_t, D_{t+1}, D_{t+2},

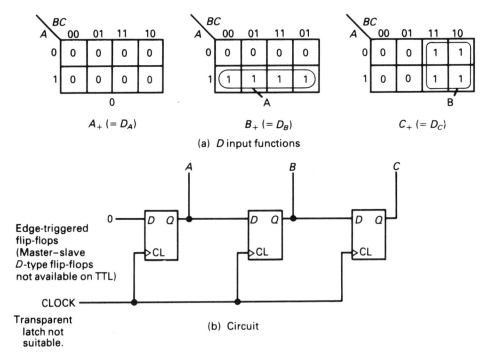

(a) D input functions

(b) Circuit

Figure 4.21   Shift register implementation

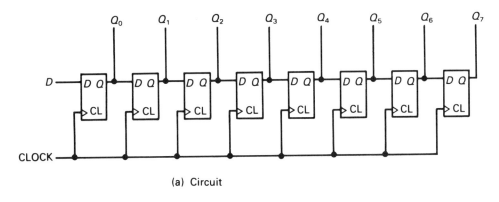

(a) Circuit

Clock pulse	D	Q_0	Q_1	Q_2	Q_3	Q_4	Q_5	Q_6	Q_7
	D_t	0	0	0	0	0	0	0	0
Φ_0	D_{t+1}	D_t	0	0	0	0	0	0	0
Φ_1	D_{t+2}	D_{t+1}	D_t	0	0	0	0	0	0
Φ_2	D_{t+3}	D_{t+2}	D_{t+1}	D_t	0	0	0	0	0
Φ_3	D_{t+4}	D_{t+3}	D_{t+2}	$D_{t.1}$	D_t	0	0	0	0
Φ_4	D_{t+5}	D_{t+4}	D_{t+3}	D_{t+2}	D_{t+1}	D_t	0	0	0
Φ_5	D_{t+6}	D_{t+5}	D_{t+4}	D_{t+3}	D_{t+2}	D_{t+1}	D_t	0	0
Φ_6	D_{t+7}	D_{t+6}	D_{t+5}	D_{t+4}	D_{t+3}	D_{t+2}	D_{t+1}	D_t	0
Φ_7	D_{t+8}	D_{t+7}	D_{t+6}	D_{t+5}	D_{t+4}	D_{t+3}	D_{t+2}	D_{t+1}	D_t
Φ_8	D_{t+9}	D_{t+8}	D_{t+7}	D_{t+6}	D_{t+5}	D_{t+4}	D_{t+3}	D_{t+2}	D_{t+1}

(b) Data flow

Figure 4.22   Serial-in parallel-out shift register

D_{t+3}, ... It is assumed that all the flip-flops in the register are first set to zero. Notice that because all the flip-flops are activated simultaneously, the data transferred from one flip-flop to the next is the data present at that time, not the subsequent data, and all digits are moved one place right simultaneously.

Shift registers can be formed with $J–K$ flip-flops, by connecting the Q and $\bar{Q}$ outputs of one flip-flop to the J and K inputs of the next flip-flop. The data can be also taken from the shift register in serial form from the final flip-flop if desired. Consequently, there are three variations, namely the serial-in serial-out register, the serial-in parallel-out shift register, and the parallel-in serial-out shift register. Shift registers in the TTL family include the 74LS194 4-bit parallel-in parallel-out bidirectional shift register, the 74165/6 8-bit parallel-in serial-out shift register, the

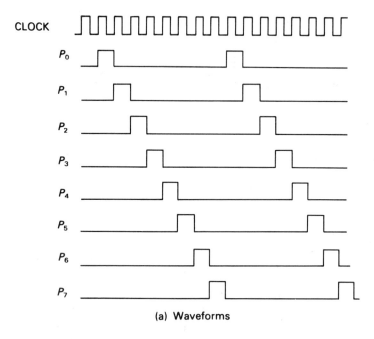

(a) Waveforms

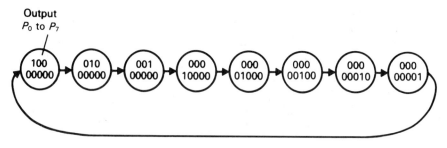

(b) State diagram

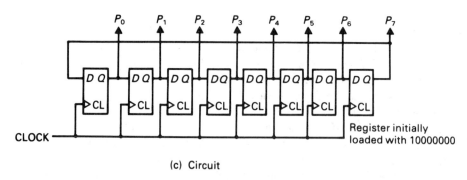

(c) Circuit

Figure 4.23 Generating timing pulses using a ring counter

74LS164 8-bit serial-in parallel-out shift register and the 7491 8-bit serial-in serial-out shift register.

When the output of the most significant (final) flip-flop of a shift register (i.e. the serial data output) is connected to the input of the least significant (first) flip-flop (i.e. the serial data input), the shift register is called a *ring counter*.

4.4.3 Generating control pulses using a shift register

A digital system is frequently controlled by sequences of timing pulses. Typically, a timing signal is required to activate a particular operation, say to transfer the contents of one register into another register. Suppose eight separate timing signals are required, each occurring in sequence and of one clock duration as shown in Fig. 4.23(a).

One design solution for generating these pulses is to initially load a 8-bit shift register with the pattern 10000000 and then shift the data right on application of a clock pulse. To achieve repetitive sequences, after 00000001 is reached we need to create the pattern 10000000 as shown in the state diagram in Fig. 4.23(b). This can be implemented with a ring counter as shown in Fig. 4.23(c). The 1 in the pattern will continually move from one position to the next on application of a clock signal, generating the required pulses.

A variation of the recirculating shift register is with the inverse output of the most significant flip-flop passed to the input of the least significant flip-flop. This arrangement is known as a *Johnson counter* or *twisted ring counter*, as shown in Fig. 4.24, with J–K flip-flops. (D-type flip-flops can be used by connecting the most significant flip-flop $\bar{Q}$ output to the least significant flip-flop D input.) The sequence followed begins with all 0's in the register. The final 0 will cause 1's to be shifted into the register from the left-hand side when clock pulses are applied. When the first 1 reaches the most significant flip-flop, 0's will be inserted into the first flip-flop because of the cross-coupling between the output and the input of the counter.

We notice now there are 16 different patterns generated with the eight flip-flops as opposed to eight different patterns with the ring counter holding a single 1. We can obtain 16 separate timing pulses by implementing the following functions:

$$
\begin{aligned}
P_0 &= \bar{Q}_0\bar{Q}_7 & P_8 &= Q_7 Q_0 \\
P_1 &= \bar{Q}_1 Q_0 & P_9 &= Q_1 \bar{Q}_0 \\
P_2 &= \bar{Q}_2 Q_1 & P_{10} &= Q_2 \bar{Q}_1 \\
P_3 &= \bar{Q}_3 Q_2 & P_{11} &= Q_3 \bar{Q}_2 \\
P_4 &= \bar{Q}_4 Q_3 & P_{12} &= Q_4 \bar{Q}_3 \\
P_5 &= \bar{Q}_5 Q_4 & P_{13} &= Q_5 \bar{Q}_4 \\
P_6 &= \bar{Q}_6 Q_5 & P_{14} &= Q_6 \bar{Q}_5 \\
P_7 &= \bar{Q}_7 Q_6 & P_{15} &= Q_7 \bar{Q}_6
\end{aligned}
$$

as each is true only during the associated clock duration. Sixteen 2-input AND gates would be needed and hence there is a trade-off between number of flip-flops and additional decode gates.

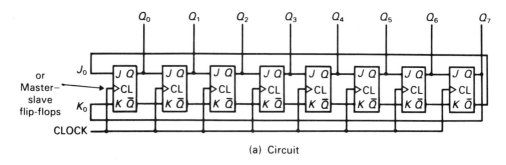

(a) Circuit

Clock pulse	Q_0	Q_1	Q_2	Q_3	Q_4	Q_5	Q_6	Q_7
Φ_0	0	0	0	0	0	0	0	0
Φ_1	1	0	0	0	0	0	0	0
Φ_2	1	1	0	0	0	0	0	0
Φ_3	1	1	1	0	0	0	0	0
Φ_4	1	1	1	1	0	0	0	0
Φ_5	1	1	1	1	1	0	0	0
Φ_6	1	1	1	1	1	1	0	0
Φ_7	1	1	1	1	1	1	1	0
Φ_8	1	1	1	1	1	1	1	1
Φ_9	0	1	1	1	1	1	1	1
Φ_{10}	0	0	1	1	1	1	1	1
Φ_{11}	0	0	0	1	1	1	1	1
Φ_{12}	0	0	0	0	1	1	1	1
Φ_{13}	0	0	0	0	0	1	1	1
Φ_{14}	0	0	0	0	0	0	1	1
Φ_{15}	0	0	0	0	0	0	0	1

(b) Output pattern

Figure 4.24 Twisted ring (Johnson) counter

When decode gates are used, it is usually important that 'glitches' do not occur. *Glitches* are unwanted logic pulses often associated with decode circuits due to more than one change occurring at the input of the gates supposedly simultaneously, but in fact at slightly different times. The principal advantage of the Johnson counter over other counter methods (see later) is that only one flip-flop output changes state at a time and consequently decode glitches will not be generated when the counter outputs are used in decode circuits such as the above. Note that, as with all counters, noise in the system may suddenly cause incorrect operation and a method of overcoming this problem must be provided, such as by the use of reset circuitry.

4.4.4 Asynchronous binary counters

A counter is a sequential logic circuit whose outputs follow a defined sequence, such as the Johnson counter above. Another example of a counter is one whose outputs begin at 0000 and count in unit steps upwards, i.e. 0001, 0010, 0011, 0100, 0101, 0110, ..., 1111. This particular counter is called a *binary (up) counter*. The sequence moves from one number to the next after the application of a clock signal. After the maximum number is reached, the counter outputs return to the first number. Such counters play vital roles in digital systems. Whereas the D-type flip-flop is a natural choice for registers, $J–K$ flip-flops are particularly suitable for counters as counter outputs often must change from 0 to 1 or from 1 to 0 (i.e. toggle). D-type flip-flops can also be used in counters by applying appropriate signals to the D inputs.

Counters, as all sequential logic circuits, can be asynchronous or synchronous in operation. In section 4.1, we defined a synchronous sequential logic circuit as one in which a clock signal initiates all changes in state, whereas an asynchronous sequential logic circuit is one in which no clock signal exists to synchronize changes. Though all counter circuits use an external clock signal to cause the states (and thus outputs) to change, the counter itself can be synchronous or asynchronous in operation internally. In the case of an asynchronous binary counter, the clock signal should be considered not as synchronizing signal but as a single input to an asynchronous sequential circuit. Firstly, we shall present asynchronous binary counter circuits. Formal asynchronous sequential circuit design is described in Chapter 11.

A 4-bit asynchronous binary-up counter is shown in Fig. 4.25(a). This counter employs falling (negative) edge triggered flip-flops or master–slave flip-flops whose slave outputs are triggered on the falling edge of the clock signal. Each flip-flop has its $J–K$ inputs connected to a permanent logic 1, which configures the counter as a 'toggle' flip-flop. The counter clock signal controls only the first flip-flop. The output of the first flip-flop, A, complements (changes from a 0 to a 1 or from a 1 to a 0) each time there is a negative clock transition. Output A is the least significant bit of the required counter sequence shown in Fig. 4.25(b). Output A is also fed into the clock input of the second flip-flop. The second flip-flop will toggle each time there is a '1 to 0' change in A. This transition occurs on every alternate output change in A and results in the required sequence for the next least significant bit, B, as shown. Similarly, the next bit C is generated by a '1 to 0' change in B.

The arrangement can be extended to any number of stages, with outputs taken from each flip-flop. The counter is asynchronous because each output depends upon a change in the previous output, and consequently there will be a small delay between output changes. The delays are cumulative, and the overall delay between the first output change and the last output change could be significant. The timing diagram for a 4-bit asynchronous counter is shown in Fig. 4.25(c). Typical flip-flop propagation delay times are in the order of 10 ns to 30 ns for TTL logic circuits. If the propagation delay time of each flip-flop is 10 ns, there would be a delay between the first output change and the fourth output change of 30 ns, when the output changes are due to change together (e.g. from 1110 to 0001). This delay will limit the rate at which clock pulses can be applied (the maximum frequency of operation). Normally a new activating clock transition is not applied to the circuit before all the flip-flop outputs have stabilized at their required outputs. Therefore in our case,

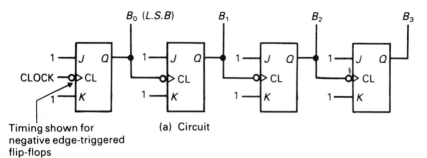

(a) Circuit

Timing shown for
negative edge-triggered
flip-flops

Clock pulse	B_3	B_2	B_1	B_0
Φ_0	0	0	0	0
Φ_1	0	0	0	1
Φ_2	0	0	1	0
Φ_3	0	0	1	1
Φ_4	0	1	0	0
Φ_5	0	1	0	1
Φ_6	0	1	1	0
Φ_7	0	1	1	1
Φ_8	1	0	0	0
Φ_9	1	0	0	1

(b) Output pattern

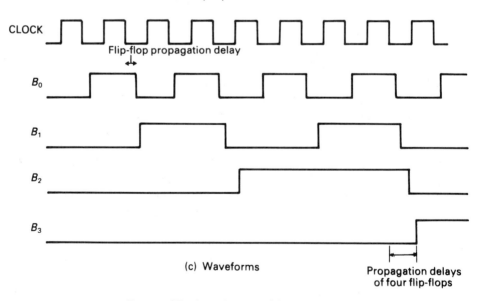

(c) Waveforms

Propagation delays
of four flip-flops

Figure 4.25 Asynchronous binary counter

activating transitions should not occur at intervals less than 40 ns (i.e. greater than 25 MHz) considering only the propagation delay alone. Flip-flops also have a maximum stated clocking frequency (closely related to the propagation delay time) which must not be exceeded. Asynchronous binary counters are sometimes called ripple counters as the clock 'ripples' through the circuit (cf. ripple carry parallel adders in Chapter 3).

A D-type flip-flop can be configured as a 'toggle' flip-flop by returning the $\bar{Q}$ output back to the D input. Hence an asynchronous binary counter can be formed in the same way as with $J–K$ flip-flops after the D to $\bar{Q}$ connections are made. Asynchronous binary counters exist in the TTL family, including the 74LS293 and 74LS197 4-bit asynchronous binary counters. Asynchronous binary counters generally require fewer internal gates than synchronous binary counters, as we shall see in section 4.4.5. However, delays between output changes may be significant (as discussed in section 4.4.8).

4.4.5 Synchronous binary counters

In the synchronous counter, the clock signal connects to all the flip-flop clock inputs. Consequently, all flip-flop output changes occur simultaneously (ignoring variations between flip-flops). Combinational logic is then provided attached to the flip-flop inputs to produce the required sequence.

The binary-up counter follows the sequence given in Fig. 4.26. The state table giving the present state and next state is derived as before. As with any counter sequence, each clock activation is required to cause one of the following 'effects' on each output:

Q to Q_+
'0 to 0'
'0 to 1'
'1 to 0'
'1 to 1'

All of these effects can be achieved by any of the major flip-flops, (i.e. $R–S$, $J–K$ and D-type flip-flops). For example, Table 4.1 gives the inputs required for the $R–S$ flip-flop. A similar table can be derived for the $J–K$ flip-flop as shown in Table 4.2. In this table, the don't care conditions result from having two possible input conditions for each output condition. To have a '0 to 0' effect, either $J = K = 0$ or $J = 0$ and $K = 1$. Therefore K could be a 0 or a 1. This is entered as an X. Similarly, to have a '0 to 1' effect, either $J = K = 1$ or $J = 1$ and $K = 0$. Therefore K is again entered as an X. To have a '1 to 0' effect, either $J = K = 1$ or $J = 0$ and $K = 1$. Therefore J could be a 0 or a 1 and is entered as an X. To have a '1 to 1' effect, either $J = K = 0$ or $J = 1$ and $K = 0$. J is entered as an X.

Let us consider the use of $J–K$ flip-flops for the counter. Three flip-flops are required for the three outputs A, B and C. There are six flip-flop inputs to consider, namely J_A, K_A, J_B, K_B, J_C and K_C. The Boolean functions for each of the six inputs

ABC

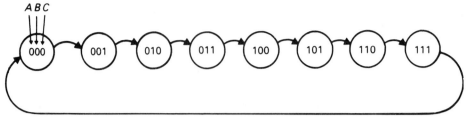

(a) State diagram

Present state			Next state		
A	B	C	A_+	B_+	C_+
0	0	0	0	0	1
0	0	1	0	1	0
0	1	0	0	1	1
0	1	1	1	0	0
1	0	0	1	0	1
1	0	1	1	1	0
1	1	0	1	1	1
1	1	1	0	0	0

(b) State table

Figure 4.26   Binary-up counter sequence

Table 4.2 Q/Q_+ table for a J–K flip-flop

Required output change		Inputs	
Q	to Q_+	J	K
0	0	0	X
0	1	1	X
1	0	X	1
1	1	X	0

can be found by deducing the required input values to achieve each new counter output from the previous counter output, using Table 4.2. For example, the first entry is $ABC = 000$, and changes to $A_+B_+C_+ = 001$. To make the required A = '0 to 0' effect, we need, $J = 0$, $K = X$, from Table 4.2. These are entered into the J_A and K_A Karnaugh maps respectively. All the entries of the six maps are entered in this way. The result is shown in Fig. 4.27(a). The circuit is given in Fig. 4.27(b).

Clearly we can extend the design procedure for any number of variables. The final design can be deduced as follows: output changes occur on the activating edge of the clock signal. Examining the binary-up sequence given in Fig. 4.28(a), we see the first stage should toggle each time an activating clock transition occurs. This is achieved by applying a permanent 1 to both the J and K inputs of the first stage. The second stage should toggle if, at the time of the activating clock transition, the B_0 output is a 1. No change will occur when the B_0 output is a 0. This is achieved by

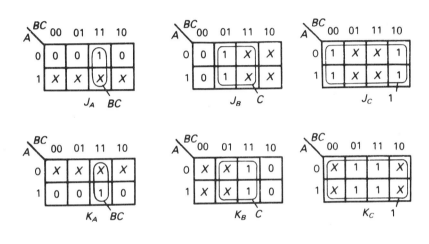

(a) J–K input functions

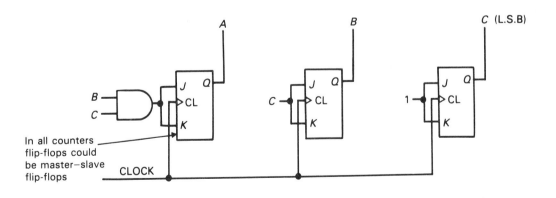

(b) Circuit

Figure 4.27 Binary-up counter implementation

Clock pulse	B_5	B_4	B_3	B_2	B_1	B_0
Φ_0	0	0	0	0	0	0
Φ_1	0	0	0	0	0	1
Φ_2	0	0	0	0	1	0
Φ_3	0	0	0	0	1	1
Φ_4	0	0	0	1	0	0
Φ_5	0	0	0	1	0	1
Φ_6	0	0	0	1	1	0
Φ_7	0	0	0	1	1	1
Φ_8	0	0	1	0	0	0
Φ_9	0	0	1	0	0	1
Φ_{10}	0	0	1	0	1	0
Φ_{11}	0	0	1	0	1	1
Φ_{12}	0	0	1	1	0	0
Φ_{13}	0	0	1	1	0	1
Φ_{14}	0	0	1	1	1	0
Φ_{15}	0	0	1	1	1	1
Φ_{16}	0	1	0	0	0	0
Φ_{31}	0	1	1	1	1	1
Φ_{32}	1	0	0	0	0	0

(a) Pattern

Figure 4.28   6-bit synchronous binary counter

applying B_0 to the J and K inputs of the second stage. The toggling action will occur on every alternate activating clock transition. It is important to note that the change in B_1 occurs because, immediately before, B_0 is a 1. Looking at the sequence, it can be seen that the third stage should toggle only when B_0 and B_1 are both 1. This can be achieved by applying B_0B_1 to the J and K inputs of the third flip-flop. Hence the first three flip-flops are configured as designed above.

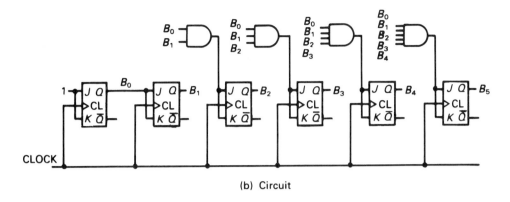

(b) Circuit

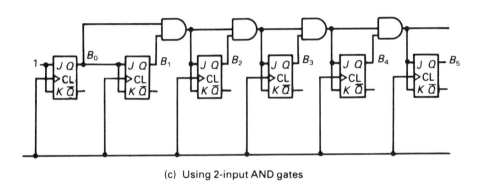

(c) Using 2-input AND gates

Figure 4.28 continued

Continuing, the toggle action for the fourth stage should occur when all of B_0, B_1 and B_2 are a 1. The combinational circuitry for the fourth stage could be one three-input AND gate. The toggle action for the fifth stage should occur when all of B_0, B_1, B_2 and B_3 are a 1 and thus requires a four-input AND gate. The sixth stage should toggle when all of B_0, B_1, B_2, B_3 and B_4 are a 1 and hence requires a five-input AND gate, and so on, as shown in Fig. 4.28(b). An alternative implementation is shown in Fig. 4.28(c) which reduces the number of inputs of the gates to two. However, this particular implementation has the disadvantage that the number of levels of gating increases with the number of stages, which will limit the speed of operation.

A *binary-down counter* is a counter whose outputs form a counting sequence in reverse order to that of the up counter, e.g. 1111, 1110, 1101, 1100, 1011, 1010, ... This can be obtained by connecting the $\bar{Q}$ output of one flip-flop to the next stage, rather than Q. Alternatively, the counter can be left connected as an up counter and the outputs taken from the $\bar{Q}$ instead of Q. (The reader may wish to confirm that complementing the output sequence, i.e changing all 0's to 1's and all 1's to 0's, will result in the count-down sequence.) If rising (positive) edge-triggered flip-flops are used in the counter circuits with the Q's taken as the counter outputs, to count up Q is fed to the next stage, while to count down, $\bar{Q}$ is fed to the next stage.

A *bidirectional counter* is a counter which can count upwards or downwards depending upon some logic control signal. One bidirectional synchronous counter is shown in Fig. 4.29. In this circuit, there are two control signals, 'count-forward'

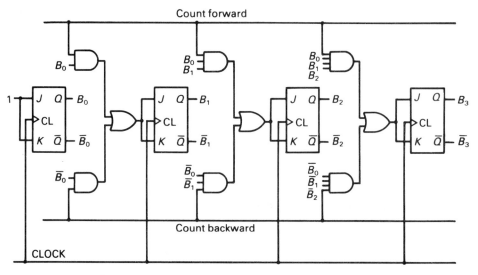

Figure 4.29 Bidirectional synchronous binary counter

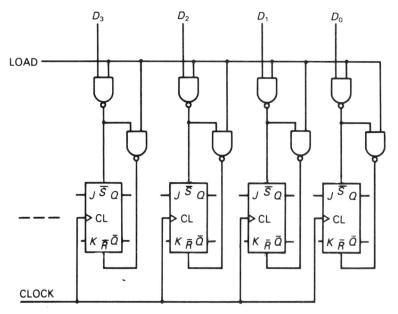

Figure 4.30 Asynchronous parallel load logic for a synchronous binary counter

and 'count-backward'. 'Count-forward' when set to a 1 selects the Q flip-flop outputs to feed to the next stage, while 'count-backward' when set to a 1 selects the $\bar{Q}$ flip-flop outputs. Counter outputs are always taken from the Q flip-flop outputs. If neither 'count-forward' nor 'count-backward' is a 1, the counter is inactive. Count-forward and count-backward are never set to a 1 together. Bidirectional counters are available as one part in integrated circuit construction, such as the TTL 74LS191/3 4-bit synchronous binary up/down counters. The 74LS191 has a single up/down control input. The flip-flops of the counters can be preset to initial values (i.e. loaded with data) using asynchronous set and reset inputs of the flip-flops activated with a 'load data' signal. Figure 4.30 shows additional logic circuitry to achieve this asynchronous load operation. The asynchronous load operation overrides any synchronous counting operation.

A synchronous load operation can be implemented as in the 74LS163 synchronous count-up counter. When the data input is a 0, $J = 0$ and $K = 1$ causing the output to become a 0, and when the data input is a 1, $J = 1$ and $K = 0$ causing the output to become a 1. The load operation takes place at the time of the activating clock transition and overrides the counting operation.

4.4.6 Design procedure for arbitrary code counters

Sometimes a counter is required which follows different sequences than simply counting in binary. Examples include binary counters which count only up to a number less than the maximum, and counters that follow specific codes sequences. It may be that an intuitive solution can be found. However, the procedure we have already presented to design binary counters can be applied to any sequence and to all types of flip-flops.

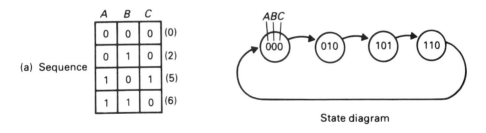

Figure 4.31 Arbitrary code counter sequence

For example, consider the sequence described in state diagram shown in Fig. 4.31(a). The corresponding state table is given in Fig. 4.31(b). The subsequent design procedure is similar to that given previously. Four numbers do not appear in the sequence, 001 (decimal 1), 011 (3), 100 (4) and 111 (7). One possible course of action is to consider these numbers as don't cares. The entries in the Karnaugh maps are then marked with X's. However, any of the unused numbers may appear upon switch-on and mapping the numbers as don't cares will mean that the subsequent behaviour of the counter will depend upon the interpretation of the don't cares during the logic minimization process. For example, if the J and K functions were minimized as though the don't care were 1's, the outputs would toggle. The subsequent sequence followed would depend upon the mapping. It is possible that a completely different and unwanted sequence could be followed. If at any time one of the required numbers in the sequence appears, the correct sequence would then be entered. To ensure that the correct sequence is followed

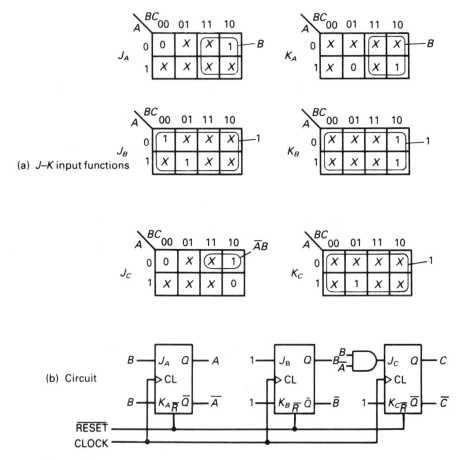

Figure 4.32   Design of an arbitrary code counter based on J–K flip-flops

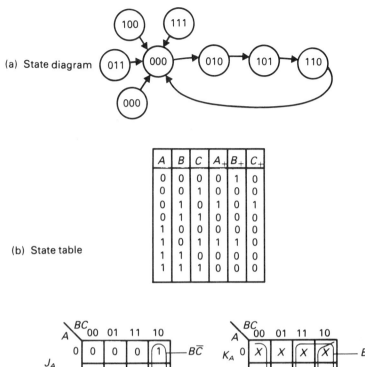

(a) State diagram

(b) State table

A	B	C	A₊	B₊	C₊
0	0	0	0	1	0
0	0	1	0	0	0
0	1	0	1	0	1
0	1	1	0	0	0
1	0	0	0	0	0
1	0	1	1	1	0
1	1	0	0	0	0
1	1	1	0	0	0

(c) J–K input functions

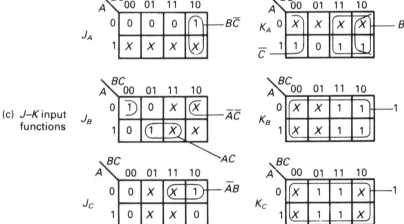

(d) Circuit

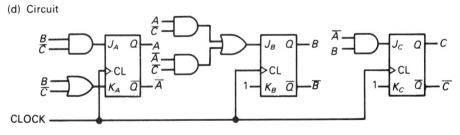

CLOCK

Figure 4.33 Arbitrary code counter design with unused codes mapped

irrespective of the start-up conditions, each don't care needs to be considered separately and interpreted in a way that the correct sequence is found eventually.

Another approach to handle start-up conditions is to force the counter outputs into one of the correct numbers when the counter is first switched on by applying a general system reset signal to the asynchronous set and reset inputs of the flip-flops (if available).

In our problem, all don't cares are considered as such and the minimal solution is obtained as shown in Fig. 4.32(a). Finally, the circuit is drawn. One implementation is shown in Fig. 4.32(b). Figure 4.33 shows the design of the counter so that the next code after an unused code is 000. If an unused code appeared upon switch-on (or due to electrical noise), after one clock pulse the counter outputs would be 000, and subsequently would remain in the correct sequence.

A D-type flip-flop implementation requires only three inputs, D_A, D_B and D_C. Table 4.3 can be used to deduce the flip-flop inputs. The problem reduces simply to entering the new Q output, either A_+, B_+ or C_+ as appropriate, into the Karnaugh maps. The design is shown in Fig. 4.34. Notice that there is a common term, $\bar{A}B$, which allows a gate to be used for both D_A and D_C inputs. In general, the D-type flip-flop expressions will be more complicated than the $J–K$ flip-flop expressions and more gates will be required for each expression. However, there are half the number of expressions so the number of gates may in fact be less. Also, larger numbers of D-type flip-flops are manufactured in one package.

4.4.7 Alternative approach for arbitrary code counter design

We have presented counter designs using flip-flops and SSI gates. In practice, MSI binary-up counters are readily available, and this influences the design approach taken. For example, an arbitrary code counter can be designed using a standard binary counter and combinational logic to convert the binary output into the required output, if the number of states in the arbitrary code counter is the same as the binary counter. As mentioned in Chapter 3, read-only memories (ROMs) can replace combinational logic. To take an example, if an 8-bit Gray code counter (counter with outputs which follow the Gray code) is required, an 8-bit binary counter could be used together with a 256 (2^8) 8-bit word ROM as shown in

Table 4.3 Q/Q_+ table for a D-type flip-flop

Required output change		Inputs
Q	to Q_+	D
0	0	0
0	1	1
1	0	0
1	1	1

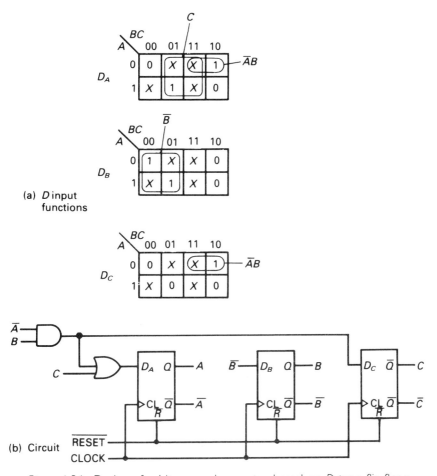

(a) *D* input functions

(b) Circuit

Figure 4.34 Design of arbitrary code counter based on *D*-type flip-flops

Fig. 4.35. The first 8-bit memory location would hold the first Gray code (00000000), the second location addressed would hold the second Gray code (00000001), the third location would hold the third Gray code (00000011), the fourth location would hold the forth Gray code (00000010), etc.

Apart from only requiring two components, a binary counter and a ROM, the method has the advantage that the sequence can easily be altered by inserting a new ROM holding a required sequence, However, the maximum speed of operation may be less than using the method in section 4.4.5 with gates because of the maximum speed of operation of the ROM.

4.4.8 Generating control pulses using binary counters

An application of binary-up and binary-down counters is to produce timing signals. Suppose the eight separate timing signals shown previously in Fig. 4.23(a) are

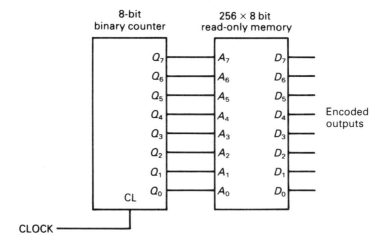

Figure 4.35 Arbitrary code counter based on a binary counter and a read-only memory

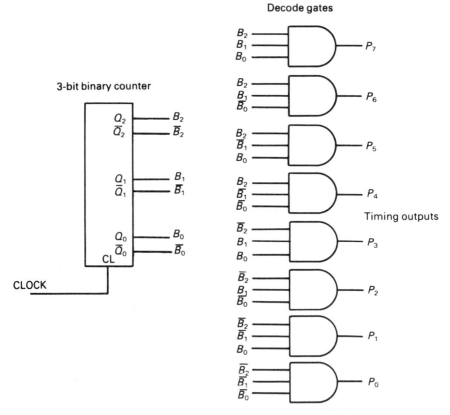

Figure 4.36 Generating timing pulses using a binary counter and decode logic

required, each timing signal occurring in sequence and of one clock duration. Figure 4.36 shows a design based around a binary counter. Here each AND gate decodes one possible binary output combination from 000 to 111 ($\bar{B}_2\bar{B}_1\bar{B}_0$, $\bar{B}_2\bar{B}_1B_0$, $\bar{B}_2B_1\bar{B}_0$, $\bar{B}_2B_1B_0$, $B_2\bar{B}_1\bar{B}_0$, $B_2\bar{B}_1B_0$, $B_2B_1\bar{B}_0$ and $B_2B_1B_0$), and produces a 1 only when the combination occurs.

If an asynchronous binary counter is used in the above circuit, glitches can occur in the outputs because of delays between counter output changes. These glitches are shown in an idealized form in Fig. 4.37 and come about when more than

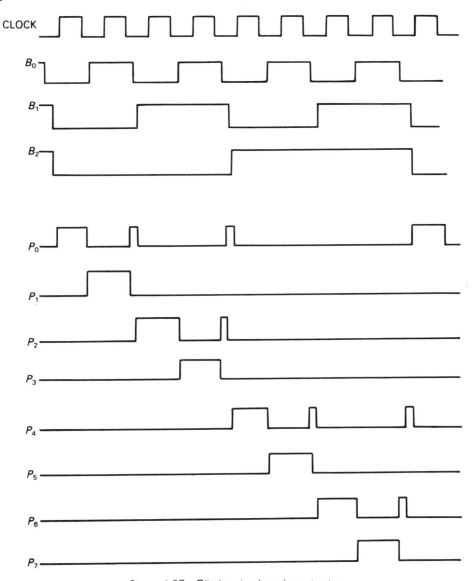

Figure 4.37 Glitches in decode outputs

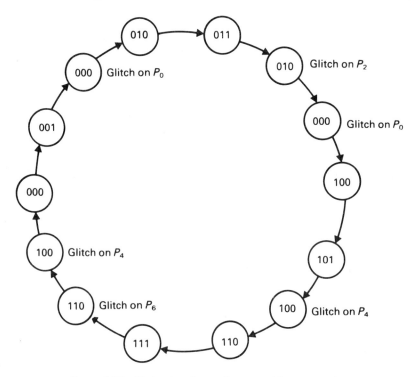

Figure 4.38 Outputs of asynchronous binary counter

one binary output must change. Figure 4.38 shows the actual patterns generated by the counter. Replacing the asynchronous counter with a synchronous counter is likely to eliminate glitches but there is still the possibility that glitches are generated due to differences between flip-flop propagation delays. For example, the 74LS78 J–K flip-flop has a low-to-high output propagation delay time of 11 ns typically, and 20 ns maximum. The high-to-low output propagation delay time is 15 ns typically, and 30 ns maximum. Minimum delay times are not quoted. Pessimistically, the minimum times could be taken to be zero. Even between typical and maximum times, it is possible to generate glitches in decode outputs should the decode gates operate at high speed. The flip-flops of complete counter parts are likely to be more closely matched though actual figures are not normally given.

The Johnson counter approach described in section 4.4.2 would overcome the problem as only one output change occurs at a time in this counter. Alternatively, an enable signal could be applied to all decode gates to produce an output only after all possible glitch combinations have passed.

4.5 ANSI/IEEE symbols for sequential circuits

The ANSI/IEEE symbols for basic flip-flops are very similar to our notation. The same input qualifying letters are used for J, K, D, S and R inputs without general qualifying symbols. However, asynchronous S and R when present in J–K and D-type flip-flops are always placed on the left edge of the symbol together with all the other inputs, rather than our method of placing them on the top and bottom of the J–K and D-type flip-flop symbols. The top and bottom places are widely used as this helps visualize the actions of set and reset. The letter C is used for the clock input with similar additional symbols to indicate the mode of triggering. Active low and active high inputs and outputs can be differentiated from negated inputs and outputs, though in most cases the distinction is not significant. A triangle is placed against the signal line and device outline to show active low inputs and outputs. The Q and $\bar{Q}$ outputs are not labelled unless to show input/output dependencies. Integers are used to show the relationship between affecting and affected inputs, as in other

Table 4.4 General qualifying symbols for common sequential circuits and memory components

Symbol	Meaning
SRGm	m-bit shift register
CTRm	m-bit counter
RCTRm	Ripple counter (count sequence = 2^m)
CTR DIV m	Synchronous counter (count sequence = m)
RAM	Random-access memory
ROM	Read-only memory
PROM	Programmable read-only memory

Table 4.5 Further input and output qualifying symbols

Symbol	Meaning
	Active low input
	Active low output
	Dynamic input (the transition from an external 0 to a 1 produces a transitory internal 1 state)
	Dynamic input with negation
	Postponed output (internal state is postponed until the input signal returns to its initial logic state/level)
D, J, K, R, S, T	Inputs of a latch or flip-flop
C	Clock input
$\rightarrow m$	Shift left to right input, m position shift
$\leftarrow m$	Shift right to left input, m position shift
$+ m$	Count-up input, increase by m
$- m$	Count-down input, decrease by m

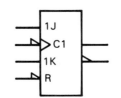

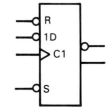

(a) Dual *D*-type latch   (b) Edge-triggered *J–K* flip-flop   (c) Edge-triggered *D*-type flip-flop

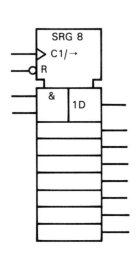

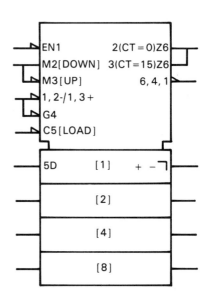

(d) 8-bit shift register   (e) 4-bit synchronous up/down binary counter

Figure 4.39 Examples of ANSI/IEEE symbols for sequential circuits

ANSI/IEEE symbols. For example, a single *J–K* flip-flop, the clock input is marked with C1 and the *J–K* inputs with 1*J* and 1*K* respectively. General qualifying symbols for counters, registers and memory are shown in Table 4.4. Input and output qualifying symbols for sequential circuits are shown in Table 4.5. Figure 4.39 shows examples of flip-flops, a shift register and a binary counter. The binary counter is given to illustrate the complexity of the notation.

Problems

4.1   Determine the truth table of the flip-flop shown in Fig. 4.40, assuming that $S = 0$, $R = 0$ cannot be followed by $S = 1$, $R = 1$, or vice versa. Comment. Modify this circuit so as to become a synchronous flip-flop.

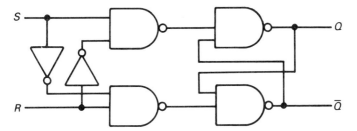

Figure 4.40 Logic circuit for problem 4.1

4.2 A design team is investigating possible new types of flip-flops and is considering a flip-flop they call an '*X−Y*' flip-flop with the truth table shown in Table 4.6. Show that the *X−Y* flip-flop can be designed around a *R−S* flip-flop by deriving the *R* and *S* input expressions.

Table 4.6 Truth table for Problem 4.2

Inputs		Output
X	Y	Q^+
0	0	0
0	1	1
1	0	$\bar{Q}$
1	1	Q

4.3 Design a logic circuit using NAND gates to convert a shift register into either a ring counter or a Johnson (twisted ring) counter. Arrange that when a control signal, *A* (say), is a 1, the configuration is a ring counter, and when *A* is a 0, the configuration is a Johnson counter.

4.4 Design an asynchronous binary-down counter using positive edge-triggered *D*-type flip-flops.

4.5 Design a synchronous binary-up counter using *D*-type flip-flops.

4.6 Design a synchronous binary counter with outputs that follow the state diagram shown in Fig. 4.41, using *J−K* flip-flops.

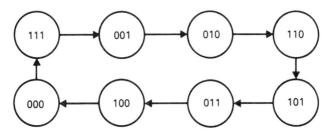

Figure 4.41 State diagram for Problem 4.6

4.7   Repeat Problem 4.6 using *D*-type flip-flops. Draw diagrams illustrating the logic levels taken by the outputs of the flip-flops for one complete cycle of the sequence.

4.8   Design a synchronous counter which follows one of the two state diagrams shown in Fig. 4.42, depending upon a control signal, *Z*. If *Z* = 1, state diagram (a) is followed. If *Z* = 0, state diagram (b) is followed. Use *J–K* flip-flops with asynchronous reset inputs and NAND gates. Numbers not in the sequences can be considered as don't cares. Use the reset inputs to initialize the circuit.

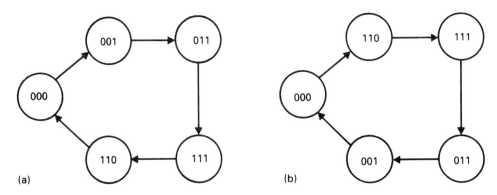

Figure 4.42   State diagrams for Problem 4.8

4.9   Design a synchronous counter to cycle repetitively through the numbers zero to five (i.e. binary 000 to 101). Ensure that the counter cannot cycle through any other sequence by mapping unused patterns to change the pattern 000 after one activating clock transition. Use *J–K* flip-flops which do not have asynchronous set or reset inputs, and NAND gates. Modify the circuit so that the number five is omitted from the sequence when a control signal, *A*, is a 1.

4.10   Determine the sequence followed by the counter shown in Fig. 4.43. Draw the state diagram.

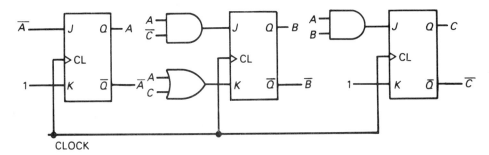

Figure 4.43   Logic circuit for Problem 4.10

4.11 Design a circuit based upon a 2-bit binary-up counter and decode gates which will generate the recurring sequence of pulses on seven outputs $P_6 P_5 P_4 P_3 P_2 P_1 P_0$ described below:

$$P_6 P_5 P_4 P_3 P_2 P_1 P_0 = 1000001, \ 0000100, \ 0011000, \ 0100010$$

Determine whether any glitches might occur if an asynchronous binary counter were used.

5 Logic Circuit Implementation

5.1 Logic gates

The circuit details of logic devices were mentioned briefly in section 2.2.4. Now we will take the subject a little further. Voltages are used almost universally to represent Boolean values and binary digits and clearly we need two voltages to represent the two Boolean/binary states. To recapitulate, if the voltage used to represent a 1 is more positive than the voltage used to represent a 0, the representation is known as positive logic representation. Conversely if the voltage used to represent a 1 is less than that used to represent a 0, the representation is known as negative logic representation. In this chapter we will assume a positive logic representation as this is most commonly chosen. It has already been noted that the representation chosen is only a convention and not intrinsic in the design of the gate.

A gate can have one input (NOT gate) or more than one input. The number of inputs is called the *fan-in*, e.g. a three-input AND gate has a fan-in of 3. The term *fan-out* is used to define the number of gates than can be connected to the output of a gate. Fan-out is limited by circuit considerations which we will consider later.

Logic gates can be designed using diodes and resistors, transistors and resistors, or diodes, transistors and resistors. Usually, the last combination of components is used. We shall firstly consider gates employing diodes and resistors as these are fundamental logic circuits. A knowledge of basic electronics would be helpful for this chapter; essential concepts will be explained only very briefly as necessary.

5.2 Diode gates

5.2.1 Diode AND gate

Let us review the *p–n* diode. Current flows in the forward direction through the diode (the same direction as the direction of the point in the symbol) when the voltage across the diode reaches about $+0.7$ V. The diode is then said to be *forward-biased* or conducting. The voltage drop across a diode does not increase substantially above 0.7 V as current is increased and is commonly assumed to be constant. Virtually no current flows when the applied voltage is less than 0.7 V or when a negative voltage is applied. When a negative voltage is applied, the diode is said to be *reverse-biased*. Figure 5.1 depicts a typical *p–n* diode voltage–current characteristic. In our analysis, we will assume an idealized characteristic in which conduction occurs at a voltage of 0.7 V and no conduction occurs below this voltage. The reader is referred to texts on electronics for a description of exactly how the diode achieves this behaviour.

A three-input diode AND is shown in Fig. 5.2. Extra inputs can be formed by adding extra diodes. We shall take the input logic levels to be 0 V for a 0 and +5 V for a 1. When all the inputs are at 0 V, all the input diodes are forward-biased and

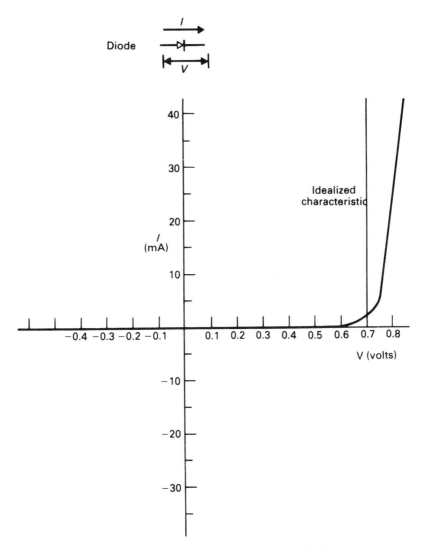

Figure 5.1   V–I characteristic of a p–n diode

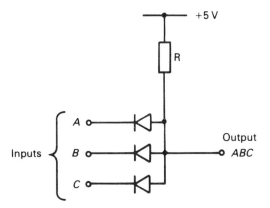

Figure 5.2   Three-input diode AND gate

current will flow from the +5 V supply through the resistor and diode and out of the input terminal. If the diodes are identical, the current will divide equally between the diodes. Therefore the output voltage must be +0.7 V above the input voltage of 0 V, i.e. 0.7 V. This voltage will be taken as the output 0 level.

If one input is raised to 5 V (representing a logic 1), the associated input diode will become reverse-biased, but the other diodes will still be forward-biased. Current will continue to flow through these diodes and the output will remain at a 0. If two inputs are raised to a 1 level, current will flow through the diodes associated with the inputs still at a 0, and the output will remain at a 0. Only when all the inputs are raised to a 1 level will this condition change. Then, the output voltage will rise. If 5 V is applied on all the inputs, none of the diodes can conduct and the output voltage will also be at 5 V (a logic 1). The circuit behaves as an AND gate since only when all the inputs are at a 1 level will the output be at a 1 level.

Notice that the output voltage representing a logic 0 is higher than the input 0 level by +0.7 V, but the voltage at a 1 is 5 V for both input and output. An extra +0.7 V at a 0 level is added to each output of similar circuits if they are cascaded, i.e. a second gate would have an output at a 0 level of 1.4 V, a third gate would have an output of 2.1 V. This is clearly unacceptable. Therefore many diode AND gates cannot be cascaded.

5.2.2 Diode OR gate

A three-input diode OR gate is shown in Fig. 5.3. Again extra inputs can be added by adding extra diodes. With all input signals at 0 V (a logic 0), the output must be at 0 V (a logic 0) since none of the input diodes can conduct. If any of the inputs rises to 5 V (a logic 1), the associated diode will conduct and the output will also rise to 0.7 V less than the input voltage, i.e. 4.3 V. This voltage will be taken as a 1. If more input signals rise to a 1 level, the output will remain at a 1 level. Consequently, the circuit behaves as an OR gate.

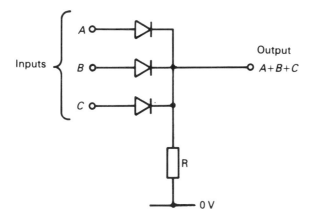

Figure 5.3 Three-input diode OR gate

Notice in this circuit that the output level at a 0 is the same at 0 V for both input and output, but the output voltage at a 1 level is lower than the input by 0.7 V. Successive output voltages of cascaded OR gates are reduced by 0.7 V, i.e. a second gate would have an output at a 1 level of 3.6 V, a third gate would have an output of 2.9 V. Therefore, many diode OR gates cannot be cascaded either.

5.3 Bipolar transistor gates

The final fundamental Boolean operation, the NOT operation, cannot be produced with diodes and resistors alone. For the NOT operation, we need to use 'active' devices, nowadays transistors. In this section, we will consider the bipolar transistor as used in logic circuits. Commonly in logic circuits, transistors are operated in either a fully conducting state or a fully non-conducting state to produce the two logic voltages. The fully conducting state is known as the *saturated* or *turned-on* state and the fully non-conducting state is known as the *cut-off* state.

5.3.1 Transistor in cut-off and saturated conditions

Let us firstly review the bipolar transistor. A transistor has three connections, a *collector* connection, a *base* connection and an *emitter* connection. There are three currents associated with the connections, a collector current, I_C, a base current, I_B and an emitter current, I_E. The direction of emitter current flow when the device is operated normally is shown by the arrow on the emitter part of the transistor symbol which may be either into the emitter terminal or out of the emitter terminal depending upon the type of transistor. In the type of transistor where the current flows out of the emitter, the current flows into the base and collector. This type is called an *n-p-n transistor*, as shown in Fig. 5.4. In transistors where the current flows

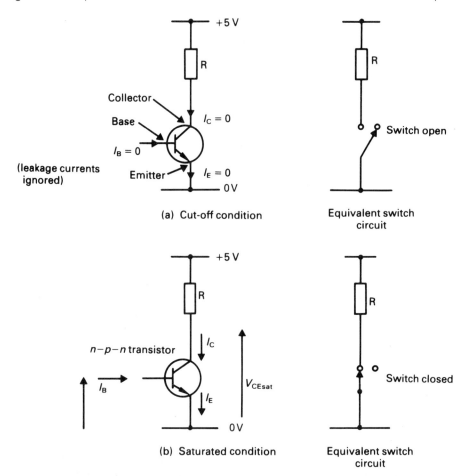

Figure 5.4   Transistor in cut-off and saturated conditions

into the emitter, the current flows out of the base and collector. This type is called a *p-n-p transistor*. The names are derived from the '*n*' type and '*p*' type semiconductor materials used in their construction. Both the base–emitter 'junction' and the base–collector 'junction' consist of diodes.

The emitter current is given by the sum of the collector current and base current, i.e.:

$$I_E = I_C + I_B \tag{1}$$

While the base–emitter voltage is between $+0.6$ V and $+0.7$ V approximately, the collector current is determined by the relationship:

$$I_C = h_{FE} I_B \tag{2}$$

where h_{FE} is the d.c. current gain, a parameter of the particular transistor. The current gain is usually more than one hundred. Therefore the base current is much smaller than the collector current and the emitter current is approximately equal to the collector current. Again, the reader is referred to electronics texts for an explanation of the actual transistor mechanism.

In Fig. 5.4, a resistor is connected between the collector and the +5 V supply to provide a path for the collector current. When the base current is zero, the collector and emitter currents are zero (except for leakage currents; see below). The device is then said to be cut off and can be considered as an electrical switch in the open position between the collector and emitter. No voltage will be produced across the resistor as no current is flowing in the resistor (by Ohm's law, $V = IR$). The voltage at the collector, i.e. V_{out}, will be the same as the +5 V supply voltage. The cut-off state is generally achieved by applying 0 V between the base and emitter, but certainly a voltage less than about 0.6 V is necessary.

When a base-emitter voltage above 0.6 V is applied, the base current increases and, according to (2), the collector current increases. The voltage across the resistor increases and the collector voltage falls towards 0 V. Clearly the collector voltage cannot fall below 0 V. In fact, there is a minimum voltage across the collector and emitter of the transistor, known as the *saturation voltage* V_{CEsat}, which is approximately 0.2 V. If the base current is increased further, the relationship between collector current and base current given above, (2), does not hold, and the collector voltage and current remains approximately constant. Then:

$$h_{FE} I_B > I_C \tag{3}$$

and the transistor is said to be *saturated*. In the saturated state, the collector current is defined by the supply voltage (+5 V) and the collector resistance (R_C) as follows:

$$I_c = (5 - V_{CEsat})/R_C \tag{4}$$

A transistor in the saturated state generates a stable, low collector voltage which can be used to represent a logic 0. The voltage varies very little with increased load if the relationship (3) is kept true to maintain saturation. We shall assume that a base–emitter voltage of 0.7 V is sufficient to saturate the transistor. In practice it may be between 0.7 V and 0.9 V.

Leakage currents are very small currents (less than 10 μA) which flow between the three transistor terminals in addition to the above currents. We can identify three leakage currents: a leakage current between the emitter and base, a leakage current between the base and collector and a leakage current between the collector and emitter. When a transistor is saturated, collector and emitter currents are typically in the region of 1 to 10 mA and base currents are in the region of 0.1 to 1 mA. Consequently the contribution due to leakage currents is not generally significant. The leakage currents can be significant in the cut-off state.

5.3.2 Transistor NOT gate

The transistor circuit shown in Fig. 5.5 is a NOT gate. If the input voltage is 0 V (or less than about +0.6 V), no base current or collector current will flow (except

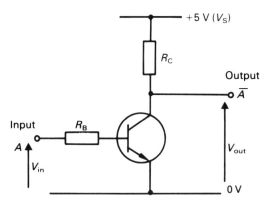

Figure 5.5   Transistor NOT gate

for leakage currents). Therefore the collector voltage will rise to 5 V. Conversely, if the input voltage is sufficiently above 0.7 V to cause the transistor to enter saturation, the output voltage will fall to 0.2 V (V_{CEsat}). Therefore the circuit can act as a NOT gate, with a 0 output represented by 0.2 V and a logic 1 output represented by 5 V. Input voltage levels can be the same.

The design values for the resistors can be calculated from Ohm's law as follows. If the input voltage is above 0.7V, base current will flow into the base of the transistor and is given by:

$$I_B = (V_{in} - 0.7)/R_B$$

The maximum collector current is with the transistor saturated and is given by:

$$I_{Cmax} = (V_S - V_{CEsat})/R_C$$

For saturation, I_B must be greater than I_C/h_{FE}, from (3). This can be achieved by choosing R_B sufficiently low for a given R_C, i.e. the following inequality must be met:

$$\frac{V_{in} - 0.7}{R_B} > \frac{V_s - V_{CEsat}}{R_C h_{FE}}$$

The calculation for R_B from the above assumes that no external load is present at the output to draw current. The effect of additional loads such as other gates is considered later in section 5.4. Typically, a choice is made for R_B and R_C to give a collector current suitable for driving a number of additional gates.

5.3.3 Diode-transistor-logic (DTL) gates

The diode AND gate of section 5.2.1 and the transistor NOT gate of section 5.3.2 can be combined to form a *diode-transistor-logic* (DTL) NAND gate. A three-input DTL NAND gate is shown in Fig. 5.6. One output logic level is with the transistor

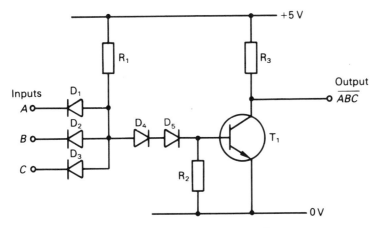

Figure 5.6 Three-input DTL NAND gate

fully conducting, i.e. saturated, and the other with the transistor fully non-conducting, i.e. cut off. When the transistor is cut off, the output voltage is 5 V which represents a logic 1 and when the transistor is saturated, the output voltage is 0.2 V (V_{CEsat}) which represents a logic 0.

    If one input signal is low (0.2 V) or more input signals are low, current will flow through R_1, the input diodes associated with the low inputs and out of the low input terminals. This current flow will cause the voltage on the lower end of R_1 to become 0.9 V (an input voltage of 0.2 V plus a voltage across the diodes of 0.7 V). One or two diodes are inserted between the input diode AND gate and the transistor NOT gate to ensure that the base of the transistor is now less than 0.7 V to cause the transistor to turn off and create a high output. R_2 is provided so that the transistor is properly kept cut off. (If one diode is provided the base voltage would be 0.2 V (0.9 V – 0.7 V). If two diodes are provided, as shown, the base voltage is 0 V as insufficient voltage is available for the two diodes to conduct.)

    If all the inputs are high (5 V), the input diodes will be reverse-biased. Current will flow through the R_1 resistor but then through the diodes D_4 and D_5 towards the base of the transistor. The current will divide at the base. Some will flow into the base and some will flow through the resistor R_2. The component values are chosen so that sufficient current flows into the base of the transistor to saturate the transistor under all load conditions. Hence the output falls to a logic 0 level.

    Because two diodes are inserted in the circuit shown here, the input voltage must rise to at least +1.4 V before there is +2.1 V on the lower end of R_1 and 0.7 V across the base and emitter of the transistor sufficient to turn the transistor on. (If one diode is used, the input must rise only to +0.7 V before the transistor turns on.) Once the threshold is passed, current will stop flowing through the input diodes and instead all the current will flow through the interstage diodes D_4 and D_5.

5.3.4 Transistor-transistor-logic (TTL) gates

Some early integrated circuit parts employed DTL designs. However, in integrated circuit construction, transistors can often be as readily fabricated as diodes. Indeed, if diodes are required, transistors are commonly fabricated and used as diodes (for example, using the base and emitter with the collector connected to the base). Circuits can employ mainly transistors used as transistors. Such gates are known as *transistor-transistor-logic* (TTL) gates. The DTL gate can be modified to the TTL version by replacing the input diodes with one multi-emitter transistor which will operate logically as the original diodes. A multi-emitter transistor is one having several emitter regions. Each emitter–base junction can behave logically as a diode in a diode AND circuit. Electrically, transistor operation occurs as described in the following.

(a) Standard TTL

Standard TTL was first introduced in 1963 and has formed the basis of many subsequent logic circuits. A standard design TTL NAND gate using a multi-emitter transistor is shown in Fig. 5.7. There are three distinct parts in the circuit, an input stage using transistor T_1, an internal stage using T_2 and an output stage using T_3 and T_4.

Comparing the TTL circuit with the DTL circuit shown in Fig. 5.6, we can see that the diodes in the diode input circuit of the DTL circuit have been replaced by a multi-emitter transistor T_1. The three emitter–base junctions of the multi-emitter transistor correspond to the diodes D_1, D_2 and D_3 and the base–collector junction of the multi-emitter transistor corresponds to the diode D_4. D_5 in the DTL circuit has been replaced by the transistor T_2 and the output transistor T_1 in the DTL circuit

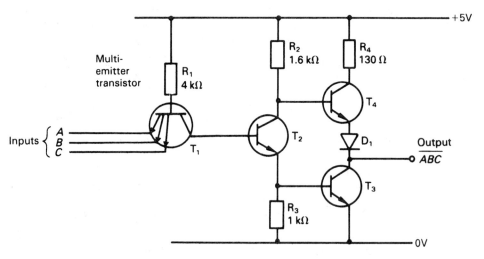

Figure 5.7   Standard TTL NAND gate

by transistor T_3 in the TTL circuit. An additional output transistor T_4 and the associated components are provided in the TTL circuit.

Firstly let us deduce the output 0 voltage level. In the DTL circuit, this level occurs when T_1 is saturated. In the TTL circuit the level occurs when T_3 is saturated and hence the logical 0 output voltage is V_{CEsat} of T_3 (say 0.2 V).

If one or more inputs are low (0.2 V), current will flow from the +5 V supply through the R_1 resistor into the base, out of the emitter (i.e. through the base–emitter 'diode') and out of the input terminals of the gate in a similar manner to the diode AND gate. However, because a transistor is used, 'transistor action' occurs and collector current will flow governed by the base current and the external circuitry. In this case, the base current is that flowing through R_1. The current flowing through the input terminals is actually an emitter current, the value of which is given by the sum of the base current and the collector current. Assuming that the base current is sufficient to saturate the transistor, the voltage across the emitter and collector is given by V_{CEsat} or 0.2 V approximately. If the input is at 0.2 V, the base of transistor T_2 is at 0.4 V which will cause this transistor to be cut off. Therefore the collector current of transistor T_2 will fall to zero and the emitter falls to 0 V. This will in turn cause transistor T_3 to be cut off as the base of this transistor will be at 0 V. Transistor T_4 will conduct (but not generally saturate) and the emitter of this transistor will be at 0.7 V below its base. In this analysis, we will ignore the base current of T_4 (and leakage currents). Hence without any current through R_2, the base of T_4 will be at +4.3 V. The only physical diode in the circuit, D_1, will conduct and this will produce an output voltage of 3.6 V (4.3 V − 0.7 V). This voltage is taken as the nominal logic 1 level.

If all the inputs are high at 3.6 V, the base–emitter junctions of transistor T_1 are all reverse-biased. However, the collector cannot rise above 1.4 V because of the base-emitter junctions of transistors T_2 and T_3. Current will flow through R_1 across the base-collector junction of transistor T_1 and into the base of transistor T_2. Transistors T_2 and T_3 will become fully saturated. Transistor T_1 is operating now in an unusual mode. The emitter voltage is 3.6 V (a logic 1), the collector voltage is at 1.4 V and the base voltage is at 2.1 V. Therefore the base–emitter junction is reverse-biased and the base–collector junction is forward-biased. In this situation, the roles of the emitter and collector are reversed. The emitter acts as a collector and the collector acts as an emitter. This is known as the *inverse mode*. The transistor may exhibit some current gain in the inverse mode, though more likely this will be base–collector current attenuation, i.e. a current 'gain' of less than unity. (Generally, the inverse gain of T_1 is reduced by suitable transistor geometry incorporating components at the base to divert the base current from the base–collector junction.)

With transistors T_2 and T_3 fully saturated, the output voltage will be at V_{CEsat} of T_3, say 0.2 V. The base of T_4 will be at 0.9 V (the base–emitter voltage of T_3 plus V_{CEsat} of T_2). This voltage is insufficient to allow both D_1 and T_4 to conduct and these devices will be fully cut off. Notice that the diode D_1 is necessary in the circuit to prevent T_4 from conducting whilst T_3 is conducting. The 130 Ω resistor limits the current available at a high output level and makes the circuit output short-circuit protected. Typically only one output of a TTL integrated circuit package can be short-circuited to 0 V at a time because of power dissipation limitations.

The circuit voltages given are only approximate. In particular, V_{CEsat} may be higher than 0.2 V. We have deduced the logic levels as 0.2 V and 3.6 V. Manufactured TTL gates have a maximum generated 0 level voltage of 0.4 V. Though not quoted, it is assumed that the minimum generated 0 level voltage is 0 V. The nominal generated 1 level voltage is sometimes quoted as 3.4 V and can fall to 2.4 V under load conditions (see later). The maximum generated 1 level voltage is $+5$ V (the supply voltage). The input circuitry will recognize a voltage of up to 0.8 V as a logical 0 and down to 2 V as a logical 1. This allows some electrical 'noise' to be acceptable on generated signals. We shall defer further discussion on noise to section 5.6.1 because it applies to all types of logic gates.

Figure 5.8 shows a TTL NOR gate circuit. The circuit without transistors T_2 and T_4 is identical to that of a TTL NOT gate (i.e. a NAND gate with a single input). Input A then generates $\bar{A}$ at the output. Similarly, the circuit with transistors T_2 and T_4 but without transistors T_1 and T_3 forms a NOT gate and the input B then generates $\bar{B}$ at the output. The circuits combine at the output stage so that if A or B or both are high, transistors T_3 or T_4 or both are conducting, causing T_5 to saturate and the output to be low. If A and B are both low, both transistors T_3 and T_4 are cut off and only transistor T_6 is conducting to produce a high output.

(b) Low-power and high-speed TTL (LTTL and HTTL)

The speed of operation and power consumption of logic devices using saturated transistors are closely related. Generally as the power consumption is increased by using smaller values of resistors, the speed of operation increases. The product

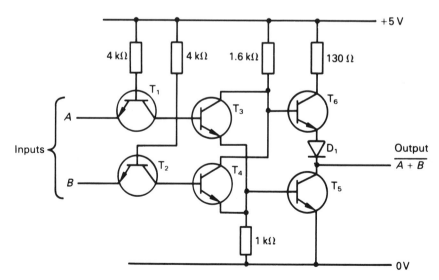

Figure 5.8 Standard TTL NOR gate

(propagation time) × (power consumption), called the *speed–power product*, is regarded as a figure of merit for a particular logic circuit family. Standard TTL has a speed–power product of 10 ns × 10 mW or 100 pJ. The component values in the basic design can be changed in order to either increase the speed of operation (i.e. reduce the propagation delay time) by decreasing resistor values, or to decrease the power consumption by increasing resistor values. The former has been done in high-speed TTL (HTTL) circuits and the latter in low-power TTL (LTTL) circuits. HTTL has a speed–power product of 6 ns × 22 mW or 132 pJ and LTTL has a speed–power product of 33 ns × 1 mW or 33 pJ. Both these circuits were introduced around 1967 but were superseded by Schottky versions in 1969–71. Schottky gates are considered in section 5.4.1.

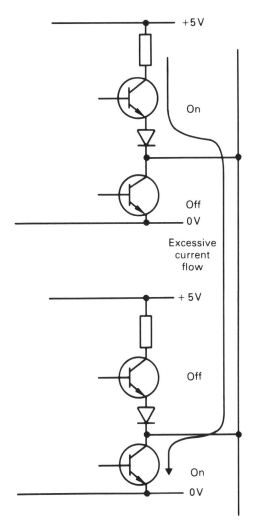

Figure 5.9 Normal TTL gates with outputs wired together

5.3.5 Open-collector TTL gates

If we join the outputs of normal TTL gates together, with the intention that one gate will drive a common line as shown in Fig. 5.9, conflict will occur if different gates attempt to drive the output in opposite states. Indeed, it is possible that excessive current will flow (because saturated transistors present a low resistance, perhaps in the region of 25 Ω, between the collector and emitter for internal TTL transistors). Wiring outputs of *open-collector* gates together enables any one of the gates to drive a common line to a logical 0 without conflict. An open-collector TTL gate is similar to a normal TTL gate except that the upper output transistor and associated diode are removed which enables two or more similar gates to have their outputs joined together without the possibility of the output transistors being damaged.

A standard TTL open-collector gate is shown in Fig. 5.10(a). Figure 5.10(b) shows a number of open-collector gates with their outputs wired together. A single *pull-up* resistor is used to produce 5 V (a logic 1) when all the individual output transistors are cut off. If at least one of the output transistors is conducting (output at a logic 0 level) the combined output will be at a 0 level (V_{CEsat}). The output will be at a logic 1 level only if all the output signals would normally be at a logic 1 level. Hence this arrangement creates an 'ANDing' operation of the output signals.

Figure 5.11 shows a logic diagram of the configuration. The value of the pull-up resistor is typically in the region 470 Ω to 4.7 kΩ. Though occasionally called a *wired*-AND configuration, the above is more commonly known as *wired*-OR, from the conceptual viewpoint that the overall operation is one of 'ORing' with active low signals. The wired-OR connection has found use in the past as it saves gates and can be expanded to incorporate perhaps up to ten gates in all without extra circuitry. Additionally, the wired-OR connection is applicable to *bus systems* in which several sources can drive the same line. Presently the wired-OR connection is not widely used for these purposes except for some particular signals in bus systems which are considered in Part 2.

The principal disadvantage of the wired-OR connection is that when the level on the output line switches from a 0 to a 1, the 1 level is brought about only by the pull-up resistor rather than an active device (transistor), which results in a slower transition. (The output capacitance must be charged to logical 1 level and the speed at which this occurs depends upon the current available. A pull-up resistor cannot generally provide the current of an active device because the minimum value of the resistor is limited by the maximum power dissipation of the open-collector output transistors.) The three-state gate overcomes this problem in bus systems.

5.3.6 Three-state TTL gates

A *three-state* (*Tri-state*†) gate has three output states, a normal logic 0 level, a normal logic 1 and a third state in which the output exhibits a very high impedance

---

† *Tri-state* is a registered trademark of the National Semiconductor Corporation.

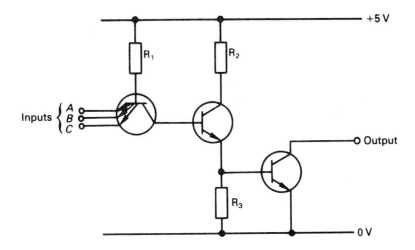

Inputs { A B C

(a) Standard TTL open-collector circuit

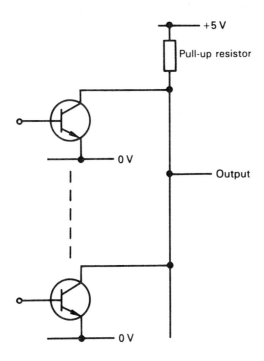

(b) Outputs wired together

Figure 5.10   Open-collector gates

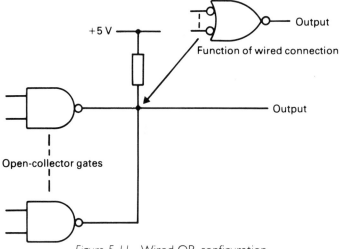

Figure 5.11   Wired-OR configuration

(a) Symbol

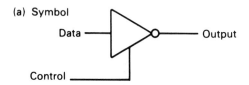

(b) Truth table

Data	Control	Output
0	0	High impedance
0	1	1
1	0	High impedance
1	1	0

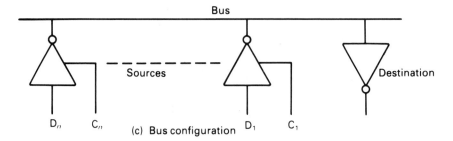

(c) Bus configuration

Figure 5.12   Tri-state gates

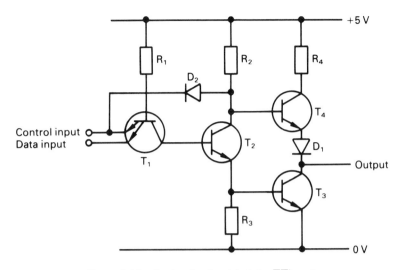

Figure 5.13   A circuit of a tri-state TTL gate

(giving rise to typically less than 10 μA leakage current). The three-state device has replaced the open-collector gate in many bus systems in which several sources transmit data to one of several destinations, such as in a microprocessor system. Only one source transmits information at any instant. Figure 5.12(a) shows a symbol for a three-state NOT state gate, Fig. 5.12(b) the truth table of the device and Fig. 5.12(c) shows the general bus arrangement. Three-state gates are used at the source. The normal inactive state of these gates is with the outputs in the third state. When the device needs to drive the line, a control signal causes the device to revert to a normal two-state gate capable of producing both logic output levels.

The third state can be created through a simple modification to the standard TTL circuit, as shown in Fig. 5.13. The control input connects to an additional input of the multi-emitter input transistor and also through a diode D_2 to the upper transistor of the output stage. When the control input is high, D_2 is reverse-biased and the gate acts as a normal two-state gate. When the control input is low, without the extra diode D_2, the output would normally become a logic 1 irrespective of the data input signal. However, with the diode, the upper transistor of the output stage is also cut off so that both output transistors are cut off. The only output current that can now flow is leakage current, and the circuit assumes a high impedance state. The circuit arrangement is enhanced in some three-state TTL gates by additional transistors.

5.4 High-speed logic circuits

The switching circuits so far described employ transistors existing in one of two states, either saturated (fully conducting) or cut off, and the transistors must switch between these two states. When a transistor is saturated, more current enters the base than is necessary to maintain the collector current and causes 'excess' charge in the device which must be removed before the device can be taken out of the saturated state. This can take some time, perhaps several nanoseconds, and limits the speed of operation of the circuit but can be avoided by arranging that the transistor does not enter saturation. The two logic states can be fully cut off at some point before saturation; such circuits are known as non-saturating logic. Before discussing the intrinsically non-saturating logic designs, we shall consider a modification made to most of the transistors in the standard TTL which prevents these transistors saturating fully. This modification was first made to TTL in 1969 and led to a series of *Schottky* TTL gates.

5.4.1 Schottky TTL

When a transistor is saturated, the base–emitter voltage is V_{BEon} (say 0.7 V) and the collector–emitter voltage is V_{CEsat}, approximately 0.2 V. A transistor can be prevented from entering saturation by preventing the collector voltage from falling to V_{CEsat} by 'clamping' the collector at a voltage above V_{CEsat}. An elegant way of doing this

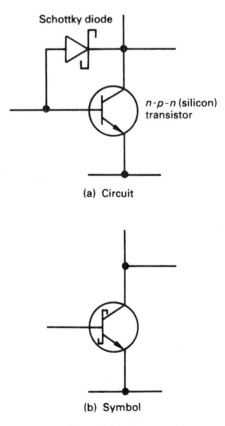

(a) Circuit

(b) Symbol

Figure 5.14　Schottky transistor

is to use a Schottky diode (a metal-semiconductor diode) as shown in Fig. 5.14(a). A Schottky diode has the special characteristic that when forward-biased (metal side more positive), there is virtually no stored charge and also the voltage drop is less than V_{BEon}, at about 0.3–0.4 V. Hence when current is injected into the base of the transistor to cause conduction, and the collector voltage falls, the diode will begin to conduct when the voltage falls to 0.4V (base voltage of transistor–forward bias of diode, 0.7 V–0.3 V) and prevent the voltage falling any further. The circuit configuration of a bipolar transistor with a Schottky diode between the base and collector is known as a *Schottky transistor*, which has the symbol shown in Fig. 5.14(b). In a Schottky TTL gate, most of the transistors are replaced by Schottky transistors. This results in a typical propagation delay (the time between the application of a new input signal which will create an output change and the resultant output change) of about 3 ns rather than 10 ns for standard TTL. Power consumption of Schottky TTL is about 19 mW compared to 10 mW for standard TTL, giving a speed–power product of 57 pJ compared with 100 pJ/100 pJ for standard TTL.

A low-power version of Schottky TTL was introduced in 1971, LSTTL, using larger internal resistor values, and resulted in a speed-power product of 9.5 ns × 2 mW = 19 pJ. A LSTTL NAND gate circuit is shown in Fig. 5.15. Notice that in this particular LSTTL circuit, the input circuitry has reverted to diode gate arrangement. Only one transistor is a non-Schottky transistor, T_5 which does not

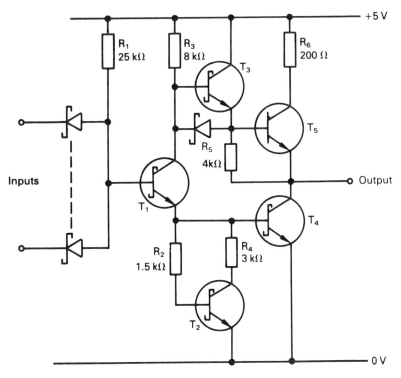

Figure 5.15   LSTTL gate

saturate because its collector keeps near $+5$ V and its emitter is always at least 1.4 V less than this. Only when the collector–emitter voltage of a transistor falls to V_{CEsat} does the transistor enter saturation. LSTTL has become the industry standard version of TTL. There have been further circuit enhancements resulting in advanced Schottky TTL (ASTTL) and advanced low-power Schottky TTL (ALSTTL), both operating at twice the speed of their predecessor. ALSTTL also has half the power consumption of LSTTL. Figure 5.16 shows an ALS NOT gate (74ALS04). In this circuit the input circuitry consists of a *p-n-p* transistor (T_1) and the low-level input current is much reduced over multi-emitter transistor and diode input circuitry as the input current constitutes a transistor base current (perhaps 20 μA). *P-n-p* input transistors are also used in some LSTTL parts to reduce low-level input currents. Table 5.1 lists the performance figures of the various TTL families.

5.4.2 Emitter-coupled logic (ECL)

Transistors are kept from saturation in *emitter-coupled logic* (ECL) designs to achieve very high speeds of operation by suitable choice of component values. Transistors in an ECL circuit are either cut off or conducting to an extent, but not saturated. A basic ECL OR/NOR circuit is shown in Fig. 5.17. Three inputs are

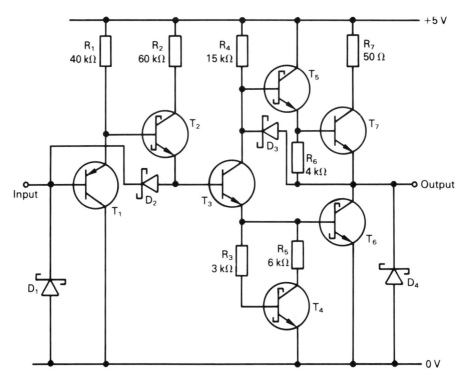

Figure 5.16   ALS NOT gate (74ALS04)

Table 5.1   Performance figures of various TTL series

Logic series	Propagation delay time (ns)	Power dissipation (mW)	Speed–power product (pJ)
74	10	10	100
74S	3	19	57
74LS	9.5	2	19
74AS	1.5	20	30
74ALS	4	1	4

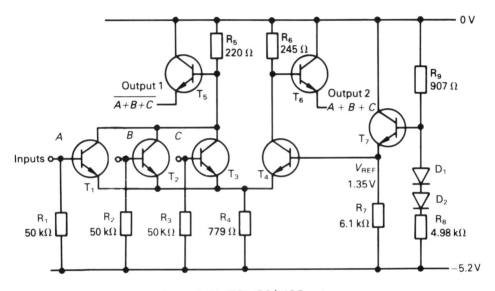

Figure 5.17 ECL OR/NOR gate

shown, A, B and C. Two outputs are provided, $A + B + C$ and $\overline{A + B + C}$. Note that the supply voltages are 0 V and -5.2 V. The logic levels are not the same as TTL logic levels.

When all the inputs are at a low voltage, the associated input transistors, T_1, T_2 and T_3, are all cut off and current flows through T_4. When one input or more inputs are taken to some high voltage, the current switches from T_4 to the input transistor and T_4 is cut off. The voltage on the base of T_4 is mid-way between the two logic levels.

Suitable input voltages can be deduced by examination of the circuit. One condition is when all the input transistors T_1, T_2 and T_3 are cut off and in this condition no current flows through these transistors and their collectors are at 0 V (ignoring any base current of T_5). V_{BE} of each transistor when conducting is in the region 0.8 V to 0.9 V. Therefore the output voltage at the emitter of T_5 must be -0.9V (assuming $V_{BES} = 0.9$ V). This is the 1 level output voltage. Since input and output voltage 1 (and 0) levels must be nominally the same, the 1 level input voltage is also -0.9 V.

If the 1 level voltage is applied to one input, A, say, there must be a 0 output level on the NOR output. Transistor T_1 will conduct but the current is limited by the resistors R_4 and R_5 to prevent saturation. The lowest voltage allowed on the collector of T_1 is -0.9 V, the same as the base voltage, as below this voltage the transistor will begin to enter saturation. Therefore the 0 level output voltage must be -1.8 V (-0.9 V $- 0.9$ V), assuming again that $V_{BE5} = 0.9$ V. In all cases, T_5 conducts dependent upon the load applied to the output 1 terminal, but the transistor is not saturated. The reference voltage on the base of T_4 is set midway between the two input voltage levels, with our values, -1.35 V (-0.9 V $- 0.9$ V/2).

ECL circuits operate at very high speed. The 10K series ECL circuit has a propagation time of 2 ns with a power consumption of 25 mW, giving a speed–power product of 50 pJ. The faster 100K series has a propagation time of 0.75 ns with a rather large power consumption of 40 mW, resulting in a speed–power product of 30 pJ. ECL has the advantage that both the true and inverse outputs are available and outputs can be wired-ORed (see section 5.3.5). The supply current is nearly constant. However, ECL consumes substantially more power than TTL circuits, limiting manufacture in dual-in-line packages to SSI/MSI (small-scale integration/medium-scale integration) and is only used for very high-speed applications.

5.5 Metal-oxide-semiconductor (MOS) gates

5.5.1 NMOS and PMOS

An alternative to employing bipolar transistors as used for TTL and ECL gates is to employ *metal-oxide-semiconductor field effect transistors* (MOSFET) particularly for LSI/VLSI (large-scale integration/very large-scale integration, more than 100/1000 gates). Because of the importance of the MOSFET in microprocessors (Part 2), let us firstly briefly review the characteristics of the MOSFET.† The MOSFET can be constructed as *n-channel* (NMOS) or *p-channel* (PMOS) and for one of two modes of operation known as *enhancement mode* and *depletion mode*. There are three connections to MOS transistors, the *source*, the *gate* and the *drain*.

An n-channel enhancement-mode MOSFET is normally operated with the drain connected to a positive voltage with respect to the source. When the gate–source voltage, V_{GS} is 0 V, no current flows between the source and drain. If V_{GS} is increased, a point is reached when conduction starts between the source and drain. The voltage at which conduction occurs is known as the *threshold voltage*, V_T. The current flow will increase as the gate–source voltage exceeds the threshold

† Significantly more detail is given in Chapter 13.

voltage. Hence the device can act as a logic device with two states, conducting and non-conducting. V_T can be about $+1$ V, allowing compatibility with TTL devices.

In the case of a depletion-mode n-channel MOSFET, V_T is negative. When $V_{GS} = 0$V, conduction already occurs between the source and drain. Conduction stops when the gate–source voltage is less than the negative threshold voltage. Therefore, a two-state device can be obtained, only now a negative voltage is required on the gate to turn the device off, with respect to the source voltage. As before, the reader is referred to texts on electronics for an explanation of the MOSFET mechanism. P-channel MOSFETs operate similarly, but the polarity of all voltages is reversed.

A simple NMOS NOT gate with a resistor load is shown in Fig. 5.18(a). The positive supply voltage is V_{DD}. NAND and NOR gates are shown in Fig. 5.18(b) and Fig. 5.18(c) respectively.† The resistor load can be replaced by an enhancement-mode MOS transistor as shown in Fig.5.19(a). The enhancement-mode load transistor has the gate connected to the drain and the positive supply which will cause the load device to conduct only when the output is low. When the output is high, there is a threshold voltage drop across the device so that the output voltage is $V_{DD} - V_T$.

The voltage drop across the device can be eliminated by using a depletion mode MOS load device with the gate connected directly to the source as shown in Fig. 5.19(b). In this case, the device will always conduct whether the output is low or high.

Separate gates are not manufactured in NMOS technology. However, the technology is used for LSI/VLSI devices such as microprocessors. PMOS was available before NMOS due to early difficulties in manufacturing NMOS, but NMOS devices intrinsically operate 2–3 times faster than PMOS and consequently PMOS is not now widely used alone for high-speed components.

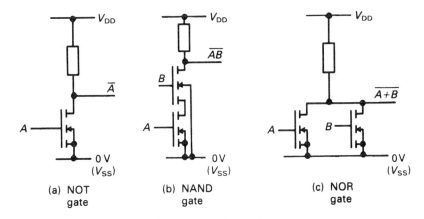

Figure 5.18 Resistor load NMOS gates

† Alternative MOS symbols introduced in Chapter 13 are more suitable for VLSI design.

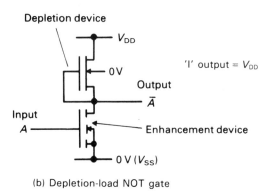

(a) Enhancement-load NOT

(b) Depletion-load NOT gate

Figure 5.19   NMOS gates with active loads

5.5.2 CMOS

Logic circuits can be implemented with *n*-channel and *p*-channel devices in a technology known as *complementary* MOS (CMOS). A CMOS NOT gate is shown in Fig. 5.20(a). An enhancement-mode *p*-channel transistor is connected to the positive supply (V_{DD}) and an enhancement-mode *n*-channel transistor is connected to 0 V. Both transistors are constructed to have similar threshold voltages of about 0.7 V, though of opposite polarities. The logic levels are 0 V and V_{DD} nominally, and V_{DD} can be typically between 3 V and 15 V.

When the input level is low (0 V), the lower transistor will be turned off as the voltage across the gate and source of this transistor is 0 V and below the threshold voltage. The voltage across the source and gate of the upper transistor is greater than the threshold voltage of this transistor. Therefore this transistor is turned on, and the output attains a high output voltage to within 100 mV of the positive V_{DD} supply. When the input is high (V_{DD}) the voltage across the source and drain of the upper transistor is 0 V. The device is turned off. The voltage across the source and drain of the lower transistor is greater than the threshold voltage of the device, so

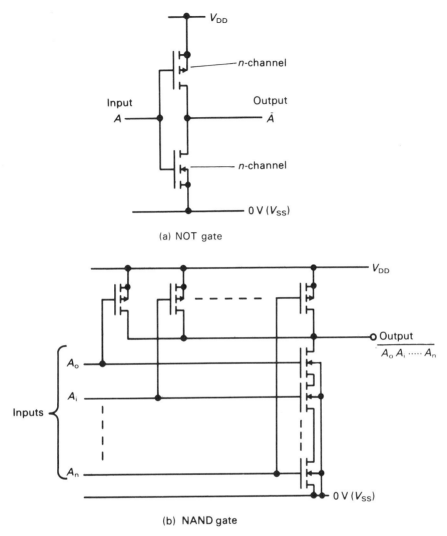

(a) NOT gate

(b) NAND gate

Figure 5.20 CMOS gates

this transistor is turned on. The output now attains a low voltage to within 100 mV of 0 V.

The switching threshold is approximately mid-way between 0 V and the supply voltage V_S, irrespective of the supply voltage (assuming this to be greater than about 1.4 V), because when the input is mid-way between 0 V and V_S, V_{GS} of the upper transistor is equal in magnitude to V_{GS} of the lower transistor. With identical characteristics, the drain source voltage of both transistors must be the same and the output must be 0.5 V_S. This represents the cross-over point, above or below which a fast transition to a stable state occurs.

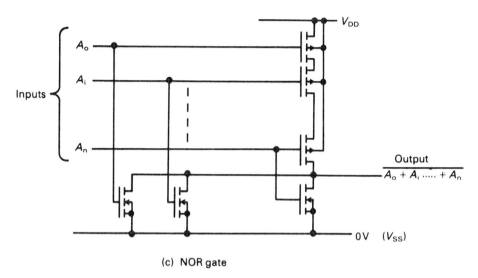

(c) NOR gate

Figure 5.20   continued

CMOS NAND and NOR gates are shown in Fig. 5.20(b) and Fig. 5.20(c) respectively. The particular advantage of CMOS circuits is that there is no d.c. current path between V_S and 0 V through the circuit in either logic state, and hence a very low static power consumption (with no logic transitions) due only to leakage currents. Unfortunately, during a logic transition both upper and lower transistors might conduct simultaneously. Also internal and external capacitances must be charged or discharged during the transition, and charging/discharging transient currents flow. This leads to the dynamic supply current and power consumption being directly proportional to the signal frequency.

CMOS versions of TTL circuits are manufactured, having similar logical characteristics and compatible input/output voltages. Many of the original 7400 series TTL gates have equivalent CMOS versions. For example the 74C00 is a CMOS equivalent of the TTL 7400 quad 2-input AND gate. In many applications, the CMOS versions can be chosen giving much lower power consumption than TTL. Power consumption of CMOS gates is in the region of 0.01 μW/gate with no logic transitions and about 1.25 mW/gate at 1 MHz. Speed of operation of CMOS versions of TTL gates has been generally slower than TTL having propagation delay times in the region of 50 ns. However, advances in CMOS technology for VLSI have resulted in improved speed.

5.6 Gate operating conditions

5.6.1 Noise margins

Noise is the term given to unwanted electrical signals occurring in a system. It can come about from the normal operation of logic devices switching, which can generate interference on neighboring devices either by electromagnetic radiation or via associated power supply variations. Less commonly, the source of the noise can be external to the system. Logic gates must be designed to accept a certain amount of electrical noise in the system and continue to operate normally.

Noise margin is the name given to the voltage present as electrical noise which can be tolerated in the system. It is given in terms of the allowable noise voltage that can be added to a generated logic signal and still be recognized as a logic level, i.e.:

Noise margin at a logic 1 = (minimum 1 output voltage generated)–
                            (minimum 1 input voltage recognized)
Noise margin at a logic 0 = (maximum 0 output voltage generated)–
                            (maximum 0 input voltage recognized)

As an example, consider the typical input/output voltage transfer characteristic of a standard TTL gate shown in Fig. 5.21. The maximum generated logic 0 output voltage is 0.4 V. The minimum logic 1 output voltage is 2.4 V which occurs under full load conditions (see later). The switching point between a logic 0 and a logic 1 is roughly 1.4 V but this can change with temperature. However, it is guaranteed that the input will always recognize a logic 0 voltage of up to 0.8 V and a logic 1 voltage down to 2 V though such voltages cannot be generated by the output of a logic device. Therefore the noise margins in this case are given by:

Noise margin at a logic 1 = 2.4 V – 2 V = 0.4 V
Noise margin at a logic 0 = 0.8 V – 0.4 V = 0.4 V

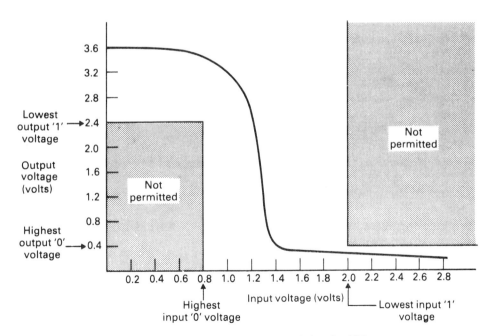

Figure 5.21   Voltage transfer characteristic of a TTL gate

The noise margins of ECL gates are much lower, at about 125 mV.

The noise margins defined are applicable to continuous, fairly low-frequency noise. The behaviour of the logic device under the influence of non-continuous or very high-frequency noise may be considerably different to that of low-frequency noise. The most likely high-frequency noise has the form of a narrow voltage pulse. If the duration of the pulse is sufficiently short, the device may not have time to respond to it. The behaviour of a logic device under high frequency noise conditions can be described by the a.c. noise margins as opposed to the (d.c.) margins.

5.6.2 Fan-out

As mentioned in the introductory section to this chapter, fan-out is the name given to the number of gates that can be attached to the output of a gate without causing the output gate to operate outside normal limits. Usually all the gates are of the same type or compatible types. Fan-out is determined by the maximum output current of the gate output stage and the maximum input currents of the gates attached to the output, together with any leakage currents of the devices. The fan-out of a gate with a low output level is not necessarily the same as the fan-out of the gate with a high output level, as the maximum output current at each level is usually different and the input currents are usually different at each level. The fan-out at each level is given by:

$$\text{Logic 1 output fan-out} = \frac{I_{OH(max)}}{I_{IH(max)}}$$

$$\text{Logic 0 output fan-out} = \frac{I_{OL(max)}}{I_{IL(max)}}$$

where

$I_{OH(max)}$ = maximum high-level (1) output current that the gate can supply
$I_{OL(max)}$ = maximum low-level (0) output current that the gate can supply
$I_{IH(max)}$ = maximum high-level (1) input current of gate connected to output
$I_{IL(max)}$ = maximum low-level (0) input current of gate connected to output.

To determine the fan-out of a particular device, the above four currents need to be known, and can be found from the appropriate data sheets. The input and output currents for members of the TTL family are shown in Table 5.2. Measurements have been taken under different conditions in different series. The standard TTL series (not now often used) has a fan-out of:

$$\text{Logic 1 output fan-out} = \frac{I_{OH(max)}}{I_{IH(max)}} = \frac{800\ \mu A}{40\ \mu A} = 20$$

Table 5.2   Input and output currents of various TTL series

Logic series	Maximum 1 level input current $I_{IH(max)}$ (μA)	Maximum 0 level input current $I_{IL(max)}$ (mA)	Maximum 1 level output current $I_{OH(max)}$ (mA)	Maximum 0 level output current $I_{OL(max)}$ (mA)
74	40	-1.6	$-0.4/-0.8^*$	16
74S	50	-2.0	-1.0	20
74LS	20	-0.36	-0.4	8
74AS	20	-2.0	-0.4	$4/8^*$
74ALS	20	-0.1	-0.4	8

*depends upon devices. Conditions under which values obtained differ slightly from one family to another; see reference [1]

$$\text{Logic 0 output fan-out} = \frac{I_{OL(max)}}{I_{IL(max)}} = \frac{16 \text{ mA}}{1.6 \text{ mA}} = 10$$

The LSTTL series, in general, has a fan-out of:

$$\text{Logic 1 output fan-out} = \frac{I_{OH(max)}}{I_{IH(max)}} = \frac{400 \text{ } \mu\text{A}}{20 \text{ } \mu\text{A}} = 20$$

$$\text{Logic 0 output fan-out} = \frac{I_{OL(max)}}{I_{IL(max)}} = \frac{8 \text{ mA}}{0.36 \text{ mA}} = 22$$

Particular devices may have different input and output currents. The smallest fan-out value would determine the number of gates that can be attached to an output. Sometimes, the extra high-level fan-out, if available, can be utilized by connecting unused inputs of gates to used inputs. (Unused inputs should not be left unconnected, but connected to a logic voltage or the supply voltage.)

Logic circuit series can be intermixed if their logic level voltages are compatible, i.e. the output voltage range of a gate must be less than the input voltage range of the gate to which the output connects for both logic levels. Usually, TTL and equivalent CMOS families can be intermixed. The fan-out in these situations depends upon the actual I_{OL}, I_{OL}, I_{IL} and I_{IH} of the gates concerned. For example, LSTTL generally has a maximum I_{IH} of 20 μA and a maximum I_{IL} of $(-)0.36$ mA. Therefore a standard TTL gate could drive 44 LSTTL gates at a low level (i.e. 16 mA/0.36 mA) and 40 at a high level (i.e. 800 μA/20 μA assuming $I_{OH(max)} = 800$ μA).

5.6.3 MOS devices

A typical output characteristic of an NMOS device such as a microprocessor is shown in Fig. 5.22. Note that the maximum output current at both low and high levels is much less than that of TTL devices and hence the number of TTL gates that

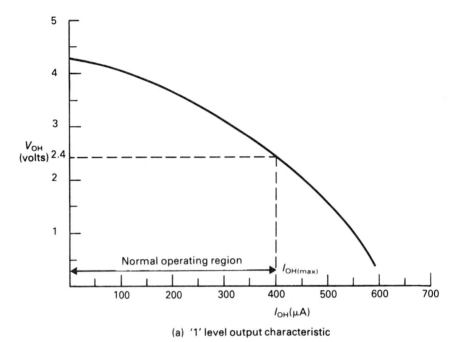

(a) '1' level output characteristic

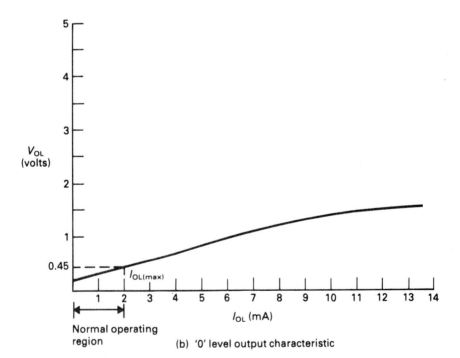

(b) '0' level output characteristic

Figure 5.22   Typical NMOS microprocessor output characteristics

can be attached to the output is very low, typically one standard TTL device or five LSTTL devices.

NMOS devices themselves present a very low current loading, normally in the region of $\pm 10\,\mu A$ for both high and low voltages. On first sight, it would seem that many NMOS devices could be attached before the loading limit is reached. However, all logic devices have an input capacitance which in the case of MOS devices, though perhaps only in the region of 10 pF, will often limit the number of MOS devices that can be connected to the output of a device. Capacitance on the output of a logic device will require the device to supply transient currents during logic transitions and will reduce the rise and fall times of the output signal. The rise and fall times each produce a delay which can be related to the capacitance by the equation:

$$dt = \frac{C_L\, dV_O}{I_O}$$

where

C_L is the load capacitance including the self-capacitance of the device
dV_O is the logic swing
I_O is the available current from the driver not taken by the d.c. load (assumed constant for the above equation).

If $dV_O = 2V$ and $I_O = 1$ mA, the delay would be 0.2 ns/pF. The delay about 0.1 ns/pF for the low-power Schottky TTL devices, 0.2 ns/pF for advanced Schottky TTL devices, and usually between 0.1 ns/pF and 0.6 ns/pF for NMOS microprocessors.

For microprocessors, stated loads in test situations are in the region of 50 pF to 150 pF, not including self-load (internal capacitance of the output). The maximum load is perhaps in the region of 300 pF and there may be different delay rates in different ranges of load capacitances. If the capacitive load is greater than the stated test conditions, the delay can be calculated from the delay rate, and the processor operated slower if necessary. However, the reliability may be adversely affected due to the greater transient currents charging and discharging the capacitances. One cannot sensibly load the output with a capacitance greater than the stated maximum.

Therefore from the above, during the design of a system, the maximum d.c. loading (at both low and high levels) and the maximum capacitive loading need to be calculated to ascertain whether the system will operate properly. Take, as an example, the following output drive specification of a microprocessor:

$I_{OL} = 2.0$ mA max.
$I_{OH} = 400\,\mu A$ max.
$C_L = 100$ pF max. without derating

Some possible combinations of devices that could be attached without exceeding the maximum load specifications are shown in Table 5.3 using the input current values given for LSTTL, assuming the input currents of each MOS device is $\pm 10\,\mu A$ and

Table 5.3 Combinations of devices that can be attached to MOS device

	Output current (mA) Logic level		Capacitance (pF)
Devices attached to output	0	1	C_L
5 LSTTL devices	2	100	50
1 LSTTL device + 9 MOS devices	0.49	110	100
3 LSTTL devices + 7 MOS devices	1.2	130	100

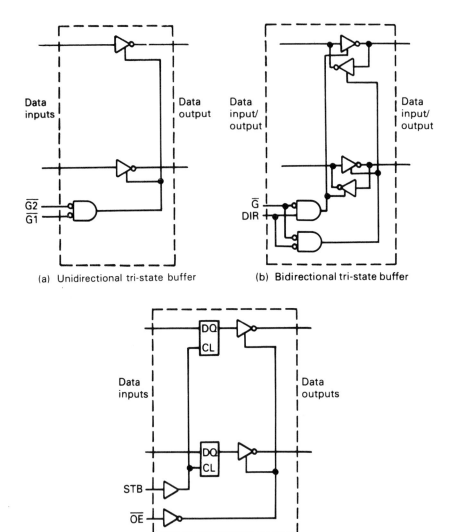

(a) Unidirectional tri-state buffer   (b) Bidirectional tri-state buffer

(c) Latched tri-state buffer

Figure 5.23   Buffers

the input capacitance of each device is 10 pF. The determining factor in the first case is I_{OL} and in the other two cases, C_L.

If the lines are loaded differently, there will be a skew in the signals in addition to the delay. The specification of a microprocessor may define a maximum differential loading to obtain given timing (for example, a maximum load difference of 50 pF might be specified). There may also be effects due to the worsening rise and fall times on particular devices. If, for example, a load of 300 pF existed and $dt/C_L = 0.2$ ns/pF, the rise and fall times would be 60 ns. Rise and fall times of this magnitude may be greater than allowed for proper operation.

The normal solution to the problem of loading is to use additional buffer gates, for example in a microprocessor system between the components of the system and the bus. This also provides a measure of protection in the event of a hardware malfunction. Integrated circuit parts are available with four, six and eight inverting or non-inverting three-state buffer gates. These buffers may be unidirectional, bidirectional or latched buffers. An 8-bit unidirectional three-state buffer is shown in Fig. 5.23(a), a bidirectional three-state buffer in Fig. 5.23(b) and a latched three-state buffer in Fig. 5.23(c). Unidirectional buffers can be used in particular when the signals can only pass from the device and not to the same device along the same lines. Bidirectional buffers can be used on all lines that carry signals to or from the device (such as data lines; see Chapter 6).

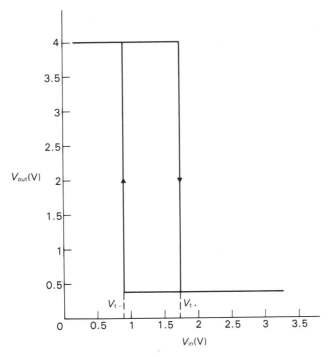

Figure 5.24   Transfer characteristic of TTL Schmitt trigger NOR gate

The differential nature of TTL input currents, I_{IL} and I_{IH}, is also reflected in the designed drive capability of all types of TTL buffers, with I_{OL} usually much larger than I_{OH}. Output stages of TTL buffers can provide currents in the region of 24 mA to 64 mA for a low output voltage and 5 mA to 15 mA for a high output voltage. The input currents of buffers are often lower than the input currents of normal TTL gates. Some buffer gates have Schmitt trigger inputs to increase the noise immunity. The characteristic of a Schmitt trigger input gate is shown in Fig. 5.24. The cross-over point for a rising input signal, V_{t+}, is higher than the cross-over point for a falling input signal, V_{t-}. This increases the effective noise immunity, that is, the maximum amount of noise allowed on the signal before it causes a transition on the output, by the amount $V_{OL} - V_{t+}$ on a low voltage, and $V_{OH} - V_{t-}$ on a high voltage. Typically $V_{t+} = 1.7$ V and $V_{t-} = 0.9$ V, which would lead to a high-level noise immunity of 1.5 V (i.e. 2.4 V − 0.9 V) and a low-level noise immunity of 1.3 V (i.e. 1.7 V − 0.4 V).

Reference

1.   *The TTL Data Book for Design Engineers* (6th European edn.), Dallas, TX: Texas Instruments, 1983.

Problems

In the following questions, assume that $V_{BEn} = 0.7$ V and $V_{CEsat} = 0.2$ V where necessary. Leakage currents can be ignored unless specified.

5.1 If the voltages applied to the diode AND gate shown in Fig. 5.2 are 2.5 V representing a logic 1 or 0 V representing a logic 0, what output voltages can be generated?

5.2 Repeat Problem 5.1 for the diode OR gate shown in Fig. 5.3.

5.3 Deduce the logical function performed by the circuit shown in Fig. 5.25 for (a) positive logic and (b) negative logic. Deduce the d.c. noise margins.

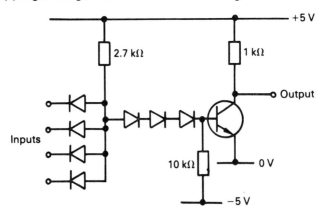

Figure 5.25 Circuit for Problem 5.3

5.4 Repeat Problem 5.3 for the circuit shown in Fig. 5.26.

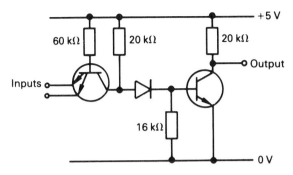

Figure 5.26   Circuit for Problem 5.4

5.5 Choose suitable values for R_B and R_C in the transistor circuit shown in Fig. 5.5 to achieve the following specification:

High-level input current, I_{IH}	= 0.5 mA
High-level output voltage, $V_{OH(min)}$	= 3.5 V
High level fan-out	= 10

Calculate the minimum value of h_{FE} to achieve a high-level noise margin of 0.5 V.

5.6 Determine the maximum value for the pull-up resistor of an open-collector TTL gate to achieve a fan-out of 10, given that $I_{IH} = 40\ \mu A$, the leakage current flowing through the collector of the TTL output transistor is $50\ \mu A$, and $V_{OH(min)} = 2.4$ V.

5.7 Determine the high-level fan-out of the open-collector gate shown in Fig. 5.27 given that the value of the pull-up resistor is 10 kΩ. What is the maximum value of this resistor to give a high-level fan-out of 5? Each diode has a maximum leakage current of $100\ \mu A$ when reverse-biased. Make, and state, any necessary assumptions.

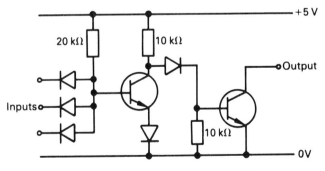

Figure 5.27   Circuit for Problem 5.7

5.8 Determine the number of LSTTL devices that can be attached to the output of a STTL device (by reference to Table 5.2).

Part 2

Microprocessor System Design

6 Computer and Microprocessor Systems

6.1 Stored program computer

In this chapter we shall describe the general features of microprocessor systems, making reference to several microprocessors. Thirty-two-bit microprocessors will be considered in Chapter 7. We firstly outline the basic features of digital computers, of which a microprocessor system is one implementation.

6.1.1 General scheme

A digital computer system contains the following fundamental parts:

 (i) Central processor unit (CPU)
 (ii) Main (or primary) memory
(iii) Input circuits and devices
(iv) Output circuits and devices

as shown in Fig. 6.1. The *main* or *primary memory* provides a means of storing binary information in the form of binary words. One word consists of a fixed number of binary digits (bits), typically 8, 16 or 32, and each word is stored in one memory location. An 8-bit word is called a *byte*. Each memory location is given a unique number, called an address, as shown in Fig. 6.2. Memory locations are numbered consecutively. With n binary digits (bits) in the address, the address range is from 0 to $2^n - 1$, i.e. 2^n unique addresses. The number of address bits provided varies from computer to computer. Sixteen bits would give the ability to address 65,536 locations. Thirty-two-bit addresses give the ability to address 2^{32} (4,294,960,000) locations.

The *central processor* is designed to obey instructions given to it. These instructions are encoded in a binary representation and stored in the main memory. Each instruction usually has between 8 and 64 bits depending upon the computer and the instruction. One or more memory locations are used to store one instruction. The instructions are called *machine instructions* and there are usually many different instructions available as defined by the *instruction set* of the computer. Operations that can be specified by instructions include data transfer

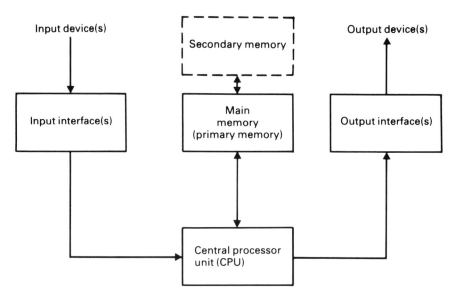

Figure 6.1   Digital computer

operations transferring numbers from one location to another, arithmetic operations such as addition or subtraction, logic operations such as AND and NOT, and control operations such as to stop all operation. The arithmetic and logic operations are performed by the *arithmetic and logic unit* (abbreviated to ALU) within the processor.

The operation specified by the instruction often requires numbers (operands), usually one or two numbers. For example, a machine instruction may specify the addition of two numbers. Generally, these numbers can be held in the main memory, or in storage registers within the central processor. The result of the operation can be placed in the main memory or in internal processor registers depending upon the computer and the instruction. A list of instructions is created by the user to produce a desired action or result. This list is known as a *machine-language program* or *machine-code program* and is held in the main memory. After the processor has executed the first instruction in the program, it proceeds to the next instruction unless directed by the executed instruction to do otherwise.

The *input circuits and devices* are used to enter the program defined by the user. Numbers can also be input during the execution of the program. The output circuits and devices are used to convey results from the program. The input and output devices can also be used to control the overall operation of the computer system. The input circuits are required to translate the signals from the input devices to the system and, similarly, the output circuits are required to translate the signals from the system to the output devices. These circuits are known as *interfaces*. Input and output for user communication is generally performed by the same device (usually a display terminal). Because input and output are often closely coupled, the two terms, input and output, are abbreviated as input/output or I/O.

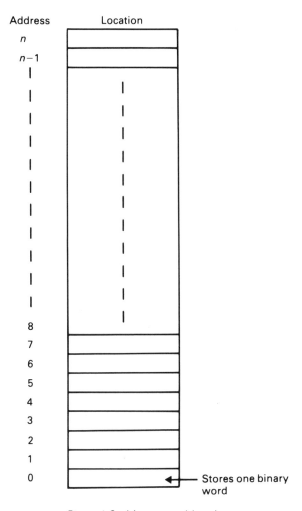

Figure 6.2 Memory addressing

The memory of the system is usually divided into two parts for economic reasons, the primary memory containing locations which can be accessed at high speed in any order, and a *secondary* memory, often based on magnetic recording (magnetic disks and tape), capable of storing much larger amounts of information but not with very high-speed access. Generally the contents of the secondary memory must be transferred to the primary memory before the processor can access the information. The term *backing store* is sometimes used for secondary memory.

Briefly, the basic mode of operation of a digital computer system is to transfer the first instruction in the program from memory to the processor during a *fetch cycle* and then the processor performs the specified operation during an *execute cycle*, as shown in Fig. 6.3. The instruction is stored in an internal processor register called an *instruction register* and decoded (its purpose recognized) during the latter

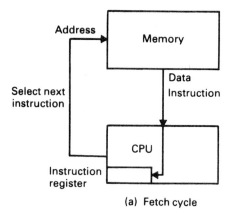

(a) Fetch cycle

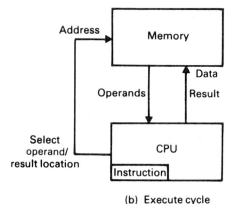

(b) Execute cycle

Figure 6.3   CPU mode of operation

part of the fetch cycle. The subsequent operations in the execute cycle depend upon the operation decoded. Should more than one memory word be necessary to hold a complete instruction, additional fetch cycles are performed to form the instruction in the processor instruction register before the execute cycle can start. (This point is taken up later.) The fetch–execute cycle sequence is repeated for subsequent instructions.

Having a list of stored instructions which are executed in a sequential manner has been the mode of operation of most digital computers since their first conception in the 1940s. The system is called a *stored program computer*. One of the fundamental aspects of a stored program computer is that the memory is used to store both the program and the data. The concept is attributed to von Neumann and his co-workers at the Moore School of Engineering of the University of Pennsylvania in the period 1946–48. Hence this stored program computer is sometimes called a *von Neumann computer*, and particularly refers to the sequential nature of program execution. It is worth noting that attempts have been made to design digital computers which do not have this sequential operation, for example data flow computers. Such computers are referred to as non-von Neumann computers, though they may still have a stored program. However, the steps taken in the program are not defined by the order in which the instructions are placed in the program. (In a data flow computer, the order depends upon valid data being made available for the instruction.)

6.1.2 Processor instructions

The first point to note on the processor instructions is that the operation specified is reduced to a simple type, and more complex operations are achieved by forming an ordered list of instructions in the program. For example, we may write an apparently simple arithmetic computation on paper as:

$$\text{Result} = (2 + 6 - 4)/ (8 \times 9)$$

However, we could not provide a unique machine instruction for this calculation and all other possible calculations. Instead, addition, subtraction, multiplication and division instructions can be provided operating upon two operands in the same manner as when using a calculator. Partial results need to be stored. Suppose all the numbers in the calculation are firstly stored in memory. A sequence might begin with an instruction to add the contents of the memory locations holding the numbers 2 and 6. Then the contents of memory location holding the number 4 would be subtracted to generate a partial result. The contents of the memory locations holding the numbers 8 and 9 would be multiplied together and the result of this operation divided into the first partial result. Clearly the same calculation using different numbers can be performed by firstly loading the appropriate memory locations with the desired numbers. Whether the described sequence could in fact be specified in practice would depend upon the computer instructions provided. As we shall see, it is often necessary to load at least one of the two operands into a processor register before an operation can be performed upon the operands.

Having accepted that (arithmetic and logic) instructions will specify a single operation upon one or two operands, we now consider the general format of processor instructions. The machine instructions are notionally split into two parts, an operation field and an operand field:

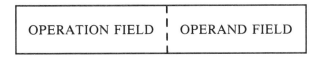

The operation field specifies the particular operation to be performed by the processor and the operand field specifies in some way the operands (numbers) that are to be used in the operation. Each of these fields contains encoded binary patterns. An operand may be given in the operand field as the actual binary number required and then it is known as a *literal*. Alternatively, the operand field may contain the address or addresses of storage locations from which the number or numbers may be obtained. This method of finding the operand is known as the *addressing* mechanism. There are various addressing mechanisms that can be invoked. It is usual to refer to the operand field as the address field even though in the case of a literal it contains the actual number to be used rather than an address. The number obtained for the operation can always be regarded by the processor as an integer, for example an 8-bit integer, 16-bit integer or 32-bit integer. More advanced processors can also operate upon floating point numbers.

The most general machine instruction format is one with four addresses specifying the following:

(i) Address of one operand
(ii) Address of second operand
(iii) Address of where the result of the operation is to be stored
(iv) Address of where the next instruction may be found.

Thus an instruction would be in the form:

OPERATION FIELD	FIRST OPERAND ADDRESS	SECOND OPERAND ADDRESS	RESULT ADDRESS	NEXT INSTRUCTION ADDRESS

The fourth address is always eliminated for machine instructions by arranging that the next instruction to be executed is immediately following the current instruction. The general movement of operands is shown in Fig. 6.4, assuming that all operands are stored in the main memory. To allow for non sequential instruction execution, instructions are introduced into the instruction repertoire which can alter the sequence of instruction execution. Whether the sequence is altered may depend upon the results of arithmetic of logical operations. This leads directly to the decision-making power of computers because it permits programs to be executed which choose different instructions depending upon immediately preceding computations. (Four-address instruction formats are used in microprogrammed control units; see Chapter 12.)

The third address above can be eliminated by always placing the result of arithmetic or logic operations in the location where the first operand was found. The computer would then be a *two-address* machine with the implication that the result overwrites one of the original numbers. It leads to the instruction format:

OPERATION FIELD	FIRST OPERAND/RESULT ADDRESS	SECOND OPERAND ADDRESS

and the operand movement shown in Fig. 6.5.

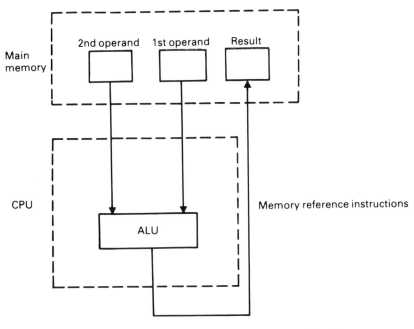

Figure 6.4   Data flow with three-address instruction format

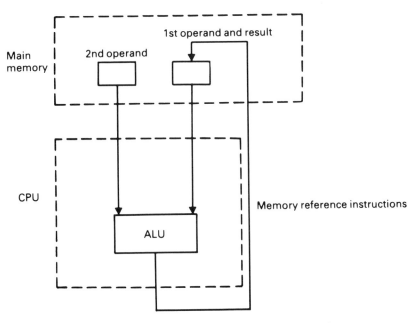

Figure 6.5   Data flow with two-address instruction format

The second address can be eliminated by also having only one place for the first operand which would be within the processor itself rather than in the memory. This location is known as an *accumulator*, as it accumulates the results. The computer would then be a *single address* or accumulator type of machine. The operand movement is shown in Fig. 6.6. However, having only one location for one of the operands and for the subsequent result is rather limiting, so a small group of locations within the processor can be provided, i.e. processor registers. The term *one and a half address* machine has been used to cover this case but we shall simply call the architecture a *register file type*. The operand movement is shown in Fig. 6.7. Notice that once a set of registers is provided, it is desirable to be able to perform calculations between contents of registers rather than one register and a memory location. This results in a substantial increase in speed of operation because internal processor registers can usually be accessed much quicker than main memory locations. Also, although the registers used in the instructions need to be specified in some manner, they can be identified with a small *register address*, e.g. a 2-bit address for four registers, or 4-bit address for 16 registers, compared with 16 or more address bits usually required for main memory locations.

All the addresses in the operand field can be eliminated by using two specific locations. These locations are specified as the first and second locations of a group of locations known as a *stack*. Usually the stack consists of a group of memory locations and the first location, or top of stack, is specified by a processor register known as the *stack pointer*. The computer using the 'top' two locations of a stack for storing the operands is called a *zero-address* machine. The operand movement using the top two locations of a stack is shown in Fig. 6.8. A zero-address machine has some advantages in some types of programming such as evaluating arithmetic

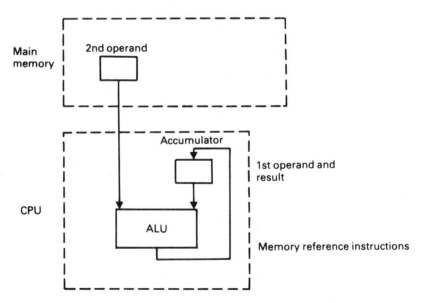

Figure 6.6 Data flow with one-address instruction format

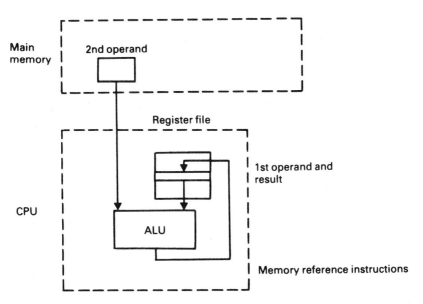

Figure 6.7   Data flow with 1½-address instruction format (register file instruction format)

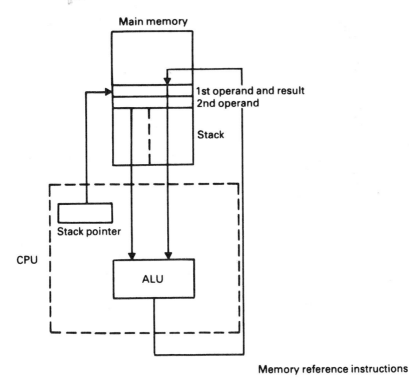

Figure 6.8   Data flow with zero-address instruction format

expressions, but has generally lost favour in preference to register machines. Stack operations are incorporated into register machines, but primarily for interrupt and subroutine handling (see Chapter 7).

There can be several hundred different instructions in the instruction set of the computer. Broadly speaking, instructions can be categorized into one of a number of groups (assuming one-, two- or three-address format):

(a) Transfer (also known as load/store and move)

Here the contents of one location are copied to another location. The locations may be memory locations or processor register locations, though direct transfer between memory locations is not always provided. The word 'transfer', though widely used, is misleading as the data is not removed from the source location, but left intact. The data held in the destination location before the execution of the transfer instruction is lost when the new data is transferred to the location.

(b) Arithmetic and logical

The arithmetic operations addition and subtraction are always in the instruction set. Logical operations are the Boolean operations AND, OR, NOT, exclusive-OR, exclusive-NOR, etc. AND, OR, NOT and exclusive-OR are often provided, operating upon pairs of bits in the two binary numbers held in the selected locations to produce the bits in the result.

(c) Shift and rotate

Shift and rotate operations involve moving each bit in a single binary number one or more places left or right in the same manner as the shift operation in a shift register. The rotate operations correspond to the operation of a ring counter (see Chapter 4, section 4.4.2).

(d) Jump/branch

These instructions alter the sequence of instructions executed. Some jump/branch instructions only alter the sequence if a specified condition prevails within the processor when the instruction is executed. Conditions normally relate to the last arithmetic/logical result before the jump/branch instructions.

(e) Input/output

Input instructions provide a means of transferring numbers from input interfaces/devices to processor registers. Output instructions provide a means of transferring numbers held in processor registers to output interfaces/devices.

(f) Control

A control instruction causes the processor to perform an operation such as stop completely, move automatically to the next instruction, wait for an external event to occur, or set a selected bit in a designated register used by the processor in connection with jump/branch operations or external events.

It is convenient to describe machine instructions using abbreviations for each field in the instruction, for example:

ADD R1, R2

could represent the instruction to add the contents of processor register R2 to processor register R1, placing the result in R1. The abbreviation ADD corresponds to the operation defined in the operation field. R1 and R2 correspond to the addresses in the operand address fields. These abbreviations form part of an *assembly language*. We will use assembly language notation in Chapter 7 for identifying specific instructions.

Apart from specifying within the instruction:

(i) The operand as a literal
(ii) The memory address of an operand and
(iii) A register holding the operand,

we can specify a register which holds the address of a memory location of the operand. We will defer discussion of this addressing method (*addressing mode*) and its variations to Chapter 7.

6.1.3 Reduced instruction set computers (RISCs)

The choice of instructions in the instruction set of a processor is a major design factor. Though operations in instructions are reduced to a simple form, throughout the development of computers, until the 1980s, more complex instructions have been provided to aid the software development and close the so-called *semantic gap* between the hardware and software. Mostly, a simple instruction format was retained with one operation, one or two operands and one result, but specialized operations and addressing modes were added. The general argument for providing additional operations and addressing modes is that they can be performed at greater speed in hardware than as a sequence of primitive machine instructions. Computers with these instructions are called *complex instruction set computers* (CISCs). CISCs often have between 100 and 300 different instruction operations with complex encoding and 8 to 20 addressing modes.

The policy of providing complex machine instructions has been questioned, and an alternative design resurfaced in the early 1980s, that of having very simple instructions with few operations and few addressing modes. Computers with few specially chosen instructions are called *reduced instruction set computers* (RISCs). RISCs often have 50 to 100 different instruction operations with regular instruction length encoding, and only two to five addressing modes. All arithmetic operations operate only on register operands. Various factors have led to this design choice, which we will summarize here.

(a) The effect of the inclusion of complex instructions

Complex instructions necessitate long instruction encoding and consequently more program memory and complex instruction decoding within the processor. However, some instructions are more frequently used than others. Some simple instructions, such as register transfer instructions, are used very frequently. The CISC solution is to have shorter instruction length for commonly used instructions which actually complicates the instruction decoding further and reduces the execution speed of all instructions, even simple frequently used instructions; the RISC solution is not to implement the infrequently used instructions at all.

(b) VLSI implementation

A decision has to be made as to the best way to utilize the newly available space in VLSI components. Is it to add complex instructions at the risk of decreasing the speed of other operations, or should the extra space on the chip be used for other purposes such as a large number of processor registers, local program/data memory or additional execution units which can operate simultaneously? The RISC proponents argue for the latter.

(c) Microcode

In Chapter 12, we will describe the conventional approach to designing the control circuitry of a processor using microinstructions held in a control memory. Micro-instructions are at a level below that of the machine instructions. A sequence of microinstructions (*microcode* or *microprogram*) is executed to execute one machine instruction. CISCs often rely heavily on microcode. Microcode was first used at a time when the main memory was based upon magnetic core stores, and faster 'read-only' memory could be provided to hold the microcode. With the move to semiconductor memory complete, the gap between the achievable speed of operation of main memory and microcode memory narrows. Also the concept of local program/data memory has been developed. Now, a considerable overhead can appear in a microprogrammed design, especially when a simple operation might correspond to one microinstruction. RISCs have often abandoned microcode in favour of direct logic gate implementation to obtain extremely fast operation.

(d) Compilers

There is an increased prospect for designing optimizing compilers if there are less instructions in the instruction set. Some of the more exotic instructions are rarely chosen by compilers which have to select an appropriate instruction automatically. It is difficult for a compiler to identify the situations in which they can be used effectively. A key part of the RISC development is the provision of an optimizing compiler which can take over some of the complexities from the hardware and make the best use of the registers.

6.2 Microprocessor system

6.2.1 General

A microprocessor system is a stored-program digital computer system with the four major parts described previously, but with an integrated circuit central processor called a *microprocessor*. The main memory is also usually fabricated in integrated circuit technology (i.e. semiconductor memory). The first microprocessor, the Intel 4004 introduced in 1971, was a 4-bit accumulator type. Second-generation microprocessors, typified by the Intel 8080 introduced in 1973, the Motorola 6800 introduced in 1974 and the Zilog Z–80 introduced in 1975, are 8-bit accumulator types. In all cases, additional registers are incorporated for particular purposes and some registers can be used to accumulate results. However, the true register type of processor in which instructions can operate on the contents of one of many registers were not widely found until later 16-bit microprocessors, for example the Motorola MC68000 introduced in 1978.

The microprocessor, memory and input/output interfaces are interconnected via a common set of electrical lines known as a *bus*, as shown in Fig. 6.9. The signals are TTL compatible, i.e. the signal voltages are within the range of TTL; (see Chapter 5, section 5.6.1). Early microprocessors (e.g. Intel 4004) were not TTL compatible and required support devices to convert their signal voltages to TTL levels.

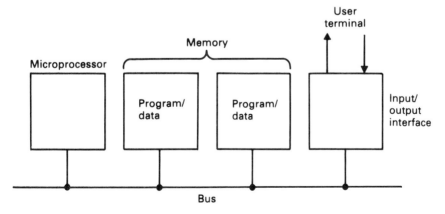

Figure 6.9 Fundamental parts of a microprocessor system

The main memory is semiconductor memory which employs a circuit arrangement to maintain one of two electrical states for each binary digit stored. *Reading* the memory, i.e. examining the states and passing this information from the memory device to the processor, does not destroy the information stored. *Writing* to the memory, i.e. storing new information of course destroys the original information. In a *random access memory*, RAM, information can be read from or written to the memory in any order with equal high speed.

It is essential that the main memory of a computer uses memory with the random access feature for both the program stored and and associated data. The main memory generally needs to be capable of both high-speed reading and high-speed writing in the case of program operands. However, the main memory may only need the feature of high-speed reading for program storage as instructions in a program are not altered when the program is being executed. This has led to the development of random access memory which is capable only of being read. The memory patterns held are defined either during manufacture of the device, or later by the user. Such devices are naturally called *read-only memories* (ROMs) although they are also random access. Thus to differentiate between the two types, the term RAM is limited to read–write memories.

The memory can comprise various types, *random access memory* (RAM), *read-only memory* (ROM), *programmable read-only memory* (PROM) and *erasable programmable read-only memory* (EPROM). Random access memory and at least one of the three types of read-only memory exists in most systems. Read-only memory is usually employed to store the *bootstrap program*, a program executed automatically when the computer is switched on. Memory may also include additional secondary memory such as *floppy disk storage*. EPROM devices use an electrical process to write information, allowing the user to 'program' the device. Ultra-violet light is used to remove the information (or an electrical process in electrically erasable PROM's). Further description of memory devices can be found in Chapter 8.

Thirty-two-bit processors can manipulate 8-, 16- and 32-bit words (and possibly larger word sizes depending upon the processor), and the memory is arranged to be able to access 8-bit words, 16-bit words and 32-bit words directly. Memory addresses are allocated to 8-bit words (bytes). Sixteen-bit words are of course held in two consecutive 8-bit locations, and 32-bit words are held in four consecutive 8-bit locations. There is a design choice of having the least significant byte of the 16- and 32-bit words in the lowest addressed byte, or the most significant byte in the lowest addressed byte. The term *big-endian* is used when the most significant byte is in the lowest address byte (i.e. big end first). The term *little-endian* is used when the least significant byte is in the lowest addressed byte (i.e. little end first). In either event, the 16- and 32-bit words are referred to by the lowest byte address. Motorola 68000 family processors use the big-endian convention, whereas the Intel 8086 family uses the little-endian convention. The choice between big-endian and little-endian does not matter if consistency is maintained within the system. However, the convention may matter if the data is transferred between processors or systems using the different conventions.

6.2.2 The microprocessor

The internal architecture of a microprocessor using a single bus to interconnect the components is shown in Fig. 6.10. For register instructions, the registers specified are held in the register file. In early single accumulator processors, the accumulator register was moved to be close to the ALU as this would be the only source of one operand and the destination of the result, but in a general register architecture, any two registers in the register file can be chosen by the instruction for the sources of the operands. The destination would either be one of the two source registers or, in the case of three-address instruction processors, potentially a different register in the register file. The number of bits in each operand is that fundamentally associated with the processor, 4, 8, 16, 32, etc. Negative numbers are considered in the 2's complement notation.

Other internal parts of the microprocessor include a control unit to generate the internal and external control signals and various control registers. The *condition code register* consists of a number of single-bit *flags* which indicate some particular aspect of the result. For example, the zero flag is set to a 1 if the result of an arithmetic operation is zero and set to a 0 if the result is not zero. Other flags found include the *negative flag* (result negative), *even parity flag* (result having an even number of 1's) and the *overflow flag* (result out of range and hence invalid). The *program counter* is an internal processor register existing in computers to hold the memory address of the next instruction to be executed. Generally, the contents of the program counter are automatically incremented (value increased by 1) after a

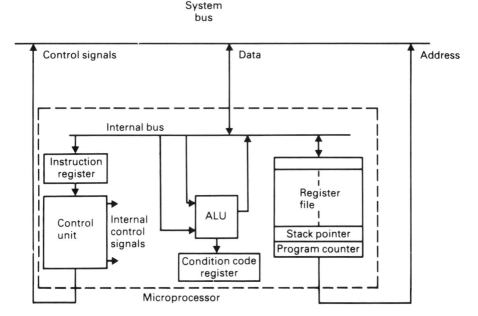

Figure 6.10 Internal architecture of simple microprocessor

memory location holding the next instruction or next part of an instruction has been taken into the processor. The *stack pointer* holds the memory address of the top of the stack, for use in stack instructions (see Chapter 7). In addition to the program counter and stack pointer, other registers in the so-called *register file* can often address the memory to access data.

The single internal bus shown in Fig. 6.10 limits one transfer between the register file and the ALU at a time. In processors with 2- and 3-address instruction formats, potentially two operand transfers are required simultaneously from the register file and two internal buses could be provided. A third bus could be provided to transfer the result back to the register file, releasing the other buses for carrying operands for the next instruction. Multiple buses imply that the register file must be able to handle multiple accesses simultaneously which may be read or write accesses. There are several other variations in the internal architecture. Three internal operand buses can be found in the Motorola MC88100 32-bit microprocessor and other 3-address microprocessors. Such high performance processors also have multiple functional units to enable more than one operation to take place simultaneously. The MC88100 is a so-called *reduced instruction set computer* (RISC), having a limited number of instructions encoded in a fixed 32-bit word for high performance. We shall have more to say about such fixed length instruction processors in Chapter 12.

6.2.3 Multiple length instructions

A characteristic of all early microprocessors and many subsequent microprocessors is that a single instruction cannot always be totally specified in one memory word. For example, 8-bit words of early 8-bit microprocessors would be insufficient to specify both the operation and the operands of even a single address instruction, not to mention two address instructions. In such cases, more than one consecutive word is used, perhaps between 1 and 5 bytes for an early 8-bit processor depending upon the instruction specification. Even more recent 32-bit microprocessors often use more than one 16-bit or 32-bit word to hold instructions. For example, instructions of the Motorola 68030/40 processors [1, 2] can be between one 16-bit word and eleven 16-bit words.

In all processors with multi-byte/word instructions, the first byte or word will specify the operation with an *operation code*, abbreviated to *op-code*. During the fetch cycle, the op-code is fetched from the program memory. This is achieved by using the contents of the program counter to address the program memory and initiating a memory read cycle. The processor decodes the op-code when received and determines whether further bytes/words must be fetched. Bytes/words are then obtained in sequence from the memory as necessary. The contents of the program counter are used to address the memory and hence the value stored is incremented by one after each byte is fetched, or by two if 16-bit words are fetched, or by four if 32-bit words are fetched. Once the complete instruction has been assembled, the processor can start the execute cycle. The addresses of any operands stored in memory are generally obtained in the second and subsequent bytes/words of the instruction, these addresses having been obtained during the overall instruction fetch cycle. The execute cycle will include reading addressed operand locations in memory as required, as well as performing the internal operation upon the operands obtained, and any final write operation. The simple division into an instruction fetch cycle and an instruction execute cycle in multi-byte/multi-word instruction microprocessors, or any computer system in which instructions are of variable length, becomes a sequence of read cycles and a possible final write cycle. Sometimes the term *op-code fetch* is used for the first read cycle which fetches the op-code.

6.2.4 Bus

The bus signals contained in the external bus can be divided into the three groups:

  (i) Data lines
 (ii) Address lines
(iii) Control lines.

(a) Data lines

The data lines are used to transfer binary words between the processor, memory and input/output interfaces. The binary words may be machine instructions from the memory to the processor prior to performing the operation specified by the instruction, or may be data to or from the processor during the execution of the operation.

Microprocessors are described as 4-bit, 8-bit, 16-bit or 32-bit if the data operands are manipulated fundamentally in units of 4, 8, 16 or 32 bits respectively. The first microprocessors were 4-bit microprocessors and four data lines were provided (actually the same lines were also used for address signals). Instructions needed to be longer than four bits so multiple data transfers were necessary to obtain one instruction. For example, a 16-bit instruction could be obtained by four successive 4-bit transfers. Early 4-bit microprocessors had some 8-bit and 16-bit instructions, necessitating two and four 4-bit transfers respectively.

Eight-bit microprocessors have eight data lines. Commonly instructions of 8-bit microprocessors are between one and five bytes, requiring one to five data transfers to obtain the instruction. Normally, 16-bit microprocessors have sixteen data lines, and each instruction consists of one or more 16-bit words. It may be advantageous in some cases to design 16-bit microprocessors with eight data lines to reduce the number of lines. Using eight data lines also allows memory and input/output devices operating on eight bits to be easily accommodated. When 16-bit data is being processed with eight data lines, two successive 8-bit data transfers are necessary. Thirty-two bit microprocessors have 32 data lines (unless reduced in the same manner to 16 or 8 lines).

(b) Address lines

The address lines carry the address of the memory location being accessed during an instruction fetch or during the execution of data transfer to or from the memory location. Whereas the data signals may originate at the processor, memory devices or input/output interfaces, for simple instruction processing address signals always originate at the processor. (There are some instances when address signals originate elsewhere, i.e. when another device controls the bus lines; see Chapter 9, section 9.4.)

It is possible to combine the address lines or to combine some of the address lines with data lines to reduce the number of connections on the microprocessor device, though address and data are usually separated for connection to the other components. (An exception to this is in a microprocessor system using specially designed components to match combined address/data lines of the microprocessor.) The early 4-bit 4004/4040 microprocessors used four combined data/address lines. A 12-bit address was generated by the unusual arrangement of passing three consecutive 4-bit addresses along the bus. The address range was subsequently increased and the next generation of 8-bit microprocessors provided 16-bit addresses on 16 address lines, normally separate from the 8 data lines, though in one instance (the Intel 8085), the lower 8 address lines were shared with data. Figure 6.11 shows the use of a latched buffer to separate the data and address. The signal $\overline{\text{ALE}}$ is activated (set to 0) when the data/address bus carries an address.

Sixteen-bit addresses give the capability to address up to 65,536 (2^{16}) locations. The early 16-bit microprocessors had 20 or 24 address lines. Trends have been to increase the number of address lines. For example, 32-bit microprocessors can have 32 address lines providing the capability to address the 4,294,960,000 (2^{32}) locations.

(c) Control lines

The control lines provide signals to synchronize the operation of the system, in particular the transfer of data along the data bus. There can be twelve or more control lines, each with a particular purpose. Most of the control signals originate at the processor, though one or two may be generated by the other components attached to the bus and sent to the processor.

The signals which originate at only one source device and pass to one or more destination devices can be generated by two-state logic circuits. For the components in addition to the microprocessor, semiconductor memory and MOS input/output parts, standard TTL gates can be used. MOS microprocessors and other MOS parts use equivalent MOS two-state circuits with active pull-up and active pull-down MOS transistors. In a simple system with no other device being able to address the memory or input/output, the address signals can be generated with two-state circuits. The control signals with one source (usually those from the processor) can also employ three-state circuits.

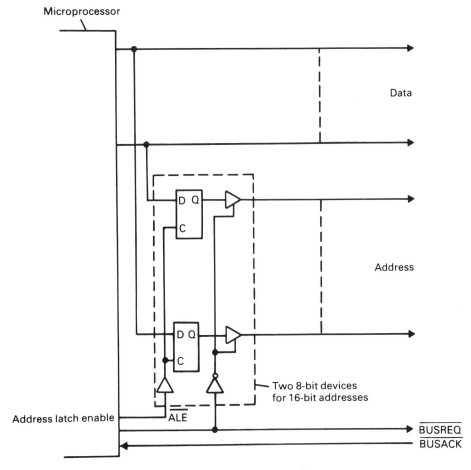

Figure 6.11 Demultiplexing data/address

Those signals which may have more than one source and one or more destinations need to employ either open-collector gates or three-state gates The data signals always employ three-state gates. The control signals with more than one source (generally those to the processor from the other bus devices) can use open-collector circuits. Open-collector signals must be active low, i.e. normally at a high level and brought low to indicate or cause some action. Open-collector signals would be used when multiple separate or simultaneous signal activations are possible, while three-state signals would be used when simultaneous activation is not allowed, such as passing data to and from the processor simultaneously. Note that the microprocessor itself is often of MOS technology and thus would use the equivalent MOS circuits. Usually MOS devices have a very low fan-out capability (about one TTL load) so additional TTL buffer gates are used between MOS microprocessors (and other MOS devices) and the bus, as described in Chapter 5, section 5.6.3.

6.2.5 Bus information transfer techniques

We now consider the techniques used to control the transfer of information in a bus system and the corresponding control signals. There are two basic information transfer techniques used. We shall call these methods the *synchronous bus transfer method* and the *asynchronous bus transfer method*:

(a) Synchronous transfer method

In the synchronous bus transfer method, a request signal together with data if appropriate, and address signals are generated by the source device, normally the processor. These signals are received by the appropriate destination device, normally a memory unit or input/output interface, whereupon data is accepted or generated. The time required for the transfer is known in advance and is taken into account by the source device before the next request is generated. The simple data transfer technique with one memory or input/output request timing signal and one active data direction signal (say read or write) is in this synchronous transfer category. Often it is arranged that all data transfers are of a fixed period, all memory operating with a common maximum access time and all the input/output interfaces operating within the same constraints.

The basic operation of synchronous data transfer requires the following information to be transferred along the control lines:

 (i) Direction of the data transfer, either to the processor or from the processor
(ii) Timing of the transfer
(iii) Whether the transfer involves a memory location or input output interface (if these are differentiated).

Data (or an instruction) transferred to the processor is called a *read* cycle or transfer. Data transferred from the processor is called a *write* cycle or transfer. One signal may be generated to indicate a read transfer and another to indicate a write transfer. With separate signals for different transactions, the time of the transaction can be when the signal is generated. If the signals are combined, for example a combined read/write signal which is true for a read transfer and false for a write transfer (true = 1, false = 0), additional signals must be generated when the operation is to occur. Control signals are often active low, as indicated by a bar over the signal name.

There are various signals that can be used to carry the three types of information, and several approaches have been tried. Software-compatible microprocessors of the same family might not use the same signals. For example, the Motorola 68030 and 68040, though essentially software compatible 32-bit processors, use fundamentally different control signals. Also, even the same approach by different manufacturers has led to different signal names. We will consider generic names which do not relate to a specific processor; however they are representative.

The direction of transfer could be differentiated with two signals:

$\overline{\text{RD}}$ Read enable
$\overline{\text{WR}}$ Write enable

or more commonly by a single signal:

R\\$\overline{\text{W}}$ Read/write. A combined read–write signal, 1 for a read, 0 for a write.

The timing of the transfer is usually established with additional control signals. A timing signal is usually necessary to indicate when all the address lines have stabilized, called $\overline{\text{AS}}$ (address strobe) say. This signal would be used in conjunction with the address signals within the memory address decode logic. (With separate $\overline{\text{RD}}$ and $\overline{\text{WR}}$ signals, it is possible to combine read/write selection with timing, for example 'memory read request', $\overline{\text{MEMR}}$, say, and 'memory write request', $\overline{\text{MEMW}}$, say.)

The bus connects to both memory and input/output interfaces. Sometimes these are differentiated, with certain instructions only operating upon memory locations and a few others operating only upon input/output interfaces. The address generated refers either to locations within memory or to locations within the input/output interface depending upon the instruction. To differentiate between memory addresses and input/output addresses in this case requires at least one additional signal, say:

M/$\overline{\text{IO}}$ Memory-input/output, a signal indicating whether the read or write transfer is to memory or input/output devices

as used on Intel processors such as the 80386 processor. Processors which do not differentiate between memory and input/output interfaces, for example Motorola processors, do not of course need these signals. Then memory is allocated certain addresses and input/output interfaces certain other addresses (memory mapped I/O see Chapter 9).

Timing is always related to the processor clock signal. Sequences of consecutive clock periods are indicated by, for example. T1, T2, T3.... Usually particular clock transitions from a 0 to a 1 or from a 1 to a 0 cause a specific control signal to be generated by the processor or other actions to take place. Some time is necessary after these clock transitions to allow the signals to establish their values on the bus.

Figure 6.12 shows representative memory write and memory read timing using a central clock signal. In both cases, the address lines are set up on the 1-to-0 transition of the first clock period and stabilize shortly afterwards. At the same time, a read/write signal indicates the direction of transfer. For a write operation, the data to be written is also presented on the data bus by the end of the first clock period. In this example, the memory is given until the third clock period to accept the data, and the signals are removed on the 1-to-0 transition of the third clock period. For a read operation, the memory is expected to provide the data on the data bus by the beginning of the third clock period which is accepted by the processor on the 1-to-0 transition of the third clock period.

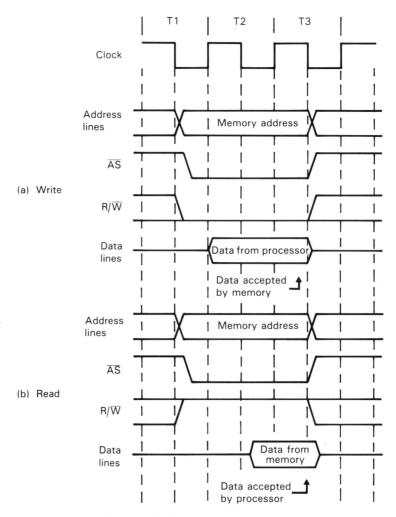

Figure 6.12 Synchronous bus timing

With the synchronous transfer technique, the processor must be operated at a frequency not greater than the speed which matches the slowest device. It may be that this clock frequency is not the maximum for the processor and the potential speed of the processor is not then being utilized. The problem can be alleviated with the introduction of a signal variously called *ready*, *wait* or *transfer acknowledge*, emitted from the destination device (memory or input/output interface) to the processor. This signal, when activated, causes the processor to add dummy processor clock cycles (known as *wait states*) to extend the data transfer period. The address, data and control signals from the processor remain activated until the transfer has been accepted. If the wait signal is not activated, the processor generates an unmodified sequence of control signals and clock periods. Hence it is not necessary to generate the wait signal if the devices attached to the bus can respond in the minimum time allowed by the processor, about two cycles in the previous example.

Figure 6.13 shows the previous example with a wait signal activated for one clock period to cause one wait state to be inserted as shown. The memory interface (or input/output interface) generates the wait signal after its address has been

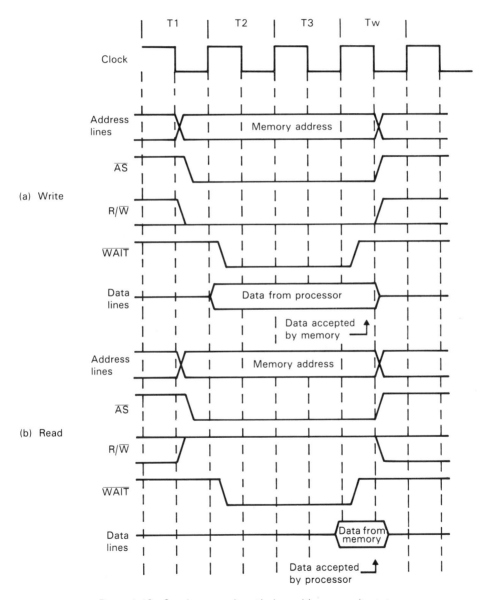

Figure 6.13 Synchronous bus timing with one wait state

recognized. It is necessary to know how much extra time is required so that the wait state generator hardware within the interface can be designed to activate the wait signal appropriately. The extra time actually given will be in multiples of one clock cycle. The processor will sample the wait line during each clock cycle to ascertain whether another dummy cycle is necessary. Memory or input/output units attached to the bus needing extra time are provided with separate wait state generators arranged to generate the wait signal as required for the unit, as shown in Fig. 6.14.

Many microprocessors (Intel 80x86, Motorola 68040, etc.) use the bus data transfer mechanism described, though each with slight variations in timing. It is possible to reduce the basic timing to two cycles by having data accepted or generated during T2 rather than T3. This would be especially applicable for a processor designed to be attached to a very high-speed memory. Sometimes the processor clock is driven by a multiple (usually double) frequency clock and signals are related to transitions of the higher frequency clock. This technique enables finer timing of the signals but requires internal circuits to operate at this higher frequency.

In the bus mechanism described (Fig. 6.12 and Fig. 6.13), the bus lines are effectively occupied for the duration of the transfer. However long the transfer takes, the address signals and other signals are established for the total duration. In an alternative scheme (as used by the Motorola 88100 processor), two phases are identified, an address phase in which the address signals are established, followed by a reply phase in which the the data and acknowledge signals are generated. Figure 6.15 shows the signals for write and read transactions. The acknowledgement takes the form of the particular code on encoded reply lines. Possible replies include success (the operation has been completed), wait (insert a wait state or otherwise handle a delay in the transaction) and fault (an error has occurred during the transaction). Assuming that each transaction is successful, a series of overlapped transactions can be performed, with the address of the next transaction presented during the reply phase of the previous transaction. This technique (a form of pipelining, see Chapter 12) requires that the memory or input/output interface has an internal latch to hold the address while it is processing the transaction.

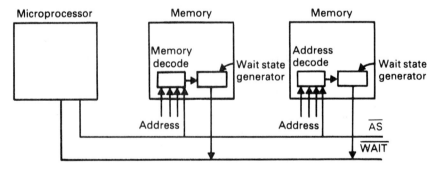

Figure 6.14 Generating wait states

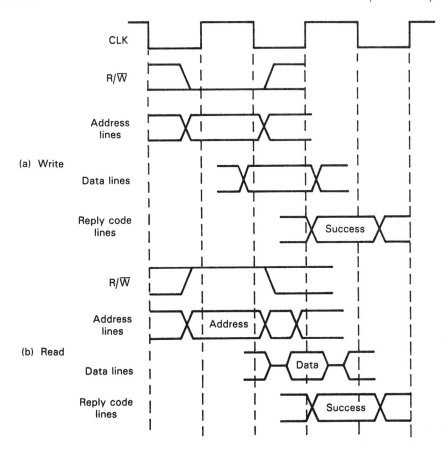

Figure 6.15 Synchronous bus timing using 'pipelining'

(b) Asynchronous transfer method

The asynchronous bus transfer method uses two signals for timing the data transfer. The first signal from the source (the processor generally) to the destination (memory or input/output interface) signifies the start of a data transfer. The transfer operation is only terminated by a second signal emitted from the destination, indicating that the transfer has been completed. This two-signal approach, as shown in Fig. 6.16, is known as handshaking and is similar to the synchronous mechanism modified with wait signal returned by the destination. However, a true asynchronous bus would allow acknowledge signals to be generated at any time and be totally unrelated to the processor clock signal. The duration of the transfer is always dictated by the returning acknowledge signal. This signal must be activated for the transfer to be completed, whereas in the wait mechanism the transfer is always completed unless delayed by receipt of a wait signal.

For data operations, there would be a data transfer acknowledge signal produced by the memory or input/output interface to indicate that the data transfer

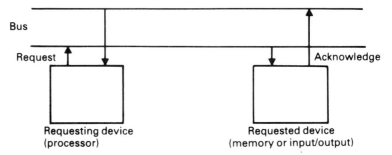

Figure 6.16   Asynchronous 'handshake' operation

is complete, in addition to the 'direction' and 'type' control signals of the synchronous method. If the asynchronous approach is taken to its logical conclusion, each control signal would have an acknowledge signal. For example, an address strobe timing signal would have an address strobe acknowledge signal. This is not done, but there may be handshaking on certain key control signals, for example the bus grant signal in DMA operation (Chapter 9) may have a bus grant acknowledge signal.

Generally, if an acknowledge signal is not received within a fixed time specified by the bus design, a 'time-out' error sequence is started automatically to ascertain the identity of the fault. (A microprocessor with a wait mechanism may also have a maximum allowed period for waiting for a unit to be ready, maybe 10 μs.)

Asynchronous bus transfer systems have the advantage of matching the speed of data transfer between the source and destination. They also have a mechanism for detecting a fault in the destination or a non-existent destination, since if an acknowledge is not received there must be a fault or the destination does not exist. (Not receiving a wait signal does not indicate a fault.) However, the method has the disadvantage of requiring more signals (the acknowledge signals), which must be allowed time to be generated and travel along the bus, so it may be that the overall speed of operation is slower. Also, the processor must synchronize asynchronous acknowledge signals for internal use, and this may incur significant logic circuit complexity, delay, and occasional malfunction (see Chapter 11). The original processor in the Motorola 68000 family, the 68000, was provided with separate asynchronous and synchronous buses, the latter to interface with 6800 peripheral devices. The 32-bit 68030 is also provided with both synchronous and asynchronous mechanisms but this duplication was not continued with the 68040. Some standard buses use asynchronous mechanisms.

6.3 Embedded controllers

A very important area recognized for microprocessors at the early stage of their development was *embedded* control applications. An embedded application is one in which a system is directly controlled by an integral computer. Embedded controllers can be found in domestic appliances (washing machines, etc.) and entertainment products (VCRs, etc.), avionic systems, industrial control systems, telecommunications equipment, automobiles, and most computer peripherals (printers, etc.). Previously, the internal electrical control signals would be generated with specific logic designs. Embedded controllers offer a cost-effective solution and enhance the functionality of the system. They have also created new products with their built-in programmability, for example electronic games products.

The architecture of an embedded controller resembles the conventional microprocessor system in Fig. 6.9. A common bus connects the major components. The main difference is that there is no user terminal interface. In its place are interfaces to the system being controlled. These interfaces often take the form of registers holding the values of signals from the system, and signals to be sent to the system. The microprocessor and its interfaces and memory are often integrated into a single integrated circuit microcontroller chip, as shown in Fig. 6.17, and replace much of the specially designed logic. Notice the concentration upon input/output interfaces. These interfaces can be programmed to operate in various modes (input, output, bidirectional). At least one timer is usually provided to enable an accurate measurement of time. The required sequence of external signals is generated at the interface under program control. The complete program is permanently held in the internal read-only memory.

Processors are designed specially for embedded applications. Embedded control places different requirements upon the processor than does general-purpose computing. First and foremost in most embedded applications, systems size and cost is critical, as is reducing the time to the marketplace. Embedded processors offer potential advantages in these areas. Second, mechanisms should be in an embedded processor for handling external signals including analog signals and also unpredictable signals, which we will discuss in Chapter 9. For an application such as a washing machine, the actual computational power required to generate the

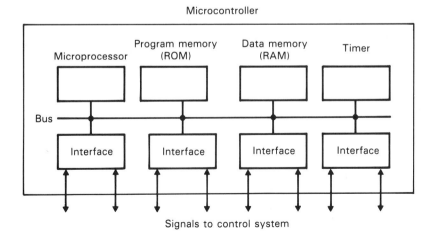

Figure 6.17 Embedded controller

external signals is very low, and processing in, say, 4-bit or 8-bit words may be sufficient. However, in some embedded applications, significant computational power may be required to obtain a sufficiently high speed of response from external events.

In the general computing arena, the trend has been for increased numbers of bits in each word processed and for increased computational power. Processors designed for embedded applications have followed this trend, albeit rather more slowly as the cost of the device and its level of system integration has often been more important than pure computational power. Eight-bit embedded controllers such as the Intel 8048 and 8051 became very popular in the 1970s and 1980s, being quite sufficient for simple tasks, and very cost-effective. Increased level of integration was used to add features, for example timers, additional on-chip program and data memory and special-purpose interfaces. We note that the designers of general-purpose processors used increased integration to improve the processor's computational power rather than for on-chip timing and interface circuits, a clear example of the trade-offs that must be made by the designer. However, with higher levels of integration becoming available, 16-bit and 32-bit controllers are possible and have been introduced, including embedded controllers based upon a reduced instruction set computer (RISC), for example the Intel 80960.

It is possible to base an embedded controller on a microprocessor already available for a wider general-purpose computing market, which has the major advantage of immediately making available all of the software support developed. An example of this approach is in the Intel 80186/80188 embedded controllers, actually complete 8086/88 processors with interface, timers and memory control circuits put on-chip. Another example is the 32-bit Intel 376 embedded controller based upon the 32-bit 80386 processor.

References

1. *Enhanced MC68030 32-bit Microprocessor User's Manual*, Englewood Cliffs, NJ: Prentice Hall, 1990.
2. *MC68040 32-bit Microprocessor User's Manual*, Phoenix, AZ: Motorola, Inc., 1989.

7 Microprocessor Instructions

7.1 General

In this chapter, we will discuss microprocessor instructions, looking at the instructions prevalent in most microprocessors. Instructions are usually written using an *assembly language* notation in which the various fields of the instruction are described by mnemonics and numbers. An *assembler* converts the assembly language program into machine instructions. The appropriate assembly language mnemonics will be used here. However, the purpose of this chapter is not to study assembly language programming; that is a separate topic of study outside the scope of this text. We are interested in the instructions from the point of view of instruction formats and processor design. We will concentrate upon 32-bit microprocessors, that is, microprocessors with complete 32-bit arithmetic capability 32-bit registers and at least 32-bit data paths. Thirty-two-bit microprocessors now generally have at least 32-bit addresses, and the trend is to increase the address space further.

The 32-bit Motorola MC88100 RISC microprocessor will be used as our primary microprocessor example. Many RISC microprocessors are actually very similar, so what is said about the 88100 often applies to other RISCs. For examples of CISCs, we will draw upon the 32-bit Intel 80386/80486 microprocessor family and the 32-bit Motorola MC68020/68030/68040 microprocessor family. For the sake of brevity, we will call the Intel family the 80x86 and the Motorola family the 680x0, unless we refer to a feature not present in all 32-bit members of the family.† No attempt is made to present all aspects of the microprocessors used as examples. The reader is referred to the users' manuals referenced [1] to [4] at the end of the chapter for full details.

7.2 Data and address registers

Almost all microprocessors are register-based; internal registers are provided to hold operands used in computations and control, and addresses of memory operands.

---

† The notation 80x86 does not include the 16-bit 8086/80286 processors; these processors only have 16-bit general-purpose registers.

The total set of registers is normally formed into an internal *register file*. Each register within the file has an identification number (register address) which is used internally to select the register. The registers are given names for reference, e.g. A, B, ..., R1, R2, ..., etc., depending upon the designers. These names are used in the assembly language.

There are two approaches to organize the data and address registers:

(i) A common set of general-purpose registers can be provided to hold operands for computations and memory addresses or
(ii) A set of registers is provided for operands, and a separate set of registers for memory addresses.

There are arguments for each approach. Memory addresses held in registers specify locations of operands. Certain specific address computations might be done on the addresses to alter the selection of operands, whereas data held in registers are used as the actual operands and a much wider range of arithmetic might be done on data; hence there is a distinct difference in these two uses of the contents of the registers. Separate data and address registers enable functional units within the processor to select registers from the appropriate set. Also, the number of bits actually in data registers and address registers need not be the same. Finally, it might enforce a structure on the use of registers within programs. However, program structure can probably be achieved by programmer conventions, and it seems more flexible to provide a general-purpose set of registers, except that separate registers are often provided for floating point operands as these operands can have a greater number of bits and a distinct format.

The actual number of registers provided in a processor is dictated somewhat by the fabrication technology and the amount of space the designer is willing to set aside for registers rather than for other circuits. The potential advantages of more registers need to be evaluated. (It has been argued that compilers cannot make good use of a very large number of registers.) With a larger number of registers, more bits will be required within the instructions to specify the registers. Also, more registers need to be saved on a *context switch* (a change from one program to another). The number of registers in processors has often been in the range 32 to 64.

The 88100 has 32 'general-purpose' registers labelled r0 through r31 for the user operands and memory addresses. About 30 other accessible registers exist for control and the operating system usage. Register r0 holds the constant zero and cannot be altered. Reading r0 returns zero. This is a technique found in RISCs for clearing locations by copying the contents of r0 to the desired location to be cleared. The other registers, r1 through r31, can be used to hold 32-bit integers (signed or unsigned) and 32-bit floating point numbers. Pairs of registers are used to hold 64-bit floating point numbers. (Single and double precision IEEE 754 standard floating point arithmetic can be performed by the 88100.) Notice that separate registers are not provided for floating point numbers as in some processors, and hence, on occasion, the number of registers may be restrictive.

Early microprocessors had few registers; indeed only one accumulator or A register would be the primary register for arithmetic operations. One or two registers were provided specifically for holding addresses (address registers). The 16-bit 8086/80286 processors continued this tradition by having four accumulator-type data registers identified by letters (AX, BX, CX, DX), and four address registers called source index register (SI), destination index register (DI), base register (BP) and stack pointer (SP). BX and DX can be used for memory addresses, and are in this sense 'general-purpose'. BP and SP address locations in the stack and are really dedicated for this purpose The eight registers are extended to 32 bits in the 80386 and are called EAX, EBX, ECX, EDX, ESI, DI, EBP, and ESP. The least significant 8 bits and 16 bits of the A, B, C and D registers can be accessed separately, but not the other registers, which are expected to hold addresses. However, with so few registers, there is a great temptation to use the address registers for operands, as many arithmetic operations can be performed upon the contents of the address registers. Many instructions can only use a defined subset of the registers (a *non-orthogonal* instruction set).

The 68020/30/40 (and indeed the 16-bit 68000) are provided with two sets of 32-bit registers, the data registers D0 to D7, and the address registers A0 to A7, Register A7 is used as a stack pointer register. Data registers can only be used to hold operands, and address registers can only be used to hold addresses.

Figure 7.1 illustrates the data/address registers of the three processors under consideration. The names given within the registers of the 88100 are suggested uses.

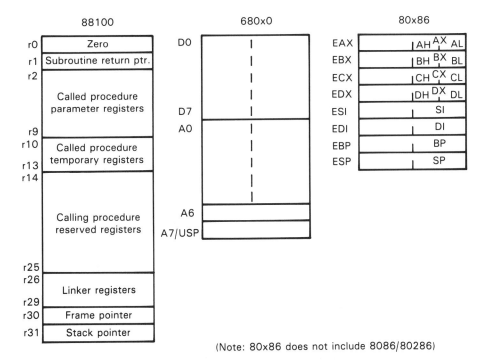

(Note: 80x86 does not include 8086/80286)

Figure 7.1 Processor registers

7.3 Operand addressing

7.3.1 Register direct addressing

Given a register-based processor, the fundamental operand addressing method entails specifying a register holding the operand, as shown in Fig. 7.2. This method is known as *register direct* addressing. The registers holding the operands are specified by register addresses within the instruction.

88100
In the 88100, all arithmetic operations operate upon operands held in registers (i.e. with register direct addressing). Operands are first loaded from memory into registers and if necessary stored back in memory afterwards. For now, let us assume that operands from memory have already been loaded into the registers; we will look at the means of achieving that later. In common with all 32-bit RISC processors the 88100 has a fixed 32-bit instruction length with a 3-register address format. All instructions have a simple regular format, five different formats in total. In all cases the first six bits specify the op-code. Five bits are needed to specify each register used in an instruction. Hence 15 bits are needed to specify the three registers, leaving 11 bits to specify a sub-operation. Actually only 51 distinct operations are provided, and some do not use all three registers.

Register-to-register instructions have the fields shown in Fig. 7.3 where op-code specifies the class of operations in this case 'triadic', sub-op-code specifies the operation within the class such as addition, S1 and S2 specify the source registers holding the operands, and D specifies the destination register where the result will be placed.

Notice that there is no possibility of increasing the number of registers in future implementations of the architecture (unless the sub-code field were used). Had 64

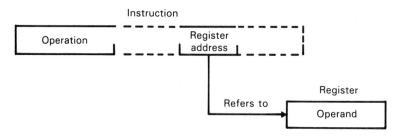

Figure 7.2 Register direct addressing

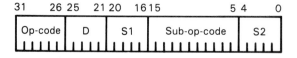

Figure 7.3 88100 triadic (register-to-register) instruction format

registers been accommodated, for example, three extra bits would have been needed, and three bits less available in the sub-op-code field. Problem 7.1 explores this possibility. In the 88100, not all the possible values in the two op-code fields are used. The pattern 100001 is used in the main op-code field to indicate 'triadic' floating point operation, and the pattern 111101 in the op-code field for 'triadic, non-floating point operations. (The 11101 code is also used for triadic indirect addressing, see section 7.3.3)

Other processors
Register direct addressing is provided in all other processors. Both the 80x86 and 680x0 families are two-register processors, i.e. one source register is also the destination register, and hence one operand is destroyed in many arithmetic operations.

7.3.2 Immediate addressing

In *immediate addressing*, the actual operand is specified within the instruction, as shown in Fig. 7.4. Sometimes the term *literal* is used to describe the operand in immediate addressing because the number is 'literally' used. The literal is usually at the end of the instruction and 'immediately', follows the operation word in memory.

88100
The 88100 supports immediate addressing in the 'immediate' op-code. Because all instructions are limited to 32 bits, the natural 32-bit literal cannot be specified in one instruction. The basic immediate mode for integer arithmetic operations specifies a 16-bit literal. The 16-bit literal immediate addressing op-code uses the instruction format given in Fig. 7.5(a) where op-code, S1 and D register specifications occupy the same fields as previously. The 16-bit immediate constant is zero extended into a 32-bit positive number, except for logical operations. Logical operations do not use the upper 16 bits of the constant. There is a slight inconsistency in the 'regular' encoding. Op-code specifies the arithmetic operation (addition, etc.) whereas in triadic operations, the sub-op-code specifies the arithmetic operation. The actual number of operations available is different. Ten-bit immediate addressing (Fig. 7.5(b)) appears in certain triadic bit operations.

Other processors
All other processors also have immediate addressing. In addition to normal 8-bit, 16-bit, and 32-bit literals, the 680x0 has special 'quick' add, subtract, and move

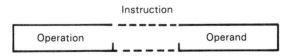

Instruction

| Operation | Operand |

Figure 7.4 Immediate addressing instruction format

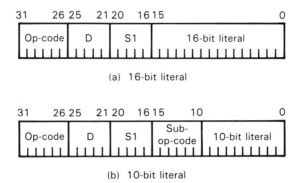

(a) 16-bit literal

(b) 10-bit literal

Figure 7.5 88100 immediate addressing instruction format

instructions for small literals that can be contained within a 16-bit instruction encoding. Otherwise, the instruction length has to be extended to hold the literal (and further if a memory location is addressed).

7.3.3 Memory addressing

(a) Absolute addressing

There are various methods of identifying a memory location holding an operand. The actual address of an operand location is called the *effective address*. The most basic method of obtaining the effective address entails specifying the address of a memory location in the instruction as shown in Fig. 7.6. This method is known as *absolute addressing*.

88100
The 88100 does not support absolute addressing, nor do other RISCs. Full 32-bit absolute addressing would necessitate an extra long instruction to hold the address.

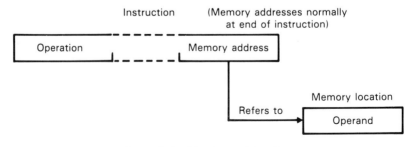

Figure 7.6 Absolute addressing

Other processors
All CISC microprocessors support absolute addressing. The 680x0 has two forms
of absolute addressing, one using a *short* absolute address and one a *long* absolute
address. The short address has a maximum of 16 bits and the long address has a
maximum of 32 bits. The short address can be encoded into an instruction with one
less word. The address is sign extended to 32 bits which results in the address range
being the bottom 32K bytes and the top 32K bytes of the addressable memory.

(b) Indirect addressing

Considerable extra flexibility would be achieved in addressing operands if an
addressing mode were provided in which the address was computed using operands
provided as data in the program. Since all computations give results in registers (or
memory locations), a useful addressing mode would be one which takes the contents
of a register (or memory location) as the address of the operand. This method is
known as *indirect addressing*. Some early microprocessors did not have any form
of indirect addressing, but all subsequent microprocessors have indirect addressing
using the contents of a register, i.e. *register indirect addressing*, as illustrated in
Fig. 7.7
    Sometimes, specific registers are allocated for register indirect addressing. The
contents of the register and a number held in the instruction are added together to
form the effective address. (Notice that the contents of the register are not affected.)
In *index register (indirect) addressing*, the specific register used is called an *index
register*, as shown in Fig. 7.8. Index register addressing is provided particularly to
access consecutive memory locations. For this application, the address of the first
memory location could be provided by the number in the instruction, and the index
register could hold the number of locations from the first location to the required
location. Hence any item in the list of locations could be accessed by modifying the
contents of the index register. To access the locations in consecutive order, the index
register would be incremented after each access.
    In *base register (indirect) addressing*, the effective address is computed in the
same way as index register addressing except that in this case the content of a register
called a *base register* is used. The principal difference is in the interpretation of the
values held in the register and in the instruction. In base register addressing, the

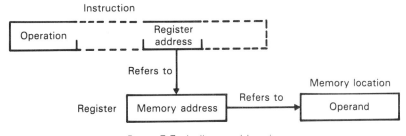

Figure 7.7 Indirect addressing

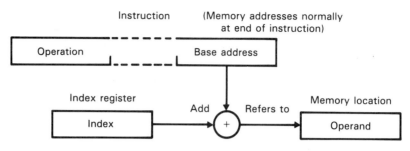

Figure 7.8 Index register addressing

register holds the address of the first location and the instruction holds the distance from the first location to the required location, whereas in index register addressing, the instruction holds the address of the first location and the register holds the distance from the first location to the required location. It may be that the value held in the instruction need not be as large in base register addressing. In base register addressing, the number held in the instruction becomes a *displacement* or *offset*.

Index and base register addressing can be combined. The value read from the base register is added to the value read from the index register together with a number held in the instruction to form the effective address, as shown in Fig. 7.9.

88100

All memory addressing modes of the 88100 are register indirect addressing. There are three variations, *register indirect with zero-extended immediate index, register indirect with index*, and *register indirect with scaled index*. Register indirect with zero-extended immediate index addressing adds together the value from a register and a 16-bit constant held in the instruction to create the effective address. This addressing mode has a similar instruction format as a register with 16-bit immediate addressing, except that now the register holds an address rather than the actual

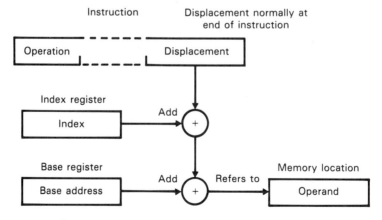

Figure 7.9 Base register–index register addressing

operand. Register indirect with index addressing adds together the values held in two registers to create the effective address. This addressing mode uses the triadic instruction format. The third addressing mode, register indirect with scaled index, is similar except that the value from one register is multiplied by 1, 2 or 4, as specified in the sub-op-code, before being added to the value from the other register. In this way, sequences of 8-bit bytes, 16-bit words or 32-bit words can be accessed. The addressing mode also uses the triadic addressing format. There are only four memory-register transfer access instructions and any one of the three memory addressing modes can be used.

7.3.4 Assembly language addressing mode notation

An assembly language notation is required to show the addressing mode of an instruction. There is no particular consensus between microprocessor manufacturers on this notation. Sometimes, the assembly language notation for immediate addressing is simply to write the literal. Then an additional notation is required for absolute addressing. One notation to show absolute addressing is to enclose the address in parentheses, i.e. [ ] means 'contents of'. This would lead to register indirect addressing being represented by enclosing the register name in parentheses, e.g. the notation, [rl], indicates that the memory operand address is held in rl. Motorola chose to prefix literals in immediate addressing with the # symbol to differentiate immediate addressing from absolute addressing (which does not have a special symbol). Intel chose to use parentheses for both absolute and register indirect addressing.

7.4 Instructions

7.4.1 General

Armed with the principal operand addressing modes, we now examine the fundamental operations provided in instructions. Operations will be specified using the appropriate assembly language. The order of the operand specification in the assembly language can either be destination on first and then source(s), or vice versa depending upon the microprocessor/assembly language. Motorola chose the source first in the 680x0. Intel chose the destination first in the 80x86.

Thirty-two-bit microprocessors always have the option of accessing an 8-bit word, a 16-bit word or a 32-bit word in memory (and often bytes/words within 32-bit registers), though the memory is organized as individually addressed 8-bit words. Recall that each 8-bit, 16-bit and 32-bit memory word is identified by an address which is not unique; one address could refer to an 8-bit word, 16-bit word or 32-bit word (see Chapter 6). Hence a notation is necessary to specify an 8-bit word, 16-bit word or 32-bit word. If it is not clear from the operands, an additional mnemonic or letter is attached to the op-code mnemonic, or preceding the location name.

Separate instructions are provided in the instruction set for each transfer size, usually differentiated by size bits in the machine instruction.

88100

The 88100 uses the following postfix option notation attached to specific op-code mnemonics to specify the memory operand size:

.b   for 8-bit byte operation
.bu   for unsigned 8-bit byte operation
.h   for 16-bit (half) word operation
.hu   for unsigned 16-bit word operation
.s   for 32-bit (single) word operation
.d   for 64-bit (double) word operation

No postfix indicates a 32-bit operation. The postfix notation, .s and .d is also used to identify single and double precision floating point numbers for each of the two operands and the result, i.e. dss identifies a double precision destination, and two single precision sources.

680x0

The 680x0 uses a postfix notation attached to the op-code mnemonic. The postfix .B is used for an 8-bit byte operation, .W for a 16-bit word operation and .L for a 32-bit long word operation.

80x86

The 80x86 uses an operand prefix notation attached to the operand name. The prefix BYTE PTR is used for 8-bit byte operations, WORD PTR for 16-bit operations, and DWORD PTR for 32-bit word operations if the size of transfer cannot be deduced by the assembler in the declaration of the names/labels used.

7.4.2 Move instructions

Clearly, it is necessary to provide a means of loading registers and memory locations with numbers. It is also necessary to be able to transfer the contents of memory locations to processor registers and vice versa. Depositing numbers in processor registers is often a prerequisite before any subsequent operation can be performed on the numbers, and transfer operations are necessary to rearrange the location of numbers for various computations. Transferring the contents of one location to another does not affect the source location, i.e. it is a copying operation. Traditionally, when the source location is a memory location and the destination location a processor register, the operation is classified as a *load* operation. Copying between processor registers is classified as a *move* operation. When the source location is a processor register and the destination is a memory location, the operation is called a *store* operation. However, a single move classification could be used for all three.

88100

The 88100 has load (ld) store (st) and exchange memory contents (xmem) using any of the three register indirect addressing modes. For example:

>   ld   r2, r3, r4

the memory address is given by the summation of the contents of r3 and r4. The contents of this memory location will be copied into register r2. Scaled index addressing uses the notation of square brackets around the index, together with the size postfix option to determine the scale factor. For example:

>   ld.h   r6, r7, [r8}

will use a scale factor of 2 (16-bit half word) on r8. The value read from r8 is shifted two places left before adding it to the value read from r7.

Store (st) performs the reverse process of load, i.e. it copies the contents of a register into a memory location. In this specific case, the first register specified in the instruction becomes the source, not the destination.

Other processors

In contrast to the 88100, both the $80x86$ and the $680x0$ have a large number of addressing modes and operations that can be applied directly to memory operands. The $680x0$ uses a single 'move' mnemonic for all register and memory transfers. Unusually, the $680x0$ has certain direct memory to memory transfer instructions.

The following program segment to transpose the contents of two 8-bit memory locations 200 and 201 is given as a simple programming example involving load instructions:

88100		*80x86*	*680x0*
ld.b	r2, r0, 200	mov al, 200	move.b 200, dl
xmem.b	r2, r0, 201	xchg 201, al	move.b 201, 200
st.b	r2, r0, 200	mov 200, al	move.b dl, 201

Notice that the 88100 code uses r0 (holding zero) in register indirect addressing. The $680x0$ has an exchange instruction, exg, but this instruction can only operate upon registers

7.4.3 Arithmetic instructions

One of the fundamental operations of any digital computer is to add two numbers and perform other arithmetic operations using two numbers. The instruction must specify the arithmetic operation, together with information regarding where the two numbers can be found. Arithmetic operations normally include:

>   Addition, with and without carry
>   Subtraction, with and without carry
>   Multiplication, both with signed and unsigned numbers

Division, both with signed and unsigned numbers
Increment (usually add 1)
Decrement (usually subtract 1).

Arithmetic operations generate certain condition flags which are often recorded in an internal processor register called the *condition code register* (which itself is often part of a larger *processor status register*). Common flags include:

(a) Carry (C) flag

If a carry signal has been generated by an arithmetic operation such as addition, the carry flag is set, otherwise the carry flag is reset. The carry flag is usually a combined carry/borrow flag. If a borrow is generated after subtraction, the carry flag is set, otherwise the flag is reset. The generation of a carry/borrow signal does not necessarily indicate an error. For this, an overflow flag is provided.

(b) Overflow (O or V) flag

The overflow flag indicates that the result of an arithmetic operation has exceeded the allowable range. For 32-bit processors using 2's complement representation, the range is from -2^{31} to $+2^{31} - 1$. If the result is outside this range, the overflow flag is set. The overflow condition usually relates only to integer 2's complement representation. (Remember that it is possible to generate a carry and produce a correct result, see Chapter 1, section 1.3.2 for proof.)

(c) Zero (Z) flag

This flag is set if the result of the arithmetic operation is zero, otherwise the flag is reset. This can be interpreted as the two operands being equal if a subtraction operation had been performed.

(d) Sign (S or N) flag

This flag is set if the result of the arithmetic operation is negative (most significant bit = 1), otherwise the flag is reset. This can be interpreted as one operand being greater than another operand if a subtraction operation had been performed (2's complement number representation).

It is important to note that the flags are not set or reset after every instruction but only after selected instructions, normally only the arithmetic instructions, other instructions not affecting the flags. In particular, the load instruction (except on the condition code register itself) does not normally affect the flags. The increment/decrement instructions may not affect the C flag. This allows counters to be used in loops without affecting other arithmetic operations that use the carry flag.

Instructions are always provided which use a previously generated carry value in the operation. The *addition with carry* instruction adds the two specified operands together with the value of the stored carry. The *subtraction with carry* instruction subtracts the two specified operands and subtracts the value of the stored carry. These instructions allow multi-word arithmetic to be performed.

The unsigned and signed arithmetic operations consider the numbers as pure positive numbers and as 2's complement notation numbers respectively. The unsigned version provides approximately double the range of positive numbers to be represented (from 0 to 2^n instead of from -2^{n-1} through 0 to $2^{n-1}-1$, given n digits), at the expense of not representing negative numbers at all. One might like to consider the possibility of not providing unsigned arithmetic in the processor and the consequent simplification that can be made (Problem 7.3). However, all processors known provide both signed and unsigned arithmetic and many high-level languages cater for both forms by having signed and unsigned types. Signed and unsigned addition/subtraction operations are in fact the same operation and may not be differentiated. The only differences are in the interpretation of the sign of the result and overflow. Signed and unsigned multiply and divide operations are often differentiated because the algorithms are different.

Instructions performing floating point arithmetic can be provided either as part of the basic instruction set, or as an extension of the instruction set and executed by a co-processor. The IEEE standard representation (Chapter 1) is always used in microprocessors. Floating point numbers match the float/double/real data types in high-level languages. One might like to consider the rather radical possibility of not using floating point arithmetic at all in the processor. Instead, extended integer arithmetic, or even variable length integer arithmetic could be used, or, conversely, having only floating point arithmetic (Problem 7.4).

In floating point numbers, the range is divided into two distinct regions, one positive and one negative (see Chapter 1). The treatment of floating point results outside the allowable range is much more complicated than simply setting an overflow bit because of the various non-floating point bit patterns, rounding and normalization errors. Therefore if the processor has floating point arithmetic, separate condition flags are set up and internal interrupts are usually generated when an overflow/error condition occurs.

Thirty-two-bit multiplication can create a result which has 64 digits. Similarly, division could use a 64-bit digit dividend divided by a 32-bit digit divisor to create a 32-bit quotient and a 32-bit remainder. Sixty-four-bit numbers could be stored in special 64-bit registers, or in pairs of 32-bit registers. Of course, another solution and one used in RISCs is to accommodate integers having only 32 bits. Any larger integer numbers are considered as 'out-of-range'.

88100

The 88100 has a reasonable complement of arithmetic operations, with the minor exception that unsigned multiply is not supported. Also, separate increment and decrement instructions are not provided. The carry is stored in the processor status register (PSR), together with other information regarding the current state of the processor. Addition and subtraction can optionally include the carry from the PSR (op-code postfix .ci), store the carry out in the PSR (op-code postfix .co), or both (op-code postfix .cio). One bit is used in the instruction format for specifying the carry in and one bit for specifying the carry out. The optional carry out storage is unusual and is not found in CISC microprocessors.

The signed and unsigned versions of addition and subtraction are provided which is very unusual as normally the results would be the same for both signed and unsigned numbers. Most processors only have one version of these instructions. It appears that the only difference is that the signed version can cause an overflow condition when the result cannot be represented in a 2's complement representation 32-bit number, whereas the unsigned version never generates an overflow condition, even when the result cannot be represented as a positive 32-bit number.

Multiplication and division can only handle 32-bit numbers. Division does not store the remainder. Most other processors store the remainder which can then be used for a modulo operation. Floating point arithmetic is performed in hardware, but only 32-bit and 64-bit IEEE floating point numbers.

Other processors
Most CISC processors have addition, subtraction, multiplication and division including the 16-bit 8086 and 68000 microprocessors which implement 32-bit × 32-bit multiplication giving a 64-bit result, and 64-bit/32-bit division giving a 32-bit result in processor registers pairs. Earlier microprocessors did not have multiplication and division because of the limited component densities.

7.4.4 Logic instructions

Logic operations, i.e. Boolean operations such as AND, OR and NOT, are always provided. Each logical operation is performed on pairs of corresponding bits in the two operands to produce a result word. For example, the AND operation would logically AND together the most significant bits of the two operands to produce the most significant bit of the result. The next most significant bit would be generated from the logical AND operation on the next most significant bits of the two operands, and so on. This corresponds to bit-wise logical AND in high-level languages.

Logical AND can be used to extract a field from a word by logically ANDing the word with the 'mask' $00 \ldots 011 \ldots 110 \ldots 00$ where the 1's in the mask correspond to the field to be extracted. The result can be shifted right to get the word right justified.

One purpose of logical operations was to provide a mechanism to set up Boolean conditions and to test the conditions. The conditions are represented by single bits (flags) within the binary word. Different flags are assigned to represent different conditions. The Boolean OR operation can be used to set particular bits in a word by performing the logical OR operation of the data word with a mask pattern $00 \ldots 010 \ldots 000$ where the 1 is in the position corresponding to the bit to be set. If this is in the position corresponding to D_3, the operation is performed as shown in Table 7.1. Thus D_3 is set to a 1 but all the other bits are left unchanged.

Table 7.1   OR logical operation

Data word:	D_n	D_{n-1}	...	D_4	D_3	D_2	D_1	D_0
Mask pattern	0	0	...	0	1	0	0	0
Result of OR operation:	D_n	D_{n-1}	...	D_4	1	D_2	D_1	D_0

(To set the bit to a 0, leaving the other bits unchanged, the mask $11 \ldots 10 \ldots 11$ is used with a logical AND operation.)

An AND operation can be used subsequently to test whether the flag bit, D_3 in the above, is a 1 or a 0. Using the mask pattern, $00 \ldots 010 \ldots 00$, if the result of the AND operation is zero numerically, the bit must be a 0, otherwise the bit must be a 1, as shown in Table 7.2. Typically, we now need to cause different sequences of program instructions to be executed depending upon whether a word is zero or not zero. This can be provided in the 'conditional jump' instruction (see section 7.4.6).

Some microprocessors, in addition to possessing logical operations, are also provided with separate instructions to set, reset and test a specified bit within a binary word. In these instructions, each bit in the addressed location is identified by number, bit 0, bit 1, etc.

88100

The 88100 has AND, OR, exclusive-OR and mask logical operations with the triadic addressing, and a register with 16-bit immediate addressing. An unusual combination can be specified with triadic addressing. A NOT operation can first be applied to the second source operand of AND, OR and exclusive-OR logical operations, by including the postfix .c to the op-code mnemonic. A register with 16-bit immediate addressing uses the lower 16 bits of the register operand with a 16-bit literal. The upper 16 bits of the source register are copied to the destination unchanged. If the postfix .u is included, the upper 16 bits of the register operand are used with the 16-bit literal. The lower 16 bits of the source register are then copied to the destination unchanged. Hence, a full 32-bit AND operation with a 32-bit constant could be obtained with two instructions:

```
and     r2, r3, lowermask
and.u   r2, r3, uppermask
```

where lowermask and uppermask are the least significant and most significant 16-bit words of a 32-bit mask.

Table 7.2   AND logical operation

Data word:	D_n	D_{n-1}	...	D_4	D_3	D_2	D_1	D_0
Mask pattern	0	0	...	0	1	0	0	0
Result of OR operation:								
if $D_3 = 0$	0	0	...	0	0	0	0	0
if $D_3 = 1$	0	0	...	0	1	0	0	0

A 'mask' logical instruction is available using a register with 16-bit immediate addressing, and is similar to the logical AND operation except that it clears the upper 16 bits of the destination (or alternatively the lower 16 bits, with the postfix .u).

The 88100 possesses a group of bit-field addressed instructions. A field within a 32-bit word is identified by a 5-bit width, W5, and a 5-bit offset from the least significant end of the word, O5. A width of zero specifies all 32 bits. W5 and O5 are held either in the instruction as literals (register with 10-bit immediate addressing) or held in a second source register (triadic addressing). The instruction, clr, clears bits in the field to zero. The instruction, set, sets all the bits to 1. The extract instruction copies the bit field into the least significant end of the destination. Two forms are provided, extu, which zero extends the extracted field, and ext which sign extends the extracted field according to the most significant bit of the field. The instruction, ext, fills out the new most significant bits with 0's. The instruction, extu, fills out the new most significant bits with a copy of the original sign bit. The mak (make bit field) instruction performs the reverse process of ext by taking a number of the least significant bits of a source location and copying the bits in the specified place in the destination as given by the offset. Other bits in the destination are set to zero.

The instructions are provided to search for the first bit of the source register reset to a 0 (ff0) or set to a 1 (ff1), starting at the most significant end and producing the bit number of the 0 or 1 found in the destination. Only one source register is specified.

Other processors
Both the 80x86 and 680x0 have the logical operations AND, OR, exclusive-OR and NOT instructions.

7.4.5 Shift instructions

Sometimes we need to move bits in a word left or right as shown in Fig. 7.10. Such operations can be achieved by shift left and shift right instructions respectively. Shift instructions are usually provided in the instruction set.

The shift right instruction known as a *logical right shift instruction* causes all the bits in the addressed location (processor register or a memory location) to be moved one place right so that the contents of B_1 moves into B_0, B_2 into B_1, etc. The

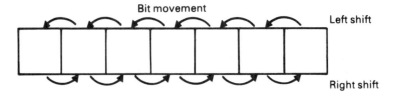

Figure 7.10   Shift operation

most significant bit is set to a 0. An alternative shift right instruction is one which keeps the most significant bit at its original value as well as shifting a copy into the next most significant bit. This shift right instruction, known as an *arithmetic right shift instruction*, would result in the number being divided by two (except for one specific case which is often forgotten, Problem 7.5).

A shift left instruction, known as a *logical shift left instruction*, causes all the bits of the addressed location to be moved one place left so that the contents of bit B_{n-1} are moved into B_n, B_{n-2} into B_{n-1}, B_{n-3} into B_{n-2}, etc. This shift left instruction causes the number to be multiplied by two and consequently is also known as an *arithmetic left shift instruction*. It is possible to differentiate between an arithmetic shift left and a logical shift left in the manner in which the flags are altered. Otherwise, only one instruction need be provided (though two mnemonics may be used). Shift instructions can be used to obtain multiplication or division by powers of two more rapidly than using standard multiplication/division instructions.

Shift instructions can include the carry flag in their shift operation, i.e. a shift right instruction can shift the least significant bit into the carry flag, and a shift left instruction can shift the most significant bit into the carry flag. Shift operations can also be circular, that is, bits shifted out of one end of a location are inserted into the other end of the location. In a rotate left instruction, information shifted out of the most significant location (or out of the carry register) is placed in the least significant location. Similarly, a rotate right instruction transfers the contents of the least significant bit (or the carry flag) into the most significant bit. Rotate instructions have applications in dealing with packed data such as packed BCD numbers. Figure 7.11 shows the actions of typical shift and rotate instructions.

88100
Unusually, the 88100 does not have specific non-circular shift instructions. However, the ext, extu and mak bit field instructions achieve shift right arithmetically, shift right logically, and shift left logically, respectively, by specifying a width of 32 and an offset given by the number of shifts, as illustrated in Fig. 7.12. The 88100 does have a specific rotate right instruction, rot.

Other processors
Both the 680x0 and 80x86 have a full range of shift and rotate instructions. In the 680x0, there is a difference between a logical shift left instruction and an arithmetic shift left instruction in the manner in which they affect certain internal flags. This is unique to the 680x0 family.

As an example of the use of arithmetic shift instructions, consider the problem of multiplying a 4-bit number, n, by 10. This can be achieved at very high speed by performing the following computation:

$$\text{Result} = (2 \times n) + (8 \times n) = 10n$$

The first product, $2n$, can be obtained by shifting n one place left arithmetically, and the second product $8n$ by shifting n three places left arithmetically ($2n$ shifted two

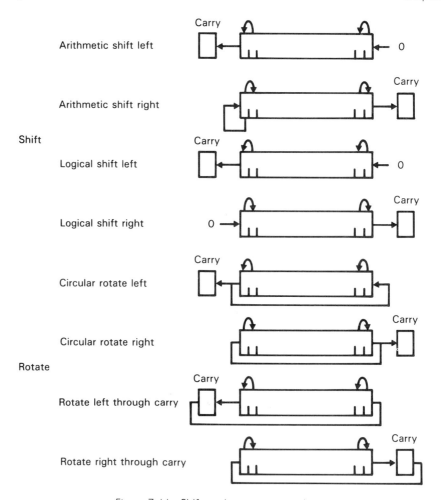

Figure 7.11   Shift and rotate operations

places). Hence if the number n is in a general-purpose processor register (say r2 in the 88100, EAX in the 80x86, and D1 in the 680x0) and the result is to be placed in a register (say r4 in the 88100, EDX in the 80x86 and D4 in the 680x0) and the original number is not to be lost, programs could be:

88100	*80x86*	*680x0*
mak r3, r2, 30⟨1⟩	mov ebx, eax	move.1 d1, d2
mak r4, r3, 30⟨2⟩	sar ebx, 1	asl.1 #1, d2
add r4, r4, r3	mov edx, ebx	move.1 d2, d4
	sar edx, 2	asl.1 #2, d4
	add edx, ebx	add.1 d4, d2

In the 88100 mak instructions, 30⟨1⟩ specifies an offset of 1 and the whole 32-bit word to obtain a shift one place left, and 30⟨2⟩ specifies an offset of 2 and the whole

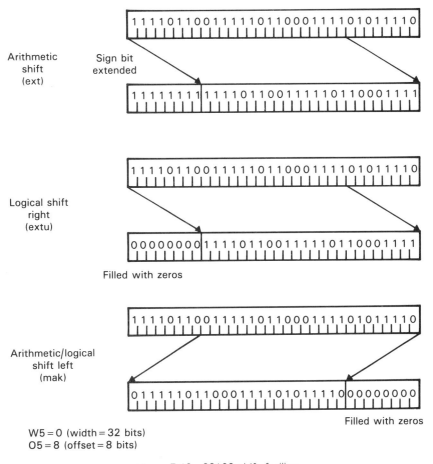

Figure 7.12   88100 shift facility

32-bit word to obtain a shift two places left. Notice that the 3-register instruction format of the 88100 results in less code than the 2-register CISC code.

An application of the technique is in the computation of the video memory address of a character displayed on a screen. A display screen typically displays 24 lines with 80 characters on each line. Suppose an arbitrary place is specified in terms of the x and y co-ordinates of the screen. The number of character positions from the upper top corner position ($x = 0$, $y = 0$) is to be computed and added to the start location in the video memory to address the correct location, i.e.:

Video memory address = base address + $(80*y) + x$

The term $80*y$ can be computed as $64*y + 16*y$ using shift operations as previously (n shifted six places plus n shifted four places respectively). It is left as a simple exercise to write the program to compute the video memory address (Problem 7.6).

7.4.6 Jump and branch instructions

Instructions are normally executed in consecutive order, i.e. instructions are executed in the order in which they are placed in the memory. To obtain any real computational power, we need to change the execution sequence, often dependent upon conditions set up within the program. Jump and branch instructions are provided for this purpose. The terms *jump* and *branch* are sometimes used synonymously. Alternatively, jump can refer to a definite change of sequence to a location a considerable distance away, and branch can refer to a change of sequence to a location not too far away. We will use this convention.

The *unconditional jump instruction* produces a change in the sequential execution by causing the next instruction to be taken from the memory location specified in the instruction. The format of the jump instruction differs from that of other instructions. The first field still specifies the operation, in this case, 'jump', but the second field specifies the address of the next instruction to be executed (not the address of an operand), as shown in Fig. 7.13. Only one address field is necessary. Certain addressing modes can be applied to obtain the address of the next instruction, including absolute addressing in which the address is stored in the instruction.

The *conditional jump/branch instruction* only changes the normal sequential execution if a particular condition is satisfied. If the condition is not met, the next instruction executed is the instruction following the jump/branch instruction. The term *target address* will be used for the address of the instruction executed if the condition is met. The conditional branch instruction finds wide application, for example to create loops.

There are various conditions, all based upon the results of a previous arithmetic operation, such as the result being zero, positive, negative, a final carry being generated, or an overflow occurring. Conditions such as one number being greater than, greater than or equal to, equal to, equal to or less than, and less than can usually be specified and it can be assumed that one number has been subtracted from another prior to the test. In these cases, signed and unsigned arithmetic is treated with separate conditions. The usual relationship between the condition codes and the arithmetic conditions tested after a compare/subtract instruction is shown in Table. 7.3. (N refers to the sign flag, V refers to the overflow flag, Z refers to the zero flag and C refers to the carry flag.) The conditional branch instruction can incorporate the unconditional branch by having the condition 'true' in its list of conditions.

An addressing mode which is convenient for conditional branch instructions is *program counter relative addressing*, a form of base register addressing used only

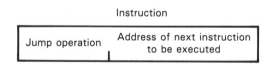

Figure 7.13 Unconditional jump instruction format

Table 7.3 Condition tests for branch instructions

Condition	Logical test
Branch if greater than	$N.V.\overline{Z} + \overline{N}.\overline{V}.\overline{Z}$
Branch if greater or equal	$N.V + \overline{N}.\overline{V}$
Branch if less than	$N.\overline{V} + \overline{N}.V$
Branch if less than or equal	$Z + N.\overline{V} + \overline{N}.V$
Branch if overflow	V
Branch if no overflow	$\overline{V}$
Branch if carry clear	$\overline{C}$
Branch if carry set	C
Branch if equal	Z
Branch if not equal	$\overline{Z}$

Considering numbers as unsigned binary numbers	
Branch if higher	$\overline{C}.\overline{Z}$
Branch if lower or same	$C + Z$
Branch if minus	N
Branch if plus	$\overline{N}$

with branch instructions. In program counter relative addressing, the 'base' register is the program counter (which holds the address of the instruction). The instruction holds the distance from the instruction to the target address, as a 'displacement' or 'offset'. The displacement is added to the contents of the program counter to create the address of the target instruction and a jump to the target instruction, as shown in Fig. 7.14.

All of the conditions in conditional branch instructions are based upon condition code flags which are set after an arithmetic operation. In fact, the

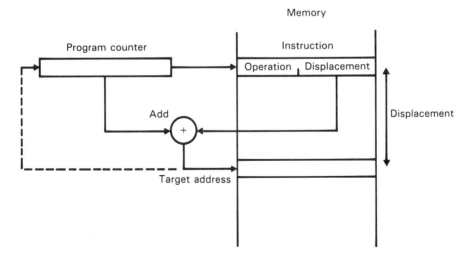

Figure 7.14 Program counter relative addressing

principal reason for having condition codes in addition to the carry flag is to hold conditions to be used in conditional branch instructions. Often, we wish to compare two operands, and this implies that we would subtract one operand from another prior to the conditional branch instruction. Since the conditional branch instructions use flags rather than the actual values of operands in the processor or memory, it is convenient to have an arithmetic operation which affects the flags but does not overwrite either of the addressed operands, particularly for two address instruction formats. One particular arithmetic instruction of this type is the *compare instruction*. The compare instruction performs a subtraction operation affecting the flags as appropriate, but without storing the result.

We have said that the condition code flags are held in the condition code register which itself is part of an internal processor status register. An alternative to using a designated condition code register to hold the conditions is to deposit the condition code flags in a general-purpose register which can be examined later. One advantage of using a general-purpose register is that the stored flags can be examined, not necessary immediately after they are generated but at other times. This feature can be useful in processors which can complete their operations in a different order from that in which they started. In effect, the data dependency of the carry and other flags on the previous arithmetic operation is removed, allowing the order of execution to be changed.

88100

The 88100 has twelve instructions which can alter the execution sequence (categorized as flow-control instructions). Unconditional jump, unconditional branch instructions and conditional branch instructions are provided. The jump instruction, jmp, uses register indirect addressing to compute the target address, i.e. the address of a general-purpose register holds the address of the next instruction to be executed. The triadic addressing format is used with the S1 and D fields ignored. The unconditional branch instruction, br, uses program counter relative addressing with a signed extended 26-bit displacement stored in the instruction. This displacement represents the number of 32-bit instruction words from the current instruction to the target instruction. The remaining six bits in the instruction form the standard op-code field, as shown in Fig. 7.15. The 26-bit displacement represents a displacement in units of 32-bit words because instructions must align on 32-bit word boundaries. Twenty-six bits allow a very large branch (a displacement from -2^{25} to $+2^{25} - 1$ 32-bit word locations).

The 88100 has three program counters, the *execute instruction pointer*, XIP, the *next instruction pointer*, NIP, and the *fetch instruction pointer*, FIP. This idea was borrowed from earlier RISC processors and comes about because the processor

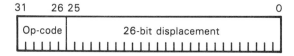

Figure 7.15 88100 unconditional branch instruction format

can fetch instructions before previous instructions have been executed completely. XIP points to the instruction currently being executed in the integer, floating point or data unit. NIP points to the instruction currently being accessed from memory. FIP points to the memory location holding the next instruction to be accessed. Branch instructions modify the FIP register. In the case of the 26-bit displacement branch instruction, the displacement from the instruction is shifted two places left, added to the value obtained from the XIP register, and the result is loaded into the FIP register.

Conditions for conditional branch instructions are held in any general-purpose register (i.e. the traditional condition code register is not used for this purpose, though a processor status register does exist in the processor). Hence conditional branch instructions need to select specific bit(s) within the selected general-purpose register which are then interpreted as condition flags. These *bit-test* branch instructions use a register with 16-bit displacement addressing. The format is similar to a register with 16-bit immediate addressing (Fig. 7.3(c)) except that the D field now specifies the condition. There is also a conditional branch instruction (bcnd) which tests for a specified source register being zero.

All the jump/branch instructions mentioned so far have the option of delaying the jump/branch by one instruction so that the instruction immediately following the jump/branch is executed whether or not the jump/branch is taken. After this instruction has been executed, the jump/branch operation, if it is to be done, is put into effect. The delayed version is selected with the postfix .n (setting bit 26 in the op-code field). The instruction following the delayed jump/branch must not be one which alters the instruction execution sequence (jmp, etc). Delayed instructions are discussed in Chapter 12.

Other processors
Both the 80x86 and 680x0 have jump and branch instructions. They both use the traditional CISC approach of a condition code register holding various primitive conditions (sign, carry, overflow, etc.). Both differentiate between signed and unsigned numbers and have separate conditions for each, i.e. jump if greater than for signed numbers and jump if above (80x86) or high (680x0) for unsigned numbers.

7.4.7 Subroutine instructions

Sometimes we wish to be able to jump to a 'subprogram' and return afterwards to the original program, and to repeat the process at different places in the main program, jumping to the same subprogram. This would eliminate the need for multiple copies of the same subprogram and make the overall program better structured. Such subprograms correspond to procedures or subroutines in high-level languages.

The overall scheme is shown in Fig. 7.16. The main program 'jumps' to the reusable subprogram from several places, each time returning to the main program

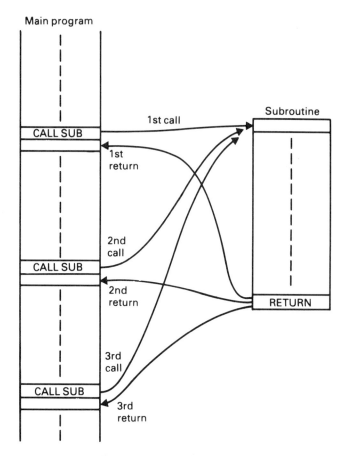

Figure 7.16 Subroutine calls

immediately after the corresponding jump. The reused subprogram is known as *subroutine* (as in FORTRAN), and the instruction which causes the jump to the subroutine is called a *subroutine jump* or, more usually, a *call instruction*. (The main program 'calls' the subroutine using the call instruction.) To be able to return to the main program, we need to store the *return address* at the time of the subroutine call. The return address is the address of the instruction in the memory immediately following the call instruction. This address is stored automatically during the execution of the call instruction, and used by a subroutine *return* jump instruction to jump back to the main program at the end of the subroutine (or whenever the return is made). Notice that the return address will depend upon the address of the location of the subroutine call instruction and this will change with different calls.

Normally the return address is kept on a *stack*. A stack is a number of consecutive storage locations almost always in the main memory. (Registers can be used, were used in the very first microprocessors and have reappeared in RISCs.)

Information such as the return address can be placed in order in the stack and
retrieved in reverse order, i.e. the first item put in the stack is the last out, and the
last in is the first out (first-in last-out queue, or FILO). A *stack pointer* holds the
address of the next location to be accessed (the top of the stack) as shown in
Fig. 7.17. Most stacks 'grow' downwards. i.e. new information is added to locations
with decreasing addresses. The contents of the stack pointer are decremented as
information is added to the stack and incremented as information is taken off the
stack. The stack mechanism, in particular, allows subroutines to call subroutines
(*nested subroutines*). This includes a subroutine calling the same subroutine
(*recursive calls*). Nested subroutines are shown in Fig. 7.18.

The subroutine call instruction has a similar format to a normal jump
instruction, though the addressing modes allowable to compute the call address may
be restricted. For example, only the actual call address might be allowed. The
mnemonic CALL is often used. The return instruction often has the mnemonic
RET. Return instructions do not have address fields.

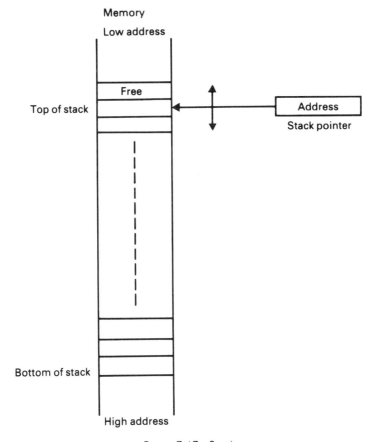

Figure 7.17 Stack

Main program

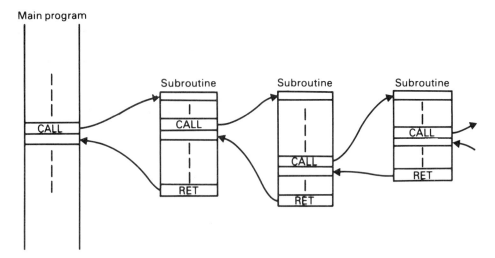

Figure 7.18 Nested subroutines

The stack is also used to hold parameters which are passed to a called subroutine and results passed back from the called subroutine routine. This is a technique commonly used by high-level language compilers, and various conventions exist for specifying the way numbers are stored on the stack. Two types of instruction are commonly available for the user to manipulate the stack called PUSH and POP instructions. The PUSH instruction causes the contents of an addressed location (normally a general-purpose processor register) to be copied onto the stack, while the POP instruction copies the top location of the stack into an addressed location. Locations on most stacks are considered as word locations, at least 16-bit words, and in this case the stack pointer has to be adjusted by two after each access. In general, it is necessary to adjust the stack pointer when returning from a subroutine call to skip over stored parameters.

It is important to remember to load the stack pointer with the appropriate starting address before the first subroutine is called or the stack is used in any other way. A suitable address must be sufficiently distant from the program to prevent the stack overwriting the program.

88100
Unconditional subroutine jump (jsr) and unconditional subroutine branch (bsr) instructions are provided. The subroutine jump instruction uses the same addressing as other jump instructions, and the subroutine branch instruction uses the same addressing as other branch instructions (section 7.4.6). Very unusually, a stack is not used. The return address for the subroutine jump/branch is automatically stored in register r1. A subroutine return instruction is not necessary. A simple jmp r1 instruction is sufficient to return from a subroutine call. Nested/recursive subroutine calls cannot be handled with this mechanism and presumably r1 has to be explicitly stored in a memory stack for nested/recursive calls.

Other processors

Both the 80x8 and 680x0, and other CISCs provide conventional subroutine call
and return instructions using the stack in memory. The 680x0 has two types of
subroutine call instruction, a jump to subroutine (jsr) which allows a full address
to be used, and a relatively addressed branch to subroutine (brs) instruction. There
are two forms of return instruction which can be used with either call instruction,
return from subroutine (rts), and return from subroutine and restore condition
codes (rtr).

The 80x86 has special support for passing parameters between routines through
the stack. The base pointer (BP) is specially provided as an additional stack address
register. (It should be mentioned that the 80x86 separates the stack address space
from the other dedicated memory spaces using the stack segment register, see
Chapter 10.) The BP register would typically be set to point to the top of the stack.
Indirect register addressing with displacement can be used to reach parameters
within the stack. In addition to a normal return instruction, a return instruction, ret
n, is provided which increments the stack pointer by a specified amount as given in
the return instruction. For example, ret 4 increments the stack pointer by an
additional four bytes. This example enables two words to be skipped over on
returning to the calling routine.

7.4.8 Input/output

There clearly needs to be a mechanism for transferring data from input/output
interfaces and devices to the program, and from the program to input/output
interfaces and devices. The classical approach at the machine-language level is to
provide special machine instructions which specify transfers between processor
registers and the input/output interfaces. These instructions are inserted into the
program where the transfers are to take place. The instructions are known as
input/output instructions and the technique is known as *programmed input/output*.
Locations within input and output interfaces are given identification input/output
numbers (known as *port addresses* or *port numbers*) in much the same manner as
memory locations are given addresses. Input/output instructions can take the same
instruction format as memory reference instructions except that the address of the
location to be accessed is an input/output port address rather than a memory
address. Since the number of input/output devices is usually quite small, the address
may be much smaller than memory addresses. For example, an 8-bit port address
would provide up to 256 independently addressed input/output locations.
Consequently input/output instructions can be shorter than memory reference
instructions in variable-length instructions.

The actions of input/output instructions can be very similar to memory
reference instructions. Some computers, including some microprocessors, use
normal memory reference instructions to transfer data between processor registers
and input/output locations. In this case, some of the memory addresses are allocated
to input/output interfaces rather than to memory locations. The appropriate address

decode circuitry has to be provided within the input/output interface. The method is known as *memory mapped input/output*, as the input/output devices are given memory addresses instead of input/output addresses (*I/O mapped*).

A particular advantage of memory mapped input/output is that all instructions available to reference memory are also available to reference input/output interfaces. Also, additional instructions do not need to be included in the instruction repertoire for input/output. A particular disadvantage is that some of the memory address space is taken by the input/output locations and generally a block of memory address space much larger than that required for the input/output locations becomes unavailable for memory. (Problem 7.8 explores the possibility of overlaying input/output addresses over existing memory addresses using a memory disable signal to stop the memory responding to input/output addresses.) Also, any special types of input/output devices can be accommodated with input/output instructions. For example, input/output devices usually have a slower speed of operation than memory, and input/output instructions could automatically wait a little longer during the transfer to allow the device time to respond.

Often before an input/output instruction can be executed, it is necessary for the input/output interface to be ready, either to accept data or with valid data available. Some very simple interfaces may always be ready, but mostly interfaces have internal registers whose contents indicate their readiness. These registers are known as (device/peripheral) *status registers* and their contents are usually read under program control prior to an input or output data transfer. For example, a typical status register for a display terminal is shown in Fig. 7.19. This register is sited in the terminal interface and indicates various conditions, notably that data will be

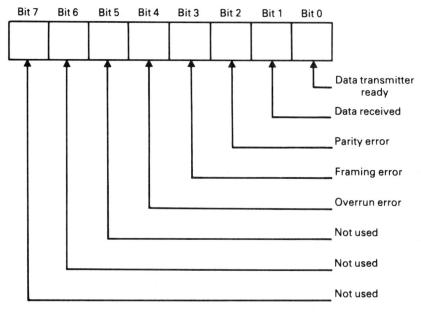

Figure 7.19 Terminal interface status register assignment

accepted by the interface if sent by the processor (in this example, bit 0 set to a 1), and data has been received at the keyboard and may be read by the processor (bit 1 set to a 1). Error conditions are also indicated with this register. The data received bit (bit 1) is automatically reset when the data is read by the processor and is only set again when new data is received (a key is pressed again) and the interface is ready. The three error conditions shown are related to the usual type of data transmission between the terminal and the interface, namely asynchronous serial transmission, which is described in Chapter 9.

A typical programmed input sequence begins with a loop of instructions which tests whether the interface/device has data ready to be taken by the processor, as indicated by the data received bit in the status register being set to a 1. In the case of the keyboard of a terminal, the condition will be true if a key has been pressed after the last time the data was read (and the subsequent new data is ready). A typical programmed output sequence begins with a loop of instructions which tests whether the interface/device is ready to receive data as indicated by the data transmitter ready bit in the status register being set to a 1. Once this test becomes true, the loop is terminated and the program proceeds to an instruction to output the required data.

88100

The 88100 uses memory mapped input/output and special instructions are not provided for input/output devices.

Other processors

The 680x0 also uses memory mapped input/output. There is one little-used special input/output instruction (MOVEP, move peripheral data) which allows bytes to be moved between alternative memory locations and registers. The 80x86 continues the Intel tradition of providing input/output instructions.

References

1. *MC88100 RISC Microprocessor User's Manual* (2nd edn.), Englewood Cliffs, NJ: Prentice Hall, 1990.
2. *MC68000 16/32-bit Microprocessor Programmer's Manual* (4th edn.), Geneva, Switzerland: Motorola, Inc., 1984.
3. *MC68040 32-bit Microprocessor User's Manual*, Phoenix, AZ: Motorola, Inc., 1989.
4. *Enhanced MC68030 32-bit Microprocessor User's Manual*, Englewood Cliffs, NJ: Prentice Hall, 1990.
5. *386 DX Microprocessor High Performance 32-bit CHMOS Microprocessor with Integrated Memory Management*, Santa Clara, CA: Intel, 1989.

Problems

7.1 Redesign the 88100 instruction set formats to accommodate 64 registers. Repeat for 512 registers. Discuss the consequences.

7.2 Explain in detail the instructions necessary to read a memory location in the 88100, given that the location has a full 32-bit address.

7.3 Discuss the effects of only providing signed arithmetic in a processor.

7.4 Investigate the possibility of providing variable-length integer arithmetic instead of floating point arithmetic.

7.5 In what specific case will an arithmetic right shift not result in the number being divided by 2? How could this situation be detected so that the result could be corrected?

7.6 Write an assembly language program (any processor) to compute the video memory address of a character at position (x, y) on the screen using shift instructions (see section 7.4.5).

7.7 Prove that the conditions given in Table 7.3 are correct.

7.8 Design the bus interface logic (any processor) for overlaying input/output addresses over existing memory addresses using a memory disable signal to stop the memory responding to input/output addresses.

7.9 Identify all the types of operations that can be done in one instruction on the $80x86$ or 680×0 but require more than one instruction in the 88100. (You may need to refer to the manufacturers' reference books cited at the end of the chapter.)

8 Semiconductor Main Memory Devices

8.1 Memory requirements

The memory in a microprocessor system, or indeed in any computer system, serves one of two principal purposes. Firstly, it is used to store the machine language programs to be executed, and secondly it stores any data to be used in the program. The requirements for the memory can be summarized as follows:

(i) The memory needs to be able to store (memorize) binary patterns (0's and 1's) by electrical, magnetic or other means.
(ii) The memory needs to be able to store many binary patterns, arranged as binary words in accessible locations.
(iii) For storing a program currently being executed and storing its associated data, we need to be able to access any program/data location in the memory at will in any order with high speed, i.e. the memory must be *random-access*.
(iv) We need the capability of both reading and writing information in the case of data storage.
(v) For program execution, the capability of reading is sufficient.

Because random-access memory is relatively expensive, additional secondary memory is also employed in most computer systems. This memory is cheaper per bit but usually is not random-access and leads to a memory system divided into two parts:

(i) Main or primary random-access memory holding programs currently being executed, together with its data
(ii) Secondary memory, not necessarily and not normally random access, for holding further information.

The secondary memory is sometimes called *backing memory* or *backing store*. The processor has a direct connection to the primary memory and a connection is made between the primary memory and the secondary memory, in the case of a microprocessor system through the system bus, to enable information to be transferred between the primary memory and the secondary memory. This transfer is done in groups of binary words, typically 128, 256 or 512 words at a time as required. In this chapter, we will look at the main memory. Chapter 10 discusses the integration of the main memory and secondary memory.

The random-access memory widely used for almost twenty years until about 1970 was the so-called *core store* which used very small rings of magnetic ferrite material, magnetized in one of two circular directions to represent the two binary states. One ferrite ring or core was necessary for each binary digit and wires threaded the ferrite cores in order to magnetize the core (write information) or to sense the state of magnetization of the core (read information).

Since 1970, *semiconductor memory* has been increasingly used. Semiconductor memory is based on transistors and associated electronic components fabricated in integrated circuit construction and is always used as the main memory of a microprocessor system. There are two basic classes of components used in semiconductor memory, namely:

(i) Bipolar transistors (*n-p-n* and *p-n-p*) and diodes
(ii) Metal-oxide-semiconductor (MOS) transistors

which leads to two classes of semiconductor memory, bipolar semiconductor memory and MOS semiconductor memory. Most semiconductor memory in microprocessor systems is of the MOS variety, though bipolar semiconductor memory is used for particular applications.

Semiconductor memory devices consist of a large number of individual memory cells of a common design, each of which maintains one of two states to represent the two binary values of one bit. The memory cell itself must have the following attributes:

(i) Two states
(ii) A method of selecting the memory cell from many fabricated on one integrated circuit together with:
(iii) A method of setting the two binary states, i.e. writing
(iv) A method of sensing the two binary states, i.e. reading.

We shall look at the ways the various cells achieve the above, but firstly we consider the common organization of these cells within the device.

8.2 Memory organization

Generally the cells are organized in a two-dimensional array and one or more cells are selected from the array. Once selected, the write or read process may be performed. One organization is to select one cell from the array for reading or writing. This is known as the *3-D organization*. As one bit is read or written at any instant, the organization is also given the notation ×1. For example, a 1024 × 1 memory would indicate a memory in which any one bit from the 1024 bits stored can be accessed and one bit of information passed to or from the memory.

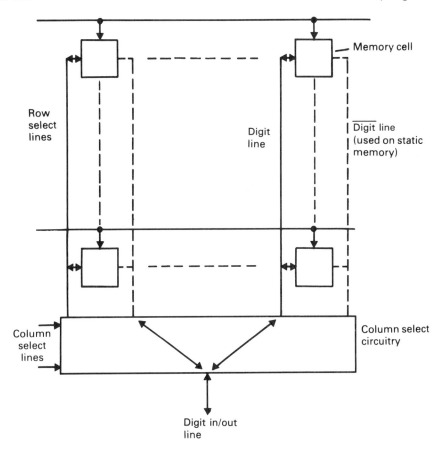

Figure 8.1 × 1 semiconductor memory organization

The × 1 organization is shown in Fig. 8.1. A row select signal selects a complete row of memory cells. A digit column line connects to the cells as shown and is used to present new data to the cells or to obtain the existing data (write and read). *Static memory* cells (which will be described later) generally employ two digit lines connecting to each cell, one for the true binary value and one for the complement value. One cell on the selected row is chosen by selecting one of the column digit lines (or pair in the case of static memories). This enables either a writing process or a read process to be performed. Each cell is given a unique address which is divided into two parts, a *row address* which selects the row and a *column address* which selects a column. If the array is square the row and column addresses would have the same number of bits. The array need not be square, but a square array would give the least number of row and column circuits in total.

If we wish to read and write binary words consisting of several binary digits simultaneously, as would be normal, several memory devices of the × 1 organization could be used, each storing one digit of each word. For example, a 1024-word memory in which each word contains eight bits could be formed with eight 1024×1 bit memory devices. An alternative organization is the $\times n$ organization which achieves simultaneous reading and writing of a complete word in one device. The usual arrangement for semiconductor memory is shown in Fig. 8.2. Here the memory array is arranged as before with a row select line connecting to a row of cells but rather than select one column digit line, n column digit lines are selected where n is the required number of digits to be read or written simultaneously. The columns are formed into n groups with one column select circuit for each group. Each select circuit selects the corresponding column in its group. Typically n is 4 or 8. A 1024×8 bit memory device would hold 1024 bytes and all the bits of any one byte can be read or written simultaneously. Of course more than one memory device of this organization can also be used to increase memory capacity. Memory capacities of semiconductor memories are manufactured in large powers of 2. Since 2^{10} is 1024 or approximately 1000, the letter K is used to indicate the multiple of 2^{10}. For example, a $64K \times 1$ bit memory holds 64×2^{10} (2^{16}) bits.

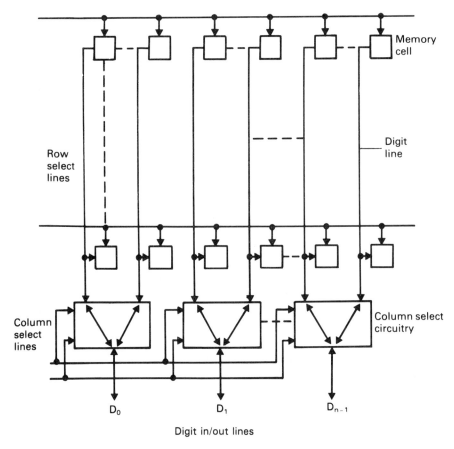

Figure 8.2 $\times n$ semiconductor memory organization

8.3 Metal-oxide-semiconductor random access memory

There are two classes of metal-oxide-semiconductor (MOS) random access memory, namely:

(i) Static MOS random access memory
(ii) Dynamic MOS random access memory

classified by the type of internal memory cell circuit used.

8.3.1 Static MOS random access memory

Figure 8.3 shows a static MOS memory cell consisting of two 'cross-coupled' MOS transistors, T_1 and T_2, two load resistors and two separate MOS transistors, T_3 and T_4, to connect the memory cell to the digit and $\overline{digit}$ lines for selection, reading and writing. In this circuit, all the MOS transistors are enhancement types. (See Chapter 5, section 5.5 for details of MOS transistors.) When one of the two cross-coupled

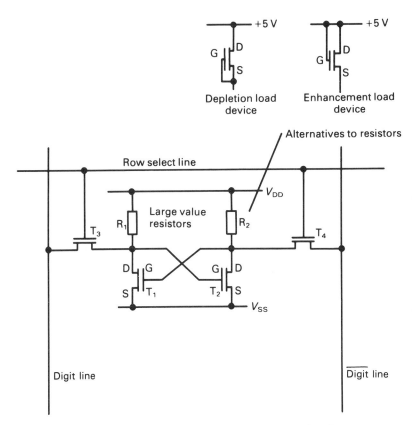

Figure 8.3 Resistor load static MOS RAM cell

transistors is fully conducting, say T_1, the voltage of its drain falls to approximately 0V. This causes the other transistor of the pair, T_2, to become non-conducting and its drain voltage rises to the supply voltage, 5V. This voltage is applied to the base of T_1. As the voltage is above the threshold voltage of T_1, T_1 is maintained in the conducting state.

The circuit can be maintained in one of two states, either with T_1 conducting and T_2 not conducting, or with T_1 not conducting and T_2 conducting. These two circuit states represent the two binary values of one digit. Selection is performed using the two extra transistors, T_3 and T_4, which are placed into their conducting state by applying appropriate voltages on the row select lines. When selected, the information can be read from or written into the cell. One read amplifier is provided for each pair of digit lines sensing the voltage difference between the two outputs of the selected cell. To write to a selected cell, one side of the cell is brought down to 0V and the other to $+5$V using a differential output write amplifier with true and inverse outputs driving the digit and $\overline{\text{digit}}$ lines respectively.

The resistors in the static MOS memory cell are fabricated as part of the integrated circuit construction and can have a very high value to reduce the power dissipation of the cell. (The power dissipation of each cell is given approximately by V_S^2/R where V_S is the supply voltage.) Resistor values as high as 500 MΩ have been used. However, very high values result in slower operation because of the long time the output circuit then takes to charge the output capacitances. To counter this, sensitive read amplifiers can be used which record the state of the memory cell before the final output voltage has been reached. A 100 mV change may be sufficient to deduce the state of the circuit.

There are several variations in the static MOS memory cell described above. The load resistors can be replaced with either enhancement MOS transistor loads or depletion MOS transistor loads in a similar fashion as the MOS logic gates described in Chapter 5. In each case, the source of the load device is connected to the appropriate cross-coupled transistor and the drain is connected to the supply voltage.

Enhancement MOS load transistors have their gates tied to the supply voltage. When one cross-coupled transistor is conducting, the voltage between the gate and the source of the enhancement load device is greater than its threshold voltage, and current will flow through the load device. Conversely, when the cross-coupled transistor is not conducting the load device becomes non-conducting. It was noted in Chapter 5 that this results in the high output voltage being $V_S - V_t$ where V_t is the threshold voltage of the load device, perhaps 1.5 V.

The depletion load has its gate connected to its source and to the cross-coupled transistors. Because the gate-source is always 0 V, the depletion device is always conducting, though only with leakage currents when the associated cross-coupled transistor is non-conducting.

8.3.2 Dynamic MOS random access memory

The second class of semiconductor MOS random access memory is the dynamic memory which uses a capacitor charged to a potential to represent one state and uncharged to represent the other state. The approach can be traced back to the early 1970s when methods were sought to reduce the number of components in the memory cell. This would clearly increase the number of memory cells that could be fabricated in one device. A characteristic of MOS transistors is that the gate current, due to the leakage across the gate electrode and the surrounding silicon dioxide, is extremely small. Therefore once the gate electrode is charged to some potential and then disconnected, it takes several milliseconds for the potential to decay. For example, if the load resistors or devices were removed from the static MOS design, the binary state of the device would be maintained for a few milliseconds due to the charge of the capacitance of one of the cross-coupled transistors. If, before the state is lost, the memory cell is refreshed, i.e. read and a full state reinstated, and repeated at regular intervals, a practical memory cell can be formed. One of the first dynamic MOS memory cells was of this type, using the two MOS cross-coupled transistors without load devices, and two select devices, four transistors in all. This approach can be developed using the charge on the gate-source capacitance of a single MOS transistor to maintain the conducting state of the MOS transistor and additional transistors to select the memory cell for reading and writing. This requires one MOS transistor as the storage element, one to select the cell for reading and one to select the cell for writing, three transistors in all.

The memory cell can be reduced to a specially formed capacitor and one select MOS transistor as shown in Fig. 8.4. This form was introduced in 1973. The select transistor, when conducting, allows both reading and writing to take place using a single digit line. The select signal selects a row of cells as in other memory designs described. One digit line is provided for each column of cells ($\overline{\text{digit}}$ not required in dynamic cells). Each digit line has a read amplifier and write amplifier attached. There were some problems to overcome with this particularly attractive design with regard to reading. To create a small memory cell, the storage capacitor needs to be physically very small and hence with a small value of capacitance. When the cell is selected and the capacitor connects to the digit line, the voltage originally on the storage capacitor reduces because of the capacitive attenuator formed by the storage

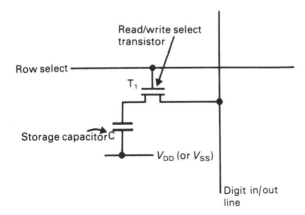

Figure 8.4 Dynamic memory cell

capacitor and intrinsic capacitance of the digit line which is connected in parallel. Designs in the 1970s called for storage capacitances in the order of 0.04 pF. The capacitance of the digit line may be in the order of 0.5 pF giving an attenuation of $0.04/0.54 = 1/13.5$ or a reduction to 7.4% of the original storage voltage. The original voltage is usually between 3.75 V and 5 V. With these voltages the final read voltage is between 278 mV and 370 mV. The voltage must be allowed to decay from these values. To sense such low voltages, sensitive read amplifiers were necessary, and generally these amplifiers needed to be fabricated using MOS technology.

The general read amplifier design often chosen has a central portion consisting of two MOS transistors configured in a similar way to the static memory cell, with their drains and gates cross-coupled. A simple example is shown in Fig. 8.5. Outputs are taken from both drains of the read amplifiers. Columns of memory cells are divided into two halves and one read amplifier is placed between the two halves for each column. Let us consider the action of one read amplifier which is repeated for

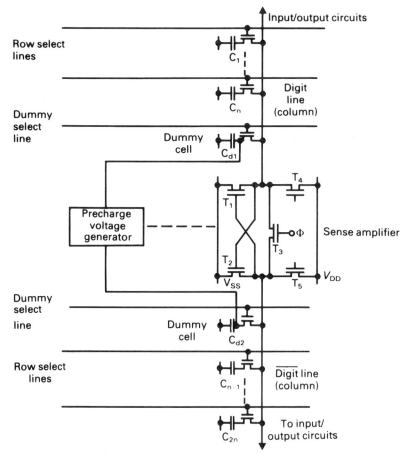

Figure 8.5   Simple dynamic memory sense amplifier

all the read amplifiers simultaneously. One row line is selected on one side of the read amplifier to select a memory cell. The cell connects to one output of the read amplifier. One *dummy* memory cell is provided on each side of the read amplifier. The dummy cell on the other side to the selected cell is connected via the column line to the associated read amplifier output. The dummy cell has been charged so as to create a voltage half-way between the two possible voltages of store cells, i.e. $\frac{1}{2} V_{storage}$ where $V_{storage}$ is the 1 level voltage and 0 V is the 0 level voltage.

The read amplifier is placed in an unstable state by, in this case, joining both outputs together temporarily using additional MOS transistors. One single transistor, T_3, is used in the simple design shown. When the outputs are released, the cross-coupled transistor circuit relaxes into a stable state with one transistor conducting and the other not conducting. If the selected memory cell is in a charged state (representing a 1), the voltage on that side of the read amplifier will be higher than on the other side having the dummy cell and the read circuit will relax with high output voltage on the selected memory cell side and low on the dummy cell side. If the selected cell is at an uncharged state (representing a 0), this is followed by the read amplifier and 0 V re-imposed. In fact the regenerative action will result in the selected cell being recharged to the starting voltage, say 5V, or discharged to 0 V and thus a read operation will also perform an automatic refresh action.

Notice that the use of dummy memory cells takes into account the voltage attenuation because both the selected memory cell and the dummy cell have the same (half) column line capacitance and each voltage will be attenuated by the same factor. Writing is performed by using the same read amplifier as these also fully charge or discharge the selected cells.

Dynamic memories will lose their information over a period of time as the charge on the storage capacitors discharges. Early dynamic memory devices had a worst-case time for the charge to decay to a level at which it cannot be distinguished of 2 ms, and all of the cells would need to be *refreshed* within this period. The longest period between refresh operations on a single cell has increased with further development of the device. Refreshing the cells means reading and rewriting the same information. With the read amplifier design above, a refresh operation can be the same as a normal read operation without any need to look at the read outputs from the device, and all the cells on a row can be refreshed together. This would need to be repeated for all the cells, and the whole process repeated every refresh period. Refresh represents an overhead to the memory system as while the memory is being refreshed, it cannot be used for normal read or write operations. However, it is usually an insignificant fraction of the overall available time. For example, if a read/refresh operation takes 100 ns, there are 1024 rows and the maximum refresh period is 8 ms, the percentage of the available time spent in refresh is:

$$\% \text{ time in refresh} = (100 \times 1024 \times 100\%)/8 \text{ ms} = 1.28\%$$

Often, it can be arranged that refresh can take place at times when the memory is not being used for normal read/write operations. If this is done, there is no overhead to the use of dynamic memories whatsoever.

8.3.3 Memory signals

(a) Memory data standards

There are various notations used by manufacturers to describe memory timing signals. A standard has been laid down by the IEEE Task Force, P662, on Semiconductor Memory Terminology and Specifications, in co-operation with the JEDEC JC42 Committee on Semiconductor Memories [1], and some but not all memory manufacturers have followed this standard. In the IEEE standard, upper case letters are designated for particular signals. For example, the data input is D and the data output is Q. A bidirectional data input/output line is labelled DQ. The time between two timing signals is described by a mnemonic consisting of a series of upper case letters, beginning with the letter T. The next letter or group of letters refers to the leading (first) timing signal. This is followed by a letter indicating the type of logic transition of the leading signal. The next letter or group of letters refers to the following (second) timing signal, and this is followed by a letter indicating

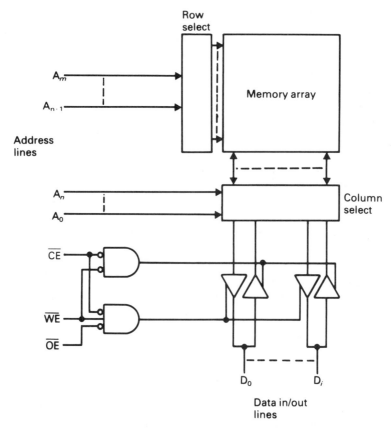

Figure 8.6   Internal architecture of static memory

the type of transition of this signal. The following types of transitions are identified:

      L   to a low logic level
      H to a high logic level
      V   to a valid state
      X to an invalid state
      Z   to high impedance (tri-state)

For example, the timing parameter TDVWL is the time from the data signal D becoming valid to the write strobe W going to a low state. The bar over an active low signal is omitted in the timing parameter name. In the following memory timing waveforms, we will give the IEEE signal names in parentheses where other names are very common. Timing parameters will use the IEEE notation.

(b) Static memory

A number of logic signals need to be applied to semiconductor memory parts. For a write operation, the following basic information needs to be passed to the part:

(i) The address of the memory cell(s)
(ii) The data to be written into the memory cells
(iii) A write strobe signal to initiate the operation.

For a read operation, the following information needs to be present:

(i) The address of the memory cell(s)
(ii) A read data strobe signal to initiate the operation

together with a data path for the resultant information read from the selected cells. Figure 8.6 shows the internal arrangement of a typical static memory and Fig. 8.7 the timing signals. A general chip enable, $\overline{CE}$, is also present. The enable signal must be activated before the part will respond to any other signal.

    The write strobe is labelled $\overline{WE}$, write enable. To activate a write transfer, the chip is selected by setting $\overline{CE}$ low. A high to low transition is applied to $\overline{WE}$. (A write transfer will also be activated if $\overline{WE}$ is set low before $\overline{CE}$. Then a high to low $\overline{CE}$ transition activates a write transfer.) These signals are applied after the address has been presented to the part and the signals have stabilized. The data entered into the addressed cells will be that present on the data lines at the time of the low to high write enable signal transition (or $\overline{CE}$ high to low transition if this occurs later).

    The read strobe is called $\overline{OE}$, output enable. For a read transfer, the chip is selected by setting $\overline{CE}$ low after the address is applied and then an $\overline{OE}$ high to low transition is applied. Some time later, the data from the addressed memory cells appear on the data output lines. In some memory devices $\overline{OE}$ is not present. In these cases, $\overline{CE}$ acts as a read strobe when $\overline{WE} = 1$.

    In the timing waveforms shown, it is assumed that the address must remain valid throughout the memory cycle. This type of memory is known as *asynchronous memory*. Some memories, known as *synchronous memories*, incorporate internal address latches which are activated by the falling edge of $\overline{CE}$. In these memories,

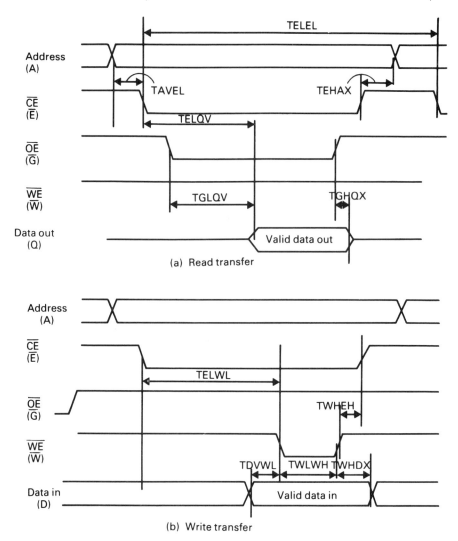

(a) Read transfer

(b) Write transfer

Symbol	Parameter
TELEL	Cycle time (of $\overline{CE}$)
TAVEL	Address to $\overline{CE}$ set-up time
TEHAX	$\overline{CE}$ to address hold time
TELQV	$\overline{CE}$ to data out valid time ($\overline{CE}$ access time)
TGLQV	$\overline{OE}$ to data out valid time ($\overline{OE}$ access time)
TGHQX	$\overline{OE}$ to data invalid time
TELWL	$\overline{CE}$ to $\overline{WE}$ set-up time
TDVWL	Data in to $\overline{WE}$ set-up time
TWLWH	$\overline{WE}$ pulse width
TWHDX	$\overline{WE}$ to Data in hold time
TWHEH	$\overline{WE}$ to $\overline{CE}$ hold time

Figure 8.7   Representative static memory read and write timing

the address needs remain valid only till the hold time from the falling edge of $\overline{\text{CE}}$. Similarly, other applied signals can be latched internally, including the data input. The data input latch would be activated by the falling edge of $\overline{\text{WE}}$.

(c) Dynamic memory

Dynamic memories require the same information and control but this is usually provided in a different way. The memory address is split into two parts, a row address and a column address corresponding to the rows and columns of the required cells. Since the row address can be selected before the column address, the two addresses are arranged to enter the part on the same address lines at different times to reduce the number of address lines. This technique is known as *address multiplexing*. The general arrangement is shown in Fig. 8.8. Two address strobe

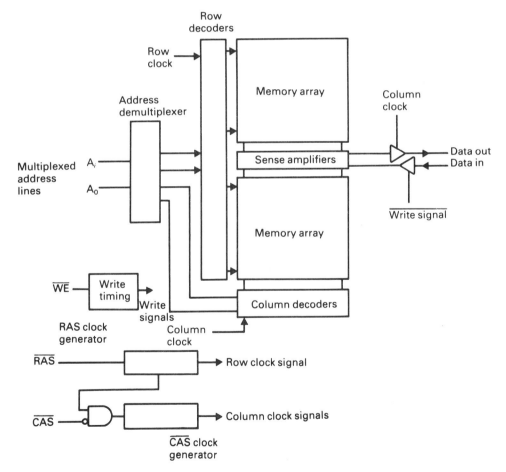

Figure 8.8 Internal architecture of dynamic memory device

signals are provided:

> $\overline{\text{RAS}}$ Row address strobe signal
> $\overline{\text{CAS}}$ Column address strobe signal

Only one other control signal is shown:

> $\overline{\text{WE}}$ Write enable

with independent data input and output. Using the $\times 1$ organization, dynamic memories up to 256 K $\times$ 1 bit can be contained in 16-pin dual-in-line packages. The $\times 8$ dynamic memories normally do not employ address multiplexing and use larger 24–28 pin packages.

Each address strobe signal is activated when the appropriate row or column address is stabilized on the address lines, first the $\overline{\text{RAS}}$ signal and then the $\overline{\text{CAS}}$ signal, as shown in Fig. 8.9. Notice that the action is triggered on the falling edge of the two strobe signals and both $\overline{\text{RAS}}$ and $\overline{\text{CAS}}$ are kept low to the end of the memory cycle.

The read cycle is selected by ensuring that $\overline{\text{WR}}$ is set to a 1 when the $\overline{\text{CAS}}$ becomes low. The time before the data bit appears on the data output line is dependent upon the $\overline{\text{CAS}}$ transition to a low (but see below). When the output becomes valid, it remains valid while $\overline{\text{CAS}}$ is low and becomes high impedance (tri-state) when $\overline{\text{CAS}}$ is brought high (outputs are not usually latched internally).

For a write operation, $\overline{\text{WR}}$ is set to a 0. If this is done before the $\overline{\text{CAS}}$ signal transition to a low, the data bit on the data line is strobed (entered) with $\overline{\text{CAS}}$ so the data must be valid then. If $\overline{\text{WR}}$ is set to a 0 after the $\overline{\text{CAS}}$ transition, the data bit is strobed with $\overline{\text{WR}}$, so that the data must be valid then. The latter case is known as *late* or *delayed write*, and the former case is known as *early write*. These mechanisms provide greater flexibility in read–write operations. The normal microprocessor memory operation is early write, which allows the data-in and data-out lines to be joined together. In both modes, $\overline{\text{RAS}}$ must be maintained at a low throughout the cycle.

Certain timing factors must be satisfied. Generally the signals $\overline{\text{RAS}}$ and $\overline{\text{CAS}}$ are internally gated so that the time relationship of these signals is not critical for the memory to operate. In particular, $\overline{\text{CAS}}$ may be applied before the device is ready to select the column, and the signal is internally inhibited until the correct time. This is known as *gated CAS*. Assuming that the delay between $\overline{\text{RAS}}$ and $\overline{\text{CAS}}$ is not greater than some maximum value, typically 50 ns, and not less than some minimum value, typically 20 ns, the access time is measured from the falling edge of $\overline{\text{CAS}}$. If, however, $\overline{\text{CAS}}$ is applied later, the access time will be determined by the 'access time from $\overline{\text{CAS}}$', plus the delay between the two strobes. To achieve the minimum access time, $\overline{\text{CAS}}$ must be applied within the window above (for example 20 ns to 50 ns), but the device will still operate, though slower, if $\overline{\text{CAS}}$ is applied later.

Set-up times and hold times as in flip-flops need to be satisfied. Typically the row address set-up time is zero and the row hold time 20 ns. To give the maximum

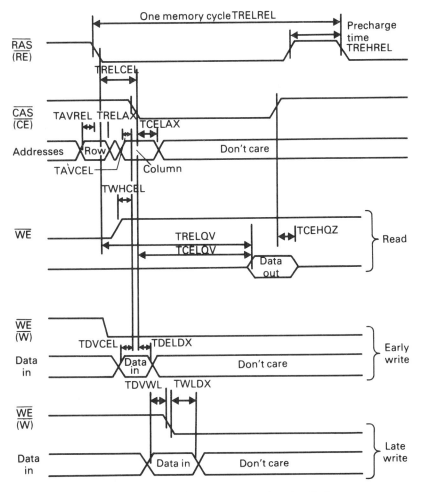

Figure 8.9   Dynamic memory read–write timing

possible time to establish the column address, the column address set-up time is often negative, for example − 10 ns, which means that the column address need not be stable until 10 ns after the $\overline{CAS}$ has been applied. The column address hold time is typically 45 ns. The WR set-up and hold times referenced to the falling edge of $\overline{CAS}$ are zero. This means that $\overline{WR}$ may be applied before or after $\overline{CAS}$ though this results in different modes of operation (early write and late write). Also the device requires time to precharge internal circuits before the next memory operation can take place, typically 100 ns. However, the data remains valid during this time while $\overline{CAS}$ is low.

Refresh operations can be initiated by one of several methods. The usual method is to use the falling edge of $\overline{RAS}$ to cause a refresh as this causes the read amplifiers to refresh a selected row. A number of refresh operations can be initiated in succession by $\overline{RAS}$ low transitions with $\overline{CAS}$ kept high. This is known as $\overline{RAS}$-

only refresh. The level on $\overline{WR}$ is irrelevant. A row address has to be provided for each refresh operation.

An alternative mode, known as *hidden refresh*, utilizes the fact that while $\overline{CAS}$ is low, valid data once appearing will remain on the data output line. Subsequent refresh cycles can be initiated by falling transitions of $\overline{RAS}$ while $\overline{CAS}$ is low, without disturbing the output data. The usual plan is to perform one or more refresh cycles immediately after each memory reference cycle while keeping the original data output valid. The first cycle consists of a normal $\overline{RAS}$–$\overline{CAS}$ cycle but with $\overline{CAS}$ remaining low at the end of this cycle. One or more $\overline{RAS}$ cycles are then performed, with refresh addresses provided to refresh rows of memory. The timing of $\overline{RAS}$-only and hidden refresh modes are shown in Fig. 8.10.

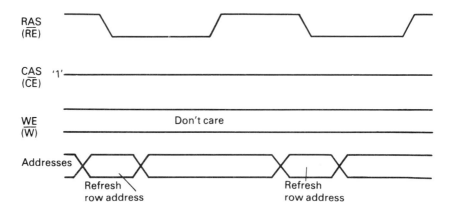

(a) RAS only refresh

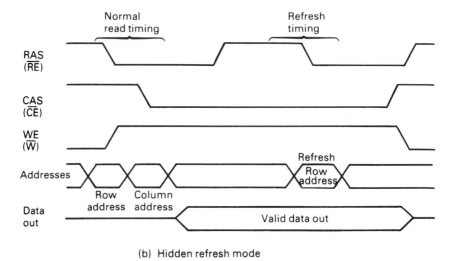

(b) Hidden refresh mode

Figure 8.10 Dynamic memory refresh timing

8.3.4 Dynamic memory subsystem design

Dynamic memories pose additional problems over static memories when designed into a memory subsystem, for two reasons:

(i) Multiplexed address inputs (when used)
(ii) Necessity of refresh.

We firstly consider the additional circuitry for multiplexed address input parts. The circuitry required needs to perform the following sequence:

1. Gate row address from processor to the memory address inputs
2. Set row address strobe, $\overline{RAS} = 0$
3. Gate column address from the processor to the memory address inputs
4. Set column address strobe, $\overline{CAS} = 0$
5. Set $\overline{CAS}$ and $\overline{RAS} = 1$
6. Allow a precharge time before next cycle.

The row and column addresses are the lower and upper parts of the full address (or vice versa). For a 1 M (i.e. 1024 K) memory device, both the row and column addresses are ten bits. The row could be the processor address signals A_0 to A_9 and the column address could be the processor signals A_{10} to A_{19}. Each ten-bit address could be connected to the memory address lines using ten 2-to-1 line multiplexers (typically two integrated circuits). Let us firstly assume that the processor address does not extend beyond A_{19}. Figure 8.11 shows the arrangement. The memory request signal, $\overline{AS}$, is used as the row address strobe with the multiplexer set to choose the row address. After one processor clock period, the multiplexer select signal is changed to select the column address and after a suitable delay, a column address strobe signal is generated from the multiplexer select signal. Signals to the memory devices have series resistors to limit signal reflections (see Chapter 14, section 14.2).

    If the processor address space is larger than one memory device (e.g. greater than 2^{20} with 1 M $\times$ 1 devices), the memory device selection needs to be performed in addition to the above. The normal approach is to connect higher address lines to the $\overline{RAS}$ inputs of individual devices, or sometimes both $\overline{RAS}$ and $\overline{CAS}$ for a two-dimensional decode.

    Now consider the second aspect, that of memory refresh. Except for self-refresh devices (see page 279) it is necessary to provide all row refresh addresses, usually in succession, to the devices within the refresh period of, say, 2 ms. Without processor support, an external refresh counter needs to be provided, which is periodically incremented and gated on to the address lines in place of the normal read–write address. If no particular regular occasion is known when the processor is not requiring the memory, the normal approach is to use the wait mechanism of the processor to hold up the processor periodically, as necessary, to perform a refresh activity.

    There are support devices available called *dynamic memory controllers* which provide most of the required circuitry, including the address multiplexer, refresh counter, processor and refresh request arbiter and row/column address strobe

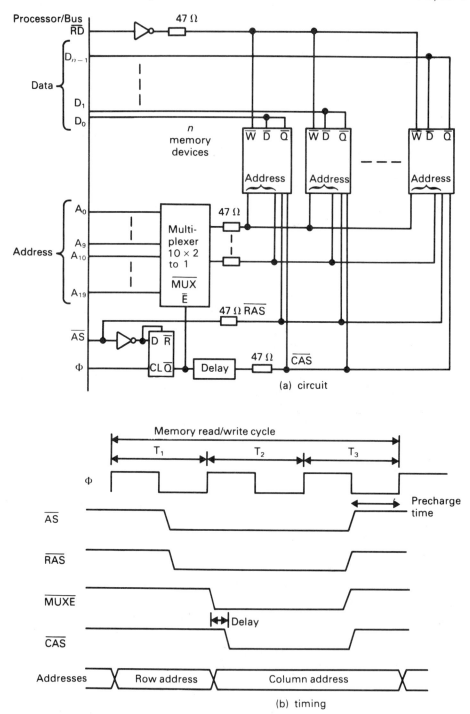

Figure 8.11   Simplified dynamic memory system

circuitry. These devices are bipolar because of the required high speed of operation, and all read, write and refresh operations are handled by the device. If a read or write request is received while the controller is performing a refresh operation, a wait request is generated, delaying the processor until the refresh operation has been completed. Refresh operations occur regularly and at sufficiently short intervals to maintain the stored information. If a refresh operation is requested by the controller after a processor read or write cycle has been accepted, the refresh operation will be held in abeyance until the read or write operation has been completed. Then the refresh operation takes place. In the event of simultaneous requests, special arbitration logic resolves the conflict.

(a) Self-refresh memories

Additional circuitry can be incorporated into dynamic memory parts to provide automatic or assisted refresh capability. The simplest form is known as *pin 1 refresh*. Pin 1 on 16-pin dual-in-line packages is used by some manufacturers to activate an internal refresh mechanism with a signal $\overline{\text{RFSH}}$. When $\overline{\text{RAS}}$ is high, $\overline{\text{RFSH}}$ is taken low to perform a refresh operation. Each low-going transition of $\overline{\text{RFSH}}$ causes the outputs of an internal refresh counter to be connected to internal row address inputs and a refresh operation take place (basically a read operation). On the subsequent rising edge of $\overline{\text{RFSH}}$, the counter is incremented by one in preparation for the next refresh operation which is initiated as required. With repeated use of $\overline{\text{RFSH}}$, either in burst or distributed between normal memory cycles, all rows in the memory can be refreshed. This mechanism is sometimes known as *automatic refresh*. Hidden refresh can be accomplished with $\overline{\text{RFSH}}$ in place of $\overline{\text{RAS}}$.

Pin 1 refresh may include a true *self-refresh* feature whereby successive refresh operations take place if $\overline{\text{RFSH}}$ is held low for, say, longer than 8 μs. From then on, refreshes with refresh counter increments take place automatically every 12–16 μs to ensure that the whole memory is refreshed totally within the specified time interval. Self-refresh is generally useful for power-down situations where the memory is powered by a battery while the normal supply is unavailable. It is simply necessary then to keep $\overline{\text{RFSH}}$ low in order to maintain the data stored. Note that when $\overline{\text{RFSH}}$ has returned to a high level, a refresh cycle may just have started and thus a period needs to elapse before a new memory cycle can begin, to allow the refresh cycle to complete. Typically this period will be the same as for a normal memory read or write operation.

Pin 1 refresh, though convenient, does require a previously unused pin. An alternative which leaves pin 1 free and available for a multiplexed address input is to use a previously unused combination of $\overline{\text{RAS}}$ and $\overline{\text{CAS}}$, namely $\overline{\text{CAS}}$ low and $\overline{\text{RAS}}$ going low to trigger an internal refresh mechanism.

A *pseudo-static* or *quasi-static* memory is a dynamic memory with additional internal circuitry providing automatic or self-refresh and with an organization which gives the device the external attributes of a static memory, so that it can be treated as such in a system design. Address multiplexing is not done. Pseudo-static memories offer higher capacity and lower cost than static memories, without the overhead of the external refresh and address multiplexer circuitry.

8.4 Read-only memory

8.4.1 General

Read-only memory is a type of memory which is capable of having its stored information read but not altered (written to). Such memory is non-volatile, that is, the stored information is not lost if the power is removed. When the power is returned to the memory device, the previous stored information is still available. Consequently, read-only memory finds applications where the program or unalterable data needs to be available when the computer is first switched on. Examples include:

(i) *Bootstrap memory,* the memory used to store the program which is first executed when the computer is switched on. This program is usually fairly short and causes a larger program to be brought into the primary memory from the secondary memory.

(ii) *Control memory* storing the processor microprogram. In a microprogrammed design of processor, a microprogram is created which defines the sequence of steps which are necessary to execute the machine instructions of the processor. This microprogram is stored in a fast memory which needs only to be read-only for the basic microprograms of the processor, but must be non-volatile. Most microprocessors, if microprogrammed, have internal read-only control memory. See Chapter 12 for further details of microprogrammed processor designs.

In addition to the above applications, read-only memory is used particularly in microprocessor-based systems where the microprocessor is applied in dedicated applications such as in washing machines or cash dispensers. In these applications, the whole program can be kept in a read-only memory. Similarly, video terminals are usually microprocessor based. The microprocessor program controlling the operation of the terminal can be kept in read-only memories within the terminal. The dot-matrix pattern of each displayable character is kept in another read-only memory.

Locations in a read-only memory can still be accessed in any order at high speed, i.e. read-only memory is still random-access, though the term random-access is normally associated with memory capable of both reading and writing. If it is necessary to differentiate clearly between memory capable of both reading and writing, and read-only memory, the term *read–write memory* (RWM) can be used for the former. There are several classes of semiconductor read-only memory. We shall firstly consider the class of read-only memory called *fixed read-only memory* in which the information is incorporated during manufacture and cannot be altered subsequently.

8.4.2 Fixed read-only memory

The memory cell in a fixed read-only memory (ROM) can use bipolar transistors or diodes or MOS transistors. A memory using bipolar transistors or diodes is a bipolar memory. Both bipolar memory and MOS memory employ the same basic technique. The memory cells are arranged in a two-dimensional array with row select lines and column output lines in the X direction and Y direction respectively, as in the previous semiconductor memories except there is no data input. One row of memory cells is selected using a row select signal. If a 1 is to be stored in a memory cell, a direct connection is made between the row select line and a column digit output line in that memory cell. Therefore after selection is made, a signal will appear on the column output lines. If a 0 is to be stored, no direct connection is made between the row and column lines and no signal appears on the column line when the cell is selected. The configuration for a 0 and a 1 can, of course, be reversed.

Figure 8.12 shows a typical MOS fixed read-only memory. In this particular

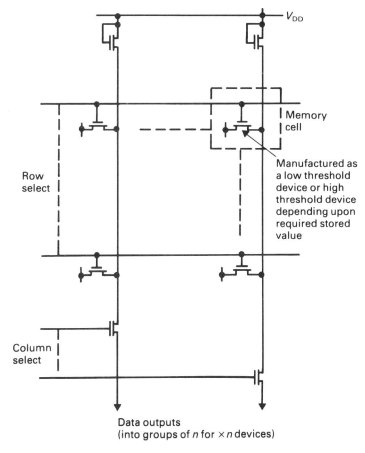

Figure 8.12 An MOS read-only memory array

case, rather than make a direct connection physically, an electrical connection is made by manufacturing the cell transistor with a low threshold voltage. For no electrical connection, the transistor is manufactured with a high threshold voltage. Bipolar transistor fixed read-only memories are also available, which use actual links in series with diodes or transistors.

8.4.3 Programmable read-only memory

In a *programmable read-only memory* (PROM), the connection is broken during a programming sequence. The devices can be supplied to the customer with all the connections left intact. The customer can then perform the programming sequence to blow selected fuses. A Schottky diode programmable read-only memory is shown in Fig. 8.13. The connection between the row and column lines is made through a Schottky diode and a semiconductor fuse. This fuse is blown intentionally in those

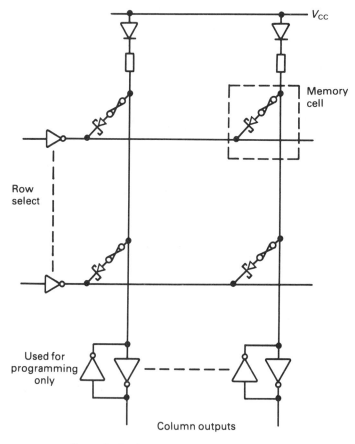

Figure 8.13 Schottky diode PROM array

cells which are to have a 0 stored, and left intact if a 1 is to be stored (assuming a 1 is represented by a direct connection and a 0 is represented by no connection). The fuse is composed of a material such as polysilicon. It is blown by selecting the cell and passing a relatively high current, perhaps 50 mA, through the cell using the row and column lines. Special programmer units are available for this purpose. Programmable read-only memories of this type are always bipolar because of the high currents involved during programming. Programmable read-only memories which can be programmed by the user are known as *field-programmable read-only memories*, FPROMs.

8.4.4 Erasable programmable read-only memory

Erasable programmable read-only memories, EPROMs, are programmable read-only memories which have a mechanism for altering the stored information. There are several mechanisms that can be used. Often the mechanism is such that the memory cannot be used for high-speed writing and thus cannot be regarded as normal read-write memory. A very successful type of erasable programmable memory uses ultra-violet light shone on to the surface of the integrated circuit to erase the information and an electrical programming sequence to reprogram the memory with new information. This type of erasable programmable read-only memory is normally associated with the term EPROM, but may be differentiated from other types by the term U-V EPROM. The U-V EPROM has had an extremely significant effect on the development of microprocessor systems.

The original U-V EPROM was developed by Intel using PMOS technology and introduced in 1971. The memory cell consists of one enhancement-mode MOS transistor with no connection made to the gate electrode. The gate is surrounded completely by a silicon dioxide insulating layer. In the natural unprogrammed state (in this case representing a logic 1), no conduction occurs between the source and drain of the device. In the programmed 0 state, charge is placed on the isolated gate and causes the transistor to conduct as the voltage on the gate is above the threshold voltage of the device.

To program the device, -30 V is applied between the source and drain. This causes electrons to avalanche through the drain towards the source. The silicon dioxide layer between the gate electrode and the drain-source channel is made only about 1000 Å thick. Electrons travel through this silicon dioxide layer on to the isolated gate, giving the gate electrode an electrical charge. The gate electrode is charged sufficiently to produce conduction between the drain and source. Then, the programming voltage can be removed. Because of the very good insulation properties of silicon dioxide, the charge on the gate leaks away very slowly and the conducting state will remain for a very long time. It is expected that at room temperature, the charge will keep the device in a recognized 0 state for decades. In manufactured devices, the condition is guaranteed for 10 years at $125°$C, and 70% of the charge is then expected to remain.

The charge can be removed by exposing the integrated circuit chip to ultra-violet light which gives the built-up charge sufficient energy to leak away. The package is provided with a transparent quartz lid so that the radiation from a U-V lamp can penetrate and reach the chip. For sufficient energy to be imparted to the electrons, the radiation needs to have a wavelength of less than 4000 Å, and typically a wavelength of 2537 Å is used. The dosage required may be 15 W-sec/cm^2 (U-V intensity × exposure time) which could be achieved with a 10,000 μW/cm^2 rated lamp for 15 seconds. Selection of the memory device is performed using an additional MOS transistor in series with the device and driven by X and Y select lines. For programming, appropriate programming voltages are applied to both X and Y lines for about 1 ms. For reading, lower voltages are used.

Subsequent developments have taken place. The original PMOS devices have been replaced with NMOS devices (except for some CMOS EPROMs) and a more compact design developed. The separate MOS selection transistor can be combined with the storage device into a single structure as in the NMOS U-V EPROM design shown in Fig. 8.14. The memory cell consists of an MOS transistor with two gate electrodes, one stacked above the other. The row select signal connects to the upper electrode. The lower electrode is unconnected and totally electrically isolated by the silicon dioxide. The column output is taken from the drain of the MOS transistor. In the unprogrammed state, which is taken to represent a 1, the MOS transistor is conducting because the row select voltage is chosen to be greater than the natural threshold voltage of the MOS transistor. Programming a 0 into the memory cell involves charging the lower electrode negatively. This is achieved by applying a voltage of + 16 V on the drain of the transistor with respect to the source and + 26 V on the select electrode. The drain–source potential causes electrons to flow from the source to the drain. As electrons cross the channel between the source and drain, some acquire sufficient energy to pass through the silicon dioxide layer between the channel and the lower floating electrode, finally reaching the floating electrode. The process will slow down as more electrons land on the floating electrode and an equilibrium state is reached. (The voltages quoted are for 64K byte devices; larger 'scaled-down' devices have lower voltages.)

When the programming voltages are removed, the charge on the lower electrode will decay very slowly indeed, as before, because the insulating properties of silicon dioxide are extremely good and it takes many years for the charge to decay significantly. The effect of a charged lower electrode is to alter the threshold voltage of the overall MOS transistor by an amount given by:

$$\Delta V_T = -\Delta Q_{FG}/C$$

where ΔQ_{FG} is the added charge on the floating gate and C is the capacitance between the floating gate and the select gate [2]. The threshold voltage becomes larger than the row select voltage, and the transistor will not conduct when selected. The charge is removed by shining ultra-violet light on to the top of the exposed integrated circuit which gives the electrons on the floating gate sufficient energy to return to the channel of the memory cells. The charge will be removed in all the cells simultaneously. Special U-V EPROM programmer units and eraser units are

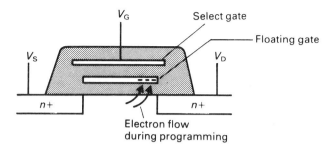

(a) Construction

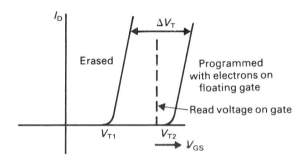

(b) Characteristic

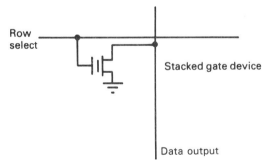

(c) Memory cell

Figure 8.14 Stacked-gate FAMOS memory cell

manufactured. Typically, it takes 300 ns to program one word of the memory and 15–20 minutes to erase the whole contents.

Clearly the necessity of ultra-violet light to erase the memory prevents in-circuit reprogramming and may be inconvenient at times. This is eliminated in the *electrically erasable programmable read-only memories*, EEPROMs. One

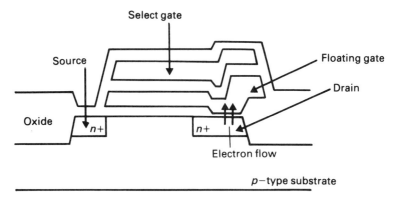

Figure 8.15   Floating-gate tunnel oxide memory cell

EEPROM design is a modification of the above U-V EPROM to allow electrons to tunnel through the silicon dioxide. Tunnelling with reasonable voltages requires a very thin oxide layer. The thin oxide layer can be placed directly underneath the two gate electrodes or, as shown in Fig. 8.15, with the electrodes extended to cover the drain, it can be placed above the drain. The term *flash memory* is applied to EEPROMs in which all of the cells in the memory are erased simultaneously.

References

1. *Memory Applications Handbook*, Santa Clara, CA: National Semiconductor Corp., 1978.
2. Woods, M. H., 'An E-PROM's Integrity Starts With its Cell Structure', *Electronics International*, 53, no. 18 (August 14, 1980).
3. Johnson, W. S., G. L. Kuhn, A. L. Renninger, and G. Perlegos, '16-K EE-PROM Relies on Tunneling for Byte-erasable Program Storage', *Electronics International*, 53, no. 5 (February 28, 1980).

Problems

8.1 A matrix of semiconductor memory cells has a $\times n$ organization with the same number of rows as columns. The memory stores 1024 words with each word having 16 bits. Draw a suitable memory layout giving the overall number of rows and columns, and the internal divisions.

8.2 The memory cells in a $16\,\mathrm{K} \times 1$ bit static RAM consist of two cross-coupled MOS transistors and two resistive loads connected to 5 V. Determine the minimum resistance of the loads if the total power dissipation of the device is not to exceed $\frac{1}{4}$ watt. The voltage across an MOS transistor when conducting can be taken as 0 V. Internal circuits apart from the memory cells need not be considered.

8.3 The value of the storage capacitors of a dynamic memory device is 0.01 pF. Each digit line has a capacitance of 0.5 pF. The voltage on a capacitor is $+4.5$ V before it is selected. Determine the voltage after the cell is selected.

8.4 The refresh period of a dynamic cell is given by the empirical equation:

$$t_{\text{refresh}} = Ae^{-BT}$$

where T is the device junction temperature ($^{\circ}$C)

    A is a constant

    $B = 0.05/^{\circ}$C (a constant)

The refresh period is to be 2 ms when the ambient temperature is 70°C which creates a junction temperature of 100°C in the device. Determine the necessary refresh period measured at an ambient temperature of 25°C if this temperature creates a junction temperature of 27°C in the device.

8.5 A 64K $\times$ 1 bit dynamic MOS RAM is organized internally as 256 row $\times$ 256 column matrix of memory cells. There is one sense amplifier per column. The cycle time (read, write or refresh) is 300 ns and the maximum period between refresh operations of one column is 2 ms. What is the percentage time that must be spent in the refresh activity? How much of this type of memory can be employed with a microprocessor that automatically produces one refresh cycle every 1.5 μs without using additional refresh circuitry?

9 Input/Output Circuits and Operation

9.1 General

We have described a microprocessor system as having three major parts, namely the microprocessor proper, the main program/data memory and the input/output circuitry. In this chapter, we will consider the last of these, the input/output circuitry together with methods of controlling this circuitry. The input/output circuitry is necessary to interconnect the system to components outside the system, collectively called the peripherals of the system. In particular, the peripheral used by the user to communicate with the system is essential in all systems and must be connected. Usually in a computing application, the user communication peripheral is the video display terminal. There may be other peripherals in the system. For example, a printer is essential in most computing applications. Peripheral devices and circuits are necessary to connect the system to experimental equipment in laboratories or industrial equipment in industrial control applications.

In Chapter 7, section 7.4.8, we identified one method of transferring information between the input/output interface and the microprocessor called *programmed input/output*. In programmed input/output, input machine instructions are used to transfer data to processor registers (or possibly to memory locations) from an input interface, and output machine instructions are used to transfer the contents of processor registers (or possibly memory locations) to output devices. We also noted that it is often necessary to check that the input device has data ready before an input instruction to read the data is issued. Similarly, it is often necessary to check that an output interface can accept data before issuing an output instruction to send data to the output interface. These checks are done by examining particular bits of the *status register* of the interface, which indicate the readiness of the interface to supply or accept data. The process of checking the readiness of individual input/output interfaces is known as polling. Some very simple interfaces may always be ready, and hence will not need polling.

In this chapter, we will firstly describe some common interfaces, and then alternative methods to polling for transferring data between the processor or memory and the input/output interfaces.

9.2 Input/output interfaces

9.2.1 Parallel interface

In a *parallel interface*, data is transmitted with one wire assigned to one bit of data. For 8-bit transfers, 8 data wires are provided between the parallel interface and the device. If data is transmitted to and from the device, 16 lines could be provided,

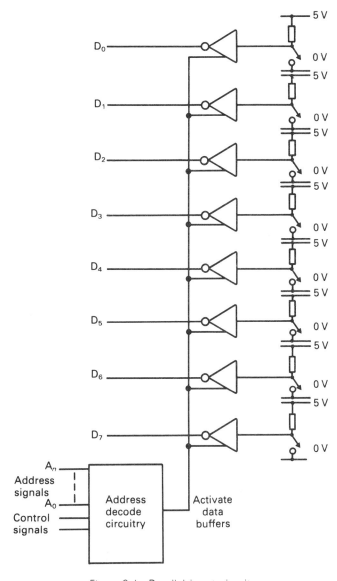

Figure 9.1 Parallel input circuit

8 for transmission to the device and 8 for transmission from the device. A simple application of a parallel input interface would be to connect to switches such as shown in Fig. 9.1. A switch arm in one position would result in a 1 being read and, in the other position, a 0 being read. In the particular circuit shown, when a switch is closed, a 0 is generated at the input of the data buffers, and when a switch is open, the pull-up of the resistor to +5 V causes a valid 1 to be generated. During the execution of an input instruction, the interface address together with the timing signals are generated in much the same way as in a memory read operation (in exactly the same way for memory mapped systems). The address and timing signals are recognized by the interface address decode circuit which causes the interface to place a binary word on the data bus. The bits of the word are set according to the state of the switches. The processor then accepts the data.

A simple application of a parallel output interface would be to drive indicator lamps. Each output line would drive one lamp. When the appropriate output instruction is executed, a binary word is sent to the interface. A 1 could specify the illumination of the lamp and a 0 could specify the lamp not to be illuminated (or vice versa). The scheme would necessitate a flip-flop to be associated with each lamp to maintain the specified state after the instruction has been completed.

An appropriate parallel output interface is shown in Fig. 9.2. The data of the output instruction is sent to the interface via the data bus together with the timing signals via the control bus, and the output address via the address bus. The address decode circuit responds to the address and the timing signals, and causes the data to be placed in the flip-flops that drive the indicator lamps. In Fig. 9.2, the indicators are light-emitting diodes and each diode is connected to the Q output of a flip-flop, such that when $Q = 1$ the diode will not emit light and when $Q = 0$ the diode will emit light. The input data is complemented by inverters so that a 1 sent to the interface causes a light-emitting diode to emit light.

The data output lines of a parallel output interface can be used to control a variety of components. For controlling a.c. mains-operated devices such as motors and solenoids, solid-state switches such as triacs and thyristors can be interfaced to the outputs of the interface. It is normal practice to switch on triacs and thyristors only when the a.c. mains is at zero volts to reduce radio-frequency interference to a minimum. A comparator can be used to detect the zero-crossing which occurs twice in every mains cycle. Composite solid-state switches or solid-state relays (SSRs) are manufactured incorporating zero-crossing detection circuitry in sealed modules for industrial applications. Sealed modules are also available for opto-isolated digital inputs, which provide electrical isolation between the logic inputs and the a.c. mains.

Commonly, parallel interfaces are designed using special LSI devices known as *parallel input/output* devices (PIOs) (or *peripheral interface adapters*, PIAs), which incorporate most of the necessary circuits to interface to a microprocessor except a full address decode circuit. Typically, two or three separate 8-bit parallel interfaces (*ports*) can be fabricated in one integrated circuit. Each port can be pre-programmed as input or output or bidirectional, or in some cases with individual lines as input or output. To effect this, the contents of internal control registers of

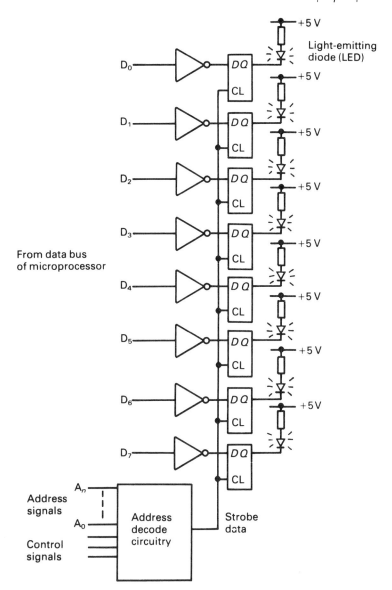

Figure 9.2 Parallel output circuit

the interface device are set to particular values during a software initialization process prior to the port being used for data input and output.

Figure 9.3 shows a simplified implementation of one line of the interface to produce programmable input/output lines. The circuit would be repeated seven more times for a typical 8-bit input/output port. The control flip-flop, FF1, is used to set up the line as input or output as required prior to normal data transfer operations. For input (FF1 Q output = 1), the data from the peripheral device is

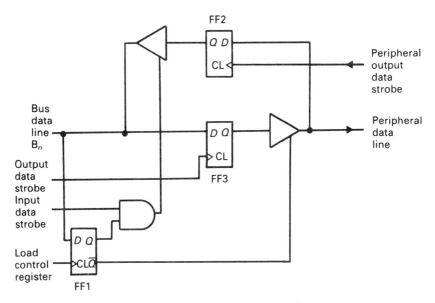

Figure 9.3   One data line of a parallel input/output device

loaded into a data input flip-flop, FF2, and enters the system bus via a tri-state buffer when enabled by an input data strobe. In some applications, the data input flip-flop is not used and the input data is not held permanently within the port. For output (FF1 $\bar{Q} = 1$), data generated by an output machine instruction enters the port from the bus and is loaded into the data output flip-flop , FF3, using the output data strobe. The output to the peripheral device is via a buffer.

A typical LSI PIO device consists of two 8-bit ports as shown in Fig. 9.4. Each port can be programmed for input, output, bidirectional or control, and has ready/strobe handshaking signals available.

Each port of the PIO has two I/O addresses, one associated with the input/output data and one associated with control registers within the PIO as governed by two inputs *B/A Sel* (select port B or port A) and *C/D Sel* (select control or data). Typically *C/D Sel* would be driven by the least significant address bit from the processor, A_0 and *B/A Sel* would be driven by the next least significant bit, A_1. Other address bits would be used by the address decode circuitry which enables the chip generally. Prior to using the port of the PIO for data transfers, the operating mode must be selected by loading control words.

9.2.2 Serial interface

In a *serial interface*, information is transmitted along one wire. The information usually consists of more than one bit, and the bits are sent along the single wire one after the other, i.e. separated in time rather than in 'space' as in a parallel interface.

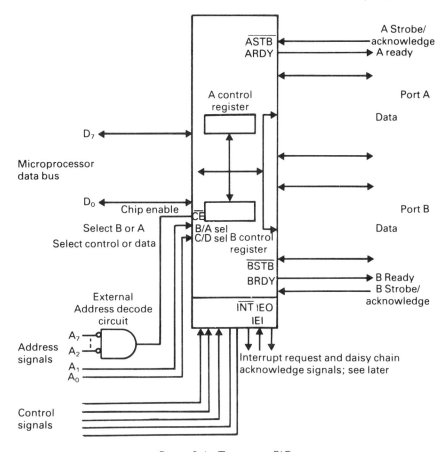

Figure 9.4 Two-port PIO

The term *full-duplex* is used to describe the transmission system where transmission occurs in both directions simultaneously, such as a serial transmission system with one line for each direction. The *half-duplex* describes the transmission system where transmission occurs in both directions but only one way at a time, as would be constrained by a single shared line. If transmission can only be in one direction the term *simplex* is used. Serial transmission in particular finds application for peripherals such as video terminals and printers connected locally or at some distance, and is also a widely used method of connecting computers in a network.

(a) Asynchronous serial transmission

The form of serial interface used for local connections to terminals and some printers is the *asynchronous* serial interface which transmits units of one binary character. A character consists of a fixed-size data word, usually between 5 bits and 8 bits, which is prefixed with a 0 level *start bit* and terminated with one 1 level *stop bit*. (One and one-half stop bits or two stop bits can also be used.) Multiple characters are sent in this format and any time may elapse between the end of one character and the beginning of the next character. The quiescent logic level is a 1. A single character to be sent to the peripheral device is first sent to the system interface, usually by the execution of a programmed output instruction. The character is converted into the asynchronous serial format by the interface and then transmitted along one wire to the device (with a 0 V return path provided by another wire). The interface within the device converts the serial format back to parallel form for internal use. A single character sent from the device is converted into asynchronous serial format by the device interface and transmitted along another wire to the system interface. The system interface converts the serial form back to parallel form which is usually read under programmed control.

From a programmer's point of view, it does not matter whether a parallel or serial interface is employed; it is just a means of transmitting the data between the device and the system. Clearly the parallel method should be faster than the serial method and, for high-speed devices, a parallel interface may be mandatory.

The data bits are usually encoded in 7-bit ASCII code shown in Chapter 1, Table 1.4. A parity bit is attached, making an 8-bit word. The asynchronous serial transmission format for the transmission of the ASCII code for the letter R (1010010) with even parity and one stop bit is shown in Fig. 9.5. The least significant bit is sent after the start bit. Speeds of transmission may be typically 9600 bits/sec for video terminals which are usually connected to the system via an asynchronous serial interface. At 9600 bits/sec, 960 characters could be transmitted in one second, assuming one start bit, eight data bits, one stop bit and no delay between character transmissions. One stop bit is widely used except for very slow mechanical devices and transmission rates (usually only for the obsolete printing terminal known as the Teletype operating at 110 bits/sec, i.e. 10 characters/sec with two stop bits). Sometimes the term *baud* is used to mean bits/sec. Strictly the baud rate is the number of pieces of information per second.

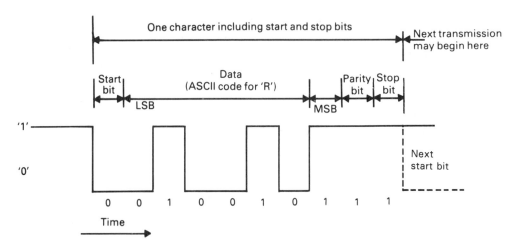

Figure 9.5 Asynchronous serial transmission format

The electrical connection between the device and the serial interface usually conforms to a standard known as RS232C/V24. In this standard, a logic 0 is represented by a voltage greater than $+3$ V (typically between $+5$ V and $+15$ V) and a logic 1 is represented by a voltage less than -3 V (typically between -5 V and -15 V). By not having 0 V to represent either level, an unconnected line can be differentiated from a connected line. The normal quiescent state with no information being transmitted is that of a logic 1. The RS232C standard not only specifies the voltages to be used but also connectors, allocation of pins on connectors and definition of signals. This enables all RS232C asynchronous serial interfaces to be compatible and peripherals with RS232C interfaces to be interchangeable electrically. Table 9.1 lists the signals and the pins numbers on the RS232C 25-way connector [2]. On simple systems, only pins 2, 3 and 7 are used for transmitted data, received data and the earth return respectively.

Special integrated circuit parts known as *universal asynchronous receiver/transmitters* (UARTs) are available to convert the parallel data as would be handled by the processor and memories to serial data in the described asynchronous format, and vice versa. These parts can be considered as having two internal sections, a transmitter to convert parallel data presented to it into asynchronous serial data, and a receiver to accept asynchronous serial data and convert this to parallel data. The transmitter inserts the start, stop and parity bits prior to transmission and the receiver checks the format and parity of the received data. The transmitter and receiver can operate simultaneously. UARTs are available to suit particular microprocessors. (These parts are also known as *asynchronous communications interface adapters*, ACIAs, or *asynchronous communications elements*, ACEs.) The serial output of a UART is converted from TTL levels to RS232C levels using an RS232C driver, and an RS232C receiver is used to convert RS232C levels to TTL levels for the UART.

Table 9.1 RS 232C signals

Contact	Description	Contact	Description
1	Protective earth	13	Secondary CTS
2	Transmitted data	14	Secondary transmitted data
3	Received data	15	Transmitter signal element timing
4	Request to send (RTS)	16	Secondary received data
5	Clear to send (CTS)	17	Received signal element timing
6	Data set ready	18	Unassigned
7	Signal earth	19	Secondary RTS
8	Received line signal detector	20	Data terminal ready
	(RLSD)	21	Signal quality detector
9	Unassigned	22	Ring indicator
10	Unassigned	23	Data signaling-rake selector
11	Unassigned	24	External transmitter clock
12	Secondary RLSD	25	Unassigned

In a UART designed for microprocessor applications, options for the number of stop bits (1, $1\frac{1}{2}$ or 2), odd, even or no parity and size of the data word are set by loading internal registers of the UART under program control. The transmitting and receiving data rates are governed either by an external oscillator or internal oscillator, operating at some multiple of the data rate. Frequently, the data rate can be modified under program control. An internal status register is provided which can be read under program control. The contents of the status register indicate the readiness to transmit and receive data and any errors.

Dual asynchronous receiver/transmitter (DART) components are available consisting of two independent receiver/transmitters (port A and port B) as shown

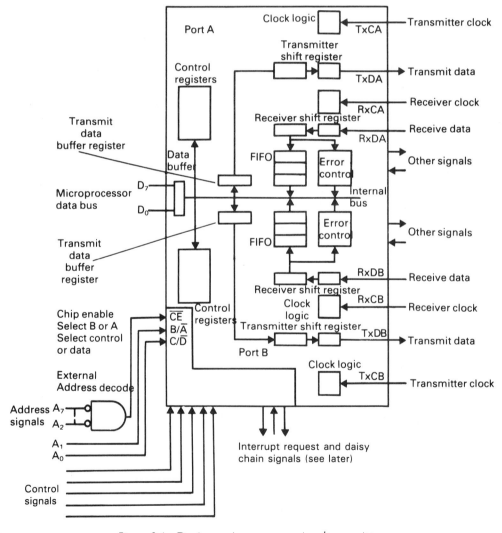

Figure 9.6 Dual asynchronous receiver/transmitter

in Fig. 9.6. One port of the DART might be used for a user terminal, and the other port might be used for a printer (if connected via an asynchronous serial method). The receiver section of each port incorporates a three-stage, first-in first-out buffer in addition to a holding buffer, which allows up to four characters to be received in succession and stored awaiting the processor to read the first character. As with the PIOs, control registers must be set up prior to using a port for data transfers. The address decode is similar to that of the PIO, having B/A port select and C/D (control/data) select inputs.

General-purpose UART parts exist for microprocessor and non-microprocessor applications. The data format of the general-purpose UART is not set under program control but by applying the appropriate logic levels to inputs of the UART. A general-purpose UART is shown in Fig. 9.7. In this UART, there are three strobe inputs, one to read data from the UART, one to write data to the UART, and one to enable separate three-state status outputs. The status outputs form a status word and can be connected directly to the data bus. The external address decode circuitry generates each of the three strobe signals when the corresponding machine instruction is executed. The data format can be altered by using switches as shown. The particular advantage of the general-purpose UART is that the switches provide a convenient manual means of selecting the data format.

(b) Synchronous serial interface

In *synchronous serial transmission*, a block of characters is transmitted one bit at a time without start or stop bits. This technique is used when the time of transmission is important as it does not carry the overhead of two or three non-data bits on each character and consequently is 20% or 27% (2/10 or 3/11) quicker for the same bit rate. The actual rate at which data is sent is reduced slightly because it is necessary to insert extra 'synchronization' characters in the transmission for the receiving circuitry to accept the data correctly. Various formats are possible. One is to insert three 'sync' characters at the beginning and at the end of the transmission and periodically between data characters during the transmission. Naturally, these 'sync' characters must not be valid data characters otherwise they would be mistaken for data. In ASCII transmissions, the control code 0010110 (SYN) can be used.

As with asynchronous serial transmission, there are LSI parts for implementing synchronous serial interfaces, which are known as *universal synchronous/asynchronous receiver and transmitters*, USARTs. As the name suggests, such parts can be programmed for either synchronous or asynchronous transmission. Microprocessor parts may be called *serial input/output* parts, SIOs (cf. PIOs) or *programmable communications interface* parts.

9.2.3 Analog interface

Digitally represented quantities can vary only in discrete steps, i.e. the smallest difference between two values is given by the least significant bit. Although

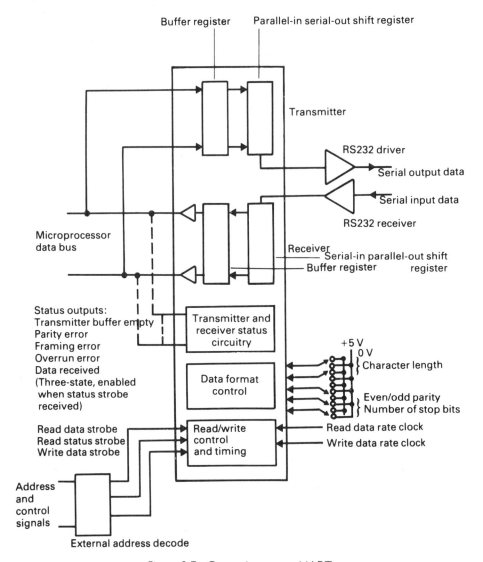

Figure 9.7   General-purpose UART

microprocessor systems, as all computer systems, are inherently digital and operate on digital quantities, there are instances when inputs and outputs are not digital in nature, but are totally variable quantities such as continuously variable voltages. Such quantities are known as *analog* quantities.

For every digital number, there must be a corresponding nominal voltage (assuming the analogy quantity is a voltage). If the binary number is an unsigned binary number with n digits, the range of numbers is from 0 to $2^n - 1$. Each of the distinct numbers is equivalent to one analog voltage. The number 0 will correspond to the minimum voltage, usually 0 V, and the maximum number, $2^n - 1$, will correspond to the maximum voltage, and there are 2^n increments.

If the binary number is a signed number using the 2's complement representation, generally negative and positive numbers correspond to negative and positive voltages respectively. The maximum negative number that can be represented in binary is -2^{n-1} which would generally correspond to maximum negative voltage. The maximum positive voltage corresponds to the maximum positive number $2^{n-1} - 1$. Again there are 2^n increments. Notice that the maximum negative number is one greater in magnitude than the maximum positive number.

An *analog output interface* is one which generates analog quantities, usually voltages, which are proportional to the digital numbers transferred to the interface. Applications for such interfaces include connections to variable speed motors and variable position valves for computer control of industrial plant. An *analog input interface* is one which accepts analog quantities, again usually voltages, and converts these to proportional digital values which can be transferred to the system by program control or otherwise. Applications for such interfaces include connection to measuring equipment.

The circuit to translate a digital quantity to its equivalent voltage or current is known as a *digital-to-analog converter* (*D/A converter* or *DAC*), and the circuit for the reverse process of translating a voltage or current to the equivalent digital quantity is known as an *analog-to-digital converter* (*A/D converter* or *ADC*). The electrical methods of achieving D/A conversion are not considered here; the reader is referred to texts on electronic circuits for details. The most common method of A/D conversion in microprocessor systems is the *successive approximation method*.

Notice that because the analog voltage of an input can take on any value within the allowable range, this range must be divided into subranges, one for each binary value. All the voltages within each subrange will convert to the same binary value. Typically each subrange extends from $\frac{1}{2}$ LSB (least significant bit) below the nominal value to $\frac{1}{2}$ LSB above the nominal value. A generated analog output will nominally be the exact equivalent of the binary input. In practice, some variation is present and allowable but not to extend beyond $\pm\frac{1}{2}$ LSB.

The outputs of the A/D converter are presented to the system data bus in parallel form via a parallel input interface, and the system data bus is presented to a D/A converter via a parallel output interface as shown in Fig. 9.8. Programmed input/output is commonly used to transfer data to a D/A converter and from an A/D converter. D/A conversion to produce an analog signal typically requires 1 to 10 μs depending upon the *settling time* of the converter. A/D conversion usually takes longer than D/A conversion. After an output instruction is issued to a D/A interface, it will be some time before the required voltage is generated, and similarly when an input instruction is issued to an A/D interface, it will be some time before the digital result is available. These factors are usually accommodated in a programmed input/output environment by the use of a status register whose contents hold single-bit flags indicating when the conversion is complete.

The number of bits in a converter is chosen to provide the required accuracy. Integrated circuit D/A and A/D converters are readily available with 8, 10 and 12

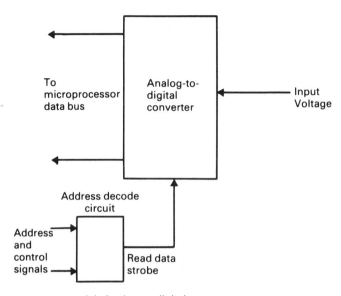

(a) Analog-to-digital converter

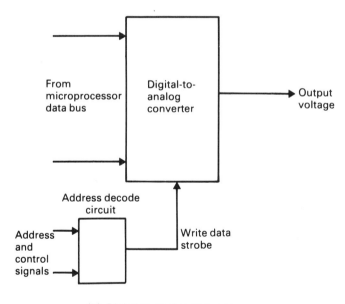

(b) Digital-to-analog converter

Figure 9.8   Analog/digital and digital/analog converters

bits. An 8-bit converter would suit an 8-bit microprocessor system if the converter is of sufficient accuracy (say $\pm\frac{1}{2}$ LSB or $\pm 0.2\%$). Converters can be designed with 14 and even 16 bits, but with increasing numbers of bits, increments in voltage steps become smaller and become difficult to distinguish from unwanted electrical noise in the system. For an 8-bit system, the data would need to be transferred in two parts for converters having 9 to 16 bits. Generally, the conversion becomes slower as more bits are provided in the converter.

In the above, we have assumed that the analog input has remained constant while the conversion is taking place. If the input varies, the conversion may not be performed correctly. Often, there is a maximum rate of change of the input signal for the converter to function correctly, and hence the corresponding maximum input frequency can be calculated (see Problem 9.8). To convert higher-frequency signals, an additional circuit known as a *sample and hold circuit* is inserted before the A/D converter. The sample and hold circuit accepts the analog input signal under program control and subsequently holds the signal constant at the output of the circuit for a period required to perform the conversion.

Finally, to prevent loss of information in the sampling process, it is necessary to perform the sampling at a frequency at least twice the greatest frequency within the sampled signal (Shannon's sampling theorem). Generally, a low pass filter is inserted to attenuate frequencies above those of interest and then the signal is sampled at greater than twice the maximum frequency of interest.

9.3 Interrupts

9.3.1 Mechanism

We have described the programmed input/output approach as one involving the use of machine instructions to cause data transfer between processor registers (or memory) and input/output devices, and one which usually necessitates a status check before the transfer. We have shown the status check in a loop of instructions which are continuously repeated while waiting for the device to become ready. If we wished to execute another program while waiting for the device to become ready, we could insert status check instructions at various places in the program and at a sufficient frequency to ensure no new input data is lost (if transferring data from an input device) or the required output rate is achieved (if transferring data to an output device).

An alternative method is the *interrupt mechanism*, so called because the device or input/output circuit interrupts the normal program execution when it is ready, rather than waiting to be serviced. This interruption is done using special signals between the processor and the input/output interface. The two basic signals necessary to implement an interrupt scheme are shown in Fig. 9.9(a), namely an *interrupt request* signal from the interrupting device to the processor and an *interrupt acknowledge* signal from the processor to the device. The interrupt request signal is generated by the device interface when it is ready either to receive data or

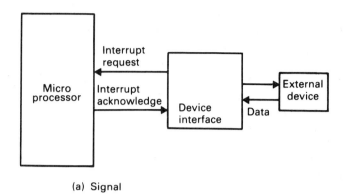

(a) Signal

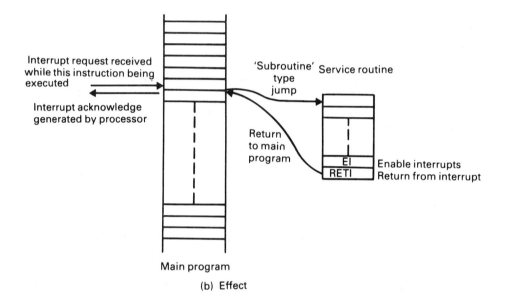

(b) Effect

Figure 9.9 Interrupt mechanism

to part with new data. The interrupt acknowledge signal is generated by the processor when it is willing to respond to the interrupt.

For example, if the interrupt mechanism is used in a keyboard interface, when a key is pressed, input data is produced and transmitted to the interface. Subsequently, the data is ready to be accepted by the processor. An interrupt request signal is generated by the interface and sent to the processor. The processor will accept an interrupt usually at the end of the execution of the current instruction and will then act in a prescribed manner. (The precise time that the interrupt acknowledge is issued and the moment the processor will act in other ways depends upon the processor.)

The basic action that must take place once the interrupt has been accepted by the processor is to provide a mechanism to cause the execution of a routine performing relevant actions associated with the interrupting device. Typically, the routine will transfer data to or from the interrupting device and is known as a *service routine* as it services the interrupt device. In all cases, when the processor accepts the interrupt request, it automatically stores the address of the instruction it would have next executed (the *return address*) on the stack and then executes the service routine. After the service routine has been executed, control is returned to the program being executed before the interrupt occurred by the use of an *interrupt return* instruction, sited at the end of the service routine in Fig. 9.9(b). The return-from-interrupt instruction (RETI) retrieves the return address from the stack for the jump back to the main program.

The process can be compared to a subroutine call, except that the jump is caused by an asynchronous hardware event. In the scheme shown, interrupts are automatically disabled immediately an interrupt is received, and must be enabled as required by a machine instruction (given in Fig. 9.9 as the enable interrupt instruction, EI). The interrupt enable instruction only takes effect after the next instruction, which allows it to be placed before the return instruction. As with a subroutine call, interrupts can cause nested routines to be executed which would occur should interrupts be enabled during the body of the service program and further interrupts occur before the return to the main program.

The interrupt mechanism is particularly suitable if the input/output device or circuitry external to the processor is ready at a time which is indeterminate and not synchronized with the processor. It would usually be at a time that the processor is performing other duties. The interrupt scheme is also especially suitable in a multi-programming environment (one which interleaves the execution of several logically separate programs). Though the interrupt scheme is described for external devices, it can be used for internal hardware conditions of the processor, for example a particular arithmetic overflow condition.

9.3.2 Finding the interrupt service routine

The interrupt acknowledge sequence is generally accompanied by one of several additional mechanisms which cause the processor to perform a specified interrupt service routine. A simple mechanism is one which creates an unconditional jump to a known memory location. The jump address may be fixed by the design of the processor. Several interrupt request inputs may be provided for more than one device, each with a different jump address.

A more flexible mechanism is the *vectored interrupt mechanism*. Here the address of the service routine (the jump address) is provided to the processor in some manner. It can be done by using a defined memory location to hold the service routine address (i.e. memory indirect addressing).

In another vector method, the device itself provides the service routine address (vector) along the data lines when requested by the processor. The implementation of this interrupt scheme could use three-state gates at the device interface with the processor bus reading the data lines. The inputs of the gates can be connected permanently to a logic 1 or logic 0 according to the required vector address, as shown in Fig. 9.10. The outputs are brought out of high impedance into two-state by the interrupt acknowledge signal together with the device request being activated. Then the data is read automatically by the processor. (Multiple interrupting devices require additional circuitry and signals to identify the jump address; see section 9.3.3.)

For an 8-bit vector, the service address would be limited to the first 256 locations. Additional jump instructions can be placed here. As such instructions are multi-byte instructions, the number of usable service addresses would be reduced. To avoid this problem, the 8-bit address can be multiplied by, say, four (i.e. two extra least significant 0's are added) by the processor before being used as the service address. The scheme can be further refined by concatenating the address sent by the device with the contents of a processor register before being used. Rather than sending the interrupt service address, other information could be sent, for example the input/output address of the device.

Finally, the processor can be designed to use the vector sent by the device to identify a memory location which holds the start address of the service routine (for example the 68000 microprocessor). Upon receipt of the vector, the address is fetched from memory and a jump operation to the service routine occurs automatically.

9.3.3 Multiple interrupting devices

If more than one interrupt device is to be connected to the system, an interrupt request line can be provided by the processor for each device (but see later). It is

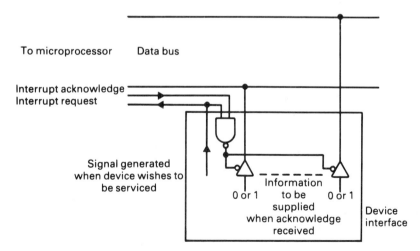

Figure 9.10   Device-supplied interrupt information scheme

possible for two or more devices to request service simultaneously, or a second and subsequent devices to request service while the first is being serviced. These situations can usually be accommodated in the hardware after assigning a particular level of priority to each device. Each device is given a *priority number*. Frequently, the lower the priority number, the higher the priority of the device. The interrupt device with the lowest priority number (highest priority) is accepted first. Those interrupts with the same priority will be accepted according to the time they are received. Actual simultaneous requests are resolved by the hardware, which makes a choice. Once a device interrupt is accepted, all other device interrupts at the same or lower priority that may occur are ignored by the processor automatically resetting a processor interrupt enable flag, unless subsequently altered by the programmer. There are various ways by which the priority can be established.

(a) Polled interrupts

The *polled interrupt* method is perhaps the simplest method of handling multiple devices with different or the same priorities. In the polled method, a single interrupt request is generated from the group of possible interrupting devices by, say, a single wired-OR (open-collector) interrupt request signal. The acknowledge sequence involves interrogating each device in turn by programmed instructions to determine whether the device has an interrupt request outstanding. One possible hardware implementation of this method is to provide one addressable interrupt request flag in each device interface capable of an interrupt request. Each flag is set if an interrupt is requested. The flags are read under program control in priority order, the highest-priority device first. The process of reading a flag resets it. An alternative scheme is to have a centralized interrupt request register with bits set in this register if the appropriate interrupts are requested. The least significant bit could be assigned the lowest-priority request and the most significant bit the highest-priority request. A program sequence can identify the interrupt request and its priority.

(b) Daisy chaining interrupt signals

An interrupt request/acknowledge pair of signals can be used with more than one device by using a *daisy chain* method. In the daisy chain method, one of the signals is passed through all the devices in a sequence dictated by the priority of the devices. A system of a daisy chained acknowledge signal and a common wired-OR request signal is shown in Fig. 9.11. The highest-priority device is closest to the processor and the lowest-priority device is farthest away. When a request is generated by a device, the request is received by the processor directly. The processor generates an acknowledge signal which is sent to the first device on the daisy chain. This device, if not the interrupting device, passes the acknowledge signal on to the next device. The process continues until the device causing the interrupt is reached. This device prevents the signal passing any further and responds accordingly. If more than one device generates an interrupt signal, the highest-priority device obtains the acknowledge signal first and is selected. After this device has been serviced, the next

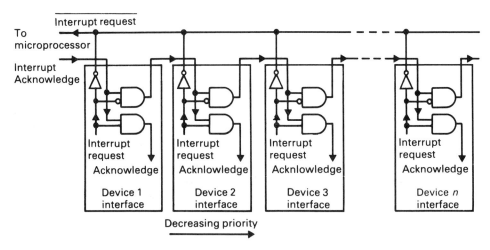

Figure 9.11 Interrupt priority scheme using daisy chained interrupt acknowledge signals

device receives the acknowledge signal and is serviced. The device-supplied vector scheme can be used to cause the correct service routine to be selected in each case.

The system with a daisy chained request signal and a common acknowledge signal has the lowest-priority device closest to the processor and the highest-priority device farthest away. When a device makes a request, the request is passed along the daisy chain and reaches the processor. The processor issues an acknowledge signal which is received by all devices. The highest-priority device making a request has an inactive request daisy chain input (say a logic 0) and an active daisy chain request output (say a logic 1). This condition causes the device to respond to the acknowledge signal. Lower priority devices issuing requests will have both daisy chain request input and output lines active (a logic 1), which inhibits the requesting device from responding to the acknowledge.

(c) Interrupt mask register

Added flexibility and speed can be incorporated into priority schemes by selectively enabling certain, usually higher-priority, devices immediately after a request has been accepted. This is often done by using an interrupt mask register arranged as shown in Fig. 9.12. The interrupt requests accepted are those with the corresponding mask register bit set. This scheme is an extension of a single interrupt enable flag mentioned previously which causes all interrupts to be accepted.

(d) Interrupt controllers

An interrupt controller is a device for handling multiple interrupts outside the processor. A typical device can support up to eight randomly occurring interrupts, and devices can be cascaded to provide more inputs. Devices normally have the ability to set priority levels for inputs and various programmable options are

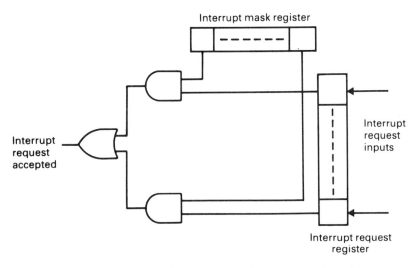

Figure 9.12   Interrupt scheme using an interrupt mask register

provided, including programmable interrupt vectors. Apart from assigning a fixed priority to inputs, interrupt controllers have the ability to assign *rotating priority*, as shown in Fig. 9.13. With rotating priority, the inputs can be considered as forming a ring. When an interrupt is received and acknowledged, the input immediately assumes the lowest priority, and those following it in the ring assume linearly increasing higher priority, with the highest priority assigned to the input immediately behind the current one. When another request is received, the same procedure is taken with this input assigned the lowest priority, and all other inputs reassigned. This scheme prevents any one input from taking a permanent or dominant portion of the available time and all inputs have a chance of being

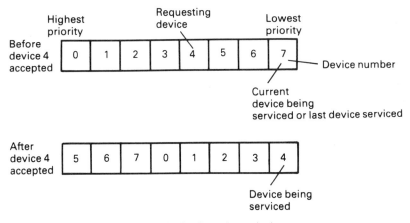

Figure 9.13   Rotating priority

serviced. The maximum time that any one input request need wait is that given by seven other service cycles if there are eight inputs.

Interrupt inputs can generally be one of two types, *level-triggered* or *edge-triggered*. With level-triggered inputs, the presence of a logic state, say a 1, causes an interrupt request to be generated and the request will remain as long as the input is activated. Consequently, if after the first interrupt acknowledge cycle is complete and the input is still activated, a second request is generated. This will continue until the input is deactivated, which may or may not be a desirable feature depending upon the application. For example, repetitive interrupts could be used to continually re-execute a service routine until the interrupt is released. It also allows for wired-OR interrupt requests. In edge-triggering, interrupts are activated by a logic transition, say a 1 to a 0 transition, and cannot be reactivated until the input returns to a 1 and another transition to a 0 occurs.

9.4 Direct memory access (DMA)

9.4.1 Mechanism

In programmed input/output, the processor initiates the data transfer to or from the input/output device, and takes full control of the transfer. There are two major disadvantages with this approach. Firstly, the processor cannot generally do any other meaningful processing while the data transfer is taking place. Secondly, the speed of transfer is limited by the speed of executing machine instructions. For multiple transfers, several machine instructions normally need to be executed between each data transfer to load the data into memory if input, or to read data from memory if output. These disadvantages can be overcome by the direct memory access (DMA) mechanism. The DMA mechanism uses additional hardware to take full control of the multiple transfers after initial activation by the processor.

The general scheme is shown in Fig. 9.14. A part known as a *DMA controller* is instructed by the processor to transfer a consecutive sequence of memory locations to the input/output device or vice versa. Once so instructed, the DMA controller uses the microprocessor bus to transfer data at a rate dictated by the input/output device without any further control from the processor. The mechanism requires that before the transfer command is received by the DMA controller, the controller is given the address of the starting location in memory (and possibly in the input/output device) and the number of transfers. This is done by loading internal registers of the controller, usually under program control. Once loaded, the DMA controller is allowed to take over the bus and initiate the first and subsequent data transfers. After the first transfer has taken place, the DMA controller increments the stored address(es) and the next transfer is initiated. The process continues until the number of transfers is reached as specified. Then, the DMA controller signals the processor that the transfers have been completed.

Notice that while the DMA transfer is occurring on the bus, the processor cannot use the bus. Similarly, if the processor is using the bus when the DMA

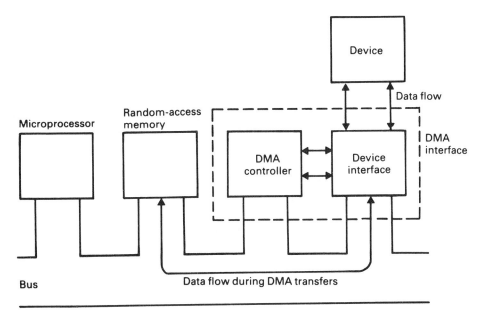

Figure 9.14   Direct memory access system

controller requires it, the controller must wait until the processor has finished using the bus. The processor then relinquishes control of the bus to the DMA controller and must then wait for the bus to be free again. Normally the processor will be executing a program while the DMA transfer mechanism is in progress and the DMA controller will 'steal' processor cycles to use the bus at intervals (*cycle stealing*). The effect on the processor is to slow its execution, by an amount dependent upon the frequency of the cycles stolen.

There are variations on this general approach. For example, the set-up addresses and count may be held in memory and the controller may be sufficiently intelligent to fetch them. The controller may have additional modes, for example a *scan* mode in which data is taken from the source, but rather than being transferred to the destination, the data is compared with the contents of a previously loaded DMA register. If a match is found, the DMA controller signals the processor accordingly. An alternative scan mode may signal the processor when a match is not found. This latter mode could be useful in testing memory, by loading a block memory location with the same value as the internal DMA register. Any discrepancy in this scan would indicate an error in the memory circuits.

The DMA mechanism is particularly applicable to input/output devices such as magnetic disk memory units as the transfer of information between the central system and these devices requires that a block of data is transferred as an uninterrupted stream of bytes at a speed dictated by the speed of revolution of the disk. In this case, the device interface shown in Fig. 9.14 typically incorporates a special-purpose device controller (e.g. a floppy disk controller) which generates the required signals for the disk unit, and works in conjunction with a general-purpose DMA controller.

9.4.2 Processor-DMA controller signals

There are two or three special signals between the processor and the DMA controller to handle the mechanism, in addition to the normal data and address signals. In particular, it is necessary that at any instant, only one device is controlling the bus, either the processor or the DMA controller. This leads to a pair of *handshaking* signals between the two devices, one to the processor from the DMA controller to request the use of the bus and one from the processor to the DMA controller granting use of the bus. DMA requests for the bus are presented for each data transfer. Each request must be granted quickly when the DMA mechanism is used with time-critical devices such magnetic disk memory units.

Suppose the two signals to transfer the control of the bus are called:

$\overline{\text{BUSRQ}}$ Bus request, for the requesting device to the processor
$\overline{\text{BUSAK}}$ Bus acknowledge from the processor to the device

A bus request will be accepted only at the end of a machine cycle and the acknowledge issued then. At the same time as the acknowledge is issued, the processor releases the bus (into tri-state). The timing is shown in Fig. 9.15. Whenever $\overline{\text{BUSRQ}}$ is brought low, this is only noticed by the processor on the rising edge of the last clock cycle of a read/write cycle, and the acknowledge signal, $\overline{\text{BUSAK}}$, is brought low on the rising edge of the next clock cycle when the bus is released into tri-state. The DMA controller may then use the bus and the bus control signals

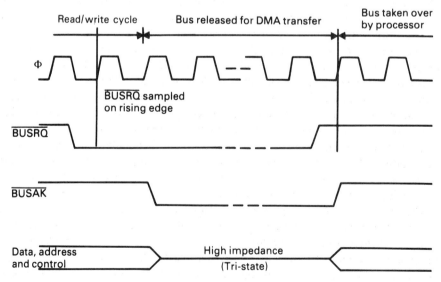

Figure 9.15 Bus request/acknowledge cycle

for data transfers. The bus is available for any duration. The DMA controller indicates that it has finished with the bus by returning $\overline{BUSRQ}$ to a high level. This is recognized by the processor on the rising edge of the next clock cycle, and returns $\overline{BUSAK}$ to a high level. At the same time the bus is taken over by the processor.

References

1. *MOSTEK Microcomputer Components Data Book*, Carrollton, TX: Mostek, 1979.
2. Wilkinson, B., and D. Horrocks, *Computer Peripherals*, London: Hodder and Stoughton, 1980.

Problems

9.1 Is it possible to use the same input/output addresses for both input and output? Explain.

9.2 A microprocessor-based combinational lock on a safe employs four switches of the parallel input interface shown in Fig. 9.1 to enter the combination to open the safe. The lock itself is controlled by bit 1 of a parallel output interface shown in Fig. 9.2. The lock is to open only after the following sequence has been entered:

> All switches are set in the open position
> Switch 0 is set in the closed position
> Switch 0 is set in the open position
> Switch 3 is set in the closed position
> Switch 2 is set in the closed position
> Switch 2 is set in the open position
> Switch 3 is set in the open position.

Any other sequence will set an alarm using bit 2 of the output interface. Design a suitable interface decode circuitry allocating addresses to the input and output interfaces, and write a suitable control program for the lock (for a microprocessor of your choice).

9.3 Identify the asynchronous serial input/output interface parts available for a microprocessor of your choice (by looking through manufacturers' catalogues) and design suitable decode circuitry to match the processor bus. Write a suitable program to read data from the serial input and output characters back to the output (i.e. echoplexing).

9.4 Design suitable address decode logic for the general-purpose UART shown in Fig. 9.7, assigning port address 25 for data and port address 26 for the status register (your choice of processor).

9.5 Determine the maximum negative and maximum positive voltages in a 2's complement 8-bit A/D converter if the incremental steps are 10 mV.

9.6 If the input to an n-bit A/D converter must not change by more than $\frac{1}{2}$ LSB, determine an expression for the maximum input signal frequency.

9.7 Sketch the logic required to pass an interrupt request signal through interrupt devices in a daisy chained request and common acknowledge interrupt scheme.

9.8 Assuming that the interrupt mask register shown in Fig. 9.12 is used in a system with the mask register and the request register given input/output addresses, write a program to implement the rotating priority service policy (Fig. 9.13). Choose any microprocessor.

10 Memory Management

10.1 Main-secondary memory management

10.1.1 Memory management schemes

In a computer system, the memory is often composed of a main memory and a secondary memory (backing store). In a microprocessor system, the main memory is always semiconductor memory and the secondary memory is usually disk memory. This memory hierarchy needs schemes to arrange that the required information is in the main memory when it is to be read or altered. The general term for the schemes is known as *memory management*.

The simplest memory management method is to employ *overlaying*, in which programs or sections of programs are transferred into main memory as required, overwriting existing programs. Each transfer is specifically programmed. Overlaying is used in microprocessor systems, particularly small floppy disk based systems. For example, one of the first widely used microprocessor operating systems,† CP/M [1], and similar subsequent operating systems such as MS-DOS, generally employ overlaying. A large software package which could not reside in the main memory in a complete form because of the limited available main memory would be divided into a main file and one or more overlay files. The overlay files would be called from within the main file, and would typically overwrite the main file when transferred into the main memory. This process would be repeated with other files as they were required. It is necessary to copy files in the disk memory before they become overwritten if true copies are not already present on the disk. The overlay method normally places a heavy burden on the programmer, since interaction between sections in different overlays can cause continual and excessive disk transfers ('disk thrashing') and errors can be very difficult to locate.

A better approach is to have an automatic process of transferring blocks of words into and out of the main memory, which relieves the burden of programming transfers specifically, and preferably takes into account the likely blocks required in the near future, to limit disk thrashing. Automatic transfer mechanisms were

---

† An operating system is the controlling program of a computer system.

devised for computers well before microprocessors were developed, and rely on having two addresses associated with each word stored, the actual address used by the memory units and another address which is produced by the processor when executing the user programs. A translation mechanism is provided in hardware (with software back-up support) to perform the translation of program addresses into the actual addresses used in the memory units. Each program address has a corresponding memory address somewhere in the memory system but the memory address may change as programs are transferred into and out of the memories, which allows programs to be transferred automatically without alteration of program addresses. There are two basic schemes, namely:

 (i) Paging system
(ii) Segmented system.

Firstly we will consider the paging system.

10.1.2 Paging system

In a paging system, the actual address in memory is called a *real* address and the program address is called a *virtual* address. The term *virtual (paged) memory system* is used to describe the system. The memory space is divided into blocks of equal size, typically 128 words, 256 words, 512 words or 1024 words. Each block is called a *page*. An address is composed of a page number and a line number. The virtual and real addresses have the same line number but a translation is necessary to convert a virtual page number to a real page number. Page numbers are concatenated with the line number to form the complete address. A hardware mechanism is provided to translate the virtual page number into the real page number. The hardware mechanism operates only on pages in the main memory. If the required real page number is not found in the translation mechanism, a software replacement algorithm (method) must be executed to find the required page in secondary memory, to transfer this page into the main memory, and to choose the best existing page to be transferred back into secondary memory providing space for the new page.

Figure 10.1 shows how the virtual and real pages might be allocated. In this example, each page contains 512 words. There are 8 pages in the main memory and 24 pages in the secondary memory; in a real system, there would be many more pages in each memory, but a small number is chosen here to clarify the assignment of addresses. The main page address range is from 0 to 7 inclusive, and the secondary memory page address page is from 8 to 31 inclusive.

Both the real and virtual addresses are divided into two fields, a page field and a line (within a page) field. Since there are 512 words in a page, both line fields contain 9 bits. The page field of the real address contains 5 bits to enable any of 32 pages to be specified. The virtual page field can have a different number of bits. In our example the virtual page field has the same number of bits as the real page field, and hence there are 32 possible virtual pages.

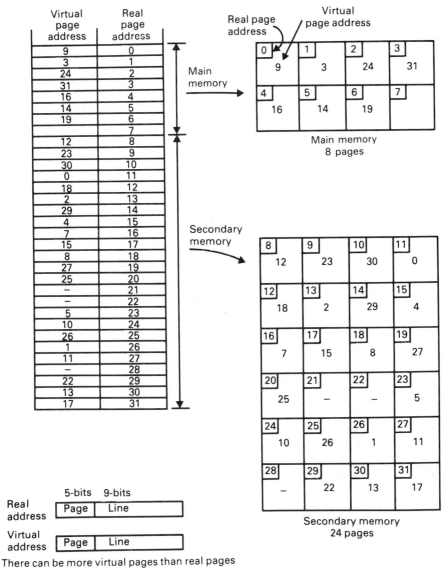

There can be more virtual pages than real pages

Figure 10.1 Real and virtual addresses in a paged system

In an assignment of virtual pages to real pages shown in Fig. 10.1, some virtual pages are unassigned (not used). Real page 7, the last page in the main memory is currently free. Suppose virtual page 3 is requested by the processor. First, hardware is activated to check whether the page is in the main memory. The hardware finds the page currently residing in real page 1 and the page can be referenced. However, suppose virtual page 7 is now requested by the processor. The check shows that the page is not currently residing in the main memory. Then, a software mechanism is activated to search for the location in the secondary memory. In this case, the page is found in real address 16 in the secondary memory. The page is transferred into the free (real) page 7 in the main memory, and subsequently referenced by the processor. Now the main memory is full. If a reference is made to another page in the secondary memory, an existing page in the main memory must be returned to the secondary memory before the new page is transferred into the main memory. Hence, a free page must always be maintained either in the main memory or in the secondary memory (unless a copy is always held in the secondary memory).

There are two basic hardware methods to translate the virtual page into a real page:

(i) Direct mapping
(ii) Associative mapping.

The *direct mapping* approach is shown in Fig. 10.2(a). All the real page addresses are stored in a high-speed random access memory in locations whose addresses are the virtual addresses of the associated real addresses. Consequently, a real address can be found directly from the memory.

The associative mapping approach is shown in Fig. 10.2(b). A special type of memory, is used called an *associative memory*, also called a *content addressable memory* CAM. In a content addressable memory, a location is identified by its contents rather than an assigned address. The binary word applied to the data inputs of the CAM is compared with all the stored words simultaneously by the internal logic of the device. If any word is found to be the same as the applied word, an appropriate match signal is generated by the device. CAMs are designed to operate at high speed using bipolar technology. Delays from data input to match output can be less than 30 ns, but the devices are relatively expensive.

When used for associative mapping, the content addressable memory is coupled to normal random access memory, giving two parts to the memory. If a match is found in the first part, the corresponding second part is read out. Each location in the first part stores the virtual page address and the second the corresponding real page address. When the virtual address is generated by the processor, it is compared with all the first parts simultaneously using the logic within the associative memory. If a match is found, the corresponding real address held in the second part is read out. The real address is then sent to the main memory. A *page fault* occurs whenever the page referenced is not already in the main memory.

10.1.3 Replacement algorithms

There are various replacement algorithms that can be used to select the page to remove from the main memory to make room for the incoming page.

(a) Random replacement algorithm

In the *random replacement algorithm*, pages to be taken out of the main memory are chosen in a random order. This method would not be really suitable for most

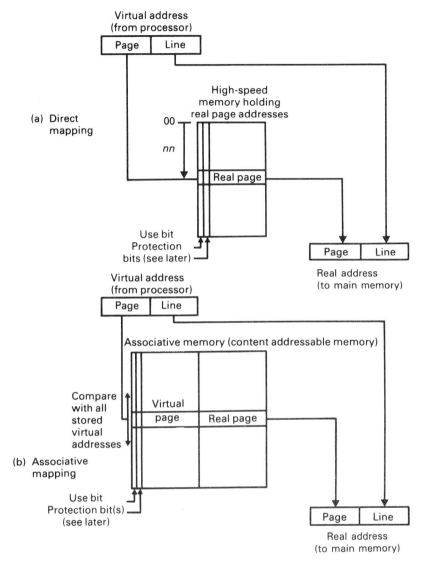

Figure 10.2   Translation of virtual addresses into real addresses in a paged system

programs which normally access locally, i.e. the next location required is usually near the last.

(b) First-in-first-out replacement algorithm

In the *first-in-first-out replacement algorithm*, the page existing in the main memory for the longest time is transferred out. A list of pages current in the main memory is maintained in a (first-in-first-out) queue. As a new entry is inserted all the entries move down one place and the last is taken out to be used for replacement.

For example, suppose the following pages are requested in the order shown:

3, 4, 3, 6, 8, 3, 7, 6, 8, 3, 2, 6

and the main memory can only hold four pages at any instant. The pages in the main memory when a page fault occurs are shown in Fig. 10.3. Initially, the main memory

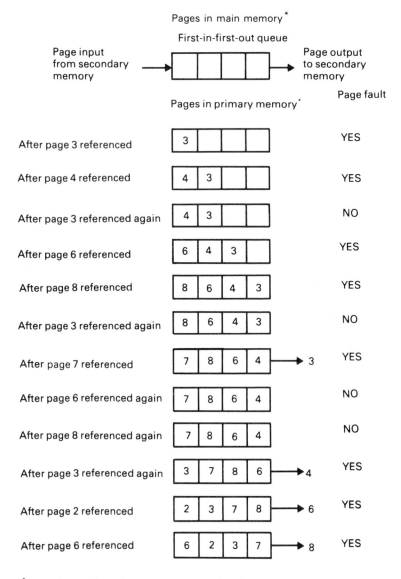

* Actual pages in main memory not reordered

Figure 10.3 Pages in main memory using first-in-first-out replacement algorithm

is empty, and page faults occur when pages are first referenced. Each time a new page is referenced, the page entries are moved one place right (conceptually, not actually). When the memory is full and a page fault occurs, the page returned to the secondary memory is the page at the rightmost end of the queue. (Free space is left in the secondary memory.) We see that with our sequence of page references, the first-in-first-out algorithm produces eight page faults.

The algorithm can be implemented using a circular list holding the page entries as shown in Fig. 10.4. A pointer indicates the current rightmost end of the queue

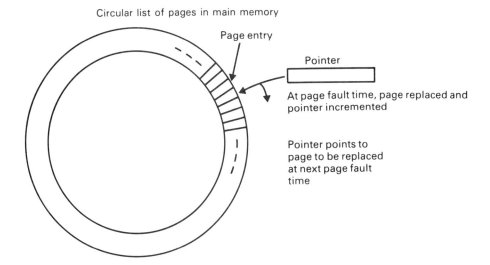

Figure 10.4   First-in-first-out replacement algorithm using a circular list

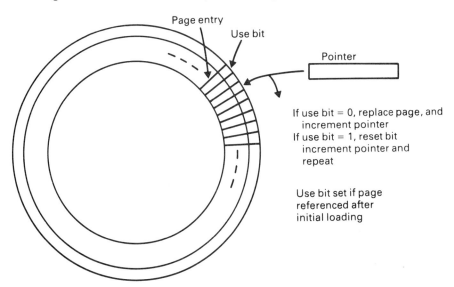

Figure 10.5   First-in-not-used-first-out replacement

and the leftmost entry of the queue is immediately before the pointed entry. At page fault time, the page replaced is that indicated by the pointer. The pointer is then incremented to point to the next entry.

The first-in-first-out algorithm can be modified to avoid unnecessary transfers by moving over pages in the queue which have been referenced (and hence are likely

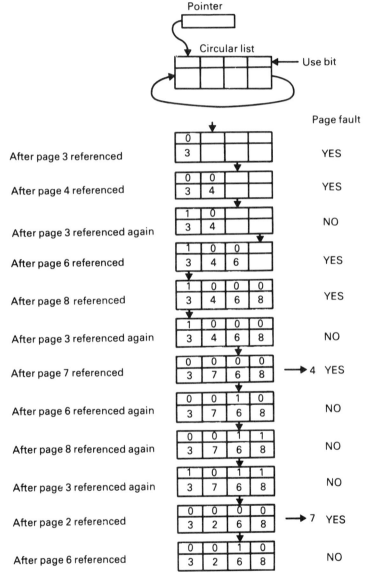

Figure 10.6 Pages in main memory using first-in-not-used-first-out replacement algorithm

to be accessed again especially if in program loops). This is known as *first-in-not-used-first-out*. It requires the addition of a *use* bit set by hardware when the page is referenced. A pointer points to a page in the circular list. When a replacement is necessary, the use bit is examined. If the use bit = 0, the page is replaced and the pointer advanced to the next page. If the use bit = 1, it is reset and the pointer advanced to the next page. This is repeated until a use bit is already reset. The corresponding page is then transferred out of the main memory and replaced with the incoming page. The pointer is then advanced one place. Whenever a page is referenced subsequently, the associated use bit is set. The bit is not set upon first loading the page. The algorithm using a circular list is shown in Fig. 10.5.

The first-in-not-used-first-out algorithm applied to the previous sequence is shown in Fig. 10.6. Here we see that there are six page faults.

(c) Least recently used (LRU) replacement algorithm

In the *least recently used replacement algorithm*, the page which has not been used for the longest time is transferred out. One implementation of the least recently used algorithm is to hold the list of pages in the main memory in the order in which they have been referenced. Whenever a reference is made, the order of the list has to be updated. This means that the page is placed at the top of the list and all the other pages are moved down one place. The algorithm applied to our sequence is shown in Fig. 10.7. Again we have six page faults. The number of page faults with each algorithm, of course, depends upon the actual sequence.

The LRU algorithm poses some practical problems for a true implementation if there are very many pages in the main memory, as would be the case in a virtual memory system. For example, a counter could be associated with each page and incremented at regular intervals. Every time a page is referenced, the associated counter is reset. Hence the counter holding the largest number identifies the least recently used page. This approach would necessitate very many counters and substantial logic and would not be feasible for a large system. Alternatively, an associative memory could be used to record the main memory pages. (It is left as an exercise to devise an associative memory solution.) Again, the associative memory would need to have substantial capacity. As associative memory is expensive, the top portion (say 16 or 32 entries) could be in an associative memory and the rest maintained by software.

The use bit of each page, if necessary for the replacement algorithm, is incorporated into the virtual address/real address hardware translation table, together with additional bits for memory protection. (Protection bits might, for example, make pages read-only or prevent a page being removed from the main memory if the page is part of an active user program in a multi-programming environment.)

The page size is typically 512 words. If a small page size is chosen, the time taken in transferring a page between the main memory and secondary memory is short and a large selection of pages from various programs can reside in the main memory. However, a small page size necessitates a large page table for any

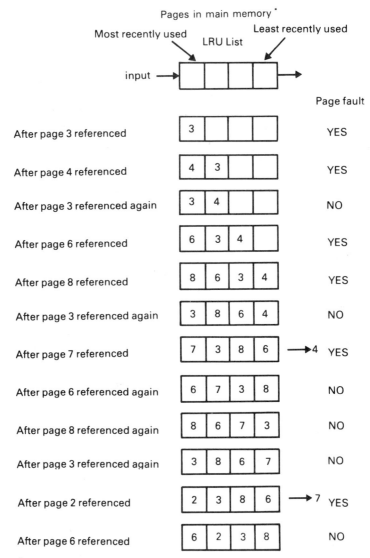

Figure 10.7   Pages in main memory using least recently used (LRU) replacement algorithm

particular main memory size, and information to link pages to programs increases. The secondary memory, if a disk memory, as normally, also constrains the page size to that of a sector or a multiple of a sector (unless additional sector buffer storage is provided to enable one page from several in a sector to be selected). Making the sector small increases the proportion of recorded information given over to sector identification on the disk. A large page size requires a small page table but the transfer time is generally longer and unused space at the end of each page is likely

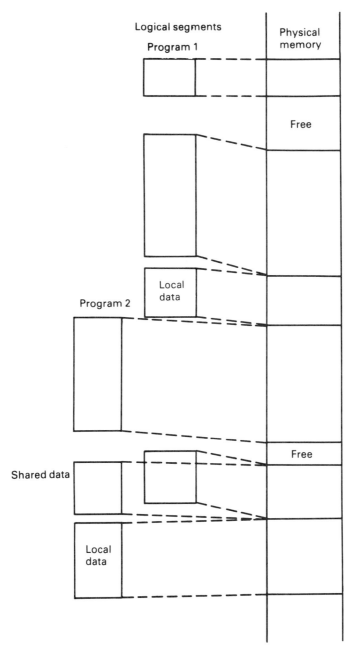

Figure 10.8 Mapping of segments onto available memory

to increase. (This is known as the *internal fragmentation*.) The number of words in each page chosen is a compromise between the various factors.

10.1.4 Segmented system

In a *segmented* system, the memory space is not divided into equal sized pages but into variable sized blocks of contiguous locations called *segments*. This approach may be better for programs and data which are naturally generated in various sizes. Segments may be allowed to overlap. Each address is composed of a segment number and a displacement within the segment (called an *offset*). Rather than concatenate the two, in a segmented scheme the segment and the offset are added together to form the read address. The term *logical* address is sometimes used in segmented systems to describe the virtual address, and the term *physical* address is used to describe the real address. Figure 10.8 shows how segments in two programs might be assigned space in the memory. Segments can be shared between different programs. Segments can also partially overlap if required.

Figure 10.9 shows the usual method of translating logical addresses into

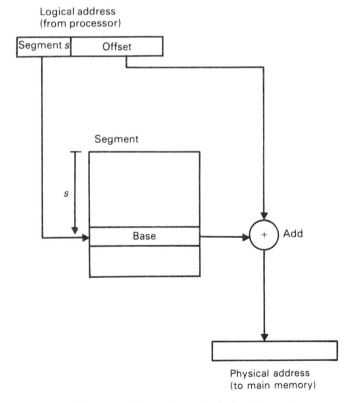

Figure 10.9 Translation of logical addresses into physical addresses in a segmented system

physical addresses. The logical address is divided into two fields, a segment number field and an offset field. The segment number field specifies the logical segment and the offset specifies the number of locations from the beginning of the segment. The logical segment field selects a physical segment from a segment table using direct mapping here. The selected location in the table holds the address of the first location in the physical memory. This address is called the *base*. The base is added to the offset to form the physical address.

The 16-bit 8086 microprocessor introduced in 1978 is perhaps the first example of a microprocessor to incorporate segmentation within the device [2]. This microprocessor contains four segment registers called the code segment register (CS), the data segment register (DS), the stack segment register (SS) and the extra segment register (ES) respectively. The address generated by the program is a 16-bit offset, without a segment number. A 16-bit offset allows segments up to 64K bytes. The particular segment is selected by context. Instruction fetch cycles always use the code segment register with the offset provided by the program counter (called instruction pointer, IP). Most data operations normally assume the use of the data register, though any register can be selected. Stack instructions always use the stack register. The extra segment is used particularly for results of string operations. The

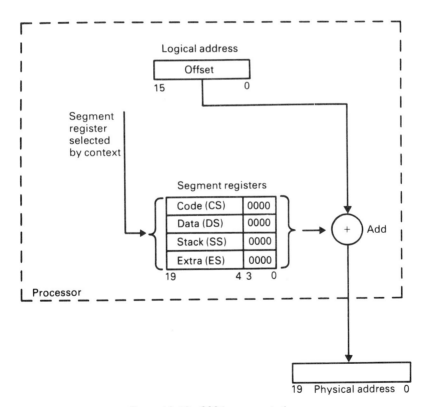

Figure 10.10 8086 segmentation

translation mechanism is shown in Fig. 10.10. The segment register has 16-bits. Four least significant 0's are added, giving a 20-bit base address, and a 20-bit physical address.

The segment table can incorporate additional information, for example use and protection bits. Protection from referencing a location beyond the end of a particular segment can be achieved by adding a segment length field in the table. Also several segment tables can be provided. A system with these features is shown in Fig. 10.11. In this system, the contents of a segment table pointer (a register) are first added to the logical segment number before accessing the segment table. The segment table holds the base together with the length of the segment, flags to enable replacement algorithms to be implemented, and memory protection flags. The length is compared with the displacement to check that a valid logical address is present. The displacement must not be greater than the length, otherwise a segment error signal is generated. The base is extracted and added to the displacement to form the full physical address. As with the paged system, all processor-generated addresses must be translated before a memory location can be accessed and hence the mechanism must operate at high speed.

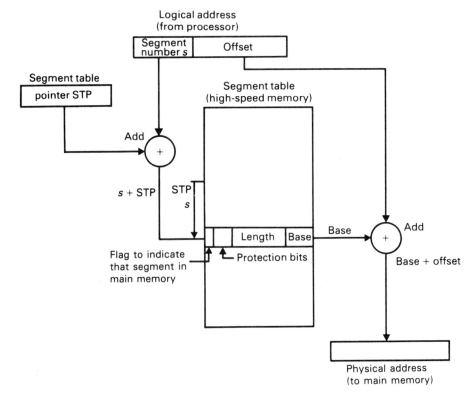

Figure 10.11 Translation of logical addresses into physical addresses in a segmented system incorporating more than one segment table

The replacement algorithm in a segmented system can be similar to the replacement algorithms in a paged system, but the algorithm needs to take the varying size of the segments into account when allocating space for new segments. Too small spaces which cannot be used should not be generated. This is known as *external fragmentation*. The *first-fit* algorithm [3] for finding space in the primary memory requires two items to be associated with each segment:

(i) Pointer to next free space, NEXT
(ii) Length of free space between segment and next segment, LENGTH

as shown in Fig. 10.12. These two items are stored at the beginning of each free space in memory. The algorithm to find a space for a segment from the secondary memory is as follows:

Step 1   Set a memory pointer, P, to select the first free space.
Step 2   If length of free space, LENGTH, is greater than incoming segment, insert segment in space, followed by LENGTH specifying remaining free space and NEXT. Alter previous NEXT to point to new free space. Leave algorithm.

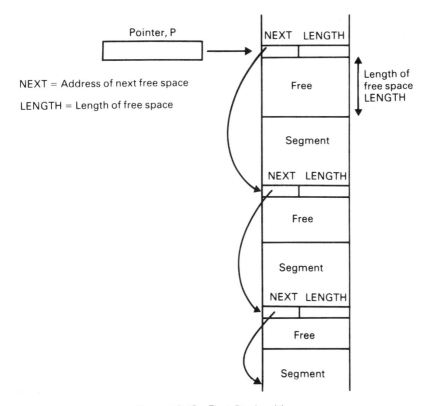

Figure 10.12 First-fit algorithm

Step 3   If length of free space is equal to the segment, as step 2 but update information relating to free space. Leave algorithm.

Step 4   If length of free space is less than segment, move to next segment and repeat step 2 or 3.

To prevent external fragmentation, step 2 can be modified to:

Step 2   If length of free space is greater than incoming segment + size of space not usable (perhaps 8–16 words), insert segment in space, alter length of free space accordingly and leave algorithm.

10.1.5 Memory management units

We now turn our attention to how a memory management scheme, either a paged memory management scheme or a segmented memory scheme, can be implemented in a computer system. We shall concentrate on a microprocessor system in particular. The hardware to implement a memory management scheme is known as a *memory management unit* (MMU). An MMU may be a processor support device or an integral part of the processor, and provides two principal functions:

(i) Memory translation
(ii) Memory protection.

As we have seen, memory address translation involves taking the address emitted from the processor, the virtual or logical address, and converting this address to a different address known as the real or physical address. The physical address is passed to the memory units. Memory protection involves stopping this translation and preventing any address or address strobe signals being passed to the memory units if there has been a violation of an accepted memory operation. For example, some areas of memory may be designated as read-only and a write operation would be an invalid operation; there are several other possible invalid operations.

Consider a segmentation system (though much is also true for a paged system). The processor provides a logical address given by a segment number together with an offset (displacement). The MMU converts this logical address into a physical address, for example as shown in Fig. 10.13. First the segment number 'points' to an MMU register holding the segment starting address, the base address. The offset address is added to this base address to obtain the physical address. The base address generally has its lower significant digits set to zero so that the lower part of the offset need only be concatenated with the address formed by the addition of the base address and the higher significant part of the offset address. In our example, the lower 8 bits of the base address are all zero.

Since every memory access requires the logical-to-physical address translation in this scheme, the translation must be very fast within the MMU. If the segment number is 7 bits, there are 128 base addresses possible. These base addresses are stored in internal MMU registers and accessed directly through the segment number. The resultant base address is added to the upper offset internally and the physical

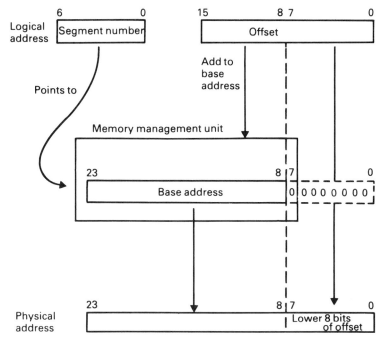

Figure 10.13 Generating a physical address using a segmented MMU

address is produced at the output of the MMU. The lower offset address need not pass through the MMU for this operation.

The second function of the MMU, that of memory protection, requires additional fields in the internal MMU memory. A limit (segment length) field is provided to enable a maximum segment size to be specified. If the offset is greater than the limit size, an error flag in the MMU error-condition register is set and the processor informed. MMU and processor status information is saved automatically to enable recovery from error conditions. Typically, any segment can be assigned as:

(i) Read-only
(ii) Execute-only
(iii) System-only.

Assigning a segment as read-only allows data to be protected from alteration. Assigning a segment as execute-only means that it can only be referenced during a fetch cycle, which prevents, for example, unauthorized copying of programs since execute-only code is unable to be read as data.

For the system-only assignment, it is necessary for the processor to have two operating modes, a normal mode which is for ordinary users and a system mode dedicated to the operating system. Generally when in the normal mode, there will be certain instructions which cannot be executed and the only method to enter the system mode is through a system call to the operating system, either intentionally or via a software or hardware interrupt, or error condition. Hence, functions such as input/output can be totally controlled by the operating system without interference from user programs.

Rather than having an 'only' assignment, it is possible to have an 'excluded' assignment, for example:

(i) CPU excluded
(ii) DMA excluded.

In CPU excluded, the segment cannot be accessed by the central processor, leaving all other possible 'bus masters' such as DMA controllers. In DMA excluded, the DMA controllers are excluded. This leaves the central processor and other bus masters, generally other processors in a multiprocessor system.

Any attempted violation of the above assignments would cause the MMU to set the appropriate error flags in the MMU error condition register and to signal the processor, generally with a special 'segment trap' signal. Information such as segment number and offset of the violation and of the current processor instruction and status information will be saved.

There may be other error conditions indicated. For example, if a segment is being used as a stack, it is convenient to know when the end of the allocated memory space is being reached before the end is actually reached. Since stacks generally grow downwards, access to, say, the first 256 locations in the segment would indicate an approach to the end of the stack. A flag may be set accordingly by the MMU which would be used to prevent a stack overflowing its memory space.

There is the possibility of multiple violations. For example, a central processor violation might occur and while this is being handled, a DMA violation might occur during an autonomous transfer. To cater for this situation, DMA violations are sensed and indicated but the status information not saved because this might overwrite status information being used by the central processor violation service routine. Similarly, if a second error condition or violation occurs while the first is being serviced, an additional 'fatal error' flag is set.

Typically two flags are associated with each logical/physical address entry in the MMU segment table to help in choosing segments for returning to the secondary memory, namely:

(i) Written flag
(ii) Accessed flag.

The written flag is set if a write operation has taken place to the segment. Thus if this flag is not set when the segment is considered for returning to the secondary memory, the transfer need not be done (assuming a copy is kept on the secondary memory when it was transferred to main memory). It is only necessary to delete the main memory copy.

The accessed flag indicates that a memory access has been made to the segment. This can be used to determine which segments are active and which are dormant and not used. The dormant segments would be returned to the secondary memory first when space is needed in the primary memory for incoming active segments. All accessed flags can be reset when a transfer is made.

The interconnection of a separate MMU to a processor involves all the data lines (for loading control registers) and at least the higher significant bits of the address lines. The lower address lines are not used for address translation if base addresses are used with the lower significant bits set to zero. Processor status information needs to be passed to the MMU and this may use a dedicated group of status lines from the processor. The usual data transfer control signals will be needed.

There are two possible methods of treating the MMU, as part of the processor or as part of the memory as shown in Fig. 10.14(a) and (b). An MMU which is an integral part of a processor must be configured as (a). If the MMU is part of a particular memory block as shown in (b), each memory would have its own MMU and all MMUs together with non-managed devices, such as input/output interfaces, connect through the processor bus or a derivative. However, if the MMU is considered as part of the processor, all memory and input/output devices connect to the physical address side of one or more MMUs and the processor connects to

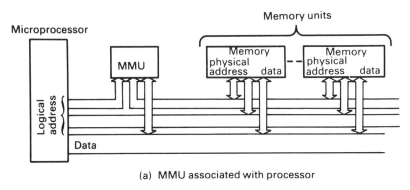

(a) MMU associated with processor

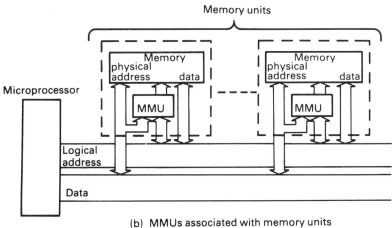

(b) MMUs associated with memory units

Figure 10.14 Connection of memory management units (MMUs) to processor

the logical address side of the MMU. This means that address translation also applies to input/output devices. In either case, each MMU is set up in a similar fashion to programmed input/output interfaces. Input/output instructions are used to load the command registers, load the MMU memory or read the status register.

10.2 Processor–main memory management

10.2.1 Cache memory

In the last section we considered the problem of efficiently handling the transfer of information between main and secondary memory. A significant factor is the difference in speed of operation of main and secondary memory. Secondary memory is often several orders of magnitude slower than main memory. There is also a mismatch between the speed of operation of the processor and that of the main memory; processors (except early microprocessors) are generally able to perform operations on operands faster than the access time of the main memory. Though semiconductor memory exists which can operate at speeds comparable with the operation of the processor, it is not economical to provide all the main memory using very high-speed semiconductor memory. The problem can be alleviated by introducing a small block of high-speed memory called a *cache* between the main memory and the processor. The general scheme is shown in Fig. 10.15. The cache consists of semiconductor memory operating at the speed required by the processor. The cache might hold, say, 512 words. Program and data are first transferred to the cache and then the processor accesses the cache. Any new data is first written to the cache and either written at same time to the main memory or subsequently when the location is replaced with new information from the main memory.

A cache is generally successful because programs usually exhibit a feature that memory references for instructions are near previous memory references for instructions and, to a lesser extent, memory references for data are near previous memory references for data (*principle of locality*), and particular instruction and data references are often repeated. For example, a purely sequential list of instructions which is executed only once is rare; more often, loops of instructions are programmed and the loop is executed many times. The length of a loop is usually quite small. Therefore once a cache is loaded with information from the main

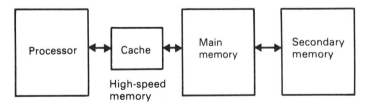

Figure 10.15 Cache memory scheme

memory, it is used more than once before new information is required from the main memory.

The principle of locality also makes main memory—secondary memory management schemes efficient. However, the principle is particularly significant in cache systems. If every memory reference to the cache required a transfer of one word between the main memory and the cache, no increase in speed would be achieved; in fact the speed would probably drop. However, suppose the reference is repeated n times in all during a program loop and after the first reference, the location is always found in the cache, then the average access time would be:

$$\text{Average access time} = (M + nm)/n$$

where M = time to transfer the word between main memory and cache

    m = time to access the cache
    n = number of references

If $M = 400$ ns, $m = 50$ ns, and $n = 10$, the average time would be 90 ns rather than 400 ns without the cache, i.e. 444% increase in speed with a cache operating at eight times the main memory, assuming no additional timing factors with the introduction of the cache, and that the processor can handle the increased speed.

We have assumed that it is necessary firstly to reference the cache before a reference to the main memory is made to fetch a word. It may be necessary to make a second reference to the cache after the word is fetched into the cache, though for a read operation it is likely that the word can be sent to the cache and processor simultaneously. Write operations require an additional scheme which we shall describe later. Also, any word altered must be transferred back to the main memory eventually and this transfer will reduce the average time.

The main memory can be and is usually interleaved to match the speed of transfer of the main memory with the cache. In interleaving, the memory is divided into modules and one word from each module is transferred to or from the memory and, in this application, the cache simultaneously. An interleaved system is shown in Fig. 10.16. Normally, the number of modules is a power of two to simplify the memory addressing. The main memory addresses are numbered across the modules. For example, with four modules, the addresses in the first module would be 0, 4, 8, 12,16, etc. The addresses in the second module would be 1, 5, 9, 13, 17, etc. The addresses in the third module would be 2, 6,10,14,18, etc., and the addresses in the fourth module would be 3, 7,11,15,19, etc.

The number of modules is chosen to produce a suitable match in the speed of operation of the memories. For example, if the cache has an access time of 50 ns and the main memory has an access time of 400 ns, eight blocks would allow eight words to be transferred to or from the cache in 400 ns, and subsequently be accessed in sequential order by the processor in another 400 ns. Hence the average access time of these words when first referenced would be 800 ns/8 = 100 ns. Should the words be read ten times in all, the average access time would be:

$$\text{Average access time} = (100 + 9 \times 50)/10 = 55 \text{ ns}$$

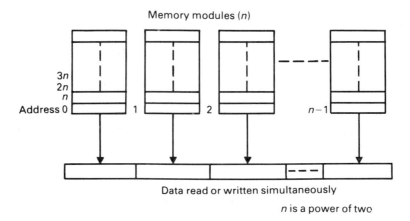

Figure 10.16 Memory interleaving

making the same rather broad assumptions as before. However, it does indicate that substantial speed improvements can be achieved by using the cache.

The probability that the required word is already in the cache depends upon the program; typically 80–90% of references will find their words in the cache. A *hit* occurs when a location is immediately found in the cache, otherwise a *miss* occurs and a reference to the main memory is necessary. The *hit ratio* is defined as:

$$\text{Hit ratio} = \frac{\text{number of times required word found in cache}}{\text{Total number of references}}$$

For example, if the hit ratio is 0.85, the main memory access time is 400 ns and the cache access time is 50 ns, then the average access time is:

$$1 \times 50 + 0.15 \times 400 = 110 \text{ ns}$$

assuming again that the first access must be to cache before an access is made to the main memory.

10.2.2 Mapping schemes

The problem of mapping the information held in the main memory into the cache is similar to main–secondary memory virtual memory systems, though any cache mapping scheme must be totally implemented in hardware to achieve improvement in the system operation. Various strategies are possible.

(a) Direct mapping

In *direct mapping schemes*, the least significant bits of the memory address in the main memory and the cache are the same. The most significant bits of the address are stored in the cache and read after the least significant bits have been used to access the cache word.

Firstly, consider the example shown in Fig. 10.17. The address from the processor is divided into two fields, a *tag* and an *index*. The tag identifies a page in the main memory and the index identifies the word within the page. Upon a memory reference, first the index is used to access a word in the cache. Then, the tag stored in the accessed word is read and compared with the tag in the address. If the two tags are the same, indicating that the word is the one required, the access is made to the addressed cache word. If, however, the tags are not the same, a reference is made to the main memory to find the required word. The word is then transferred into the cache and the access made to the word.

In the above scheme, one word is transferred to the cache at a time. In Fig. 10.18, several words are transferred together by interleaving. We shall call the words transferred a *block*. The main memory address is composed of a tag, a block, and a word within a block. All the words within a block in the cache have the same stored tag. The block/word part of the address is used to access the cache and the stored tag compared with the required tag address. If the tags are not the same the block containing the required word is transferred to the cache. In this scheme, the corresponding blocks in every page would map into the same block in the cache.

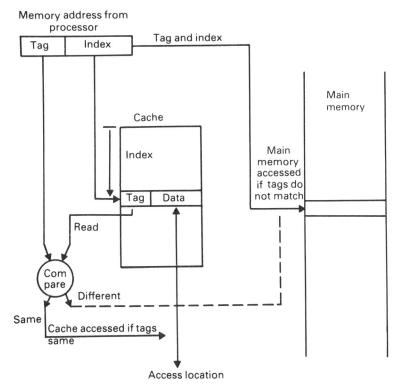

Figure 10.17 Cache with direct mapping

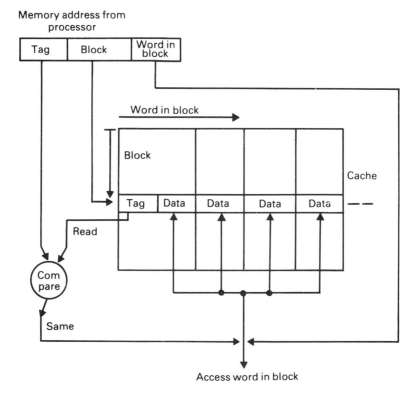

Figure 10.18 Direct mapped cache with block organization

(b) Associative mapping

Associative mapping requires the cache to be composed of associative memory as also used in the main memory–secondary memory associative mapping scheme (section 10.1.2). The incoming memory address is compared with all the stored addresses simultaneously using the internal logic of the associative memory as shown in Fig. 10.19. If a match is found, the corresponding data is read out. When used as a cache, single words from anywhere within the main memory could be held in the cache (assuming that the associative part of the cache is capable of holding a full memory address).

(c) Set-associative mapping

In the direct scheme above (Fig. 10.17), all words stored in the cache must have different indices. The tags may be the same or different. The *set-associative mapping* scheme allows more than one word in the cache with the same index and different tags as shown in Fig. 10.20. Each word has a stored tag completing the identification of the word. The tags are stored in associative memory. First the index of the address from the processor is used to access the words. Then, all tags are compared

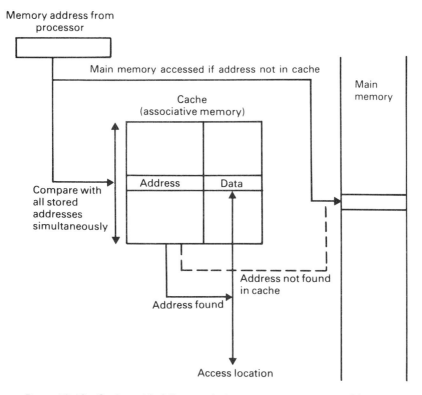

Figure 10.19 Cache with fully associative memory to store addresses

with the incoming tag associatively. If a match is found the location is accessed, otherwise, as before, an access to the main memory is made.

10.2.3 Write mechanism and replacement policy

As reading the required word in the cache does not affect the cache contents, there can be no discrepancy between the cache word and the copy held in the main memory after a memory read instruction. However, writing can occur to cache words and in these cases it is possible that the cache word and copy held in the main memory may be different. It is necessary to maintain both the cache and the main memory copy identical if input/output transfers (such as DMA, Chapter 9, section 9.4) operate on the main memory contents. There are two mechanisms to update the main memory during a memory write instruction.

(a) Write-through

In the *write-through* mechanism, every write operation to the cache is repeated to the main memory. The additional write operation to the main memory will of course

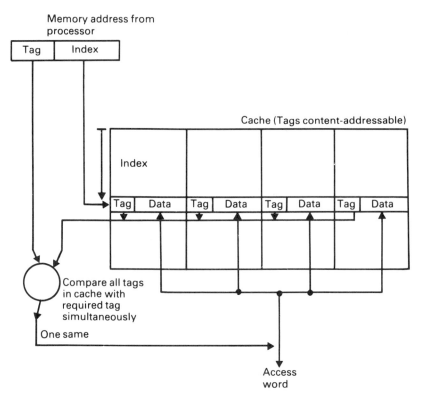

Figure 10.20 Cache with set-associative mapping

take much longer than to the cache. Fortunately, there are usually several read operations between write operations (typically between 3 and 10) and these read operations to the cache can take place while the main memory write operation is in progress.

(b) Write-back

In the *write-back* mechanism, the write operation to the main memory is only done at a block replacement time. A tag (bit) is associated with each cache word, which is set whenever the word is altered. At replacement time, the tags are examined to determine whether it is necessary to write the block back to the main memory.

When the required block or word is not held in the cache, it is necessary to transfer the block or word needed from the main memory into the cache, displacing an existing block or word. The existing block or word in the cache can be chosen by a random replacement algorithm, first-in-first-out algorithm, or least recently used algorithm as used in virtual memory systems. The least recently used algorithm can be implemented fully because the number of blocks involved is small. The replacement mechanism must be implemented totally in hardware, and additional tags in the cache are provided to assist the replacement algorithm.

References

1. *An Introduction to CP/M Features and Facilities*, Pacific Grove, CA: Digital Research, 1978.
2. *The 8086 Family User's Manual*, Santa Clara, CA: Intel Corp., 1979.
3. Bear, J. L., *Computer System Architecture*, Rockville, MA: Computer Science Press, Inc., 1980.

Problems

10.1 In a paged system, suppose the following pages are requested in the order shown:

$$3, 4, 6, 10, 3, 5, 3, 5, 4, 5, 3$$

and the main memory can only hold four pages at any instant. List the pages in main memory after each page is transferred using the first-in-first-out replacement algorithm and the least recently used replacement algorithm. How many page faults occur in each case?

10.2 In the *working set algorithm*, the last n pages referenced are kept in memory, where n is the 'working set'. At replacement time, the page deleted from the working set and transferred to secondary memory is the one not referenced in the last n references. It is possible to have less than the full set held. For example, if the last four references were pages 2, 6, 8 and 2, the pages in the set would be 6, 8 and 2. Apply the working set algorithm to the sequence:

$$3, 4, 3, 6, 8, 3, 7, 6, 8, 3, 2, 6$$

(also used in section 10.1.3), assuming the maximum number of pages in the main memory is four.

10.3 A computer employs a 64K 16-bit word main memory and a cache of 512 words. Determine the number of bits in each field of the address, in the following organizations:

(a) Direct mapping with a block size of one word
(b) Direct mapping with a block size of eight words
(c) Set-associative mapping with a set size of four words.

10.4 Determine the average access time in a computer system employing a cache, given that the main memory access time is 500 ns, the cache access time is 75 ns and the hit ratio is 90%. The write-through policy is used. 20% of memory requests are write requests.

10.5 Repeat Problem 10.4 assuming a write-back policy is used, and the block size is 16 words fully interleaved.

Part 3

Further Aspects of Digital System Design

11 | Formal Sequential Circuit Design

A method of developing a sequential logic circuit beginning with a state diagram was introduced in Chapter 4 to obtain the basic J–K flip-flop circuit configuration and to design synchronous binary counters. The method will be considered further in this chapter.

11.1 Synchronous sequential circuit design

11.1.1 General model

The general model for a synchronous sequential circuit is shown in Fig. 11.1. There are a number of inputs to the circuit, x_0, x_1, ..., x_n and a number of outputs, Z_0, Z_1, ..., Z_m. In addition, internal signals are generated, Y_0, Y_1, ..., Y_k which are stored (shown using D-type flip-flops) and fed back to the input. The signals fed back to the input are labelled here y_0, y_1, ..., y_k. Thus the sequential circuit is divided into two parts, a combinational logic section and a storage section. The internal Y variables are combinational functions of the y variables and the system input variables.

   The whole circuit exists in a particular state as defined by the y variables, and hence these variables are called *state variables* or *present-state variables*. With three state variables and three flip-flops, there could be eight different states. The present state variables and applied input variables produce the Y signals which will produce a change in the present state variables after the activating clock transition has occurred. Hence the Y variables could be called the *next-state variables*. The output variables are combinational functions of the present state variables, and the applied input variables in some cases. Sometimes state variables are also the system outputs, as in the case of synchronous counters.

   We expect the system input changes, if any, to occur at one instant between the activating clock transitions, perhaps just before a transition. There must be a sufficient delay between the occurrence of new input values and the clock transition to allow the next-state variables to be set up in time for the clock transition. Multiple changes in the inputs between activating clock transitions have no effect on the state of the circuit; only the value of the inputs at the time of the activating clock

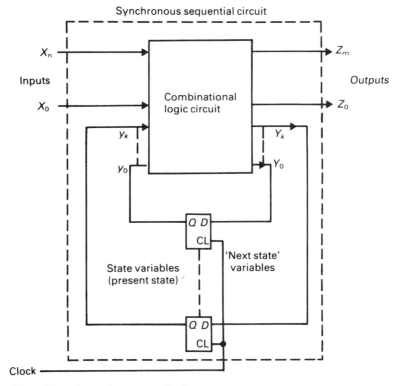

Figure 11.1   General model of a synchronous sequential circuit

transition can cause a state change. The type of clock transition (rising edge or falling edge) which causes a state change is that which activates the particular flip-flops used. However, multiple input changes between activating clock transitions may be reflected on the output if the output is a combinational function of both the state variables and the input variables.

11.1.2 Design procedure

Consider the following problem: a synchronous sequential circuit has one output, Z, and one input, x. The output is to be at a logic 1 whenever the sequence 0110100 occurs in serial form on x. The output is to become a 1 during the last bit of the sequence. Overlapping sequences are not to produce a 1 output. A synchronizing clock signal is provided. Design the circuit.

This sequence detector problem, though chosen to illustrate the formal techniques of traditional synchronous sequential circuit design, has application in computer design. For example, data transmitted along one wire one bit at a time for high-speed transmission, may use the synchronous serial format rather than the common asynchronous serial format. In the synchronous serial format, start and stop bits are not introduced and many characters are transmitted without any data gaps. Timing is achieved by inserting SYN characters at intervals. These SYN characters are intercepted by the receiving circuitry. Another area is in magnetic disk recording. Synchronization sequences are recorded at the beginning of the recording to enable the read circuitry to lock onto the read signal.

The first step we shall take is to draw the state diagram. This step is usually the most difficult because the state diagram usually needs to be deduced from the problem specification. Clearly the state diagram must be correct, otherwise the subsequent implementation will be incorrect. We can use the Moore model state diagram or the Mealy model state diagram. Recall that in a Mealy model state diagram, the output is associated with the corresponding input values on the paths connecting the present and new states. In the Moore model state diagram, the output is associated with the state only. Hence in the Mealy model, the output will generally be a combinational function of both the system input variables and the (present) state variables representing the state. In the Moore model, the output will only be a combinational function of the state variables. Here we will create two designs, one based on the Mealy model, and one based on the Moore model to show the implications of each model.

(a) Mealy model state diagram

The Mealy model state diagram of our sequence detector is shown in Fig. 11.2(a). There must be an initial state from which other states are entered when the required bits in the sequence are encountered. Since there are seven digits in the sequence, there are seven fundamental states and the move from one state to the next is after the next bit in the sequence has occurred at the input.

In the state diagram, the path caused by the occurrence of the correct sequence is from left to right except the final path from state 7 to state 1. If the input is a 0 for the final path, the output becomes a 1. This output will remain for only one clock duration (approximately, depending upon the state variable timing). The other paths in the state diagram are for incorrect sequences. Not all intermediate paths return to the initial state 1. When determining return paths, the bit patterns received at each state must be examined to see if the last part corresponds to the beginning of the required sequence. In our problem, at state 3, if a 0 is received, the circuit stays in state 3 because at least three 0's have been received, of which the last two may be the first two 0's in the correct sequence. Similarly, the return path from state 5 is to state 3, not state 1, as two 0's have been received. The return path at state 6 upon receiving a 0 is to state 2, not state 1, because the 0 received may be the first 0 in the correct sequence. It is specified that overlapping sequences are not allowed. In our case, the final 0 in the sequence cannot also be the first 0 in a new sequence. Therefore, the return path from 7 to 1 when a 0 is received is to state 1, not state 2.

The state table is obtained from the state diagram and this is shown in Fig. 11.2(b). The output is due to the present state and the new system input. The

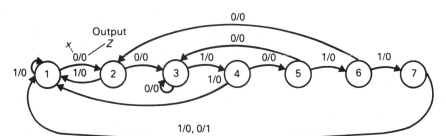

(a) Mealy model state diagram

Present state	Next state x		Output Z x	
	0	1	0	1
1	2	1	0	0
2	3	1	0	0
3	3	4	0	0
4	5	1	0	0
5	3	6	0	0
6	2	7	0	0
7	1	1	1	0

(b) State table

Present state $Y_3Y_2Y_1$	Next state $Y_3Y_2Y_1$		Output Z x	
	0	1	0	1
000	001	000	0	0
001	011	000	0	0
011	011	010	0	0
010	100	000	0	0
100	011	101	0	0
101	001	111	0	0
111	000	000	1	0

(c) Assigned state table (Y matrix)

Figure 11.2 Sequential detector using Mealy model state diagram

next step is to minimize this table if possible, i.e. to reduce the number of states in the table to a minimum. We will consider minimization separately. The state table for our problem does not minimize.

The state variables are assigned to represent the states. We need a minimum of n state variables when the number of states lies between $2^{n-1} + 1$ and 2^n. One (binary) variable is needed for two states, two variables when there are 3 or 4 variables, three variables for 5 to 8 states, four variables for 9 to 16 states, five variables for 17 to 32 states, etc. Therefore in our case, we need three variables to represent the seven states. An arbitrary approach can be used to assign the state variables to the states. Here we will make the arbitrary assignment as shown in Table 11.1. This particular

Table 11.1 State variable assignment for synchronous sequential circuit problem

y_3	y_2	y_1	State
0	0	0	1
0	0	1	2
0	1	1	3
0	1	0	4
1	0	0	5
1	0	1	6
1	1	1	7

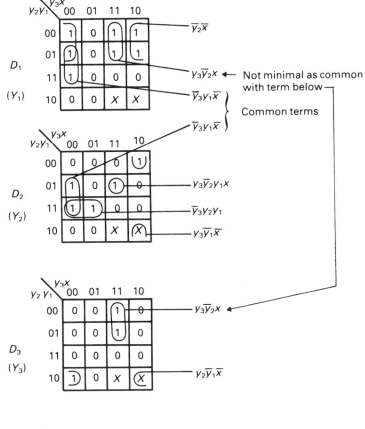

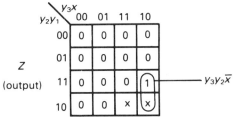

$$D_1 = \bar{y}_2\bar{x} + y_3\bar{y}_2x + \bar{y}_3y_1\bar{x}$$
$$D_2 = \bar{y}_3y_1\bar{x} + y_3\bar{y}_2y_1x + \bar{y}_3y_2y_1 + y_3\bar{y}_1\bar{x}$$
$$D_3 = y_3\bar{y}_2x + y_2\bar{y}_1\bar{x}$$
$$Z = y_3y_2\bar{x}$$

(a) Next state and output functions

Figure 11.3 Sequence detector design using D-type flip-flops (Mealy model)

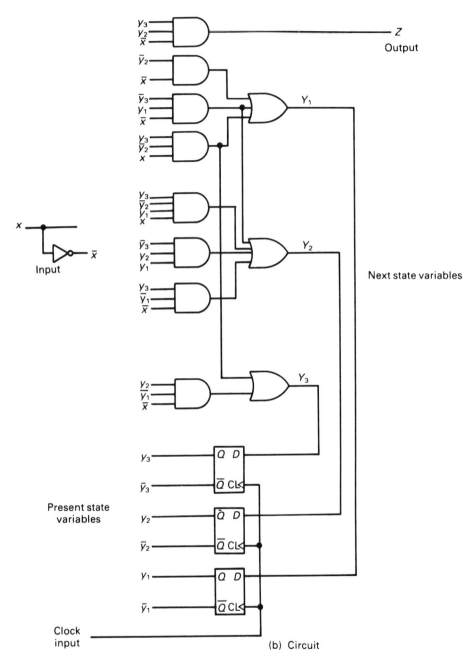

Figure 11.3 continued

choice will allow rapid translation of state variables on to Karnaugh maps. However, it may not necessarily lead to the minimum number of gates. This matter will be raised later. After an assignment is made, the state numbers in the state table are replaced by the equivalent state variables to produce an assigned state table as shown in Fig. 11.2(c). The assigned state table is known as the *Y matrix*. Note that the present states are represented by the assigned y (present-state) variables and the next states are represented by the assigned Y (next-state) variables.

We now need to decide on the implementation. Examining our model of a synchronous sequential circuit shown in Fig. 11.1, we see that flip-flops are required to store the state variables. Combinational circuits generate the next-state variables and output from the system input variables and stored state variables. We could use small-scale integrated circuits (SSI) for the combinational section and SSI flip-flops for storage.

Firstly, let us choose D-type flip-flops and gates. Three D-type flip-flops are required for the three state variables. It is necessary to determine the next-state variables, i.e. the Boolean expressions for the D inputs. Karnaugh maps can be drawn for each of D_1, D_2 and D_3. The flip-flop Q output of a D-type flip-flop is the same as the applied D input, after clock activation. Therefore, the new values of y_1 (i.e. the values of Y_1) are entered on to the D_1 map, the new values of y_2 (i.e. Y_2) are entered on to the D_2 map and the new values of y_3 (i.e. Y_3) are entered on to the D_3 map. The output expression is also derived from the state table. The Karnaugh maps for the three state variables and the output, Z, are shown in Fig. 11.3(a). The expressions are minimized. Because this is a multi-output combinational circuit, common terms are sought. One such term is found in D_1 and D_3 ($y_3 \bar{y}_2 x$) and chosen in D_1 rather than the reduced term, $y_3 \bar{y}_2$. Another common term, $\bar{y}_3 y_2 \bar{x}$, is found in D_1 and D_2. Finally, from the minimized expressions, we obtain the circuit implementation, as shown in Fig. 11.3(b). This circuit is drawn to emphasize the correspondence with the synchronous sequential circuit model.

(b) Moore model state diagram

The Moore model state diagram for our sequence detector is shown in Fig. 11.4(a). Note that an extra state (8) is introduced. States 1 to 6 and the interconnecting paths are identical to those in the Mealy model state diagram. The state table is shown in Fig. 11.4(b) and the assigned state table in Fig. 11.4(c). Three state variables are again adequate. The new state, 8, is assigned the number 110. A D-type flip-flop design based on the assigned state table is shown in Fig. 11.5. Note that the output is only a function of the state variables, $y_3 y_2$ and y_1. Compared to the Mealy model design, we observe that the number of states is increased. This is often the case, though in our particular example, no extra flip-flops are necessary. Traditionally, the Mealy model has been selected for synchronous designs because it results in the minimum number of states and hence the minimum number of flip-flops.

If the inputs only change at the time of the activating clock transition, the output will be the same in both designs. However, if the input does change (even transiently, say due to noise) at other times, the output may also change in the Mealy

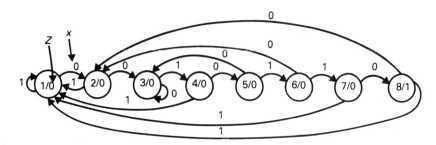

(a) Moore model state diagram

Present state	Next state x		Present output, Z
	0	1	
1	2	1	0
2	3	1	0
3	3	4	0
4		1	0
5	3	6	0
6	2	7	0
7	8	1	0
8	2	1	1

(b) State table

Present state $Y_3Y_2Y_1$	Next state $Y_3Y_2Y_1$ x		Present output, Z
	0	1	
000	001	000	0
001	011	000	0
011	011	010	0
010	100	000	0
100	011	101	0
101	001	111	0
111	110	000	0
110	001	000	1

(c) Assigned state table (Y matrix)

Figure 11.4   Sequence detector using Moore model state diagram

model design but not in the Moore model design. In the Mealy model, the output is a function of both the state variables and the system input variables. In the Moore model design, the output is only a function of the state variables which can only change at the time of the activating clock transition.

(c) Alternative implementations

Consider another problem: a synchronous sequential circuit has one output, Z, and two inputs, x_1 and x_2. The output will be at a 1 whenever the input sequence on x_1 and x_2 both consist of 0011 in the same time sequence. The output will become a 1 during the last bit period of the sequence. Design the circuit.

This problem is similar to the previous sequence detector, except that there are two synchronous inputs rather than one. The Mealy model state diagram is shown in Fig. 11.6(a) and the state table in Fig. 11.6(b). There are four states so that two state variables are adequate. The assigned state table is shown in Fig. 11.6(c). Notice that there are four next-state columns and four output columns, because there are four combinations of the two inputs. The combinations are listed in the order which corresponds to the labels of a Karnaugh map. A design using D-type flip-flops is

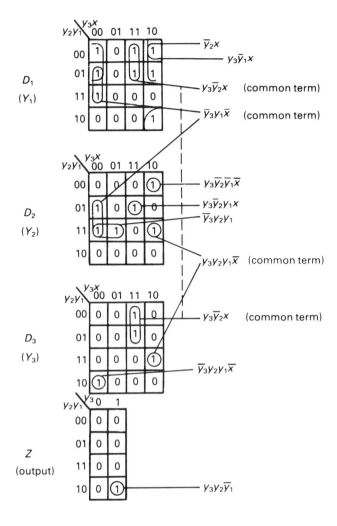

$$D_1 = \bar{y}_2 x + y_3 \bar{y}_2 x + \bar{y}_3 y_1 \bar{x}$$
$$D_2 = y_3 \bar{y}_2 \bar{y}_1 \bar{x} + y_3 \bar{y}_2 y_1 x + \bar{y}_3 y_2 y_1 + \bar{y}_3 y_2 y_1 \bar{x} + \bar{y}_3 y_1 \bar{x}$$
$$D_3 = y_3 y_2 y_1 \bar{x} + \bar{y}_3 y_2 y_1 \bar{x} + y_3 \bar{y}_2 y_1$$
$$Z = y_3 y_2 \bar{y}_1$$

(a) Next state and output functions

Figure 11.5 Sequence detector design using D-type flip-flops (Moore model)

shown in Fig. 11.7. Notice that there is a direct correspondence of entries in the assigned state table and four variable Karnaugh maps.

As a first alternative, let us choose $J-K$ flip-flops rather than D-type flip-flops. Table 4.3 in Chapter 4 lists the required input values for each of the possible output effects (0 to 0, 0 to 1, 1 to 0 and 1 to 1) and is used to deduce the required $J-K$

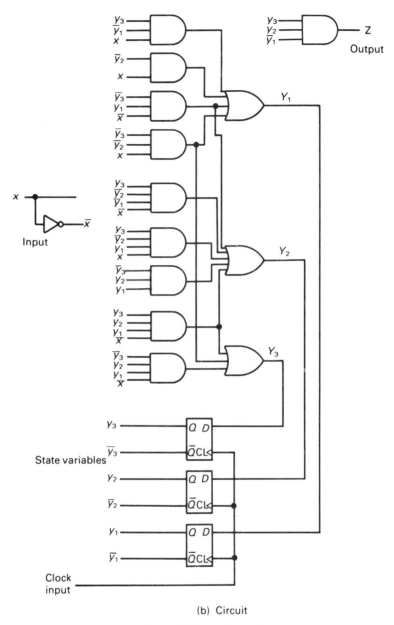

(b) Circuit

Figure 11.5 continued

inputs. There are two next-state variables for each flip-flop, one for the J input and one for the K input. For each present-state entry and each state variable, we note the present output (y) to next-stop output (Y) change. For example, in the first state, the present to next-state change is a 0 to 0 for y_1. Therefore the top left-hand entry of the J_1 Karnaugh map is a 0 and a don't care (X) for K_1 to achieve this

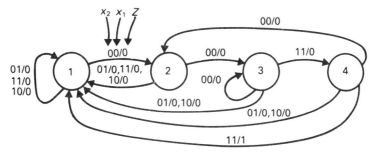

(a) State diagram (Mealy model)

Present state	Next state x_2,x_1				Output x_2,x_1			
	00	01	11	10	00	01	11	10
1	2	1	1	1	0	0	0	0
2	3	1	1	1	0	0	0	0
3	3	1	4	1	0	0	0	0
4	2	1	1	1	0	0	1	0

(b) State table

Present state y_2y_1	Next state, Y_2Y_1 x_2,x_1				Output Z x_2,x_1			
	00	01	11	10	00	01	11	10
00	01	00	00	00	0	0	0	0
01	11	00	00	00	0	0	0	0
11	11	00	10	00	0	0	0	0
10	01	00	00	00	0	0	1	0

(c) Assigned state table (Y matrix)

Figure 11.6 Two-input sequence detector

change according to the table. All other changes are examined to complete each Karnaugh map. The final realization using $J-K$ flip-flops is shown in Fig. 11.8.

We could use synchronous $R-S$ flip-flops. Then Table 4.1 in Chapter 4 is used to deduce the required $R-S$ inputs. The $R-S$ flip-flops must not be simple cross-coupled NAND/NOR gates. An edge-triggered or master–slave version is necessary for stable operation. (There is only one suitable $R-S$ flip-flop available in the TTL 7400 family, namely the old 74L71 master–slave flip-flop which has three 'S' and three 'R' AND-gated inputs.)

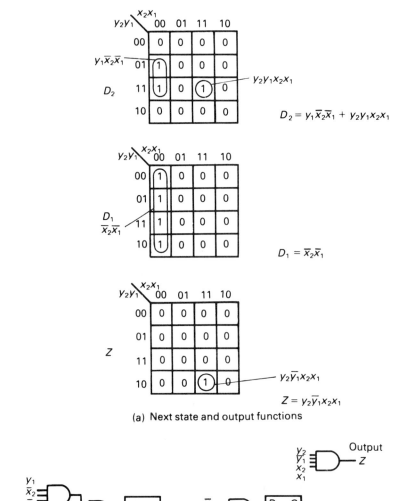

(a) Next state and output functions

(b) Circuit

Figure 11.7 Two-input sequence detector design using D-type flip-flops

A completely different approach is to replace the combinational circuitry with a read-only memory (ROM) in conjunction with a storage register (e.g. D-type flip-flops) as shown in Fig. 11.9(a). Each memory location of the ROM is addressed by the input variables, x_2x_1, and state variables, y_2y_1. The ROM outputs are the next-state variables, Y_2Y_1, and the circuit output, Z. The memory contents are found directly from the assigned state table as shown in Fig. 11.9(b). The approach is

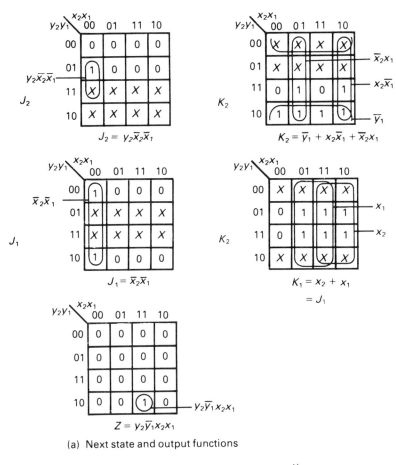

(a) Next state and output functions

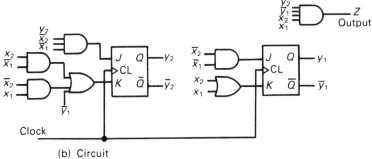

(b) Circuit

Figure 11.8 Two-input sequence detector design using *J*–*K*-type flip-flops

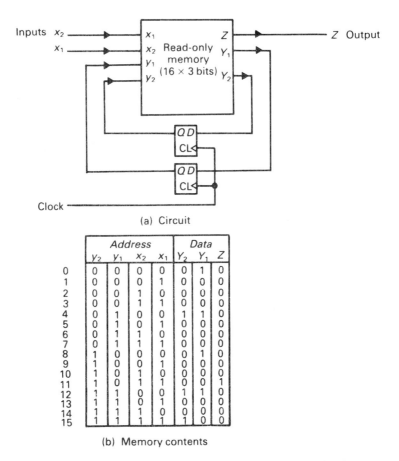

(a) Circuit

	Address				Data		
	y_2	y_1	x_2	x_1	Y_2	Y_1	Z
0	0	0	0	0	0	1	0
1	0	0	0	1	0	0	0
2	0	0	1	0	0	0	0
3	0	0	1	1	0	0	0
4	0	1	0	0	1	1	0
5	0	1	0	1	0	0	0
6	0	1	1	0	0	0	0
7	0	1	1	1	0	0	0
8	1	0	0	0	0	1	0
9	1	0	0	1	0	0	0
10	1	0	1	0	0	0	0
11	1	0	1	1	0	0	1
12	1	1	0	0	0	1	0
13	1	1	0	1	0	0	0
14	1	1	1	0	0	0	0
15	1	1	1	1	1	0	0

(b) Memory contents

Figure 11.9 Two-input sequence detector design using a read-only memory

particularly elegant and one which is easy to check or modify by ROM replacement. Since large-capacity read-only memories are manufactured, state minimization may be unnecessary, and indeed undesirable because it then masks the original sequence.

11.1.3 State minimization

The minimum number of states is usually a requirement for SSI/MSI implementation, to reduce the number of gates. State minimization methods are available which depend upon recognizing states which are identical or can be made identical.

Consider the state table given in Table 11.2 based on a Mealy model. Here there are two input variables, x_1 and x_2, eight states and one output, Z. States cannot be the same or made the same if their outputs are different for the same conditions. For example, state 5 has a 1 in the $x_2 x_1 = 11$ output column whereas all other states

Table 11.2 State table; candidate for minimization

Present state	Next state x_2x_1				Output Z x_2x_1			
	00	01	11	10	00	01	11	10
1	1	2	2	4	0	0	0	0
2	1	3	1	4	0	0	0	0
3	1	3	2	4	0	0	0	0
4	1	8	1	5	0	0	0	0
5	1	5	6	5	0	0	1	0
6	3	8	7	5	0	0	0	0
7	2	8	6	5	0	0	0	0
8	3	8	7	8	0	0	1	0

have a 0 in that column. This is known as an *output incompatible state*. Therefore state 5 cannot be combined with any other state. All the other states have compatible outputs and it may be possible to combine some of these states.

A procedure is to look at every combination of pairs of states which are output compatible and note, for each pair, the required states which must be identical for the pair to be equivalent. This is shown in Table 11.3 for our problem. Then the required equivalent pairs are examined. All output incompatible pairs are identified and the associated possible equivalent pair is deleted. If this results in other pairs being incompatible, these are also deleted. The process is continued until all incompatible pairs are deleted, leaving possible equivalent pairs.

Table 11.3 Equivalent pairs in Table 11.2

Possible equivalent pairs	Required equivalent pairs	Incompatible
1, 2	(2, 3)	
1, 3	(2, 3)	
1, 4	(2, 8), (1, 2), (4, 5)	x
1, 6	(1, 3), (2, 8), (2, 7), (4, 5)	x
1, 7	(1, 2), (2, 8), (2, 6), (4, 5)	x
2, 3	(1, 2)	
2, 4	(3, 8), (4, 5)	x
2, 6	(1, 3), (3, 8), (1, 7), (4, 5)	x
2, 7	(1, 2), (3, 8), (1, 6), (4, 5)	x
3, 4	(3, 8), (1, 2), (4, 5)	x
3, 6	(1, 3), (3, 8), (2, 7), (4, 5)	x
3, 7	(1, 2), (3, 8), (2, 6), (4, 5)	x
4, 6	(1, 3), (1, 7)	x
4, 7	(1, 2), (1, 6)	x
5, 8	(1, 3), (6, 7)	
6, 7	(3, 2)	

Creating a state diagram in which states are equivalent may occur because the state diagram is deduced intuitively from the problem specification. There can be more than one state diagram which describes a circuit, some with more states than others.

In our state diagram, the following pairs are equivalent:

$$1 \equiv 2$$
$$1 \equiv 3$$
$$2 \equiv 3$$
$$5 \equiv 8$$
$$6 \equiv 7$$

The remaining state, 4, is incompatible with any other state. Since $1 \equiv 2$, $1 \equiv 3$ and $2 \equiv 3$, we can say that $1 \equiv 2 \equiv 3$. In fact, if only two of these equivalent pairs are found, say $1 \equiv 2$ and $1 \equiv 3$, it is correct to deduce the third pair, 2 is equivalent to 3 and hence all three are equivalent, if every next state is specified in the state table. This produces three identical entries. It is not allowable to make this deduction if the state table has don't cares. State tables with don't cares are discussed in section 11.1.5.

We now need to select a group of equivalent states which as a set includes all the original states. There may be more than one selection which will cover all the states. In our case, the minimization procedure results in only one possible selection:

$$(1 \equiv 2 \equiv 3),(4),(5 \equiv 8),(6 \equiv 7)$$

which could be called, say:

$$A, B, C, D$$

Then a new reduced state table is drawn in terms of these states, as shown in Table 11.4. Each occurrence of 1, 2 or 3 has been replaced by A, each occurrence of 4 by B, each occurrence of 5 or 8 by C and each occurrence of 6 or 7 by D. The design procedure then follows the usual pattern using the reduced state table to form the Y-matrix.

11.1.4 State assignment

So far, the assignment of state variables to states has been done arbitrarily. It may

Table 11.4   Minimized state table

Present state	Next state $x_2 x_1$				Output, Z $x_2 x_1$			
	00	01	11	10	00	01	11	10
A	A	A	A	B	0	0	0	0
B	A	C	A	C	0	0	0	0
C	A	C	D	C	0	0	1	0
D	A	C	D	C	0	0	0	0

be that one particular assignment will result in less components in the final design. However, there is no known method to obtain directly an assignment which will result in a minimum component count for every problem. It even differs for different implementations. The number of assignment combinations grows very rapidly with the number of states and it is impractical to try every combination except in very small problems. After choosing the minimum number of state variables, we can employ two rules of thumb which tend to lead to fewer components:

(i) Choose codes which differ by one variable (are adjacent on a Karnaugh map) for states that lead to the same next state.
(ii) Where (i) is not possible, choose codes which differ by one variable for next states of a present state.

Usually neither of these rules can be applied completely. By applying the rules to the first Mealy model sequence detector problem, one assignment becomes as shown in Table 11.5. It is left to the reader to rework the design procedure.

11.1.5 Incompletely specified systems

An incompletely specified system is one in which there is at least one condition that cannot occur, or if it does occur, the response of the system is irrelevant. This is the same as 'cannot happen' or don't care conditions in combinational circuits. As an example, consider the following incompletely specified problem.

A synchronous sequential circuit has a single input, x, and a single output, Z. A binary sequence is applied to the input and the output is required to become a 1 only when the serial input sequence 00110010 is detected and then only during the last clock pulse period of the sequence. The sequence 0010 cannot occur except as part of the sequence to be detected. Design the circuit.

A Mealy model state diagram for this problem is shown in Fig. 11.10(a), deduced in a similar manner as previous diagrams (and purposely not minimal to

Table 11.5 State assignment using empirical rules

State	Assignment $y_3 y_2 y_1$
1	000
2	001
3	011
4	010
5	101
6	110
7	100

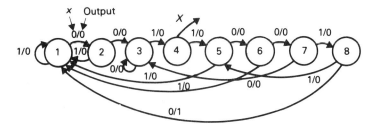

(a) State diagram

Present state	Next state x		Output x	
	0	1	0	1
1	2	1	0	0
2	3	1	0	0
3	3	4	0	0
4	X	5	X	0
5	6	1	0	0
6	7	1	0	0
7	3	8	0	0
8	1	5	1	0

(b) State table

Present state	Next state x		Output x	
	0	1	0	1
1/5	2	1	0	0
2/6	3	1	0	0
3/7	3	4	0	0
4/8	1	1	1	0

(c) Reduced state table

(d) Reduced state diagram

Present state Y_2Y_1	Next state Y_2Y_1 x		Output x	
	0	1	0	1
00	01	00	0	0
01	11	00	0	0
11	11	10	0	0
10	00	00	1	0

(e) Assigned state table

Figure 11.10 Incompletely specified problem

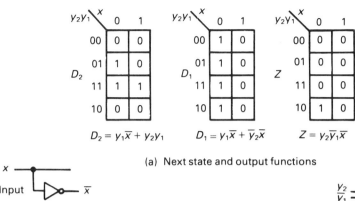

$$D_2 = y_1\bar{x} + y_2 y_1 \qquad D_1 = y_1\bar{x} + \bar{y}_2\bar{x} \qquad Z = y_2\bar{y}_1\bar{x}$$

(a) Next state and output functions

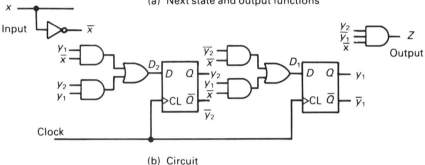

(b) Circuit

Figure 11.11 Implementation of incompletely specified problem using D-type flip-flops

illustrate the technique of minimizing incompletely specified systems). As in the previous sequence detector, the main flow is from left to right with incorrect numbers causing paths backwards, not all of which return to state 1. Because the sequence 0010 cannot occur except as the latter part of the correct sequence, there is a 'cannot happen' situation at state 4. A 0 cannot occur here since this would form 0010. The state table is given in Fig. 11.10(b). The cannot happen condition at state 4 with x input at a 0 is marked in both the next state and the output columns as an X. Minimizing results in the following equivalent pairs, interpreting the X's differently in the cases where state 4 is involved:

$$
\begin{array}{llll}
1 \equiv 2 & 2 \equiv 3 & 3 \equiv 4 & 4 \equiv 5 \\
1 \equiv 3 & 2 \equiv 4 & 3 \equiv 5 & 4 \equiv 6 \\
1 \equiv 4 & 2 \equiv 5 & 3 \equiv 6 & 4 \equiv 8 \\
1 \equiv 5 & 2 \equiv 6 & 3 \equiv 7 &
\end{array}
$$

Generally in incompletely specified systems, it does not follow automatically that if $A \equiv B$ and $B \equiv C$, then $A \equiv C$ because the don't care/cannot happen conditions might be interpreted differently for $A \equiv B$ and $B \equiv C$. Therefore only pairs are formed. In our case, there is a completely circular equivalence of $1 \equiv 4$, $1 \equiv 5$ and $4 \equiv 5$. Consequently we can say that $1 \equiv 4 \equiv 5$. The X in the state table is interpreted as either 6 or 2 and one equivalent pair is $2 \equiv 6$.

We need to choose those pairs which as a set cover all the original numbers, and also do not require other pairs to be equivalent which are not in the selection. This leads to the following selection (by trial and error):

$$(1 \equiv 5), (2 \equiv 6), (3 \equiv 7), (4 \equiv 8)$$

The reduced state table with these four states is shown in Fig. 11.10(c), the reduced state diagram in Fig. 11.10(d) and the assigned state table in Fig. 11.10(e). A solution using D-type flip-flops is shown in Fig. 11.11.

The original state diagram was deduced intuitively using more than the necessary number of states so that the formal minimization techniques can be shown. Clearly, it is possible (and desirable) to deduce the minimal state diagram (Fig. 11.10(d)) directly without needing to minimize formally. For more complex problems, the minimal state diagram may not be obvious.

11.2 Asynchronous sequential circuit design

11.2.1 Asynchronous circuit design difficulties

The general model of an asynchronous sequential logic circuit is shown in Fig. 11.12. As opposed to a synchronous sequential logic circuit, a general

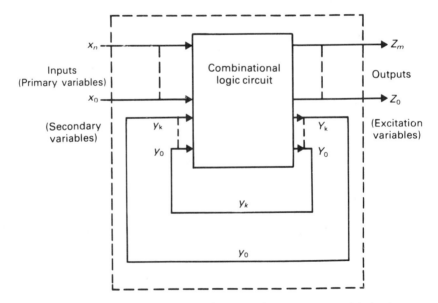

Figure 11.12 General model of an asynchronous sequential circuit

asynchronous sequential logic circuit does not use a clock signal to time all events. The system inputs are called *primary variables*. The inputs may change at any time unless some restriction is placed on them. An asynchronous sequential logic circuit, as a synchronous sequential logic circuit, can exist in a particular state, though in an asynchronous sequential circuit some of the states only last for a short time between changes from one permanent or *stable* state to another stable state. The transitory states are called *unstable* states. The states are indicated by the y state variables, called here the *secondary variables*. The Y signals generated from the combinational circuit part of the system cause a change in the state and are called here the *excitation variables*. The excitation variables are fed back into the combinational logic, and enter the combinational circuit as secondary variables. The circuit is in a stable state when the primary inputs are stable and all internal signals have been established. In the stable state, the excitation variables and the secondary variables are the same. The excitation variables can be imagined to be generated with no delay through the combinational logic circuit and a lumped delay introduced between the excitation variables and the secondary variables. The terms primary variables, excitation variables and secondary variables derive from relay switching circuit design [1].

Though the design of asynchronous sequential logic circuits follows similar lines to those of synchronous sequential circuits, the lack of any synchronization presents additional constraints and design problems over the synchronous circuits. If, for example, two excitation signals are fed back to the inputs and it is intended that both these signals should change together, say from 00 to 11, after an input change, it is most likely in practice that one signal will change before the other due to different delays in the circuit. For a short period we may have the combinations 01 or 10. One of these combinations may be sufficient to cause the circuit to enter an unwanted state, producing new excitation signals and subsequent incorrect operation. Similarly, if the system primary inputs change together, an incorrect sequence could be followed. To avoid this problem, asynchronous sequential circuits are designed so that internal signals fed back to the input do not change simultaneously. In addition to disallowing simultaneous changes, sufficient time must elapse between any changes to allow the system to settle.

Preventing simultaneous changes in system inputs is more difficult as this may occur naturally. It is necessary to assume that simultaneous input changes do not occur (or to prevent such changes) to be able to design an asynchronous sequential circuit that will work reliably. In some cases, we might be able to consider a change of two inputs from, say, 00 to 11, as either a change from 00 to 01 and then from 01 to 11, or as a change from 00 to 10 and then from 10 to 11, i.e. limiting the change to one signal at any instant. If so, it is still necessary that the time between the changes is sufficient for the circuit to distinguish the input changes. We can compare the problem to the input set-up and hold times that must be satisfied in a flip-flop such as a D-type flip-flop (which internally can be considered as an asynchronous sequential circuit). If we applied a signal change on the D input at exactly the same time as the activating clock transition, the operation of the flip-flop would be indeterminate. If simultaneous input changes are likely to occur in a problem, asynchronous sequential circuit design should not be used [2].

An asynchronous sequential circuit design must also not generate *critical race hazards*. As mentioned in Chapter 3, section 3.2.9, a race hazard is a logic configuration which leads to the unwanted generation of logic spikes due to signals passing through different paths to the output and experiencing different delays. A critical race hazard is one which subsequently causes the system to operate incorrectly (i.e., to enter unwanted instable states). Race hazards can be tolerated in an asynchronous sequential circuit if they cause perhaps different unstable states to be entered but finally the same stable state to be reached; indeed, allowing non-critical race hazards can give reduced logic components.

Race hazards can be classified into three types:

  (i) Static race hazards
 (ii) Dynamic race hazards
(iii) Essential race hazards.

A *static race hazard* can be created by a race between a signal and its complement and is considered in Chapter 3. It was noted that these race hazards can be completely eliminated by the introduction of all the prime implicants in the Boolean expression being implemented. Note, however, that static race hazards are concerned with 1-to-0 logic transitions on input signals (in sum-of-product expressions) and not with 0-to-1 transitions. In an asynchronous sequential circuit, it is only necessary to correct for a static race hazard if a 1-to-0 change will occur. Often, there are several transitions that cannot occur if the circuit is functioning correctly. We can of course correct for all static race hazards, but this would often lead to more components than are actually necessary [3].

A *dynamic race hazard* results in three transitions in a signal when only one is intended, for example a change from 0 to 1 to 0 to 1 instead of a 0-to-1 change. Such hazards may be due to multi-level gate implementations in which signals interact as they pass through several gates between the input and output. If circuits are designed with only two levels of gating and static hazards have been eliminated, dynamic hazards do not occur.

Both static hazards and dynamic hazards are combinational circuit hazards, but generally are only significant in asynchronous sequential circuits (as opposed to purely combinational logic circuits or synchronous sequential circuits). In contrast, an *essential race hazard* is found only in asynchronous sequential circuits, and is caused, as we shall see, by the interaction between a primary and a secondary signal change. Essential race hazards can be eliminated by introducing delays in the circuit.

11.2.2 Design procedure

For our first example of an asynchronous sequential circuit design, consider a circuit with one input, x, and one output, Z. A series of pulses is applied to the input and

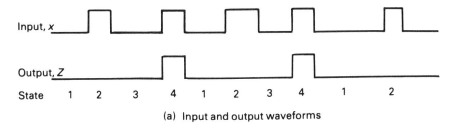

(a) Input and output waveforms

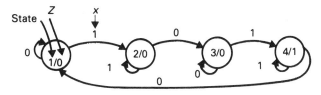

(b) State diagram (Moore model)

Present state	Next state x		Output Z
	0	1	
1	①	2	0
2	3	②	0
3	③	4	0
4	1	④	1

(c) Primitive flow table

(d) Transition map

Present state Y_2Y_1	Next state Y_2Y_1		Output Z
	0 x	1	
00	00	01	0
01	11	01	0
11	11	10	0
10	00	10	1

(e) Assigned primitive flow table

Figure 11.13   Asynchronous sequential circuit

every alternate pulse is to be passed to the output. This is shown diagrammatically in Fig. 11.13(a). The pulse duration and separation are variable.

A Moore model state diagram for this circuit is shown in Fig. 11.13(b). A Moore model state diagram is often used for asynchronous sequential circuit design because a stable state is clearly identified in the Moore model by a 'sling' path around the state. A transition from a stable state will only occur when the input changes from the sling value.

The next step is to draw the state table giving the information in tabular form. The asynchronous sequential circuit state table, as shown in Fig. 11.13(c), is known a *primitive flow table*.† The stable states are indicated by circles around the stable state numbers in the next-state columns. The circled stable states will be the same as the number in the present-state column. The output pertains to the stable state. The primitive flow table should then be minimized where possible. We will consider the minimization methods later. Our table does not minimize.

Then secondary variables are assigned. In doing this assignment, we must take care not to make an assignment which results in more than one variable change between states. A *transition map* may help us here. A transition map is a map labelled in the same way as a Karnaugh map, and using the secondary variables. States are chosen for each square on the map. Then, the transitions from one state to another are marked on the map and if any show a diagonal path across two variable changes, a new assignment must be made. A transition map for our problem giving a satisfactory assignment is shown in Fig. 11.13(d), and the assigned flow table in Fig. 11.13(e). Swapping state assignments for 1 and 2 would result in an unsatisfactory map. It may be necessary in some problems to introduce dummy states, i.e. to have a non-minimal number of states, in order to achieve a satisfactory assignment.

Finally a circuit is developed. There are two principal circuit implementations, one using purely combinational logic gates and one using combinational logic with asynchronous R–S flip-flops. (The asynchronous R–S flip-flops are implemented with combinational logic gates, e.g. a pair of cross-coupled NAND gates.)

(a) Combinational logic gate implementation

For a purely combinational logic gate implementation, the Boolean expressions for the excitation variables, Y_2 and Y_1, are obtained directly from the assigned primitive flow table, as shown in Fig. 11.14(a). Redundant prime implicants are added to eliminate static hazards.

The output function can be obtained in a three-step procedure. First the stable states are identified in the primitive flow table and mapped onto a Karnaugh map. The unstable states (transitions between stable states) can then be included as either the same as the present stable state output or the same as the next stable state output. If there is a change, a don't care could be mapped. If an early output change is

---

† The word *primitive* is used to indicate that there is only one stable state in each row; the table can sometimes have more than one stable state per row, as we shall see.

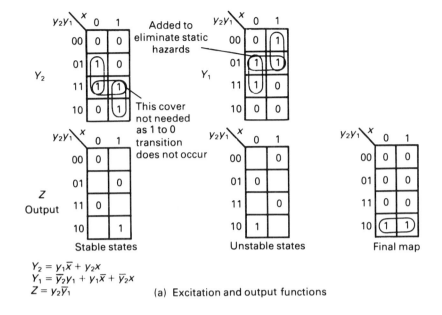

$$Y_2 = y_1\bar{x} + y_2x$$
$$Y_1 = \bar{y}_2y_1 + y_1\bar{x} + \bar{y}_2x$$
$$Z = y_2\bar{y}_1$$

(a) Excitation and output functions

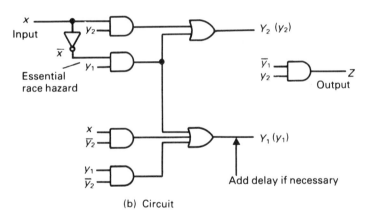

(b) Circuit

Figure 11.14 Asynchronous sequential circuit design using gates

desired, the next output value can be chosen so as to produce the final output during the transition between stable states. If a late change is desired, the present output value can be chosen, causing the output during the transition to be the same as the output before the transition. Our unstable outputs are mapped to be the same as the next stable state outputs. The final map is then minimized, taking care to eliminate static hazards if spikes must not occur in the output.

The complete logic circuit is shown in Fig. 11.14(b). Notice that the Y (excitation) outputs are fed back to the inputs of the gates as the y (secondary) variables. In a stable state, $Y = y$.

We must now consider essential race hazards. A possible critical essential race hazard is found in the circuit as a race between primary input, x, and the secondary variable, y_1, as indicated in Fig. 11.14(b). A change in x from 0 to 1 causes y_1 to change from 0 to 1, and if this returns before $\bar{x}$ is generated, incorrect operation will result. The particular circuit implementation shown makes this unlikely (but not impossible). If required, a delay circuit can be added to the y_1 output.

The essential race hazard can be identified on our primitive flow table as occurring during the transition from stable state 1 to stable state 2. The hazard will cause a transition from stable state 1 to stable state 4 rather than the required change to stable state 2. Stable state 4 would, in fact, normally be entered after a change in the input from 0 to 1, then back to 0 and again to 1. If, in any primitive flow table, three changes in an input (for example 0 to 1 to 0 to 1) result in a different state after the final change than after the first change, an essential race hazard is present, which is known as Unger's rule [4]. We may apply Unger's rule to detect the presence of essential race hazards, though it is then necessary to locate the problem and add the appropriate delay if necessary.

Since essential race hazards (as all race hazards) are due to gate propagation delays and their variations, we should examine the specification of the gates used. Often typical and maximum propagation delays are given but not the minimum delays. For example, typical LSTTL gates (such as the 74LS00, 74LS04, 74LS10 and 74LS20) have the following propagation delay times:

	Typical	*Maximum*
t_{PLH} Propagation delay time low-to-high level output	9 ns	20 ns
t_{PHL} Propagation delay time high-to-low level output	10 ns	20 ns

If we were to assume a minimum propagation delay time of 0 ns for the gates in our circuit except the inverters, and a non-zero propagation delay time for the inverter, the secondary variables would always arrive back to the input before the inverter had generated its output and a critical essential race hazard would exist. The appropriate delay in this case would be the same as the maximum propagation delay time of the inverter. Occasionally, a minimum propagation delay time is given (e.g. the Fairchild Advanced Schottky TTL type 74F00 quad 2-input NAND gate has a stated minimum T_{PLH} and T_{PHL} of 1.5 ns (maximum $T_{PLH} = 3.9$ ns and maximum $T_{PHL} = 3.6$ ns)) [5]. In addition to gate propagation delays such as the above, interconnection delays should also be considered (about 2 ns/ft).

(b) Designing with combinational circuits and asynchronous R–S flip-flops

The $R–S$ flip-flop design approach assigns one flip-flop for each secondary variable. The inputs to these flip-flops are determined by the required change of y to Y. Using Table 4.1 with y as Q and Y as Q_+, we obtain one function for each flip-flop input as shown in Fig. 11.15(a). The final circuit shown in Fig. 11.15(b) uses cross-coupled NAND gate $R–S$ flip-flops. A particular advantage of the $R–S$ flip-flop method is that it is not necessary to correct for static hazards because all the prime implicants are present in both the set and reset functions, which will be

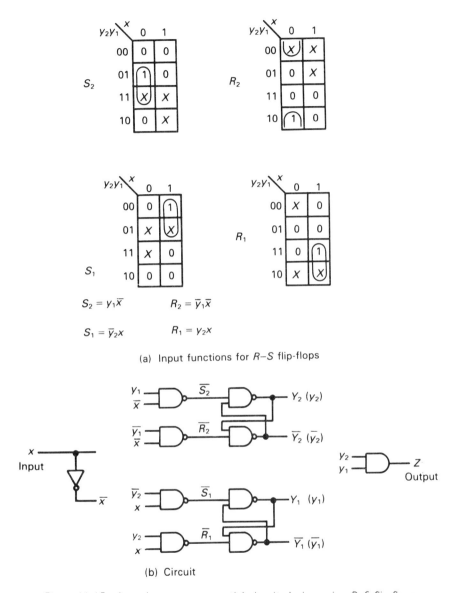

$S_2 = y_1\overline{x}$ $R_2 = \overline{y}_1\overline{x}$

$S_1 = \overline{y}_2x$ $R_1 = y_2x$

(a) Input functions for R–S flip-flops

(b) Circuit

Figure 11.15 Asynchronous sequential circuit design using R–S flip-flops

the case in all problems. Hence, the R–S flip-flop method often requires less components.

In the R–S flip-flop method, both true and inverse y outputs are available for feeding back to the flip-flop inputs. If the set and reset functions of the flip-flop include true and inverse variables, it is possible that both set and reset are a 1 together during a transition, causing both the y and $\overline{y}$ outputs both to be 0. This might create a critical race hazard, though this is unlikely with two-level circuits. The inverse y output can be generated using a separate gate if necessary [6].

11.2.3 State minimization

Consider a second asynchronous circuit problem. An asynchronous sequential circuit has two inputs, x_1 and x_2, and one output, Z. The output is to change state (from a 0 to a 1 or from a 1 to a 0) if any change from 0 to 1 occurs on either of the two inputs. Design the circuit assuming that the input signals never change simultaneously.

As before, the first step is to draw the state diagram. A Moore model state diagram for the problem is shown in Fig. 11.16. The primitive flow table is shown in Fig. 11.17(a). The dashes indicate disallowed conditions (requiring simultaneous changes in two primary variables).

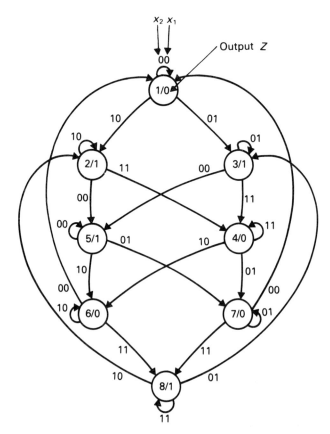

Figure 11.16 Asynchronous sequential circuit Moore model state diagram requiring minimization

Present state	Next state x_2x_1				Present output
	00	01	11	10	
1	①	3	–	2	0
2	5	–	4	②	1
3	5	③	4	–	1
4	–	7	④	6	0
5	⑤	7	–	6	1
6	1	–	8	⑥	0
7	1	⑦	8	–	0
8	–	3	⑧	2	1

(a) Primitive flow table

Present state	Next state x_2x_1			
	00	01	11	10
A	①	3	⑧	2
B	5	③	4	②
C	⑤	7	④	6
D	1	⑦	8	⑥

A = 1/8
B = 2/3
C = 4/5
D = 6/7

(b) Merged flow table

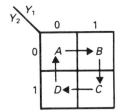

(c) Transition map

Present state Y_2Y_1	Next state Y_2Y_1 x_2x_1			
	00	01	11	10
00	00	01	00	01
01	11	01	11	01
11	11	10	11	10
10	00	10	00	10

(d) Assigned flow table

Figure 11.17 Asynchronous sequential circuit minimization and design

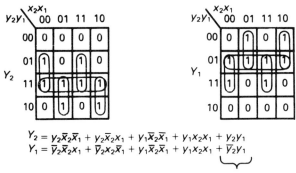

$$Y_2 = y_2\bar{x}_2\bar{x}_1 + y_2\bar{x}_2x_1 + y_1\bar{x}_2\bar{x}_1 + y_1x_2x_1 + y_2y_1$$
$$Y_1 = \bar{y}_2\bar{x}_2x_1 + \bar{y}_2x_2\bar{x}_1 + y_1\bar{x}_2\bar{x}_1 + y_1x_2x_1 + \bar{y}_2y_1$$

Added to eliminate static hazards

(e) Secondary variables

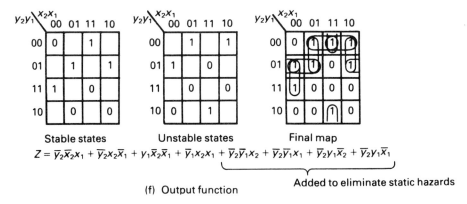

Stable states   Unstable states   Final map

$$Z = \bar{y}_2\bar{x}_2x_1 + \bar{y}_2x_2\bar{x}_1 + y_1\bar{x}_2\bar{x}_1 + \bar{y}_1x_2x_1 + \bar{y}_2\bar{y}_1x_2 + \bar{y}_2\bar{y}_1x_1 + \bar{y}_2y_1\bar{x}_2 + \bar{y}_2y_1\bar{x}_1$$

Added to eliminate static hazards

(f) Output function

Figure 11.17 continued

Next we can minimize where possible. As in synchronous sequential circuits, we look for states which are equivalent. Following the same procedure as in the synchronous design of examining pairs of states with the same output, and listing the required equivalent pairs, we find that two pairs are equivalent without any required equivalent pairs, namely (2, 3) and (6, 7). These pairs are the same (rather than equivalent). No other pairs can be found as equivalent.

Next, we can use a technique known as *merging* which utilizes the disallowed conditions in the next-state columns. A disallowed condition is a form of can't happen condition and can assume any state for minimization. For example, in our primitive flow table, states 2 and 3 can also be combined by merging:

Present state	Next state				Output		Present state	Next state			Output
2	5	–	4	2	1	=	2/3	5	3	4	2	1
3	5	3	4	–	1							

Similarly, states 6 and 7 can be combined. But in addition, states can also be merged even if their outputs are different because the outputs are uniquely defined by the inputs and the secondary variables. Consequently, states 1 and 8 can be combined and states 4 and 5 can be combined. This leads to the reduced flow table shown in Fig. 11.17(b). More than two states can be merged, but all the corresponding can't happen conditions (dashes) must be equivalent. The merging procedure results in four states:

$$(1, 8), \ (2, 3), \ (4, 5), \ (6, 7)$$

which we shall call A, B, C, and D respectively. The original state numbers are kept in the merged state diagram.

The subsequent procedure is the same as outlined previously. A transition map for assignment is given in Fig. 11.17(c), the assigned flow table in Fig. 11.17(d), secondary variables in Fig. 11.17(e) and output function in Fig. 11.17(f). We can identify several possible essential race hazards by Unger's rule. For example, starting at stable state 1 (A), one change in x_1 leads to stable state 3 (B), while two further changes in x_1, lead to state 7 (D). It is left to the reader to find the other essential race hazards by using Unger's rule.

In the above problem, a satisfactory secondary variable assignment can be made for the merged flow table. Often this is not possible, and either the original primitive flow table must be used, or dummy states introduced between state transitions so that only one secondary variable changes at a time. For example, consider the merged flow table shown in Fig. 11.18(a) which has three states (1, 2), (3, 4) and (5) given the letters A, B and C respectively. A satisfactory assignment cannot be made without modifying the state table. A transition map is shown in Fig. 11.18(b). We note that the transition from state A to state C, with the assignment chosen, requires both secondary variables to change. In two cases (the first and final next-state columns), there is only one stable state in the next-state column and any race hazard is not critical. In the third next-state column, there are two stable states and a hazard exists. One solution is to generate a fourth state D as shown in Fig. 11.18(c). The A–C transition when $x_2 x = 11$ now passes through state D. The other A–C transitions are similarly mapped through state D to maintain race-free transitions. The remaining entry is considered as can't happen.

If we do have a final state table which does not use all combinations of secondary variables, the next states of any unused row should be mapped with suitable unstable states to lead to a used state, so that a predicted action occurs upon switch-on.

11.2.4 Pragmatic approach to asynchronous sequential circuit design

The above design techniques are really only suitable for designs with relatively few components. Once the problem requires several state variables (secondary variables), obtaining a satisfactory race-free design can become difficult. The difficulties of

Present state	Next state $x_2 x_1$			
	00	01	11	10
A	①	3	②	5
B	1	③	④	5
C	1	–	2	⑤

(a) Merged flow table

(b) Transition map

Present state	Next state $x_2 x_1$			
	00	01	11	10
A	①	3	②	5
B	1	③	④	5
C	1	–	2	⑤
D	1	–	2	5

(c) Assigned flow table

Figure 11.18 Introducing a dummy state into the flow table

asynchronous sequential circuit design have led design engineers to avoid asynchronous designs when possible. Generally, asynchronous designs would be used if the required speed of operation could not be achieved with a synchronous design.

One approach is to convert the asynchronous signals into synchronous signals using a timing or clock signal. An asynchronous signal can be synchronized with a clock signal using a *D*-type flip-flop (clock signal to clock input of flip-flop and asynchronous signal to *D* input). However, this suffers from the disadvantage that the set-up and hold times of the flip-flop must be satisfied for proper operation. For example, if the set-up and hold times of a flip-flop used to synchronize an asynchronized signal were 20 ns and 5 ns respectively and the asynchronous input changed between 20 ns before and 5 ns after the clock signal being applied, the output could not be predicted. Worse, the flip-flop might enter a non-stable state with the output not at a defined logic level but at some intermediate point. This condition could, theoretically, last for ever, but in practice lasts for a considerable time (tens of nanoseconds). To reduce the probability of this output, two flip-flops

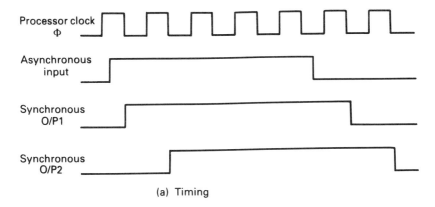

(a) Timing

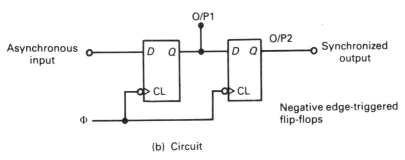

(b) Circuit

Figure 11.19 Double flip-flop synchronization circuit

Table 11.6 Set-up and hold times of various TTL flip-flops

Flip-flop	Type	Set-up time (ns)	Hold time (ns)
7474	D	20	5
74109	J–K	10	6
74111	J–K	0	30
74LS74	D	20/25	5
		(D = 1/D = 0)	
74LS76/78/112/114	J–K's	20	0
74LS109	J–K	20	5
74S74	D	3	2
74S112	J–K	3	0
74ALS74	D	15	0
74ASL109	J–K	15	0

in cascade can be employed as shown in Fig. 11.19, though there is still a finite probability of the circuit entering an unstable state. Once the asynchronous inputs have been synchronized with the clock signal, the design can be synchronous. Set-up and hold times of some flip-flops in the TTL family are listed in Table 11.6.

A microprocessor application of the above technique is in the synchronization of asynchronous ready signals from memory units to the processor, the processor being a synchronous device internally. External interrupt signals can also be synchronized for the processor. Similarly, the asynchronous bus transfer technique described in Chapter 6 for communication between units in a microprocessor system is an example of handshaking in which units operate synchronously internally, but with no synchronization between them. Synchronization circuits can be used to capture the external asynchronous signals.

11.3 Designing with programmable logic devices (PLDs)

11.3.1 Configurations

A *programmable logic device* (PLD) is an integrated circuit containing logic components which can be interconnected internally in various restricted ways by using fusible links or other selectable interconnection methods. One type of programmable logic device was introduced in section 3.3.3, the *programmable logic array* (PLA). Such PLAs contain a set of AND gates connecting to a set of OR gates. There are selectable links from the device inputs into the AND gates and between the AND gates and OR gates so that combinations of sum-of-product expressions can be realized. Other types of PLDs have been developed. Figure 11.20 gives the names of various types of PLDs.

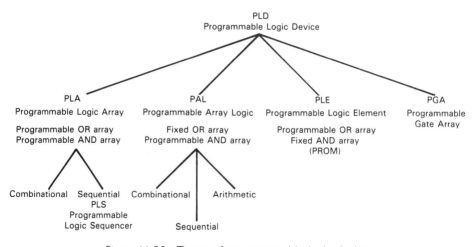

Figure 11.20 Types of programmable logic devices

Some PLDs are purely combinational circuits and some have flip-flops. Some PLDs are specifically designed to implement Mealy model or Moore model state machines. Apart from PLDs using bipolar fuses, CMOS electrically programmable PLDs using the technology of EEPROMs (Chapter 8, section 8.4.4) have been produced which allow the interconnection patterns to be altered through a programming sequence. In a similar fashion to ROMs, fixed patterns can be manufactured for large quantities. Software has been provided which converts a description of the logic required (Boolean equations, state equations, etc.) into 'fuse' patterns which can be transmitted to a PLD programmer unit. First, though, let us outline the various common PLDs given in Fig. 11.20.

Advanced Micro Devices Inc. [7] manufacture a family of AND-OR gate PLD devices which they call *programmable array logic* devices (PALS).† PALS are similar to PLAs having AND and OR gates interconnected to form AND-OR functions, except that the connections between the AND gates and the OR gates are fixed; only the connections into the AND gates are programmable. Hence AND gate outputs cannot be shared between AND-OR functions and must be duplicated if common terms exist. However, the device is less expensive generally and easier to program, and has found wide usage. The *programmable logic element* (PLE) identified in Fig. 11.20 has all combinations of fixed links into the AND gates and programmable links to OR gates. A PLE corresponds to a PROM since there will be a particular output binary pattern for each input combination (as with the data outputs for each address input pattern in a PROM). In the *programmable gate array*, each gate (or various types) can be programmed to connect to nearby tracks.

Figure 11.21 shows the general arrangement of a PAL device. There may be various numbers of inputs and outputs. Some output pins may be shared with some inputs, as shown, to conserve pins and allow convenient feedback connections (though not all output pins are shared with inputs in a particular device). The input/output lines can be used as inputs when the outputs are disabled, outputs, or as outputs fed back as inputs. The OR gate outputs reach the device outputs through three-state inverting buffers which can be enabled by a product combination of the inputs and feedback signals. A permanent enable condition will occur if none of the inputs and feedback signals are selected across the enable row (i.e. all the associated links are 'blown'). A permanent disable condition will occur if all of the inputs and feedback signals are selected across the enable row. An output will be permanently disabled if the line is required for input only and not an input fed back from an output. Sharing certain inputs and outputs has the disadvantage of reducing the number of independent variables that can be applied to each AND gate. Not using an output releases the line for extra input variables, and hence there is some flexibility between having more outputs or more input variables.

A representative combinational PAL device using the circuit shown in Fig. 11.21 is the AMD PAL16L8 which can create, subject to certain shared input/output line limitations, eight sum-of-product functions each having seven product terms and each product term having 16 variables. This device consists of eight OR gates,

†PAL is a registered trademark of Advanced Micro Devices Inc.

Input and feedback signals

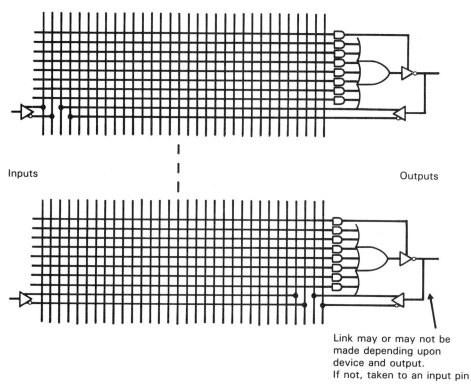

Inputs

Outputs

Link may or may not be
made depending upon
device and output.
If not, taken to an input pin

Figure 11.21   Programmable array logic circuit

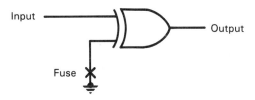

Input ———

Output

Fuse

Figure 11.22   True/inverse output circuit

one for each sum-of-product output function. Each OR gate has seven AND gates
at its input, one for each product term. Each AND gate can use any combination
of 16 variables or their complement. Ideally, the circuit would have 16 independent
inputs and eight independent outputs which could be fed back to the inputs if
required. In the 20-pin packaged PAL16L8, six of the eight outputs are also shared

with six of the inputs and may be fed back. The ten remaining inputs and two remaining outputs have separate pins. As with other logic components, PAL are manufactured to different specifications. For example, the (TTL) PAL16L8-7 has a propagation delay time of 7.5 ns (max.). Slower-speed devices are available with low-power consumption, including CMOS versions.

Notice that the natural function of each PAL output in Fig. 11.21 is an AND-NOR function (i.e. inverted or active low outputs, which is indicated by the L in the 16L8 mnenomic). Of course, PAL can be designed with active high outputs, and with programmable high/low outputs. Programmable outputs can be implemented using exclusive-OR gates as shown in Fig. 11.22. The fuse left intact will program a true output, the fuse blown will program an inverted output. Alternatively, a multiplexer can be used, selecting low or high signals if both are naturally available (as the outputs of flip-flops, for example).

The output–input feedback connection can be used to good effect in multi-level combinational functions, and in sequential circuits. Flip-flops can be created by implementing their characteristic equations, as described in Chapter 4, section 4.3. Each flip-flop created would require at least one feedback link.

A synchronous sequential circuit state machine can be created as shown in Fig. 11.23, in this example using external flip-flops to hold the state variables. A natural

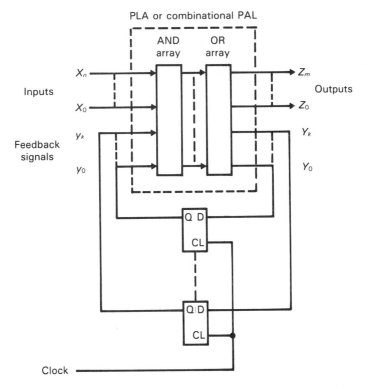

Figure 11.23 Synchronous sequential circuit model using PLA/PAL

extension would be to incorporate the flip-flops into the PAL, and PLDs also exist which incorporate these flip-flops. A general arrangement is shown in Fig. 11.24 using D-type flip flops. J-K and S-R flip-flop designs also exist. Such devices with outputs stored in flip-flops and synchronized to clock signals are called *registered PLDs*. Registered PLDs are capable of implementing general state machines, with the flip-flops holding the state variables. Of course, ordinary counters and shift registers can also be implemented. Not all outputs may have flip-flops, depending upon the design, and these outputs could be used as Z outputs (see Fig. 11.1). Both Mealy model and Moore model state machines are possible.

A representative registered PAL with some flip-flop outputs is the AMD PAL16R6, which is similar to the 16L8, but with the addition of six edge-triggered D-type flip-flops storing six of the outputs, and a common clock input for activating the flip-flops. (In fact, the 16R6 family contains the 16L8 as an option.) Other registered PLD families include the AMD PAL20X10, which has AND-OR-exclusive-OR gate combinations as shown in Fig. 11.25. The X series is particularly suitable for counters. PLAs with output flip-flops also exist, that is, AND-OR gates with selectable connections into both the AND gates and OR gate, and registered

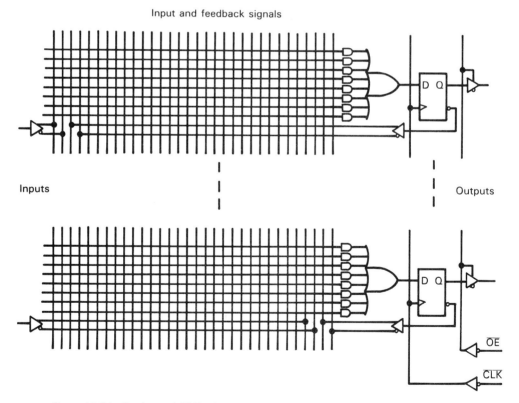

Figure 11.24 Registered PLD circuit using AND-OR gates and D-type flip-flops

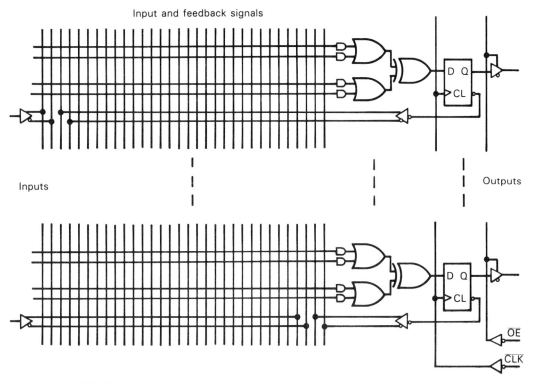

Figure 11.25 Registered PLD circuit with AND/OR/Exclusive-OR gates and D-type flip-flops

outputs. These devices are called *programmable logic sequencers* (PLSs), see Fig. 11.20.

Further flexibility can be incorporated into PLDs by having selectable bypass paths around the flip-flops to create either a combinational function output or a registered function output. There may also be selectable feedback paths. *Macrocells* are repeated circuits which have such selectable paths between the OR gates, flip-flops and feedback paths. Flip-flops whose outputs do not pass to the device outputs are called *buried* flip-flops. An example of a macrocell with a buried flip-flop is shown in Fig. 11.26. In this example, one multiplexer is used to select either the combinational OR gate function or the flip-flop to be output from the device, depending upon the fuse S1. Typically, both true and inverse device outputs can also be programmed. Another multiplexer is used to select either the flip-flop output or device output to be fed back into the AND array depending upon the fuse S2. Examples of PALs with macro cells include the PAL22V10 and PAL32VX10. Macrocells containing convenient combinational and sequential circuits can be formed into arrays with two-dimensional programmable interconnects (*logic cell arrays*).

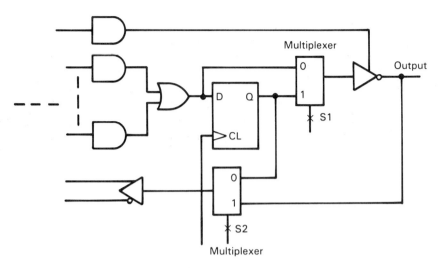

Figure 11.26 Macrocell with buried flip-flop

11.3.2 PLD programming languages

It is not usually necessary to specify the required connection patterns in a PLD directly. Software exists for programming PLDs, taking Boolean expressions or other descriptions of the required circuit and producing interconnection patterns for hardware PLD programming units. Such software includes logic simulation so that the circuit can be modelled and tested prior to creating a blown PLD. Industrial standard software includes PALASM2 (PAL assembler) from AMD Inc. and ABEL (Advanced Boolean Expression Language) from Data I/O Inc. The expressions describing the circuit are written in a 'high-level language' notation. Various symbols are used for logic operators. For example, in PALASM2, the OR operation is indicated by the symbol + , and the AND operation by the symbol *, as one would expect. The exclusive-OR is indicated by the symbol : + :. The NOT operation is difficult to represent as an overbar in computer print-out, and instead a symbol is often prefixed to the signal name, for example the symbol / in PALASM2. In ABEL, the default symbols are # (OR), & (AND), $ (exclusive-OR) and ! (NOT). In both systems, the = symbol indicates a combinational function. Registered outputs are indicated with the := equality. For example:

$$Z := A * B + /C;$$

specifies the output Z stored in a flip-flop and given by the expression $A.B + \bar{C}$. Expressions need not be two-level sum-of-product expressions; Boolean minimization can be performed. The names of signals need to be associated with the physical input and output pins of the device to map the minimized function onto the device. Such allocation is also done in the PLD program in the form of declarations. The complete PLD program consists of such declarations; other declarations, for example, indicating the device type and optional symbols, and the Boolean equations. Additional features include substitution strings for frequently used sequences and a notation to specify a group of related signals as might be found on a bus. ABEL allows, among other things, input to be entered as a state diagram description.

Perhaps the most common real application for PLDs is in the interface logic of a microprocessor system to reduce the component count. For example, the combinational logic problem of decoding the memory can easily be implemented with a combinational PLD. Suppose the memory addresses in a 32-bit microprocessor system are divided into four areas:

Read-only memory	00000000–001FFFF
Random access memory	00200000–005FFFF
MMU registers	FFF00000–FFF7FFFF
Serial I/O registers	FFF80000

The RAM has two adjoining areas from a decode point of view, from 00200000 to 003FFFFF and 00400000, to 005FFFFF. (This example is derived from a MC88100/88200 system design [9].) Figure 11.27 shows a PAL solution with a PAL16L8 specification. Device inputs are associated with signal names in the pin-out declaration which assumes that each signal name is assigned to the next pin in sequential order. (Another form of declaration found assigns specific names to specified pins.) A processor–memory interface design problem which could be implemented with a registered PLD will be described in the next section.

11.4 State diagrams using transition expressions

In this section, an alternative form of a state diagram will be introduced which is particularly suitable for problems with large numbers of variables such as in microprocessor systems. An alternative state assignment method will also be introduced. To describe these methods, we shall use a second processor–memory interface example, the design of memory interface timing logic for responding to processor memory request signals.

Suppose the control signals derived from the processor:

R/W   Read/write (0 for read, 1 for write)
REQ   Request (1 for memory request)

(The signal REQ is active high for simplicity.) The signal:

ADDR   address decode signal

is generated by the memory address decode logic when the address of the particular memory module has been presented by the processor. The memory interface timing logic accepts R/W, REQ and ADDR and should generate two signals:

REN   Read enable (1 for data being transmitted from memory)
WEN   Write enable (1 for data being transmitted from processor)

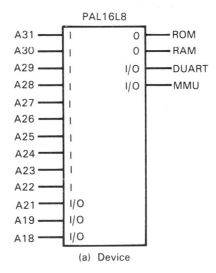

(a) Device

```
;PAL program for address decode
;pin-out

A31 A30 A29 A28 A27 A26 A25 A24 A23 GND
A22 /ROM A21 A20 A19 NC /MU /RAM /DUART VCC

;ROM addresses
ROM = /A31*/A30*/A29*/A28*/A27*/A26*/A25*/A24*/A23*/A22*/A21*/A20*/A19

;RAM addresses
RAM = /A31*/A30*/A29*/A28*/A27*/A26*/A25*/A24*/A23*/A22*A21+
      /A31*/A30*/A29*/A28*/A27*/A26*/A25*/A24*/A23*/A22*/A21

;MMU addresses
MMU = A31*A30*A29*A28*A27*A26*A25*A24*A23*A22*A21*A20*/A19

;DUART addresses
DUART = A31*A30*A29*A28*A27*A26*A25*A24*A23*A22*A21*A20*A19
```

(b) PAL program

Figure 11.27 Address decode using combinational PAL

according to the timing shown in Fig. 11.28. Din indicates the data transmitted from the memory to the processor, and Dout indicates data transmitted from the processor to the memory. (These signals do not correspond to any particular system but are representative.) During a memory read operation, REN is generated when data is provided by the memory. During a memory write operation, WEN is generated when data is provided by the processor. These signals could be used, for example, to control three-state bus buffers. Both read and write operations require at least two periods, R1 and Rw for read and W1 and Ww for write. The final 'wait' states are repeated until the processor completes its operation by releasing REQ. In

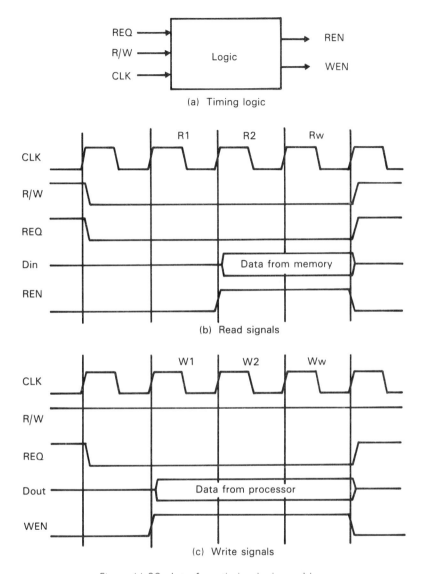

(a) Timing logic

(b) Read signals

(c) Write signals

Figure 11.28 Interface timing logic problem

addition, the read sequence can include one optional extra period, R2, selected if R2cycle is true during the R1 period. Similarly, the write sequence can include one optional extra period W2, selected if W2cycle is true during the W1 period. This mechanism allows the logic to account for slow memory. R2cycle and W2cycle could be permanently set to 1 to always include the extra cycles. Figure 11.28 shows these extra cycles.

A state diagram for the timing logic is shown in Fig. 11.29(a). This state diagram uses an alternative notation to that used previously; each arc is marked with

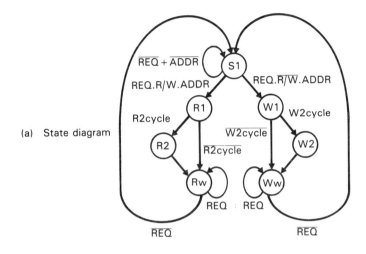

(a)   State diagram

(b) Output table

State	Output	
	REN	WEN
S1	0	0
R1	1	0
R2	1	0
Rw	1	0
W1	0	1
W2	0	1
Ww	0	1

Figure 11.29 State diagram and output table for interface timing logic problem

a Boolean expression which must be true for the transition. All expressions associated with each arc must be exclusive of each other (i.e. no combinations of variables make more than one expression true). Also, the set of expressions must cover all combinations of variables (i.e. all combinations of variables are represented in the expressions). For example, if there are two variables A and B, such that a transition from one state to another is to occur when $A = 1$ and $B = 1$, otherwise the present state remains, the arc leaving the state would be marked with AB, and the arc around the state (a 'sling') would be marked with $\bar{A} + \bar{B}$ (or $\overline{AB}$).

The notation is particularly suitable if there are many variables; the previous notation would require all Boolean combinations to be marked separately. (We would have marked the AB transition with 11 and the sling with 00,01,10.) Also, it becomes quite easy to derive the state transition variables. However, care is needed to ensure that all expressions are mutually exclusive and, as a set, are inclusive. Outputs have not been marked on the state diagram. With this form of state diagram, it is convenient to list the outputs in a separate output table as shown in Fig. 11.29(b).

In Fig. 11.29, the initial state S1 remains until a request is received and the correct address has been decoded. For a read operation, R1 is entered, and for a write W1 is entered as indicated by the arc expressions. Note that the expressions, REQ.$\overline{R/W}$.ADDR, REQ.R/W.ADDR, and $\overline{REQ} + \overline{ADDR}$ cover all combinations of variables. Transitions to R2 and Rw depend only upon R2cycle and transitions to W2 and Ww depend only upon W2cycle. Hence REQ, R/W and ADDR need not be specified; these are 'don't cares'. This assumes that the signals REQ, R/W and ADDR cannot change during these periods or that it does not matter if they do. We could incorporate an error state for such occurrences (Problem 11.7). However, if such an error condition does occur, as defined in Fig. 11.29 the system will simply follow the normal sequence and terminate normally. Termination occurs when REQ is released. (ADDR could also be added to the termination condition if required.)

Table 11.7 shows a state table for Fig. 11.29, giving both the states and their assignment. The state assignment is somewhat arbitrary, though an attempt has been made to minimize the state variable changes from one state to the next. The next states from a particular state are given vertically (together with the

Table 11.7   State table for state diagram in Fig. 11.29 using encoded state variables

Present state			Transition expressions	Next state				Present outputs	
	y_3	y_2	y_1			Y_3	Y_2	Y_3	REN	WEN
S1	0	0	0	$\overline{REQ} + \overline{ADDR}$	S1	0	0	0	0	0
				REQ.$\overline{R/W}$.ADDR	R1	0	0	1		
				REQ.R/W.ADDR	W1	1	0	0		
R1	0	0	1	R2cycle	R2	0	1	1	1	0
				$\overline{R2cycle}$	Rw	0	1	0		
R2	0	1	1	1	Rw	0	1	0	1	0
Rw	0	1	0	REQ	Rw	0	1	0	1	0
				$\overline{REQ}$	S1	0	0	0		
W1	1	0	0	W2cycle	W2	1	0	1	0	1
				$\overline{W2cycle}$	Ww	1	1	0		
W2	1	0	1	1	Ww	1	1	0	0	1
Ww	1	1	0	REQ	Ww	1	1	0	0	1
				$\overline{REQ}$	S1	0	0	0		

Next state equations:
$Y_3 = (\overline{y_3}.\overline{y_2}.\overline{y_1}).REQ.R/W.ADDR + (y_3.\overline{y_2}.\overline{y_1}).W2cycle + (y_3.\overline{y_2}.\overline{y_1}).\overline{W2cycle} + (y_3.\overline{y_2}.y_1)$
$\qquad + (y_3.y_2.\overline{y_1}).REQ$
$Y_2 = (\overline{y_3}.\overline{y_2}.y_1).R2cycle + (\overline{y_3}.\overline{y_2}.y_1).\overline{R2cycle} + (\overline{y_3}.y_2.y_1) + (\overline{y_3}.y_2.\overline{y_1}).REQ + (y_3.\overline{y_2}.\overline{y_1}).\overline{W2cycle}$
$\qquad + (y_3.\overline{y_2}.y_1) + (y_3.y_2.\overline{y_1}).REQ$
$Y_1 = (\overline{y_3}.\overline{y_2}.\overline{y_1}).REQ.\overline{R/W}.ADDR + (\overline{y_3}.\overline{y_2}.y_1).R2cycle + (y_3.\overline{y_2}.\overline{y_1}).W2cycle$

Output equations:
$REN = \overline{y_3}.y_2.y_1 + \overline{y_3}.y_2.\overline{y_1}$
$WEN = y_3.\overline{y_2}.\overline{y_1} + y_3.\overline{y_2}.y_1 + y_3.y_2.\overline{y_1}$

corresponding transition expressions), rather than horizontally as in previous state tables. We can quickly obtain the next-state equations using the general form:

$$Y_i = \Sigma \text{ (present state leading to } Y_i = 1) \cdot \text{transition expression}$$

The results are shown in Table 11.7 together with output equations. In this particular case, the outputs are functions of the states only (i.e. a Moore model). Generally the next-state equations can be reduced using conventional minimization techniques.

As an alternative state assignment, let us redesign the circuit using the *one-hot assignment*. In one-hot assignment, each state is assigned one unique state variable which is a 1 when the system is in that state. Hence with seven states in Fig. 11.29, seven state variables would be needed. Though the one-hot assignment leads to more state variables, it usually requires less complicated next-state expressions, and may be a good choice for small numbers of states. Table 11.8 shows the state table using one-hot assignment, except that the initial state is assigned to 00 ... 00 rather than an additional one-hot state variable. This is a convenient modification to the strictly one-hot assignment, since it is easy to initialize the state flip-flops to 00 ... 00, and

Table 11.8 State table for state diagram in Fig. 11.29 with one-hot assignment (except for initial state)

Present state R1 R2 Rw W1 W2 Ww	Transition expressions	Next state R1 R2 Rw W1 W2 Ww	Present outputs REN WEN
S1 0 0 0 0 0 0	$\overline{REQ} + \overline{ADDR}$	S1 0 0 0 0 0 0	0 0
	REQ.$\overline{R/W}$.ADDR	R1 1 0 0 0 0 0	
	REQ.R/W.ADDR	W1 0 0 0 1 0 0	
R1 1 0 0 0 0 0	R2cycle	R2 0 1 0 0 0 0	1 0
	$\overline{R2cycle}$	Rw 0 0 1 0 0 0	
R2 0 1 0 0 0 0	1	Rw 0 0 1 0 0 0	1 0
Rw 0 0 1 0 0 0	REQ	Rw 0 0 1 0 0 0	1 0
	$\overline{REQ}$	S1 0 0 0 0 0 0	
W1 0 0 0 1 0 0	W2cycle	W2 0 0 0 0 1 0	0 1
	$\overline{W2cycle}$	Ww 0 0 0 0 0 1	
W2 0 0 0 0 1 0	1	Ww 0 0 0 0 0 1	0 1
Ww 0 0 0 0 0 1	REQ	Ww 0 0 0 0 0 1	0 1
	$\overline{REQ}$	S1 0 0 0 0 0 0	

Next state equations:
R1 = $(\overline{R1}.\overline{R2}.\overline{Rw}.\overline{W1}.\overline{W2}.\overline{Ww})$.REQ.$\overline{R/W}$.ADDR
R2 = R1.R2cycle
Rw = R1.$\overline{R2cycle}$ + R2 + Rw.REQ
W1 = $(\overline{R1}.\overline{R2}.\overline{Rw}.\overline{W1}.\overline{W2}.\overline{Ww})$.REQ.R/W.ADDR
W2 = W1.W2cycle
Ww = W1.$\overline{W2cycle}$ + W2 + Ww.$\overline{REQ}$

Output equations:
REN = R1 + R2 + Rw
WEN = W1 + W2 + Ww

it reduces the number of state variables/flip-flops by one. Wakerly [10] called this assignment *almost one-hot assignment*. The next-state equations are derived in the same way as previously. Because of the state assignment, the expressions reduce considerably; in fact knowing that each state variable can only be a 1 in one instance reduces the expressions significantly. The almost one-hot assignment does slightly increase the complexity of the next-state equations over fully one-hot assignment. Problem 11.8 explores one-hot assignment and other state assignments fully.

References

1. Lewin, D., *Design of Logic Systems*, Wokingham, England: Van Nostrand Reinhold, 1985.
2. Lind, L. F., and C. C. Nelson, *Analysis and Design of Sequential Digital Systems*, London: Macmillan, 1977.
3. Fletcher, W. I., *An Engineering Approach to Digital Design*, Englewood Cliffs, NJ: Prentice Hall, Inc., 1980.
4. Unger, S. H., 'Hazards and Delays in Asynchronous Sequential Switching Circuits', *IRE Trans. Circuit Theory*, CT6 (1959), 12–25.
5. *Fairchild Advanced Schottky TTL*, Mountain View, CA: Fairchild Corp, 1979.
6. Dunderdale, H., *An Introduction to Formal Methods in Logical Design, Sequential Systems*, University of Salford (UK), 1970.
7. *PAL® Device Data Book Bipolar and CMOS*, Sunnyvale, CA: Advanced Micro Devices, Inc., 1990.
8. Lala, P. L., *Digital System Design Using Programmable Logic Devices*, Englewood Cliffs, NJ: Prentice Hall Inc., 1990.
9. Motorola Inc., *MC88200 Cache/Memory Management Unit User's Manual*, Englewood Cliffs, NJ: Prentice Hall Inc., 1990.
10. Wakerly, J. F., *Digital Design Principles and Practices*, Englewood Cliffs, NJ: Prentice Hall Inc., 1990.

Problems

11.1 A synchronous sequential logic circuit has two inputs, x_1 and x_2, and one output, Z. The output is required to become a 1 only during the presence of the final number in the sequence 00, 01, 10,11 applied to the two inputs.

Draw a Mealy model state diagram for the circuit and derive the state table. Hence design a circuit to perform the desired function using the minimum number of $J-K$ flip-flops and combinational circuits.

11.2 A synchronous sequential circuit has one input, x, and one output, Z. The output will be a 1 whenever the input sequence consists of 0110 or 1001, otherwise the output will be a 0.

Draw a state diagram for this circuit and construct a state table. Simplify where possible and design the circuit using D-type flip-flops and combinational circuits.

11.3 A synchronous sequential circuit has two inputs, x_1 and x_2, and one output, Z. The output is to be set to a 1 only when a group of four bits on one input is identical to the group of four bits on the other input, occurring in the same clock sequence.

Draw a Mealy model state diagram for the circuit and a state table. Determine a suitable state variable assignment by considering present and next states. Derive input equations for D-type flip-flop realization, and an output equation. Then give a complete circuit diagram.

Show how the combinational circuit can be realized using a read-only memory (ROM). List the contents of the ROM and give the overall circuit configuration.

11.4 Minimize the synchronous sequential circuit state table given in Table 11.9. Draw the reduced state table and sketch the equivalent state diagram. Assign state variables and obtain input and output equations for synchronous R–S flip-flop realization. Draw the logic circuit.

Table 11.9   State table for Problem 11.4

Present state	Next state $x_2 x_1$				Output, Z $x_2 x_1$			
	00	01	11	10	00	01	11	10
1	1	2	2	4	0	0	0	0
2	1	3	1	4	0	0	0	0
3	1	3	2	4	0	0	0	0
4	1	8	7	5	0	0	0	0
5	1	5	6	5	0	0	1	0
6	3	8	7	5	0	0	0	0
7	2	8	6	5	0	0	0	0
8	3	8	7	8	0	0	1	0

11.5 An asynchronous sequential circuit has one output, Z, and two inputs x_1 and x_2. An output logic pulse is generated when a logic pulse has occurred on x_1 and a logic pulse has occurred on x_2 (in either order). The input pulses are of variable width and occur at undefined intervals but cannot overlap. The output pulse has the same duration as the last input pulse that occurs. Second and subsequent pulses on one input before a pulse on the other input has activated the output do not have any effect.

Draw an annotated Moore model state diagram for the circuit and derive the primitive flow table. Minimize the table where possible.

Modify the state diagram to generate a single output pulse if overlapping input pulses occur. Describe the modification. State any assumptions considered necessary.

11.6 An electronic door switch is controlled by two 'push-button' switches, A and B. The door will open after switch A has been depressed and released twice and subsequently switch B has been depressed and released once. Any other sequence will cause an alarm to be activated. The sequence to open the door will also switch the alarm off if it has been activated. Switch A is depressed and released once to lock the door.

Draw an annotated Moore model state diagram for the door lock.

11.7   Incorporate all possible transitions from each state in Fig. 11.29 if all variables can change at any time between clock transitions. Re-work the state tables for both the minimum number of state variables (Fig. 11.7) and almost one-hot assignment (Fig. 11.8).

11.8   For the processor-memory interface problem (Fig. 11.29), re-work the state table and equations for 4, 5, and 7 state variables (fully one-hot assignment), making your own assignment choices. Comment upon the trade-off between the number of state variables and circuit complexity.

12 Processor Design

In Chapter 6, the internal operation of a microprocessor was briefly described. Now we shall consider the internal operation in greater detail. The techniques described apply to processors in general.

12.1 Internal operation of processor

12.1.1 Fetch/execute cycles

Let us recapitulate the mode of operation of a central processor. As noted in Chapter 6, section 6.1.1, the operation of a processor can be divided into two parts:

(i) Fetch cycle
(ii) Execute cycle

In the fetch cycle, the instruction to be executed is brought from the memory into an internal processor register known as the *instruction register*. (In the first instance, we will assume that the whole instruction is held in one memory word and is transferred in one action.) The fetch cycle itself may require several distinct steps. Referring to Fig. 12.1(a), a typical internal architecture of a register type of processor, the program counter holds the address of the instruction at the beginning of a fetch cycle. First, the contents of the program counter are placed on the address lines and the appropriate control signals are generated by the processor when the address signals are stable. The address signals, together with the control signals, are fed to all the memory units. The unit holding the memory location whose address coincides with the address transmitted is activated and the contents of the addressed location are placed on the data lines some time later. The delay before the data is presented depends upon the access time of the memory but is typically 20–100 ns. The processor waits either a set time unless modified by a wait signal from the memory, or it always waits until an acknowledge signal is received from the memory, depending upon the design. The former is assumed here.

After the data signals have settled on the bus, i.e. after all transients have died down and valid logic levels have been established, the processor accepts the data. This 'data' is the required machine instruction and is placed in the internal

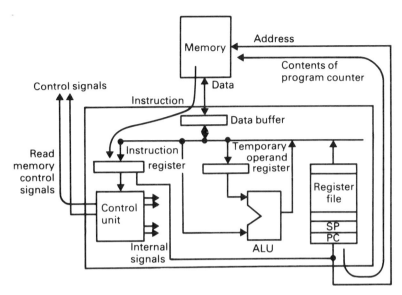

(a) Fetch cycle

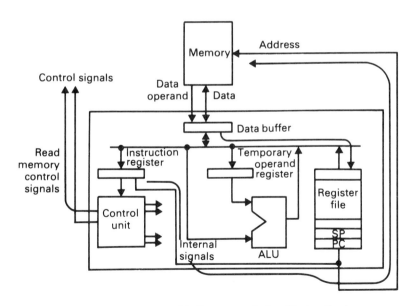

(b) Execute cycle (load instruction)

Figure 12.1   Processing operation

instruction register. Generally, the program counter is then incremented by one in preparation for the next instruction fetch cycle.

We have noted in section 6.2.3 that the instruction may be composed of more than one byte or word, each byte/word requiring a memory read operation. If this is the case, the fetch cycle is repeated for each byte or word of the instruction. The first byte or word specifies the operation and will indicate how many further bytes/words are necessary to fetch to complete the instruction fetch cycle. In 8-bit microprocessors, the first byte fetched is the op-code and the first fetch cycle is the op-code fetch cycle. The op-code fetch cycle would be followed by memory read cycles to obtain additional bytes of the instruction, when necessary. A similar process occurs in 16-bit microprocessors, but the transfers are often in 16-bit words. The fetch cycle is complete when all the bytes/words have been transferred into the processor, and the fetch cycle is then followed by the execute cycle.

Referring now to Fig. 12.1(b), in the execute cycle the operation specified in the instruction is executed. This may involve several distinct steps which will be different for different instructions. As an example, consider the instruction:

LD A,(100)   ;copy the contents of location 100 into the A register

To execute the instruction, firstly location 100 is addressed by placing the address 100 on the address lines together with, at the correct time, the control signals. The appropriate memory unit becomes activated and some time later the contents of the addressed location are placed on the data lines. The contents of the memory location are accepted by the processor and directed to the A register, whereupon this simple read instruction has been executed, and the next instruction can be fetched.

In the write instruction:

LD (100), A   ;copy the contents of the A register into memory
              ;location 100

the execute cycle begins by placing the contents of the A register on to the data line and the address 100 on the address lines. The appropriate control signals are generated. Some time later the memory unit addressed will accept the data, whereupon the instruction execution cycle is complete.

In general, the execution phase will involve an effective address calculation which may involve extra steps. For example, indirect addressing involves an extra memory read cycle to obtain the address of the operand from memory before the operand itself can be accessed. Therefore, the execute cycle may be composed of several memory read cycles or read cycles and a write cycle. It is convenient to divide the execute cycle into several subcycles, each of which is either a read cycle or a write cycle. The op-code fetch cycle is simply a special case of a read cycle.

The processor operates using a periodic clock signal. All internal operations are initiated by the clock and all timing is related to the clock. A microprocessor clock signal is either generated internally or externally using a crystal to create the correct frequency. There are two basic design approaches to activate read or write cycles using the processor clock. The simplest arrangement is to have one clock period for each cycle, either the instruction fetch, read or write cycle. A direct transfer instruction would need two clock periods whereas a complex indirect addressing instruction may require many clock cycles.

An alternative is to have a number of clock periods for each of the fetch, read or write cycles. The division of major cycles into subcycles has the advantage of being able to activate the various steps within each cycle in sequence and to time the steps more finely.

12.1.2 Register transfer logic

An essential part of the mechanism described is the transfer of the contents of one register to another register. We can specify this action in a register transfer notation. For example:

$$A \leftarrow B$$

means transfer the contents of register B into register A. The notation specifies a *data flow* action. Obviously, some control signal must be generated to initiate the action. We shall specify the control signal within the register transfer notation by prefixing the data flow action with a symbol identifying the control signal and a colon. For example:

$$T:A \leftarrow B$$

indicates that when a control signal, T, is true (1), the data flow occurs. The control flow component could be a Boolean expression, for example T_1T_2, which would indicate that the data flow occurs when both T_1 and T_2 are true.

To transfer the contents of one register to another register requires gating between the registers. The transfer can be activated by the control signal alone. Alternatively, the transfer can be synchronized with a central clock signal which could be specified as:

$$T\Phi:A \leftarrow B$$

where Φ is a clock signal. In this example, the transfer occurs when both T and Φ are true. The transfer mechanism might be implemented as shown in Fig. 12.2. Here, register B is composed of rising edge-triggered D-type flip flops, and hence the transfer occurs on the rising edge of the last signal to become true.

Since commonly a number of registers will exist in the system and many if not all combinations of transfers are to be provided, an internal bus configuration is convenient. A single bus can connect all inputs and outputs of the registers with the appropriate gating on the inputs and outputs of each register. The data flow component can include operations between stored operands. The operations are performed by one or more units in addition to registers. The most common additional unit is the arithmetic and logic unit (ALU) which performs the arithmetic

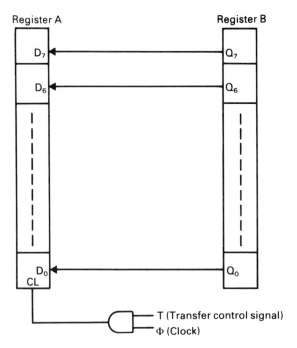

Figure 12.2 Register transfer mechanism

and logical operations on data operands within the processor. Arithmetic addition would be specified by:

$$T:A \leftarrow B + C$$

which specifies two operations, firstly the addition of the contents of the B and C registers, and secondly the transfer of the result to the A register. All this occurs when T is activated. We now need to differentiate between arithmetic addition and the Boolean OR operation. Here, in the data component, we will use the $+$ symbol to indicate arithmetic addition. The symbols $\vee$ and $\wedge$ can be used to indicate the Boolean OR and AND operations respectively. The Boolean symbols $+$ and $\cdot$ can be used to indicate the OR and AND Boolean operations in the control component. The $\cdot$ can be implied.

There are various other notations apart from the $A \leftarrow B$ notation used here, including the development of high level language constructs (for example in [3]). Notice that $\leftarrow$ is effectively the 'becomes equal' symbol $:=$ used in some high-level languages.

In general, a sequence of transfers is required to complete each machine instruction. Each transfer can be performed in a specified period, say T_1, T_2, T_3, etc. Figure 12.3 shows a simple sequence of T signals derived from the processor clock. We shall use the term *micro-operation* to describe each operation specified to occur at a particular time. It may be that several elementary operations are

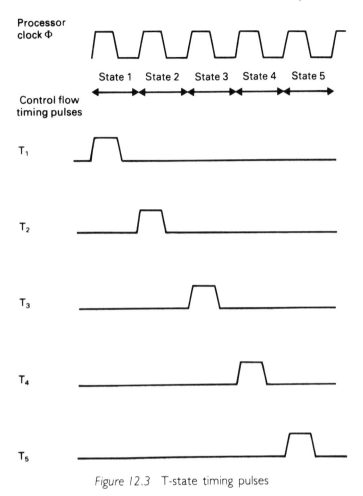

Figure 12.3 T-state timing pulses

specified within the micro-operation. Concurrent actions during one T period will be listed together and separated by commas.

Let us now apply the register transfer notation to a very elementary processor only having a single internal bus connecting the main internal components as shown in Fig. 12.4. We shall also assume that the instructions have a fixed single word length (c.f. RISCs, Chapter 6). A single internal bus restricts the transfers between attached registers to one at a time, but reduces the space required for the interconnections. Early microprocessors had this architecture, though with variable-length instructions as the data paths were often limited to 8 or 16 bits. Most recent processors provide more than one bus, for example three buses (see shortly in Section 12.2.3).

The external data and address buses connect to the main memory. An internal address buffer, ABF, and an internal data buffer, DBF, are introduced. The

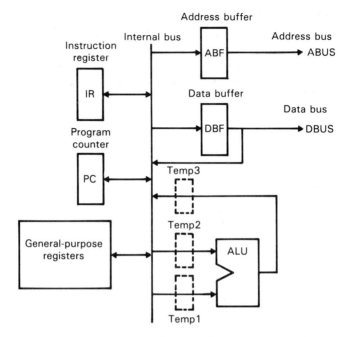

Figure 12.4 Simple processor architecture with a single internal bus

function of ABF is to hold the address that is to be placed on the external address bus. The transfer:

ABUS ← ABF

will be an implicit action which happens automatically when ABF is loaded. DBF holds data to be placed on the data bus. The transfer:

DBUS ← DBF

is also an implicit action which happens automatically when DBF is loaded. The transfer of data from the external data bus to the internal bus does not use DBF, though such transfers use internal buffer gates. ABF and DBF would be expected to exist in most microprocessors, but are not visible to the programmer. The inclusion of ABF and DBF enables the address and data on the external bus to remain stable while the internal bus is used for other purposes. Other 'invisible' registers also exist in most designs for holding values temporarily. For a single internal bus, temporary registers are needed at the input of the ALU for holding operands, since both operands need to be present before the ALU can operate (for two-operand operations). Also, the internal bus must be free to pass the results to the specified destination.

The register transfer notation can be extended to include the generation of external control signals such as read ($\overline{\text{RD}}$), write ($\overline{\text{WR}}$), and memory address strobe

($\overline{AS}$, say). One approach is to hold the control output signals in flip-flops. Then each flip-flop can be considered in the register transfer notation as an addressable single-bit register. For example, $\overline{RD} \leftarrow 0$ micro-operation would set the $\overline{RD}$ output to a 0, which would remain until a $\overline{RD} \leftarrow 1$ micro-operation occurred. An alternative approach is to generate the control signal when specified in the micro-operation, so that to maintain the signal at a 1, $\overline{RD} \leftarrow 1$ micro-operation would need to appear in each T cycle. We will take this latter approach. If the micro-operation to set a control signal does not appear, the signal will be reset to 0.

(a) Instruction fetch

A representative instruction fetch cycle specified in our register transfer notation is shown in Table 12.1. The control signal F signifies that a fetch cycle is activated. The address lines are given one cycle T_1, to settle, and then control signals, $\overline{RD}$ and $\overline{AS}$, are set to a 0 during T_2 and T_3. The instruction is transferred from the external data bus to the internal instruction register during the last cycle, T_3. Notice that the program counter is incremented after the contents have been placed on the address bus and well before the end of the cycle. This will have a particular significance and will be taken into account in instructions that use the contents of the program counter, principally relative jump instructions. Memory is assumed to be able to respond in one T cycle. Additional Tw cycles could be included if necessary, dependent upon an external $\overline{WAIT}$ signal.

(b) Execute cycle

(i) Move instructions
The execute cycle of the register-to-register move instruction might simply be implemented in a single micro-operation:

$$E_{MOVRR}T_1: Ri \leftarrow Rj$$

where E_{MOVRR} indicates that a register–register move instruction has been decoded. The execute cycle of a move instruction copying a constant into a register can also be implemented in a single micro-operation:

$$E_{MOVRn}T_1: Ri \leftarrow IRn$$

where E_{MOVRn} indicates that a literal–register move instruction has been decoded. The literal is held in the instruction indicated with IRn, suggesting that a path is necessary from the literal field of IR to the internal bus.

Table 12.1 Instruction fetch cycle

FT_1:	ABUS $\leftarrow$ PC
FT_2:	RD $\leftarrow$ 1, AS $\leftarrow$ 1, PC $\leftarrow$ PC + 1
FT_3:	RD $\leftarrow$ 1, AS $\leftarrow$ 1, IR $\leftarrow$ DBUS

These two implementations assume that the register file read and write can be done in one micro-operation on the specific architecture. However, for our single internal bus architecture, two separate micro-operations would be required, one to read the register file into a temporary register, and one to write from the temporary register into the register file.

The move instruction copying the contents of an absolutely addressed memory location into a processor register, i.e. MOV Ri, [nn], usually requires more than one micro-operation. It generally has a similar format to the fetch cycle except that the address of the memory is provided by the operand address field in the instruction. Table 12.2 lists the micro-operations. IRaddr represents the address field on the instruction. It is assumed that this address field can be accessed.

(ii) Arithmetic instructions

To execute arithmetic (and logical and shift) instructions, the operands are read from the specified locations and transferred to the ALU, which is set up to perform the operation. The result is generated and passed back to the specified destination. This suggests several sequential steps. For our single internal bus architecture, temporary registers are needed to store the operands after they are passed to the ALU in sequence. Table 12.3 shows one possible sequence of micro-operations. In this example, two registers are provided on the input of the ALU, Temp1 and Temp2, and Temp3 is an ALU output register. In fact, these registers are the only registers that this ALU can use. The T_3 micro-operation step orders the ALU to perform an addition, and transfer the result to the destination.

In Table 12.3, each step is assumed to take the same time; each register transfer operation requires the same time as the ALU operation. Clearly, it is possible to combine steps. Table 12.4 shows only two micro-operations for the addition

Table 12.2   MOV Ri, [nn] execute cycle

$E_{MOVRi(nn)}T_1$:	ABUS ← IRaddr
$E_{MOVRi(nn)}T_2$:	RD ← 1, AS ← 1
$E_{MOVRi(nn)}T_3$:	RD ← 1, AS ← 1, Ri ← DBUS

Table 12.3   ADD Ri,Rj execute cycle with three temporary registers

$E_{ADDR}T_1$:	Temp1 ← Ri
$E_{ADDR}T_2$:	Temp2 ← Rj
$E_{ADDR}T_3$:	Temp3 ← Temp1 + Temp2
$E_{ADDR}T_4$:	Rj ← Temp3

Table 12.4   ADD Ri,Rj execute cycle with one temporary register

$E_{ADDRR}T_1$:	Temp1 ← Ri
$E_{ADDRR}T_2$:	Rj ← Rj + Temp1

instruction, using only one temporary register. Now the T_2 step is significantly more complex but is still only given the same time as a register transfer step.

Whether Table 12.3 or Table 12.4 or some other sequence is used will depend upon the actual hardware design. In fact it may even be possible to specify the arithmetic operation in one step, i.e. $Rj \leftarrow Ri + Rj$.

We note in passing that transfers through the internal bus could be decomposed into two operations. For example, from Ri to Temp1:

> Intbus $\leftarrow$ Ri
> Temp1 $\leftarrow$ Intbus

where Intbus represents the internal bus, though this decomposition will not be made. Note also, the inclusion of temporary registers may slow down the system unnecessarily.

Incrementing the program counter in the instruction fetch cycle, $PC \leftarrow PC + 1$ (Table 12.1) could be done by the ALU as with other arithmetic operations, or intrinsically by constructing the PC as a counter. If so constructed, the PC would be separate from the general register file as shown, otherwise it would be convenient to place the PC within the register file.

(iii) Conditional micro-operation

So far, we have omitted wait states. Wait states are introduced if the memory is not ready to read or write. They provide a delay until the memory is ready. We need a notation to describe a micro-operation which is executed if $\overline{WAIT} = 0$, but not otherwise, i.e. a conditional micro-operation. For example:

> If Boolean condition THEN micro-operation

In this notation, if the Boolean condition has been satisfied, the stated micro-operation is performed, but not otherwise. However, this is not sufficient, as we need to be able to repeat a micro-operation until a Boolean condition becomes false (i.e. until $\overline{WAIT} = 1$). One approach would be to introduce a 'conditional jump' operation, i.e.:

> T_2: IF $\overline{WAIT} = 0$ THEN $T_{next} = T_2$

Here we are controlling the next T cycle to be executed. If $\overline{WAIT} = 0$, then the next T cycle after the first T_2 is another T_2 cycle. Alternatively, since it is not desirable to allow continuous wait states to be generated, as would occur if the memory never responded, a fixed number of conditional operations could be included, say ten. If after this time the wait line is still a 0, an error flag could be set.

Conditional micro-operations are also necessary to implement conditional machine instructions, i.e. conditional jump/branch/call instructions. These conditions are indicated in the F register. All conditions, whether externally or internally generated, need to be made available for the control unit (see next section).

12.2 Control unit design

We have seen generally that the processing of every machine instruction consists of an instruction fetch cycle and an execute cycle. Each cycle consists of a number of fundamental micro-operations. Each of these micro-operations requires signals to be generated by the control unit of the processor to initiate the micro-operations. There are two basic approaches to the design of a control unit:

(i) Random logic design
(ii) Microprogrammed design.

12.2.1 Random logic design

In the random logic approach, gates and counters are interconnected to generate the signals. Each design requires a unique set of gates and counters and interconnections. One implementation is to use a ring counter or shift register holding a circulating 1 to generate the T state signals as shown in Fig. 12.5. A signal sets the first flip-flop of the shift register to a 1 output and the remaining flip-flops to a 0 output. Then the clock pulses may be applied (at twice the frequency of Φ to achieve the waveforms given in Fig. 12.3). Further gating is then necessary to produce the required control signals.

12.2.2 Microprogrammed design

The microprogrammed approach utilizes the fact that each step in itself is a basic 'instruction' and these instructions need to be executed in sequence. Each step is encoded into a *microinstruction*. A sequence of microinstructions is formed for each machine instruction and stored in a control memory within the internal control unit

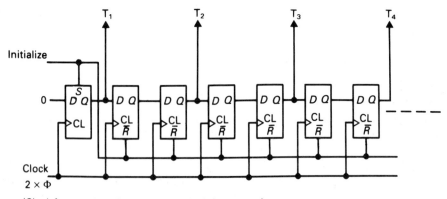

(Clock frequency twice processor clock frequency)

Figure 12.5 Using a shift register to general control pulses

of the processor. The sequence of microinstructions is known as a *microprogram* and a sequence is executed for each machine instruction. The method leads to a clear-structured and flexible design and has been adopted in the design of some microprocessors (e.g. Motorola 68000, National Semiconductor 16032) but not all (e.g. Motorola 6809 and Zilog Z8000 use a random logic design). A combination of the two approaches can be taken (e.g. Intel 8086).

The technique of microprogramming was first suggested by Wilkes in the early 1950s [1], though it was not commonly put into practice for the design of digital computers until the 1960s. The original Wilkes scheme used a microinstruction encoded into two fields, one known as a *micro-order* (or *microcode*) giving the signals to be generated for the step, and one giving the address of the next microinstruction to be executed. The general arrangement of a microprogrammed control unit is shown in Fig. 12.6. The instruction is fetched into the instruction register using a standard microprogram. The machine instruction 'points' to the first microinstruction of the microprogram for that machine instruction. This microinstruction is executed and subsequent microinstructions in the microprogram. The sequence can be altered by conditions occurring within or outside the processor. In particular, microprogram sequences of conditional branch machine instructions may be altered by conditions indicated in the processor condition code register. One scheme causes the next microinstruction to be skipped over if a condition prevails, i.e. a microprogram counter is incremented by two

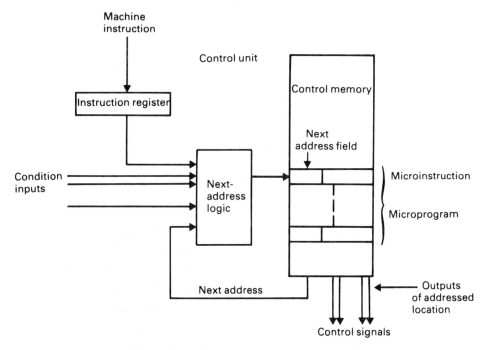

Figure 12.6 Microprogrammed control unit

rather than by one. Also subroutine microinstructions can be provided to reduce the size of the microprogram. Just as a stack is used to hold the return address of machine instruction subroutines, a control memory stack can be provided to hold the return address of a microinstruction subroutine return.

There are two basic types of micro-order format:

(i) Horizontal micro-order format
(ii) Vertical micro-order format.

In the *horizontal* micro-order format (the original Wilkes scheme), one bit is provided for each logic signal that can be generated by the microinstruction, as shown in Fig. 12.7(a). For example, if there were 100 possible signals, there would be 100 bits in the micro-order. To generate a particular signal, the corresponding bit in the micro-order would be set to a 1. More than one signal could be generated simultaneously if required by setting more bits to a 1.

In the *vertical* micro-order format, the bits are encoded into fields to reduce the number of bits in the micro-order, as shown in Fig. 12.7(b). Bits are formed into groups specifying signals that cannot be activated together. For example, if four data transfer request signals, memory read, memory write, input read and output write, were provided, these would be all mutually exclusive and could not occur

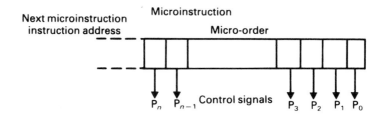

(a) Horizontal micro-order format

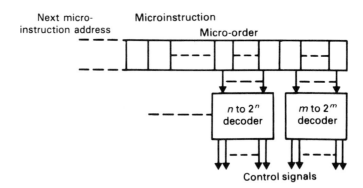

(b) Vertical micro- order format

Figure 12.7 Micro-order formats

together. These together with up to three other signals could be encoded into three binary digits. One encoded pattern, say 000, must be reserved for no signal at all.

The horizontal method is the most flexible but results in a long micro-order whereas the vertical method is more efficient but requires logic to decode the patterns and hence the speed of operation is reduced. Examples can be found of both approaches. Texas Instruments' 99000 microprocessor uses an almost totally unencoded microinstruction word of 152 bits, while Intel's 8086 uses an encoded field of 21 bits. Motorola's 68000 uses a two-level approach in which a 10-bit microinstruction points to a 70-bit 'nano' instruction. The horizontal and vertical formats can be used in one microinstruction, if desired.

Since a complete microprogram must be executed for each machine instruction, it follows that the speed of operation of executing each microinstruction must be much faster than that of the required machine instruction. Therefore, the control memory must operate much faster than that of the main memory holding the machine instruction. In a processor with a fixed set of machine instructions, the control memory can be read-only memory (see Chapter 8). If a read–write memory (or programmable read-only memory) is used for the control memory, the possibility exists of altering the machine instruction set through writing new microprograms (a technique known as *microprogramming*) which leads to the concept of *emulation*. In emulation, a computer is microprogrammed to have exactly the same instructions set as another computer and behave in exactly the same manner, so that machine instruction programs written for the emulated computer will run on the microprogrammed computer. Emulation is not applicable to complete microprocessor devices.

12.2.3 Microprogrammed processor design

In this section, we will consider the main components of a processor designed using the microprogrammed approach. In section 12.2.4, we will relate the general design to specific commercial microprogrammable devices.

The first step is to establish the machine instruction formats. For simplicity, let us choose a fixed 32-bit-length machine instruction having a three-register format for register–register operations, a one-register-constant format for literal operations, and a one-register–memory address for register–memory operations. Figure 12.8 (a), (b) and (c) shows the formats with selected field sizes. A key feature is that the op-code and operand fields remain in the same place in both formats, which greatly simplifies the design.

The op-code field occupies eight bits, enabling up to 256 different operations to be specified. Op-codes could be divided into two equal halves, say one for formats (a) and (b) and one for format (c), using bit 31 = 0 for format (a)/(b), and bit 31 = 1 for format (c). If the memory reference operations are limited to load and store as in most RISCs, a more complicated decode would be necessary to utilize all possible op-code patterns. In our design, it does not matter how the three formats are differentiated within the op-code, as a full 8-bit decode can easily be accommodated.

(a) Register-to-register instruction format

(b) Register-literal instruction format

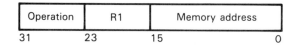

(c) Register-memory instruction format

Figure 12.8 Instruction formats for microprogrammed processor

The register fields are allocated eight bits each, enabling one of 256 different internal processor registers to be specified for each of the sources and the destination. This is greater than the number of processor registers found in many existing processors (which is often in the range 32–64), but allows the register and op-code fields to remain in the same place in each format with a 16-bit literal in format (b) and a 16-bit memory address in format (c). A 16-bit literal implies that two operations will be necessary to load a 32-bit register, which is always necessary with 32-bit fixed-length instruction sets. The 16-bit address field is also somewhat smaller than is found in all but RISC processors. To counter this limitation, register indirect plus displacement addressing can be provided. The address would then be relative to the R1 register specified in the instruction. In addition, 16-bit absolute addressing can be accommodated. (Other possibilities are studied in Problem 12.6.) For branch instructions, rather than using the R1 register as the base register, the program counter is of course a more appropriate base register. The actual instructions will be left unspecified at this time. One advantage of the microprogrammed approach is that there is flexibility in the selection of instructions within the instruction set.

Figure 12.9 shows a block diagram of a microprogrammed processor. The design can be compared to the concept in Fig. 12.6. The main parts are:

(a) Machine instruction register, IR, and op-code decode
(b) Sequencer
(c) ALU
(d) Register file
(e) Control memory and microinstruction register
(f) Interface to external data/address/control bus.

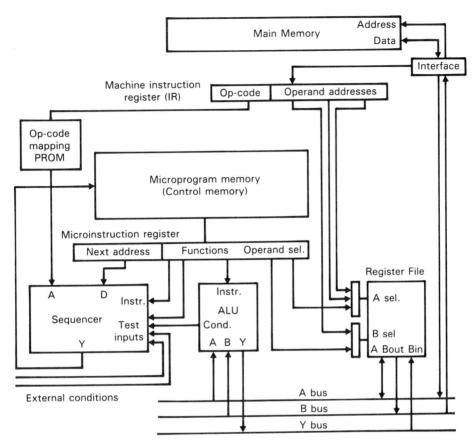

Figure 12.9 Microprogrammed processor

(a) Machine instruction register and decode

Upon switch-on, the first machine instruction fetch cycle should start and fetch the machine instruction from a defined location (say location zero). All instruction fetch cycles could be performed by special hardware as, mostly, instruction fetch cycles are similar and are not influenced by the actual instruction (unless multiple-length instructions are involved). Alternatively, the fetch cycle could be performed by one or more microinstructions held at the beginning of the microprogram control memory. We will provide for the microprogrammed approach. In either case, the fetch cycle causes the machine instruction to be loaded from the main memory into the machine instruction register, IR.

The next step is to decode the fetched instruction. This could also be done by a sequence of microinstructions decoding individual bits in the op-code. However, the decode step is best done by hardware for speed, and a common approach is to use a read-only memory look-up table. Figure 12.9 shows the use of a PROM. (An alternative solution is to use PLDs.) The look-up table holds the addresses of the first microinstruction in the control memory for each possible op-code. For an 8-bit op-code, a 256-word look-up table is necessary. The size of the word will depend upon the size of the control memory, assuming that the first microinstruction can be placed anywhere in the control memory. For example, a 64K microinstruction control memory would require a look-up-table word size of 16 bits.

(b) Sequencer

The next address logic in Fig. 12.6 is identified in Fig. 12.9 as a (microprogram) *sequencer*. The sequencer generates the next microinstruction address from one of various sources. The principal sources that can be expected in a design are:

(i) Op-code mapping PROM
(ii) Next address field of the current microinstruction
(iii) Microinstruction program counter within the sequencer
(iv) Address stack within the sequencer
(v) Interrupt logic.

The actual source chosen by the sequencer to output as the next microinstruction address is defined by a *sequencer instruction* (function code) and *condition select code* presented to the sequencer. These codes are held in fields of the current microinstruction.

The sequencer contains an address multiplexer and an instruction decoder to control the multiplexer, together with the internal sources of addresses. The address output of the sequencer passes to the control memory to select the next microinstruction. The initial address is provided by the mapping PROM and this address enters the sequencer via one address input (input A in Fig. 12.9).

Various sequencer instructions are provided to select each address input for output, perhaps 16–64 different instructions. The internal microinstruction program counter is provided for sequential microinstruction execution. Many sequencer instructions are for non-sequential microinstruction execution. Unconditional and conditional jump and call instructions are provided. The unconditional jump instruction simply selects a particular source to output. Conditional jump instructions select the source if certain conditions occur on external test inputs or in an internal counter. An internal counter is provided to control microinstruction loops. The counter can be loaded (by a sequencer instruction) with a loop count, and subsequentially decremented during the execution of specific sequencer instructions. Specific conditional jump instructions can recognize when the counter reaches a termination value. For conditional instructions that fail the conditional and unconditional instructions, the contents of the microprogram counter are passed to the address output, thus causing a sequential instruction execution.

The sequencer subroutine call instruction behaves like a subroutine call at the machine instruction level; the return address is stored on a stack at the time of the call, though in this case using a sequencer stack. A sequencer stack is also very useful for storing parameters, notably counter values for nested loops. For speed, a small internal register stack is provided within the sequencer, 20–40 locations would probably be sufficient.

(c) ALU

The ALU in Fig. 12.9 performs the normal arithmetic, logical and shift operations expected at the machine instruction level of a processor. The ALU is also available for other arithmetical, logical and shift operations needed at the microinstruction level only. It has two source operand inputs (A and B in Fig. 12.9) and one result operand output (Y in Fig. 12.9). Condition codes are also generated and used as some of the test inputs of the sequencer. The ALU responds to an ALU function code held in the microinstruction. There may be 64–128 different operations implemented within the ALU, arithmetic, logical, and single-bit shift operations certainly being provided. Other more specialized operations such as parity generation/checking may be provided. High-speed multi-bit shift is useful, especially if provided at the machine instruction level. In some designs, a separate shifter is provided at the output or input of the ALU, rather than, or in addition to, any built-in shift operations. This has applications in multiplication and division implemented with multiple microinstructions.

According to our machine instruction format, we must handle register–register operations and register–memory operations. Hence paths are provided between ALU, the register file, and the main memory. A convenient arrangement, especially if more than one arithmetic unit is included in the system, such as floating point or multiply/divide units, is to have internal buses connecting the units to the register file and the interface to external memory. This type of internal organization has been seen earlier, and is commonly employed. Figure 12.9 shows three such internal buses, A, B and Y, corresponding to the A, B inputs and Y output of the ALU.

(d) Register file

The register file contains the principal registers visible to the programmer at the machine instruction level, such as:

(i) General-purpose accumulator registers
(ii) Special-purpose data and address registers
(iii) Program counter (a special-purpose address register).

Also, some of the registers in the register file can be reserved for internal use only, for example as temporary registers for the microcode. It would be possible to include the machine instruction register (IR) in the register file, which might be convenient if the instruction decode is done by microcode, but we choose to separate this particular register. (Problem 12.9 investigates the design with the IR register as part of the register file.) Placing the PC in the register file implies that this register is incremented by microcode after each machine instruction is fetched from memory. Jump machine instructions will further modify the PC register.

In all machine instructions having the formats shown in Fig. 12.8, one or more register file addresses are provided in the instruction. Hence paths are provided for directly addressing the register file from the IR register as shown. In addition, the register file can be directly addressed by microinstructions during the execution of the microprogram. Hence we see address paths from the microinstruction register to the register file. Whether the register address is provided by the machine instruction or microinstruction is determined by the microinstruction, and a select bit is necessary within the microinstruction.

The register file needs to be at least dual access, providing the capability of reading two different locations at the same time so that both operands can be presented to the ALU at the same time along the A and B buses. Dual-access register file chips are available and provide independent simultaneous accesses to two separately addressed locations within the register file. Each access can be read or write, and the same or different locations can be selected. Separate read and write ports can be provided. Figure 12.9 shows a dual access register file with the read and write ports for A combined into a bidirectional port for the A bus. The read and write ports for B (Bout and Bin) are used separately for the B bus and Y bus respectively.

(e) Control memory and microinstruction register

The control memory is a conventional, very-high-speed, read-only semiconductor memory. Some of this memory could be read/write memory for user micro-programming, though interest has diminished in this possibility. However, during the development phase, read/write memory can be provided in a prototype system attached to a host computer system used for loading the control memory. The read/write control memory would be replaced with read-only memory when the design was finalized. The microinstruction read from the control memory is commonly held in a *microinstruction register* as shown. (In some designs, using a register here also enables the next microinstruction to be read from the control memory while the currently held microinstruction is being executed, see Section 12.3 for a discussion of this so-called overlap/pipelining technique.)

Each microinstruction provides in individual fields:

   (i) Sequencer instruction
  (ii) Sequencer condition input select code
 (iii) ALU function code
 (iv) Register file operand addresses when held in microinstruction
  (v) Various single-bit flags indicating for example:
      Direction of operand transfer
      Source of register file addresses
 (vi) Next microinstruction address for non-sequential operation

and effectively controls all parts of the system. Notice that many fields are vertically encoded and control specific units. The decoding is done within each unit.

(f) Interface to external data/address/control bus

An interface is necessary between the internal buses and the external address/data/control bus. In our design, the external memory data and memory address are shown connecting to the A and B buses respectively. The memory address generated by the processor can be held in any register in the register file, and similarly for memory write operations, the data provided can be in any register. Normally it would be a different register. Notice that it is possible to read the contents of two registers simultaneously given the dual-access register file. Often, though, the data can be issued to the memory later (see, for example, the external bus timing in Chapter 6). For memory read operations, data from the memory can be accepted by any selected register within the register file. We have chosen to use a bidirectional bus connecting to A port of the register file for passing data from memory to the register file. A possible alternative design would be to use the A read and write ports of the register file separately (Problem 12.7).

The design does not show other features generally necessary such as circuits to handle external interrupts and external interface logic.

12.2.4 32-bit microprogrammed processor – an example

In the previous section, we described a microprogrammed processor architecture and the general component requirements. Now we will identify specific available components for the architecture from the Am29C300 microprogrammable family of devices [2], and highlight their features. Three family members, a program sequencer (Am29C331), a full 32-bit integer ALU (Am29C332), and a four-port dual-access register file (Am29C334), form the main special elements of the systems.† Other available components include separate floating point processors and a high-speed 32-bit multiplier.

The Am29C334 is a 64 word × 18-bit dual-access register file with separate read and write ports. Typically, two devices would be used to obtain 64-bit words plus eight parity bits. In our system, we have specified 256 general-purpose registers. In addition, we need to provide for the program counter and possibly some temporary registers for the microcode. Several design options appear including:

 (i) Provide 512 registers, all available by the microcode using 9-bit select addresses in the microinstruction, and 256 selectable at the machine instruction level
 (ii) Provide 320 registers (256 + 64), all available by the microcode using 9-bit select addresses in the microinstruction (not all codes used), and 256 selectable at the machine instruction level
(iii) Provide 256 registers available to both machine instruction and microcode.

† Historical note: The earlier Am2900 family [3], an industry standard during the 1970s and 1980s, included the Am2910 sequencer and the Am2901 ALU. The Am2901 ALU integrated the register file into the ALU into one chip but only as a 4-bit unit (4-bit slice), four of which had to be cascaded to form 32 bits.

Option (iii) would mean that less than the full 256 general-purpose registers were provided, say 254 general-purpose registers, plus the program counter and one register for the microcode. However, some mechanism should then be placed to prevent the machine instruction addressing the microcode register (i.e. detecting an unused code). Addressing the program counter directly may be useful, and special machine instructions could be provided for this purpose. Detecting unused codes significantly complicates the design (Problem 12.10) and instead we will choose option (ii). Ten Am29C334 devices are thus needed. Option (ii) can easily be upgraded to option (i) by adding memory.

Figure 12.10 shows the Am29C331 sequencer architecture, somewhat simplified for our purposes. The Am29C331 microprogram sequencer generates a 16-bit address on the Y output from one of five sources:

(i) Primary external 16-bit address input labelled D
(ii) Second external 16-bit address input labelled A
(iii) Internal microinstruction program counter (incrementer)
(iv) Multiway jump address logic
(v) Internal 33-word address microprogram stack.

A facility to jump to one of several defined locations dependent upon external inputs is very convenient as it eliminates a sequence of steps to identify a target

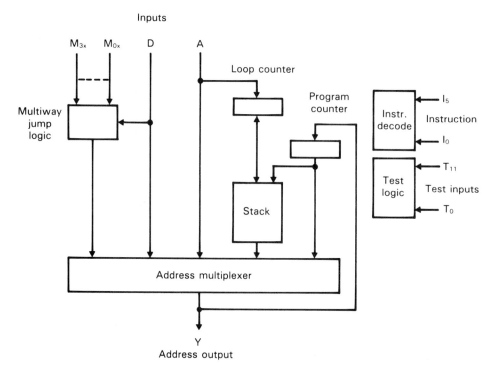

Figure 12.10 Microinstruction sequencer

address when there are several possible identifiable outcomes. The multiway jump mechanism in the Am29C331 uses the D inputs and sixteen inputs labelled $M_{3,3} \dots M_{3,0}$, $M_{2,3} \dots M_{2,0}$, $M_{1,3} \dots M_{1,0}$, and $M_{0,3} \dots M_{0,0}$. The mechanism enables one of four different target addresses to be generated, selected by the least two significant bits of the D input, $D_1 D_0$. Each of the target addresses is formed by the bits $D_{15} \dots D_4$ concatenated with one group of four M inputs, namely $M_{3,3} \dots M_{3,0}$ if $D_1 D_0 = 11$, $M_{2,3} \dots M_{2,0}$ if $D_1 D_0 = 10$, $M_{1,3} \dots M_{1,0}$ if $D_1 D_0 = 01$, and $M_{0,3} \dots M_{0,0}$ if $D_1 D_0 = 00$. Each group of four M inputs can select one of 16 consecutive locations. Since the possible jump locations are consecutive, each of these locations will need to hold a further jump to a new location in most applications.

There are various design possibilities for using the multiway mechanism. A group of M inputs could be connected to an addressable register. A group of M inputs could be connected directly to the condition outputs of the ALU. (However, the Am29C331 does have a separate mechanism for handling the ALU condition codes.) Separate M groups could come from status outputs of other arithmetic processors such as floating point processors. A group of M inputs could be used as address modifier bits in the machine instruction directly, say as the first four bits of the 8-bit op-code, to be effective in certain operations.

The Am29C331 responds to a 6-bit instruction ($I_5 \dots I_0$). The instruction set is shown in Table 12.5, and can be divided into three groups:

(i) Unconditional jump ($I_5 I_4 = 10$)
(ii) Conditional jump ($I_5 I_4 = 00$ and $I_5 I_4 = 01$) and
(iii) Special functions ($I_5 I_4 = 11$).

One of four possible sources can be explicitly specified in the unconditional and conditional jump groups, namely, the D input, the A input, a multiway address obtained from D and M inputs as described previously, and the top of the internal stack (TOS). The source is indicated with an $\times$ in Table 12.5. Each possibility has a unique instruction encoding.

The conditional jump group has two subgroups, one for true conditions ($I_5 I_4 = 00$) and one for false conditions ($I_5 I_4 = 01$). Conditions are based upon twelve test inputs $T_{11} \dots T_0$. External test select inputs, $S_3 \dots S_0$, select either an individual test input $T_0 \dots T_{11}$ to be used in conditional instructions ($S_3 \dots S_0 = 0000$ to 1010), or a logical combination of T_8, T_9, T_{10} and T_{11} for typical conditional jump tests. (Normally $T_8 =$ carry flag, $T_9 =$ negative flag, $T_{10} =$ overflow flag, and $T_{11} =$ zero flag.)

The Am29C332 32-bit ALU chip accepts two 32-bit operands, A and B, on external pins, and generates a 32-bit result, Y, on external pins. Parity is checked on the A and B inputs using one parity bit for each byte, and parity is generated on each byte of Y. The device responds to an externally presented 9-bit instruction word ($I_8 \dots I_0$). Instructions are divided into fixed operand length and variable operand length instructions. In either case, bits $I_6 \dots I_0$ of the instruction specify the operation in a fully encoded 7-bit op-code giving 124 different operations (four codes not used). The upper two bits, $I_8 I_7$, are interpreted differently depending upon whether the op-code specifies a fixed-length operation or a variable-length operation.

Table 12.5 Microinstructions of Am29C331 Microprogram sequencer

$I_4 \ldots I_0$ (Hex) Source, $\times$				
D	A	M	TOS	Description
	$I_5 I_4 = 10$			Unconditional jump instructions
20	24	28	2C	Goto $\times$
21	25	29	2D	Call $\times$ (return address pushed onto stack)
22	26	2A	2E	Exit to $\times$ (Unconditional jump and pop stack)
23	27	2B	2F	Loop Termination $-$ If Cnt$\neq$1, THEN Cnt:= Cnt $-$ 1, GOTO $\times$ ELSE Cnt:= Cnt $-$ 1 {if $\times$ = TOS pop stack}
	$I_5 I_4 = 00$ and 01			Conditional jump instructions
00	04	08	0C	IF CC THEN Goto $\times$
01	05	09	0D	IF CC THEN Call $\times$
02	06	0A	0E	IF CC THEN Exit to $\times$
03	07	0B	0F	IF CC AND Cnt$\neq$1 THEN Cnt:= Cnt $-$ 1, Goto $\times$ ELSE Cnt:= Cnt $-$ 1
10	14	18	1C	IF NOT CC THEN Goto $\times$
11	15	19	1D	IF NOT CC THEN Call $\times$
12	16	1A	1E	IF NOT CC THEN Exit to $\times$
13	17	1B	1F	IF NOT CC AND Cnt$\neq$1 THEN Cnt:= Cnt $-$ 1, Goto $\times$ ELSE Cnt:= Cnt $-$ 1
	$I_5 I_4 = 11$			Special function with implicit continue
	30			Continue
	31			initialize FOR loop $-$ Push addr. reg. + 1 onto stack, Cnt:= D
	32			Cnt:= Cnt $-$ 1
	33			Initialize REPEAT/WHILE loop $-$ Push address reg + 1 onto stack
	34			Pop stack onto D
	35			Push D onto stack
	36			Reset stack pointer to zero
	37			Initialize FOR loop $-$ Push addr. reg. + 1 onto stack, Cnt:= A
	38			Pop stack into Cnt
	39			Push Cnt onto stack
	3A			Exchange Cnt and top of stack
	3B			Push Cnt, Cnt:= D
	3C			Cnt:= D
	3D			Cnt:= A
	3E			Comp. Reg:= D, Enable Comparator
	3F			Disable Comparator

Notation:
D = D input
A = A input
M = $D_{15} \ldots D_4 + M_{x3} \ldots M_{x0}$ (multiway)
TOS = Top of stack
Cnt = Counter
CC = condition TRUE. Condition given by test condition inputs $T_{11} \ldots T_0$ and select inputs, $S_3 \ldots S_0$. If a jump is not selected, the next instruction taken (i.e. 'continue')

Fixed-length instructions perform the specified operation on the lower 8 bits, 16 bits, 24 bits or full 32 bits of the operands. The upper two bits, $I_8 I_7$, specify the operand size (8 bits, 16 bits, 24 bits or 32 bits). The 24-bit operand size is definitely very unusual for a 32-bit processor, and is probably only included because four operand sizes can be encoded in two bits. Three-quarters of the instructions (op-codes 00 hex to 5F hex) use the fixed-length format, and familiar arithmetic, logical and single-bit shift operations are provided operating on the selected operand size. Reverse subtraction (B−A rather than A−B), is provided as well as BCD operations. Somewhat unusually, prioritize operations are provided which return the bit position of the most significant 1 of the operand field.

Variable-length instructions (op-codes 60 hex to 7F hex) select a specified field in each operand to perform operations such as multi-bit shift, rotate, bit set/reset, and logical (Boolean) operations on bits of the fields. Now the upper two bits, $I_8 I_7$ specify how the position of the start of the field and the width of the field can be found. The position and width are either held in an internal status register or supplied on external pins to the device, $P_5 \ldots P_0$ and $W_4 \ldots W_0$ respectively. Typically $P_5 \ldots P_0$ and $W_4 \ldots W_0$ would be obtained from microinstruction words in the microprogram control memory. Full details of the instruction set can be found in [3].

Figure 12.11 shows a suitable encoding for the microinstruction. The sequencer instruction is labelled $\mu I_5 \ldots \mu I_0$ to differentiate it from the ALU function code.

12.3 Overlap and pipelining

Overlap and the associated concept, *pipelining*, are methods of increasing the speed of operation of the central processor and are applied to the internal design of more advanced microprocessors. Overlap and pipelining really refer to the same technique, that of dividing a *task* into a number of *operations* which need to be performed in sequence. Each operation is performed by its own logical unit rather than a single unit performing all the operations. The units are connected together in a serial fashion with the output of one unit connecting to the input of the next unit. The overall operation is such that while one unit is performing an operation on the nth task, the preceding unit is performing an operation on the $(n + 1)$th task. The unit attached before that is performing the operation on the $(n + 2)$th task, as shown in Fig. 12.12.

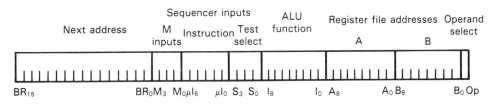

Figure 12.11 Microinstruction format

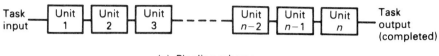

(a) Pipeline scheme

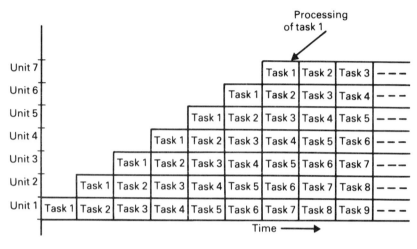

(b) Processing of tasks

Figure 12.12 Pipelining

The mechanism can be compared to a conveyor belt on an automobile assembly line, in which automobiles are in various stages of completion. Each automobile must pass through all stages to be completely assembled. Similarly in overlap/pipelining, tasks are presented in succession to the first unit. After the first operation on the first task is completed, the second task is presented, then the third, in the same way as parts enter an assembly line. Results from one operation are passed to the next unit as required. One complete task is completed after all the units have processed the operations of the task.

Suppose each unit has the same operating time to complete an operation, the first task is complete and a succession of tasks is presented. Then the time to perform one complete task is the same as the time for one unit to perform one operation of the task, rather than the summation of all the unit times. Ideally, each operation should take the same time, but if this is not the case, the overall processing time will be that of the slowest unit, with faster units having to be delayed.

Let us take a specific example, that of the overlap of the fetch and execute cycles of the processor. In the first instance, we shall assume one fetch cycle fetching a complete instruction and one execute cycle, without further decomposition. The technique requires that there are two separate units, a fetch unit and an execute unit, which are connected together as shown in Fig. 12.13(a). The address of the first

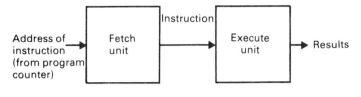

(a) Fetch and execute units

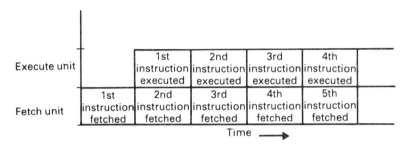

(b) Fetch/execute timing

Figure 12.13 Fetch/execute overlap scheme

instruction is presented to the fetch unit (by the program counter) and the fetch unit proceeds to fetch the first instruction. Once this is complete, the instruction is passed to the execute unit which decodes the instruction and proceeds to execute it. While this is being done, the fetch unit fetches the next instruction. The process is continued with the fetch unit fetching the nth instruction while the execute unit is executing the $(n - 1)$th instruction, as shown in Fig. 12.13(b). The overall processing time is given by:

$$\text{Processing time} = \sum_{i=1}^{n+1} \text{Max}(T(F_i), T(E_{i-1}))$$

where:

$T(F_i) = $ time of ith fetch unit
$T(E_i) = $ time of ith execute unit

and

$$T(F_{n+1}) = T(E_0) = 0$$

Clearly, the execute unit may operate at a different time to the fetch unit. In particular, it is likely to require more time for complicated instructions, and this will dominate the overall processing time. To reduce this effect, the execute unit could be split into further separate units. Firstly, a separate instruction decode unit could be provided after the fetch unit, followed by an execute unit. This scheme is known as a *three-level overlap*. However, it is usually not possible for the fetch unit to fetch an instruction and an execute unit to fetch any required operands of the previous instruction at the same time if the program and data are held in the same memory, as only one unit can assess the memory at any instant.

One method to overcome this problem is to fetch more than one instruction at a time using memory *interleaving*. In memory interleaving, the memory is divided into modules which allows one word from each module to be accessed simultaneously (see also Chapter 10, section 10.2.1). Memory addresses of individual locations are numbered across the modules as shown in Fig. 10.16. The number of modules is a power of two, so that the memory addresses in the first module, which identify all the words accessed, might be obtained from any memory address by setting the least significant bits to 0 (one bit for two modules, two bits for four modules, etc.).

To fetch two instructions simultaneously, two memory modules are required. The two instructions can then be used in three-level overlap as shown in Fig. 12.14(a). In three-level overlap, there are three units, a fetch unit which fetches two instructions, a decode unit which decodes one of the instructions and fetches any operands, and an execute unit which executes one instruction as shown in Fig. 12.14(b). After the memory bus has been used by the fetch unit to fetch two instructions, it is available to the decode unit for fetching operands. The execute unit does not now use the bus.

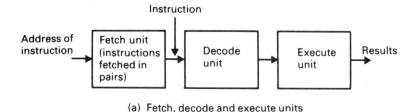

(a) Fetch, decode and execute units

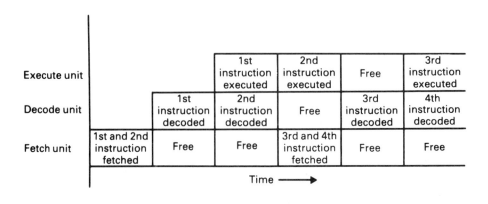

		1st instruction executed	2nd instruction executed	Free	3rd instruction executed
Execute unit					
Decode unit	1st instruction decoded	2nd instruction decoded	Free	3rd instruction decoded	4th instruction decoded
Fetch unit	1st and 2nd instruction fetched	Free	Free	3rd and 4th instruction fetched	Free	Free

Time ⟶

(b) Timing

Figure 12.14   Three-level instruction fetch/decode/execute overlap

Further decomposition can be made. For example, we could have five stages:

(i) Fetch instruction
(ii) Decode instruction
(iii) Fetch operand(s)
(iv) Execute operation (ADD, etc.)
(v) Store result.

The term 'pipelining' is usually applied when several units are connected together.

Complex arithmetic operations could be decomposed further, into several separate operations. Floating point arithmetic, in particular, can naturally be decomposed into several sequential operations. Consider the addition of two floating point numbers A and B, where A and B are each represented by a mantissa and exponent and the addition produces a floating point result. The addition requires a number of steps:

(i) Normalization, if not already done (remove leading 0's in mantissas and adjust the exponents accordingly)
(ii) Compare exponents and determine which is larger
(iii) Adjust small exponent to become the same as the larger exponent and adjust mantissa accordingly
(iv) Add mantissa
(v) Normalize result.

We can provide a separate unit for each step with the units connected in a pipeline. With this scheme, a series of floating point additions can be performed at increased speed over a single floating point unit. For example, suppose the processing time of each unit is:

(i) Pre-normalization $t_1 = 200$ ns
(ii) Comparison $t_2 = 100$ ns
(iii) Exponent adjustment $t_3 = 150$ ns
(iv) Mantissa addition $t_4 = 250$ ns
(v) Post-normalization $t_5 = 200$ ns

The processing time if the operations are performed within a single unit would be $t_1 + t_2 + t_3 + t_4 + t_5 = 900$ ns. With the pipeline and a series of floating point additions, the processing time is 250 ns (the processing time of the slowest unit). To gain full use of a pipeline system in an ALU, all the arithmetic operations would need to be integrated into a single pipeline. Units not necessary for a particular operation could be switched out of the pipeline temporarily.

Two methods of implementing the control mechanism of a pipeline (or overlap) can be identified, namely:

(i) Asynchronous method
(ii) Synchronous method

as shown in Fig. 12.15. In the asynchronous method, a pair of handshaking signals is used between each unit and the next unit. One signal is a ready signal from a unit

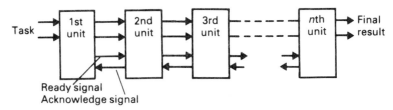

Ready signal
Acknowledge signal

(a) Asychronous method

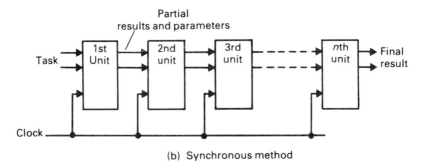

Partial
results and parameters

(b) Synchronous method

Figure 12.15 Transfer of information between units in a pipeline

to the next unit which informs the next unit that it has finished its present operation and is ready to pass the task and any results onwards. The second signal is an acknowledge signal from the unit receiving the ready signal back to the previous unit generated when it is ready to accept the task and results. In the synchronous method, one timing signal causes all outputs of units to be transferred to the succeeding units. The timing signal occurs at fixed intervals. In the floating point addition pipeline shown above, this would be every 250 ns.

The asynchronous method provides the greatest speed of operation. Also, in the synchronous method, *clock skew* can cause mal-operation. Clock skew is the variation in the delay of a clock signal arriving at different units, due to the time it takes for signals to pass along interconnection tracks (about 5–7 ns/m). In the example shown in Fig. 12.16, a pipeline consists of several D-type flip-flops, and the CLOCK signal is increasingly delayed before it reaches successive flip-flops. It is possible that CLOCK will be delayed sufficiently to cause subsequent data to be passed across to the next flip-flop, rather than present data.

Overlap and pipelining assume that there is a sequence of tasks to be performed in one order and that there is no interaction between tasks, other than passing the results of one unit on to the next unit. However, although programs are written as a linear sequence, the execution of one instruction will often depend upon the result of a previous instruction, and also the order of execution may be changed by jump/branch instructions. In addition, with multiple units operating simultaneously in the pipeline, situations can arise in which more than one unit wishes to access a shared 'resource' such as external memory. Therefore, we have three main causes

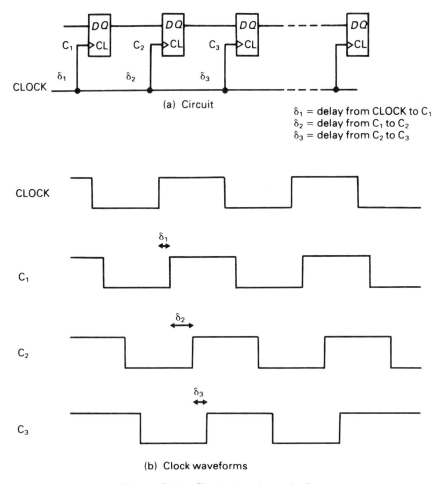

δ_1 = delay from CLOCK to C_1
δ_2 = delay from C_1 to C_2
δ_3 = delay from C_2 to C_3

(a) Circuit

(b) Clock waveforms

Figure 12.16   Clock skew in a pipeline

for breakdown of the pipeline, namely [4]:

(i) Data dependencies between instructions
(ii) Conditional instructions
(iii) Conflict in use of shared hardware resources.

As regards (i), suppose we wish to compute the value of $C = 2 \times (A +$ contents of memory location 100) with the program sequence (given in 8086 code) as:

```
ADD AX,[100]   ;AX:= A + contents of location 100
SAL AX,1       ;AX:= 2AX (Shift AX one place left)
MOV CX,AX      ;CX:= AX
```

and these instructions are in a five-stage pipeline, as shown in Fig. 12.17. This figure also shows memory contention. (The 8086 does not have the pipeline shown.) It

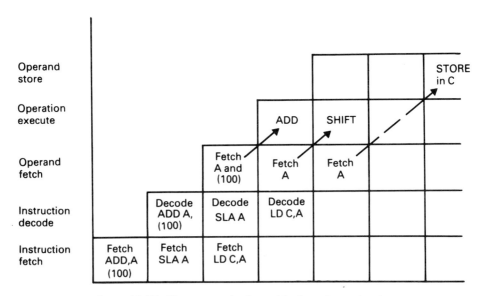

Figure 12.17 Five-stage pipeline with data dependencies

would be incorrect to begin shifting the value in AX before the add instruction, and similarly, it would be incorrect to begin loading CX before the shift operation. Hence, in this program each instruction must produce its result before the next instruction can begin.

Should the programmer know that a specific pipeline organization exists in the processor used, it may be possible to rewrite some programs to separate data dependencies. The process could be automated to some extent within special compilers. Otherwise, when a data dependency does occur, there are two main pipeline design strategies:

(i) Hold up the pipeline at the point at which a data dependency occurs until the part of the pipeline in front has processed the data dependency

(ii) Block instructions within the pipeline which are held up by data dependencies, but allow subsequent instructions to proceed, i.e. to overtake the blocked instructions.

Both strategies require a mechanism to detect the data dependencies.

A relatively simple method of maintaining a proper sequence of register read/write operations is to associate a 1-bit tag with each operand register. This tag indicates whether a valid result exists in the register or new data will be loaded by a pending instruction within the pipeline. The register is only accessed by any instruction within the pipeline if the data is indicated as valid. A form of this technique (known as a *scoreboard* technique) is used in the Motorola MC88100 RISC microprocessor.

As regards (ii) one approach is to allow the branch instruction, and other instructions that follow, to be processed as normally. When the branch instruction is completely executed, it would be known which instruction to process next. If this instruction is not the next instruction in the pipeline all the instructions in the pipeline are abandoned and the pipeline is cleared. The required instruction is fetched and must be processed through all the units in the same way as when the pipeline is first started.

Jump/branch instructions might typically occur every 10–20 instructions and would reduce the speed of operation accordingly in the above mechanism. For example, if a seven-stage pipeline operated at 100 ns steps and an instruction which subsequently cleared the pipeline occurred every 10 instructions, the average instruction processing time would be:

$$(9 \times 100 \text{ ns} + 1 \times 700 \text{ ns})/10 = 160 \text{ ns}$$

Methods to alleviate this problem include:

(i) Prediction logic to fetch the most likely next instruction after a jump/branch instruction
(ii) Instruction buffers to fetch both possible instructions.

The first method is generally successful because normally jump/branch instructions are used in program loops and cause a repetition of branching back to the same instruction many times before leaving the loop. After the first branch, it can be predicted with a good probability that the next time the instruction is encountered, the branch will be to the same location.

The instruction fetch/execute overlap technique is now applied to the many microprocessors, including 8-bit microprocessors, to substantially increase the speed of operation. The bus timing described earlier needs to be modified if the processor uses overlap/pipelining because the instruction and the associated operand transfers on the bus will not be in sequence. It may be possible to have a number of instruction fetch cycles between operand transfers.

References

1. Wilkes, M. and C. Stringer, 'Micro-progamming and the Design of Control Circuits in an Electronic Digital Computer', *Proc. Camb. Phil. Soc.*, 49 (1953), 230–38.
2. *Am29C300/29300 Data Book*, Sunnyvale, CA: Advanced Micro Devices, Inc., 1988.
3. *Am2900 Family Data Book*, Sunnyvale, CA: Advanced Micro Devices, Inc., 1985.
4. Wilkinson, B., *Computer Architecture: Design and Performance*, London: Prentice Hall, 1991.

Problems

In Problems 12.3–12.9, the objective is to study the design process to create a microprogrammed processor in sections 12.2.3 and 12.2.4, given the various trade-offs between cost, simplicity and performance. The answers should include both hardware and software implications.

12.1   Write a microprogram using the register transfer notation in section 12.1.3 to perform the move instruction LD rl, [r2] (register indirect addressing).

12.2   Write a microprogram for the Am29000 system described in section 12.2.3 to perform the following machine instructions:

(i) ADD R1,R2,R3   ;R1 := R2 + R3
(ii) ADC Rl,R2,R3   ;as ADD but with carry
(iii) BR 100   ;branch to location with displacement
                     ;100 locations from current instruction

Make but state any necessary assumptions.

12.3   Investigate the use of two instruction lengths, 32-bit and 64-bit, rather than the fixed 32-bit instruction used in section 12.2.3.

12.4   Investigate the following methods of increasing the address field in a fixed 32-bit instruction:

(a) Memory load/store operations only operating with one specific processor register.
(b) Variable-length op-codes, with a very short length for memory load/store operations.

Compare to having register-indirect addressing mode as the only memory addressing mode.

12.5   Investigate the possibility of designing Fig. 12.9 with separate memory–register file port rather than using a bidirectional A bus.

12.6   Investigate the possibility of having two microinstruction formats, one for sequential instructions without the next address field, and one for conditional jump instructions having the next address field. Draw the major components of a processor design.

12.7   Investigate the possibility of moving the IR register into the register file in Fig. 12.9. Determine the relative advantages and disadvantages of this design.

12.8   Investigate all the ramifications of each of the three options listed for choosing the size of the register file. Suggest other possibilities and their advantages.

12.9   Providing a 256 general-purpose register gives a sufficient number of registers for holding return addresses and passing parameters between procedures rather than using a memory stack. Discuss the potential limitations of not also providing machine instruction memory stack operations.

12.10 A microprocessor has two internal units, an instruction fetch unit and an instruction execute unit, with fetch/execute overlap. Compute the overall processing time of eight sequential instructions, in each of the following cases:

(a) $T(F_i) = T(E_i) = 1$ μs for $i = 1$ to 8
(b) $T(F_i) = 0.5$ μs, $T(E_i) = 1$ μs for $i = 1$ to 8
(c) $T(F_i) = 1$ μs, $T(E_i) = 0.5, 0.75, 1.25, 1.50, 1.25, 1, 0.75$ and 0.5μs for $i = 1, 2, 3, 4, 5, 6, 7$ and 8 respectively

where $T(F_i) =$ the time to fetch the ith instruction, and $T(E_i) =$ the time to execute the ith instruction.

13 Introduction to VLSI Systems Design and Testing

13.1 Introduction

Recent advances in microelectronics process technology have been nothing short of astounding. It is now possible to manufacture integrated circuits with integration levels as high as several million transistors on a single chip. Very large scale integration (VLSI) refers to the process technologies which are capable of such high levels of integration. Design engineers are now faced with the challenge of exploiting these awesome technological achievements in designing digital systems that are faster, occupy less space, dissipate less power, and perform larger amounts of computation. In order to meet this challenge, the digital designer must acquire some knowledge in device electronics, process technology, circuit design techniques, performance estimation, and testing. It is the purpose of this chapter to provide an introductory overview of the above areas. It is not the purpose of this chapter to provide expert-level knowledge of VLSI design, but to be a foundation for further in-depth study. None the less, this chapter does present the important issues of VLSI design and testing in readable layman's terms.

13.2 MOS transistor basics

The silicon MOS (metal-oxide-semiconductor) transistor consists of a SiO_2 insulating layer sandwiched between a doped silicon layer and a conducting layer typically formed of polysilicon. The silicon layer is said to form the substrate and the conducting layer is said to form the gate. Depending on the polarity of the substrate, the transistor can be classified as either n-type or p-type. Figure 13.1(a) shows an n-type MOS transistor and Fig. 13.1(b) shows a p-type MOS transistor. The n-type transistor is characterized by a diffusion of heavily doped n-type material into a lightly doped p-type substrate. The transistor has three main terminals: gate, source, and drain. The area directly under the gate is called the channel area. Current flows from source to drain conditionally under the influence of the gate voltage. In the n-type transistor, the majority carriers are electrons and in the p-type transistor, the majority carriers are holes. The MOS transistor can be further classified as either enhancement mode or depletion mode. In the enhancement

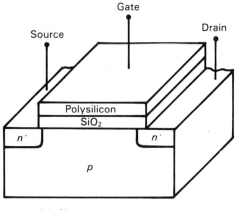

(a) *N*-type transistor

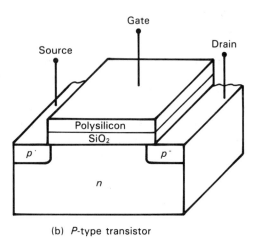

(b) *P*-type transistor

Figure 13.1   Profile of MOS transistors

mode, the transistor is normally off with no gate bias, and in the depletion mode it is normally on with no gate bias. In this chapter we will consider enhancement-mode transistors only.

We will next briefly explain the workings of the *n*-type MOS transistor. Figure 13.2 shows a cross-section of a transistor where V_{GS} represents the gate-to-source voltage and V_{DS} represents the drain-to-source voltage. One can visualize the transistor as a voltage-controlled switch. In this scenario, the gate voltage controls the switch. The switch is said to be 'on' if a connection is made between the source and the drain. Otherwise, the switch is said to be 'off'. Remember that the source and drain are made up of *n*-type materials which are insulated from each other by a *p*-type material. When an *n*-type material comes into intimate contact with a *p*-type material, a natural barrier called a depletion layer is formed between the two. The depletion layer is basically an area which is devoid of carriers. If somehow,

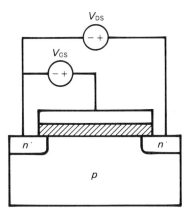

Figure 13.2 Cross-section of an *n*-type transistor showing normal biasing conditions

under voltage control, we can change the area directly under the gate (which is between the source and drain) from *p*-type to *n*-type, then we would form a path for the current to flow between the source and the drain. In this manner the switch can be turned on. Such a mechanism can be achieved as follows:

If a positive voltage is applied to the gate, it will repel the positive charges in the *p* substrate and attract negative charges from the substrate to the surface directly under the gate. Further increases in the gate voltage will attract more and more negative charges to the surface. At a certain point, there will be enough negative charges in this channel area to provide a connection between the source and the drain. This point is referred to as the point of inversion because the surface has been effectively inverted from *p*-type to *n*-type. The gate voltage level at which inversion is achieved is called the threshold voltage V_T.

We have now seen how the gate voltage can be used to turn the transistor on or off. The MOS transistor has three regions of operation:

Cutoff: In this region $V_{GS} < V_T$

Linear: In this region $V_{GS} > V_T$ and $V_{DS} < V_{GS} - V_T$

Saturation: In this region $V_{GS} > V_T$ and $V_{DS} > V_{GS} - V_T$

In the cut-off region, the transistor is off, but it is on in the other two regions. The difference between the linear and saturation regions is in the geometry of the inversion layer under the gate which influences the amount of current that can pass through the channel. In digital circuits, we switch the transistors very rapidly between the cut-off and saturation regions without spending much time in the linear region.

13.3 **Gain**

The magnitude (first order) of the drain-to-source current I_{DS} in each of the three regions of operation of an *n*-type MOS transistor is given by equation (1).

$$I_{DS} = \begin{cases} 0; \ V_{GS} < V_T & \text{cut-off} \\ \beta[(V_{GS} - V_T)V_{DS} - V_{DS}^2/2]; \ 0 < V_{DS} < V_{GS} - V_T & \text{linear} \\ \dfrac{\beta}{2}(V_{GS} - V_T)^2; \ 0 < V_{GS} - V_T < V_{DS} & \text{saturation} \end{cases} \quad (1)$$

where V_{GS}: gate-to-source voltage

V_T: threshold voltage

V_{DS}: drain-to-source voltage and

β: gain factor.

The gain factor is dependent on the geometry of the channel region and process parameters:

$$\beta = K_p' \frac{W}{L} \quad (2)$$

where K_p' is the process gain factor and is a constant for a given process technology, W is the width of the channel and L is the length of the channel as seen in Fig. 13.3. The gain β is a critical parameter and can be controlled by the designer by varying the W/L ratio.

In fact, for a given process technology, a designer can control the performance of a circuit by specifying W and L for each of the transistors utilized in the circuit. In general, one would desire a larger value of β for improved drive capability. However, to obtain very large values of β one must design transistors where $W \gg L$ which in turn requires the utilization of additional silicon area and power. Thus designers are often faced with a trade-off between performance and silicon area and power dissipation.

In analyzing equation (2), it is clear that our ability to obtain large values of β within a given area of silicon is limited by how short we can make L. The smaller the value of L the larger the value of β. In general, one can regard the degree to which L can be made short as the limit of the process technology in terms of the resulting performance. This is related to the so-called '*minimum feature length*' that can be delineated through photolithography. As of the date of publication of this book, the state-of-the-art in silicon technology is 0.5 μm.

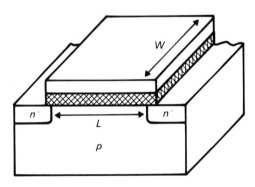

Figure 13.3 N-type transistor showing channel area dimensions

13.4 CMOS circuits

The acronym CMOS stands for complementary MOS and refers to the fabrication of both n-type and p-type transistors on a common substrate, as we shall see in section 13.5. CMOS logic refers to logic functions that are evaluated via a mix of n-type and p-type transistors implemented in CMOS technology. Let us first examine the reasons for employing such a technology.

We now know that both n-type and p-type transistors can be utilized as voltage-controlled switches. The voltage-controlled switch is the foundation of logic circuits because it allows us to represent the '1' and '0' states of Boolean logic by simply turning the switch 'on' and 'off'. Note that when a transistor is in the 'off' state it is non-conducting and represents the high impedance state. Now, in order to specify and distinguish between a '1' state and a '0' state, one requires two distinct voltage levels. In positive logic, one assigns a high-voltage value to the '1' state and a low-voltage value to the '0' the state. Typically, the high-voltage value is achieved from a power source V_{DD} and the low-voltage value is achieved from a ground source GND. In a given logic circuit, some of the nodes are at either the high-voltage state or the low-voltage state. For best operation one would like the high and low states of every node to be as close as possible to V_{DD} and GND respectively. This is where the use of CMOS technology can pay big dividends.

By optimizing the use of n-type and p-type transistors in the same circuit, one can achieve good high-(logic 1) and low-(logic 0)voltage levels. As it turns out, n-type transistors can conduct and preserve low-voltage levels well and p-type transistors can conduct and preserve high-voltage levels well. In CMOS logic, one utilizes p-type transistors to pull a node high (i.e. bring it up to logic 1). This portion of the circuit will be referred to as the pull-up network. Furthermore, we will use n-type transistors to pull a node low (i.e. bring it to logic 0). This portion of the circuit will be referred to as the pull-down network. Figure 13.4 illustrates the use of pull-up and pull-down networks to implement a combinational function.

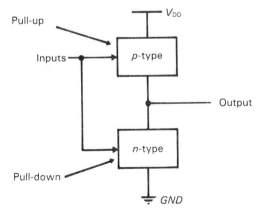

Figure 13.4 CMOS logic gate where p-type transistors are utilized in the pull-up network and n-type transistors are utilized in the pull-down network

Another advantage of CMOS technology is low power dissipation. Much power is dissipated when a circuit path is established between V_{DD} and *GND*. In most CMOS designs, this path is established only during switching (dynamic) and thus power dissipation is reduced.

13.5 CMOS technology

In order to design VLSI circuits we need to acquire some basic knowledge of the process technology which is employed. As stated earlier, the basic premise here is that we have both *n*-type and *p*-type transistors in the same IC chip. There are several different types of CMOS technologies available today. Here, we will take a brief look at one such process, known as the *p*-well process.

Figure 13.5 illustrates some of the major process steps. First, we start with an *n*-type substrate and form a passivation layer (Fig. 13.5(a)). This is where we will form the *p*-type transistors. Next we form a *p*-type well in the *n*-type substrate (Fig. 13.5(b)). This is where the *n*-type transistors will be formed. Next is the formation of the gate oxide regions (Fig. 13.5(c)), followed by the formation of the polysilicon regions representing the gate electrodes (Fig 13.5(d)). Then the $n+$ and $p+$ regions are defined by diffusion or ion implantation processes (Fig. 13.5(e)). Wiring between two nodes can be achieved by using polysilicon or metal (aluminium). Today's processes can accommodate two or more levels of metallization for wiring purposes. In order to connect two nodes, we first apply a passivation layer (typically SiO_2). Then contact cuts are made to the desired nodes (Fig. 13.5(f)), followed by a metal deposition (Fig. 13.5(g)).

Although the transistors of Fig. 13.5 are MOS transistors, there exist lateral parasitic *npn* and *pnp* bipolar junction transistors. These parasitic transistors can cause a problem called *latch-up*. Latch-up occurs when the parasitic transistors draw large currents and lock the logic state of the gate. Fortunately, the latch-up problem has been overcome by surrounding the MOS transistors with $n+$ and $p+$ regions known as *guard-rings*. A $p+$ guard-ring connected to V_{DD} is diffused in the *p*-well, and an $n+$ guard-ring connected to *GND* is diffused in the *n*-substrate. This effectively neutralizes the ability of the parasitic transistors to draw large currents.

In order to form each of the above layers in a specific region, an elaborate process is used known as patterning. Patterning is composed of several major steps. Let us examine the patterning of SiO_2 in a specific region, as shown in Fig. 13.6.

Step 1   Grow a layer of SiO_2 on the wafer by placing the wafer in an open-tube furnace system and passing the oxidant over the wafer.

Step 2   Coat the wafer with negative photoresist which is a material that becomes insoluble when exposed to light. Photoresists are photosensitive materials (polymers) that exhibit chemical resistance, have film forming properties, and adhere well to various surfaces.

Step 3   In this step, a pattern is transferred from a mask to the wafer. This is known as *photolithography*. The mask is an emulsion plate containing

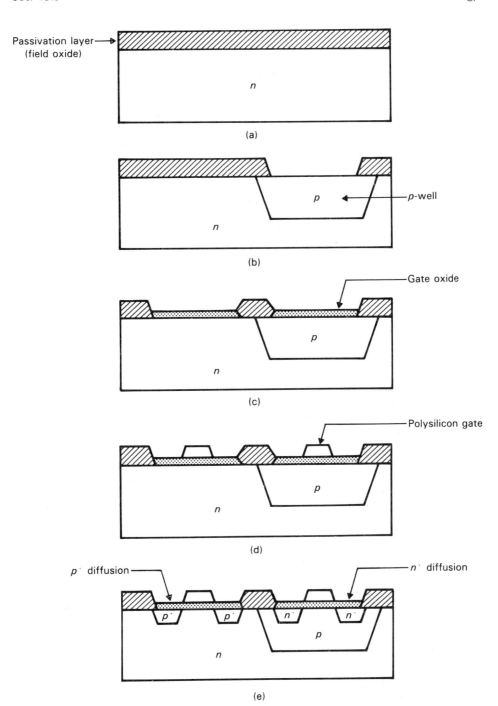

Figure 13.5 Major steps of a p-well CMOS process

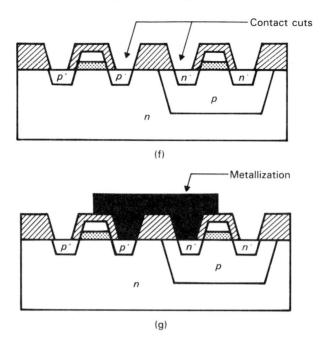

Figure 13.5   continued

the geometry of the layout for a given layer (in this case SiO_2). The mask must be aligned to the wafer with great precision ($<0.5\ \mu$m). The mask is then exposed to ultraviolet light. The exposed areas of the photoresist become insoluble. The unexposed areas are soluble in chemicals.

Step 4   The unexposed areas of the photoresist are dissolved away, exposing the SiO_2 underneath. This step is called *developing*.

Step 5   An etchant is used to remove the exposed SiO_2 but not the Si underneath. This step is called *etching*.

Step 6   Finally, the remaining photoresist is removed via a technique called *photoresist stripping*.

Other layers such as polysilicon and metal are patterned in a similar manner. It is the task of the designer to specify the geometry (two-dimensional) of the following layers:

p-well
n+ diffusion, and *p*+ diffusion
transistor channel area
polysilicon
metallization
contact cuts

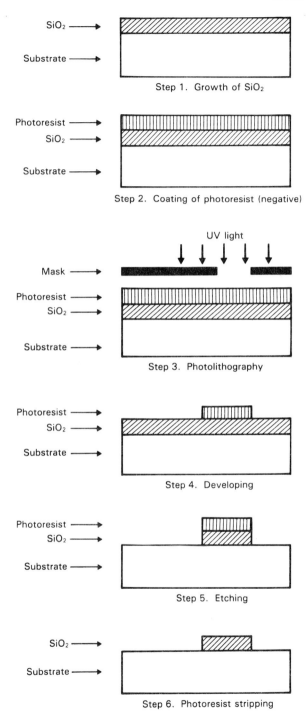

SiO₂ →

Substrate →

Step 1. Growth of SiO₂

Photoresist →
SiO₂ →

Substrate →

Step 2. Coating of photoresist (negative)

UV light

Mask →

Photoresist →
SiO₂ →

Substrate →

Step 3. Photolithography

Photoresist →
SiO₂ →

Substrate →

Step 4. Developing

Photoresist →
SiO₂ →

Substrate →

Step 5. Etching

SiO₂ →

Substrate →

Step 6. Photoresist stripping

Figure 13.6 Basic processing steps for patterning of SiO₂

13.6 Basic CMOS components

We now have a basic understanding of the principles of operation and technology of MOS transistors. In this section we will model the MOS transistor at a higher level of abstraction and use it as the principal building block for implementing combinational functions. Within this context the MOS transistor will have two main modes of operation as shown in Fig. 13.7. The n-type transistor is said to be 'on' if a logic 1 is applied to its gate. It is said to be 'off' if a logic 0 is applied to its gate. The p-type transistor is said to be 'on' if a logic 0 is applied to its gate, and is said to be 'off' if a logic 1 is applied to its gate. For either transistor, the 'on' state implies a connection or path between the source and the drain. In the 'off' state no path exists between the source and the drain which can be modelled as an open circuit.

In the 'on' state both types of transistors pass whatever logic value is present on the source to the drain. For example, if the source of the n-type transistor is connected to ground (logic 0 state), the drain will also be at that level if the transistor is switched on. In the 'off' state both transistors present themselves as infinite resistances. What does this mean? Well in MOS technology, each of the terminals of a transistor is capacitive, implying a capacity to store charge. This is the case even though we do not explicitly show a capacitor hanging off every terminal. When a transistor is in the 'off' state, its drain will retain whatever charge was previously

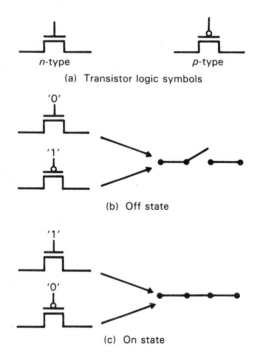

(a) Transistor logic symbols

(b) Off state

(c) On state

Figure 13.7 Switch-level representation of MOS transistors

stored on it for a few milliseconds. Thus the MOS transistor is a tri-state device as its drain can be at logic '0', logic '1', or high impedance.

13.6.1 Inverters

Recall that in CMOS logic, *n*-type transistors are used to conduct low-voltage levels and *p*-type transistors are used to conduct high-voltage levels. This is due to the ability of *n*-type transistors to preserve low-voltage levels and the ability of *p*-type transistors to preserve high-voltage levels without voltage degradation. This implies that we can pass these logic values from the source to the drain efficiently without loss of voltage.

A CMOS inverter is shown in Fig. 13.8. It consists of a *p*-type transistor whose source is connected to V_{DD} (which represents logic high or 1) and an *n*-type

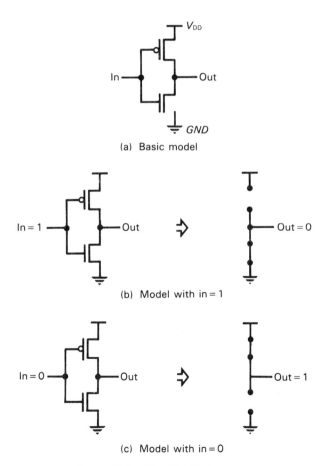

(a) Basic model

(b) Model with in = 1

(c) Model with in = 0

Figure 13.8 The CMOS inverter

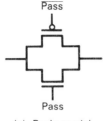

(a) Basic model

(b) Logic symbol

Figure 13.9   The CMOS switch (transmission gate)

transistor whose source is connected to *GND* (representing logic low or 0). The gates
of the two transistors are connected to each other and form the input. The drains
are connected together and form the output. Figure 13.8(b) shows a model of the
inverter when the input is at logic 1. In this case the *n*-type transistor is 'on' and
the *p*-type is 'off'. Thus a connection is established between *GND* and the output.
Physically, this discharges the capacitance on the output node (not shown) and
brings it down low to the logic 0 state. Figure 13.8(c) shows the inverter with a logic
0 applied to its gate.

13.6.2 CMOS switch

Another important CMOS component is the CMOS switch (Fig. 13.9). This is
composed of a parallel connection of *n*-type and *p*-type CMOS transistors. The
CMOS switch can be used for conducting both low- and high-voltage levels without
voltage degradation. The *n*-type transistor is used because of its capability to
conduct logic 0 values well and the *p*-type transistor is used because of its capability
to conduct logic 1 values well.

13.7 Building combinational circuits

In building a combinational circuit, one has to determine the logic conditions which
cause the output to be 1 and the logic conditions which cause the output to be 0.

In keeping with our earlier discussion, these conditions correspond to the make-up of the pull-up and pull-down networks. In general, each network is composed of AND and/or OR functions. Let us examine these functions more closely. The AND function can be realized by a series connection of transistors and the OR function can be realized by a parallel connection of transistors, as shown in Fig. 13.10. The type of transistor (p or n) which is deployed depends on its location relative to the pull-up and pull-down networks. We will use p-type transistors in the pull-up network and n-type in the pull-down network for the reasons delineated earlier.

13.7.1 NAND gate

Consider the NAND function

$$F = \overline{A \cdot B} = \bar{A} + \bar{B}$$

The condition under which $F = 1$ is $(\bar{A} + \bar{B})$. The condition under which $F = 0$ is $(A \cdot B)$.

It is obvious that the pull-up network $(\bar{A} + \bar{B})$ is the logical complement of the pull-down network $(A \cdot B)$. Now the pull-up network is an OR function and the pull-down network is an AND function, as shown in Fig. 13.11(a). Note that the p-type transistors are switched on when the gate is 0. Thus, the function $(\bar{A} + \bar{B})$ is realized by using two p-type transistors; one whose gate is driven by A (not $\bar{A}$), and one whose gate is driven by B (not $\bar{B}$).

In order to fully implement the NAND gate, we need to supply the power and ground sources which are connected to the pull-up and pull-down networks as shown in Fig. 13.11(b). This type of logic implementation is known as *FCMOS*

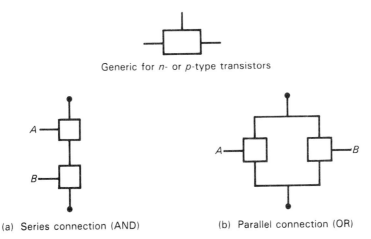

Generic for *n*- or *p*-type transistors

(a) Series connection (AND)   (b) Parallel connection (OR)

Figure 13.10 Transistor connections for implementing AND and OR functions

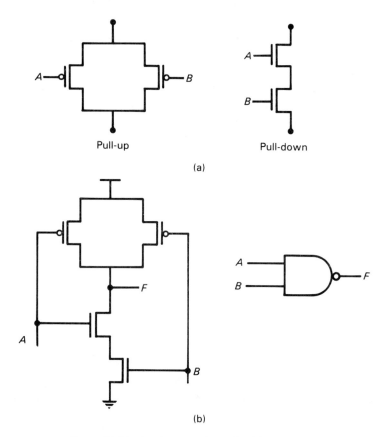

(a)

(b)

Figure 13.11   Implementation of a NAND gate

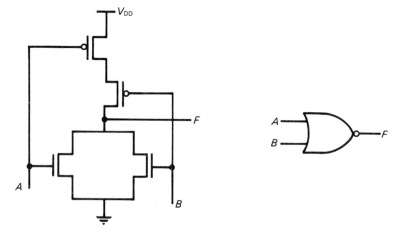

Figure 13.12   Implementation of a NOR gate

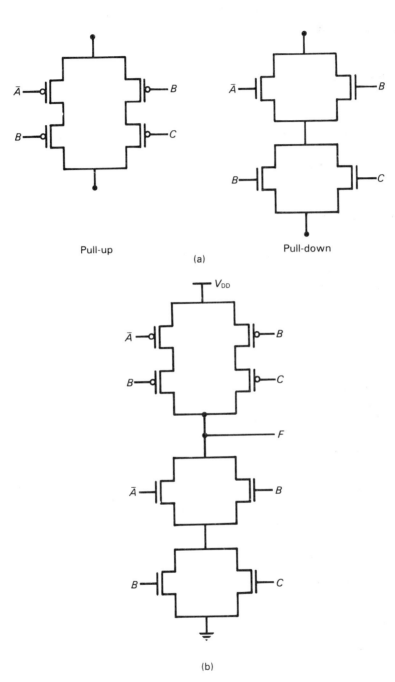

Figure 13.13 Implementation of $F = A \cdot \bar{B} + \bar{B} \cdot \bar{C}$

(fully complementary MOS) because the pull-up and pull-down networks are logical complements of each other.

13.7.2 NOR gate

A NOR gate is shown in Fig. 13.12. In this case we have a parallel connection in the pull-down network and a series connection in the pull-up network. When either A or B is 1, a path is established between the output F and GND and thus F goes low. However, it takes both A and B to be 0 to cause F to go high.

13.7.3 Combinational functions

Let us now turn our attention to more complex combinational functions. In this case we may have a combination of series and parallel connections in each of the pull-up and pull-down networks. None the less, the implementation of more complex

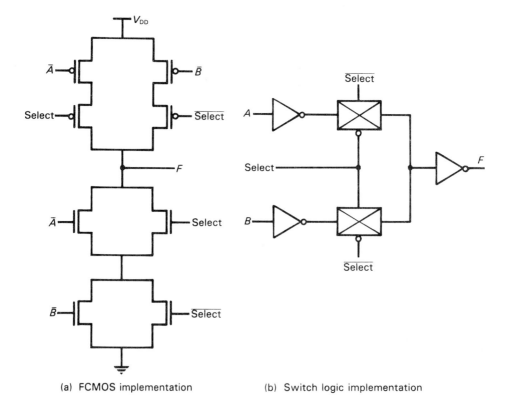

(a) FCMOS implementation   (b) Switch logic implementation

Figure 13.14 Implementation of a 2-to-1 multiplexer

functions is no more difficult than what we have seen for the NAND and NOR gates. Basically, we need to determine the conditions that make the output high and those that make the output low.

Consider the following function:

$$F = A \cdot \bar{B} + \bar{B} \cdot \bar{C}$$

The condition that makes $F = 1$ is $(A\bar{B} + \bar{B}\bar{C})$. The condition that makes $F = 0$ is

$$\overline{A\bar{B} + \bar{B}\bar{C}} = (\bar{A} + B) \cdot (B + C)$$

The pull-up and pull-down networks are shown individually in Fig. 13.13(a) and the full implementation is shown in Fig. 13.13(b). Note that an inverter is required to obtain $\bar{A}$ from A.

13.7.4 Multiplexers

The multiplexer is a component that often comes in handy and we will conclude this section by examining it. A two-to-one multiplexer

$$F = A \cdot \overline{\text{select}} + B \cdot \text{select}$$

can be implemented using the above techniques, as shown in Fig. 13.14(a). It can also be implemented, as shown in Fig. 13.14(b). The inverters are used in order to introduce a supply of power to the circuit.

13.8 Flip-Flops

In this section we will examine several implementations of D flip-flops. A simple D flip-flop is shown in Fig. 13.15. It consists of two inverters and two transmission gates. The inputs ϕ_1 and ϕ_2 constitute a two-phase non-overlapping clock, as defined by Fig. 13.15(b). Note that at no time do the high portions of ϕ_1 and ϕ_2 overlap. This is a very important aspect of the flip-flop of Fig. 13.15 and is crucial to achieving correct operation. The two phases can be coded as

$$\phi_1 = 0100$$

and

$$\phi_2 = 0001.$$

A single clock cycle would encompass all four portions of ϕ_1 and ϕ_2, as shown in Fig. 13.15(b). This flip-flop can be divided into two identical stages. During the first phase of the clock, the logic level on the D input is loaded into the first stage. During the second phase of the clock the logic level is transferred to the output. The non-overlapping phases of the clock ensure a disciplined clocking scheme. The clock

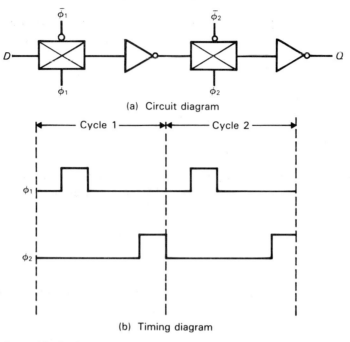

(a) Circuit diagram

(b) Timing diagram

Figure 13.15   D-type flip-flop with 2-phase non-overlapping clock

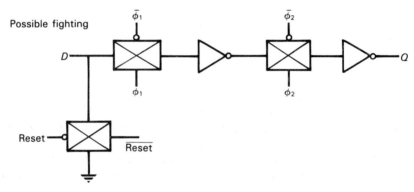

(a) *D* flip-flop with synchronous reset

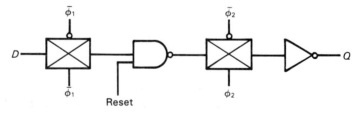

(b) Alternate *D* flip-flop with synchronous reset

Figure 13.16   Two methods for employing a reset for a D flip-flop

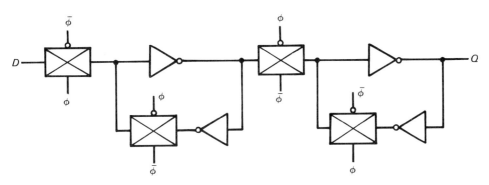

Figure 13.17 Two-stage D flip-flop with feedback

period must be of sufficient duration to satisfy the worst-case delay path through the circuit.

It is important to have the means to initialize any sequential circuit. This can be accomplished by incorporating a reset facility to the *D* flip-flop, as shown in Fig. 13.16. Figure 13.16(a) utilizes a CMOS switch which is connected at one end to *GND*. A low signal on the reset input will activate the switch and synchronously (with the clock) reset *Q* to 0. A problem could occur if *D* is at logic 1 while attempting to reset the flip-flop. This can result in having both a logic 1 and a logic 0 fighting on the highlighted node of Fig 13.16(a). As a consequence the final value of the node is indeterminate. A better way to incorporate a reset facility is shown in Figs 13.16(b). A low signal on the reset input will reset *Q* to 0 upon the arrival of ϕ_2 of the clock.

One disadvantage of the flip-flops shown in Figs. 13.15 and 13.16 is the need for continuous recharging of the flip-flops. Figure 13.17 shows a *D* flip-flop with a feedback mechanism that can provide such recharging. This particular flip-flop utilizes two phases of a single clock. During the high portion of ϕ, the logic level on *D* is transferred into the first stage of the flip-flop and is reinforced (during $\bar{\phi}$) along the feedback path. During the low portion of ϕ, the logic level is transferred to the output *Q* which in turn is reinforced (during ϕ) along the feedback path.

13.9 CMOS logic structures

An FCMOS circuit utilizes a pull-up network to pull the output high and a pull-down network to pull the output low. The pull-up and pull-down networks are derived by computing the output function and its full complement respectively. Logic circuits can also be implemented by utilizing other circuit techniques that result in less transistors, as compared to FCMOS, at the cost of additional design complexity. In this section, we will examine some of these circuit techniques.

13.9.1 Pseudo-NMOS

The general model of a pseudo-NMOS circuit is shown in Fig. 13.18(a). It consists of a pull-down network which is derived by computing the logic conditions that pull the output low, and a pull-up network consisting of a single p-type transistor which is permanently on. The p-type transistor acts as a resistor and thus the output is always connected (through the p-type transistor) to V_{DD}. The output is conditionally discharged if the pull-down network is true, providing a connection to *GND*. In such a situation the output will be connected to both V_{DD} and *GND*. This presents two problems. First, we need to resolve the fighting at the output node so that we can bring it low. This can be accomplished by choosing the appropriate transistor dimensions so that the pull-down network could effectively be stronger than the pull-up transistor. The second problem presents itself as additional power dissipation (whenever the pull-down network is true) because of the direct path between V_{DD} and *GND*. This is the main disadvantage of pseudo-NMOS logic. Figure 13.18(b) shows the pseudo-NMOS implementation of a logic function. Note that the function of Figure 13.18(b) can be implemented using one less transistor by factoring out the term $\bar{B}$.

13.9.2 Dynamic CMOS

Dynamic CMOS gates utilize a disciplined clocking strategy whereby the output is precharged high during one phase of the clock and conditionally discharged during

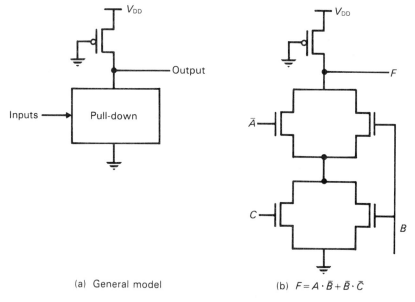

(a) General model   (b) $F = A \cdot \bar{B} + \bar{B} \cdot \bar{C}$

Figure 13.18 Pseudo-NMOS logic

another phase of the clock. Figure 13.19(a) shows the general model of a dynamic CMOS circuit that utilizes two phases of a single clock. When $\phi = 0$, the output is precharged high. Figure 13.19(b) shows the implementation of a logic function. When $\phi = 1$, the pull-up transistor is off and the output is conditionally discharged through the pull-down network. Note that this type of circuit does not suffer from the problems that plague pseudo-NMOS; however it does require careful timing analysis when cascaded with other clocked logic. For example, consider Fig. 13.20, which shows a cascade of two dynamic CMOS logic gates. During $\phi = 0$, both $F1$ and $F2$ are precharged high. During $\phi = 1$, both $F1$ and $F2$ are conditionally discharged. However, $F2$ is a function of $F1$ and there is a finite propagation delay time associated with the evaluation of both $F1$ and $F2$. At the instant when ϕ goes to 1, $F1$ is still at logic 1 and thus $F2$ may be erroneously evaluated. This problem can be alleviated by using more complex clocking strategies which are outside the scope of this chapter, or by using domino logic, which is presented next.

13.9.3 Domino logic

The general model of a domino logic circuit is shown in Fig. 13.21(a). Note that the circuit model is very similar to clocked CMOS with the exception of the inverter. During the precharge phase, the output of the inverter is low. In a cascade of domino

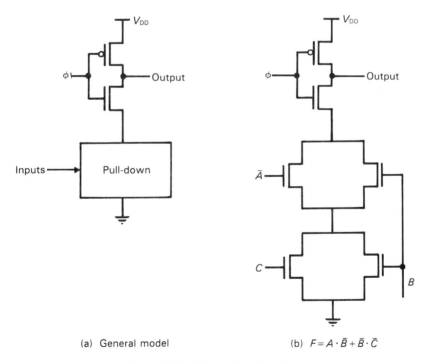

(a) General model   (b) $F = A \cdot \bar{B} + \bar{B} \cdot \bar{C}$

Figure 13.19 Dynamic CMOS logic

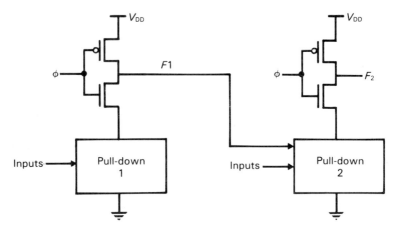

Figure 13.20 Problem associated with cascading of dynamic CMOS logic circuits. The output F2 might be erroneously evaluated due to the propagation delay time of pull-down network I

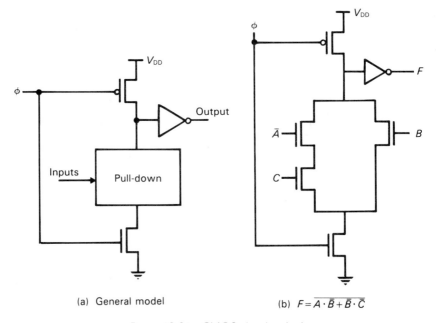

(a) General model   (b) $F = \overline{A \cdot \overline{B} + \overline{B} \cdot \overline{C}}$

Figure 13.21   CMOS domino logic

logic structures, the output of one stage feeds inputs to subsequent stages. Thus during the precharge phase, the transistors which are fed from the previous stages are turned off. When a domino logic circuit is conditionally discharged, the output of the inverter goes high thus enabling subsequent stages to conditionally discharge also. A stage is thus evaluated only after the preceding stage has been evaluated.

This discipline allows for correct logic operation in a cascade of logic circuits. However, it requires the use of an additional inverter and cannot support non-inverting structures. Domino logic can also suffer from a problem called *charge sharing*. Charge sharing is a process by which charge is redistributed in a logic circuit, causing a shift in the output voltage level. For example, if an output node which is initially charged high is connected via a transistor to an internal node which is discharged, the output voltage level will be degraded as a result of charge flowing from the output node to the internal node. Figure 13.21(b) shows the domino logic implementation of a combinational function.

13.10 Layout

In section 13.5, it was mentioned that the designer specifies the geometry of various layers such as polysilicon, diffusion, and metallization. This is known as the *layout*. Each layer is assigned a colour code. Typically, the designer specifies polysilicon in red, first-level metal in blue, second-level metal in purple, *n*-diffusion in green, and *p*-diffusion in brown. The geometry of each layer is then translated into a representation which is suitable for manufacturing the associated mask pattern. The mask pattern is then used in the process of photolithography (see section 13.5).

The layout is governed by a number of rules known as *design rules*. The design rules reflect the limitations of the fabrication technology as well as electrical and reliability constraints. The design rules are affected, in part, by the following.

(i) *Minimum geometry* that can be resolved in the photoresist. The minimum geometry metric changes from layer to layer because of the non-planar nature of the surface. Higher layers such as second-level metal experience stiffer design rules (i.e., larger minimum geometries) because the degree of non-planarization increases at higher levels.

(ii) *Etching* requirements for prevention of shorts between adjacent layers as well as prevention of line openings.

(iii) The *alignment* accuracy for the various layers. The choice of alignment sequence affects design rules because each layer is typically aligned to the previous layer.

The design rules are specified in terms of *minimum linewidths* and *minimum spacings*. The minimum linewidth reflects the smallest width of a line that can be reliably patterned on a layer. The minimum spacing requirements specify the minimum separation between lines on the same layer and between lines on different layers. This, too, reflects the limitations of the process technology as well as electrical and reliability constraints. For example, *n*-diffusion must be separated from *p*-diffusion by a given distance to ensure correct electrical operation.

Associated with each fabrication process line is a unique set of design rules which provides a measure of the integration density. However, a set of general design rules has been developed which can be, in principle, tailored to a given process line. This general set has been developed using a fundamental design parameter λ. The parameter λ is a measure of the minimum geometry that can be resolved by a given process line. In the general design rule set, all minimum dimensions are integer multiples of λ. Table 13.1 provides a partial list of general design rules for a CMOS process.

Figure 13.22 shows a possible layout for an inverter. The V_{DD} and *GND* sources are distributed to the inverter in metal. Metal-to-diffusion contact cuts are specified to connect V_{DD} to *p*-diffusion and *GND* to *n*-diffusion. The drains of the two transistors are connected via metal to form the output. The gates of the two transistors are also connected to form the input.

In general, *n*-type transistors switch faster than their *p*-type counterparts because the effective mass of electrons is smaller than that of holes. The gain of an *n*-type transistor whose channel is of dimensions *W* and *L* is approximately twice as large as a *p*-type transistor having the same channel dimensions. As a result, the fall time of an inverter is faster than the rise time. To compensate for this asymmetry, designers choose *p*-type transistors with a *W/L* ratio twice that of the *n*-type transistor. However, at very high switching speeds, near the saturation

Table 13.1   Partial list of design rules for a typical CMOS *p*-well process

Layer	Dimensions
p-well	
width	4λ
spacing (different potential)	10λ
Active (channel area)	
width	2λ
spacing	2λ
Poly	
width	2λ
spacing	2λ
poly overlap of active	2λ
active overlap of poly	2λ
Contact	
square	$2\lambda \times 2\lambda$
poly overlap of contact	λ
metal 1 overlap of contact	λ
Metal 1	
width	2λ
spacing	3λ
maximum current density	$0.8 \text{ mA}/\mu\text{m}$
Metal 2	
width	3λ
spacing	3λ
maximum current density	$0.8 \text{ mA}/\mu\text{m}$

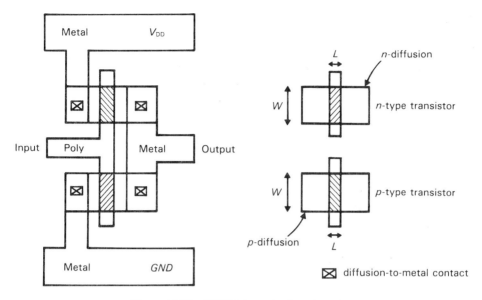

Figure 13.22 CMOS layout of an inverter

velocities of the majority carriers, the performance of the *p*-type transistors rivals that of the *n*-type transistors because the saturation velocities for *n*- and *p*-type transistors are similar. Consequently, it would not be necessary to use larger *p*-type transistors in such situations.

13.11 Performance issues

For a given process technology, parameters such as the thickness of the layers and the doping concentrations are predetermined and, in general, cannot be controlled by the designer. These parameters influence the value of the threshold voltage. However, the designer can control the performance of the circuit by specifying the width and length of the various layers such as the channel region. Facilities are also available, in some processes, to directly bias the substrate, which alters the value of V_T.

Bounded by the design rules, a designer can specify the geometry of every layer in the circuit so as to achieve the desired performance. Performance issues generally fall into three categories: *delay*, *area*, and *power dissipation*. In order to attain a given performance level, the designer attempts to manipulate the following parameters:

(i) The size of every transistor. Specifically, the gain which is directly proportional to the ratio W/L is specified so as to provide the proper drive capability.
(ii) The width of the interconnect layers is specified so as to provide the capability to handle a given amount of current.

(iii) The amount of capacitance represented by layer-to-layer such as diffusion-to-substrate, and inter-layer, such as metal-to-metal, is sought to be minimized for improved performance.
(iv) The amount of resistance represented by the resistance of the various layers as well as the resistance of the transistors (often called *active resistance*) is sought to be minimized for improved performance.

13.11.1 Delay time

The delay time through a transistor or a wire depends on the amount of resistance embodied and the amount of capacitive load. The delay time

$$T \propto RC_L \tag{3}$$

where R is the resistance and C_L the load capacitance. We will next examine resistance estimation followed by capacitance estimation.

13.11.2 Resistance estimation

There are two types of resistors: passive and active. Passive resistors include those of the various layers such as polysilicon and metal. Active resistors refer to the resistance embodied in transistors.

The amount of resistance of a passive resistor can be determined from the following equation:

$$R_{\text{wire}} = \frac{\rho l}{A} \tag{4}$$

where R is the resistance in ohms, ρ is the resistivity in ohm/cm, l is the length of the wire, and A is the cross-sectional area (see Fig. 13.23). The area is given by

$$A = tw \tag{5}$$

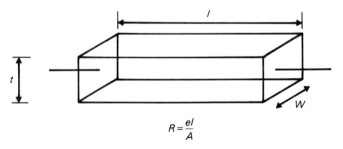

$$R = \frac{el}{A}$$

Figure 13.23 Conductor resistance estimation

where t is the thickness of the wire and w is the width. Substituting (5) into (4) yields

$$R_{\text{wire}} = \frac{\rho}{t}\frac{l}{w} = R_S \frac{l}{w} \tag{6}$$

where R_S is called the *sheet resistance* in units of ohms/square and is a constant for a given material in a given fabrication process line. Table 13.2 gives some typical values of R_S for different layers. One can also calculate the value of R for thin rectangular regions by counting the number of squares, N, that can fit in the region:

$$R_{\text{wire}} = NR_S \tag{7}$$

Figure 13.24 shows two examples for calculating R. In Fig. 13.24(a), a total of 5.5 squares can be placed in the rectangular region. Figure 13.24(b) shows a serpentine pattern. In this case the corners are each assigned an empirical value of 0.55.

The amount of resistance of an active resistor depends on the region of operation of the transistor. The channel resistance can be approximated by taking the partial derivative of I_{DS} with respect to V_{DS} as the limit $V_{DS} \to 0$. For example, the channel resistance R_C of an n-type transistor in the linear region of operation is

$$R_C = \frac{L}{WK_p'(V_{GS} - V_T)} \tag{8}$$

Now K_p' is a constant and thus R_C is directly proportional to the ratio L/W, where L is the channel length and W is the channel width. For a given silicon area, active

Table 13.2 Typical sheet resistance values for a p-well CMOS process ($\lambda = 1.5\ \mu$m)

Layer	Resistance (ohms/square)
$n+$ diffusion	35
$p+$ diffusion	80
poly	25
metal	0.03

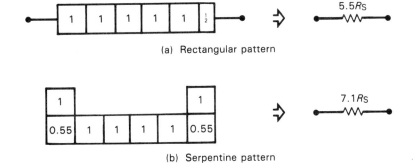

(a) Rectangular pattern

(b) Serpentine pattern

Figure 13.24 Alternative method for resistance estimation

resistors have much larger resistance values than passive resistors. This is because typical values of K'_p are around 25×10^{-6} amps/volt^2 whereas typical values of R_S are in the range 0.05 to 80 ohm/square.

13.11.3 Capacitance estimation

Capacitors can also be classified as passive or active. Passive capacitors are obtained by overlaying two conducting layers separated by an insulator such as SiO_2. This can be modelled as a parallel plate capacitor (neglecting fringing effects)

$$C_{wire} = \frac{\varepsilon_i \varepsilon_0}{t_i} A \tag{9}$$

where ε_i: dielectric constant or relative permittivity of the insulating material
$\quad\varepsilon_0$: permittivity of free space (8.85×10^{-12} Farads/meter)
$\quad A$: area (length $\times$ width of wire)
$\quad t_i$: thickness of insulating material.

Figure 13.25 shows the major capacitances associated with an MOS transistor. These include:

$\quad C_G$: gate region capacitance (gate-to-substrate, gate-to-drain, and gate-to-source capacitances)
$\quad C_D$: diffusion region capacitance (drain-to-substrate, and source-to-substrate).

The gate capacitance can be approximated by

$$C_G = \frac{(\varepsilon_{ox} \varepsilon_0)}{t_{ox}} WL = C_{ox} WL \tag{10}$$

where ε_{ox} is the relative permittivity of SiO_2 (having a value of 3.9).

$\quad t_{ox}$: thickness of SiO_2
$\quad C_{ox}$: oxide capacitance.

The diffusion capacitance consists of two components; sidewall capacitance C_S and junction capacitance C_j. The sidewall capacitance is on the periphery between the diffusion and the substrate, as shown in Fig. 13.26(a), and the junction capacitance

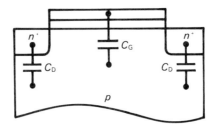

Figure 13.25 Major capacitances of an MOS transistor

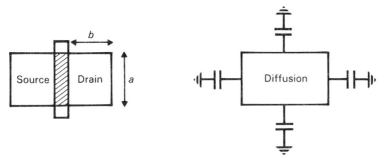

(a) Top view of diffusion area showing sidewall capacitance

(b) Side view of diffusion area showing junction capacitance

Figure 13.26 Sidewall and junction capacitance

Table 13.3 Typical capacitance values for a
p-well CMOS process ($\lambda = 1.5\ \mu$m)

Layers	Capacitance
Poly to substrate	0.045 fF/μm^2
Metal 1 to substrate	0.025 fF/μm^2
Metal 2 to substrate	0.014 fF/μm^2
Poly to metal 1	0.04 fF/μm^2
Poly to metal 2	0.039 fF/μm^2
Metal 1 to metal 2	0.035 fF/μm^2
$n+$ diffusion sidewall	2.6 fF/μm
$p+$ diffusion sidewall	3.5 fF/μm
$n+$ diffusion junction	0.33 fF/μm^2
$p+$ diffusion junction	0.38 fF/μm^2

includes the diffusion base areas, as shown in Fig. 13.26(b). The total sidewall
capacitance can be determined by $(2a + 2b) * C_S$ where a and b are the width and
extension of the diffusion region respectively (see Fig. 13.26(a)). The total junction
capacitance is $a * b * C_j$. Thus the total diffusion capacitance is

$$C_D = (2a + 2b)C_S + abC_j \tag{11}$$

Typical capacitance values are given in Table 13.3.

13.12 Design verification

Design verification is performed at a number of levels coincident with every design phase. Computer-aided design (CAD) and verification tools are utilized to cope better with design complexity. The design process can be divided into the following general phases.

High-level design. This includes the utilization of *behavioural* and *functional* specification tools. The behavioural level specification consists of a text description of what each module does from an algorithmic standpoint, but does not specify how the module is built. The functional level specification consists of decomposing the modules into functional components such as RAMS, ALUs, etc. Behavioural and functional simulation tools can be utilized to verify the integrity of the design early in the design process so as to avoid the increasingly higher cost of failure at each of the subsequent design levels.

Gate-level design. At this level, the functional modules are broken down into gates, flip-flops, logic arrays, etc. *Logic simulation* is utilized to verify the integrity of the design from a logic standpoint. Most logic simulators assign a unit delay to each gate and cannot be used for very accurate performance estimation. At this level, testability assessment aids such as *fault simulators* are used to measure the effectiveness of test vectors (see section 13.13) in detecting physical defects after circuit fabrication. A fault simulator injects defects into the circuit and uses a fault model to compute the response of the circuit to an input pattern T. This response is compared to the response of the fault-free circuit. If the two circuit responses are different, then the input pattern T is said to constitute a test for the injected defect. A number of logic and fault simulators, such as CADAT (HHB systems) and HILO (Genrad Inc.) are commercially available. The circuit can be specified using a *netlist* as shown in Fig. 13.27. It can also be specified schematically using *schematic capture* tools such as Capfast (phase three logic) and SDA (CADENCE).

Simulators that can perform simulation at different hierarchical levels are also commercially available. These are called *multi-level simulators* such as Multisim (Teredyne EDA). Simulators are also available for simulating circuits with mixed digital and analog circuits. These are called *mixed-mode simulators* such as native mixed-mode simulation (Analogy).

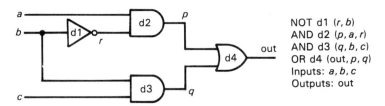

Figure 13.27 Netlist description of a two-way multiplexer consisting of a NOT gate, two AND gates, and an OR gate

Layout. Once the gate level design is completed, the transistor level design is invoked. The layout of each cell is made followed by extensive simulation. At this level, two types of simulators are used: *switch-level* and *circuit-level*. In a switch-level simulator such as Timemill (Epic Design), a transistor is modelled as a simple voltage controlled switch, whereas circuit-level simulators such as SPICE and CAzM (MCNC) utilize elaborate transistor models and give good estimates of delay time and power dissipation.

In addition to switch and circuit simulation, *timing simulation* is performed using tools such as veritime (CADENCE), so as to identify timing problems and critical shortest and longest paths.

A floor plan of the integrated circuit is made so as to specify the locations of the cells relative to one another to reduce routing area, efficiently distribute power, and efficiently distribute the clocks so as to minimize clock skew. Then the integrated circuit is assembled by incorporating special input/output and power supply pads which are bonded to external pins after packaging.

CAD tools are available to manage the complexity of the layout design and simulation. The layout can be developed using tools such as MAGIC (University of California at Berkeley). Such tools allow the designer to specify the geometry of the layout schematically where a colour code is established to represent the various integrated circuit layers. The layout CAD tool then converts this representation into an intermediate representation such as CIF which is suitable for communicating the design details to a fabrication foundry.

Over the past few years a number of tools have been introduced to perform some of the tedious tasks traditionally undertaken by the designer. These include *logic synthesis* and *silicon compilation* tools.

Logic synthesis. Automated logic synthesis of sequential machines typically refers to a process by which a high-level description of the machine is transformed into a gate-level netlist. Beginning with a state transition table, a typical synthesis process consists of the following steps:

(i) *State assignment.* A heuristic is used to assign a unique binary code to every state so as to optimize circuit parameters such as silicon area, testability, and performance. Examples of state assignment tools include MUSTANG (University of California at Berkeley) and MARS (University of North Carolina at Charlotte).

(ii) *Minimization.* This can include two-level minimization, multi-level minimization, or both, depending on the target circuit structure. For example, two-level minimization is used for PLAs whereas multi-level minimization is used for random logic. Examples of minimization tools include ESPRESSO (two-level minimization from the University of California at Berkeley) and MIS (multi-level minimization from the University of California at Berkeley).

(iii) *Technology mapping.* This refers to the process of mapping the logic equations, resulting from the minimization phase, into a set of standard components such as AND-OR-INVERT, Multiplexers, etc.

There are a number of commercially available logic synthesis tools such as Design Compiler (synopsis), and PLD synthesis (Mentor Graphics).

Silicon compilation. Silicon compilation refers to the process of translating a gate-level netlist into a complete layout. Silicon compilers perform this task in two major phases: (1) *placement*, which refers to selecting the locations for placing the cells in order to reduce routing area; and (2) *routing*, which refers to the process of defining the interconnections between the cells. There are many different heuristic algorithms in use today for performing placement and routing but these are outside the scope of this chapter. The reader is encouraged to review the reference section of this chapter for further reading. Examples of commercially available placement and routing tools include SDA (CADENCE), and Avant Gards (routing only by Silvar-Lisco).

13.13 Testing and design for test

Advances in process technology have made it possible to manufacture integrated circuits with levels of integration exceeding millions of transistors in a single chip. However, the number of available primary input/output pads on a package has not increased in proportion to the number of internal circuit nodes. As a result, testing integrated circuits has become an elaborate process. In order to better manage the testing of these complex devices, the testability issues must be addressed at an early stage in the design process itself. This is known as design-for-test (DFT). It requires that designers be well versed in test issues in order to produce circuits that can be thoroughly tested. In fact, today, DFT is not just good design practice but a necessity. Testing has a direct impact on quality control and can even help in tuning the fabrication process line. The cost associated with testing can constitute over 40% of the total development cost depending on the circuit complexity and target test coverage.

The testability of a VLSI circuit depends on the degree to which internal circuit nodes can be controlled and observed. The goal of DFT is to enhance the controllability and observability of internal circuit nodes. In this section we will give a basic introduction to the field of testing digital circuits. We will start by introducing test generation techniques for combinational circuits followed by DFT techniques.

13.13.1 Fault models

The goal of testing is to detect and locate physical defects in the integrated circuit. There exist many types of physical defects (faults) that can affect the function and/or performance of a given circuit. In order to better cope with the complexity of testing, it is convenient to provide a high-level model for these faults. In general, faults can be modelled by the effect that they have on the functionality of the circuit. Fault models can be divided into two broad categories: *logic*, and *parametric*. Logic fault models deal with faults that affect the logic function of the circuit, and parametric fault models deal with faults that affect the magnitude of circuit parameters such as voltage, current, drive, and delay. In this chapter we will only consider logic fault models.

(a) Stuck-at fault

The *stuck-at* (s-a) fault is a physical defect that causes a logic node to be permanently fixed at either the high-voltage level (s-a-1) or the low-voltage level (s-a-0), as shown in Fig. 13.28. This condition can occur if a node is shorted to one of the power supply rails. The stuck-at fault model is a gate-level fault model. It is the most popular fault model because of its simplicity and is utilized as the principal fault model in most fault simulators.

(b) Stuck-on fault

The *stuck-on* fault is a transistor level stuck-at fault. It is a fault which is difficult to detect because some test conditions cause the assertion of both the pull-up and pull-down networks, resulting in an indeterminate logic level on the output. DFT techniques have to be implemented at the transistor level in order to detect stuck-on faults. Figure 13.29 shows a stuck-on fault where the gate of a transistor is s-a-1. In this case the transistor is always on.

Figure 13.28 Example of stuck-at faults

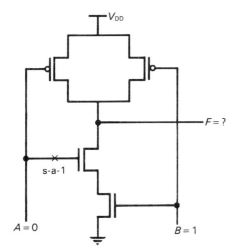

Figure 13.29 The effect of a stuck-on fault showing a short between V_{DD} and GND for the pattern $A = 0, B = 1$

(c) Stuck-open

The *stuck-open* fault is characteristic of the CMOS process. It is a defect that causes a transistor to be in the high impedence state. As a result, for some input patterns, both the pull-up and pull-down networks are off, which causes the output to retain its previous value for a limited amount of time (normally a few msec). Figure 13.30 shows an example of a stuck-open fault.

(d) Bridging

A short between two wires is modelled as a *bridging* fault, as shown in Fig. 13.31. A bridging fault can result from a breakdown in the insulating layer separating two conducting layers. The final logic value on a bridged node depends on the strengths of the logic levels on the individual wires which are bridged together.

(e) Other logic faults

The existence of several stuck-at faults in a circuit is referred to as a *multiple stuck-at* fault. There are many more multiple stuck-at faults in a given circuit than single

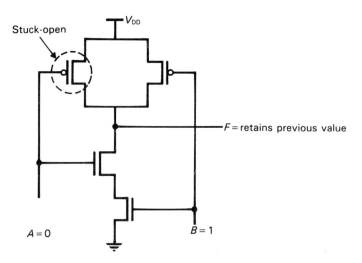

Figure 13.30   The effect of a stuck-open fault when $A = 0$ and $B = 1$

Figure 13.31   Examples of bridging faults

stuck-at faults. However, test sets which detect a high percentage of single stuck-at faults also detect a good percentage of multiple stuck-at faults.

There exists a number of fault models that are specific to circuit structures such as RAMs and PLAs. For example, RAMs can suffer from defects which depend on the applied input pattern. These are referred to as *pattern sensitive* or *disturb* faults. For example, the logic value of a RAM cell might be disturbed due to capacitive coupling with its surrounding cells.

13.13.2 Test generation (combinational circuits)

In this section we will consider techniques for generating tests to detect stuck-at faults in combinational circuits. In order to detect a fault, one must apply a test pattern which produces a different output response from the expected output response. In other words, one seeks to propagate the effect of the fault to an observable output point. Thus a test T for a fault α can be derived from the following Boolean equation:

$$T = F \oplus F_\alpha \tag{12}$$

where F is the logic function of the circuit under test and F_α is the function resulting from the fault α. For example, let $F = a.b + c.d$ and assume that b is s-a-0. Then

$$T = (a.b + c.d) \oplus (c.d)$$

which yields

$$T = a.b.\bar{c} + a.b.\bar{d}$$

Thus there are two tests for the fault b s-a-0:

$$a = 1, \ b = 1, \ c = 0, \ d = x$$

and

$$a = 1, \ b = 1, \ c = x, \ d = 0$$

Examining the first test we find that the response of the good circuit (fault-free) is $F = 1$, but the response of the actual faulty circuit is $F = 0$ because b is s-a-0. Thus the fault is detected. Note that the above test patterns also detect the faults a s-a-0 and F s-a-0. Furthermore, other faults can be detected depending on the logic values assigned to d (in the first test) and c (in the second test).

13.13.3 Path sensitization

In simple combinational circuits, test patterns can be derived by inspection using a technique called *path sensitization*. A path is said to be sensitized if the effect of a fault is propagated along the path from the fault site to an observable output.

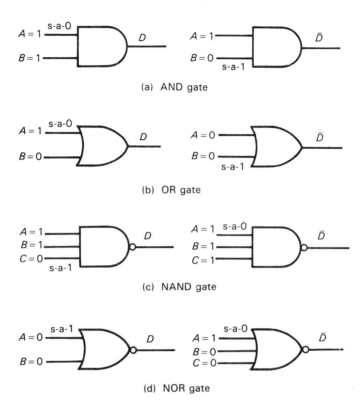

Figure 13.32 Conditions for propagating faults through basic gates

Consider the AND gate in Fig. 13.32(a). If input A is s-a-0, the fault can be detected by applying a logic 1 to A and a logic 1 to B. This input combination produces a value of 1 on the fault-free circuit output and a value of 0 on the faulty circuit output. The symbol D is used to denote logic 1 in the fault-free circuit and logic 0 in the faulty circuit. The symbol $\bar{D}$ denotes logic 0 in the fault-free circuit and logic 1 in the faulty circuit. Now the s-a-1 fault on input B can be detected by applying a logic 1 to A and a logic 0 to B which results in a $\bar{D}$ on the output. In both cases of Fig. 13.32(a), the effect of a fault was propagated from the input of an AND gate to the output by applying a logic 1 to the other input. Thus a path through an AND gate is sensitized by applying a logic 1 to the fault-free inputs. Similarly, a stuck-at fault on an input of an OR gate is propagated to the output by applying a logic 0 to the other inputs, as shown in Fig.13.32(b). Figures 13.32(c) and 13.32(d) show the sensitization of paths through NAND and NOR gates respectively.

Consider the circuit of Fig. 13.33 where A is s-a-0. In order to detect the fault, it has to be propagated through G1 and G3 to the output. The pattern $A = 1$ and $B = 1$ propagates the fault to G1. The assignment $C = 0$ produces a logic 1 on G2

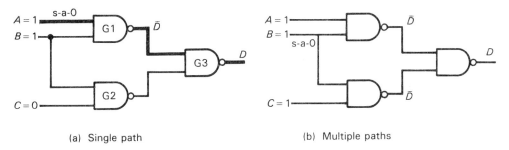

(a) Single path   (b) Multiple paths

Figure 13.33 Examples of single and multiple path sensitization

which allows the propagation of the $\bar{D}$ on G1 to G3. The resulting sensitized path is highlighted. Not only is the fault *A* s-a-0 detected, but also the faults G1 s-a-1 and G3 s-a-0. In fact, *half of the single stuck-at faults along a sensitized path are detected*. The pattern $A = 0$, $B = 1$, $C = 0$ detects *A* s-a-1, G1 s-a-0 and G3 s-a-1. By coincidence, the pattern also detects some faults in G2.

In the above example, we sensitized a single path to detect faults in the circuit. In Fig. 13.33(b), multiple paths are sensitized in order to detect the fault *B* s-a-0.

13.13.4 Automatic test pattern generation

Practical VLSI circuits may contain tens of thousands of gates. Thus there is a need to automate the procedure of test generation in order to cope better with the VLSI test complexity. Automatic test pattern generators (ATPGs) utilize an algorithmic approach to test pattern generation. A typical algorithm consists of the following steps:

Step 1 *Initial assignment*: find an input pattern to set up a D $(\bar{D})$ on the output of the faulty gate.

Step 2 *Forward drive*: propagate the D $(\bar{D})$ to an observation point via the shortest possible path.

Step 3 *Justification*: assign values to the remaining unassigned inputs so as to justify the assignments made in Step 2. Should an inconsistency arise, go back to Step 2 and choose an alternate path.

The most common ATPGs are *D-algorithm*, *PODEM*, and *FAN*. An ATPG is measured by the efficiency of its algorithms in generating the test patterns. Most bottlenecks occur in the justification phase where assignments made in the forward drive cannot be justified. This causes the ATPG to *backtrack* to the forward drive phase and try alternative paths. A good ATPG is one that requires a minimum amount of backtracks and can quickly generate test patterns for VLSI applications.

13.13.5 Design for testability

As previously mentioned, the goal of DFT is to enhance the controllability and observability of internal circuit nodes. This can be accomplished by providing access to internal circuit nodes directly from external input/output pins. Unfortunately, there is a limited number of external input/output pins available on an integrated circuit chip or printed circuit board. In general, the number of external pins is much smaller than the number of internal nodes. Thus the challenge of DFT is to improve one's access to the internal circuit nodes at a reasonable cost in terms of input/output and circuit overhead. In this section, we will describe three DFT methods: *partitioning*, *scan-path*, and *boundary scan*.

(a) Partitioning

One of the major challenges of testing digital systems is managing the complexity of the test. The complexity level of testing can be reduced by partitioning the target circuit into smaller subsystems that can easily be managed. The moral of this story

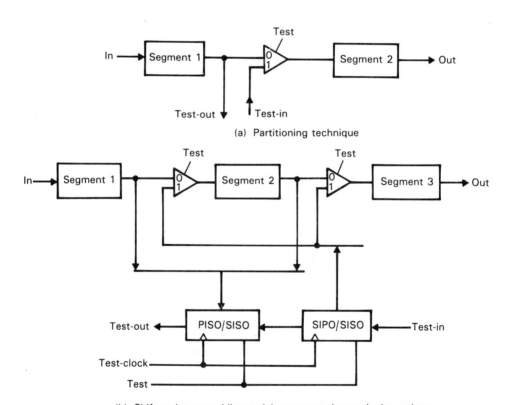

(a) Partitioning technique

(b) Shift register providing serial access to the partioning points

Figure 13.34 Partitioning of logic circuits

is: to solve big problems, think small. There are two major partitioning standards: partitioning by function, and partitioning by size.

Partitioning by function

A test strategy that targets a certain functional block can be radically different from that which targets other functional blocks. For example, a test strategy that targets a memory array has to cope with the problems of pattern sensitivity and is intrinsically different from testing for stuck-at faults in a multi-level combinational circuit. Thus it would be appropriate to partition these functional blocks from each other so that each can be accessible and tested in isolation.

Partitioning by size

It is common practice to solve a large problem by partitioning it into smaller parts, finding the solutions for the parts, and then combining the solutions of the parts into a solution of the whole. In DFT, one can partition a large circuit into smaller segments. The size of a segment can be defined relative to the number of inputs/outputs and/or the number of components stacked in it. In addition to this, however, the testability of a component in a segment is dependent on the degree to which the component inputs can be controlled and its outputs observed. In general, deeply embedded components are more difficult to test. Thus it would be desirable to partition a circuit such that, within each segment, the worst-case path crosses a maximum of N gate levels where N is user-defined.

Figure 13.34(a) shows a typical method of partitioning two segments. A multiplexer is used to allow for driving segment 2 from an external source. Furthermore, a test point is added to allow for observing the output of segment 1. This approach can be costly in terms of additional input/output pins if the number of segments becomes large. To deal with this problem, one can utilize shift registers that allow for serial access to the segments, as shown in Fig. 13.34(b). In this scheme, the test registers can be configured in one of two modes of operation. The SISO mode allows for testing the shift register itself.

(b) Scan path

The scan-path method is used to simplify the problem of testing sequential circuits. Refer to the finite state machine of Fig. 13.35(a). One of the critical problems is the limited ability to place the machine in the appropriate state so as to propagate a fault to an observation point. This problem renders the testing of sequential circuits much more complex than testing combinational circuits.

The scan-path method is basically a form of partitioning wherein the combinational portion of a finite state machine is separated from the flip-flop portion. A scan path can be incorporated into a circuit as shown in Fig. 13.35(b). In the normal mode of operation the input test = 0. In the test mode, test = 1. This

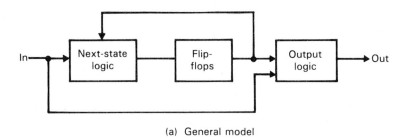

(a) General model

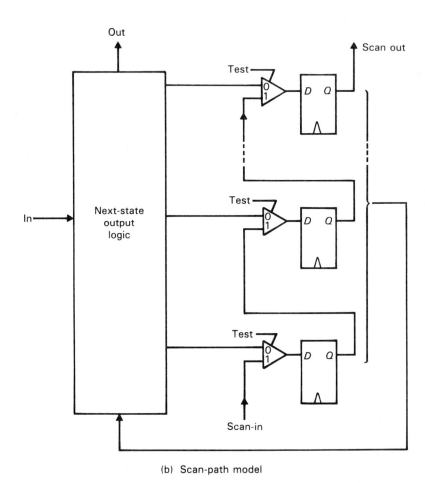

(b) Scan-path model

Figure 13.35 The use of a scan path to separate the combinational portion of the state machine from the flip-flops

allows the test engineers to load the flip-flops directly with the desired input pattern and thus provide the capability to set the finite state machine directly to the desired state. In order to test the finite state machine, the following test steps are followed:

Step 1 *Compile test vectors*: derive the test patterns for the combinational portion as if its outputs were observable.

Step 2 *Test flip-flops*: set test = 1, shift in via scan-in an alternating sequence of 1's and 0's and shift out the response via scan-out.

Step 3 *Test combinational portion*: for each test pattern, perform the following: (a) set test = 1, shift in the appropriate portion of the input pattern (this corresponds to the inputs of the combinational circuit which are fed by the flip-flops) into the flip-flops and apply the remaining portion directly to the primary inputs; (b) set test = 0, and clock the response of the combinational circuit in parallel into the flip-flops; (c) set test = 1, and shift out the contents of the flip-flops via scan-out so that they may be observed.

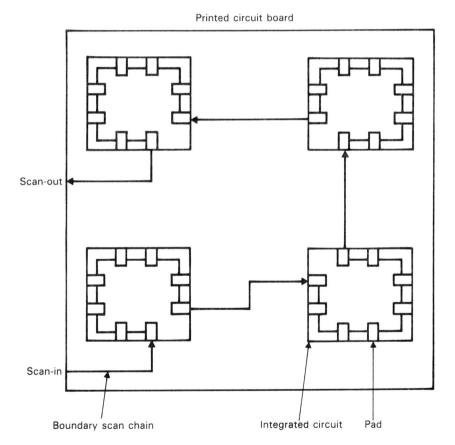

Figure 13.36 Boundary scan chain used to access internal components

(c) Boundary scan

Boundary scan is utilized at the printed circuit board level to allow access to integrated circuit chips on the board in a serial manner, as shown in Fig. 13.36. In this scheme, the inputs/outputs of each chip are connected together serially in the test mode of operation. Connections are also made, in the test mode of operation, between the various chips so that the pins of all the chips on a board can form a single scan chain. The boundary scan method is especially useful for printed circuit boards that have surface mounts. Surface mount packages are difficult to probe using conventional testers once they have been mounted on a board. The boundary scan method allows for accessing these packages directly via the edge connectors of the board.

In this section, we presented an overview of some DFT methods. However, there are many more DFT methods which deal with different test problems. For example, there are DFT methods that specifically target array structures such as PLAs. Furthermore, there are methods for generating test vectors and analysing the circuit responses on chip. These methods are classified as *built-in-self-tests* (BIST) and are used in circuits which are difficult to access in field testing and/or require periodic testing.

References

1. Weste N., and K. Eshraghian, *Principles of CMOS VLSI Design*, Reading, MA: Addison Wesley, 1985.
2. Geiger R. L., P. E. Allen and N. R. Strader, *VLSI Design Techniques for Analog and Digital Circuits*, McGraw Hill, 1990.
3. Miczo, A., *Digital Logic Testing and Simulation*, New York: Harper and Row, 1986.
4. Preas B., and M. Lorenzetti, *Physical Design Automation of VLSI Systems*, Menlo Park, CA: The Benjamin/Cummings Publishing Company Inc., 1988.
5. Chen J., *CMOS Devices and Technology for VLSI*, Englewood Cliffs, NJ: Prentice Hall, 1990.
6. Makki, R. Z., and P. Krishnan, 'Practical Partitioning for Testability with Time-Shared Boundary Scan', *Proceedings of International Test Conference*, Washington D.C., 1990, pp. 970–7.
7. *ASIC Technology and News*, March 1990.
8. Roth, J. P., Diagnosis of automat failures: A calculus and a method', *IBM J. Res. Develop.*, Vol. 10, pp. 278–91, July 1966.
9. Goel, P., 'An implicit enumeration algorithm to generate tests for combination logic circuits', *IEEE Trans. Comput.*, pp. 215–222, March 1981.
10. Fujiwara, H. and Shimono, T., 'On the acceleration of test generation algorithms', *IEEE Trans. Comput.*, vol. C–30, pp. 1137–1144, December 1983.
11. *CAzM reference manual, version 4.1*, MCNC Center for Microelectronics and Duke University, Research Triangle Park, NC, June 1990.

Problems

13.1   Given an n-type transistor with $K'_p = 32 \ \mu A/V^2$ and a p-type transistor with $K'_p = 16 \ \mu A/V^2$:

(a) Find the gain, β_n, of the n-type transistor if $W/L = 4$
(b) Find the W/L ratio of the p-type transistor which is required to produce a $\beta_p = \beta_n$ where β_p is the p-type transistor gain factor.

13.2   List and explain the major process steps associated with a p-well integrated circuit.

13.3   Implement the following functions using FCMOS, pseudo-NMOS, and clocked CMOS:

(a) $F = A + \bar{B}.C.D$
(b) $F = A \oplus B \oplus C$
(c) $F = A.\overline{B.C} + \overline{D.E}$

13.4   Minimize and implement the following multi-output function using a minimum amount of transistors:

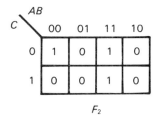

$$F_1 \qquad\qquad\qquad F_2$$

13.5   Implement the following function using an 8-to-1 CMOS multiplexer:

C \ AB	00	01	11	10
0	0	1	0	1
1	1	0	1	0

13.6   Repeat Problem 13.5 using a 4-to-1 CMOS multiplexer.

13.7   Implement the following finite state machine in CMOS. Use dynamic flip-flops:

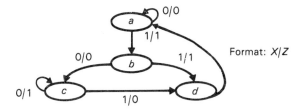

13.8   Find the total resistance of the following polysilicon wire ($R_S = 25$ ohms/square):

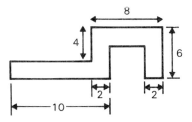

13.9   Find the total drain capacitance in the following n-type transistor. Use the parameter values of Table 13.3:

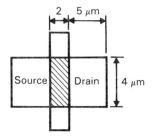

13.10   Find a minimum set of tests to detect all single stuck-at faults in the following circuit:

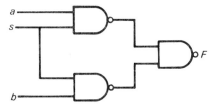

13.11   For the following circuit, list all the faults detected by the test pattern:

$T = T(abcd) = (1110)$

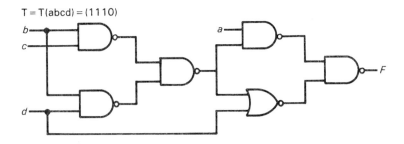

(Hint: use path sensitization.)

13.12 Implement the state machine of Problem 13.7 using a scan-path, and write the test sequence necessary to detect all single stuck-at faults in the combinational portion of the machine.

14 Engineering Aspects

14.1 General

This chapter can be considered as a continuation of Chapter 5. Three problems have been selected, each relating to obtaining a working system. In particular, we shall be concerned with problems of interconnected logic devices. A microprocessor system will be used as the example of a digital system, though most of the discussion is applicable to digital systems in general.

The first problem is concerned with *signal reflections* occurring at the ends of wires or printed circuit tracks. When a logic transition reaches a termination point, say the input of a gate, an effect known as signal reflection occurs which causes a part of the signal to travel back towards the source. The reflected signal may add to or subtract from the original signal and the process may repeat at each end several times, though over a period of time the reflected signal will decay to zero. Reflections, if too large, may cause incorrect logic operations.

The second problem is concerned with the unwanted transfer of a portion of a logic signal transition from one line to an adjacent line due to the proximity of the lines. This again may cause incorrect operation.

The final problem is concerned with the effects of electromagnetic interference or noise both externally generated and generated by the system itself. The dominant internal noise is caused by device switching which can produce a significant transient signal on the power supplies. Noise must be considered in all digital designs.

Reliability of digital systems, an additional engineering consideration, is discussed separately in Chapter 15 because of the extent of this subject.

14.2 Transmission line reflections

14.2.1 Transmission lines

Let us firstly review the electrical characteristics of interconnection wires or tracks in a digital system. The term *transmission line* is given to an interconnection path in electrical systems when the series resistance and inductance and the resistance and capacitance to earth are regarded as distributed along the length of the path.

Generally, the line carries a changing electrical signal, or a signal that can change, and the distributed nature of the inductance and capacitance of the lines has a significant effect on the signal. In a transmission line, the distributed resistance, inductance and capacitance are (normally) constant, and as a signal passes along the line, it is presented with a constant impedance called the *characteristic impedance* of the line. The characteristic impedance, Z_0, is given by:

$$Z_0 = \frac{\text{transient line voltage}}{\text{transient line current}}$$

Notice that the voltage and currents are transient values. When the signal is stable at a d.c. voltage, the corresponding line current is not defined by the characteristic impedance but by the output resistance of the source, the input resistance of the destination and the series resistance of the line (and the resistance to earth). We shall ignore the transmission line series resistance and resistance to earth as these have a negligible effect upon the analysis in our case.

The characteristic impedance of a line can be related to the distributed inductance and capacitance as follows: let the line inductance per unit length be L and the line capacitance per unit length be C. In a small element of the line, dx, the inductance is Ldx and the capacitance is Cdx. If the transient current is i, the voltage generated across the distributed inductance Ldx is given by:

$$v = Li dx/dt \quad \text{(from } v = di/dt)$$

Also the current due to the transient voltage, v, across the capacitance Cdx is given by:

$$i = Cv dx/dt \quad \text{(from } i = Cdv/dt)$$

by substituting, we get:

$$v/i = Z_0 = L/C$$

The propagation velocity of a signal, V_p, is given from the above equations as:

$$V_p = dx/dt = 1/\sqrt{LC} \quad \text{m/s}$$

or the delay, d, of:

$$d = \sqrt{LC} \quad \text{s/m}$$

The distributed inductance and capacitance of a line will depend on the dimensions and shape of the line, and the proximity to the return ground. The distributed capacitance will also depend on the relative permittivity of the surroundings. Normally the surroundings are non-magnetic so that the relative permeability is unity.

The distributed inductance and capacitance of simple line configurations, and hence the characteristic impedance, can be found from standard formulas derived by electric and magnetic field theory. We shall quote for two configurations [1] which may be of use in digital design. Firstly, a pair of round wires of radius r and separated by a distance d has an inductance, capacitance and characteristic impedance given by:

$$L = \frac{\mu_0 \ln(d/r)}{\pi} \quad \text{henries/m}$$

$$C = \frac{\pi \varepsilon_0 \varepsilon_r}{\ln(d/r)} \quad \text{farads/m}$$

$$Z_0 = \sqrt{\frac{\mu_0}{\varepsilon_0 \varepsilon_r}} \frac{\ln(d/r)}{\pi} \quad \text{ohms}$$

respectively. Secondly, a single wire of radius r separated from a ground plane by a distance h has an inductance, capacitance and characteristic impedance given by:

$$L = \frac{\mu_0 \ln(2h/r)}{2\pi} \quad \text{henries/m}$$

$$C = \frac{2\pi \varepsilon_0 \varepsilon_r}{\ln(2h/r)} \quad \text{farads/m}$$

$$Z_0 = \sqrt{\frac{\mu_0}{\varepsilon_0 \varepsilon_r}} \frac{\ln(2h/r)}{2\pi} \quad \text{ohms}$$

respectively. Z_0 is computed from $Z_0 = L/C$. The permeability constant, μ_0, is $4\pi \times 10^{-7}$. Non-magnetic surrounding media is assumed. The permittivity constant, ε_0, is approximately $1/(36\pi \times 10^9)$. The relative permittivity of the media, ε_r (also called the dielectric constant) is typically 4.5 for printed circuit material epoxy glass.

The characteristic impedance of printed circuit tracks similarly depends on the width of the track, the distance from the ground plane if any, and the dielectric constant of the printed circuit board. The characteristic impedance is typically in the region of 80 Ω to 200 Ω.

Whatever the physical configuration and track size, the propagation velocity is only dependent upon the relative permittivity of the media surrounding the track or wire according to the equation:

$$V_p = 1/\sqrt{\mu_0 \varepsilon_0 \varepsilon_r} = c/\sqrt{\varepsilon_r}$$

where c is the velocity of light in a vacuum. The propagation velocity is often in the range 5 ns/m to 7 ns/m (1.5 ns/ft to 2 ns/ft).

14.2.2 Reflections

Now, let us investigate the effects of logic signal changes from a voltage representing one logical state to another voltage representing the other logical state. To understand the effects that occur, consider a source which generates a logic transition from 0 volts to V_f volts. This transition passes along a line of characteristic impedance Z_0 to a destination with an input impedance Z_t as shown in Fig. 14.1(a). As the signal passes along the line, the equation:

$$Z_0 = V_f / I_f$$

must be satisfied, where I_f is the current flowing in the line due to V_f. The subscript f signifies the 'forward' direction. The voltage (and current) travel along the line as

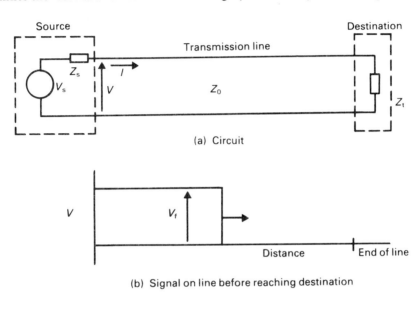

(a) Circuit

(b) Signal on line before reaching destination

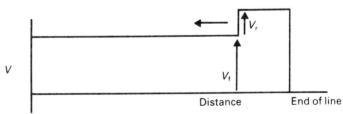

(c) Signal on line after reflection $Z_t > Z_0$

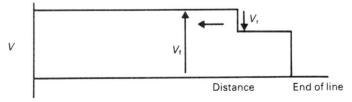

(d) Signal on line after reflection, $Z_t < Z_0$

Figure 14.1   Transmission line reflections

a step function, as shown in Fig. 14.1(b). When the transient reaches the destination, it is presented with an impedance Z_t, so then the voltage and current must be determined by Z_t. If Z_t is not equal to Z_0, the voltage and current must change immediately. The change that occurs will result in a transient signal known as a *reflection*, travelling backwards along the line towards the source. The reflection may be positive or negative and add to the original voltage or subtract from the original voltage. We shall see that it will add to the original forward signal if Z_t is greater than Z_0, as shown in Fig. 14.1(c), and subtract from the original forward signal if Z_t is less than Z_0, as shown in Fig. 14.1(d).

The amplitude of the reflected 'wave' can be obtained as follows. At the instant that the signal arrives at the destination, we have the current flowing into Z_t given as:

$$I_t = I_f + I_r$$

where I_f is the current of the forward (original) wave and I_r is the additional current producing the reflected wave. The corresponding voltages are given by:

$$V_t = V_f + V_r$$

where

$$I_t = V_t/Z_t$$

and

$$I_f = V_f/Z_0$$

and

$$I_r = -V_r/Z_0$$

Combining the above, we get:

$$V_r = V_f \left(\frac{Z_t - Z_0}{Z_t + Z_0} \right)$$

The term $(Z_t - Z_0)/(Z_t + Z_0)$ gives the fraction of the reflected wave to the forward wave and is called the *voltage reflection coefficient*, ρ. The voltage reflection coefficient has a value between -1 through zero to $+1$. It is zero when Z_t equals Z_0 and then no reflection occurs. If $Z_t = 0$ (a short-circuit), the reflection coefficient is -1 and a maximum negative reflection occurs, i.e. the reflected signal is of the same amplitude as the forward wave and subtracts from the forward wave to produce no signal. If $Z_t = \infty$ (an open-circuit), a maximum positive reflection occurs, i.e. the reflected wave is of the same amplitude as the forward wave and adds to the forward wave to produce double the original signal.

The actual voltage reflected down the line is given by V_t (which is equal to the sum of V_f and V_r). Rearranging the above equations, we get:

$$V_t = (1 + \rho)V_f = 2\left(\frac{Z_t}{Z_t + Z_0} \right)V_f$$

i.e. the final reflected signal can be between zero and double the original signal. In practice, zero or double the original signal will never occur because perfect short-circuit or open-circuit conditions cannot occur.

When the reflected wave reaches the source, a second reflection occurs if $Z_0 \neq Z_t'$, where Z_t' is the output impedance of the source. Reflections may continue at both ends of the line, though each reflection will be reduced and eventually a steady state is reached in which the line voltage and current are governed by ohmic resistances. The signal at each end will change in amplitude at t-second intervals if reflections occur, where t is the time taken for the signal to travel down the line in either direction. Often the signal changes manifest as a damped oscillation or ringing, as shown in Fig. 14.2, and it is usually necessary that this ringing does not cause the noise margins of the logic circuits to be exceeded.

14.2.3 Graphical analysis

Input and output impedances of logic devices are generally non-linear and accurate analytical prediction of the reflections is not easy. A convenient method is by graphical construction. Firstly let us consider the simple potential divider circuit shown in Fig. 14.3(a). A voltage step from 0 V to +5 V is applied to the circuit, and a current I flows through both R_s and R_1. A graphical construction to determine the voltage V_1 across R_1 is shown in Fig. 14.3(b). The two axes indicate current and voltage. Two lines are drawn, one with a slope of $-1/R_s$ and one with a slope of $1/R_1$. The intersection of these two lines defines the current I and the voltage V_1 by geometry as shown.

The technique can be applied to a transmission line circuit such as is shown in Fig. 14.4(a). A voltage step is applied to the circuit as before, and a current I_0 flows. Initially a step voltage V_0 appears at the input of the transmission line. At this time, the step voltage 'sees' the characteristic impedance of the line, Z_0. We can obtain the voltage V_0 by graphical construction, as in Fig. 14.4(b). Two lines are required, one with a slope of $-1/R_s$ and one with a slope of $1/Z_0$. The intersection of the

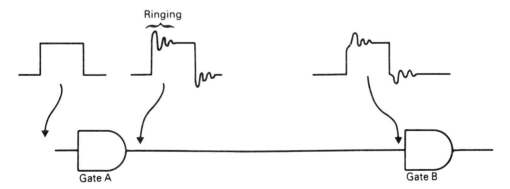

Figure 14.2 Interconnected gate suffering from transmission line reflections

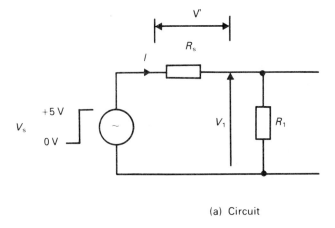

(a) Circuit

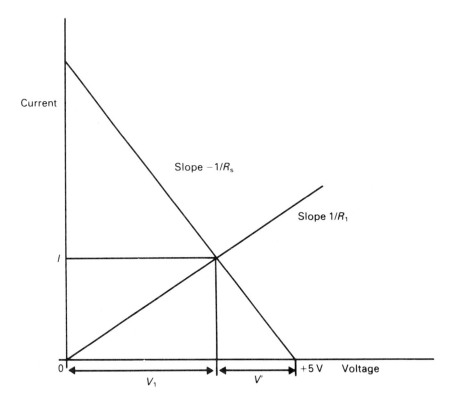

(b) Graphical construction

Figure 14.3 Graphical analysis of potential divider

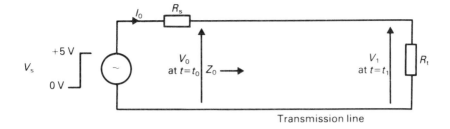

(a) Circuit

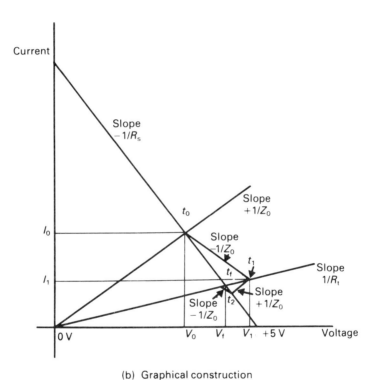

(b) Graphical construction

Figure 14.4 Graphical analysis of transmission line

lines gives V_0 and I_0. This event is marked on the graph as occurring at time t_0. The step voltage travels along the transmission line, always 'seeing' an impedance Z_0, and hence a constant amplitude is maintained. When the step voltage reaches the end of the line, it 'sees' a resistance, R_t. A change in voltage will occur if $R_t \neq Z_0$. The new voltage can now be ascertained by graphical construction using a line of slope $-1/Z_0$ and a line of slope $1/R_t$. One end of the $-1/Z_0$ line must start at the t_0 point. The intersection of the two lines is marked as occurring at t_1 and defines

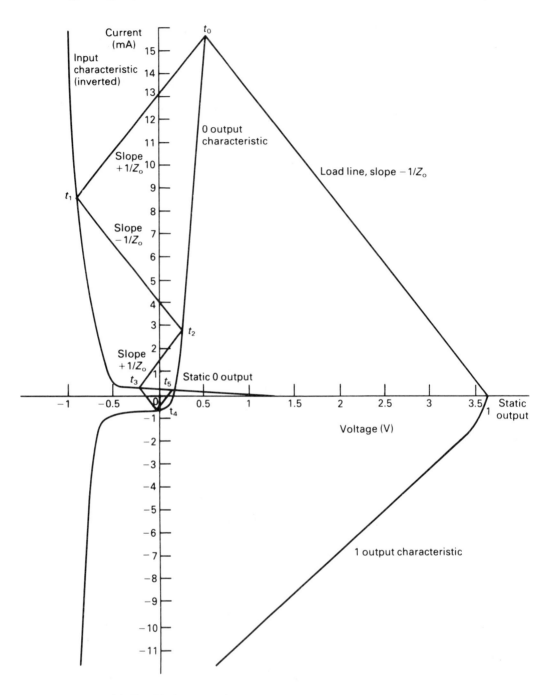

(a) Graphical construction

Figure 14.5 Graphical analysis of 1-to-0 transition with TTL gates

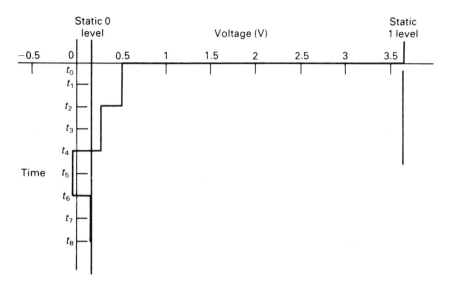

(b) Idealized waveform at source (gate A)

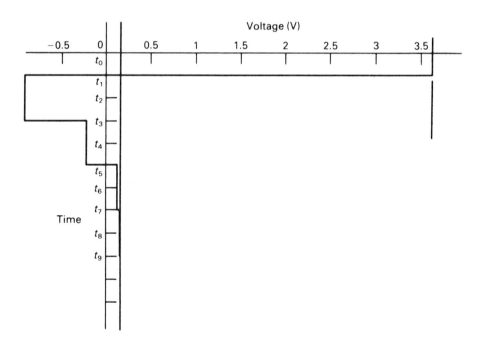

(c) Idealized waveform at destination (gate B)

Figure 14.5 continued

the new voltage at the end of the line, V_1. Assuming a different voltage is generated and hence a reflection occurs, a step waveform travels back towards the source, reaching the source at time t_2. This point is identified by drawing a line of slope $1/Z_0$ from t_1 to intersect the line of slope $1/R_t$ as shown. This process can be continued by drawing lines alternately of slope $-1/Z_0$ and $1/Z_0$, to find successive voltages at the source and destination as the signal travels forward and backward along the line until steady-state point t_f is reached.

We can now extend the technique for non-linear resistances. Take the example of a low-power Schottky (LS) TTL gate A connected to another LSTTL gate B (see Fig. 14.2). The input and output characteristics of the gates are plotted on graph paper. We shall arbitrarily choose the positive current axis for the current flowing into a device and the negative axis for the current flowing out of the device. There is one input characteristic for the destination gate B. The two output characteristics of the source gate A, one for a logic 0 output and one for a logic 1 output, are plotted separately.

Suppose firstly a 1-to-0 transition is to be investigated. Figure 14.5(a) shows the characteristics of the TTL gates and the subsequent graphical construction. The static 0 and 1 levels are identified by the cross-over of the input and output characteristics. From the static 1 point, a *load line* is drawn with a slope of $-1/Z_0$ where Z_0 is the characteristic impedance of the line. The intersection of the load line with the 0 output characteristic gives the initial low output voltage at the driving gate A. From this intersection, a line is drawn with a slope of $+1/Z_0$ to reach the input characteristic. The line is constructed for the signal as it travels from gate A to gate B, and gives the initial voltage appearing at gate B after the signal has passed along the line once. From this point on the input characteristic, a line is drawn with a slope of $-1/Z_0$ to strike the 0 level output characteristic. This gives the voltage after the first reflection at gate A. Subsequent lines are drawn between the input and output characteristics with alternate slopes $+1/Z_0$ and $-1/Z_0$ respectively until the static 0 point is reached. Each line indicates one transversal of the signal along the line.

The appropriate voltages and signal waveforms can be found from the intersection of the lines with the characteristics. These points are marked t_0, t_1, t_2, etc., in Fig. 14.5(a). The odd subscripts indicate the times when the signal is at gate A and the even subscripts the times when the signal is at gate B. The result in our example is shown in Fig. 14.5(b) and (c) for the signal at A and B respectively. We can see that the waveform at gate A falls within the 0 voltage range after t_2 seconds, i.e. after one complete transversal of the signal to the destination and back to the source. The signal at gate B initially undershoots (falls below the static 0 level) but then rises and finally settles at the static 0 voltage. In practice, the actual waveforms are not straight with abrupt changes as shown, but will have finite rise and fall times with rounded peaks and troughs.

A similar process is followed to obtain the reflections for a 0-to-1 transition starting at the static 0 point and drawing a load line to meet the 1 output characteristic. Subsequently, lines with alternate slopes of $-1/Z_0$ and $+1/Z_0$ are drawn. This has been done in Fig. 14.6(a). The resultant waveforms are shown in Fig. 14.6(b) and (c).

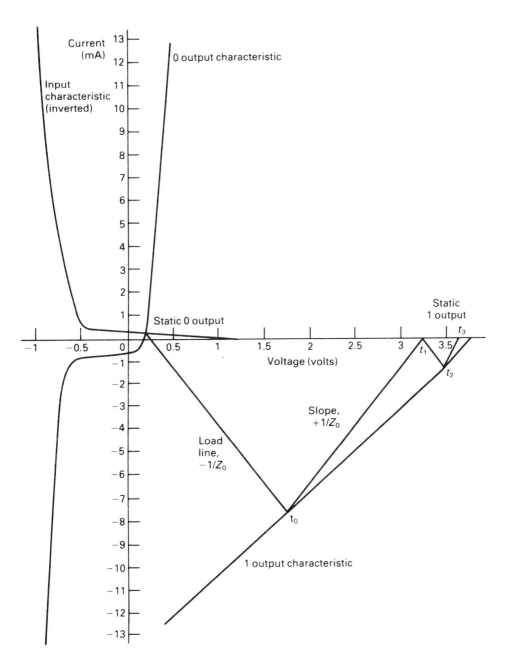

Figure 14.6 Graphical analysis of 0-to-1 transition

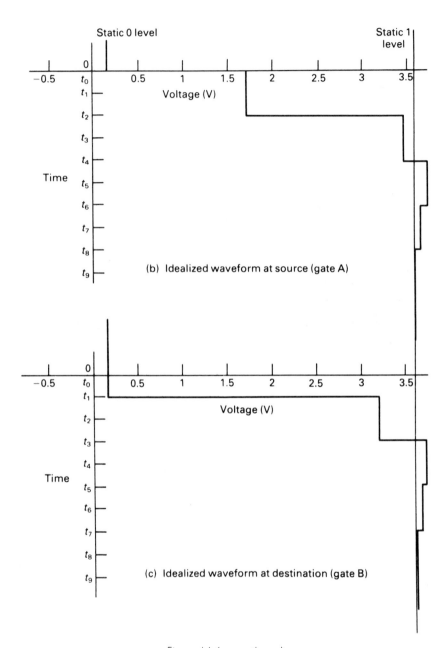

Figure 14.6   continued

The method is applicable to all types of gates including non-saturating logic such as emitter-coupled logic gates which have relatively high input and output impedances. Characteristics of gates can vary between manufactured devices and this would have a significant effect on the validity of the results. Given no additional knowledge of the actual gates in the system, the typical characteristics would be used. In some cases, individual device characteristics can be very different from typical device characteristics. For example, the LSTTL logic 1 output characteristic is significantly different from device to device within the same device type. The characteristic falls approximately in a linear fashion from the static 1 output to 0 V as the output is increasingly loaded. Zero volts occur when the output is short-circuit. The short-circuit current of an LSTTL gate is given as between 5 mA and 42 mA [2]. Typical values are not usually quoted but may be approximately 14 mA. The wide range of short-circuit current leads to very different possible characteristics in practice.

14.2.4 Methods of reducing reflections

If the driving gate has an output impedance equal to the characteristic impedance of the line and the input impedance of the receiving gate is equal to the characteristic impedance, no reflections occur at either end of the interconnection. (The reader may care to show this graphically.) Normal TTL gates do not possess these impedances. The output impedance of an LSTTL gate (including a three-state gate with its output not in high impedance) is in the region of 30 Ω for a logic 0 and 300 Ω for a logic 1 output. The logic 1 output impedance changes to about 50 Ω for currents below about 2 mA. The input impedance is about 100 Ω for input voltages less than 1.5 V and about 10 kΩ for input voltages greater than 1.5 V. The input circuitry of TTL gates usually includes clamping diodes which prevent undershoot being below about − 1 V. Without clamping diodes, a large undershoot might occur.

The output impedance of a gate can be increased artificially in an attempt to match the line characteristic impedance, by using an external series resistor as shown in Fig. 14.7(a). A typical value for the resistor is 47 Ω. Series resistors might be used for critical signals such as the ready signal in a microprocessor system.

Matching at the receiving end in bus systems can be done by line termination resistors placed at the end of the bus. For example, the bus on a multi-board system is normally laid out on parallel tracks on a motherboard. At the end of these tracks, a full-value reflection would occur if not terminated since an open-circuit line is an infinite impedance and the worst case for reflections. (Note that MOS devices exhibit very high input impedance and cause almost maximum reflections.) Termination resistors attached to the ends of the lines can take the form of a single resistor connected to + 5 V (pull-up) or to 0 V (pull-down) as appropriate. Typical values for the former case may be in the region of 2.7 kΩ and in the latter case in the region of 10 kΩ. The smallest value is determined by the drive currents available. Open-

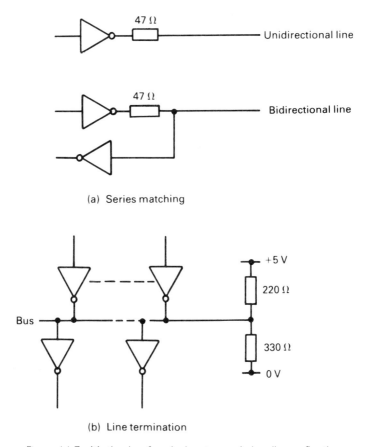

(a) Series matching

(b) Line termination

Figure 14.7   Methods of reducing transmission line reflections

collector gates naturally require pull-up resistors to +5 V. Three-state gates could use either pull-up or pull-down resistors. When the output line is in high impedance (tristate), a pull-up resistor would cause a 1 to be generated, while a pull-down resistor would cause a 0 to be generated.

An alternative approach, particularly to achieve improved matching, is to use a resistor divider network with one resistor connected to +5 V and one connected to 0 V as shown in Fig. 14.7(b). Typical values are 3.3 kΩ connected to +5 V and 4.7 kΩ connected to 0 V. Values may be lower to improve the matching with the characteristic impedance, perhaps as low as 220 Ω and 330 Ω respectively if the gates can supply the required d.c. currents (20 mA with 220/330 Ω resistors). The effective resistance of this termination is 132 Ω, close to the typical characteristic impedance of lines. More complex terminations using diodes and voltage sources are possible. Termination can be applied to critical signals or to all bus signals, but in each case, the d.c. current of the termination resistors must be taken into account when accessing the d.c. loading.

14.3 Cross-talk

Cross-talk is the effect of one signal transition coupling on to an adjacent line due to the capacitance and mutual inductance between the lines. Suppose a gate A is connected to gate B with a line close to a line connecting gate C to gate D. A logic pulse is generated by gate A to pass to gate B. The connection of A to B runs close, in the worst case parallel, to the connection of gate C to gate D as shown in Fig. 14.8(a), and causes a signal to appear on the C–D line. The signal coupled on to C–D is backward wave, i.e. a current flows in the opposite direction to that caused by the signal on A–B. This can be deduced by considering the two lines as inductors with a mutual inductance between them and capacitors as shown in Fig. 14.8(b). The current flowing in the coupled inductor opposes that flowing in the 'primary' circuit. When a logic transition is generated on the A–B line, a current (and voltage) transition appears on the C–D line starting with the A–B transition and lasting for the time it takes for the A–B transition to propagate down the A–B line, ignoring reflections.

The detailed analysis is rather complicated. We shall restrict our analysis to a simple single lumped impedance [3]. Consider two lines with a mutual impedance,

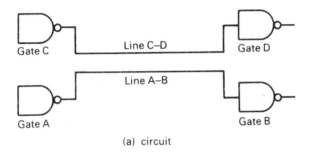

(a) circuit

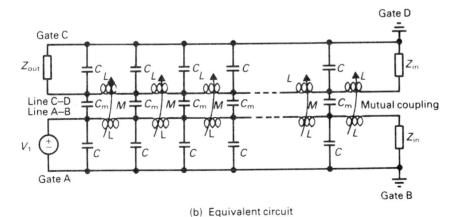

(b) Equivalent circuit

Figure 14.8 Cross-talk between signal lines

Z_m, between them sited in one place at the middle of the two lines as shown in Fig. 14.9(a). The characteristic impedance of each line is Z_0. Gate A has an output impedance of Z_{out} and a voltage source V_{out}. The gate is connected to the A–B line which presents the output with a load impedance Z_0 as in the equivalent circuit for transient signals shown in Fig. 14.9(b). The actual voltage generated by gate A is thus:

$$V_1 = \left(\frac{Z_0}{(Z_0 + Z_{out})}\right) V_{out} \tag{1}$$

Note that when the transient starts at A it is presented with an impedance Z_0 irrespective of the termination impedances.

Now referring to the transient signal equivalent circuit shown in Fig. 14.9(c), two characteristic impedances in parallel are shown for the C–D line, one to the left of the middle point of the line and one to the right of the middle point. The voltage at the middle point of line C–D becomes:

$$V_2 = \left(\frac{Z_0}{2(Z_0 + Z_m)}\right) V_1 \tag{2}$$

Combining the equations (1) and (2), we obtain:

$$V_2 = \left(\frac{Z_0}{2(Z_0 + Z_m)}\right) \left(\frac{Z_0}{(Z_0 + Z_{out})}\right) V_{out} \tag{3}$$

The voltage V_2 is that at the middle point of line C–D. The signal travels towards gate C. Then it is reflected and travels towards gate D. The reflected signal at C is given by the transmission line coefficient of reflection multiplied by the forward signal. Therefore the final equation for the signal at gate D (before any further reflections) is:

$$V_2' = \left(\frac{Z_0}{2(Z_0 + Z_m)}\right) \left(\frac{Z_0}{(Z_0 + Z_{out})}\right) \left(\frac{(Z_t - Z_0)}{(Z_t + Z_0)}\right) V_{out} \tag{4}$$

where Z_t is the output impedance of gate C. It is important to note that the above equation is approximate; in practice the problem is much more complex. However, it gives us a suitable equation to obtain a guide to the reflections that may be encountered.

EXAMPLE

Suppose, all four gates in Fig. 14.8 are TTL gates. A falling 1-to-0 transition occurs on the output of gate A. Gate C has a static 0 output and an output impedance of 50 Ω. Gate A has an output impedance of 10 Ω. The connections are via two surface printed circuit tracks 1 mm wide running parallel and 1 mm apart with a ground place 2 mm distant. The characteristic impedance of the lines is 100 Ω and the mutual impedance is 200 Ω. Determine the crosstalk.

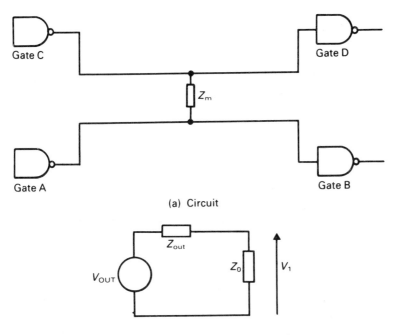

(a) Circuit

(b) Equivalent circuit for gate A driving line

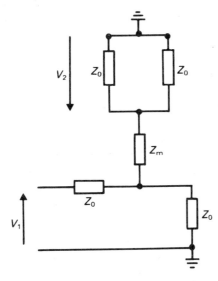

(c) Line equivalent circuit (see text)

Figure 14.9   Cross-talk analysis; lumped impedance approach

Using equation (3), we obtain the cross-talk as:

$$\frac{V_2}{V_{out}} = \left(\frac{100}{2(100 + 200)}\right)\left(\frac{100}{(100 + 10)}\right) = 10.15$$

i.e. cross talk of -15%. If the logic swing is 2 V, the cross-talk is 300 mV, in the same direction as the initial transition. From equation (4), the cross-talk after reflection at gate C is -5%. If the output impedance of gate C is 10 Ω, the reflection becomes worse at -12.4%.

14.4 Noise and decoupling

We defined noise in Chapter 5 as unwanted electrical signals occurring in a system. Noise becomes significant when it is imposed on logic signals to such magnitude as to affect the system. Some noise can be tolerated at the inputs of gates as defined by the noise margins of the gates. Excessive noise must be eliminated. Noise on logic signals within the system can come from various sources. The predominant source of noise in complex digital systems is caused by individual logic devices switching from one binary state to the other binary state, leading to voltage transients along power supply lines and noise on the device outputs. We have also seen the cross-talk effect described in section 14.3. External noise can be induced into the system by electrostatic or electromagnetic fields. The source may itself be an electronic device such as an SCR (silicon controlled rectifier) or an electromechanical device such as a relay. Radiated noise can be reduced by shielding (enclosing the digital system with metal). The shielding material must be magnetic for electromagnetic shielding.

As regards noise due to switching of logic devices, three factors can be identified, namely:

(i) The d.c. supply current is different for each output logic level (e.g. an LSTTL 7400 part containing four NAND gates has a total supply current of 2.4 mA when all the outputs are at a 0 and a supply current of 0.8 mA when all the outputs are at a 1).

(ii) During the time that the output changes state, either from a 0 to a 1 or vice versa, the output line capacitance (and internal capacitances) must be charged or discharged. This results in a transient current demand to the supply.

(iii) Also during the time that the output changes state in logic circuits such as TTL, significant additional transient currents are generated if both output transistors at any time conduct simultaneously.

The current changes are depicted in Fig. 14.10. Both static changes and transient changes cause the supply voltage to vary and clearly any variation of the supply voltage will have an adverse effect on the operation of the gates. Supply variations are reduced by the use of smoothing or decoupling capacitors which are connected across the supply at various places within the system (C_1 and C_2 in Fig. 14.11).

An estimate of the values of the capacitors can be made for each of the effects separately. Firstly, consider (i) above. To take a simple example, consider a system

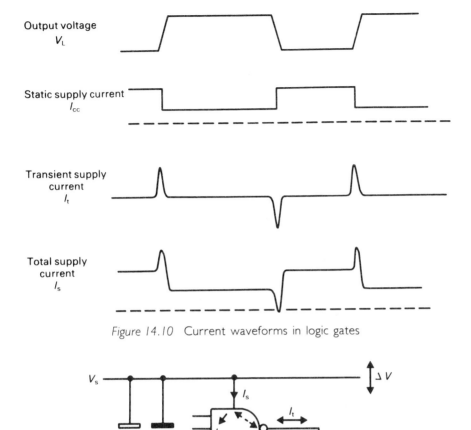

Figure 14.10   Current waveforms in logic gates

Figure 14.11   Smoothing capacitors

with one LSTTL 7400 part with all the inputs joined together and a 1 MHz square-wave signal applied to the inputs. Let the specification call for a maximum change of 5% on the +5 V supply. Over the period that the outputs are at a 1, a current will be demanded from the supply, and when the outputs change to a 0, a different current will be demanded. The minimum value of the smoothing capacitor for a given maximum supply voltage change over the period of charging or discharging can be found from the equation:

$$I = C \; \mathrm{d}v/\mathrm{d}t$$

where I is the difference between the 0 and 1 level currents. Entering the values given, we get:

$$(2.4 \text{ mA} - 0.8 \text{ mA}) = C(0.25 \text{ V})/(0.5 \text{ } \mu\text{s})$$

or

$$C = (1.6 \times 10^{-3} \times 0.5 \times 10^{-6})/0.25 = 3.2 \times 10^{-9}\text{F} = 3.2 \text{ nF}$$

The exact maximum switching frequency might not be known in practice. Clearly a very large value of capacitor can be used assuming it will operate at the switching frequency. In typical systems comprising many gates, electrolytic capacitors with values in the range 50 μF to 200 μF are generally used on individual printed circuit boards.

Now consider (ii) and (iii) which generate transients only at the time of switching. To calculate a value of capacitor to control the transients, the various capacitances and inductances in the circuits need to be considered. We can identify the capacitance at the output of gates as a source of transient current when output logic transitions occur. We can also identify the inductances associated with the power supply lines which consume transient currents when changes in the power supply voltage occur. Inductances include the track inductance, internal inductance of the power connections of the devices, and the self-inductance of smoothing capacitors. All these inductances exist for (i) but can be neglected at lower frequencies. At very high frequencies, the inductance effect dominates. Also the resistances in the power circuits become significant.

Firstly though, let us perform a rather naïve calculation for the transients due to discharging/charging load capacitors ignoring inductance and resistance. Suppose that the total load capacitance applied to the output of each of the four NAND gates is 50 pF which includes the track capacitance, input capacitance of logic devices attached to the outputs, and output self-capacitance. The output signal transition from a 0 to a 1 and from a 1 to a 0 follow non-linear relationships, but let us assume linear transitions with slopes of 0.25 V/ns for a rising transition and 0.4 V/ns for a falling transition with a 50 pF load and a logic swing of 3.6 V. These are typical values for LSTTL.

Using $I_t = C_L \, dV_{out}/dt$, where I_t is the transient current, dV_{out} the output logic swing and dt the time that the transition occurs, we obtain the transient currents as:

Rising transition: $I_t = 4 \times 50 \times 10^{-12} \times 0.25 \times 10^9 = 50 \text{ mA}$
Falling transition: $I_t = 4 \times 50 \times 10^{-12} \times 0.4 \times 10^9 = 80 \text{ mA}$

These would be step functions of period dt. The rising transition occurs over 14.4 nsec (3.6/0.25) and the falling transition occurs over 9 nsec (3.6/0.4). We can obtain the value of the smoothing capacitor, C_S from $C_S = I_t \, dt/dV_S$, where dV_S is the allowable supply voltage change. Thus:

Rising transition: $C_S = (50 \times 10^{-3} \times 14.4 \times 10^{-9})/0.25 = 2880 \text{ pF}$
Falling transition: $C_S = (80 \times 10^{-3} \times 9 \times 10^{-9})/0.25 = 2880 \text{ pF}$

In fact, the transient current and the time dt are not needed for the calculation of C_S as $C_S/C_L = dV_{out}/dV_S$. The 9 ns current pulse has an equivalent frequency in excess of 100 MHz (389 MHz using the formula $f = 3.5/t$). The capacitor would need to operate at this frequency. This rules out electrolytic capacitors.

High-frequency capacitors such as ceramic types must be used. These are not manufactured in very large values such as would be needed in systems employing many gates. Therefore, two types of capacitor are used, connected in parallel across the supply lines, at least one large value electrolytic capacitor and several smaller valued high-frequency capacitors distributed around the components.

The above calculation is not normally valid, especially for dynamic memory devices which have very high current transients. Let us perform a more realistic calculation by considering the effect of inductance. For this, we need to know the rate of change of the supply current, i.e. dI_S/dt. This is rarely given in the specification of logic devices, but suppose it is 20 mA/ns. Using the equation $V = L \, dI/dt$ the maximum allowable inductance with the values given would be:

$$L = 0.25/20 \times 10^6 = 12.5 \text{ nH}$$

To keep the inductance to 12.5 nH requires care in the circuit layout. For example, a normal ceramic 0.1 μF capacitor mounted very closely around each integrated circuit would typically have an inductance of around 5 nH to 6 nH, not including the self-inductance of the capacitance. The self-inductance of the capacitor is in the region of 3 nH to 4 nH. Dynamic memories have rather large values for dI_S/dt, perhaps 50 mA/ns. The total inductance in this case would need to be not more than 5 nH.

References

1. Shepherd, J., A. H. Morton and L. F. Spence, *Higher Electrical Engineering*, London: Pitman, 1967.
2. *The TTL Data Book for Design Engineers* (2nd ed.), Dallas: Texas Instruments, Inc., 1976.
3. Morris, R. L., and J. R. Miller, eds., *Designing with TTL Integrated Circuits*, Texas Instruments Electronics Series, New York: McGraw-Hill, 1971.

Problems

14.1 The output of a TTL NAND gate is connected to the input of a similar gate with a cable 3 m long. Estimate the time required for a 0-to-1 transition to settle to 0.2 V of steady-state value, given the following.

Input characteristic of gates:	V_{in} (V)	I_{in} (mA)
	5	+1
	1.4	0
	0.4	−1.6

Output characteristic of gates:

V_{out} (V)	I_{load} (mA)
5	+ 1
3.6	0
2.4	− 10
0.4	+ 16
0.05	0

Characteristic impedance of cable = 100 Ω
Velocity of propagation in cable = 2×10^8 m/s.

Employ the graphical method of determining transmission line reflections, and piece-wise linear models for the input and output characteristics.

14.2 The output of a TTL gate, A, is connected to the input of an NMOS device, B. A resistor, R, is connected from the input of device B to the supply (+5 V) to reduce transmission line reflections. Estimate the minimum value of R to give a maximum undershoot of − 1 V on the interconnecting line at device B, for 1-to-0 logic transitions, given the following:

Gate A   1 level open-circuit output voltage = 3.5 V
         0 level open-circuit output voltage = 0.05 V
         0 level output impedance   = 30 Ω

Characteristic impedance of line = 150 Ω

The input current of device B can be ignored. Obtain a value for R assuming that the 1 level output impedance of device A is zero, and then repeat assuming that it is 750 Ω.

The resistor, R, is replaced by a pair of resistors, R_1 and R_2. R_1 is connected between the line and + 5 V and R_2 is connected between the line and 0 V, at device B. Determine suitable values for R_1 and R_2 to give the same undershoot as above and a steady-state 1 voltage of 3.5 V on the line. Clearly indicate the steps taken to reach your solution. What is the principal advantage of using the pair of resistors?

14.3 (a) Why is it common practice to insert a low-value resistor in series with memory driver gates on large memory boards?

(b) A TTL logic gate is connected via a printed-circuit track to the input of an MOS memory device. The output impedance of the TTL gate is 25 Ω for both high and low logic levels and the input current of the MOS device is 10 μA. The low logic level is + 0.5 V and the high logic level is + 3.5 V. The printed-circuit track has a characteristic impedance of 100 Ω. Estimate, by graphical means, the maximum overshoot and undershoot for fast logic transitions.

(c) Estimate the minimum spacing of two parallel printed circuit tracks each arranged as above if the coupling between tracks is to be less than 10%. Take the mutual impedance between printed-circuit tracks to be proportional to the distance between tracks, and 100 Ω at 0.1 cm spacing.

14.4   The following relates to a single TTL inverted logic gate:

Logic low output voltage level	=	0.4 V
Logic high output voltage level	=	2.4 V
Rise time of output	=	7 ns
Fall time of output	=	5 ns
Propagation delay, low to high level	=	22 ns
Propagation delay, high to low level	=	15 ns
Input capacitance	=	15 pF
Logic low output supply current	=	5 mA
Logic high output supply current	=	2 mA
Supply voltage	=	+5 V

Three inverters are connected in cascade and driven by a 10 kHz square wave logic signal. Sketch the supply current variations. Estimate suitable minimum decoupling capacitors if the supply voltage is not to vary by more than 5%. Neglect inductances. Make any other necessary assumptions.

15 Reliability

15.1 Definitions

In a system of electrical components, there is always a likelihood that over a period of time one or more components will suddenly fail to function. This will often cause the system itself to fail. In this chapter, we shall look at the likelihood that a failure will occur and possible designs to make the system resilient to failures such that the system will continue to function properly in the presence of one or more component failures. Firstly we need to define a number of terms.

15.1.1 Failure rate

Suppose a number of identical components are operated in a test. Over a period of time, components will fail at intervals. When a component fails, it is not replaced with a working component, i.e. it is a *non-replacement* test. We might obtain the decrease of working components shown in Fig. 15.1. (A continuous curve is shown: actually there will be step changes as a component fails.) At an instant in time, the slope of the curve is given by dN/dt, and there are dN failures in time dt. The parameter *failure rate*, λ, is associated with the components and can be defined as:

$$\lambda = -\frac{dN/N}{dt}$$

i.e. the fractional rate of decrease of N, where N is the number of components still working.

An alternative test is the *replacement* test. In the replacement test, when a components fails, it is replaced with another component. This leads to slightly more failures during the test and a slightly higher value for failure rate. In the following, we will assume a non-replacement test.

Failure rate is not necessarily a constant; commonly it takes the form shown in Fig. 15.2. When a component is first operated, there is a greater likelihood that it will fail due to factors such as manufacturing defects, stress and internal temperature changes. Usually after perhaps 500 hours of operation, the failure rate settles down to a constant value. This is the normal operating period. At the end

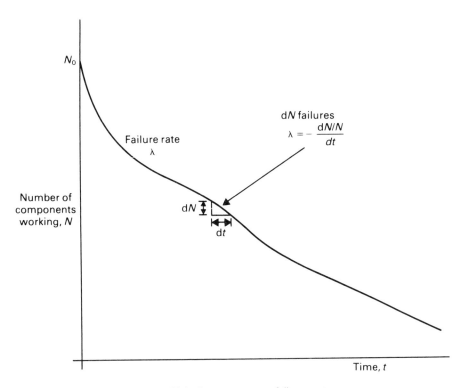

Figure 15.1   Instantaneous failure rate

of the component's life, perhaps after a few years but depending upon the operating conditions, the failure rate begins to increase. This is the *wear-out* period. We can define an 'instantaneous' failure rate given by:

$$\lambda(t) = -\frac{dN(t)/N(t)}{dt}$$

In many cases, we can assume that component failure rates under fixed conditions are constant. Constant failure rates are normally given in terms of $\%/1000$ hr or failures/10^6 hr. For example, a constant failure rate of $5.6\%/1000$ hr can be written as $56/10^6$ hr.

Integrated circuits typically have failure rates in the region 1 to 1000/hr depending upon the complexity of the component, among other factors. For example, a 4-gate 74LS00 part has a failure rate of approximately $2/10^6$ hr while a 2200-gate Z-80 microprocessor has a failure rate of approximately $100/10^6$ hr (computed from reference [1]). Failure rates normally refer to the normal operating period.

For a constant failure rate component, we have:

$$\lambda \, dt = -\frac{dN(t)}{N(t)}$$

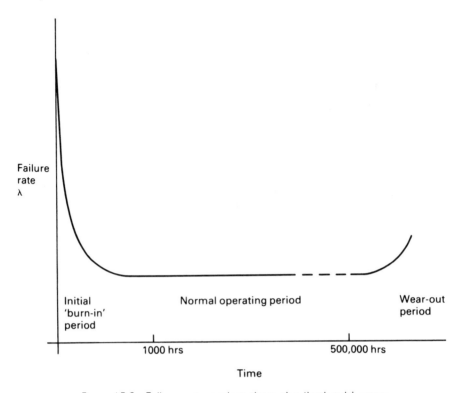

Figure 15.2 Failure rate against time; the 'bath-tub' curve

$$\int \lambda \, dt = - \int \left(\frac{1}{N(t)} \right) \, dN(t)$$

$$\lambda t = - \log N(t) + K$$

$$N(t) = K' e^{-\lambda t}$$

where K and K' are constants. At $t = 0$, $N = N_0$ (the initial number of components). Therefore $K' = N_0$ and

$$N(t) = N_0 e^{-\lambda t}$$

i.e. the rate of decrease of working components is an exponential function for a constant failure rate component, as shown in Fig. 15.3.

15.1.2 Reliability

The term *reliability* is defined as:

$$R = \frac{\text{number of components working at time } t}{\text{number of components working initially}}$$

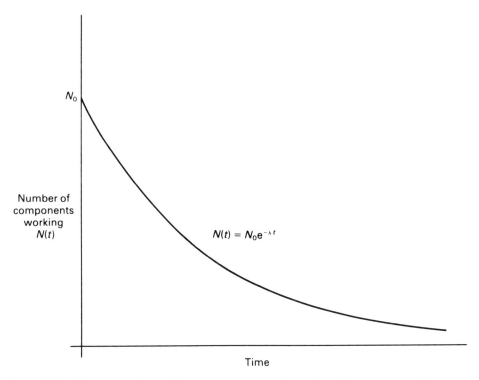

$$N_0$$

Number of
components
working
$N(t)$

$N(t) = N_0 e^{-\lambda t}$

Time

Figure 15.3 Decrease of working components against time for constant failure rate
components

Reliability has a value of unity at $t = 0$. For a constant failure rate component, we
have:

$$R(t) = \frac{N(t)}{N_0} = e^{-\lambda t}$$

Hence reliability is also an exponential function for a constant failure rate
component, as shown in Fig. 15.4. Reliability can be given as a ratio, say 0.999, or
as a percentage, 99.9%.

For a constant failure rate system, after an operating time equal to $1/\lambda$, the
reliability has reduced to 0.37 or 37%. After a time of $2/\lambda$, the reliability has
reduced further to 0.135 or 13.5%. After a time $3/\lambda$, the reliability has reduced to
0.05 or 5%.

15.1.3 Mean time between failures

The term *mean time between failures*, MTBF, is the mean time between successive
failures [2]. If a system is repaired, the system MTBF would include the repair time.

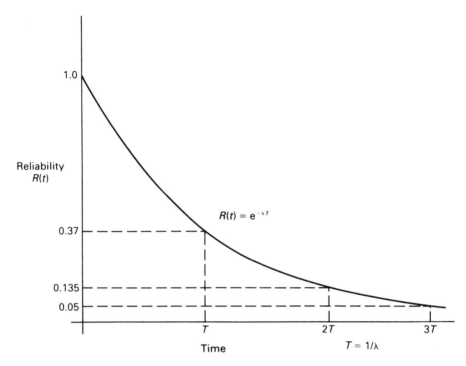

Figure 15.4 Reliability of a constant failure rate system

The MTBF of a batch of components could be obtained by measuring the time that each component operates, and computing the mean operating time, i.e.

$$\text{MTBF} = \frac{\text{Summation of the component operating times}}{\text{Initial number of components}}$$

Ideally, we would like to perform the test until all the components have failed. Then all the operating times would be added together and the result divided by the original number of components, giving a mean value for the batch of components. MTBF is a constant (whether or not the failure rates are constant).

In the general case, over a period of time from t to $t + dt$, $N(t)$ components are operating. The cumulative operating time over the period dt is given by $N(t)\,dt$. Integrating from $t = 0$ to $t = \infty$, we obtain the expression for the MTBF given by:

$$\text{MTBF} = \frac{\int_0^\infty N(t)\,dt}{N_0} = \int_0^\infty R(t)\,dt$$

The integration is performed to infinity to ensure that all of the components have failed.

For constant failure rate components, $N(t) = N_0 e^{-\lambda t}$ and MTBF is given by:

$$\text{MTBF} = \frac{\int_0^\infty N_0\, e^{-\lambda t}\, dt}{N_0} = \int_0^\infty e^{-\lambda t}\, dt$$

$$= 1/\lambda$$

i.e. the reciprocal of failure rate gives the mean time between failure but only for a constant failure rate system.

15.1.4 Non-constant failure rate

When the failure rate is not constant but a function of time, i.e.

$$\lambda(t) = -\frac{dN(t)/dt}{N(t)}$$

we get by multiplying by N_0/N_0:

$$\lambda(t) = -\left(\frac{dN(t)}{N_0}\right)\left(\frac{N_0}{N(t)}\right)\frac{1}{dt}$$

$$= -\frac{dR(t)/dt}{R(t)}$$

since $R(t) = N(t)/N_0$. Therefore:

$$\lambda(t)\, dt = -\frac{1}{R(t)}\, dR(t)$$

Integrating, we get:

$$\int \lambda(t)\, dt = -\int \frac{1}{R(t)}\, dR(t)$$

At $t = 0$, $R(t) = 1$. Therefore:

$$-\int_0^t \lambda(t)\, dt = \log R(t) - \log 1 = \log R(t)$$

$$R(t) = \exp\left(-\int_0^t \lambda(t)\, dt\right)$$

This expression can only be evaluated if the function $\lambda(t)$ is known. If it is constant, the expression reduces to that obtained before, i.e.

$$R(t) = \exp(-\lambda t)$$

Using the previous definition, MTBF is given by

$$\text{MTBF} = \frac{\int_0^\infty N(t)\ dt}{N_0}$$

$$= \int_0^\infty \exp\left(-\int_0^t \lambda(t)\ dt\right) dt$$

which will be a constant but can only be evaluated if we know the function $\lambda(t)$. (With a constant failure rate, we get the previous value, i.e. $\text{MTBF} = 1/\lambda$.)

15.2 System reliability

The terms we have introduced in section 15.1 regarding components under a test can be applied to the components in a functional system and for the system. Let us consider the reliability of a system composed of several components. Firstly we define the terms *probability of working* and *probability of failure*.

15.2.1 Probability of working and probability of failure

The probability of a system (or component) working, P, is the same as reliability (see definition of reliability). The probability of a system (or component) failure, Q, is given by:

$$Q = 1 - P$$

For example, if the probability of working is 0.9 (90%), the probability of failure is 0.1 (10%). The reliability of a constant failure rate system after an operating time equal to the MTBF is 0.37 (see Fig. 15.4), or expressed alternatively, the probability of a system working at this time is 37%. In the following, we shall often use probability terms to obtain the probability of working expressions, though of course reliability terms can be substituted.

15.2.2 Series configuration

A series configuration is one in which the complete system will fail if any one component in the system fails. Most computer systems are of this form. A system with a series configuration can be illustrated diagrammatically as one in which the components are connected in series electrically, as shown in Fig. 15.5. The probability of the system working must be the product of the probabilities of working of the individual components, i.e.

$$\text{Probability of system working, } P_s = P_1 \times P_2 \times P_3 \times \cdots \times P_n$$

where P_n is the probability of the nth component working. The reliability of the

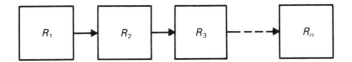

Figure 15.5 Components in a series configuration

complete system is given by the product of the reliabilities of the individual components, i.e.

Reliability of system, $R_s = R_1 \times R_2 \times R_3 \times \cdots \times R_n$

where R_n is the reliability of the nth component. Replacing the reliability with the constant failure rate exponential form, we get:

$$\exp(-\lambda_s t) = \exp(-\lambda_1 t) \times \exp(-\lambda_2 t) \times \cdots \times \exp(-\lambda_n t)$$
$$= \exp[-(\lambda_1 + \lambda_2 + \cdots + \lambda_n)t]$$

i.e. the failure rate of the system, λ_s, is given by the summation of the individual failure rates. Therefore if the component failure rates are constant, the system failure rate must also be constant.

For a system of n identical components, we have:

$$P_s = (P)^n$$

where P is the probability of an individual component working. The probability of system failure, Q_s, is given by:

$$Q_s = 1 - P_s = 1 - (P)^n = (1 - Q)^n$$

where P is the probability of each component working and Q is the probability of each component failure.

EXAMPLE

If the series system is composed of 100 components, each with a reliability or probability of working of 99%, the reliability of the system is:

Reliability of system $= 0.99^{100} = 0.366$

or expressed another way, if the components have a 99% chance of working, the system has a 36.6% chance of working. With 200 components, the reliability falls to 0.134 (13.4%). This illustrates that components need to have a very high reliability to give high system reliability.

15.2.3 Parallel configuration

A parallel configuration is one in which the system fails only if all the components in the system have failed, as opposed to a series configuration in which only one component need fail for the system to fail. Clearly a parallel configuration will lead to a greater reliability than a series configuration and is the basis of many fault-tolerant systems (section 15.4).

A system with a parallel configuration can be illustrated diagrammatically as a system of components connected in parallel as shown in Fig. 15.6. The probability of a system failure is given by the product of the individual probabilities of failure:

$$\text{Probability of system failure, } Q_s = Q_1 \times Q_2 \times Q_3 \times \cdots \times Q_n$$

where Q_n is the probability of failure of the nth component. (This equation may be compared to a series configuration in which the system works only if all the components are working.)

The probability of the system working can be found by substituting $Q_s = 1 - P_s$ into the above relationship, i.e.

$$1 - P_s = (1 - P_1)(1 - P_2)(1 - P_3)\ldots(1 - P_n)$$

Substituting the component failure rates as before, we find that the system failure rate is generally not a constant, even if the component failure rates are constant.

For n identical components, we have:

$$Q_s = (Q)^n = (1 - P)^n$$

or

$$P_s = 1 - Q_s = 1 - (1 - P)^n$$

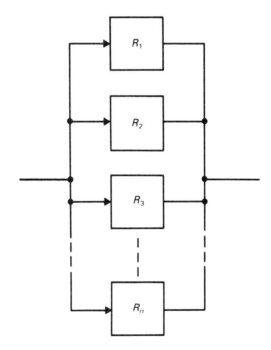

Figure 15.6 Components in a parallel configuration

EXAMPLE

If a parallel system is composed of 100 components, each with a reliability of 99%
as in the series system example, the reliability of the system is:

$$R_s = 1 - (1 - 0.99)^{100} = 1 - 10^{-200}$$

i.e. the system has a 99.99...99% chance of working. It is unlikely that a 100-
component parallel system would be feasible. However, even with 3 components
configurated in parallel, we obtain:

$$R_s = 1 - 10^{-6}$$

or a 99.9999% chance of working.

15.2.4 Reliability assessment

Many systems fall into the series category and then the overall failure rate is given
by the summation of the failure rates of the individual components. As the overall
system has a constant failure rate, the MTBF is given by the reciprocal of the system
failure rate. The probability of working (reliability) can also be calculated from the
constant failure rate exponential equation $R(t) = e^{-\lambda t}$, if the operating time is
known. In a system of many different components operating under different
electrical and perhaps different environmental conditions, we should take the
different reliabilities under different conditions into account. The general approach
is to incorporate *weighting factors* which modify the basic failure rate according to
the conditions that the components experience. Typical conditions are operating
power, temperature and mechanical stress. Each component failure rate is
multiplied by the appropriate weighting factor and the results summed to obtain the
overall system failure rate.

    A comprehensive reference giving the failure rates of all types of electrical
components, comprehensive weighting factors and procedures is given in *Reliability
Prediction of Electronic Equipment*, MIL-HDBK – 217B US Department of
Defense, [1]. Two reliability assessment treatments are identified. One is called the
parts count method which gives a general idea of the system reliability during the
system design phase. The other is called the *parts stress analysis* method which is
a thorough treatment done when the design is finished and all the operating
conditions are known. Firstly we outline the parts count method.

(a) Parts count method

In this method, each failure rate is multiplied by two weighting factors, a quality
factor and a learning factor, leading to the system failure rate:

$$\lambda_s = \sum_{i=1}^{n} N_i(\lambda_G \pi_Q \pi_L)$$

where:

λ_s = total system failure rate (failures/10^6 hr)
λ_G = generic failure rate of the ith component (failures/10^6)
n = number of different components' categories
N_i = number of components in the ith category
π_Q = quality factor of the ith component
π_L = learning factor of the ith component (for microelectronic devices only)

This failure rate applies if the whole system is operating in one environment, as would be usual. Failure rates are given for different environments and the appropriate failure rates chosen accordingly. Nine different physical environments are listed in reference [1]: ground benign (nearly zero stress), ground fixed, ground mobile, naval sheltered, naval unsheltered, airborne inhabited areas, airborne uninhabited areas, space flight and missile launch.

The quality factor refers to the manufacturing and testing methods employed for the component. More stringent testing will lead to a lower factor and a lower failure rate. Quality factors are used in both the parts count method and the parts stress method. There is a factor of 300 between the highest testing procedure (most stringent military specification) and the lowest (normal commercial testing with epoxy or similar packaging).

The learning factor can have a value of 1 or 10. The value of 10 is applied if the component is new and has been placed into initial production or where there have been major changes in design or production or where there has been an 'extended interruption in production or a change in line personnel (radical expansion)'.

Failure rates are given for types of components, not particular components. Bipolar digital devices are separated from others including MOS devices, digital or linear. Within each group, a range of internal gate numbers are categorized together at each environmental condition and the same generic failure rate listed. For example, a bipolar digital device with 1 to 20 gates has the same failure rate (0.029 for fixed ground conditions, 0.21 for missile launch), 21 to 50 gates the same failure rate, 51 to 100 gates the same failure rate, 101 to 500 gates the same failure rate, etc. A similar table is produced for MOS devices. Read-only memories are categorized according to the number of bits. Random access memory is quoted as having 3.5 times the failure rate of read-only memory.

Table 15.1 lists the generic failure rates for bipolar and MOS devices operating at ground-fixed environment (G_F). This environment is defined as 'conditions less than ideal to include installation in permanent racks with adequate cooling air, maintenance by military personnel and possible installation in unheated buildings' [1]. Separate tables are provided for discrete components. Table 15.2 lists some common components, again under a ground-fixed environment.

Table 15.3 shows an example of the computation for digital system (having a series configuration). The result, 567.5044 failures/10^6, would normally be rounded to, say, 570 failures/10^6. The MTBF is given by $1/570 \times 10^6 = 1750$ hr. This rather

Table 15.1 Generic failure rate, λ_G, of bipolar and MOS devices [1]. G_F environment (ground fixed)

Circuit complexity	TTL	Bipolar beam lead, ECL, Linear, MOS
1–20 gates	0.029	0.048
21–50 gates	0.062	0.19
51–100 gates	0.094	0.31
101–500 gates	0.22	0.82
501–1000 gates	0.34	1.4
1001–2000 gates	0.78	3.1
2001–3000 gates	2.1	8.4
3001–4000 gates	5.7	23.0
4001–5000 gates	16.0	62.0
ROM* ⩽ 320 bits	0.022	0.87
321–576 bits	0.033	0.13
577–1120 bits	0.052	0.20
1121–2240 bits	0.078	0.30
2241–5000 bits	0.12	0.46
5001–11000 bits	0.18	0.70
11001–17000 bits	0.28	1.1
Linear ⩽ 32 transistors		0.052
33–100 transistors		0.11

* RAM failure rate $= 3.5 \times$ ROM failure rate
$\pi_Q = 75$ for commercial part hermetically sealed
$\pi_Q = 150$ for commercial part packaged in organic material (e.g. epoxy).

low MTBF could be substantially improved by using component screening procedures (which would reduce π_Q from 75 to 45 for MIL-STD-883, method 5004, class C, or to 2.5 if class B. The highest screen procedure MIL-M − 38510 class A produces $\pi_Q = 0.5$).

(b) Parts stress method

In parts stress analysis, several weighting factors are incorporated into the calculation to accommodate the operating conditions. Two types of conditions are identified: failure over a period of time due to mechanisms accelerated by temperature or electrical bias, and failure due to mechanical causes (including thermal expansion). These are summed together into one equation. The equation depends on the type of component. Monolithic MOS and bipolar digital devices have a similar general equation:

$$\lambda_P = \pi_L \pi_Q (C_1 \pi_T + C_2 \pi_E) \pi_P$$

Table 15.2 Selection of component generic failure rates [1] G_F (ground fixed)

Component	Generic failure rate (failures/10_6 hr)
Resistors	
Composition, style RCR	0.002
Film, style RL	0.075
Film power, style RD	0.96
Capacitors	
Paper/plastic, style CHR/CPV/CQR	0.0006
Ceramic, style CKR	0.022
Tantalum solid, style CSR	0.026
Aluminum dry electrolyte, style CE	0.41
Transistors	
Si NPN	0.18
Si PNP	0.29
Diodes	
Si, general purpose	0.12
Zener and avalanche	0.16
Connectors	
Circular, rack and panel, Printed wiring board	0.45
Switches	
Toggle	0.57
PC wiring boards	
Two-sided	0.0024
Multi-layer	0.30
PC wiring board connections	
Solder, reflow lap to PC boards	0.00012
Solder, wave to PC boards	0.00044
Other hand solder	0.0039
Crimp	0.0073

Table 15.3 Example of parts court method

Component	N_i	λ_G	π_Q	π_L	$N_i(\lambda_G\pi_Q\pi_L)$ (failures/10^6 hr)
Resistors	6	0.002	1	1	0.012
Capacitors	10	0.022	1	1	0.22
TTL 1–20 gates	2	0.029	75	1	4.35
TTL 21–50 gates	5	0.062	75	1	23.25
MOS 1001–2000 gates	2	3.1	75	1	465.0
MOS 16K RAM	1	0.98	75	1	73.5
PC board	1	0.0024	1	1	0.0024
PC connections	300	0.0039	1	1	1.17
				Total	567.5044

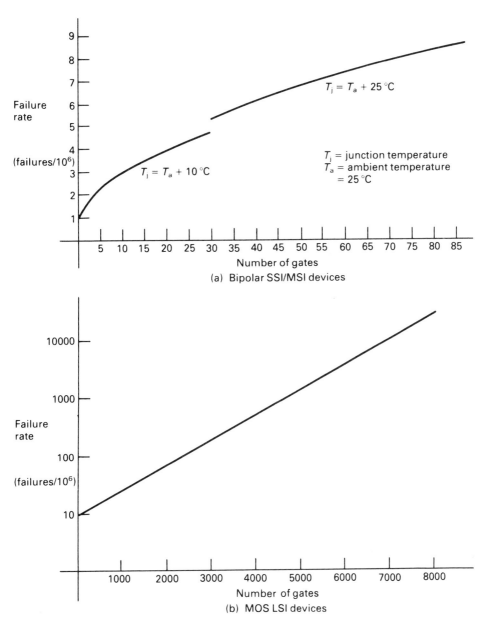

Figure 15.7 Failure rates of integrated circuits computed from parts stress method

where:

λ_p = device failure rate (failures/10^6)

π_L = device learning factor

π_Q = device quality factor

π_T = temperature acceleration factor (technology dependent)

π_E = environment factor
C_1 = circuit complexity factor (exponential function of number of gates)
C_2 = circuit complexity factor
π_P = pin factor (1 to 1.3 depending on the number of pins on package and device)

The above equation is used in subgroups, bipolar and MOS digital SSI/MSI and bipolar and MOS LSI and microprocessor. Bipolar and MOS memories are treated separately because of the high 'gate to pin' ratio. MOS includes all types including NMOS, PMOS and CMOS with normal integrated circuit processes.

Components within each type are classified more finely than in the parts count method. Digital devices are classified according to the number of internal gates (1, 2, 4, 6, 8, 10, 12, etc.) and the number of gates in a particular device, for example a 74LS00 (4 gates), Z-80 (2200 gates). Figure 15.7(a) and (b) gives the failure rates for bipolar SSI/MSI and MOS LSI calculated from the data provided in the parts stress method of MIL-HDBK – 217B.

15.3 Reliability of complex systems

Systems may have a configuration that is neither series nor parallel. If they can be divided into parallel sections and series sections, the reliability of each of these sections can be calculated separately and the results combined as appropriate. However, if this reduction cannot be performed or there are additional aspects such as multiple failure modes, alternative methods need to be employed. We shall describe two methods that are suitable for all configurations, one using Bayes's probability theorem (section 15.3.1) and one using Boolean truth tables (section 15.3.2). Multiple failure mode problems are discussed in section 15.3.3 and solved using Bayes's theorem.

15.3.1 Using Bayes's probability theorem

To explain Bayes's theorem, consider a pack of playing cards. The probability of drawing a card of the club suit is 13/52 (1/4), as 13 of 52 cards are of the club suit. This is the *marginal* (or *simple*) *probability* of an event occurring. The probability of drawing a card which is both of the club suit and a court-card (either jack, queen or king) is 3/52 as there are three cards in the court group, jack of clubs, queen of clubs and king of clubs. This probability is known as the *joint probability* as it depends upon the joint event of drawing a club and a court-card. If it is known that a club has been drawn, the probability that it is also one of the court cards is 3/13. This probability is known as the *conditional probability* and is related to marginal and joint probability in our example by:

$$3/13 = \frac{3/52}{13/52}$$

or more generally:

$$\text{Conditional probability} = \frac{\text{joint probability}}{\text{marginal probability}}$$

This relationship is known as Bayes's probability theorem [2].

Also, the summation of all the possible joint probabilities is equal to the marginal probability. For example, the (marginal) probability of drawing a court-card of any suit is given by the summation of the joint probability of drawing a court-card and club (3/52), the joint probability of drawing a court-card and spade (3/52), the joint probability of drawing a court-card and diamond (3/52) and the joint probability of drawing a court-card and heart (3/52), i.e. $3/52 + 3/52 + 3/52 + 3/52 = 12/52$. Generally:

$$P_a = P_{a1} + P_{a2} + P_{a3} + \ldots + P_{an} \tag{1}$$

where

P_a = marginal probability that event a occurs

and

P_{an} = joint probability that both event a occurs and event n occurs

All n events must be mutually exclusive and form a complete list.

Replacing each joint probability by the product of marginal probability and conditional probability (Bayes's theorem) provides the equation:

$$P_a = P_{a/1}P_1 + P_{a/2}P_2 + P_{a/3}P_3 + \ldots + P_{a/n}P_n \tag{2}$$

where

$P_{a/n}$ = conditional probability that a occurs given that event n has occurred

and

P_n = marginal probability that event n occurs.

We can use this expression to determine the probability of a system working. Suppose a system consists of two or more units. One unit is called A. Two mutually exclusive events are identified, one of which must occur, namely a system with A working and a system with A not working. We can write:

Probability of system working = (probability of system working assuming A works) × (probability of A working) + (probability of system working assuming A not working) × (probability of A not to working)   (3)

Let us now apply equation (3) to various system configurations, starting with a system having two components A and B.

(a) Two-component series configuration

Suppose A and B are in a series configuration. We shall arbitrarily choose component A for our expression. The various probabilities need to be determined.

The probability that the system works if A works depends upon B, i.e. the probability that B works. The probability that the system works if A does not work is zero because the system cannot work if A does not work. Therefore the probability of the system working is given by:

$$P_s = P_A P_B + 0$$

where

P_A = probability of A working
P_B = probability of B working

This result is the same as previously, i.e. the probability of system working or reliability is given by the product of the individual component working probabilities or reliabilities.

(b) Two-component parallel configuration

Suppose A and B are in a parallel configuration. From (3), we get:

$$\text{Probability of system working} = 1 \times P_A + P_B \times (1 - P_A)$$
$$= P_A + P_B - P_A P_B$$

This result is equivalent to that obtained previously.

(c) More complex configurations

Figure 15.8 shows a system configuration in which the system can work if some of

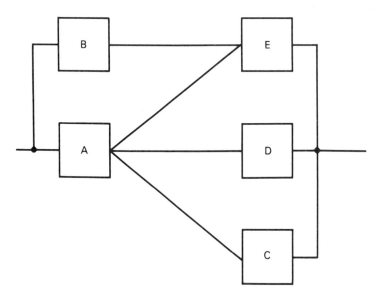

Figure 15.8 System which does not decompose into simple series or parallel configurations

the components are working. In particular, the system works if:

A and C are working; or
A and D are working; or
A and E are working; or
B and E are working.

We shall apply equation (3) with A again chosen as working or not working. When A is working, we have the parallel combination of C, D and E as shown in Fig. 15.9(a) and the probability of this working is given by:

$$P = 1 - (1 - P_C)(1 - P_D)(1 - P_E)$$

as a simple parallel combination. It does not matter whether B is working and so B does not need to be considered. When A is not working, the system reduces to a series combination of B and E as shown in Fig. 15.9(b), which has the probability of working of:

$$P = P_B P_E$$

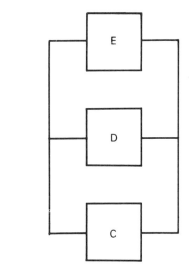

(a) System if A works

(b) System if A does not work

Figure 15.9 Reduction of system using Bayes's theorem

Substituting these results into (3), we get:

$$P_s = (1 - (1 - P_C)(1 - P_D)(1 - P_E))(P_A) + P_B P_E (1 - P_A)$$

EXAMPLE

If $P_A = 0.95$, $P_B = 0.90$, $P_C = 0.85$, $P_D = 0.80$ and $P_E = 0.75$, $P_s = 0.976625$.

15.3.2 Boolean truth table method and probability maps

In the Boolean truth table method, a truth table is formed which lists all the possible combinations of components working or not working in a system and whether the complete system works in each case, determined by examination of the system configuration. A component working is indicated by a Boolean 1 and a component not working by a Boolean 0.

To take an example, consider the previous problem shown in Fig. 15.8. There are five components, A, B, C, D and E. Hence, there are 32 combinations of components working or not working, as shown in the A-B-C-D-E columns of Table 15.4. The next column indicates whether the particular combination leads to a working system or a system failure. For example, the condition of A working ($A = 1$), B working ($B = 1$), C not working ($C = 0$), D working ($D = 1$) and E not working ($E = 0$) leads to a working system because A and D are working. The probability of this particular event is given by:

$$P_A P_B (1 - P_C) P_D (1 - P_E)$$

Given the actual probabilities, the system probability of the event occurring can be calculated. In our example, $P_A = 0.95$, $P_B = 0.90$, $P_C = 0.85$, $P_D = 0.80$ and $P_E = 0.75$ and the probability for $A = 1$, $B = 1$, $C = 0$, $D = 1$, and $E = 0$ is $(0.95) \times (0.90) \times (1 - 0.85) \times (0.80) \times (1 - 0.75) = 0.02565$. The other system working probabilities can be calculated similarly. All the probabilities are given in the final column of Table 15.4. The probability that the system will work is given by the summation of the individual probabilities given in the last column. With the values here, the summation is 0.976625 as before.

We can write the Boolean expression for P_s in terms of A, B, C, D and E:

$$\begin{aligned} P_s = &\bar{A}\bar{B}C\bar{D}E + \bar{A}\bar{B}CDE + \bar{A}BC\bar{D}E + \bar{A}BC\bar{D}E + \bar{A}BCD\bar{E} \\ &+ \bar{A}BCDE + A\bar{B}\bar{C}\bar{D}E + A\bar{B}\bar{C}D\bar{E} + A\bar{B}\bar{C}DE + A\bar{B}C\bar{D}E + A\bar{B}CD\bar{E} \\ &+ A\bar{B}CDE + AB\bar{C}\bar{D}E + AB\bar{C}D\bar{E} + AB\bar{C}DE + ABC\bar{D}E \\ &+ ABCD\bar{E} + ABCDE \end{aligned}$$

where

> A = component A working

and

> $\bar{A}$ = component A not working.

Table 15.4 Probability table

A	B	C	D	E	System	Probability
0	0	0	0	0	Fails	
0	0	0	0	1	Fails	
0	0	0	1	0	Fails	
0	0	0	1	1	Fails	
0	0	1	0	0	Fails	
0	0	1	0	1	Fails	
0	0	1	1	0	Fails	
0	0	1	1	1	Fails	
0	1	0	0	0	Fails	
0	1	0	0	1	Works	0.0010125
0	1	0	1	0	Fails	
0	1	0	1	1	Works	0.00405
0	1	1	0	0	Fails	
0	1	1	0	1	Works	0.0057375
0	1	1	1	0	Fails	
0	1	1	1	1	Works	0.02295
1	0	0	0	0	Fails	
1	0	0	0	1	Works	0.0021375
1	0	0	1	0	Works	0.00285
1	0	0	1	1	Works	0.00855
1	0	1	0	0	Works	0.0040375
1	0	1	0	1	Works	0.0121125
1	0	1	1	0	Works	0.01615
1	0	1	1	1	Works	0.04845
1	1	0	0	0	Fails	
1	1	0	0	1	Works	0.0192375
1	1	0	1	0	Works	0.02565
1	1	0	1	1	Works	0.07695
1	1	1	0	0	Works	0.0363375
1	1	1	0	1	Works	0.109012
1	1	1	1	0	Works	0.14535
1	1	1	1	1	Works	0.43605

Total: 0.976625

This expression can be simplified algebraically using the equality $A + \bar{A} = 1$ (i.e. probability of working + probability of failure = 1), in the same way as simplifying Boolean expressions using the identical Boolean equality. However, care must be taken not to use Boolean equalities which are not valid for probability expressions. In particular, the Boolean equality $A + A = A$ which allows us in Boolean algebra to use a term repeatedly in simplifying expressions, is not allowed in simplifying probability expressions.

An alternative process to algebraic simplification uses the equivalent of a Karnaugh map, called a *probability map*. The probability map is labelled as a

Karnaugh map with adjacent squares representing terms which have one variable
different (variable true in one term and false in the other term). The probability
function is mapped onto the probability map using 1's to indicate a working system
and 0's to indicate a non-working system. The probability map for our problem is
shown in Fig. 15.10. Note that each term describes an exclusive product of component probabilities. Groups of 1's are formed as in a Karnaugh map except that
overlapping groups are not allowed. There may be more than one selection of groups
which will cover the 1's and these will give equivalent solutions. One solution is:

$$P_s = AD + \bar{A}CE + A\bar{D}E + \bar{A}B\bar{C}E$$

Substituting the probability values, we get the same result as previously (0.976625).

15.3.3 Multiple modes of failure

So far we have considered a component which either works or fails completely. Now
we will develop the technique further to cover components which have more than
one type of failure, in particular components which have a mode of failure not
leading inextricably to a system failure. A simple example is a circuit consisting of
two semiconductor diodes D_1 and D_2 connected in series. A diode may work, fail
producing a short-circuit connection, or fail producing an open-circuit connection.
(Of course it is possible to have an intermediate failure.) We need to define what
constitutes a working system. Let us say in this case that the system works if it has
a rectifying action, i.e. has electrical conduction in one current direction but not in
the other direction, and any voltage drop across the circuit is irrelevant. If one diode
fails with a short-circuit, the system will still behave in this manner, while if one
diode fails with an open-circuit, the system fails.

Equation (2) in section 15.3.1 (derived from Bayes's theorem) can be used to
calculate the overall probability of working as follows:

Probability of system working =
(probability of system working if D_1 works)(probability of D_1 working)

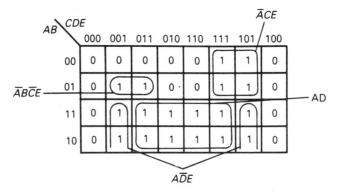

Figure 15.10 Probability map

+(probability of system working if D_1 short-circuit)

(probability of D_1 short-circuit)

+(probability of system working if D_1 open-circuit)

(probability of D_1 open-circuit)

Letting:

P = probability of diode working
$Q_{s/c}$ = probability of diode short-circuit
$Q_{o/c}$ = probability of diode open-circuit

and assuming both diodes are identical, we obtain:

Probability of system working, $P_s = (P + Q_{s/c})(P) + (P)(Q_{s/c}) + 0$
$$= P^2 + 2PQ_{s/c}$$

Note $P = 1 - Q = 1 - (Q_{o/c} + Q_{s/c})$. We could deduce P_s from considering all combinations which produce a working system, i.e. with both diodes working (P^2), plus two combinations of one diode working and one diode short-circuit $(2PQ_{s/c})$.

Taking another example more closely related to digital system design, consider the logic circuit shown in Fig. 15.11. Suppose each gate has two modes of failure, failure with a permanent 1 output and failure with a permanent 0 output. The failures are independent of the input conditions. The circuit is assumed to be working if the system output = 1 when the system input = 1, and the system output = 0 when the system input = 0. Selecting gate A, we get:

Probability of system working =
(probability of system working if A works)(probability of A working)

+

(probability of system working if A output permanent 1)(probability of A output permanent 1)

+

(probability of system working if A output permanent 0)(probability of A output permanent 0)

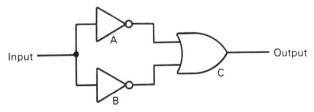

Figure 15.11 Logic circuit; gates have two modes of failure, with permanent 1 and with permanent 0 output

Letting

P_A = probability of A working
P_B = probability of B working
Q_{A0} = probability of A output permanent 0
Q_{B0} = probability of B output permanent 0

we get:

Probability of system working $= (P_B + Q_{B0})P_C P_A + 0 + P_B P_C Q_{A0}$

Generally, we will expect the probability of a system working to be higher if the system can continue to operate with particular failures. Such arrangements form the basis of a *fault-tolerant system*.

15.4 Design of reliable systems

In this section we shall examine some possible ways of improving the reliability of a system. The reliability of a system can be increased by adding component parts to the system which though redundant for normal operation lead to a parallel or semi-parallel system configuration. Reliable systems can also be designed by incorporating error checking and correcting circuits into the system so that when an error occurs, the error is corrected and the system continues to operate. Firstly, though, we consider adding redundant parts to a system.

15.4.1 System, gate and component redundancy

We can duplicate parts at:

(i) System level (extra systems)
(ii) Gate level (extra gates)
(iii) Component level (extra capacitors, resistors, transistors, etc.).

One arrangement of system redundancy is to use three systems together with a *voter* circuit as shown in Fig. 15.12. Only one output from each system is shown. (For multiple outputs, a separate voter would be necessary for each output.) The voter chooses the outputs which are the same. If all three systems are working, all the outputs will be the same. If only two of the three systems are working, the voter chooses the two identical outputs. If more than one system is not working, the system fails. It is assumed that there is a negligible probability of two faulty systems producing the same output. Firstly, with the voter working, there are four conditions for the system to work:

(i) All three systems working
(ii) System 1 and 2 working and system 3 not working
(iii) System 1 and 3 working and system 2 not working
(iv) System 1 and 2 working and system 3 not working.

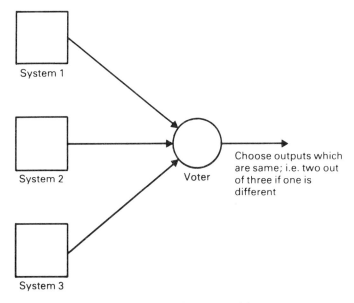

Figure 15.12 Triplicated system with a voter

Therefore the probability of the system working is given by the probability of all three systems working plus the probabilities of the three combinations of two working systems and one failing system, i.e.:

$$\text{Probability of system working} = P^3 + 3P^2Q$$
$$= P^3 + 3P^2(1 - P)$$
$$= 3P^2 - 2P^3$$

or in terms of reliability and failure rate:

$$\text{System reliability} = 3R^2 - 2R^3 = 3e^{-2\lambda t} - 2e^{3-\lambda t}$$

This expression can be compared with the reliability of a single system, $R = e^{-\lambda t}$, as shown in Fig. 15.13. We find that indeed the reliability of the triplicated system is higher than the single system, but only for a period. The triplicated system reliability function crosses over the single reliability function at a time, t_0. This time can be found by equating the two reliabilities:

$$e^{-\lambda t} = 3e^{-2\lambda t} - 2e^{3-\lambda t}$$

or $e^{-\lambda t} = 0.5$ or $t_0 = 0.7/\lambda$. Before $t_0 = 0.7/\lambda$, the triplicated system has a higher reliability than the single system but after this time, the single system has a higher reliability. Therefore the triplicated system can be used to increase the overall reliability during an operating period less than $0.7/\lambda$ or $0.7 \times$ (one system MTBF).

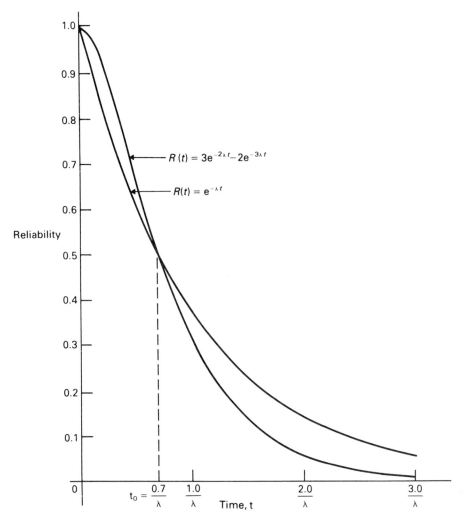

Figure 15.13 Reliability of single and triplicated systems

The MTBF of the triplicated system (not a constant failure rate system) is found by integrating $R(t)$ i.e.:

$$\text{MTBF}_{\text{triplicated system}} = \int_0^x (3e^{-2\lambda t} - 2e^{-3\lambda t})\ \mathrm{d}t = 5/(6\lambda)$$

which is slightly less than the MTBF of a single system $(1/\lambda)$.

We have not considered the reliability of the voter. The voter can be included into the probability equation as follows:

$$\text{Probability of triplicated system working} = (3P^2 - 2P^3)P_v$$

where P_v is the probability of the voter working. Hence the value for the reliability decreases if the effect of the voter is included. The probability of failure can of course be obtained by substituting $Q = 1 - P$ into the above equations.

An alternative method is to derive the probability of failure equations. The system will fail if:

(i) All three systems fail
(ii) Any two systems fail (with one working).

There are three combinations of two systems failing with one system working. Therefore:

> Probability of system failure,
> Q_s = (probability of all three systems failing
> $\quad$ + 3(probability of two failing)(probability of one working)
> $\quad = Q^3 + 3Q^2 P = 3Q^2 - 2Q^3$

Including the voter, we get:

> Q_s = (probability of triplicated system failing)(probability of voter working)
> $\quad$ + (probability of voter failing)
> $\quad = (3Q^2 - 2Q^3)(1 - Q_v) + Q_v$

The triplicated technique would normally be applied to (computer) systems rather than at the gate or component level. Then the voter would be a much simpler system than the triplicated systems and of much higher reliability. In such a case, it may have a negligible effect on the overall reliability. If the voter has a significant effect, one could take the extreme measure of three voters and a super-voter taking two out of three voter outputs. The triplicated system accepts the presence of one error without causing an overall system failure. To handle two errors, five systems and a voter which selects three out of five outputs would be necessary.

It is possible to connect components or gates in parallel to increase the reliability of the system. A direct application of the parallel configuration is shown in Fig. 15.14(a) and (b). In (a), n components are connected in series and these are connected in parallel. Each series arm has a probability of working of P^n. Therefore the probability of the complete system working is given by:

$$P_s = P^n + P^n - P^n P^n = 2P^n - P^{2n}$$

Alternatively, the probability of a system failure can be derived, i.e.:

$$Q_s = (1 - (1 - Q)^n)^2 = n^2 Q^2 \qquad \text{as } Q \text{ approaches zero}$$

In Fig. 15.14(b), pairs of components are connected in parallel and these are then connected in series. The probability of each pair working is given by $2P - P^2$ and the probability of the system working is given by:

$$P_s = (2P - P^2)^n$$

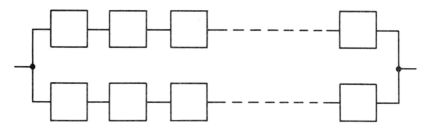

(a) Two series configurations in parallel

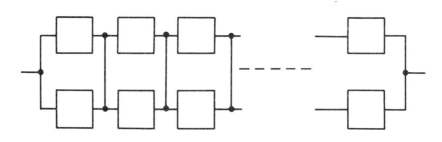

(b) Parallel pairs in series

Figure 15.14   Series-parallel configurations

The probability of failure is given by:

$$Q_s = (1 - (1 - Q^2)^n) = nQ^2 \qquad \text{as } Q \text{ approaches zero}$$

From the two failure expressions, we can see that configuration (b) has a higher reliability than configuration (a) (an 'unreliability' of nQ^2 as opposed to n^2Q^2). This assumes that the components have only one mode of failure.

An example of an implementation of series-parallel configurations at the component level would be four series-parallel connected diodes. It can be shown that configuration (a) produces a higher reliability than configuration (b) if the probability of a short-circuit is higher than the probability of an open circuit. Conversely, if the probability of an open-circuit is higher than the probability of a short-circuit, configuration (b) produces a higher reliability (Problem 15.8).

Gates can have three possible modes of failure, failure with a permanent 1 output, failure with a permanent 0 output, and failure with an intermediate output level. To increase gate level reliability, gates can be connected in series–parallel configurations utilizing the fact that a permanent 0 on the input of an OR gate will not inhibit the OR gate, and a permanent 1 on the input of an AND gate will not inhibit the AND gate. However, it is arguable whether fault tolerant design at this level is worthwhile. The reader is referred to [3] for further information on fault-tolerant design and the associated topic of design for fault testing.

15.4.2 System incorporating error detection and correction

An alternative approach to the design of reliable systems is to provide a means of detecting faults (errors) due to hardware malfunction, and correct the faults immediately they occur. A simple, widely used method of error detection is the parity system as mentioned in Chapter 1. To recapitulate, in the parity system an additional bit is appended to each binary word being transmitted between systems. This bit is arranged to be a 1 or a 0, whichever is necessary to make the number of 1's in the word, including the appended bit, even (for even parity). If a single-bit error has occurred, the number of 1's in the word will become odd which can be detected by logic. The appended bit is known as the parity bit and is often appended to words transmitted between peripherals and the system. The parity system is one example of introducing unused patterns into the coding of information. Whenever one of the unused patterns occurs, an error has been introduced.

Let us consider the general case of a binary word consisting of p bits. If some patterns are not used to represent valid information, and they occur, we know an error has occurred. The greater the number of unused patterns, the greater the ability to detect errors and, as we will see, the greater the ability to correct errors that do occur. If every combination of the p bits (i.e. all 2^p combinations) is used to represent valid information, there is no possibility of detecting errors by examining the patterns.

To take this idea further, consider a number of *code words* representing information. Of the possible binary patterns used for the code words, some will represent valid information while some will be invalid. A single-bit error in a correct word results in one bit changing from a 0 to a 1 or vice versa. Two bits in error will result in two bits changing. We arrange that correct code words are separated from each other by incorrect code words, as shown in Fig. 15.15. Here the patterns 0000 and 0111 are two correct code words while 0001 and 0011 are two of the incorrect code words between the correct code words. The incorrect code word 0001 differs from the first correct code word, 0000, by one digit and indicates a single-bit error. The next incorrect code word, 0011, differs from 0000 by two bits and indicates two errors from the correct code word, 0000, or one error from the second correct code word, 0111.

If in the above, all correct code words are separated by two incorrect code words, we can detect up to two errors as these would result in distinguishable incorrect codes. Three errors would result in a correct code word and thus could not be detected. If we assume only a single-bit error has occurred in our example, the

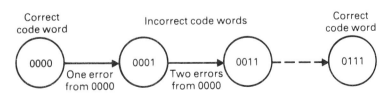

Figure 15.15 Code words

correct code would be the nearest one to the incorrect code word, and hence could be deduced. For example, if the code word 0011 has occurred, we would know that not only has an error occurred, but also that the correct code word would be 0111, the nearest correct code word. This could be chosen to replace the incorrect code word. This is therefore a method of detecting errors and correcting errors based on the ability to recognize incorrect code words. The parity system has one incorrect code word between correct code words and hence cannot be used to correct errors, only to detect one error.

We define the 'distance' between two correct code words as the *Hamming distance, d.* The Hamming distance is the minimum number of digits that are different in two code words in a set of code words. With no incorrect code words, the Hamming distance is 1 and no error detection or correction is possible. The code words in Fig. 15.15 have a Hamming distance of 3. The following conditions apply:

(i) *Detection of errors.* The necessary and sufficient condition to detect K errors or fewer is that the Hamming distance between two code words is $K + 1$.
(ii) *Correction of errors.* The necessary and sufficient condition to be able to correct K errors or fewer is that the Hamming distance between two correct codes is not less than $2K + 1$.

For the condition to correct errors, consider Fig. 15.16. A number of incorrect codes are sited between two correct codes. Let there be $2K$ incorrect codes. There are K incorrect codes closer to one correct code and K incorrect codes closer to the other correct code. K errors or fewer occurring from, say, the left-hand correct code word would result in one of the left-hand incorrect code words. This error can be corrected to the left-hand correct code word. Similarly, K errors or fewer from the right-hand code word would result in possible correction to the right-hand code word. However, more than K errors occurring in a code word could not be corrected. The overall Hamming distance between correct codes is $2K + 1$ as shown.

We could devise a coding scheme without any further information, by specifying codes with the appropriate Hamming distance for the desired detection

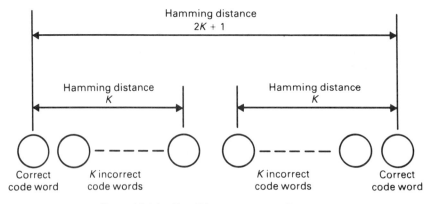

Figure 15.16 Condition to correct K errors

and correction capability. Implementation of error detection and correction could be based around a read-only memory. For example, an 8-bit code word has 256 combinations. Using a 256×1-bit read-only memory, the incoming code word can address the memory and the contents indicate whether the code word is valid or invalid. For invalid code words, an additional mechanism is necessary. One way is to increase the number of bits stored in the memory to hold the nearest valid code word which can then be read out. For simplicity, even correct code words could be stored, and in all cases the contents of the memory is read out.

Hamming [4] developed a coding system which produces a correction mechanism based on a simple calculation. We shall describe the method by example. Consider a 4-bit data word with digits D_1, D_2, D_3 and D_4. Three check digits, C_1, C_2 and C_3 are inserted between the data digits in the following positions:

| Check and data digits: | D_4, | D_3, | D_2, | C_3, | D_1, | C_2, | C_1 |
| Bit number: | B_7, | B_6, | B_5, | B_4, | B_3, | B_2, | B_1 |

leading to a seven-digit code word, B_1 to B_7. The check digits are computed as follows:

C_3 is computed to give $B_7B_6B_5B_4$ as having even parity
$$(C_3 = B_7 \oplus B_6 \oplus B_5 \oplus B_4)$$
C_2 is computed to give $B_7B_6B_3B_2$ as having even parity
$$(C_2 = B_7 \oplus B_6 \oplus B_3 \oplus B_2)$$
C_1 is computed to give $B_7B_5B_3B_1$ as having even parity
$$(C_1 = B_7 \oplus B_5 \oplus B_3 \oplus B_1)$$

The even-parity system is calculated on groups of bits, one bit of which is a check digit. Hence C_1 will check whether there is one bit in error in the set $B_7B_5B_3B_1$. C_2 will check whether there is one bit in error in the set $B_7B_6B_3B_2$ and C_3 will check whether there is one bit in error in the set $B_7B_6B_5B_4$. Listing the patterns of $C_3C_2C_1$ for single-bit errors on B_1, B_2, B_3, B_4, B_5, B_6 or B_7:

Bit in error	C_3	C_2	C_1
No error	0	0	0
B_1	0	0	1
B_2	0	1	0
B_3	0	1	1
B_4	1	0	0
B_5	1	0	1
B_6	1	1	0
B_7	1	1	1

we see that the pattern obtained, if not 000, indicates an error and also identifies the position of the bit.

If $D_4D_3D_2D_1 = 1100$, the check digits are computed as $C_3 = 0$, $C_2 = 0$, $C_1 = 1$ and the complete code word is 1100001. Suppose an error has occurred in position six (B_6). Since this can only mean that the sixth bit changes from one binary state to another, B_6 must become a 0, and the code word becomes 1000001. To detect and correct the error, the parity computation is repeated, returning a 0 if there is even parity and a 1 if there is odd parity, i.e.:

$$B_7 \oplus B_6 \oplus B_5 \oplus B_4 = 1$$
$$B_7 \oplus B_6 \oplus B_3 \oplus B_2 = 1$$
$$B_7 \oplus B_5 \oplus B_3 \oplus B_1 = 0 \text{ (least significant bit)}$$

(The computation can be viewed as performing the arithmetic summation of the digits, returning only the least significant bit of the summation.) The binary number obtained with the least significant bit as shown identifies the position that the error has occurred, in this case, position 110 or position 6. Therefore B_6 can be corrected by changing the digit from a 0 back to a 1.

The Hamming scheme can be applied to any number of data digits. The check digits are in binary power positions 1, 2, 4, 8, 16, 32, etc., as required. The data digits are inserted between the check digits. The B bits in the check digit computation can be found by listing binary numbers in an ascending order from zero upwards and allocating the first check computation (C_1) to the least significant column, the next check digit computation (C_2) to the next least significant column, the next check digit computation (C_3) to the next column and so on. Whenever a 1 appears in a column, the corresponding binary number identifies the B digit to be included in the check digit computation allocated to the column.

The overhead of check digits becomes less significant as more data digits are encoded. For example, 8-bit data needs 4 check digits (i.e. a 50% increase), a 16-bit word needs 5 check digits (31.25% increase) while a 64-bit word needs 7 check digits (10.9375% increase). One application of the Hamming code is to increase the reliability of a semiconductor memory system. Consider a 1024K × 16-bit (1 M × 16 bit) memory system using 256K × 1-bit devices. Sixty-four devices are needed for a system without error detection/correction. The probability of working (reliability) of the system, assuming the system fails when one device fails, is given by:

Probability of system working, $P_s = P_m^{64}$

where P_m is the probability of a memory device working. (Only the memory devices are considered.) The MTBF is given by:

$$\text{MTBF}_s = \int_0^\infty \exp(-64\lambda_m t) \, dt = 0.0156/\lambda_m$$

where λ_m is the failure rate of each memory device [5].

If we add five Hamming check digits and the associated detection and correction logic, the memory would need to be 1024K × 21 bits (16 data digits plus 5 check digits). The number of devices is now given by 21 × 4 (i.e. 84). This memory system would continue to operate in the presence of one memory device totally faulty out of each group of 21 memory devices. (It would be possible to have up to four faulty memory devices, each associated with different words and hence each fault could be corrected when the words were read.) The probability of working is given by:

Probability of system working,

$P_{hs} = [(\text{Probability of all 21 devices working})$
$+ 21(\text{probability of 20 devices working and probability of one device faulty})]^4$

as there are 21 combinations of 20 devices working and one device faulty. Hence the probability of working becomes:

$$P_{hs} = [P_m^{21} + 21 P_m^{20}(1 - P_m)]^4$$

and the MTBF is:

$$\text{MTBF}_{hs} = \int_0^\infty \{\exp(-21\lambda_m' + 21 [\exp(-20\lambda_m')] [1 - \exp(-\lambda_m')] \}^4 \, dt$$

$$= 0.0393/\lambda_m$$

or a 252% improvement in the MTBF over the system without correction. The calculation does not include the interface logic and clearly the extra detection/correction logic will reduce the MTBF to some extent.

References

1. *Reliability Prediction of Electronic Equipment*, MIL-HDBK-217B, US Department of Defense, 1974.
2. Smith, D. J., *Reliability Engineering*, London: Pitman, 1972.
3. Lala, P. K., *Fault Tolerant and Fault Testable Hardware Design*, Englewood Cliffs, N.J.,: Prentice-Hall, Inc., 1985.
4. Hamming, R. W., 'Error-detecting and Error-correcting Codes', *Bell Syst. Tech. J.*, 29 (1950), 147–60.
5. Lala, P. K., 'Error Correction in Semiconductor Memory Systems', *Electronic Engineering*, 51, no. 617 (Jan. 1979), 49–53.

Problems

15.1 A system consists of 500 components in a series configuration. The failure rate of each component is 0.03%/1000 hr. What is the system reliability over a period of 200 hours? What is the maximum component failure rate necessary if the system reliability is to be 0.99? In each case, calculate the system MTBF.

15.2 Prove that the reliability of a constant failure rate system after an initial operating period equal to the MTBF is approximately 37%.

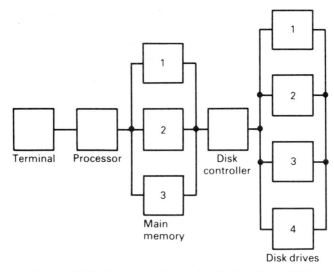

Figure 15.17   System configuration for Problem 15.3

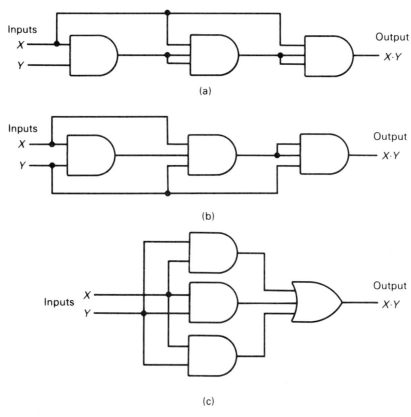

Figure 15.18   Logic circuits for Problem 15.4

15.3   A microprocessor system consists of the following units:

Unit	Number	Failure rate
Processor	1	λ_P
Main memory unit	3	λ_{MM}
Disk controller	1	λ_{DC}
Disk drive	4	λ_{DD}
Video terminal	1	λ_{VT}

each with a constant failure rate. The system configuration is shown in Fig. 15.17. For the system to operate, the processor, terminal and disk controller must function together with two of the memory units and three of the disk drives. Obtain an expression for the reliability of the system and the system MTBF.

15.4   Derive expressions for the reliability of the circuit shown in Fig. 15.18, given that each gate has two modes of failure, one with a permanent 0 output and one with a permanent 1 output. The failure rates are constant.

15.5   Apply Bayes's theorem to determine the reliability of each of the logic circuits shown in Fig. 15.19, given that the probability of an individual gate failure with a permanent

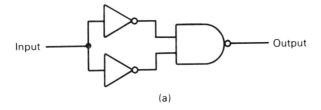

(a)

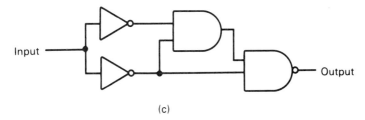

(b)

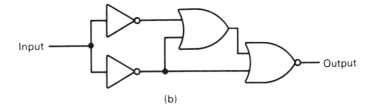

(c)

Figure 15.19 Logic circuits for Problem 15.5

0 output is 0.1% and the probability of an individual gate failure with a permanent 1 output is 0.2%. These probabilities apply for a mission time (operating time) of 1000 hours. Determine the MTBF of the circuit shown in Fig. 15.19(a). Assume that the failure rates of the gates are constant. The circuits are defined as working if the output is the same as the input for both 0 and 1 input values.

15.6   Figure 15.20 shows a logic system consisting of four identical open-collector TTL gates and a pull-up resistor, R. Each gate has two modes of failure:

(i) With the output short-circuit to 0 V
(ii) With the output open-circuit.

The corresponding failure probabilities are $Q_{s/c}$ and $Q_{o/c}$. Derive an expression for the reliability of the system in terms of $Q_{s/c}$ and $Q_{s/c}$. The failure rate of the resistor may be ignored.

15.7   Derive an expression for the overall reliability of five identical single-output subsystems with outputs connected to a voter. The overall system works if two or more outputs of the subsystems are the same. (It is assumed that the associated subsystems must be working.)

15.8   Determine the conditions required to cause a system of diodes connected in the configuration of Fig. 15.14(a) to be more reliable than diodes connected on configuration of Fig. 15.14(b) and vice versa, given that the diodes have two modes of failure, short-circuit failure and open-circuit failure, and there are four diodes.

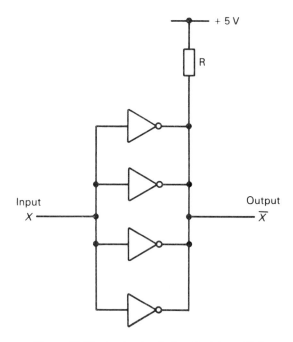

Figure 15.20 Logic circuit for Problem 15.6

15.9   Four message symbols are encoded as follows:

$$S_1 = 01101$$
$$S_2 = 10001$$
$$S_3 = 01110$$
$$S_4 = 11011$$

How many errors can be detected and how many errors can be corrected with this code? Devise a code for the four messages which allows the detection of two errors and the correction of one error using the minimum number of bits. (Do not use the Hamming code.)

15.10   Devise a Hamming code consisting of data digits and check digits to encode the 5-bit data word 10101. Show how one error can be detected and corrected.

Index